IFA DIVINATION

IFA DIVINATION

Communication Between Gods and Men In West Africa

WILLIAM BASCOM

INDIANA UNIVERSITY PRESS
Bloomington and Indianapolis

First Midland Book Edition 1991

Library of Congress catalog card number: 69-10349

Manufactured in the United States of America

ISBN 0-253-32890-X
ISBN 0-253-20638-3 (pbk.)

5 6 7 8 9 95 94 93 92 91

CONTENTS

LIST OF FIGURES

LIST OF TABLES

LIST OF PLATES

PREFACE

Ifa is the most respected, in many ways the most interesting, system of divination of five to ten million Yoruba in Nigeria[1] and millions more of their African neighbors and their descendants in the New World.

Unquestionably, the most important of the previous studies of Ifa is that of Maupoil (1943), for Dahomey. Maupoil describes initiations and other rituals, and ritual paraphernalia, in a detail that is not attempted here, where the primary emphasis is on the Yoruba, and not on the worship of Ifa as a deity, but on the method of divination, the manner in which it "works," and the Ifa verses that are of such fundamental importance to the entire system of divination. Neither study should be regarded as definitive, if only because of the thousands of Ifa verses that remain to be recorded before they are forgotten. Fortunately, this work is currently being pursued at the University of Ibadan.

The established Yoruba orthography is followed, with ẹ for ɛ, ọ for ɔ, p for kp, ṣ for sh, and with n representing nasalization except where it appears initially or between two vowels; a, e, i, o, u have continental values. In translating the verses in Part Two, I have usually taken the liberty of using sh instead of ṣ. In transcribing the Yoruba texts I have departed from convention, for example giving "n(i)-igba-ti" as "at-time-that" in the interlinear translation rather than "nigbati" as "when." Parentheses enclose elided sounds; and hyphens join parts of Yoruba compound words and their English equivalents. When two or more English words are required to translate one Yoruba word, they are joined by colons, as in "be:able" for "le."

To avoid confusion it is important to note at the outset that Ifẹ or Ile-Ifẹ is a city and Ifa is both a method of and a deity of divination. Ọni is the title of the King (Ọba) of Ifẹ, and Ọrunmila is another name for Ifa, the deity. The Ifa diviners are known in Yoruba as babalawo.

---

1. The last official Nigerian census in 1952 gave 5,079,746 Yoruba (including 32,947 Itsẹkiri, a Ỵoruba subgroup) out of a total population of 31,156,027. Only gross figures have been released for the controversial 1962 census, which gave a total population of 53,200,000 for Nigeria, but with no indication of ethnic affiliation. If one can put any faith in recent statistics, the Yoruba may number 11,000,000. This estimate is reached by multiplying the percentage of Yoruba in the Regions and Provinces of Nigeria in 1952 by the population figures given in Tables 10 and 11 of the Western Nigeria Statistical Bulletin, VI (1-2), 1964: 11-12. If recent figures are exaggerated, as may be the case, those of the 1952 census were probably underestimated and do not allow for interim growth. One recent statement gives 10,250,000 Yoruba (West Africa, December 26, 1964: 1452).

Most of the data for this study were recorded in the city of Ifẹ in 1937-38 on a predoctoral fellowship from the Social Science Research Council; six weeks were spent in Igana during that year. A Fulbright grant in 1950-51 made it possible to spend about three months each in Mẹkọ, Ọyọ, and Ileṣa and to work for a day or two in Ilaro, Ilara, Abẹokuta, Ibadan, Isẹyin, Oke-Iho, Irawọ, Ogbomọṣọ, Oṣogbo, Ṣagamu, Ijẹbu Ode, Ọndọ, and a half dozen towns in Ekiti. Further research was carried on during a two-month visit at the time that Nigeria received her independence in 1960 and during three months in 1965. This later research was financed respectively by grants from the University of California's Institute of International Studies and the Social Science Research Council. An invitation from Cambridge University and a Senior Postdoctoral Grant from the National Science Foundation provided a year in England in 1958 to analyze field notes, during which the texts and translations of the Ifa verses were typed and a preliminary draft of the first section was completed. Ifa divination was by no means the only topic of investigation during these periods of research, but without these grants this study would not have been possible. I am indebted to these institutions, and to Professor Meyer Fortes, a welcome visitor during three years spent in West Africa during World War II, who arranged the invitation to Cambridge.

I am especially grateful to Thomas A. Sebeok and to Michael A. Aronson of the Indiana University Press for facilitating the publication of this study.

The courtesies of government officials and others in 1937-38 have been previously acknowledged (Bascom, 1944: 6-7). By now the list has grown too long to name all those who have given assistance on other trips, but I should particularly like to thank Eoin M. Catto, Mr. and Mrs. John Davies, Mr. and Mrs. A. F. F. P. Newns, Ṣoba Ọyawoye of the University of Ibadan, and Nnamdi Azikiwe, the first President of Nigeria.

Thanks are again due my friend Aderẹmi, the Ọni of Ifẹ, for his assistance and cooperation, and to Agbọnbọn, Amosun, Samuel Elufiṣoye, Awodire Awoṣeemọ Ifẹ, and the many other diviners who served as informants. Special thanks go to the diviner from whom most of the Ifa verses were recorded, but who remains nameless for reasons explained in Chapter XII. Again I owe a deep debt of gratitude to the late D. O. Rufus Awojọdu, who served as interpreter in 1937-38 and whose personal fascination with Ifa divination induced me to become so deeply involved in this most important aspect of the Yoruba way of life. I had long intended to dedicate this book to him, but there is another to whom my debt is even greater.

I dedicate this book to the memory of one who contributed so much to the development of African studies in the United States; who first interested me in Africa, the Yoruba people, and the city of Ifẹ; who made his own work on Ifa in Dahomey available to me in the field before its publication; who guided my training to the Ph.D. degree; and who was a considerate chairman, helpful colleague, and staunch friend during my many years at Northwestern University.

W. B.

Berkeley, California
March 1965

To the memory of
Melville J. Herskovits

TRUTH AND DEATH

(Epega, n.d.: XI, 4; VII, 14-16)

Qsa Otura says, "What is Truth?" I say, "What is Truth?" Qrunmila says, "Truth is the Lord of Heaven guiding the Earth." Qrunmila says, "Truth is the Unseen One guiding the Earth. The wisdom of Olodumare he is using."

Qsa Otura says, "What is Truth?" I say, "What is Truth?" Qrunmila says, "Truth is the character of Olodumare. Truth is the word that cannot fall. Ifa is Truth. Truth is the word that cannot spoil. Might surpassing all. Blessing everlasting was the one who cast Ifa for Earth. They said they should come and speak the truth. Song:

"Speak the truth, tell the facts;
"Speak the truth, tell the facts;
"Those who speak the truth are those whom the gods will help."

Leaves of Ifa: We should mark this figure in the divining powder; we should mix it with cornstarch gruel and drink it, or put it in palm oil and eat it, so that it will be easy for us to speak the truth. Or we should apply idabo to the head. What is idabo? It is divining powder in which we have marked the figure of Ifa.
(Qsa Otura).

* * * * *

"The Omniscient One knows those who wickedly shoot others. People of the farm knowing people of the town; travelers of earth and travelers of heaven; we will see each other again. Termites do not scatter unless they reassemble again" was the one who cast Ifa for us humans who are mourning one who has died.

Where the people of earth have come from is where they are returning to. What are tears for? What is sorrow for? What is raising oneself up and down for? What is fasting for? He who sends one to come is he who is calling him to return home. That which pleases us on earth does not please Olodumare. The people on earth sit on earth and they do evil. Olodumare does not like it; Olodumare does not accept it. Well then, if I say come, you come.

If a child does not know his father, the earth is not right. Death is the one who takes a child to know heaven. Who is thinking of Olodumare? If there were no Eshu, who would think of those who eat sacrifices? Everyone is thinking of themselves; they are looking for food and drink. You know darkness; a child does not know his father. Speak to me that I may speak to you; by our voices we recognize each other in the darkness. If a child does not know his father, the earth is not right.

Sacrifice: four white pigeons, four ewes, and two shillings. They heard and they sacrificed so that they might remain long on earth and that they might see blessings. (Otura Qwonrin).

PLATES

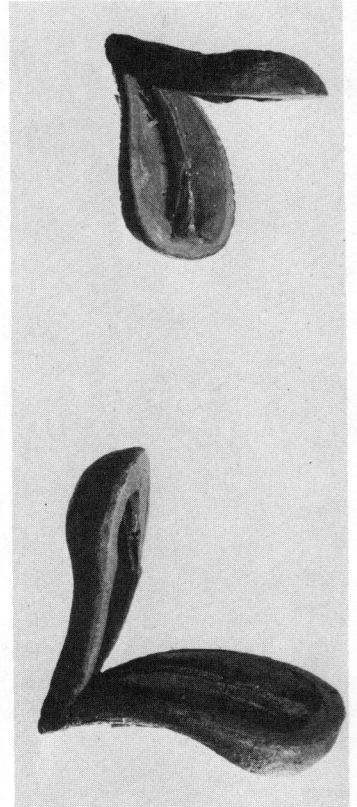

1A. (Ref. p. 28.) Two carved heads (Ẹla or irin) of ivory and of elephant bone, one of which may be kept with the diviner's set of sixteen palm nuts as a decoration. Heights: 2.75, 2.25 inches.

1B. (Ref. p. 30.) Two ọpẹlẹ pods, halves of which are widely used in making divining chains. Lengths: 1.75, 2.25 inches.

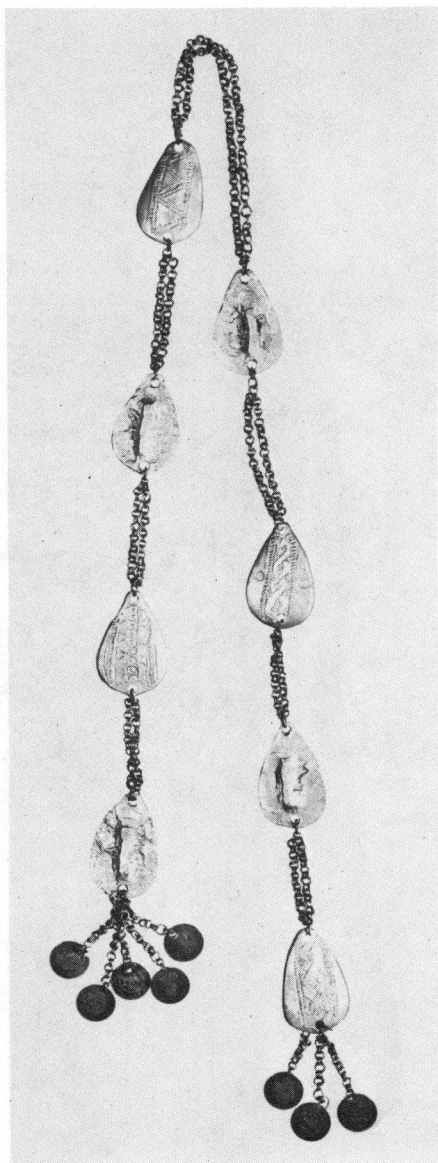

2A. (Ref. p. 29.) A divining chain (ọpẹ̀lẹ̀) from Ọyọ, made of ọpẹ̀lẹ̀ pods and the preferred kind of brass chain, with cowries at each end. The figure shown is Ọ̀ṣẹ́-Ofun. Overall length: 50 inches.

2B. (Ref. p. 31.) A divining chain from Ilara, made of replicas of ọpẹ̀lẹ̀ pods cast in a light white metal (probably aluminum) with coins at each end. As shown, the figure also reads Ọ̀ṣẹ́-Ofun, but perhaps this should be reversed (Ofun-Ọ̀ṣẹ́), since one of the coins may have been lost from the right-hand half of the chain. Overall length: 35.75 inches.

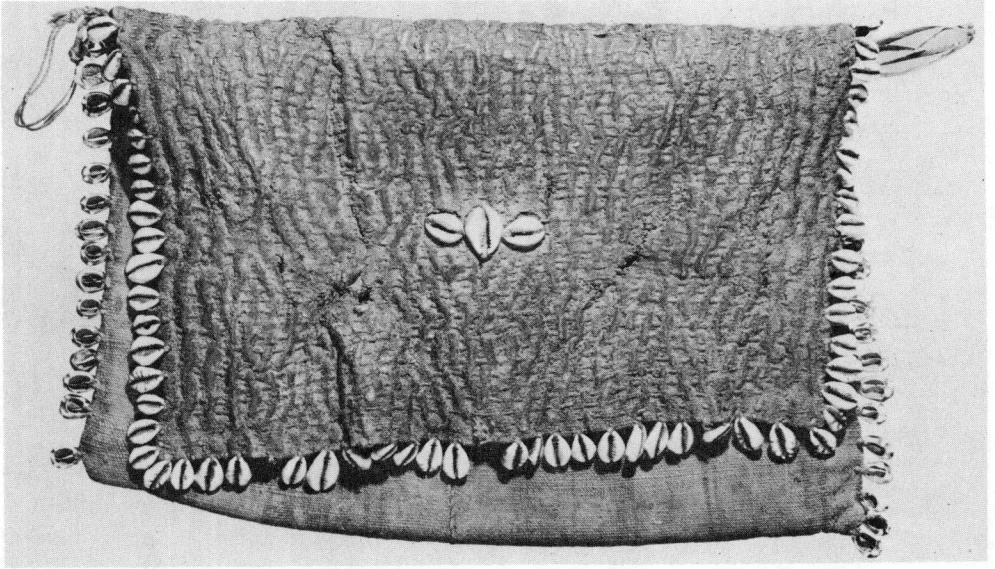

3. (Ref. p. 32.) A divining bag (apo Ifa) from Qyǫ, made of cloth and decorated with cowry shells. Width: 14 inches.

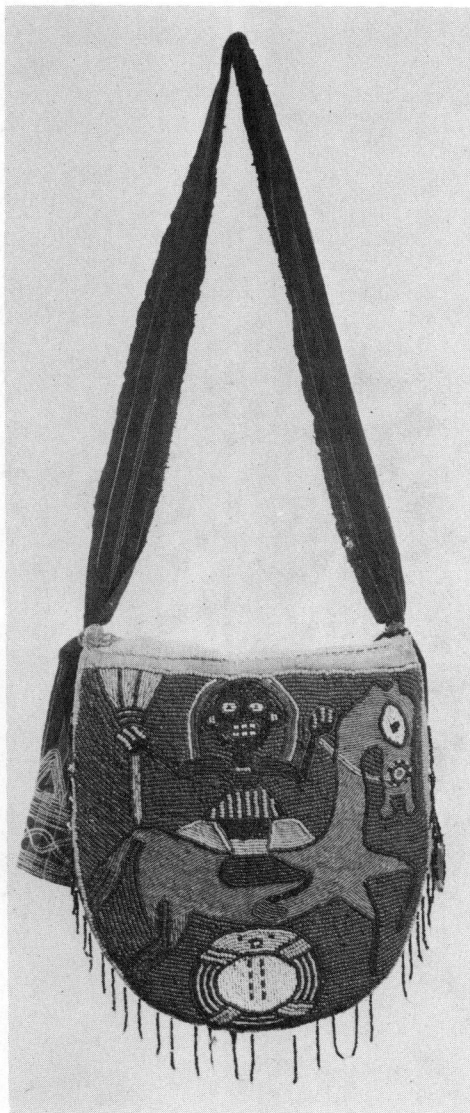

4A-B. (Ref. p. 32.) Two beaded divining bags. One from Igana, on the left, shows a diviner on horseback carrying his iron staff (ǫrẹrẹ) in his right hand and with his head covered with a cloth as protection against the sun. In the foreground is a divining tray showing the face of Eshu at the top and with the figure Ogbe Meji marked on it. The other from Ǫyǫ, on the right, shows two men, one holding a gun and the other a crown. The letters OK refer to the name of the diviner, Oke Anigbami, who made the bag about 1949. Widths: 10.75, 5.5 inches.

5. (Ref. p. 32.) A divining cup (agere Ifa, ajele Ifa) from Deyin, a Yoruba town in Dahomey. It shows a man on horseback accompanied by three drummers and an attendant with a staff. On the lid two cocks are biting two snakes who, in turn, are biting a tortoise. The cup, lid, and loop hinge are carved from a single block of wood. Height: 11.5 inches.

6. (Ref. p. 32.) A lidless divining cup showing a man on horseback accompanied by drummers and attendants. The woman on his right carries a bowl with a hinged lid. (Collection of Mr. and Mrs. William F. Kaiser, Berkeley, California.) Height: 10.75 inches.

7. (Ref. p. 52.) A brass divining cup with a hinged lid, cast by the lost wax method. It represents a man on horseback accompanied by his wife and fourteen attendants. (Collection of The Denver Art Museum.) Height: 12 inches.

8. (Ref. p. 32.) A divining cup from Ẹfọn-Alaye representing a female worshiper offering a cock whose back forms a removable lid. The woman is surrounded by attendants whose subordination to the two main figures is indicated both by their diminutive size and by the fact that their carving has not been completed. Height: 14.5 inches.

9. (Ref. p. 33.) A wooden divining bowl (ọpọn igẹdẹ) from Ifẹ, showing the central and radial compartments. The triangular designs on the separable lid are markers to indicate how the lid should be positioned on the base. Diameter: 15 50 inches.

10. (Ref. p. 33.) A divining bowl at Igana whose separable lid, decorated with four Eshu faces, serves also as a divining tray. Diameter: ca. 20 inches.

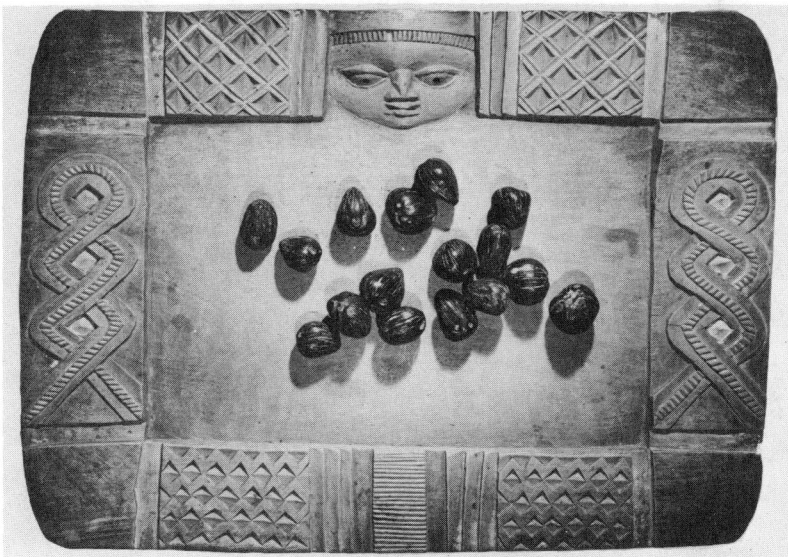

11. (Ref. p. 34.) A circular divining tray (ọpọn Ifa) carved about 1934 by Baba
Alawode of Igana. The face of Eshu is at the top, and the figures around the
edge represent porcupines, wild goats, and tortoises. The interwoven motif
is common in embroidery and beadworking as well as in carving. Diameter:
14 inches.

12. (Ref. p. 34.) A rectangular divining tray carved by Duga of Mẹkọ, on which
is a set of the sixteen palm nuts (ikin) used in divination. Length: 15.75
inches.

13A-B. (Ref. p. 36.) Three divining bells or tappers (irǫ Ifa), which are tapped
against the divining tray to call Ifa's attention. The ivory one, on the left, is
from Mękǫ and has no clapper. The brass pair from Ifę, on the right, have
clappers and were cast by the lost wax method. Lengths: 10.5, 17, 17 inches.

14. (Ref. p. 40.) Beating the set of sixteen palm nuts between the hands.

15. (Ref. p. 40.) Marking a figure (odu) in wood dust (iyẹrosun) on tne divining tray (ọpọn Ifa) which is placed so that the face of Eshu is looking at the diviner, Samuel Elufiṣoyi. He is seated on a mat which is partially covered with a locally woven cotton cloth, and holds the set of sixteen palm nuts (ikin) in his left hand. In the foreground is the seventeenth palm nut (oduṣọ or olori ikin), covered with wood dust and resting in the ring of cowry shells known as the "money of Ifa" (aje Ifa). To the left is the cow-tail switch (irukẹrẹ), and to the right is the divining bowl (ọpọn igẹdẹ).

16. (Ref. p. 68.) Before the first cast of the divining chain (ọpẹlẹ), it is dangled over the penny provided by the client as the diviner asks Ifa if he has heard the question which the client has whispered to the coin. Often, as in this case, the chain is lowered so that it coils on top of the penny. The diviner's beaded bracelet in the form of a wristwatch can be seen on his left wrist, and below his left hand is another divining chain and some of the assorted objects (abira) used as symbols of specific alternatives.

17. (Ref. p. 56.) In choosing between specific alternatives—the five kinds of
good fortune in this case—the divining chain is touched to the symbol in question before each cast. The client's penny can be seen on the diviner's bag
near the piece of china which symbolizes defeat of one's enemies.

18. (Ref. p. 56.) The divining chain is cast on the divining bag (apo Ifa) in one of the five casts to determine which of the five kinds of good fortune awaits the client.

19. (Ref. p. 89.) Samuel Elufiṣoye is divining for his two "wives of Ifa," who are seated beside him holding calabashes. Also present are a daughter, two young apprentices, and a number of spectators (standing). Divination normally takes place indoors, but an exception was made in this case in 1937 so that photographs could be taken.

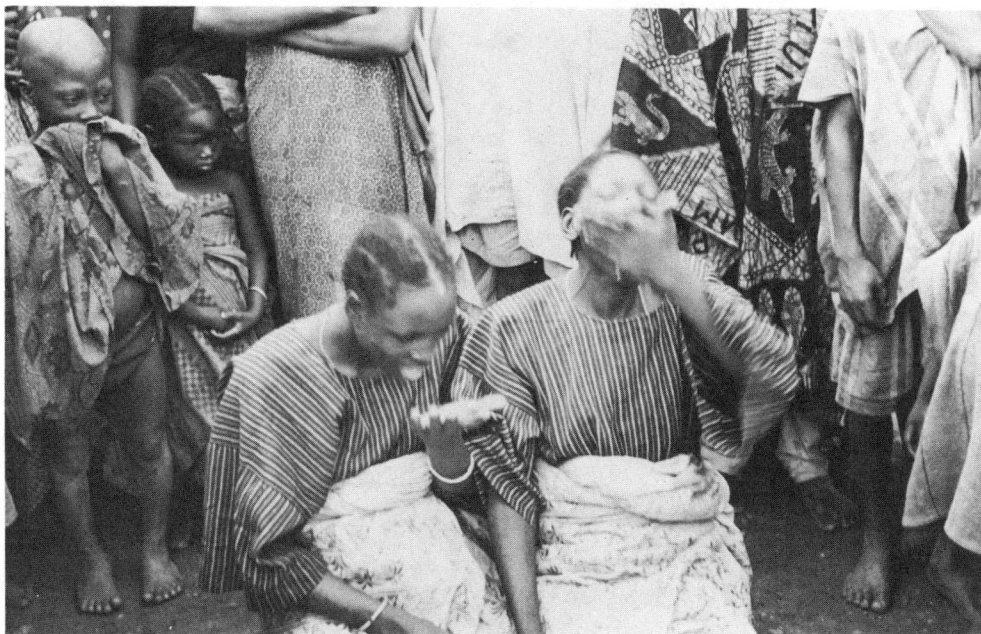

20A-B. (Ref. p. 61.) At the conclusion of the divination, the two wives took some of the wood dust from the divining tray, marked a line down the center of their heads with it, and then swallowed the remainder.

21A. (Ref. pp. 82, 95, 99.) Two cylindrical odu containers and a divining bowl
covered with cloths have been carried into the street during the Egbodo Erio
festival at Ifẹ in 1965. Note the beads (ẹdigba or ogbara) worn over the shoulder of the diviner in the center.

21B. (Ref. pp. 82, 84.) Three iron staffs (ọrẹrẹ) decorated with palm fronds have
been set into the ground behind an origi in front of an Ifẹ compound during the
Egbodo Erio festival in 1965.

Part One:

IFA DIVINATION

I. INTRODUCTION

Ifa is a system of divination based on sixteen basic and 256 derivative figures (odu) obtained either by the manipulation of sixteen palm nuts (ikin), or by the toss of a chain (ǫpǫlǫ) of eight half seed shells. The worship of Ifa as the God of Divination entails ceremonies, sacrifices, tabus, paraphernalia, drums, songs, praises, initiation, and other ritual elements comparable to those of other Yoruba cults; these are not treated fully here, since the primary subject of this study is Ifa as a system of divination. The mode of divination will be discussed in detail later, but a brief description is required at the outset.

The sixteen palm nuts are grasped in the right hand, leaving only one or two nuts in the left; if two nuts remain, a single mark is made on the divining tray; if one nut remains, a double mark is made. Repeating this procedure four times will give one of the sixteen basic figures as shown in Table 1, A; repeating it eight times gives a pair or combination of the basic figures, i.e. one of the 256 derivative figures. Alternatively, one of the 256 derivative figures can be obtained by a single cast of the divining chain, with heads and tails instead of odds and evens. The chain is held in the middle so that four half seed shells fall in a line on each side. Each half shell may fall either heads or tails; i.e. it may fall with its concave inner surface upward, which is equivalent to a single mark, or with this surface downward, equivalent to a double mark on the tray. Representing the concave inner side up as O and the convex outer side up as ⊗, the sixteen basic figures (one half of the divining chain) appear as given in Table 1, B.[1] The basic figures are listed in Table 1 in the order recognized at Ifǫ, but a slightly different order is more widely recognized (see Chapter IV, Table 3, B).

Ifa divination is practiced by the Yoruba and Benin Edo of Nigeria (Dennett, 1910: 148; Melzian, 1937: 159; Bradbury, 1957: 54-60; Parrinder, 1961: 148); the Fǫn of Dahomey, who call it Fa (Herskovits, 1938: 201-230; Maupoil, 1943); and the Ewe of Togo, who know it as Afa (Spieth, 1911: 189-225). It is also practiced under the name of Ifa by descendants of Yoruba slaves in Cuba (Bascom, 1952: 170-176) and Brazil (Bastide, 1958: 104-109). The Fǫn and Ewe acknowledge as its place of origin the Yoruba city of Ifǫ, from which the Yoruba themselves claim it has spread. It was at Ifǫ that the Ifa verses given in Part Two were recorded and that the system of divination was studied in greatest detail. Where information is based on field work in other Yoruba areas, or drawn from the literature, it is so specified.

Ifa divination may be practiced more widely than is indicated above. Thomas (1913-1914: I, 47) reports cryptically that the Ibo of eastern Nigeria "also have the well-known palm nut divination." The Kamuku and Gbari or Gwari are neighboring peoples in Niger Province, Northern Nigeria. Among the Kamuku, "to foretell the future, peas are shaken up in a tortoise-

---

1. Other conventions for representing the figures are given in Bascom (1961: 677).

3

TABLE 1

THE SIXTEEN BASIC FIGURES OF IFA

A. Using Sixteen Palm Nuts

1 Ogbe	2 Qyẹku	3 Iwori	4 Edi	5 Qbara	6 Qkanran	7 Irosun	8 Qwọnrin
1	1 1	1 1	1	1	1 1	1	1 1
1	1 1	1	1 1	1 1	1 1	1	1 1
1	1 1	1	1 1	1 1	1 1	1 1	1
1	1 1	1 1	1	1 1	1	1 1	1

9 Ogunda	10 Qsa	11 Irẹtẹ	12 Otura	13 Oturupọn	14 Ika	15 Qsẹ	16 Ofun
1	1 1	1	1	1 1	1 1	1	1 1
1	1	1	1 1	1 1	1	1 1	1
1	1	1 1	1	1	1 1	1	1 1
1 1	1	1	1	1 1	1 1	1 1	1

B. Using the Divining Chain

1 Ogbe	2 Qyẹku	3 Iwori	4 Edi	5 Qbara	6 Qkanran	7 Irosun	8 Qwọnrin
O	⊠	⊠	O	O	⊠	O	⊠
O	⊠	O	⊠	⊠	⊠	O	⊠
O	⊠	O	⊠	⊠	⊠	⊠	O
O	⊠	⊠	O	⊠	O	⊠	O

9 Ogunda	10 Qsa	11 Irẹtẹ	12 Otura	13 Oturupọn	14 Ika	15 Qsẹ	16 Ofun
O	⊠	O	O	⊠	⊠	O	⊠
O	O	O	⊠	⊠	O	⊠	O
O	O	⊠	O	O	⊠	O	⊠
⊠	O	O	O	⊠	⊠	⊠	O

shell and then gathered into the right hand or left hand. They are counted
out and according as to whether an odd or even number remains in the
hand a mark is made in the ground. This process is repeated eight times
and a meaning come to according to the combination" (Temple and Temple,
1919: 210). "Divination by peas and a tortoise-shell is common among
many tribes, notably the Gwari. The peas are shaken up in the tortoise-
shell and then gathered in the hand. According as the number is odd or
even a mark is made in the ground, and finally, by the combination of the
various odd and even marks, a meaning is obtained" (Meek, 1925: II, 70).
The Gbari also practice the widespread Islamic form of divination known
as "sand-cutting" (Temple and Temple, 1919: 210), which will be discussed
later in this chapter.

What may be the earliest report of Ifa divination comes from the coast
of what is now Ghana in a description given by Bosman, who served as factor for the Dutch at Elmina and Axim for fourteen years at the end of the
seventeenth century. After first discussing a method of divination in which
"about twenty small bits of Leather" are used, Bosman (1705: 152) says,
"The second way of consulting their Idols, is by a sort of wild Nuts, which
they pretend to take up by guess and let fall again: after which they tell
them, and form their Predictions from the number falling even or odd."

Another early account comes from Assinie in the southeastern corner
of the Ivory Coast, still farther to the west. Lòyer (1714: 248-249) describes a method of consultation with the gods which involves the moving
of palm nuts (noyeaux de palmistes) which are taken from a wooden or copper cup, making marks with the finger in wood dust on a board a foot long
and half a foot wide, and choosing between objects which are held in the
hands of an assistant and which represent the good and evil outcome of the
consultation.[2] The recent literature does not record Ifa divination west of
Togo.[3]

Hamilton describes a system of divination observed at Siwah in the
Sahara, which is "called 'Derb er raml,' or 'Derb el ful,' according to the
medium used, whether it is sand or beans; the latter (with the beans) is the
simplest, but both are in principle the same. Seven beans are held in the
palm of the left hand, which is struck with a smart blow with the right

---

2. I have been unable to locate the original, but the passage is quoted
in full by Maupoil (1943: 45) and by Labouret and Rivet (1929: 28) and is
briefly cited by Parrinder (1949: 161; 1961: 146). Tauxier (1932: 151)
and Maupoil date Loyer's visit as about 1700; Bosman (1705: 17) was in
Ghana by 1690. For the use of objects to represent good and evil, see
Chapter V.

3. Field (1937: 40) reports for the Gan of coastal Ghana "There also
attached itself to Labadi, at some time uncertain, a colony of Ewe people
from Little Popo, worshipping their own god Okumaga." She gives no details as to the nature of this deity, but as Parrinder (1949: 156) has noted,
ogumaga is the Fǫn name for the divining chain, or agunmaga according to
Maupoil (1943: 196).

half-closed fist, so that some of the beans jump into the right hand — if an odd number, one is marked; if even, two. The beans are replaced in the left hand, which is again struck with the right, and the result marked below the first. This being repeated four times gives the first figure, and the operation is performed until there are obtained four figures, which are placed side by side in a square; these are then read vertically and perpendicularly [sic!], and also from corner to corner, thus giving in all ten figures. As each may contain four odd or four even numbers, they are capable of sixteen permutations, each of which has a separate signification, and a proper house or part of the square in which it should appear. The Derb er-raml is only distinguished from this by being more complicated, fresh combinations being obtained by the addition of every pair of figures." (Hamilton, 1856: 264-265; cited in Ellis, 1894: 63).

In the use of four rather than two basic figures and in making one line for an odd number of beans and two lines for an even number, Derb el ful resembles Islamic sand-cutting rather than Ifa.

According to Frobenius (1924b: 61-62) diviners among the Nupe, who live just north of the Yoruba beyond the Niger river, use a string (ebba) of eight pieces of calabash or sometimes fruit shells fastened together, corresponding to the Yoruba divining chain. However, Nadel (1954: 39) describes "eba" as a set of eight strings of four half shells from the shea nut or the dompalm kernel.

The Jukun of eastern Nigeria employ a pair of strings or chains (noko),[4] each of which has four pieces of calabash, metal, or nuts from elephant dung. These are equivalent to the two halves of the Ifa divining chain. The divining instrument (agbendi) of the neighboring Tiv is made with pieces of seed shells of the native mango (ive) and is "identical with that used by the Jukun and all the tribes in the neighbourhood down to, and possibly below, the Cross Rivers" (Downes, 1933: 69). Parrinder (1961: 148) mentions the use of this instrument among the Ibo, as well as the use of four similar strings. According to Mansfeld (1908: 176) the Ekoi of the Cross River region also employ two chains (ewu), each composed of four half mango seeds; according to Talbot (1912: 174-175) they use four such strings, known as ebu or efa. The data are too meager to permit any reliable conclusions, but there is further evidence of an even broader distribution of the sixteen basic figures.

Divination with four strings of four markers each, as mentioned by Parrinder and Talbot, is a related but separate system which is also known by the Yoruba. It involves the same sixteen basic figures and is sometimes called Ifa, but the method of interpretation is different, and it is distinguished as Agbigba or Agbagba. Short verses comparable to the introductory phrases of the Ifa verses are associated with the figures. Ogunbiyi (1952: 50, 63) illustrates Agbigba with two strings like the Ifa

---

4. In an earlier publication, Meek (1925: II: 70) reported six strings, but this is corrected in Meek (1931: 326-327), cited here, and in Meek (1937: 82), and is correctly reported by Frobenius (1924a: 236).

divining chain (ọpẹlẹ) thrown side by side. The Agbigba sets I have seen
were of four separate strings with four markers each, but again it is of no
practical significance whether or not two are joined at the top, as illustrated by the dotted line in Figure 1, C. Effectively Agbigba is a double
ọpẹlẹ or Jukun noko, and half the Nupe eba. Among the Igbira, the Agbigba
diviners also produce a quadruple figure marked on an "Ifa board" (Ifapako,
Ifa apako) through the manipulation of sixteen ayo or warri seeds (Caesal-
pinia crista) instead of palm nuts.

The order of the basic figures differs markedly from that of Ifa, but
their names are clearly related. Listing the figures in the order given by
an Agbigba diviner at Ifẹ, and numbering them according to the most common order for the figures of Ifa (Table 3, B, below, p. 48), the order for
Agbigba reads: 1, 2, 8, 7, 11, 12, 3, 4, 13, 14, 15, 16, 10, 9, 5, 6. Two figures have distinctive names, as in the case of Oyinkan for Ika and Qtaru
for Oturupọn; two have similar names, as Oji for Edi (which is also known
as Odi) and Osa for Qsa; some have identical names, as in the case of
Qyẹku, Qbara, Otura, Irẹtẹ, and Ofun; and some have identical alternate
names, as Oṣika or Ogbe, Ogori or Iwori, Qkọna or Qkanran, Orosun or
Irosun, Qga or Qwọnrin, Ogunta or Ogunda, and Qkin or Qṣẹ. The order of
the figures and the method of interpretation differ, but the similarity in the
names for these figures and in the apparatus as well suggests a historical
relationship with Ifa.

Agbigba among the Yoruba appears to be confined to the Yagba Yoruba,
a northeastern subgroup, although Yagba diviners practice in many Yoruba
cities. Four divining chains of this type are known as afa, aha, or efa
among the Ibo; as efa among the Ekoi; as ẹba among the Idoma; as ẹva
among the Isoko Edo; and as Ogwẹga among the Benin Edo, as well as by
obviously unrelated names in these and other Nigerian societies; but the
distribution of this method need not be detailed here. Suffice it to say that
it is known in parts of Northern Nigeria and as far east as the southern
part of what was the British Cameroons, and that Talbot (1926: II: 186)
concludes: "The Awpele system, but with four strings instead of two, and
with four pieces of each string composed generally of shells of the wild
mango (Irvingia Barteri), is in use over nearly the whole of Southern Nigeria."

The significance of these sixteen basic figures extends far beyond the
Yoruba and their neighbors. They are obtained in the Sikidy divination in
Malagasy either by the manipulation of seeds or by the widespread method
of "sand-cutting." The latter involves making a random number of marks
in the sand or dust, canceling them off two by two until only one or two
marks are left, and drawing a single or double line. In Sikidy, as in Ifa, a
double line is made if a single mark remains, while a single line is made
if two marks remain. Repeated four times, this procedure yields one of
the sixteen basic figures.

Sand-cutting is a widespread form of geomancy, practiced by many Is-
lamic groups in west and north Africa. Its similarities to the Dahomean
Fa and Yoruba Ifa have been noted by Fischer (1929: 67-73), Monteil (1932),
Trautman (1940), Schilde (1940: 100-164), Maupoil (1943: 49-51), Jaulin

(1966: 156-159), and others, citing analogues in Europe, Persia, and India. As early as 1864 Burton had noted similarities between the Dahomean Fa and the "geomancy of the Greeks, much cultivated by the Arabs under the name of Al-Raml, 'The sand,' because the figures were cast upon the desert floor. 'Napoleon's Book of Fate' is a notable specimen of European and modern vulgarization" (Burton, 1893: I, 222). Napoleon brought back to Europe a manuscript found in upper Egypt by M. Sonini in 1801, and it was subsequently published under this and other titles in a dozen or more editions from about 1820 to about 1925 (Napoleon, n.d.).

Among the Yoruba, sand-cutting (iyanrin titẹ) is practiced by Muslim diviners known as alufa. They speak of it as Hati Ramli, or "Atimi" in Yoruba, distinguishing it from Ifa. The names of the sixteen basic figures (Al Káusẹji, Aláhika, Utúba dahîla, etc.) clearly differ from those of Ifa but correspond to those given in the Arabic book of Mohammed Ez Zenati, and the order in which these figures were given by an alufa at Mẹkọ, himself a native of Zaria, is identical with that in which they are listed by Ez Zenati.[5] There can be no question of a historical relationship of Atimi with Islamic geomancy, but it is probably a recent introduction among the Yoruba, who were at war with their Muslim neighbors to the north throughout most of the last century. Again, listing the figures in the order recorded at Mẹkọ and numbering them according to the most common order for the figures of Ifa (Table 3, B), the order for Atimi reads: 14, 7, 10, 12, 1, 15, 11, 8, 5, 4, 3, 6, 9, 13, 16, 2. This is completely at variance with the orders of both Ifa and Agbigba divination.

Burton, Maupoil, and others have concluded that Fa and Sikidy are derived from Islamic geomancy or earlier non-African methods of divination. The purpose here is neither to deny a historic relation between the many modes of divination employing sixteen basic figures, nor to attempt to determine the ultimate origin of Ifa. These questions require far more data than are presently available. However, as other authors have stressed the similarities between the two methods, including the fact that the figures are "read" from right to left, some of the points of difference may be mentioned.

Among the Yoruba and the Nupe of Nigeria (Nadel, 1954: 57), the Sara of Chad (Jaulin, 1957: 45, fig. 1), the Teda of Tibetsi (Kronenberg, 1958: 147), and the Fulani of Macina (Monteil, 1932: 96, fig. 8), when canceling the random marks in sand-cutting, a single line is made if one mark remains and a double line if two remain; this is the opposite of Ifa and Sikidy. The sixteen basic figures have a very different order and completely different names. A quadruple figure is obtained (as in Agbigba), which is read crosswise to give a second quadruple figure, and additional figures are derived through further computations,[6] rather than interpreting a double figure as in the two halves of the Ifa divining chain. Ifa is not

---

5. Monteil (1932: 89-90). Beyioku (1940: 34-35) and Ogunbiyi (1952: 84-88) simply list the names in the order of the Ifa figures.

6. Cf. Nadel (1954: 54-61). The procedure is similar among the Yoruba.

A. *Opele*   B. *Noko*   C. *Agbigba*   D. *Eba*

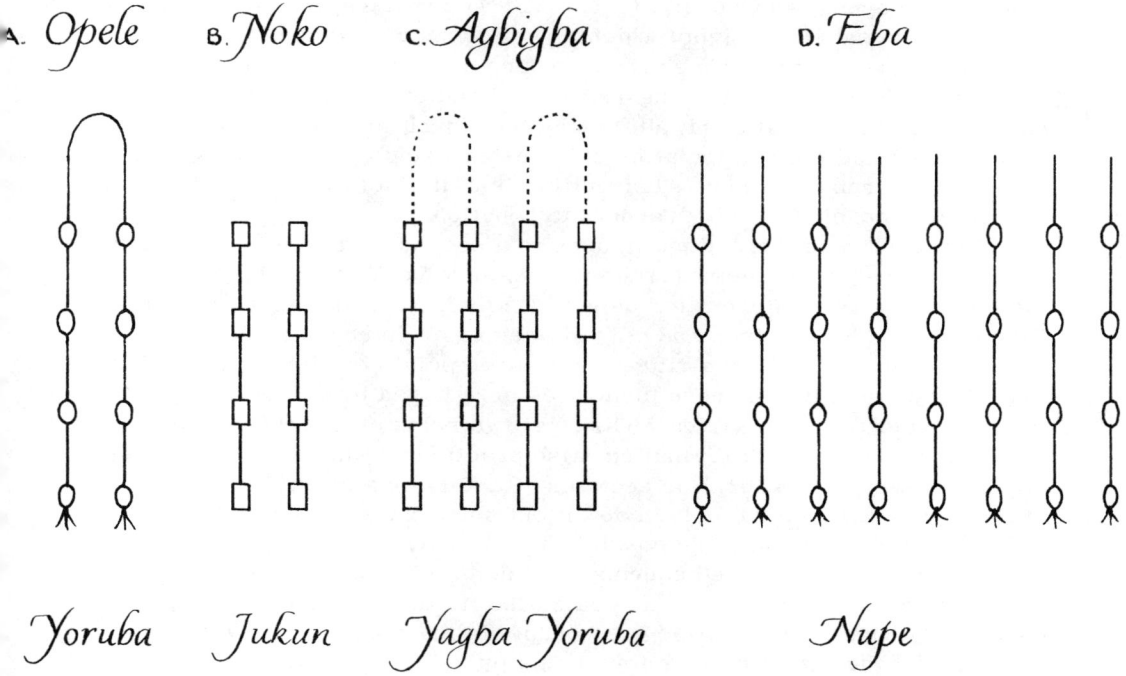

Yoruba   *Jukun*   *Yagba Yoruba*   *Nupe*

FIGURE 1. ỌPẸLẸ, NOKO, AGBIGBA, AND EBA

associated with astrology, as Burton first observed, but rather with a series of memorized verses and stories upon which their interpretation depends. Islamic geomancy has no verses, at least as practiced by alufa among the Yoruba, as Ogunbiyi (1952: 83-84) confirms; and he also states that it has no sacrifices (ẹbọ) which are of such importance in Ifa. The method of sand-cutting differs from tossing a chain or manipulating palm nuts; but it does involve the question of odd and even numbers, and it should be recalled that at Siwah, among the Gbari, and in Malagasy both sand-cutting and the manipulation of seeds are employed. This is also true among the Yoruba, but here sand-cutting is a distinct system of divination and in all probability a very recent introduction.

The identity of the sixteen figures is a necessary and inevitable derivative from three principles: (1) the figures involve four items; (2) each of them can take two different forms; and (3) their sequence is significant. Given these rules, sixteen and only sixteen basic figures are possible. Accordingly, this identity constitutes only three points of similarity, rather than sixteen, and two of these principles are shared by forms of divination that are widespread in Africa. The first two rules characterize the common African methods of divination, also practiced by the Yoruba, of casting four cowry shells, or four sections of a kola or a bitter kola nut. Each of these can fall face up or face down; but since the sequence is not controlled, only five figures are possible: 4, 3, 2, 1, or 0 facing up.

One might control the sequence in which four cowries are read by casting them one at a time. One could also tie them on a string, which is essentially what is done in the case of the Ifa divining chain. One might also control the sequence with four coins by using a penny, nickel, dime, and quarter, casting them all at once but reading the heads and tails in that order. In effect this is what is done in the Hakata divination of the Karanga, Zezeru, Korekore, and other Shona subgroups, some Bushmen groups, and the Venda, Ila, Tonga, Pedi, Leya, Rhodesian Ndebele, and other peoples in southern Africa. Here four pieces of bone or wood with distinguishing marks are identified as man, boy, woman, and girl and are read heads and tails in that order. Here again sixteen "figures" result, which can be equated with those marked with single and double lines.

The Chinese system of I Ching involves the second and third principles stated above, as well as figures composed of single and double lines. However, as it is based on three items rather than four, there are only eight basic figures or "trigrams" and sixty-four derivative figures or "hexagrams," whereas Ifa and the other African systems involve sixteen quadragrams and 256 derivative octagrams. The I Ching figures are obtained by tossing three coins, or by manipulating forty-nine yarrow stalks, which are counted off by fours in a manner somewhat reminiscent of Islamic sand-cutting (Wilhelm and Cary, 1951: I, 392-395). As far distant as Micronesia a system of knot divination, which is also based on counting off by fours, produces sixteen basic figures and 256 derivative figures (Lessa, 1959: 194-195).

Names related to those of the figures of Ifa are also employed for a different set of figures in still another Yoruba system of divination (owo mẹrindinlogun), in which sixteen cowries are cast on the ground. As in casting four cowries, n + 1 figures are possible because sequence is of no significance; in this case there are seventeen figures, with zero to sixteen cowries facing mouth up. Some of these are known by names of the basic Ifa figures, like Odi or Edi, Irosun, Qwọnrin, Qkanran, Ogunda, Qsa, Qṣẹ, and Ofun; and some have the names of the derivative figures, such as Eji Ogbe and Ogbeṣẹ (Ogbe Qṣẹ). Some of the names employed in this system are also used to designate the five figures derived from the cast of four cowries. As in Ifa the seventeen figures are associated with memorized verses which contain myths and folktales that aid in their interpretation. This method is regarded as a derivative from Ifa by many Yoruba, including the Ifa diviners, who cite a myth according to which the method is based on what the River Goddess Qṣun learned about divination while she was living with Ifa.

Of all the methods of divination employed by the Yoruba, Ifa is regarded as the most important and the most reliable. The honesty or knowledge of individual babalawo may be questioned, but most are highly esteemed, and the system itself is rarely doubted. The number of babalawo is a reflection of the patronage they receive and a measure of the influence they wield. In comparison there are only occasional Agbigba diviners among the Yoruba outside the Yagba area. Whereas Ifa is open to the public in the sense that the babalawo are consulted by the worshipers of any deity, divination with sixteen cowries is usually performed on ritual occasions within the cults of particular deities. This is also true of divination with four cowries, four sections of kola nuts, or four sections of bitter kola nuts; and these three methods are restricted in what they can forecast, primarily because they lack the verses associated with Ifa and the casting of sixteen cowries. Since the end of the Yoruba wars against their Muslim neighbors in the last century, the number of Muslim alufa has increased, but it still does not compare with the number of babalawo. Dreams and other omens are significant, but the babalawo or other diviners are usually consulted to interpret them; in recent years several dream books have been published. Utterances made while under possession by one of the deities are regarded as important, but possession is less widespread and less frequent than Ifa divination. Water-gazing and a few other methods of divination are also practiced by the Yoruba, but compared with Ifa they are of negligible significance.

The real core of Ifa divination lies in the thousands of memorized verses by means of which the 256 figures are interpreted, but their significance has not been fully appreciated. As for the working of the system of divination, these verses are of far greater importance than either the figures themselves or the manipulations from which they are derived. The verses form an important corpus of verbal art, including myths, folktales, praise names, incantations, songs, proverbs, and even riddles; but to the Yoruba their "literary" or aesthetic merit is secondary to their religious significance. In effect these verses constitute their unwritten scriptures.

The verses embody myths recounting the activities of the deities and justifying details of ritual, and they are often cited to settle a disputed

point of theology or ritual. A babalawo is expected to know a larger number
of verses than other Yoruba diviners, and he is accepted as an authority on
Yoruba religion. He is a professional whose business involves learning
about all the deities, not merely the one he himself worships. He functions
for the general public, and is consulted by the worshipers of the many different Yoruba deities as well as by many Muslim and Christian converts.

The babalawo constitutes a focal point in the traditional Yoruba religion,
channeling sacrifices and worshipers into different cults, recommending
sacrifices to the dead or means of dealing with witches and abiku (children
who do not wish to live), and preparing protective and retaliatory "medicines."
He helps his clients deal with the wide range of personalized and impersonal
forces in which the Yoruba believe, and to achieve the individual destinies
assigned to them at birth. An indication of the importance of Ifa to the religious system as a whole is the fact that the most striking religious syncre-
tisms resulting from European contact are to be found in a church established in Lagos in 1934, the Ijọ Qrunmila Adulawọ, which was founded on
the premise that the teachings of Ifa constitute the Yoruba Bible.

The rules of Ifa divination can be defined as precisely as those of the
simpler methods using four or sixteen cowries. In many other types of divination, in Africa and elsewhere, the subjective element in interpretation
leaves room for dispute, even among diviners. This would seem to be true
in the interpretation of the fall of bones or other divining objects in terms
of their relative positions, of the angles at which sticks protrude from holes
in joint bones into which they are inserted, of the designs of lines on shoulder
blades cracked by fire, of the conformation of the entrails of a fowl or animal, as well as of the patterns of tea leaves or lines of the palm. In crystal-
or water-gazing, where no one can confirm or contradict what the diviner
says he sees, and in shamanistic performances or states of possession,
where a familiar spirit or deity speaks to or through his medium only, interpretations are not subject to check either by the client himself or by other
diviners.

In contrast, the babalawo follow a regular system of rules, deviation
from which is criticized by their colleagues and condemned by their clients.
At least the elementary rules are understood by their regular patrons and,
even when they are not known, clients are provided with recognized tech-
niques to prevent a babalawo from departing from the rules in order to employ his personal knowledge of their affairs to his own or any one else's advantage. A client need not even reveal to the diviner the nature of the problem which prompts him to seek his advice. In view of this fact, some of the
early descriptions of Ifa are amusing reflections of the naïveté, prejudices,
and superstitions of the observers who recorded them.

II. PREVIOUS STUDIES

The two earliest known descriptions of Ifa divination among the Yoruba date from the same year. Speaking of the Yoruba deities, Tucker (1853: 33) says: "One of the principal of these is Ifa, the god of palm-nuts, to whom they ascribe the power of healing, and to whose priests they apply in times of sickness. On these occasions the friends of the sufferer procure a sheep or a goat for sacrifice, and send for the babbalawo or priest, who begins the ceremony by tracing a number of uncouth devices with chalk upon the wall. Then taking a calabash, he puts into it some cowries or some palm-nuts, and placing it in front of the figures he has made, performs his incantations, which are supposed to prevail on the god to enter the palm-nuts or the cowries. The sacrifice is then brought in, its throat is cut, and the priest sprinkles some of the blood on the calabash and on the wall. He then smears it across the sick man's forehead—thus, as they imagine, conveying the life of the creature into the patient."

Irving (1853: 233) says: "Ifá, the god of palm-nuts, or the god of divination, is said to be superior to all the rest. He is consulted on every undertaking—on going on a journey, entering into a speculation, going to war, or on a kidnapping expedition, in sickness, and, in short, wherever there is a doubt of the future. To him are dedicated palm-nuts, as by these the oracle is consulted. Various acts of adoration and prostration, touching the nuts with the forehead &c., initiate the performance. The babbalawo then, holding the nuts, sixteen in number, with the left hand, grasps as many as he can with the right, and according to the number—there are certain rules for this, of course—the answer is favourable or unfavourable: a tally is kept of these, and the result made known. Pieces of crockery-ware, &c., held by the bystanders, are also introduced in the process. If the responses be unfavourable, a sacrifice has to be made; and under these circumstances, it will be readily supposed the answer is very often so."

In view of later accounts, which so often repeat earlier errors, Irving's statement is remarkably accurate. The description of the manipulation of the sixteen palm nuts is correct; and the pieces of crockery held by bystanders are readily recognizable as a reference to the choice between specific alternatives, discussed in Chapter V.

Bowen (1857: 317), usually a good observer, reports only briefly: "The next and last órisha which I shall notice, is the great and universal honored Ifa, the revealer of secrets, and the guardian of marriage and child-birth. This god is consulted by means of sixteen palm nuts. The reason of this is not assigned, but sixteen persons founded Yóruba; the palm nut which they brought produced a tree with sixteen branches; and there is said to be a palm tree with sixteen branches on Mt. Adó, which is the residence of the chief priest of Ifa. The worship of Ifa is a mystery into which none but men are initiated. Neither have I been able to collect much information in regard to the nature of the idol or the ceremonies of his worship."

13

Later Bowen (1858: xvi) adds that Ifa "is called Banga, the god of palm-nuts." Banga means a "head" or bunch of fruit of the oil palm, but its use as a name for Ifa is not confirmed by informants; Dalziel (1937: 499) concurs: "the word does not seem to be so used at the present."

Campbell (1861: 75-76) says: "Ifa, one of their inferior deities, is much resorted to as an oracle. He has a numerous corps of priests, who realize great profit from the offerings made the god, to induce favorable responses. He is consulted by means of a sort of checkerboard, covered with wood-dust, on which the priest traces small squares. The party consulting the god hands him sixteen consecrated palm-nuts, which all the votaries of Ifa carry constantly. He throws them into a small urn, from which taking a few, the number being left to accident, he disposes them at random on the board, and from the order they assume, determines first whether the offering shall be a goat, a sheep, or otherwise; next he ascertains whether the god is satisfied with the offering; if not, he manipulates further to ascertain whether a pair of pigeons or fowls should not be added. The preliminaries being thus arranged, he enters into his business, all the time holding a free and easy conversation with the applicant, through which he is sure to ascertain the kind of responses most welcome."

This inaccurate description is paraphrased many years later by Stone (1899: 88-89), who disregarded what Burton, Baudin, and Ellis had contributed meanwhile: "All devotees of that god carry sixteen consecrated palm-nuts. The priest takes these nuts and puts them into a wooden urn. He then takes a number at random and scatters them at random on a board covered with wood-dust and marked into small squares. From the position that the palm-nuts take on the board, the priest pretends to find out what kind of a sacrifice Efa demands. This ceremony is repeated to find out if a chicken or something else must not be added to the first thing to be offered as a sacrifice. The priest in the meantime talks to the person consulting the oracle and finds out pretty well what kind of answer is desired. Sometimes the applicant wishes him to interpret a dream or to assist him in a business or a matrimonial enterprise. Priests of Efa are very numerous and they rob people of much of their income."

What might be called the "standard" version of Ifa divination, as given most recently by Abraham (1958) and Lucas (1949), goes back through Farrow (1926) and Dennett (1910) to J. Johnson (1899), and before that through Ellis (1894) to Baudin (1885) and to Burton's works on Dahomey (1864) and the Yoruba (1863).

Burton (1863: I, 189-190), after paraphrasing Bowen, adds: "The priests are known by their bead necklaces, small strings twisted together, with ten large white and green beads, some inches apart. They officiate in white, and constantly use a fly-whisk. Their deity being called Bángá, God of Palm-nuts, they choose as his symbols those that are placental with four holes. The operation of casting lots is intricate, and is variously described by different observers: odd and even, and 'heads or tails,' appear to be the ruling principles.

"The priest brings his nuts in a rhinoceros horn from the upper country. Holding the sixteen in his left hand, he takes them up at random—as we do at a 'bean club'—in his right, and the operation is repeated till either

two, called 'ofu,' or one, called 'ossa,' remains. The chosen nut is then
rolled, with the middle finger, over the earth, or over a board whitened
with the dust made by tree-worms. Finally, it is marked with certain lines,
which, by deciding the value and the nature of sacrifice, procure success.

"An old converted priest thus performed the ceremony in my presence.
He counted sixteen nuts, freed them from dust, and placed them in a bowl
on the ground, full of yam half boiled, crushed, and covered with some ac-
rid vegetable infusion. His acolyte, a small boy, was then called, made to
squat near the bowl, resting his body on the outer edge of the feet, which
were turned inwards, and to take from the fetish-man two or three bones,
seeds, and shells, some of which are good, others of bad omen. Elevating
them, he rested his hands upon his knees. The adept cast the nuts from
one hand to the other, retaining some in the left, and while manipulating
dropped others into the bowl. He then stooped down, drew with the index
and the medius lines on the yam, inspected the nuts, and occasionally referred to the articles in the boy's hand. Thus he was enabled to pronounce
an opinion upon what was to happen.

"I cannot flatter myself that the modus operandi has been made quite
intelligible to the reader, for the best of reasons—I do not quite understand it myself. The system is far more simple in Dahomey, and at some
future time I may explain it."

This Burton did in the following year, explaining in a footnote that
"When fate is consulted the 16 nuts are thrown from the right hand to the
left; if one is left behind, the priest marks two; if two, one (the contrary
may be the case, as in European and Asiatic geomancy); and thus the sixteen parents are formed" (Burton, 1893: I, 220). Burton was the first to
record the figures of Fa and their names (in Fǫn), referring to the paired
figures as the sixteen "mothers" and to the combinations as their children;
but there is no evidence that the Dahomean Fa is simpler than the Yoruba
Ifa.

Baudin (1885: 32-35) paraphrases Bowen and then adds several Ifa
myths and other data of his own: "When they wish to consult fate or to
make a grand ceremonious feast in honor of Ifa in the grove sacred to this
god, the mother or wife of him for whom the god is consulted carries in a
cloth on her back the sixteen sacred nuts, and the fetich-priest before com-
mencing the ceremony salutes Orungan and his wife, saying, Orungan ajuba
ô! ('Orungan, I salute you.') Orichabii ajuba ô! ('Orichabii, I salute you.')

"Then he offers sacrifice to Ifa, of which the dates[1] are the symbol.
Finally he places before the god a small board on which are marked sixteen
figures, each having a certain number of points. These figures are very
similar to playing-cards used by fortune-tellers. The fetich-priests use
them in almost the same way, bringing out at will good or bad fortune according as they deem it expedient to better dupe the fool who comes to consult them. When he has found the desired figure, he begins to explain
whether the enterprise in question will succeed or not, the sacrifices to be

---

1. This is an error of the translator; Baudin (1884: 224) gives palm
nuts (noix de palme) in the original.

offered, the things to be avoided. It is well understood that the higher the
price paid the greater the inspiration of the fetich-priest, for there are
large and small games.

"Ifa is the most venerated of all the gods; his oracle is the most consulted, and his numerous priests form the first sacerdotal order. They
are always dressed in white, and shave the head and the body."

Bouche (1885: 120) treats divination briefly: "Ifa est l'oricha des
sorts et de la divination. Ses prêtres sont des devins: on les appelle babbalawo, pères du secret, du mystère (awo). Ifa est né, comme Chango,
dans la ville d'Ifè. Il a reçu le surnom de Banga ou fétich des amandes de
palme, parce que les babbalawos se servent ordinairement dans leurs
pratiques de divination de seize amandes de palme qu'ils jettent à terre.
Ils augurent par la position dans laquelle tombent ces amandes."

Teilhard de Chardin (1888: 158) gives an abbreviated account of Ifa
based on Baudin and Burton: "La consultation a lieu au moyen de seize
noix de palme, et d'une planchette sur les deux faces de laquelles sont
marqués seize figures ayant chacune leur nom, leur symbole, et un certain
nombre de points. La réponse plus ou moins favorable dépend de certaines
combinaisons des points et des signes, obtenues par le féticheur en jetant
les noix d'une certaine façon. En règle générale, plus les honoraires sont
forts, plus favorable est l'oracle."

Ellis (1894: 56-64) copies without acknowledgment most of what
Baudin, Burton, and Bowen have said. Of the divination itself he says: "For
the consultation of Ifa a whitened board is employed, exactly similar to
those used by children in Moslem schools in lieu of slates, about two feet
long and eight or nine inches broad, on which are marked sixteen figures.
These figures are called 'mothers.' The sixteen palm-nuts are held loosely
in the right hand, and thrown through the half-closed fingers into the left
hand. If one nut remains in the right hand, two marks are made, thus ‖;
and if two remain, one mark, |. [Footnote: This process is repeated eight
times, and the marks are made in succession in two columns of four each.]
In this way are formed the sixteen 'mothers,' one of which is declared by
the babalawo to represent the inquirer, and from the order in which the others are produced he deduces certain results. The interpretation appears to
be in accordance with established rule, but what that rule is is only known
to the initiated. . . . From these sixteen 'mothers' a great many combinations can be made by taking a column from two different 'mothers,' and the
figures thus formed are called 'children.'"

Cole (1898), a Sierra Leone Yoruba, discusses Ifa in a work which I
have never been able to locate but which is quoted in Dennett (1906: 269-
271); the quotation is based on Ellis (1894: 58-59) and ultimately on Baudin
(1885: 33-35).

J. Johnson's work, published both in Yoruba (1899a) and in English
translation (1899b), is important as the first independent account of Ifa divination by a Yoruba author, which has been frequently quoted by subsequent
writers. It is also important because he is the first to record the Yoruba
names and order of the Ifa figures, though the figures themselves are not
represented; and he is the first to note the use of the divining chain and the

importance of the Ifa verses or "stories." Both publications are extremely
rare, but very useful extracts from the English edition are included in
Dennett (1906: 243-269). The passages of greatest relevance to the method
of divination are quoted below:

"The great Oracle of the Yoruba country is Ifa. He is represented
chiefly by 16 palm nuts each having from four to 10 or more eyelets on
them. Behind each one of these representative nuts are 16 subordinate Divinities. Each one of the whole lot is termed an Odù — which means a chief,
a head. This makes the number of Odùs altogether 256. Besides these,
there are 16 other Odùs connected with each of the 256, and this makes the
whole number of Odùs 4,096. Some increase this large number still by an
addition of 16 more to each of the last number of Odùs, but the 16 principal
ones are those most frequently in requisition.

"There is a series of traditional stories, each of which is called a road,
a pathway, or a course, and is connected with some particular Odù. Each
Odù is supposed to have 1,680 of these stories connected with it, and these,
together with those of the other Odùs, every one aspiring to the office of 'A
Babalawo,' who is a divining or sacrificing priest, is expected to commit to
memory, though scarcely has any one been found to perform the feat. Many
learn by heart a very considerable number, rather an appreciable number
connected with the principal Odùs. Upon the appearance of an Odù on the divining or consulting bowl, the 'Babalawo' thinks of some of the stories attached
to it, and from any of them that appears to him to suit the case upon which
he is consulted, he delivers his Oracular response, and prescribes the sacrifice that would be accepted" (Dennett, 1906: 246-247).

"Divination is taken by a Babalawo on a highly esteemed broad circular
bowl or four cornered fan of a moderate size, which is generally covered
with white flour from a dry tree, and upon which he works, and with one of
the fingers of the right hand imprints certain signs, representing such Ifa
representatives as may be left on the palm of his left hand, after he has attempted with one grasp of the palm of his right hand to take up all the 16,
where they were all held. These small signs or marks which would represent a number of efforts, and would be placed one after another horizontally
would, according to their number and respective positions, represent one
or the other of the principal or subordinate Odùs, or Divinities. From that
Odù or Divinity, and one or other of the traditional stories connected with
it, and with the aid of lot casting and of Ọpèlè, divination is taken and de-
livered" (Dennett, 1906: 249).

"Ọpèlè, or Ọpẹpẹrẹ, is an Oracle of inferior rank to Ifa, and who is
regarded as his constant attendant and is commonly spoken of as his slave.
He is always represented by eight flat pieces of wood, or metal, or something else, strung together in two rows of four on each side, placed at equal
distances from each other and joined together. The disposition of one or
other of these pieces when the whole ensign is thrown and made to spread
out upon the ground would represent at once a particular Odù, and one of
Ọpèlè's chief duties is to show to the Babalawo what particular Odù he
should consult upon a case referred to him.

"Ọpẹlẹ is often and frequently thus independently consulted by Babala-wos, who usually carry about them its ensigns, because, consulting it carries with it less labour than, and is not so difficult as the work of consulting the Master, Ifa himself; but this would be on matters of minor importance, and its response would be that of a servant for his master, and which is not always absolutely relied upon" (Dennett, 1906: 250-251).

In his own work on the Yoruba, Dennett (1910: 146-150) quotes, rather than simply repeating without acknowledgment, from Ellis, J. Johnson, and others on the method of divination, adding no new information except for his own list of the names of the figures, which he compares with those of earlier writers.

Frobenius appears to be the first to have recorded the figures of Ifa, as well as their names and order, for the Yoruba, ascribing them to the "Central Yoruba," by which he apparently means Ibadan. His description of the divination process follows that of Ellis, J. Johnson, and Burton. Quoting from the English translation (1913: I, 244) of his work, he says that after strewing finely powdered wood upon the divining tray, "The odd or even number of nuts[2] caught up in falling is recorded in a series of double or single lines, marked on the flour, four of which make up an Odu." This is later amplified by a passage, part of which is confusing both in English and in the German original: "He strews white flour on it, takes all the seeds and throws them up towards his left hand, in which he catches some of them. If the number caught is odd, two vertical lines are drawn thus: ||. If even, a single line is drawn with the right hand finger thus: |. Four throws are made and the marks placed beneath each other. The resulting figure of four such signs is called 'Medji,' or a 'pair'. This proceeding is repeated eight times, so that two Medjis are always marked next to, and also 4 x 2 above, each other. [Achtmal wird dies Verfahren wiederholt, und zwar werden immer zwei Medji nebeneinander, also 4 x 2 untereinander, gezeichnet.] The numbers so noted are the Odus, laid out before the oracle for the day. The picture so drawn upon the flour is read from right to left. . . . Each Medji stands for one Odu, assumed to consist of sixteen Odus, each of which is again composed of sixteen and so on" (Frobenius, 1913: I, 251-252; 1912-1913: I, 280).

"And, lastly, there is the Oquelle. This is a string connecting eight halved palm-nuts,[3] and its ends are usually prettily tasselled with beads. The High Priest at Ifé had one with yellow nut-pieces in place of the halved nuts, and would-be adepts in divination mainly used an Oquelle in which pieces of gourd were substituted for the palm-seeds. In fortune-telling by the Oquelle, it is taken by the middle, so that four of the nuts hang down on either side. When it falls, an Odu or figure is formed by the number of convex and concave positions assumed" (Frobenius, 1913: I, 250).

---

2. The original says kernels (Kerne). Frobenius (1912-1913: I, 271-280) repeatedly says this, palm kernels (Palmkerne), or Ifa kernels (Ifa-kerne), and only occasionally palm nuts (Palmnüsse).

3. The original again says palm kernels (Palmkerne). Frobenius (1912-1913: I, 278).

"The foundation of the prophecies alone is said to consist of no less than one thousand six hundred and eighty dicta for each of the four thousand and ninety-six different Odus. Of course, no one can remember such an enormous total and, as a prophecy in question naturally depends upon the various positions of the different Odus, there is an absolute freedom of interpretation of this which is no less mysterious than the Pythian or Ammonite Oracle" (Frobenius, 1913: I, 246).

Wyndham (1919: 151-152; 1921: 65-67) gives a brief, but independent description of the method of divination. Ifa's "priests (called Babaláwo) profit considerably by divination, which they perform with sand on a circular board, or with a charm called Okpéllè. Okpéllè consists of eight pieces of bark on a string. These eight are arranged in fours. Each of the pieces of bark may fall either with the outside or the inside showing. Consequently each set of four may fall in sixteen different ways, having different names and meanings." Wyndham then lists these sixteen figures and their names, the names of the sixteen paired figures, or "Messengers of Ífa" and discusses the combinations: "These combinations are called children of the Messenger who appears on the right. Thus, Ogbe Yeku is a child of Ogbe; Oyeku Logbe is a child of Oyeku. From this it will be seen that Okpéllè can show 256 combinations.

"Procedure. — A man comes to a Babaláwo to consult Ífa. He places a gift of cowries (to which he has whispered his needs) before the Babaláwo. The latter takes Okpéllè and places it on the cowries. He then says, 'You, Okpéllè, know what this man said to the cowries. Now tell me.' He then lifts Okpéllè and lays it on the floor. From the messenger or child which appears the Babaláwo is supposed to deduce that his client wants a son, has stolen a goat, or has a toothache, as the case may be. He then tells him what he must bring as a sacrifice to achieve his ends."

S. Johnson (1921: 33) describes the method very briefly. "To consult Ifa, in the more common and ordinary way, 16 palm nuts are to be shaken together in the hollow of both hands, whilst certain marks are traced with the index finger on a flat bowl dusted with yam flour, or powdered camwood. Each mark suggests to the consulting priest the heroic deeds of some fabulous heroes, which he duly recounts, and so he goes on with the marks in order, until he hits upon certain words or phrases which appear to bear upon the matter of the applicant before him."

Meek (1925: II, 69-70) gives a less accurate account: "Ifa can be approached through his priests on certain days. The god uses as his medium sixteen strings of palm-kernels, which have been consecrated to his use by certain elaborate rites. Each string represents some minor divinity and has sixteen kernels attached to it — the total number of kernels being thus 256. With the kernels are associated a great many stories of the gods, and according to the combination of the number of kernels, after they have been passed through the hand, so is the priest able to apply these various tales to the case in point."

Talbot (1926: II, 185-186) draws mainly on J. Johnson: "The actual divining is practised with the help of sixteen palm nuts from the Awpe-Ifa tree, each of which usually possesses four or more eyelets. Everyone of

these palm nuts represents sixteen subordinate powers, called Odu, and
each of these latter another sixteen . . . . All are associated with parables
or traditional stories with which the Babalawo is supposed to be acquainted.
A whitened, flat and generally circular wooden bowl or platter, sometimes
finely carved, called Opon-Ifa, is used by the diviner, who makes on it certain marks in accordance with the number of nuts remaining in his left
palm after he has seized as many as he can hold in his right. This action
is repeated eight times, so that a very large number of combinations and
permutations is possible. Each grouping has its appropriate story, decoded
or translated by the priest into the awaited response.

   "Ifa, however, cannot be consulted unless the counsel of an inferior
oracle, called Awpele or Awpepere, who is regarded as his attendant, is
first taken. This is represented by eight pieces of wood, metal, bone or
calabash, which are strung loosely together in two rows, and involves
much less thought and knowledge than the first method. The answer depends
upon the disposition and the number of the various pieces which fall face up-
wards, when the two strings are flung upon the ground. Awpele is, however,
consulted only on minor matters and by anyone who has learnt the procedure
from the Babalawo."

   Farrow (1926: 38-39) draws on both Ellis and J. Johnson: "In consulting the oracle, the babalawo uses sixteen palm-nuts, from a special palm-
tree (the Opelifa), and a divining bowl, i.e. an engraved circular board, or a
rectangular one, with a handle, similar to a Mohammedan writing tablet . . . .
Sometimes a fan is used, of a square shape. This divining bowl is called
Opon-Ifa. Its surface is covered with white flour (iyerosu), or dust, from
the irosu tree. Upon this the priest works, and with one of the fingers of
the right hand imprints certain signs, to indicate such Ifa representatives
as may be left in the palm of his left hand, after he has attempted with one
grasp of the palm of his right hand to take up all the sixteen nuts which were
held therein. Or, he may hold these sixteen nuts loosely in the right hand
and throw them through his half-closed fingers into the left hand. If two
nuts remain in the right hand, he makes one mark, thus |, on the board; but
if only one remains, he makes two such marks, ||. This process is repeated
eight times, and the marks are made in two columns of four each. The complicated nature of this process is shown by the fact that behind each of the
sixteen nuts are sixteen subordinate deities. Each such deity is termed an
Odu, i.e. a 'chief' or 'head.' There are thus $16 \times 16 = 256$ leading Odus,
and each of these 256 has 16 subordinates again, bringing the total number
of Odus to 4096. Some increase this again by multiplying each of these by
16 lesser subordinates! Add to these figures the fact that in the 8 throwings, or drawings, of the 16 nuts, there is a possibility of a vast number of
different results, and that in connection with each Odu there are supposed
to be 1680 traditional stories, each of which is represented by a brief cou-
plet, which must be memorized, and it will be seen that the task of a babalawo is no light one, even if he confines his attention, as is usually the case,
to the 16 principal Odus. Most babalawos commit to memory a large number of the couplets, or stories in brief, connected with each of the principal
ones. Then, when an Odu appears on the consulting bowl, the diviner thinks

of the most appropriate story attached to it, suitable to the case about
which he is consulted, and so gives the oracular response and prescribes
the appropriate sacrifice.

"Opele is the name of a lesser oracle, who is regarded as a messenger
of Ifa. He is represented by eight small laths of wood, and as it is a far
easier task to consult him, the babalawos do so each day and in all lesser
causes" (Farrow, 1926: 42).

Southon (n.d., c. 1931: 25-26) draws primarily on Farrow: "Removing
the cloth before the wonder-filled eyes of Adebiyi, Fatosin revealed an
elaborately carved calabash. Opening the top of this, the priest put his
hand inside and brought it out again with several small oblongs of ivory
loosely clasped within it. Shaking these through his partly opened fingers,
so that they fell upon the ground within the circle of light thrown by a hur-
ricane lamp, Fatosin stooped and studied the carved markings upon the
various ivory 'nuts'. The side of his divining bowl had been dusted with
white powder from the sacred tree used for the purpose, and the Babalawo
now made a mark upon the dust with his finger. Again the ivory nuts were
shaken out, and the marks noted, with a second mark placed upon the divining bowl. Eight times in all, to fulfil the prescribed number, Fatosin cast
his ivory nuts. Then he noted carefully the marks he had placed upon the
bowl, and behind his impassive face worked out a complicated sum involving a prodigious feat of memory.

"There were sixteen ivory nuts, each called an 'Odu' or chief, each of
which has a subordinate deity, each of these again having an attendant deity
of its own, making a total of over 4,000 Odus. Attaching to each of these
Odus is a brief story or parable, which every Babalawo is supposed to learn
and be able to quote.

"The casting of the ivory nuts eight times resulted in fixing one of thousands of possible numbers. Fatosin's task now was to work out the exact
number which was indicated by the throw of the nuts, and to recall the story
associated with that number, for this was the answer of Ifa to Adebiyi's request for help."

Delano (1937: 178-179) gives a brief independent account: "'Ifa' priests
are called 'Babalawos.' Their work is difficult and they must possess a
very powerful and retentive memory. There are numberless recitals, dealing with every sphere of life, which they have to memorize by listening to
a senior 'Babalawo.' These recitals are called 'Odu.' Inasmuch as human
ailments, human anxieties and human goodness vary, and are numberless,
so there has not been a single 'Babalawo' who could cover the whole sphere
of 'Ifa.' Every sphere of life has an 'Odu' applicable to it. . . .

"When a child is sick and the parents go to a 'Babalawo' to find out the
cause of the illness and its remedy, they appear before him without the
child and without telling him the cause of their anxiety. When he is asked
to be consulted there is no fee payable. He takes out his 'Ifa.' looks at the
parents, and begins the recitals while he throws the 'Opele' and makes
signs and impressions with his hand on the sand before him. 'Opele' is the
guidance by which he arrives at his deductions. Then he looks up and tells
the parents that the child is sick. Again he looks up and says: 'It is ap-
pendicitis,' or whatever the sickness is."

Price (1939: 134), who served as District Officer in Ifẹ, gives another brief, independent account of the babalawo: "They learned to read omens and give advice to clients from far and near regarding their future. I cannot vouch for the accuracy of these prophets, but I have watched them at work. They use a round wooden platter decorated with carvings at the edge, on which is evenly sprinkled a layer of sand, and sixteen palm-nuts, half of which have four natural holes in them, while the other half only have three. Some of these are shaken like dice and thrown on the ground. In accordance with the way they fall, certain marks are made in the sand with the priest's fingers. After several repetitions of this, he reads the final pattern on the platter and discloses its meaning as regards the question on which he is being consulted. It takes years of hard study to become an efficient babalawo; there being, it is said, ninety-nine degrees to pass before reaching the highest rank." Later he repeats, "The palm-nuts are then shaken and thrown down, just as dice are thrown, and the verdict is read from the way they fall" (Price, 1939: 138-139).

Clarke (1939: 239-252) describes four consultations with diviners which he witnessed, one with palm nuts and three with the divining chain, in addition to giving the figures of Ifa and two listings of their names. Earlier sources are cited, but this is an independent and important account. The divining chain and its use are correctly described, and the choice between specific alternatives "called igbigbo or Obtaining the Ibo" is noted. In using the divining nuts, the diviner took a divination tray and "sprinkled upon it some powder obtained from a tree called Irosun (Baphia nitida). Then, after throwing sixteen palm-kernels from the right to the left hand, he had two kernels remaining in his right hand, so with the second finger of his right hand he pressed one mark in the powder on the right-hand side of the tray. Then he again threw the nuts from the right to the left hand and, having one nut remaining, he made a double mark with his first and second fingers on the left-hand side of the tray. This he repeated eight times in all, always making the marks first on the right hand and then on the left of the tray. In this way he obtained a pattern on the tray which corresponded to the patterns made by the Ọpẹlẹ — two rows of four things — in this case double or single marks instead of concave or convex pods" (Clarke, 1939: 240).

Since that time there have been several brief accounts by myself (1941; 1942; 1943; 1944: 25-29; 1952; 1961; 1966); a recapitulation of Farrow by Lucas (1948: 75-79); accounts by Parrinder (1949: 152-161; 1953: 31-36; 1954: 119-120; 1961: 137-147) and Abraham (1958: 275-276), who draws on Lucas and other sources; Idowu's work (1962), which says little about divination but cites thirty-one Ifa verses; and articles by Prince (1963) and McClelland (1966). Over the years there has also developed a significant body of literature in the Yoruba language by authors such as Lijadu, Epega, Ogunbiyi, Şowande, and others cited in the bibliography and in Bascom (1961: 681-682). Most of these say little about the technique of divination, which they tend to take for granted, but they are very important because of the many Ifa verses which they record. Unfortunately many of them are ephemera, locally published, and are not widely available for scholarly research.

Meanwhile, a number of studies were being made in Dahomey and Togo. Following Burton (1864) there were the works of Skertchly (1874), Grandin (1895), Spieth (1911) for the Ewe, Le Herisse (1911), Monteil (1931), Quenum (1935), Gorer (1935), Bertho (1936), Herskovits (1938), Trautman (1940), the monumental work by Maupoil (1943), Alapini (1950), Garnier and Fralon (1951) for the Ewe, and a collection of Fa myths in Herskovits and Herskovits (1958). There were errors and repetitions in these works also, but they include a number of important, independent studies. Several drew on published accounts of Ifa divination among the Yoruba; but the related studies among the Yoruba have seldom paid attention to the Dahomean sources except for Burton, whose account is the earliest.

The essentials of the method of divination have been described in the earlier literature, but a number of discrepancies remain to be sorted out. The tedious repetitions in these previous accounts, many of which have been excluded here, show how often prior accounts have been repeated or paraphrased, usually without acknowledgment. The number of times that a statement is made is no measure of its reliability, as in the case of the 16 x 4096 figures and the 1680 verses for each figure, for which there is no indication of any independent verification by subsequent writers of J. Johnson's original statement.

Most of the discrepancies will be dealt with later in the discussions of divining apparatus and procedure, but a few can be resolved here. The statements of Campbell, Stone, Bouche, Southon, and Price that the palm nuts are scattered at random on the divining tray or tossed on the ground and their positions then interpreted, which suggests East African divining bones, is inaccurate. The manipulation of the nuts as given by Meek, Farrow, Southon, Lucas, and Abraham derives from Ellis, who says that they are "thrown through the half-closed fingers," whereas other writers from Burton to Clarke speak only of throwing the palm nuts from one hand to another. Most accurate is the description of J. Johnson, who says that the diviner attempts "with one grasp of the palm of his right hand to take up all the 16."

Baudin's description of the client's wife or mother carrying the palm nuts on her back to the diviner, though repeated by Ellis and Farrow, is not confirmed by subsequent writers and was denied by informants; nor do all devotees of Ifa carry their consecrated palm nuts constantly, as Campbell and Stone maintain. Though a sheep or a goat may be required as a sacrifice, these and other items are not brought in advance, as Tucker and Southon state; the purpose of divination is to determine the nature of the sacrifice which will ensure a blessing or avert an impending misfortune.

References to the use of a Muslim "slate" (wala) as a divining tray stem from Ellis' misinterpretation of Burton's account (1893: I, 220-222), which at no point states it was so employed. What Burton describes is one of the carved tablets or the calendars employed in Dahomey as shown by Maupoil (1943: 209-218); although their origin is ascribed to Ifẹ, they have not been reported for the Yoruba. Statements that sixteen figures are permanently marked on the divining tray also derive from Burton's description of these Dahomean calendars. Campbell's description of the divining tray as a checkerboard is inaccurate, as is Stone's statement that it is a board covered with wood dust and marked into small squares. Tucker's description of marks made on the wall can refer only to protective medicine made by the diviners (see Chapter VI), and not to the method of divination.

Suspicion of the diviners and skepticism of their methods appear in many of these accounts, and several explanations are offered of the manner in which they arrive at their "predictions." Frobenius maintains that the diviner has an absolute freedom of interpretation of the various positions of the different Odu. Baudin compares the method to fortune telling with playing cards, by which the diviners bring out "at will good or bad fortune according as they deem it expedient to better dupe the fool who comes to consult them." Campbell and Stone state that the diviner talks to the client to find out the kind of answer he would like to hear. None of these statements is correct.

Southon (n.d.: 23-25) offers his readers the choice of two inaccurate explanations: "Neither Fatosin nor his teachers had ever heard the word 'psychology,' but they understood very clearly what the word connotes. To be successful in his chosen calling, and by means of it to rise to wealth and power, he had to understand the minds and hearts of those who come to him in their need. Through assiduous practice and close observation Fatosin could read the minds of those who came to him as clearly as one could read a printed page, and played upon their hopes and fears with the skilled touch of a master of men.

"Such was the priest—half-convinced of the possession of the powers he claimed, half-charlatan—to whom the simple Adebiyi came in her desperate need. . . . Fatosin greeted her in a cold, level voice, which somehow made the difference between them seem still vaster, and asked her what she desired that she sought him at this hour. . . . Adebiyi came at last to her tale of the sick Abiodun, and her belief that 'a worm was eating into his head,' put there by the magic employed by an unknown enemy. . . . A few questions about the beginning and history of Abiodun's sickness told the astute priest that Abiodun was suffering from nothing more serious than a bad attack of fever, which his herbs could swiftly relieve. . . ."

Wyndham seems to have been the first to state that the client does not reveal his question to the diviner, who is expected to learn it for himself through divination, though he does not suggest how this is done. Delano (1937: 179), who also realized this, offers a somewhat mystical explanation: "It is wonderful how a 'Babalawo' finds out the germ of the matter brought to him. The connections in life, the similarities in nature, and the commonness in humanity are what he puts together, and from them he makes a correct deduction." Gorer (1935: 197-198), who records that in Dahomey the client whispers his request "as quietly as he can" to a palm nut, says of the Fa diviners (bokonon): "I do not think the bokonon are on the whole conscious cheats; it seems to me more probable that they have a hypertrophied sense of hearing, such as is not uncommon with 'telepathic mediums,' and possibly unconsciously overhear the whispered request to the lucky palm nut."

Parrinder (1961: 137) offers much the same explanations: "The secrets of diviners are closely guarded, and it is difficult to tell the extent
and manner of their knowledge. They maintain, and some serious writers
believe them, that they have esoteric secrets of which modern science is
ignorant. It is certain that they sometimes seem to gain knowledge of people's deeds, or the whereabouts of their lost or stolen goods, by methods
which are not easily explicable. Some would say that they have secret
agents to listen to village gossip and watch suspected people; others claim
that they practise telepathy and have powers of prevision." In the first edition of this work, the final sentence is less noncommital: "There is need of
careful investigations into the phenomena of telepathy, prevision, and spir-
itualism" (Parrinder, 1949: 152).

Clarke (1939: 251) concludes: "If they are honest, we must exclude the
hypothesis that, through their associates, they inquire into the affairs of
their clients and thus know the probable subject of an enquiry and are enabled to prescribe the measures which should be taken. Perhaps, either by
means of telepathy or, as has been suggested, by means of some hyper-
aesthesia, the Babalawo may know consciously or unconsciously what the
enquirer has whispered to the Ọpẹlẹ." A less mystical explanation, which
has been suggested earlier (Bascom, 1941: 51-52), will be given in Chapter
VII; but before we leave the earlier accounts, it is worth noting that according to J. Johnson, S. Johnson, Meek, Farrow, and Lucas, the appropriate
verse is selected by the diviner.

III. THE APPARATUS OF IFA DIVINATION AND THE PRELIMINARY INVOCATIONS

This chapter is concerned with the palm nuts and the divining chain; the bags, plates, cups, and bowls in which these are kept; and the tray, the powder, and the bell used in divination. It concludes with a description of the morning invocation that precedes the first divination each day. The diviner's cow-tail switch and other materials that serve primarily as insignia of status or as ritual paraphernalia are discussed briefly in Chapters X and XI. In divining with either the palm nuts or the chain, the diviner is seated on a mat (ẹni); and Epega (n.d.: I, 77) records a verse from Otura Meji which accounts for this usage. However, as any kind of mat will serve, it requires no special description.

The Palm Nuts (ikin)

Sixteen palm nuts are the most important objects employed in Ifa divination, and in Ifa ritual as well. They also distinguish Ifa divination from other systems using different numbers or other kinds of seeds, from Agbigba, sand-cutting, and other systems of divination in which the same sixteen basic figures are employed. Ritually, the sixteen palm nuts symbolize Ifa as the God of Divination, as the prehistoric celts or "thunder stones" symbolize Şango, the God of Thunder. As sacrifices to Şango are offered to these celts, so sacrifices to Ifa are offered to his sixteen palm nuts. In divination, ritual, and myth, Ifa is associated with a special variety of the oil palm.

The oil palm (ọpẹ) or <u>Elaeis guineensis</u> bears fruit (ẹyin) in large bunches (idi ẹyin, banga); each fruit consists of a palm nut covered with a reddish-orange pericarp from which palm oil (epo) is extracted for cooking and for export. The nuts (ekurọ) themselves are about an inch long, ovoid or egg-shaped, with hard black shells marked with lengthwise grooves. Inside are white kernels which are exported and from which the Yoruba extracted palm kernel oil (adin, adi) for making soap and other purposes. Frobenius to the contrary, palm kernels are not used in place of palm nuts. Both palm nuts and palm kernels are ordinarily known as ekurọ, but the palm nuts used in Ifa divination are distinguished by a special term (ikin, iki, ẹkẹn). They are sometimes referred to as the palm nuts of Ifa (ikin Ifa), and the tree from which they come is called the oil palm of Ifa (ọpẹ Ifa) or the oil palm of ikin (ọpẹ ikin).

Dalziel[1] lists this as a distinct botanical variety (<u>Elaeis guineensis idolatrica</u>) known as the King Palm, Juju Palm, Tabu Palm, and Palmier Fetiche; he says that it is easily recognizable by its half-furled leaves,

---

1. Dalziel (1937: 501). This book is the best source available for the botanical identification of Yoruba terms; identifications are based on it unless otherwise indicated. It should be noted that Dalziel's orthography differs from that used here. He gives ĕ (ẹ), ŏ (ọ), and sh (ş).

and its foliage is usually darker and less drooping than in the common
types. An Ilara diviner said that its leaves all are straight and point
upward because they are "folded," which makes them stiff. He added that
if the fruit from this tree is mixed with ordinary fruit in making palm oil,
the oil will be spoiled, because it mixes with the water instead of rising to
the surface; when this happens, they know that there is at least one ikin
among the palm nuts. It is with reference to this that informants say that
Ifa's palm nuts are not eaten.

Some Ifẹ diviners maintained that only nuts with four or more indenta-
tions or "eyes" (oju) at their bases can be used for divination or for ritual
purposes, and that those with three eyes are unacceptable to Ifa. One of
the Ifa verses (175-2) recorded in Ifẹ accounts for the four eyes on Ifa's
palm nuts. Burton (1863: I, 189) refers to the use of palm nuts with four
eyes, and Talbot (1926: II, 185) and Ataiyero (1934: 6) to those with four
or more eyes. J. Johnson (Dennett, 1906: 246) says that Ifa is represented
by palm nuts with from four to ten or more eyelets. Elsewhere he says:
"There is a particular Palm tree that is known by the name of Ọpẹ̀-Ifa, or
the Ifa Palm tree, because that class of palm trees commonly yield nuts
carrying four eyelets each, and these are the only nuts employed in Ifa
worship, and are devoted to it. They are regarded sacred to this purpose,
and are often spoken of as Ekurọ-aijẹ, i.e. 'Nuts that are not to be eaten';
and if nuts carrying two or three eyelets should be found among these
yielded by such trees, these would be called Ekurọ-Òṣọ̀ṣà — i.e. the palm
nuts whose beauty has deserted them through the loss of one or more eyelets — ọṣọ-ṣá" (Dennett, 1906: 257).

There is general agreement that palm nuts with four eyes are especially appropriate to Ifa, but many diviners find those with other numbers of
eyes acceptable. According to an Ileṣa diviner, each set should have eight
nuts with four eyes and eight with three, as Price (1939: 134) also reports.
An Ilara diviner explained that nuts with three, four, and five eyes are
found growing on the same tree, and in the same bunch of fruit. Those with
four eyes are female and are called awẹnrẹn Ifa; those with three or five
eyes are male and, although they have no special name, may be referred to
as leopard (ẹkun) because they are "strong." Male and female nuts can be
mixed either eight and eight, seven and nine, or nine and seven. Maupoil
(1943: 180) says that the nuts have from two to six eyes and that in Dahomey
those with four eyes are preferred by Fa; those with three eyes are given
to initiates, and those with six eyes are saved for chiefs and other wealthy
initiates. Epega (n.d.: I, 29) refers to the use of palm nuts with three to
six eyes. Nuts with an odd number of eyes were included in most sets of
ikin examined; one set in Ifẹ had three palm nuts with three eyes and thirteen with four eyes; and another set acquired in Ọyọ has seven palm nuts
with three eyes, five with four, and four with five eyes.

A diviner must have at least two sets or "hands" (ọwọ) of palm nuts.
One set is buried with him when he dies, and another is inherited by one of
his sons if the son becomes a diviner or a worshiper of Ifa. If none of the
sons becomes a worshiper, the second set of palm nuts is hung over the
father's grave, and if none becomes a diviner, the other apparatus may be
discarded. Both sets of palm nuts are ritually consecrated, which involves

washing them in an infusion of the leaves of Ifa (ewe Ifa), and they are
washed again each year during Ifa's annual festivals. Some diviners have
three, four, or more sets of consecrated palm nuts for divination. They
may acquire additional "hands of Ifa" (ọwọ Ifa) through inheritance or by
being directed to do so through divination; as an Ifẹ diviner explained, Ifa
likes to have several sets of palm nuts, as a man likes to have more than
one suit of clothes.

S. Johnson (1921: 33) states that according to Yoruba tradition, the
first Ifa diviner employed small pebbles and that "In process of time palm
nuts, pieces of iron and ivory balls were successively used instead of pebbles." Neither pebbles nor pieces of iron were observed by me, but some
Ifẹ informants said that a wealthy diviner may have his set of nuts carved
of ivory (ike). A set of sixteen spheroids carved from the bone, not the
tusk, of an elephant and marked with crosses to distinguish them readily
from palm nuts was seen in Ifẹ; their owner said he used them occasionally
for divination but that their main purpose was in the preparation of a good-
luck charm (awure). They are known as irin, a term which resembles the
word for iron (irin), but which is also applied to the bone and ivory objects
used in the worship of the God of Whiteness.

Only sixteen palm nuts are manipulated in divining, but in Ifẹ the diviner has a seventeenth nut that he places opposite him beyond the divining
tray on a ring of cowries known as the money of Ifa (aje Ifa) (see Plate 15).
Before divining, he sprinkles a small amount of powder from the divining
tray on its top because, as with Yoruba kings, "no one should see its bare
head." This seventeenth palm nut is known in Ifẹ as the chief of the palm
nuts (olori ikin) and as oduṣọ, which is derived from figure (odu) and "to
watch, to guard" (ṣọ). J. Johnson (Dennett, 1906: 248), who gives "akin" as
a variant of "ikin," cites an aphorism referring to the fact that this nut is
never manipulated with the other sixteen in divination: "An Akin is the one
we may strike for divination: we have no right to strike an Oduṣọ" (Akin
li a i pà; a kĩ lu Odùṣọ́). Frobenius (1913: I, 251) describes the oduṣọ as
carved of ivory and recognizable as the head of Eshu by its long pigtail,
and says that it is used to stand "sentinel over the Baba-lawo's actions and
the fall of the sixteen Ikis" (ikin). One of these is illustrated by Frobenius
(1913: I, 231, no. 3). In Ifẹ these small heads are known as Ẹla (see Chapter XI) or as irin, like the elephant bone "nuts"; one is kept with the set of
palm nuts "as a decoration," but it is not set out like the oduṣọ or otherwise employed in divination (see Plate 1 A).

J. Johnson (Dennett, 1906: 248) also refers to a palm nut that is left
in the bag or cup as "a keeper of the house both for himself and his comrades, till they should be returned to their place again." He calls this the
"Watch Akin" or àdèlé, which would mean that which watches or guards the
house (a-de-ile). This was not observed or referred to by informants in
Ifẹ, who considered the second set of palm nuts to be the adele; but Maupoil
(1943: 182-183) confirms the use of two additional nuts in Dahomey which
are known as adele or adele of Ifa (adelefa); and Mẹkọ diviners have eighteen palm nuts in a set, two of which are replaced in the bag before beginning to divine.

The Divining Chain (ọpẹlẹ, ọpẹlẹ Ifa)

The divining chain is said to "talk more" than the palm nuts, but it is regarded as an inferior instrument, less reliable than palm nuts for deciding important questions. It is also spoken of as Ifa's servant. Nevertheless it is more commonly used in divination, and a number of Ifẹ diviners employ only the chain, because they dislike using the palm nuts. The reason for this is that the divining chain arrives at the same interpretation through the same set of figures and verses more rapidly, and answers more questions than are usually asked when the slower method with palm nuts is employed.

The divining chains are most commonly and most widely referred to as ọpẹlẹ. The name ọpẹpẹrẹ, given by J. Johnson (Dennett, 1906: 250), was recognized in Ifẹ but not in Mẹkọ. One Mẹkọ informant claimed that ogumaga was another Yoruba name for it; but this represents influence from Dahomey, where the chain is known in Fọn by this name (Parrinder 1949: 156) or as agunmaga or gumagan (Maupoil, 1943: 197). The chains are made by the diviners for themselves and for their pupils.

The divining chain, which is about three to four feet long, usually consists of eight halves of seed shells or pods joined together by short sections of chain three to four inches long (see Plate 2). The middle section of the chain, by which it is held, is somewhat longer. The other sections are of equal length, so that when the chain is held in the middle, the four shells on the right and the four on the left hang down side by side. The chain is thrown with the right hand, which is said to be used consistently in Ifa divination, even by left-handed individuals. It is tossed away from the diviner in such a way that the two open ends fall nearest to him and the two sides fall parallel (see Plate 18). If the shells or pods do not fall side by side in straight lines so that the figures can be easily read, the chain may be adjusted by drawing the two ends toward the diviner, with care taken not to overturn any of the pods. Each half seed shell can fall with either the concave inner surface or the convex outer surface facing up. It is essential that the two surfaces of the shells, or of other materials used in place of them, can be distinguished.

Various objects — including beads, cowries, shells, coins, buttons, rings, small bells, and bits of metal — are attached to the bottom of the pods at either end of the chain. Their purpose is to enable the diviner to distinguish the right and left half of the chain, so that the same half is always cast on the same side, and so that the figure will not be misread — for example, by mistaking Ogbe Ọyẹku for Ọyẹku Ogbe. Often an odd number of cowries (one or three) marks the right half and an even number (two or four) marks the left.

In place of a chain, a simple cord of beads of various colors strung on threads may be used to join the seeds together. A single cord is often used on the instruments with which apprentices practice while they are learning divination, but as some cords interfere with the free fall of the seeds, they are considered unsuitable by diviners for actual consultation. The type of chain most highly prized in Ifẹ in 1937, though infrequently available in the markets in 1951 or 1965, was of European manufacture; it consisted of circular brass links set at right angles to each other, permitting the seeds to fall freely in either the concave or the convex position. With a good divining chain the probability of each of the figures appearing is equal (1 in 256). This is desirable from the point of view of the diviners as well as the clients, though not expressed by either in terms of probability. From their point of view, the fall of the seeds is not left to chance but is controlled by Ifa, the deity of divination, and any interference with the free fall of the seeds, by the instrument or by the diviner, garbles the message which Ifa wishes the client to receive.

In both Ifẹ and Ileṣa the shells of an unidentified dark-colored seed (egbere), said to come from a large tree (igi epú), is most commonly used and most highly regarded; neither is listed in Dalziel. These seeds resemble almond shells in their general shape and markings but are darker, smaller, and much harder. They are found by hunters in elephant dung and sold in the markets, but they have become increasingly rare and expensive since the early trade in ivory. When split open, they show a smooth, slightly concave inner surface readily distinguishable from the roughly wrinkled, convex, outer surface. A small hole is burned through each end of a half of a seed shell with a hot iron, so that the sections of chain may be attached by thread. This seed was unknown in Igana and Mẹkọ, and other materials are often used in place of it.

Most common is the seed pod known as ọpẹlẹ, from which the divining chain takes its name. It comes from the ọpẹlẹ tree, identified by Clarke (1939: 239) as <u>Schrebera golungensis</u>.[2] In Ileṣa this pod is referred to as ewe's foot (ẹsẹ aguntan, ẹsẹ agutan). Mẹkọ informants claimed that these are the only seeds found in elephant dung, and that they are obtained either from hunters or directly from the tree. This seed pod has a distinctive pear shape and naturally splits open at the base, with the two halves splaying out from the top where they are joined until broken apart (see Plate 1 B). On the concave inner surface of each half is a marked medial ridge, and when two halves are placed side by side with this surface upward they are considered to resemble the figure Ogbe Meji as marked on the tray after the single lines have been joined together (see Figure 2, Chapter IV). According to an Ifẹ diviner, when Ogunda Meji died[3] at the town of Oko, a tree called ọpẹlẹ ọga Oko sprang up on his grave, and from it fell a fruit that split open, revealing the figure Ogbe Meji "written" inside.

The use of halves of apọn seed shells from the oro tree, the wild or African mango (<u>Irvingia</u> <u>gabonensis</u> or <u>I</u>. <u>barteri</u>, according to different classifications) was mentioned by informants at Mẹkọ and Ileṣa; and an Ifẹ diviner maintained that Ifa himself originally used them, with egbere shells having been introduced by Ọramfẹ, the Ifẹ God of Thunder, during his reign

---

2. Opele (not ọpẹlẹ) is given as the Yoruba name of <u>Schrebera golungensis</u> and <u>S</u>. <u>arborea</u> by Ainslie (1936: 30) and Dalziel (1937: 365).

3. The figures of Ifa are said to have been named after men who lived when Ifa was on earth.

as the Ọni of Ifẹ. It will be recalled that these seed shells are widely used
in Nigeria in the system of divination employing four strings; according to
Talbot (1912: 174), they too are found in elephant dung. They are also used
in Dahomey, as are the seeds of Mangifera gabonensis (Maupoil, 1943: 198;
Alapini, 1950: 53). Mangifera indica, the only species listed by Dalziel, is
the mango, known to the Yoruba as mangoro. Informants say that it is not
used, but some said that it could be, as well as any seed shell that can be
split in half.

Epega (n.d.: I, 42) reports the use of an unidentified fruit, apuraga.
Frobenius describes the divining chain as made of halved palm nuts, but
Arrien's sketch of one so identified clearly represents ọpẹlẹ shells.[4] No
chains made of halves of palm nuts have been observed, although an Ileṣa
diviner said they could be used. There is no evidence to support the statements of Frobenius (1912-1913: I, 278) and Meek (1925: II, 69) that palm
kernels are used, and Meek's statement that the babalawo uses sixteen
strings each having sixteen kernels is obviously erroneous.

A divining chain purchased from an Ilara diviner has markers cast
from a light white metal in the shape of ọpẹlẹ pods with the outer surfaces
decorated with simple geometric patterns (see Plate 2B). A similar chain,
with markers cast in brass (idẹ) in the shape of ọpẹlẹ seeds, was seen in
Ibadan; these and other metals may be used to form other shapes that can
serve as markers. Maupoil (1943: 199) refers to a chain in the Musée de
l'Homme with copper markers in the shape of avini or avavini seeds (unidentified), and the use of copper (baba) was confirmed by Mẹkọ and Ileṣa
informants. A Mẹkọ diviner mentioned the use of silver (fadaka), lead (oje),
and iron (irin), but according to an Ileṣa diviner these three metals can be
used only for the chain and not as markers. He also said that in ancient
times cowry shells were used in place of seed shells.

Pieces of calabash strung together by pieces of cord are commonly
employed in Ifẹ and elsewhere by apprentices when they are learning divination; Frobenius (1913: I, 247) illustrates one of these strings, which are
spoken of as "older" than the regular divining chain because a diviner begins with them. Pieces of wood or ivory may also be substituted for seed
shells. According to Mẹkọ diviners scales of the Pangolin or Scaly Anteat-
er (akika, aika, aka, ayinka)[5] are used, though this was denied in Ileṣa.
Maupoil (1943: 198-199) reports the use of crocodile scales, head bones of
a fish, head bones of the crocodile, and sea turtle shell. Mẹkọ and Ileṣa
informants both confirmed the use of crocodile scales (ipẹpẹ ọni, ipẹ ọni),
and the head bones of the large-headed fish (abori; sacred to the River Goddess Ọṣun in another context), but denied the use of the head bones of the
crocodile. A Mẹkọ diviner confirmed the use of pieces of the shell of the
sea turtle (ajapa ewiri), but this was denied in Ileṣa. There may be regional differences in the materials regarded as suitable.

---

4. Frobenius, 1913: I, 250, 247. Cf. the larger sketch in Frobenius,
1926: 179.

5. Uromanis longicaudata Briss. See Maupoil (1943: 280).

The Divining Bag (apo, apo Ifa)

The divining chain is kept and carried in a shoulder bag usually about
nine inches deep and fifteen inches broad, with a full-sized flap. It is made
of locally woven cloth or sometimes of leather, and it may be decorated
with cowry shells or beads. Beaded bags are often smaller (see Plates 3
and 4). A babalawo is one of the very few nonroyal persons permitted to
use solidly beaded materials; these are usually reserved to the Yoruba
kings, who had beaded cushions, slippers, and gowns, and who alone may
wear beaded caps and crowns. Beaded bags, knife handles, hangings for
the shrine, and other objects may be made by the diviners themselves, or
by the beadworkers who work for the kings.

The divining bag also contains an assortment of miscellaneous objects
that serve as symbols of specific alternatives (see Chapter V), including
cowries and other kinds of shells, vertebra and other small bones, horns
and teeth, broken bits of china and glass, pebbles, and different kinds of
seeds. The whole of these objects and the divining chain are referred to
as abira, and the divining bag is called apo abira or apo Ifa, the bag of ac-
cessories or the bag of Ifa. The divining chain is often cast on this bag
(see Plate 18), which is laid out on the mat on which the diviner is seated.
The palm nuts, divining tray, and bell may be carried in this bag if it is
large enough, but for palm nuts other types of containers are usually provided, which remain at the shrine for Ifa most of the time.

Divining Vessels: Plates, Cups, and Bowls

Several types of containers for the palm nuts are commonly employed,
the simplest of which is a pottery plate (awo, awo Ifa). In place of the
earthenware black plates (awo dudu) produced by Yoruba women, imported
chinaware is often used. In Mękǫ palm nuts were sometimes stored in a
small cloth bag containing cowry shells. All these are considered perfectly adequate by diviners at Ifę, and at Mękǫ and Ilara; but if he can afford it,
a diviner may wish to have a carved wooden cup or bowl to decorate his
shrine and show his gratitude to Ifa.

The carved wooden divining cup (agere Ifa, ǫgęrę Ifa, ajęrę Ifa, ajele
Ifa), has been widely illustrated because of its aesthetic qualities; and indeed it is probably the most versatile of all the sculptured forms produced
by Yoruba woodcarvers (see Plates 5-8). Twenty of these vessels are illustrated in Frobenius (1913: I, 233, 235, 237, 239). They are decorated
with various birds, animals, or fish, with human beings engaged in ritual
and other activities, or with combinations of these figures; the decorative
elements may become so elaborate that any resemblance to a cup is lost.
It may be uncovered or provided with a lid, either hinged or separable,
which may be the setting of an independent scene or incorporated into the
total composition.

Several divining cups portray a woman kneeling before a chicken
whose head, back, and tail form a removable lid. A common motif, particularly in Igana and in the area of the old Ketu kingdom in the West, is that
of a chicken biting a snake, with the snake striking back at the chicken's

leg. A particularly complex example from Ḍeyin in the Ketu area depicts
a chief on horseback surrounded by four attendants on foot, with a hinge
and lid carved from the same piece of wood; the lip of the cup and the inside of its circular lid are carved with incised geometric design, and the
top of the lid is ringed with two snakes, each being bitten by a chicken, and
each in turn biting a tortoise. One from Abẹokuta shows a babalawo marking a figure of Ifa on a divining tray while holding a sacrificial chicken in
the other hand, and with his female client kneeling beside him (Bascom and
Gebauer, 1953: 32). The designs occasionally are derived from the Ifa
cult, as in this instance, but more often they are not. They are considered
simply as decorations which the purchaser may specify or which he may
commission the woodcarver to execute as suits his individual fancy. A few
divining cups are cast in brass.

Although divining cups are found in Mẹkọ, Abẹokuta, Igana, Ọyọ, Ileṣa,
Ekiti, and other parts of Yoruba country, they are not employed in Ifẹ, where
the divining bowl is preferred; however, divining cups are known in Ifẹ and
are referred to in one of the verses (175-2) recorded there.

The divining bowl (ọpọn igẹdẹ), which in Ifẹ is used in place of the cup,
is also known in other areas by various names. Aesthetically it is much
more formal and restricted, generally taking the shape of a circular covered bowl about fifteen inches in diameter and nine inches deep, with decorations usually in low relief or incised designs (see Plates 9 and 15). Frobenius (1913: I, 257) illustrates five of these, one square in shape, one with
high relief carving and three short legs, and one elaborately carved in low
relief with geometric and representational designs. In other respects they
are more complex than the divining cups, which have only a single cavity;
if several sets of palm nuts are to be stored in the same cup, plate, or bag,
it is necessary to wrap each in a small cloth bag to keep them apart. The
interiors of the divining bowls are usually divided by raised partitions into
a round or square central section, surrounded by four, six, or eight radial
sections. The "chief palm nut" (olori ikin, oduṣọ) and one set of palm nuts
are kept in the central compartment, while the rest are used for other sets
of nuts, for divining chains, kola nuts, cowries, and other small accesso-
ries. Informants denied Frobenius' statement (1913: I, 254) that they are
used to store sulphur, charcoal, chalk, and camwood. Similar bowls are
used in Ọyọ, where they are known as igbajẹ Ifa or ọpọn Ifa; in Mẹkọ, where
they are known as awẹ Ifa; and in Dahomey, where Maupoil (1943: 184, 217)
gives their Yoruba name as awofa, meaning "plate of Ifa" (awo Ifa).

A variant form, owned by diviners in Ifẹ and in Igana, combined a bowl
of this type with a divining tray (see Plate 10). The interior of the Igana
bowl was divided into two concentric circular compartments, surrounded
by a number of radial sections. The top of the flat lid was in the form of a
circular divining tray and was used as such.

The Divining Tray (ọpọn Ifa)

When divining with palm nuts, the figures of Ifa are marked in powder
on the divining tray and, even when the divining chain is used, the tray is

often employed in the course of making the sacrifices or the medicines
which are prescribed. It is flat and usually circular in shape, though it
may be rectangular or approximate a square or a semicircle. Its dimen-
sions range from about six to eighteen inches (see Plates 11-12). The
outer edge is slightly raised and carved in a variety of geometric designs
or representations of human and animal forms and objects; these are almost always in low relief, but a divining tray with two snails sculptured on
the edge was seen in Mękǫ, and Wescott (1958: pl. V) illustrates a tray
with sculptured birds and animals.

The raised edge of the tray has at least one stylized face, identified
as Eshu (Eşu), the messenger of Ifa and the other deities. Trays with one,
two, four, and eight such faces have been seen, and Maupoil (1943: pl. VIII)
illustrates one from Dahomey with sixteen faces. Where two or more faces
of Eshu appear on a divining tray, one must be recognizable by its size or
position, or be marked in some way so that it can be placed opposite and
facing toward the diviner. For this purpose a bunch of cowries is sometimes attached to the tray opposite it, and the burned hole by which it is attached may serve to orient the tray after the string has broken and the
cowries have been lost. The bunch of cowries is used also to spread the
divining powder on the tray so as to "erase" a figure marked on it; according to an Ifę diviner, it should include at least fifty cowries.

In using the divining tray it is as important to distinguish the right and
left hands of a figure as in the case of the divining chain. It is believed
that Ifa controls the figures marked on the tray, as he does the fall of the
seeds of the chain, and that he sits opposite the diviner watching over the
proceedings from the same viewpoint as that of the client. Frobenius (1913:
I, 252) states that the diviner "always turns to the East"; and an Ifę informant said that long ago diviners faced East; now they can sit facing in any
direction so long as Eshu is placed opposite them (see Plate 15; and
Maupoil, 1943: plates III and IV).

The divining tray is known as the "tray of Ifa" (ǫpǫn Ifa) in Ifę and elsewhere, though the name atęfa or atę Ifa is recognized in Mękǫ and in Dahomey. A basketry tray used for displaying small merchandise in the market is known as atę, but it is not employed in divination, and the Mękǫ term
may be derived from the verb tę, "to press," which is used to refer to the
manner in which the diviner marks the figures of Ifa on the tray; or it may
be of Fǫn origin. In Ileşa the divining tray is known also as a plank or
board (apako) or as the board of Ifa (apako Ifa). All the divining trays seen
were made of wood except one at Ifę carved of quartz, like the looped-han-
dled quartz stools of ancient Ifę; it was said to have been the tray used by
Ifa himself. One verse (175-2) refers to a brass tray (ǫpǫn idę), which Ifa
used, and this is also mentioned in a myth. There was no mention of using
a fan, or bowl, as reported by J. Johnson.

The Divining Powder (iyęrosun)

The figures of Ifa are marked on the tray in a powder which is scattered
on its surface. This probably comes from Baphia nitida or camwood, as

Clarke (1939: 240) says. There are problems in botanical classification and apparently regional variations in the name of the tree, but iyẹrosun as the name for the powder is widely recognized. Ifẹ informants explained that this name means iyẹ irosun, or wood dust (iyẹ) made by termites from the irosun tree. Clarke (1939: 240) also gives irosun as the name of the tree, and Farrow (1926: 38) gives irosu. Diviners in Mẹkọ, however, knew of no tree named irosun, saying that the termite dust came from the osun tree (igi osun); they explained the term iyẹrosun as a combination of iyẹri or ọyẹri (termite dust) and osun. Abraham (1958: 334) gives both ìyẹ̀ as "wood-dust from tree eaten away by borer-insects" and ìyẹ̀rẹ̀ òsùn = irosun as "powdered wood of the tree ìròsun sprinkled on the divining board."

Dalziel gives irosun as the name both for Camwood, Baphia nitida, and for Barwood, Pterocarpus osun, which is also known as osun or red osun (osun pupa); Pterocarpus erinaceus is known as black or dark osun (osun dudu). Significantly, he begins his discussion of Pterocarpus with the statement: "Much confusion exists as to the botanical identification of various specimens of Redwoods known as Barwood and Camwood, and, as the native names are not distinctive, they give little assistance to collectors. It is proposed to confine the term Barwood to species of Pterocarpus, and Camwood to species of Baphia" (Dalziel, 1937: 256).

In Ifẹ divining powder is often kept on hand in a bottle or other container. When more is needed, the diviner or his assistant takes a termite-infested piece of irosun wood, pounds it on a flat stone to knock out the dust, and "pans" it on a divining tray so that larger bits of wood can be removed. Mẹkọ diviners bring home a piece of the trunk of the osun tree during the dry season and leave it on the ground so that termites can eat it, but not near the spot where they divine. The termites, they explain, eat only the whitish outer parts of the wood, and powder from the reddish heartwood is never used. The heartwood produces osun, the reddish wood powder commonly known in English as camwood, but which would be barwood according to Dalziel's classification if the Mẹkọ and Ifẹ terms are distinctive.

In Mẹkọ other woods may also be used, including igi ayọrẹ and igi idin (unidentified), igi iṣin (Akee apple or Blighia sapida), and powder from bamboo palm or oil palm rafters; iyẹrosun is preferred, but the kind of wood does not matter as much as the fact that the dust is made by termites. Ifẹ diviners regard termite dust from any other kind of wood as unsatisfactory, but occasionally they use dust from rafters made from the oil palm tree as a substitute.

Although marking in the sand is basic to the Islamic system of divination, and although Wyndham (1921: 69) and Price (1939: 134) refer to the use of sand on the divining tray in Ifẹ, and Gorer (1935: 196) reports its use in Dahomey, its use in place of wood dust is denied by Ifẹ diviners and is not mentioned by Maupoil. In Mẹkọ neither sand nor chalk is used; yam flour (elubọ) may be used, as S. Johnson (1921: 33) notes, but it is not considered good for the purpose of divination. Similarly Maupoil (1943: 194) was told that soot, charcoal, corn flour, and cassava did not work. Marking the figure on a crushed, half-boiled yam as described by Burton (1863: I, 190) was denied by informants and has not been suggested by subsequent observers.

The Divining Bell (irǫ, irǫ Ifa)

As the figures are considered to be not simply the result of chance but controlled by Ifa, who personally supervises each divination, the diviner may attract Ifa's attention before beginning to divine. For this purpose he may tap a bell or "tapper" (irǫ) against the divining tray. This is known as the tapper of Ifa (irǫfa, irǫ Ifa) in Ifę, as the tapper of ivory (irǫke, irǫ ike) in Ibadan and the Ǫyǫ area, and as ǫrunfa (ǫrun Ifa) or ǫrunke (ǫrun ike) in Mękǫ; but the terms irǫfa and irǫke are widely recognized. The tapper is generally about eight to sixteen inches in length and carved of wood with the lower end, which is tapped on the tray, shaped like an elephant tusk. The upper end, as it is held, may be simply decorated or carved—for example, to represent a kneeling woman; above this there is sometimes a bell-shaped end that may or may not have a clapper within it. The bell at the top is far less common than the tusklike point with which the tray is tapped. Frobenius (1913: I, 253) reproduces sketches of fourteen Ifa bells, illustrating the range of variation in their form.

Wealthier diviners have their bells carved of ivory or cast in brass. An unusual pair from Ifę, cast in brass, is illustrated in Plate 13. A simple stick covered with the tan and light green beads of Ifa is also used for this purpose in Mękǫ and is known by the same names, or the handle of the cow-tail switch may be used. Many diviners own divining bells, but they are not essential in divination, and in Ifę the more experienced diviners often do not use theirs.

The following Ifa myth accounting for the origin of the bell or tapper was told by an Ifę diviner who ascribed it to the figure Ogbe Ǫkanran:

At one time Ǫrunmila befriended Elephant and went to the forest with him. They did any kind of work to get money, but Ǫrunmila was not as powerful as Elephant and could not endure the hardships as well. They worked in the forest for three months and three years; but when they returned, Ǫrunmila had earned only enough money to buy one white cloth. On their way home, Ǫrunmila asked Elephant to hold the cloth while he went into the bush to relieve himself. Elephant did; but when Ǫrunmila returned, Elephant had swallowed it. When Ǫrunmila asked for it, Elephant denied he had ever been given it. A great dispute arose between them and continued as they walked along the road. Finally they came to the crossroad, where they parted, Ǫrunmila going on the road to Ado without his cloth, and Elephant going to Alǫ.

On the road to Ado, Ǫrunmila met Hunter, who said he was going to hunt elephants. Ǫrunmila told him that he knew where he could find an elephant, and directed him along the road to Alǫ. He said he would meet an elephant and kill it, and that when he cut it open, he would find a white cloth, which he should bring back to him. Hunter went along the road, met Elephant and killed him. When he cut Elephant open, he found the white cloth inside. He returned the cloth, with an elephant's tusk as a gift, to Ǫrunmila.

Since that time, because of the falsehood of Elephant, Ǫrunmila and the babalawo use the tusk of an elephant as irọfa. And since that time, any hunter who kills an elephant must take the ala[6] to a babalawo.

Initial Invocations

Before the first divination of the day, prayers and invocations are offered to Ifa and other deities while the apparatus is being arranged. It is convenient to describe this preliminary ritual, which is performed only once during the day, before turning to the actual mechanics of divination and the manner in which the appropriate Ifa verse is selected for the client. As recorded in Mẹkọ, the diviner sits on a mat with his tray in front of him. He spreads wood dust on the tray, and places the divining cup in the center of it. The assortment of miscellaneous objects which serve as symbols of specific alternatives are placed on the right side of the tray. Two bags of cowry shells, one of which also contains eighteen palm nuts, are placed in front of the tray.

The diviner takes the palm nuts out of the bag and places them in the divining cup; he raises this in both hands and blows spit on the palm nuts and says: "Ifa awake, oh, Ọrunmila. If you are going to the farm, you should come home, oh. If you are going to the river, you should come home, oh. If you are going to hunt, you should come home, oh." [Ifa ji-o, Ọrunmila; bi o lọ l(i)-oko, ki o wa-(i)le-o; bi o lọ l(i)-odo, ki o wa-(i)le-o; bi o lọ l(i)-ọdẹ, k(i)-o wa-(i)le-o.] This is to make sure that Ifa supervises the divination and sees that the correct figure is selected.

He then places the divining cup on the ground to the left of the divining tray, saying, "I take your foot and press the ground thus." [Mo fi ẹsẹ rẹ tẹ-(i)lẹ bayi.] He then puts it on the mat, saying, "I take your foot and press the top of the mat thus. I carry you to sit on the mat, so you can carry me to sit on the mat forever." [Mo fi ẹsẹ rẹ tẹ ori ẹni bayi. Mo gbe ọ ka l(i)-ori ẹni, ki o le gbe mi ka l(i)-ori ẹni titi lai.] He replaces the cup on the divining tray, saying, "I carry you to sit on Ifa's tray, so that you can carry me to sit on Ifa's tray forever." [Mo gbe ọ ka l(i)-ori ọpọn-(I)fa, ki o le gbe mi ka l(i)-ori ọpọn-(I)fa titi lai.] These prayers for long life are followed by prayers for children and money.

He draws a line clockwise with his finger in the wood dust around the base of the divining cup, saying, "I build a house around you, so you can build a house around me,[7] so you can let children surround me, so you can let money surround me." [Mo kọ-(i)le yi ọ ka, ki o le kọ-(i)le yi mi ka, ki o le jẹki ọmọ yi mi ka, ki o le jẹki owo yi mi ka.] He erases the line with his cow-tail switch, saying, "I pay homage, oh; I pay homage, oh. Homage come to pass; homage come to pass; homage come to pass." [Mo ju-(i)ba-o,

---

6. Ala means both a part of the intestines of an elephant, and a white cloth.

7. Or "I make a fence around you, so you can make a fence around me." [Mo sọ-(ọ)gba yi ọ ka, ki o le sọ ọgba yi mi ka.]

mo ju-(i)ba-o; iba ṣẹ; iba ṣẹ; iba ṣẹ.] He takes a little wood dust from the
tray and places it on the ground, saying, "Ground, I pay homage; homage
come to pass." [Ilẹ mo ju-(i)ba; iba ṣẹ.]

He sets the divining cup aside again and marks a line away from him
in the divining powder at the center of the tray, saying, "I open a straight
road for you, so you can open a straight road for me; so you can let children take this road to my presence, so you can let money take this road to
my presence." [Mo la ọna fun ọ tororo, ki o le la ọna fun mi tororo; ki o
le jẹki ọmọ tọ ọna yi wa s(i)-ọdọ mi, ki o le jẹki owo tọ ọna yi wa s(i)-ọdọ
mi.] He then stirs the wood dust on the ground with the end of the handle
of the cow-tail switch, saying, "I do the ground thus." [Mo ṣe ilẹ bayi.] In
the same way he stirs the wood dust on the tray, saying, "I do the tray thus."
[Mo ṣe ọpọn bayi.]

Tapping the tray with the divining bell or with the handle of the cow-tail
switch, he recites, "To climb and chatter, oh, to climb and chatter. If the
West African Grey Woodpecker mounts the top of a tree, it will chatter. To
climb and chatter, oh, to climb and chatter. If the Agbe bird[8] awakes, it
will chatter. To climb and chatter, oh, to climb and chatter. If the Woodcock awakes, it will chatter. To climb and chatter, oh, to climb and chatter." [A-gun ṣẹ-o, a-gun ṣẹ. Bi Akoko g(un)-ori igi a ṣẹ. A-gun ṣẹ-o,
a-gun ṣẹ. Bi Agbe ji a ma ṣẹ. A-gun ṣẹ-o, a-gun ṣẹ. Bi Aluko ji a ma ṣẹ.
A-gun ṣẹ-o, a-gun ṣẹ.]

He continues, "Ẹlẹgbara [i.e. Eshu], homage, oh" [Ẹlẹgbara, iba-o] and
recites several of Eshu's praise names; "Ogun chatters" [Ogun ṣẹ], followed
by praise names of the God of Iron; "Ọṣun will chatter" [Ọṣun a ma ṣẹ], followed by praise names of the Goddess of the River Ọṣun; "Ṣango, your homage, oh, homage" [Ṣango iba-ẹ-o, iba] and praise names of the God of Thunder. He continues to invoke and recite the praise names of as many deities
as he can, the order being unimportant after Eshu and Ogun. He then invokes the living and the dead kings: "Kings on earth and Kings in heaven,
your homage, oh" [Ọba aiye ati Ọba ọrun, iba yin-o] and the earth: "Ground,
your homage, oh." [Ilẹ iba-ẹ-o.]

He concludes, "Ọrunmila, sacrifice is offered; Ọrunmila, sacrifice is
satisfactory; Ọrunmila, sacrifice come to pass"[9] [Ọrunmila-bọ-ru; Ọrun-

---

8. See n. 1, verse 17-2.

9. This very widely known invocation may take the form, "Ifa, I awake,
sacrifice is offered; I wake, sacrifice is satisfactory; I awake, sacrifice
come to pass" [Ifa, mo-ji-bọ-ru, mo-ji-bọ-yẹ, mo-ji-bọ-ṣiṣẹ] or "Ifa, sacrifice is offered; Ifa, sacrifice is satisfactory; Ifa, sacrifice come to pass"
[(I)fa, bọ-ru, (I)fa, bọ-yẹ, (I)fa, bọ-ṣiṣẹ]. An Ọyọ diviner cited two myths
in which these invocations are personified as children of Ifa, one of which
gives a fanciful explanation of their meaning.

Ọrunmila was summoned before the Sky God to answer six accusations
made by the other deities. Before going, he consulted a diviner and was
told to sacrifice a monkey, which he did. He was cleared of the accusations
and later bore three sons. He called the first "Use monkey to sacrifice,"

mila-bọ-yẹ; Qrunmila-bọ-şişẹ]; he claps his hands and says, "Thank you, oh" [Adupẹ-o]. The invocation addressed to Qrunmila is a prayer that the sacrifice which is offered will be acceptable to him, and that it will achieve its purpose.

The diviner removes the palm nuts from the divining cup, replaces two of them in the bag with the cowries, and counts the remaining sixteen, saying, "To count again (and again) is how a mad man counts his money." [A tun ka li aşiwere ika owo rẹ.] As he continues to pass the palm nuts from one hand to another, he invokes the relative who was in charge of his initiation, "Homage to oluwo" [Iba oluwo] or "Honor to oluwo" [Qwọ oluwo], and to give homage to his teacher [ojugbọna],[10] to all those who have taught him anything about Ifa [a-kọ-(ẹ)ni-li-(I)fa], to the one who pressed him in the mud [a-tẹ-(e)ni-l(i)-ẹrẹ],[11] to other diviners who take thus [a-ko-bayi], who press (mark Ifa figures) thus [a-tẹ-bayi], and who do thus [a-şe-bayi]. He offers homage or honor to the termite hill (gbodipẹtẹ), ant hill (kukubọlẹ), king (ọba), Whiteman (oyinbo), police (ọlọpa), a court case (ẹjọ), loss (ofo), falling branch of a tree (ayalu igi), gun (ibọn), stone (okuta), slap (ibaju), and a deadly smoke (efin), at the farm (loko), at the river (lodo), in the grassland (lọdan), and so on. There are many such invocations, which the diviner may mention or omit as he wishes.

Finally, the diviner replaces the palm nuts in the divining cup, saying, "One word alone does not drive a diviner from home; one word alone does not drive an elder from home" [Qrọ kan şo ko şi awo n(i)-ile; ọrọ kan şo ko şi agba n(i)-ile]. This is said to ensure that the diviner will not suffer if he has neglected to mention some deity or other entity in his homages. He is then ready to divine.

---

the second "Use monkey to live," and the third "Use monkey, come to pass" [F(i)-ọbọ-ru, F(i)-ọbọ-yẹ, F(i)-ọbọ-şişẹ].

Another time Qrunmila was told to sacrifice but he had no money. He went to his children, and Ibọru gave him two thousand cowries, Ibọyẹ gave him two thousand, and Ibọşişẹ gave him another two thousand. With these he bought a she-goat, pigeons, and other things necessary for the sacrifice. After the sacrifice he invited many people to come and eat, and they praised him for spending so much money and giving a feast fit for a king. They thanked him, but he said, "Don't praise me or thank me. Praise and thank Ibọru, Ibọyẹ, and Ibọşişẹ."

10. See Chapter IX.

11. This may refer to the point when the initiate is led into a muddy part of a stream, where his head is washed. See J. Johnson (Dennett, 1906: 253).

IV. THE FIGURES OF IFA

Divination is spoken of as casting Ifa (dafa, da Ifa), using the verb that describes throwing corn to chickens or tossing out water. Casting the divining chain (dapęlę, da ǫpęlę) may be distinguished from casting the sixteen palm nuts (dakin, da ikin); more descriptive of the latter is the phrase "beating the palm nuts" (lukin, lu ikin), which employs the verb that refers to beating a drum. After selecting the sixteen nuts to be used, the diviner first rubs them together vigorously eight at a time as if to rub off loose pieces, and then inspects them carefully.

He takes them in both hands and rapidly beats them together several times, then attempts to pick up as many nuts as he can with his right hand (see Plate 14). As sixteen nuts form a large handful, and as their ovoid surfaces become polished through use, some usually remain below in his left hand. If none is left, or if more than two remain, or if the grasp is not secure and he feels that some are "trying to slip out," he beats them again and takes another grasp.

Only when one or two nuts remain in the left hand is a trial counted. If one nut remains, the diviner draws two short parallel lines in the divining powder on the tray; if two nuts remain, he makes a single line. In justification of this apparently arbitrary reversal, the diviners say only that this is how Ifa taught them to do. A single line is made using the middle finger of the right hand, and a double line with the middle and ring fingers of the right hand to push or press (tę) the powder away from the diviner so that the darker surface of the tray can be seen (see Plate 15). The process is called "to press Ifa" (tęfa, tę Ifa), and the marks are known as the eyes of the tray (oju ǫpǫn).

When this process has been repeated eight times, the diviner has made eight single or double marks on the tray. These are arranged in two parallel columns of four marks each, made in the order indicated in Figure 2 as A, giving a configuration such as is represented in B. In practice, when similar marks are vertically juxtaposed, they may be joined together as in C. Thus the figure Ogbe Meji may be represented by two long parallel lines, and Ǫyęku Meji by four such lines.

Such a pattern constitutes one of the 256 figures (odu) of Ifa, in this case Ǫkanran Irętę. These figures are also spoken of as the "roads of Ifa" (ǫna Ifa), while their more common name, odu, is explained as meaning something big or bulky. Each figure is named and interpreted in terms of its two halves, of which the right (ǫtun) is regarded as male and "more powerful" than the left (osi), which is female; for this reason the name of the right half precedes that of the left. The halves of a figure are spoken of as feet (ęsę), according to Epega (1937: 10), and as sides or "arms" (apa) or hands (ǫwǫ), according to Ifę informants, but there is no specific term to distinguish the sixteen basic figures from the 256 derivative figures.

40

A.   B.   C.

2   1 | | | | | |

4   3 | | | | | |

6   5 | | | | | | | | |

8   7 | | | |

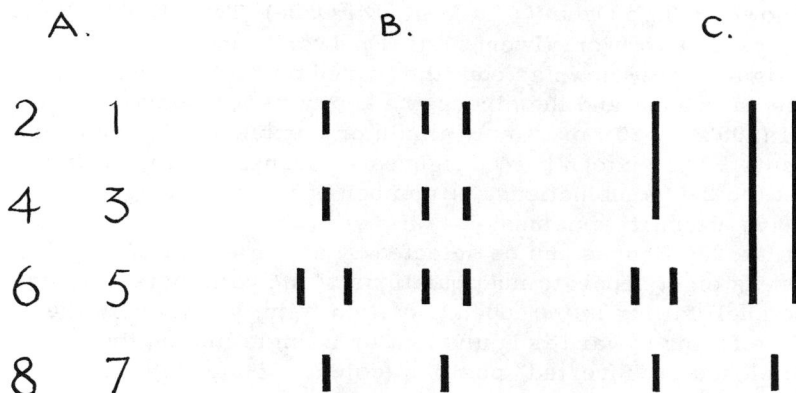

FIGURE 2. MARKING THE IFA FIGURES

Each half of a figure can take one of the sixteen basic forms shown in Table 1 A (above, page 4), according to the formula 2^n for the number of permutations of heads and tails for a coin tossed four times in succession, with 2 being the number of possible alternatives (heads or tails) and n the number of tosses. Each of these sixteen configurations may appear in either half of a figure and be associated either with the same configuration or with any of the fifteen others in the other half. If Ogbe appears on the right, for example, it may be combined with another Ogbe, or with Qyẹku, Iwori, Edi, Qbara, and so on in the left hand, giving a total of sixteen figures with Ogbe on the right. As the same holds for each of the sixteen basic configurations, a total of 16 x 16 or 256 derivative figures (odu) are possible.

Each derivative figure is given a compound name based on the names of the patterns of the right and of the left side. The name of the right side precedes that of the left side, so that in the illustration above (Figure 2) the figure is Qkanran Irẹtẹ, and not Irẹtẹ Qkanran. Because the latter is another figure, with a different set of predictions and sacrifices, it is essential to differentiate between the two halves of the figure by orienting the divining tray and the two halves of the divining chain properly. It will be noted that the diviner works from right to left in marking the lines on the divining tray, in reading the figure, and in choosing between specific alternatives as described below (cf. Chapter V). Again this is how Ifa taught the diviners to do.

In sixteen of the 256 figures, the two halves are identical, so that one finds Ogbe Ogbe, Qyẹku Qyẹku, Iwori Iwori, and so on. These paired figures are known as Two Ogbe (Ogbe Meji, Eji Ogbe), Two Qyẹku (Qyẹku Meji, Eji Qyẹku), Two Iwori (Iwori Meji, Eji Iwori), and so on. All 256 derivative figures are known as odu; the paired or double figures may be distinguished as olodu, and the others are known as amulumala, according to Ogunbiyi (1952: 9, 20), or simply amulu or combinations, according to Ifẹ informants. The sixteen paired figures are considered most important and outrank the 240 combinations. A number of the paired figures and combinations have alternative names.

One of the 256 figures can be selected by a single cast of the divining chain, whereas eight separate manipulations of the palm nuts are required. Half a seed shell falling in the "open" position (ṣiju, ṣi-oju) with the concave inner surface facing upward is equivalent to a single line on the tray; if it falls in the closed or "inverted" position (dojude, di-oju-de) with the convex outer surface up, it is the equivalent of a double mark.[1]

Divination with the chain of seeds, though regarded as inferior, is more rapid and permits the asking of questions through specific alternatives, but otherwise the two systems are identical. They employ the same set of figures with the same names and rank order, and the same verses. In both, the first figure cast—known as "post of the ground" (opolẹ, opo ilẹ) because it "stands on the ground"—is remembered by the diviner until it is time to recite its verses, which contain the prediction and specify the sacrifice which the client should make.

As we have seen earlier, many authors have claimed that the figures of Ifa number in the thousands. These claims derive from J. Johnson's account of sixteen principal odu, 256 or 4,096 odu altogether, and, "according to some" 65,536. Farrow would increase even this staggering number by "the fact that in each of the 8 throwings, or drawings, of the 16 nuts there is a possibility of a vast number of different results," a fact which is already accounted for in increasing the number from sixteen to 256. As any reader may verify for himself, however, the system permits no more and no less than 256 figures.

It has been implied by several writers that a particular figure is associated with a particular prediction, sacrifice, or deity, or that each is affirmative or negative, or favorable or unfavorable. These statements are gross oversimplifications of the system of divination, arising from a failure to understand the importance of the verses associated with the figures. Le Herisse (1911: 143-144), for example, lists the figures as "bon" or "mauvaise"; Monteil (1931: 116-117) identifies them as "favorable" or "défavorable"; and Abraham (1958: 276-277) gives them as "favourable" and "unfavourable." The verses known by a single diviner for a particular figure may be predominantly favorable or unfavorable, but predictions of both kinds are usually associated with a given figure, and may even be given in

---

1. This is the reverse of what Clarke (1939: 240) implies in the passage quoted in Chapter I; but see Clarke (1939: 244-245).

the same verse (e.g. 3-4, 35-3). Clarke's (1939: 242-243) reference to affirmative and negative figures appears to result from a misunderstanding
of the technique of specific alternatives, discussed in the following chapter.
Bertho (1936: 373-374) and Clarke (1939: 255) imply that there is a single
sacrifice for each figure, but an examination of the verses in Part Two
will show a variety of sacrifices and predictions for individual figures.

Several deities may be mentioned in the verses for any given figure,
although again one may be mentioned more frequently in the verses known
to a single diviner. It is probably on this basis that informants may associate a particular figure with a particular deity. In any event a comparison
of these associations made by informants in Ifẹ, Mẹkọ, and Qyọ with those
published by Beyioku (1943a: 1-7) for the Yoruba and by Herskovits (1938:
II, 214) for the Fọn shows little consistency, even when Fọn deities can be
readily equated (in parentheses) with Yoruba ones. Moreover, in a second
publication Beyioku (1943b: 41) gives different associations for eight of the
sixteen figures (2 Oduduwa, 5 Yemaja, 6 Ferewa, 11 Qya, 13 Egungun, 14
Oriṣa Oko, 15 Oke, 16 Oro), adding to the variation.

Each listing reflects deities of importance locally, suggesting a considerable regional variation in the Ifa verses because of their adaptation to
local belief systems. For example, Qramfẹ has not been reported outside
of Ifẹ, Ileṣa, and Qyọ, nor Agbona and Oriṣa Madoga outside of Mẹkọ.
Oṣumare, Iroko, and Nana Buruku are important as deities in Mẹkọ and in
Dahomey, but not among the eastern Yoruba, although of course both the
rainbow (oṣumare) and the iroko tree are known.

Checking these associations with the seven verses recorded in Ifẹ for
the figure Iwori Meji, for example, reveals that two of the deities (Nana
Buruku and Ṣọpọna) mentioned in Mẹkọ do not appear, nor does the deity
(Ogun) mentioned in Qyọ. Qlọrun and the personified rainbow (Oṣumare)
are mentiond in the names of the diviner in one verse (35-6). Qrunmila
or Ifa is the central character in one (35-7), with Eshu having a prominent role in this and another verse (35-3). In all verses, as usual, it is
Ifa who states the prediction and Eshu to whom the sacrifices are offered.
Eji Iwori or Iwori Meji, the name of the figure, is personified as the central character in two verses (35-1, 35-5), but no other deities are mentioned, although they might have been if more verses had been recorded.

The meanings of the names of the Ifa figures are unknown. Several
suggest similar words in Yoruba, such as the cock's comb (ogbe), camwood (irosun), lagoon (ọsa), wickedness and finger (ika), soap (ọṣẹ), and
loss (ofun); but all of these are tonally distinct from the names of the figures. Puns on some of these words occur in the verses, for example the
cock's comb in a verse of Ogbe Meji (1-6), and finger in a verse for Ika
Qwọnrin (Epega, n.d.: VII, 11). Other puns in the verses purport to explain the names of the figures such as "It befits two corpses" [o-yẹ-(o)ku
meji] in a verse for Qyẹku Meji (18-10), "Qwọn walks" [Qwọn-rin], "The
God of Iron casts" [Ogun-da], "He runs" [o-sa], and "He offends" [o-ṣẹ],[2]
but these are not to be taken seriously as etymologies.

---

2. Epega (n.d.: VII, 11, 7, 8; X, 13).

TABLE 2

THE IFA FIGURES AND THE DEITIES

1. Ogbe Meji

Beyioku: Ọbatala (Orişala)

Herskovits: Xẹvioso (Şango)

Ifẹ: Orişala or Ọşun for boy; "wife of Ifa" for girl

Mẹkọ: Şango, Ọya, Ogun, Agbona, Ọbaluaiye (Şọpọna), Buku (Nana Buruku)

Ọyọ: Şango

2. Ọyẹku Meji

Beyioku: Awọn iya mi (witches)

Herskovits: Mawu (Odua, Odudua?)

Ifẹ: Ori (head)

Mẹkọ: Ọşun, Agbona, Ọşọsi, Ọya

Ọyọ: Ọbatala (Orişala)

3. Iwori Meji

Beyioku: Ifa

Herskovits: Dan, rainbow (Oşumare)

Ifẹ: Ifa, Eşu

Mẹkọ: Buku (Nana Buruku), Babaligbo (Şọpọna), Oşumare

Ọyọ: Ogun

4. Edi Meji

Beyioku: Eşu

Herskovits: Hoho, twins (ibeji)

Ifẹ: Egungun, odu of Ifa

Mẹkọ: Ọbatala (Orişala), Şango, Iroko

Ọyọ: Ọşun

5. Ọbara Meji

Beyioku: Wọrọ

Herskovits: Dangbe, rainbow (Oşumare)

Ifẹ: Ẹgbẹ (abiku) for girl; odu of Ifa for man; wash head for old man

Mẹkọ: Erinlẹ, Arẹ

Ọyọ: Ọya

6. Qkanran Meji   Beyioku: Erikiran

Herskovits: Loko (Iroko)

Ifẹ: Ifa

Mẹkọ: Agbona, Qsọsi

Qyọ: Yemọja

7. Irosun Meji   Beyioku: Qsun

Herskovits: Lisa (Orişala)

Ifẹ: Ifa, Şango

Mẹkọ: Oşumare, Ẹlẹgbara (Eşu), Iroko

Qyọ: Ibeji (twins)

8. Qwọnrin Meji   Beyioku: Qbalufọn

Herskovits: Tọxọsu

Ifẹ: Eşu

Mẹkọ: Ẹlẹgbara (Eşu), Qsun

Qyọ: Ẹrinlẹ

9. Ogunda Meji   Beyioku: Ogun

Herskovits: Gu (Ogun)

Ifẹ: Orişala

Mẹkọ: Ogun, Qbaigbo (Orişala), Qsun

Qyọ: Qsọsi

10. Qsa Meji   Beyioku: Orişa beji, twins (ibeji)

Herskovits: All deities

Ifẹ: Orişala

Mẹkọ: Iya mi (witches), Oge

Qyọ: Şango

11. Irẹtẹ Meji   Beyioku: Qbaluaiye (Şọpọna)

Herskovits: Na

Ifẹ: Qramfẹ

Mẹkọ: Qsọsi, Agbona, Iroko, Oro

Qyọ: Iya mi (witches)

12. Otura Meji   Beyioku: Şango

                      Herskovits: Kukutǫ, the dead (oku)

                      Ifę: Qşun odo (Qşun where people draw water)

                      Mękǫ: Qlǫrun, Ogun, Qşun

                      Qyǫ: Alufa (Muslim diviners)

13. Oturupǫn Meji   Beyioku: Qya

                      Herskovits: Sagbata, smallpox (Şǫpǫna)

                      Ifę: Ifa

                      Mękǫ: Egungun, Orişa Madoga

                      Qyǫ: Ilę (earth, i.e. Ogboni)

14. Ika Meji   Beyioku: Onile (Oşugbo, Ogboni)

                      Herskovits: Hoho, twins (ibeji)

                      Ifę: Qna (road)

                      Mękǫ: Agbona, Ogun, Arę Itagun

                      Qyǫ: Ori (head)

15. Qşę Meji   Beyioku: Aje (money)

                      Herskovits: Dada Zodji

                      Ifę: Oro, Qşun

                      Mękǫ: Qsanyin, Qşun

                      Qyǫ: Orişa oke (hill)

16. Ofun Meji   Beyioku: Orişanla (Orişala)

                      Herskovits: Aido Hwedo (Oşumare)

                      Ifę: odu of Ifa

                      Mękǫ: Orişa Oluwa, Ifa, Ęlęgbara (Eşu)

                      Qyǫ: Odu (see Chapter IX)

An examination of 86 lists of the 16 basic figures of Ifa, based on 61 sources, established that these names are standard throughout Yoruba coun- try and, with some modifications in pronunciations and spelling, among the Fǫn of Dahomey, the Ewe of Togo and Ghana, and in Cuba and Brazil as well (Bascom, 1961; Bascom, 1966). It was also shown that one order for the 16 paired figures is predominant, being given in 42 of the 86 lists, in- cluding 30 of the 60 for the Yoruba, 4 of the 16 for the Fǫn, one of the 3 Ewe lists, 5 of the 6 from Cuba, and the single list available for Brazil.[3]

Although the dominant order accounts for half of the total number of lists analyzed, twenty-one other rankings have been recorded. Some of these are undoubtedly inaccurate, but others strongly suggest regional variations. For the Yoruba these variants are largely associated with the area of Ifę, Ileṣa, Ekiti, and Igbomina, in the northeast; whereas the domi- nant pattern is primarily associated with Lagos, Ode Ręmǫ near the Abęokuta border of Ijębu Province, and the provinces of Abęokuta and Ibadan in the southwest. One of these local variants, which is followed in this study, was given by four Ifę diviners and is confirmed by Wyndham (1921; 66) for Ifę, Odumǫlayǫ (1951; 13) for Ileṣa, and by Clarke (1939: 252) for Omu in the Igbomina area of Ilǫrin Province. This order, as shown in Table 1, is compared in Table 3 with the dominant order.

This ranking of the figures, which is important for answering ques- tions asked in terms of specific alternatives (see Chapter V), is said to be based on their seniority, that is, the order in which "they were born and came into the world." One diviner explained that the sixteen paired figures were sons of Ifa by the same mother, whose name he refused to divulge. Ogbe Meji was the father of Ogbe Qyęku, Ogbe Iwori, and the other com- binations beginning with Ogbe, as were Qyęku Meji, Iwori Meji, and the other paired figures. Other informants added that they lived on earth like human beings, and the figures of Ifa were named after them. They are mythological characters of the period when the deities also lived on earth, but they are not considered as, or worshiped as, deities (ębǫra, ębura, oriṣa). They appear as diviners and as central characters in the verses. One verse (35-5) for the figure Iwori Meji recounts how the other paired figures conspired against him and tried to keep him from coming to earth, and how he was able to attain his rightful position in third place by making a sacrifice.

Ofun Meji, the last of the paired figures, is an exception. It has some of the strongest medicines associated with it and, as it is a tabu for a fly to alight upon it, it is "closed" immediately by turning over one of the seed shells of the divining chain when it is cast, so as to make a different figure. Although listed sixteenth, Ofun is equal in rank with Qwǫnrin, in the eighth position.

This was explained by one diviner as due to the fact that Ofun Meji and Qwǫrin Meji were twins, and that when Ogunda Meji, the ninth figure, fought

---

3. Two additional Yoruba lists in the dominant order have been added by Prince (1963: 3) and McClelland (1966: 422), the latter verified by twenty-two informants.

TABLE 3

THE ORDER OF THE BASIC IFA FIGURES

A. Ifẹ	B. Southwestern Yoruba
1. 1111 Ogbe	1. 1111 Ogbe
2. 2222 Ọyẹku	2. 2222 Ọyẹku
3. 2112 Iwori	3. 2112 Iwori
4. 1221 Edi	4. 1221 Edi
5. 1222 Ọbara	5. 1122 Irosun
6. 2221 Ọkanran	6. 2211 Ọwọnrin
7. 1122 Irosun	7. 1222 Ọbara
8. 2211 Ọwọnrin	8. 2221 Ọkanran
9. 1112 Ogunda	9. 1112 Ogunda
10. 2111 Ọsa	10. 2111 Ọsa
11. 1121 Irẹtẹ	11. 2122 Ika
12. 1211 Otura	12. 2212 Oturupọn
13. 2212 Oturupọn	13. 1211 Otura
14. 2122 Ika	14. 1121 Irẹtẹ
15. 1212 Ọsẹ	15. 1212 Ọsẹ
16. 2121 Ofun	16. 2121 Ofun

with Ofun for his position he was peeved and went to the very end, even though he is stronger than Ogunda Meji. Two other diviners maintained that it was Ọwọnrin Meji who fought with Ofun Meji. One explained that they are equal because they are still fighting for the eighth position. The other diviner recounted the following myth (noting that today Ogbe Meji is spoken of as the father of all the figures, though this merely refers to his present rank order):

Ofun Meji was the first born of all the figures and the first to come to earth. He was the head of all the other figures and ruled them like a king, but because things went badly under his rule, they sent to Ifa in heaven to tell him how hard things were for them on earth. Then Ifa sent Ogbe Meji down to earth to take Ofun Meji's place as the head of the other figures. When he arrived, Ofun Meji gave him a house to lodge in, and he sent Ọsẹ Otura, the servant of all the paired figures, to go to welcome him.

When Ọsẹ Otura arrived, Ogbe Meji gave him food and drink, and he remained there with Ogbe Meji. Ofun Meji sent another to find out why Ọsẹ Otura had not returned, and he also stayed to eat and drink with Ogbe Meji. One after another was sent to find out what was happening, until all

the paired figures and all the combinations had gone, and Ofun Meji was
left alone.

Finally, Ofun Meji himself went and knocked on Ogbe Meji's door.
Everyone knew who it was, and he was told to wait outside. Then they
gathered the bones from their feasting and threw them outside to him, saying that he was no longer wanted. They told him that he ranked beneath
them all and should receive only the last share. Ofun Meji did not agree to
this. He came into the house and began to fight his way through the crowd
toward Ogbe Meji. He fought with each in turn, defeating all the combinations and the paired figures until he reached Qwǫnrin Meji. These two
fought and fought and fought, until the others sent to Ifa in heaven. Ifa ruled
that Ofun Meji and Qwǫnrin Meji should be equal in rank, taking turns in
priority. This is why Ofun Meji outranks Qwǫnrin Meji when Ofun Meji is
thrown first; but when Qwǫnrin Meji is thrown first, it outranks Ofun Meji
(see Chapter V).

For the same reason Ofun Ogbe and Qwǫnrin Ogbe are equals, as are
Ofun Qyẹku and Qwǫnrin Qyẹku, and so on. The sixteen paired figures out-
rank all the combinations, which also follow this modified order with Ogbe
Ofun and Ogbe Qwǫnrin sharing the twenty-third position, Qyẹku Ofun and
Qyẹku Qwǫnrin tied for thirty-eighth, and so on. According to some informants, Qṣẹ Otura, as the messenger of the paired figures, follows them
immediately and outranks all other combinations; but others regard Ogbe
Qyẹku as the senior combination, and one verse (2-1) refers to "Ogbe
Qyẹku, father of combinations." Following the latter interpretation, the effective or practical rank order of the first sixty-one figures in selecting
between specific alternatives would be as indicated in Table 4.

However, this order is by no means certain. Epega (n.d.: I, 1-28) gives
a quite different "Order of the Odu in Ifa" (Eto awǫn Odu ninu Ifa), in which
Ofun Meji is in the sixteenth place, followed immediately by Ogbe Qyẹku,
Qyẹku Ogbe, Ogbe Iwori, Iwori Ogbe — as does Ogunbiyi (1952: 14-35) and,
most recently, McClelland (1966: 425, 428). As the figures involving Ofun
rank last in each series rather than as equal to Qwǫnrin, this may be the
order in which the figures are learned, rather than their actual rank order.
Odumǫlayǫ also lists Ofun Meji in sixteenth place, followed by Ogbe Qyẹku,
Ogbe Iwori, Ogbe Edi.

Because of the uncertainties and because of apparent variations from
diviner to diviner, a simpler system has been followed here in numbering
the verses, simply as a matter of convenience. Following the Ifẹ order of
ranking the basic figures, as given in Table 1, the figures are numbered as
follows:

     1-16.   Ogbe Meji, Ogbe Qyẹku, Ogbe Iwori, Ogbe Edi . . . . . Ogbe
               Ofun;

    17-32.   Qyẹku Ogbe, Qyẹku Meji, Qyẹku Iwori, Qyẹku Edi . . . . .
               Qyẹku Ofun;

. . . . . .

    240-256. Ofun Ogbe, Ofun Qyẹku, Ofun Iwori, Ofun Edi . . . . . Ofun
               Meji.

Each verse is given a double number, the first part indicating the figure to
which it belongs, and the second indicating the order in which it was recorded.

TABLE 4

THE RANK ORDER OF THE FIRST SIXTY-ONE FIGURES

1. Ogbe Meji

2. Ọyẹku Meji

3. Iwori Meji

4. Edi Meji

5. Ọbara Meji

6. Ọkanran Meji

7. Irosun Meji

8. Ofun Meji

8. Ọwọnrin Meji

10. Ogunda Meji

11. Ọsa Meji

12. Irẹtẹ Meji

13. Otura Meji

14. Oturupọn Meji

15. Ika Meji

16. Ọṣẹ Meji

17. Ogbe Ọyẹku

18. Ogbe Iwori

19. Ogbe Edi

20. Ogbe Ọbara

21. Ogbe Ọkanran

22. Ogbe Irosun

23. Ogbe Ofun

23. Ogbe Ọwọnrin

25. Ogbe Ogunda

26. Ogbe Ọsa

27. Ogbe Irẹtẹ

28. Ogbe Otura

29. Ogbe Oturupọn

30. Ogbe Ika

31. Ogbe Ọṣẹ

32. Ọyẹku Ogbe

33. Ọyẹku Iwori

34. Ọyẹku Edi

35. Ọyẹku Ọbara

36. Ọyẹku Ọkanran

37. Ọyẹku Irosun

38. Ọyẹku Ofun

38. Ọyẹku Ọwọnrin

40. Ọyẹku Ogunda

41. Ọyẹku Ọsa

42. Ọyẹku Irẹtẹ

43. Ọyẹku Otura

44. Ọyẹku Oturupọn

45. Ọyẹku Ika

46. Ọyẹku Ọṣẹ

47. Iwori Ogbe

48. Iwori Ọyẹku

49. Iwori Edi

50. Iwori Ọbara

51. Iwori Ọkanran

52. Iwori Irosun

53. Iwori Ofun

53. Iwori Ọwọnrin

55. Iwori Ogunda

56. Iwori Ọsa

57. Iwori Irẹtẹ

58. Iwori Otura

59. Iwori Oturupọn

60. Iwori Ika

61. Iwori Ọṣẹ

V. SPECIFIC ALTERNATIVES: IBO AND ADIMU

Ifa's message to the client, which is contained in the divination verses, may be clarified and supplemented by asking a number of specific questions phrased in terms of two or more mutually exclusive alternative propositions; thus Ifa may be presented with the choice between several specific courses of action or candidates for a particular office, or he may be asked questions which must be answered either "Yes" or "No." These questions are posed in terms of two statements, the first affirmative and the second negative, such as "The venture which I am considering will be good for me," and "The venture which I am considering will not be good for me." Such questions are asked following the initial throw but before its verses are recited. The client may ask as many questions as he wishes, so long as they are phrased in terms of specific alternatives, and the answers may help in selecting the verse most appropriate to his case.

Questions of this kind are most frequently asked when the divining chain is employed, because a figure can be selected by a single cast of the chain as contrasted to the eight manipulations required when palm nuts are used. This probably accounts for the common statement that the divining chain "talks" more than the palm nuts, as the client may learn things which are not mentioned in the verses, which are the same in both cases. Nevertheless, and despite some informants' statements to the contrary, specific alternatives are also used with palm nuts, for example in selecting between candidates for an important office, for which palm nuts are preferred because of their reliability. Mękǫ diviners also maintained that palm nuts are better than the divining chain for choosing between specific alternatives, although the latter is quicker. Maupoil (1943: 203) records the use of palm nuts for this purpose in Dahomey.

The choice between these alternatives depends on the rank order ascribed to the figures, as discussed in the previous chapter. The diviner makes two casts, one for the affirmative statement and one for the negative, and the answer is that proposition for which the higher ranking figure is cast. Thus if the first is Qyęku Meji and the second is Iwori Meji, the affirmative statement is indicated by Ifa to be the correct one. Whether a figure is affirmative or negative, or favorable or unfavorable, in this situation is relative, depending upon the position in which it occurs and the figure with which it is associated. If Qyęku Meji followed Iwori Meji or if it were followed by Ogbe Meji, the answer would be negative.

The choice between two alternatives is illustrated by the examples in Table 5, in each of which the first alternative is selected. Example A again illustrates how the higher ranking of two paired figures is selected, while B illustrates the fact that any combination is outranked by any paired figure.

The important principle that, in the case of "ties," subsequent casts of the same figure confirm the first is illustrated in example C. This same principle is to be seen in examples D to H, which show its application to Ofun and Qwǫnrin, which are ranked as equal, and how they "take turns" in

TABLE 5

THE CHOICE BETWEEN TWO SPECIFIC ALTERNATIVES

First Throw	Second Throw
A. Qyẹku Meji	Iwori Meji
B. Qṣẹ Meji	Qyẹku Ogbe
C. Iwori Edi	Iwori Edi
D. Qwọnrin Qṣẹ	Ofun Qṣẹ
E. Ofun Iwori	Qwọnrin Iwori
F. Qyẹku Qwọnrin	Qyẹku Ofun
G. Otura Ofun	Otura Qwọnrin
H. Qwọnrin Meji	Ofun Meji

priority (Chapter IV). Thus when Qwọnrin Meji is followed by Ofun Meji, as in H, the first alternative is chosen because the two figures are of equal rank and the second cast confirms the first.

Similarly, if Ofun Meji were to appear on the first throw, it would also take precedence over Qwọnrin Meji on a second throw, although in actual practice this would not happen, because Ofun Meji is one of the figures that are final in the choice between specific alternatives when they appear on the initial cast. There would therefore be no occasion for making a second cast. These figures are not final in that they end the client's questioning through specific alternatives but only by answering the point in question at the moment and only if they appear on the first throw. The figures that are final in this sense, and thus select the first alternative immediately, are Ofun Meji, Iwori Ofun, Qbara Ika, Qwọnrin Ika, Ogunda Ogbe, Ogunda Iwori, Irẹtẹ Qṣẹ, Irẹtẹ Otura, and Qṣẹ Otura. To this list one diviner added Ogbe Qyẹku, and another added Otura Ogbe, Otura Qkanran, and Qṣẹ Irẹtẹ. All these informants were Ifẹ diviners, suggesting that there may be individual variation in this matter, depending upon the teacher with whom the diviner studied.

When Ifa is asked to choose between more than two alternatives — and there are several occasions in which he is presented with five — the appearance of these figures on the first throw again indicates that the first alternative is selected, and no other throws are necessary. But if Ofun Meji should appear on the second, third, or fourth throw, the series is completed; in this case Ofun Meji would be confirmed by Qwọnrin Meji on a subsequent throw, as in example I of Table 6, though it could be outranked by a higher figure on any other throw, as in J. In all the following examples the second alternative is selected, and figures that would be "final" if they occurred on the first throw are indicated by asterisks.

Example K illustrates how Ofun Qṣẹ confirms Qwọnrin Qṣẹ, provided that it is not outranked, while L shows that, however often a figure may be confirmed, it may be beaten by a higher ranking figure. As Ogbe Meji ranks

TABLE 6

THE CHOICE BETWEEN FIVE SPECIFIC ALTERNATIVES

	First Throw	Second Throw	Third Throw	Fourth Throw	Fifth Throw
I.	Ogunda Meji	Ofun Meji*	Ọsa Meji	Qwọnrin Meji	Irẹtẹ Meji
J.	Iwori Meji	Qyẹku Meji	Ofun Meji*	Qwọnrin Meji	Edi Meji
K.	Otura Edi	Qwọnrin Qṣẹ	Ogunda Iwori*	Qṣẹ Otura*	Ofun Qṣẹ
L.	Qṣẹ Ogbe	Iwori Ofun*	Qṣẹ Ogbe	Qṣẹ Ogbe	Qṣẹ Ogbe

higher than all other figures, it constitutes a "final" figure in any single set of alternatives, in whatever position it occurs, as there is no possibility of its being beaten by any subsequent throw.

Two variant patterns, described by a single diviner in each case, should be noted. One held that any of the "final" figures ended the casting for a given set of alternatives regardless of the position in which they occurred. If one appeared on the third throw, for example, the fourth and the fifth throw would not be made, and the highest ranking of the first three throws would be selected. In examples I-L there would be no further casts after the first asterisk in each row, but the figure selected would still be that in the second column.

Another diviner maintained that all combinations are ranked by the right half of the figure alone, which is male, and that it is unnecessary to examine the left or female half of the figure except to determine whether the figure was double or a combination. All double figures outrank all combinations, but all combinations beginning with Ogbe are equal; as the same holds for other combinations as well, there are only thirty-two effective rankings according to this interpretation, the sixteen paired figures and the sixteen kinds of combinations. Maupoil (1943: 203) says that in Dahomey also only the right half of a figure is considered; but Ifẹ diviners say that only diviners who do not know Ifa well do not consider both sides of a figure.

The Symbols of the Specific Alternatives

In presenting Ifa with the choice between two alternatives, a small vertebra is often used to symbolize bad, and a pair of cowries tied back to back to symbolize good. Any two objects can be used, but the bone is associated with death while cowries were formerly used as money. If the client has faith in the diviner and no reason to keep secret what he wants to find out, he may ask the question directly of the diviner. The diviner then touches the ends of the divining chain to the cowries while stating, for example, "This marriage which has been proposed will be successful" and casts the chain, noting the figure that appears. He then touches the chain to the bone and states, "This marriage which has been proposed will not be successful," after which he makes the second cast. When the bone instead of the cowries is chosen, indicating an unfavorable response, it is said that "Ifa puts the bone in his mouth" (Ifa gbe egungun ha ẹlu[1]) or "Ifa cuts the farm and eats" (Ifa ja oko jẹ).

If, on the other hand, the client wishes to conceal his question from the diviner, he asks for two objects from the diviner's bag and whispers these statements to them so that the diviner cannot hear, cupping his hands over his mouth so that the diviner cannot read his lips. To eliminate all possibility of the diviner trying to influence the answer, he may then shake the two objects in his hands, and conceal one in each hand. In so doing, he may reverse the symbols, using the bone to represent the desirable and the cowries to represent the undesirable alternative. It is understood that Ifa will hear his questions and know which object to choose, even though the alternatives that they represent are kept secret from the diviner. In this case, the diviner makes two casts to determine which hand is selected, asking first, "Is it the left hand?" and then, "Is it the right hand?" From the object held in the hand selected, the client knows the answer to his question, but the diviner does not.

It is for this reason that the specific alternatives are spoken of as ibo, meaning "covered" or concealed, or as closing or "tying" ibo (dibo, di ibo). Though ibo is given in the CMS Dictionary as "casting of lots or dice by the priests in consulting the gods" and by Abraham as "casting lots," it is derived from the verb "to cover" (bo), and refers to the fact that the alternatives presented to Ifa may be "covered" in order to conceal them from the diviner.

After the initial cast of the divining chain, the client may inquire whether the general portent is favorable or unfavorable by presenting Ifa with the choice between "Good" and "Bad" as specific alternatives. He can then ask about the particular kind of blessing or misfortune that lies in store. This again is done through specific alternatives, and in terms of a conventionalized view of the five kinds of good fortune and the five kinds of bad fortune that are to be met in the world. These were compared by one of the principal diviners of Ifẹ (Agbọnbọn) to the fronds branching from a palm tree. Five fronds on the right hand represent the five kinds of good with long life as the lowest frond, and five fronds on the left hand represent the five kinds of bad, with death as the lowest frond, because all good things come from the right hand, whereas the left hand is the source of all misfortune.

The desirable things in this world are represented by five categories, ranked in order of importance: long life or "not death" (aiku), money (aje, owo), marriage or wives (aya, iyawo), children (ọmọ), and victory (iṣegun) over one's enemies. First of all a man desires to live a long life, for if he dies all other blessings become meaningless. If he does not die, he wants to have money, because through this he can be married. If he has money, he wants wives so that he may have children. Finally, if he has children, wives, money, and good health, he will pray only to be able to overcome his

---

1. Ẹnu is the more common form for "mouth."

enemies. Each of these blessings is of little value without those which precede it.

To represent the five kinds of "good," the diviners use a small stone
(okuta), two large cowries (owo) tied together, the tip of the shell of a snail
(igbin), a small bone (egun, egungun), which is often a vertebra, and a potsherd (apadi) from a china plate or bowl. The stone represents long life because it does not die. The cowries represent money, having been used as
such before the introduction of European currency. The snail shell represents marriage because snails are a part of the gifts which precede marriage, so that a man must have snails before he can get a wife; or, according to one diviner, because a wife brings snails to sacrifice to Ifa. The
bone represents children because they are of one's own "bone," as the
Yoruba say, whereas we speak of them as of our own flesh and blood. The
potsherd represents defeat of one's enemies because, while a china plate
or bowl is something fine, it is utterly useless after it has been broken,
the implication being that one's enemies will be defeated as completely as
the plate is broken.

Similarly, there are five kinds of evil in this world: death (iku), sickness (arun, aisan), fighting (ija), the want of money (aje, owo), and loss
(ofun). Death is the most serious because it is the only one that cannot be
remedied or alleviated. Sickness is less serious because there are medicines to cure it, though these require the assistance of a specialist. Fighting is third, as anyone can stop a fight and arbitrate an argument. The
want of money is something that one can remedy by his own efforts. Finally, loss is the least serious, because if one has nothing, he cannot lose anything.

The same objects may be used to represent these five kinds of misfortune, but the symbolism is different. A vertebra or other piece of bone
represents death, because when a man dies, only his skeleton remains.
The tip of a snail shell represents sickness because in it, when the shell
is broken open, one finds filth and dirt, which are associated with illness.
Two cowries, tied together, again, not only represent money but once
served as money; some Ifẹ diviners substitute trouble (ọran), also symbolized by cowries, for want of money. A china potsherd represents loss,
because when a plate or bowl is broken, it is irretrievably lost.

Though commonly employed in Ifẹ, these symbols are not ritually
fixed or unalterable. One Ifẹ diviner sometimes used the smooth, almond-
shaped seed (ọsan) of the African Star Apple (Chrysophyllum africanum) to
represent both children and illness, because it is a tree that has many
children (i.e. much fruit), and because the fruit falls from its mother (the
tree) when it is ill. A piece of china represented marriage, because a
wife uses a plate to feed her husband. He also used a bone to symbolize
defeat of one's enemies, because of the similarities between the word
"bone" (egungun, egun) and the verb "to conquer" (ṣegun, ṣe-ogun; literally,
make-war). In other cases he employed the symbols described above.

Igana diviners similarly use a piece of china to represent wives and
marriage because women use plates to feed their husbands and are the
ones who make pottery; the star apple seed to represent children because

its tree has many "children"; a bone to represent defeat of one's enemies
because the animal from which it came had been "defeated" in the forest by
the hunter; a stone to represent long life; and cowries to represent money.
They maintained that the piece of china, the star apple seed, and the stone
always represented good, as they did not have symbols for the five kinds of
misfortune. Maupoil (1943: 205-206) gives other symbols for Dahomey.

This symbolism, which resembles in some ways that employed by the
Yoruba in the sending of messages before writing was introduced (Bloxam,
1887), is sometimes based on a play on words, as in the use of a bone (egun)
to represent the defeat of enemies (şegun), and often on the association of
similar ideas in terms of what Frazer called "imitative magic," as in the
case of the star apple seed to represent children and illness, the snail to
represent illness, or the piece of china to represent loss and the defeat of
enemies.

In choosing between specific alternatives, the diviner works from his
own right to left, as he does in asking first about the client's left hand and
then the right hand when the question is concealed from him. Before each
throw he touches the ends of the divining chain to the symbol of the kind of
good or bad fortune being investigated (see Plate 17). As viewed by the diviner, the order in which the casts are made and the order in which the
symbols are laid out, with the categories of good and evil which they represent, are shown in Table 7. The symbols representing the five kinds of
good are shown as they are viewed by the client in Plate 18.

When good fortune is indicated and its nature has been specified, the
client usually asks no further questions about it, assuming that it refers to
himself, though he could do so if he wished. However, when death or illness, for example, have been foretold, he may wish to learn the nature of
the illness or for whom it is in store. For this he uses two objects, such
as a stone and a cowry, and asks in turn whether or not the sickness is a
headache, fever, dysentery, and so on, mentioning any diseases he thinks
of in any order that he wishes, until one is designated as the correct answer. If he himself or someone closely related is ill, it is likely that he
will name his illness first. If death has been indicated as the impending
misfortune, he usually asks first whether he himself is the one concerned,
again using two ibo, and then about close relatives in turn until one name
is selected. Again he is likely to begin by naming relatives who are ill.

When a choice is made between five specific alternatives through
symbols laid out simultaneously, the chances of any of them being selected
are equal (1 in 5). They are also equal (1 in 2) when a choice is made between any two specific alternatives, as in the cast to determine whether
the portent is good fortune or bad fortune. When a series of choices are
presented in sequence through two alternatives to which "Yes" and "No" answers are given, the probabilities are determined by the order in which
they are named, being fifty-fifty for the first and less than one in a thousand for an alternative named tenth or later, as shown in Table 8.

Adimu

When the nature of the impending good or evil fortune has been ex-
plored to the client's satisfaction, the next step is to ask whether a sacrifice

TABLE 7

THE FIVE KINDS OF GOOD AND BAD FORTUNE

A. Good Fortune

5	4	3	2	1
china	bone	snail	cowries	stone
defeat of enemy	children	marriage	money	long life

B. Bad Fortune

5	4	3	2	1
china	cowries	stone	snail	bone
loss	want of money	fight	illness	death

(ẹbọ) to Eshu will be sufficient, or whether an additional offering is necessary. This asked in terms of two alternatives, ẹbọ and adimu; the latter, which is interpreted as meaning "to take refuge," being understood to mean adimu in addition to the sacrifice (ẹbọ) mentioned in the verse.

If adimu is selected, Ifa must then be asked to whom it should be offered, again in terms of a choice between five specific alternatives. The same objects are used to represent these, and are laid out before the diviner as shown in Table 9, with the numbers again indicating the order in which the divining chain is cast.

Because of the similarity in their names, though they are clearly distinguished by tone, the bone (egungun, egun) symbolizes the masked dancers (Egungun, Egun, Egigun), who themselves represent the dead during certain funerals. The snail shell represents Orişa, because snails are sacred to Orişala and to other "White Deities" (orişa funfun). Cowries represent Ifa "because it takes so much money to become a diviner," or, as clients might add, because diviners earn so much money. The small stone represents the forehead (iwaju) or head (ori) because "when a person grows old and his head turns grey, his skull turns into stone." The china potsherd represents the occiput (ipakọ, ọrun) because the back of the head resembles a china bowl.

If Egungun is indicated, the adimu is offered to an Egungun in the client's compound, if there is one; if not it can be taken to any Egungun in town. If an Orişa is indicated, two objects are used to determine which one through specific alternatives, asking in turn whether or not it is Orişa Agbala (Orişa of the Backyard), Orişala (God of Whiteness), Orişa Oko (Orişa of the Farm), Orişa Alaşe or Oluorogbo, Orişa Ikire, and any of the many other "white deities" (see Chapter XI), and the adimu is taken to its shrine. Adimu is not given to Ogun, Şango, Şọpọna, Ọramfẹ, Ọşun, or many other deities who receive offerings only when the verses direct they be given sacrifices (ẹbọ). If Ifa is indicated, the adimu is offered to the palm nuts of the diviner who is consulted. If the forehead or the back of the head are indicated, it is understood that it is the head of the client

TABLE 8

PROBABILITIES FOR TWO ALTERNATIVES PRESENTED IN SEQUENCE

Order Mentioned	Probability	Percentage
Cast 1	1 in 2	50.0
Cast 2	1 in 4	25.0
Cast 3	1 in 8	12.5
Cast 4	1 in 16	6.25
Cast 5	1 in 32	3.125
Cast 6	1 in 64	1.563
Cast 7	1 in 128	0.781
Cast 8	1 in 256	0.391
Cast 9	1 in 512	0.195
Cast 10	1 in 1024	0.098

TABLE 9

THE CHOICE OF ADIMU

5	4	3	2	1
china	stone	cowries	snail	bone
occiput	forehead	Ifa	Oriṣa	Egungun

himself to which the adimu should be given; both parts of the head are associated with the individual's multiple souls, and with the destiny assigned
him at birth (see Chapter XI).

Again there is some variation in symbolism. In place of the snail shell
one Ifẹ diviner used the tip of an elephant tusk, because the symbol (irin
oriṣa) of Oriṣala and other White Deities is a piece of bone or ivory. In
Igana, the china potsherd represents Oriṣa, because its color, white, is sacred to Oriṣa; and the hoof of a she-goat represents Ifa because she-goat
is Ifa's favorite sacrificial food. Only four alternatives are presented in
Igana: Egungun, Oriṣa, Head, and Ifa, the other two symbols being the
same (see n. 10, p. 114).

The next step is to determine the nature of the offering to be made as
adimu. This is again done in terms of five alternatives, represented by
any five objects without any symbolism. For Egungun the alternatives are
(1) a calabash of cold water; (2) two dried fish and two dried rats; (3) food
and drink, meaning lots of stew and yam loaves (4) dry meat, meaning wild
game shot by a hunter; and (5) a live animal killed at home. For Oriṣa the

alternatives are the same except that in (2) two snails are added. For Ifa, in (1) kola is added, in (2) bundles or dried fish and dried rats are speci- fied, and in (3) maize beer is added. For both the forehead and the back of the head, in (1) kola is added. If the fifth alternative is indicated, the client may determine which kind of a four-legged animal should be killed by using two alternatives. In this case a forearm of the animal may be sent to the diviner as a gift, but the diviner receives nothing as payment (eru) from adimu.

The general outline of the procedure in divination is as follows. (1) The first cast is made to determine the figure for which the verses are recited. (2) Two casts are made to determine whether the prognostication is for good or for evil. (3) Five casts are made to find out what kind of good or evil is indicated. (4) A succession of double casts may be made to find out in more detail about the evil. (5) Two casts are made to find wheth- er a sacrifice (ẹbọ) is sufficient, or whether adimu is required in addition. (6) If adimu is indicated, five casts are made to learn to whom it should be offered. (7) If adimu is to be made to a "white deity," it is identified by a succession of double casts. (8) Five casts are made to determine what is required as adimu. (9) If a live animal is required, a succession of double casts may be made to find out what kind. (10) The verses of the figure of the initial cast are recited, and the appropriate verse is selected. (11) The correct sacrifice is determined by a succession of double casts. If at point 5 ẹbọ is indicated, steps 6 through 9 are omitted; and if the client wishes, steps 2 through 9 may be skipped; and if palm nuts are used, the process may be reduced to steps 1 and 10 only.

VI. THE SACRIFICES AND MEDICINES

The objective of Ifa divination is to determine the correct sacrifice necessary to secure a favorable resolution of the problem confronting the client, whether or not an adimu is required in addition. Sacrifices are necessary to ensure that predictions of good fortune will come true, as well as to avert the misfortunes which have been foretold. As is made clear in some of the verses (e.g. 101-1, 170-1, 170-3), the failure to sacrifice when blessings are prophesied may result not only in their forfeiture, but in evil consequences.

Except for the offerings known as adimu, all sacrifices (ẹbọ) are offered (ru, rubọ, ru-ẹbọ) to the shrine of Eshu unless otherwise specified in the verses. Eshu, the divine messenger and trickster, is symbolized by a rough chunk of laterite (yangi) set outside of every Ifẹ compound and just outside the room of every babalawo. Any liquid is poured over the laterite, bits of kola nuts are placed on top of it, and the rest of the sacrifice is placed at its base. In Mẹkọ and some other Yoruba towns a crude mud image is the symbol of Eshu; each Mẹkọ diviner keeps such a figure under an inverted pot (cf. Maupoil, 1943: 179). In making the sacrifice the client prays, "Eshu, here is my sacrifice. Please tell Qlọrun (the Sky God) to accept my sacrifice and relieve my suffering."

A small part of each sacrifice is set aside for Eshu himself as a "bribe" to ensure that he will carry the rest to Qlọrun, the Sky God, for whom most sacrifices are destined. Eshu does not carry the sacrifices to the other deities; sacrifices to them are made at their own shrines; but again something is set aside for Eshu, so that he will not cause the client trouble. Several verses (6-3, 14-2, 86-2, 244-2, 255-3) state that a sacrifice should be offered to Ifa, in which case it is made to the diviner's palm nuts unless the client has a set of them at home. Some specify that sacrifices should be offered to Şango (4-3), to Olurogbo or Orişa Alaşẹ (17-1), or to a deity that uses the parrot's red tail feathers (247-5). Some instruct the client to care for his own deity (111-1) or to renovate the shrine of a neglected deity in his family (2-2). Others prescribe sacrifices to the client's head (7-4, 247-4), to the head or the grave of his father (7-1, 54-8) or mother (3-1, 170-2), depending upon whether they are alive or dead, or giving a dead person a funeral (101-1, 181-1, 184-1). Some verses instruct that the sacrifice be taken to a crossroad or fork in the path (orita mẹta), one of Eshu's favorite haunts, and it may be taken there even if this is not specifically stated in the verse (183-4). Some verses state that all or part of the sacrifice should be taken into the forest (1-10), to the farm road (86-1), to a garden by the waterside (167-1), to the bank of a river (120-1), to a flowing river (225-1), to still water (225-2), to a town gate, to a market, or into the street. Sacrifices which have to be disposed of at a specified place, such as these, are known as irabọ.

When Christians and Muslims who consult the babalawo are reluctant to sacrifice to Eshu, whom they have been taught to regard as the Devil, or to the other Yoruba deities, they are told to give alms (sara) instead. In

this case they prepare a feast (sara) with the foods prescribed and invite
relatives and passing strangers to partake of it. One verse (248-3) specifically instructs that a feast of this type be given in place of a sacrifice.

In addition to the sacrifices, some verses prescribe the preparation of
magic or "medicines" (ogun) of a type known as ayajǫ. These often include
the appropriate leaves of Ifa (ewe Ifa), which vary from verse to verse, some
of the divining powder in which the appropriate Ifa figure has been marked
on the tray, and an incantation. One Ifę babalawo maintained that all incantations (ǫfǫ) came from the Ifa verses, although other medicine men (ologun)
try to use them without knowing Ifa. The leaves and other materials are
compounded and given to the client in a drink or in food (1-8, 2-1, 239-1),
or for him to use in washing or rubbing his head or body (111-2, 225-1, 256-
1). The medicine may be rubbed into small incisions (gbęrę) cut in his skin
(1-6, 5-4, 6-4), or be used to mark the appropriate figure on the wall of his
house (239-2, 256-6). The two latter figures, Ǫsę Meji and Ofun Meji, are
commonly seen marked on the front of a house as protective medicines for
its inhabitants. Sometimes the divining powder is simply sprinkled in a
line from the client's forehead to his occiput (see Plate 20).

There may be protective and retaliatory medicines ("good and bad magic") for the same verse. For verse 1-2, for example, the proper leaves of
Ifa are gathered to make the medicine and Ogbe Meji is marked in the divining powder while pronouncing a good incantation to "open the road" for the
client wherever he goes; other leaves are prepared and Ogbe Meji is marked
while reciting a bad incantation to keep an enemy from completing anything
he undertakes. Other medicines are compounded to protect against witches,
avoid death, keep out thieves, kill one's enemies, cause them to go mad, or
simply make continual trouble at home for them.

Not all verses have medicines associated with them; but in addition to
those which do, the babalawo learn "pure ayajǫ," which have no verses but
which are considered as part of Ifa because they are associated with the Ifa
figures. Only one of these is recorded here (256-6); it consists simply of
the instructions and the incantations to give it power, and it has none of the
usual characteristics of the verses.

The figures of Ogbe Meji, Ǫyęku Meji, Iwori Meji, and Edi Meji set at
right angles to each other as reported by Frobenius (1913: I, 255), Maupoil
(1943: 187-188), and Mercier (1954: 255) was recognized by informants as
part of Ifa, but only as medicine and without any orientation to the cardinal
points of the compass. A Mękǫ diviner identified it as medicine for good
luck and success in trading, with color associations running white, black,
blue, and red. An Ifę diviner denied associations of the figures with either
colors or deities, and identified it as "mediator" (oniata), a very strong
medicine to spoil the work of one's enemy. One sits at a crossroad facing
the enemy's house, draws the four figures with Ǫyęku Meji toward it and
Ogbe Meji toward one's self, and recites the incantations.

The preparation of any of these medicines is spoken of as "making
Ifa" for or against someone. The babalawo are herbalists as well as diviners, although divining is their primary function. Clients may come to
them for medicine without having a divination, and they pay extra for its
preparation. The diviners are very reluctant to reveal these medicines,

not only because some of them are antisocial, but also because they are
purchased like other medicines (ogun) and some cost dearly. They are the
last things that the diviners learn, and they are not compounded or recited
in the client's presence. The diviner recites only to the point where the
medicine begins, and then stops.

Two verses (1-8, 239-1) prescribe the preparation of medicine without mentioning a sacrifice; some (1-1, 1-2, 18-5, 18-11, 246-1, 249-5) mention neither sacrifices nor medicine; and others (1-4, 1-5, 14-2, 183-2, 183-
3) indicate that a sacrifice is required without specifying its content. It is
possible that these verses are incomplete, but even if the sacrifice is not
recited as a part of the verse, it was memorized along with the verse when
the diviner was learning Ifa (see n. 8, verse 1-1). Of the 186 Ifa verses recorded here, only one (248-3) does not require a sacrifice; it calls for a
feast (sara) instead. No sacrifice is required for text 256-6 either, but this
is medicine and not a verse.

The diviners say that there are a few verses which state that the result
is inevitable and cannot be altered by sacrifices, although none was actually
recorded. These verses state specifically that no sacrifice is necessary
for some good fortune to come to the client, or that someone is certain to
die regardless of what he may do. This is consistent with the Yoruba belief in a destiny that controls their lives, and in a predetermined life span
that can be shortened by evil forces, but never lengthened (see Chapter
XI). Delano (1937: 180-181) describes a prediction for the daughter of a
friend: "'The illness will prove fatal.' 'Any sacrifices?' we asked him together. . . . 'There is no sacrifice. She will die,' he announced, but he advised the father to get certain medicines which might have a healing effect."
It is not clear whether these medicines were a friendly afterthought or
whether they were prescribed in the verse. With these few exceptions, every divination should end with the offering of a sacrifice, and it does not
only if the client fails to carry out his implicit obligations.

It is considered advisable to make the sacrifice as soon as possible,
and a number of verses (e.g. 14-1, 18-2) warn of the dangers of postponing
them. As several of the verses (e.g. 35-7, 54-6) make clear, if a client
cannot afford to make the prescribed sacrifice, it is wise for him to give
at least part of it in order to "appease Eshu" (pa Eşu). If a sacrifice is inexpensive and requires only materials that are readily available, it is often
made immediately. The client may send someone home to get them or give
him the money to buy them in the market, waiting with the diviner until
they arrive; or he may go for them himself. If the client has difficulty in
raising the money or in finding some of the materials, the sacrifice may be
made as much as twenty or more days later.

When postponed, a sacrifice is usually offered on the "day of secret"
(ǫjǫ awo) which is sacred to Ifa, more commonly known in Ifę as Ǫjaifę, or
the day of the market of Ifę (ǫja Ifę). On these days the babalawo divine
for each other, and in Mękǫ they prefer to cast kola nuts, because they say
that the palm nuts and the divining chain call for more expensive sacrifices.

If the sacrifice costs more than the client can afford, if he does not
trust the diviner, or if he does not believe the prediction, he simply leaves

and does not return. Even if the verse has specified that the sacrifice
must be made at once, the diviner has no way of knowing his decision, and
in any event he makes no attempt to force him to make it or to induce him
to do so by reducing the sacrifice. If the client and diviner meet in the
street, the diviner does not refer to the incident, and the client is free to
consult him again at any time about other problems. The diviner has no
further obligations in this instance, and the client assumes the full responsibility for the consequences of failing to follow Ifa's instructions.

If the client chooses not to make the sacrifice prescribed, the only
charge is the small amount of money that he lays down after whispering
his problem to it. This is usually only a penny or two or three pennies,
but a wealthy man may wish to give as much as five shillings. One or more
kola nuts or cowry shells are sufficient also, and in some verses (1-3, 1-7,
33-1, 181-1) five cowries are specified as the amount given by the mythological character. The amount given at this time is left entirely to the client, and the only factors determining it are what he happens to have at hand,
how much he can afford, and how much his social position requires him to
give. The diviner keeps these cowries and small coins, but they are an in-
significant part of his income, which is derived mainly from the sacrifices
themselves.

In most verses the things to be sacrificed are specified either in describing a sacrifice made by a mythological character under similar circumstances in the distant past, or in a statement directed to the client.
Where different sacrifices for the mythological character and for the client are mentioned, as in verse 123-1, the latter takes precedence. Some
verses (e.g. 137-1, 225-3, 247-2, 249-3) mention several different sacrifices, with the choice between them depending upon the client's particular
problem.

Some verses (33-5, 33-6) state that the prescribed sacrifice must be
complete (pipe), and others (6-3, 6-4, 183-4) say that it must not be reduced (aidin). According to one diviner the prescribed sacrifices must be
made without modification when palm nuts are employed, and their cost is
higher, suggesting that when the divining chain is used, the modifications
suggested are generally less expensive.

In other cases Ifa is usually asked whether the sacrifice is acceptable
or whether it should be modified. This is done in terms of two specific alternatives, stating, "The sacrifice is correct" (as specified) and then, "The
sacrifice is not correct." When Ifa indicates that it should be modified, it
may be either increased or decreased. Again by means of two specific alternatives, the diviner suggests a sacrifice similar to that mentioned in
the verse, but altering the quantities or the items involved, and asking
whether or not it is acceptable. A series of such variations is proposed
until one is accepted by Ifa. If a sacrifice includes two kola nuts, their
number may be increased to four, six, eight, or more, or reduced to one
or none.

In one instance, when the verse (131-1) called for the sacrifice of a
she-goat, three cocks, one hen, and one razor, Ifa first indicated that the
sacrifice should be modified, then refused the suggested addition of sixteen

shillings six pence, and finally accepted a reduction of the number of cocks to one and the amount of money to eleven shillings while retaining the other items.

Most sacrifices include money (owo), although many do not. The amounts of money are stated in the verses in terms of cowry shells (owo), which served as money before the introduction of currency. In Part Two the number of cowries required is given in the Yoruba texts and in their interlinear translations; their value is given on the opposite pages in terms of pounds, shillings, pence, and oninis. The onini was a Nigerian coin worth a tenth of a penny, which was in common use in 1937-38, when the shilling was worth $0.24. Following World War II, it largely went out of circulation as a result of inflation; and the value of the shilling fell to $0.14 as the result of the devaluation of the pound sterling. A second devaluation of the pound in 1967 reduced the value of the shilling to $0.12.

Inflation has reduced the value of cowries since the early days of the slave trade. In 1515 the King of Portugal issued a license to import cowries from India to Sao Tome, and by 1522 they were being imported to Nigeria from the Malabar Coast by Portuguese traders (Ryder, 1959: 301). During the seventeenth century the Dutch were importing cowries to Nigeria from the East Indies (Dapper, 1668: 500). During the nineteenth century the value of 2000 cowries was reported as 4 s. 6 d. by Tucker (1853: 26), and as having fallen to between 2 s. and 1 s. 5 d. by Burton (1863: I, 318-319) when still cheaper cowries were being imported from Zanzibar. The Zanzibar cowries (owo ẹyọ) drove the smaller, whiter Indian and East Indian cowries out of circulation as money, although they are still used for ritual purposes. When cowries were replaced by currency, the value of 2000 cowries was stabilized at 6 d., at least for the purposes of divination, or 80,000 cowries to the pound. Cowries were counted in strings of 40, in bunches of 200 (5 strings), in heads of 2000 (10 bunches), and in bags of 20,000 (10 heads) weighing sixty pounds. In the range of money included in the sacrifices the basic unit of counting is 2000 cowries (ẹgbẹwa, ẹgba).

When money is included in the sacrifice, it is understood that, unless otherwise specified in the verse, it is to be kept by the diviner as payment (eru). Some verses specify that he is to receive no payment at all; others say that he may not keep the money, but must give it away. Some verses (e.g. 35-7, 241-2, 248-1, 248-2) require the same amount from two or more individuals, increasing the potential income of the diviner but not the cost to the individual client. The amounts of money most commonly mentioned in the verses recorded are 7 d. 2 o. (ten instances), 1 s. 3 d. (twelve instances), 1 s. 7 d. 8 o. (fourteen instances), 3 s. (twenty-three instances), and 11 s. (twelve instances). The range is from less than a penny (7.8 oninis) to thirty shillings, with two shillings as the median.

These amounts were far more costly in earlier times before inflation reduced the value of cowries, but they still were not inexpensive in 1937-38. According to Forde and Scott (1946: 91) the daily wage of laborers on Ifẹ cocoa farms was only one shilling plus 4½ d. for food in 1938, following a very prosperous cocoa season; and in 1937 cocoa laborers were being paid as little as six pence a day by Ifẹ informants.

If Ogbe Meji or Qkanran Iwori is the first figure cast for a client, he must pay an additional six pence. Both additional fees are called 2000 cowries (ẹgba, ẹgbẹwa), and the latter is known as Qkanran, which Egan takes (Qkanran Egan gba). Egan was interpreted as referring to Eshu, but the money is kept by the diviner as part of his payment.

Instead of money, or in addition to it, the sacrifices call for domestic fowls or animals, wild animals or wild meat, dried rats or dried fish, snails, eggs, yams, palm oil, kola nuts, peanuts, beans, leaves, cooked food, maize beer, cloths or clothing, rope, bags, pots, plates, calabashes, digging sticks, hoes, axes, cutlasses, knives, razors, needles, rings, beads, chalk, whips, cudgels, mortars, drums, or other items. The total value of these may exceed that of the money called for in the sacrifice.

Unless otherwise specified in the verse, the entire sacrifice, except for money, in theory belongs to Qlọrun and should be deposited at Eshu's shrine. However, the diviner may ask Ifa through specific alternatives whether he may keep some of the sacrificial materials for himself as part of his payment; and he may suggest giving Eshu only a feather of a chicken or a hair of a goat instead of killing them, or offering only a thread in place of a cloth. In each instance the probabilities are fifty-fifty.

When an animal is sacrificed, its head is given to Eshu, but Ifa must be asked about the disposition of the body. The first question is whether it is to be eaten. If the answer is affirmative, the meat is cooked and eaten by the diviner and his family and visitors, the client receiving nothing. If the answer is negative, Ifa is asked whether it is to be given to another diviner and whether the diviner is an Ẹlẹgan or an Olodu (see Chapter IX); finally, the names of individual diviners are suggested in sequence. If it is not to be given to a diviner, Ifa is asked if the meat is to be roasted and divided among the inhabitants of the diviner's compound. If the answer is negative, Ifa is asked whether it is to be cut up and put in a potsherd with palm oil and left as an offering (ipeṣe) for witches (ajẹ) at a fork in the road, a river, and other specific places.

Because so many questions are left up to Ifa, and because the disposition of the sacrificial materials is often not specified in the verse, there is no easy formula for relating the sacrifices mentioned in the verses to the income of a diviner. The most that can be said is that the amount of money is a rough approximation of the minimum payment he receives, and that the total value of the sacrifice is a rough indication of his maximum payment and of the cost to the client. As the result of inflation, the relative value of these other items has of course increased, but because they may have to be given to Eshu while the money is kept by the diviner unless otherwise specified in the verse, the diviner's net income from individual sacrifices must have declined steadily since European contact. Certainly the worth of the money included in the sacrifice has decreased relative to the value of these other materials.

The favorite sacrificial animal of Ifa is a she-goat, and one verse (204-1) recounts how she-goats were substituted for human beings as sacrifices to Ifa. A different version of how this happened is given in an Ifa myth as told by an Igana diviner.

The King of Benin consulted the diviners and was told to make a sacrifice lest his daughter, Poye (or Poroye) lose her way. He refused to sacrifice, saying that she could never lose her way; but she got lost and wan-
dered about in the forest. At that time Qrunmila's mother had a slave
named Şiere. The slave was a harnessed antelope and its work was to cut
the facial marks of Qrunmila's children. The slave became tired of seeing
them every day, and ran away. Ifa ran after it and chased it for sixteen
days. The antelope ran into the forest, and Qrunmila drove it out. It ran
into the grasslands, and he chased it out. It ran into the dense forest of
Alabẹ and fell into a pitfall; Qrunmila followed and fell in also. Neither
could get out. After seven days in the pit, Qrunmila heard the voice of
someone passing by and called out, "Forest is the forest of fire; Grassland
is the Grassland of sun;[1] Dense forest which remains is that of Alabẹ. It
is seven days that Erigialọ has been in the pit, that Ifa has been rolling in
the pit."

It was Poye who was passing, lost in the forest. She looked into the
pit and saw Ifa. Ifa begged her to pull him out of the pit, and she agreed.
As she pulled him out, he was pulling up the thigh of the antelope. When
Qrunmila was out, he announced that the antelope thigh was his walking
stick, "My life is leopard, thigh of antelope." Ifa thanked Poye and asked
what he could do to repay her for her help. She said that she had no child,
so Ifa had intercourse with her. He told her that since his other wives
must not know that he had taken another wife, she could not live with him.
Poye became pregnant and gave birth to a daughter. They asked her who
the child's father was, and she said it was Ifa. She named the child Qlọmọ.

In those days Ifa used to sacrifice human beings. He told his people
to bring him a slave so that he could sacrifice to his ancestral guardian
soul, and they brought him Qlọmọ. He said he would make his sacrifice in
three days; meanwhile, he ordered Qlọmọ to pound cornstarch in the mortar. While she was pounding, she was saying, "I am the daughter of Poye.
If I had a father they would not have taken me as a sacrifice." Ifa's three
wives (Osu, Odu, and Osun) heard what she was saying and told Ifa that the
girl who was pounding cornstarch was strange and that he should listen to
what she was saying. When Ifa had heard her, he asked, "How did it happen
that you are the daughter of Poye?" The girl replied that her mother had
told her, "I helped your father to get out of a pit; afterward he had relations
with me and I had you as my daughter." Ifa said, "Sorry, oh! This is my
daughter."

His three wives asked, "Oh? When was this that you took another wife
and had this daughter?" Ifa replied, "It was not like that. I was in trouble
and this woman pulled me out of a pit. She begged me for a child, so I repaid her for what she had done for me." Then he sent them to buy a goat to
sacrifice, and he set Qlọmọ free.[2] He said that from that time on, they
should not bring any human sacrifices to him; that they should sacrifice
only she-goats. Since that time, she-goats have been sacrificed to Ifa.

---

1. Cf. verse 1-4.
2. Cf. the variant of this tale recorded by Frobenius (1926: 205-207).

The sacrifices are rituals in themselves, varying from one instance to another, which the diviners must learn to perform correctly during their period of instruction. In the following example the verse selected (183-4) for a client contemplating a trip named four pigeons and 16,000 cowries (four shillings) as the sacrifice, to which two lumps of cornstarch and a small quantity of palm oil were added through specific alternatives. Two dried rats and two dried fish had been selected as the adimu to be given to Ifa. The client gave the diviner four shillings, which constituted his payment, and three shillings six pence for his apprentice to purchase the other materials in the market. The four pigeons cost three shillings, though smaller ones could have been purchased for seven pence each, while six pence covered the fish, rats, porridge, and palm oil.

The figure Otura Irosun, which had been cast with the divining chain, was marked in the divining powder on the tray, and four piles of leaves provided by the diviner were laid out in front of the divining bag. The two lumps of cornstarch porridge were broken in half and one half was placed on top of each pile of leaves. The four shillings provided by the client were then placed on the tray, with eight cowries that were to represent them,[3] and were stirred intermittently in the divining powder while the diviner repeated all the verses of Otura Irosun that he had previously recited, holding the four pigeons in his left hand. Then the cowries were taken out and touched to the client's head, and the four shillings were set aside for the diviner.

Two pigeons were given to each of two assistants, who stood on either side of the diviner. After putting palm oil on the blades of the locally made knife and the imported razor which they used, each cut off the head of one pigeon, cut open its stomach, spilling out the feed, pulled out the heart, and threw it on the ground near the head. It was said that the hearts and heads would be thrown away. The two pigeons were laid on top of the two center piles of leaves and the cornstarch porridge was stuffed inside them.

The two remaining pigeons were returned to the diviner, who held them while casting the divining chain again to ask Ifa if he could keep them as part of his payment. Ifa refused, and they were killed as the others had been, stuffed with cornstarch porridge, and placed on the outer piles of leaves. Two cowries were then placed on the porridge in each pigeon, divining powder was sprinkled on them, and palm oil was poured on top of each (cf. verse 1-9). The pigeons were then touched to the client's head, two at a time, and placed in a calabash, and some of the divining powder was dropped in a narrow line from the back to the front of the client's head (cf. n. 6, verse 1-5 and Plate 20). That night, after dark, the diviner would have the sacrifice taken to a crossroad, where it would be left for Eshu. It would be avoided by people who saw it being carried there, and the first person to see it at the crossroads the next morning would receive the misfortune that had been foretold for the client.

---

3. As cowries are counted in units of two thousand, four shillings is the equivalent of eight units; each unit, worth six pence, was represented by one cowry.

VII. THE PREDICTIONS

Three principal steps are involved in Ifa divination. The first is the selection of the correct figure, associated with which is the message that Ifa wishes to have conveyed to the client. This is achieved by the manipulation of the palm nuts or by a cast of the divining chain, and can be interpreted in terms of the laws of probability, with each of the figures having one chance in 256 of appearing. As viewed by the Yoruba diviners and clients, the choice is not left to chance; rather it is controlled by Ifa himself. From our point of view, Ifa, rather than Eshu, might be described as the deity of or a personification of chance. The initial figure cast determines the group of verses that will be recited.

Secondly, the correct verse bearing on the client's problem must be selected from those which the diviner has memorized for this figure. The verses deal with a variety of problems that may confront the client, including illness and death, poverty and debt, getting married and having children, taking new land and building a new house, choosing a chief and acquiring a title, undertaking a business venture, taking a trip, and recovering lost property. The verses prescribe the sacrifice to be offered, although this may be somewhat modified, and they predict the outcome of the client's problem. The verses are the key to the entire system of divination; and the selection of the correct verse, containing the message that Ifa wishes to have conveyed to the client, is the crucial point in the procedure.

Finally, it is necessary for the client to offer the sacrifice in the prescribed manner in order to assure the blessings or to avert the evil consequences that have been foretold.

It is not necessary for the diviner to know his client's problem in order for the correct verse to be selected; in fact, clients take pains to conceal their problems from the diviner for the same reasons that they conceal or reverse the symbols of good and bad in working with specific alternatives. Taking the penny or so which they give to the diviner, they cup it in their hands so as to cover their lips and whisper as voicelessly as they can their question to it, and then put it down. Before the diviner makes his initial cast, he dangles the divining chain so that its ends touch the coin (see Plate 16) and asks, "Ifa, have you heard what has been said to the penny?"

Informants in Ifẹ agreed that the diviner's experience gives him a special understanding of human problems, as Herskovits (1938: II, 216) says, but when told that in Dahomey the position of diviner "is one in which complete frankness between him and his questioners is demanded, so that he is able to get at the facts in a given case to an extent which an ordinary adviser would find impossible," they objected. They said it was wrong for the diviner even to know the nature of the problem, because he would be tempted to lie to satisfy the client, either faking a verse bearing on the problem or reciting one which belongs to a different figure from the one cast, and the client would not receive the correct message from Ifa. Both diviners and clients in Ifẹ maintained that a good diviner does not draw upon his knowledge of the client's personal affairs, though they admitted that there are some unscrupulous diviners who do so. Araba of Igana said that after the correct verse has been selected, the diviner may draw on his knowledge of the client's affairs in advising him; but the client should not tell a diviner why he has come for a consultation, as the diviner will tell him this when he recites the verses.

Actually it is the client himself who selects the verse. The diviner simply recites the verses that he has memorized for the initial figure, while the client listens for one that bears on the problem with which he is concerned. He may either stop the diviner as soon as it has been recited or wait until the end of the verses before deciding which is most appropriate. As each figure has verses bearing on a variety of problems, there is nothing mysterious, as Delano and others have suggested, about the way that the diviner arrives at an answer to the client's problem. The client finds his own "answer," i.e. the prediction and the required sacrifice, when he chooses the verse most directly related to his own problem.

This does not mean that the diviners are charlatans or that the entire system is a fraud, as both European observers and educated Africans have sometimes concluded. What it does mean, however, is that Ifa divination is essentially a projective technique, comparable to the Rorschach Test, in that "its interpretation depends on the client's motivations and other psychological factors," as René Ribeiro (1956: 18-19) says. This parallel was recognized by a priestess of a Yoruba-derived Afrobrazilian cult in Recife, who regarded the Rorschach Test as a divinatory technique and asked Ribeiro (1956: 5-6) to "look Ifa" for her. "Finally it should be pointed out that since Ifa verses are frequently ambiguous entailing the re-structuring of loosely structured stimuli for interpretation, its rapprochement with the best projective methods becomes more than legitimate" (Ribeiro, 1956: 20). The client, depending on his own problem, selects the verse that provides his "answer," and he also interprets the problems of the mythological characters in the verses in terms of his own needs and anxieties. In this connection it is to be recalled that according to three Yoruba authors, J. Johnson, S. Johnson, and Lucas, it is the diviner rather than the client who selects the appropriate verse.

For those who expect that divination will tell them which candidate will win the next election or which horse will win in the third race, a word of explanation is required. It is possible to ask such questions through the technique of specific alternatives, but to do so would be foolish and would neither prove nor disprove the effectiveness of the system of divination, because their frame of reference is quite different from the questions that Ifa answers. These are, in essence, "Which of the candidates proposed should be selected for the best interest of all concerned?" or "Which of the suggested house sites will be best for the welfare of the people who will live there?" and "What sacrifices are necessary to ensure the most favorable outcome?" Answers to these questions are not easily evaluated, either immediately or ultimately, especially since they are given in terms of the destinies that are believed to control the lives of the individuals concerned.

As with other systems of divination, and even with Western medicine and science, the client is rarely able to decide whether the prediction is

accurate. The results are usually known for some time, and even when the
sacrifice is followed by misfortune, there is always the reasonable doubt
that the consequences might have been worse if the sacrifice had not been
made. As one diviner explained, if bad is foretold through specific alternatives and then confirmed in the verse, the sacrifice is made so that the
consequences will not be as severe as predicted; and if good is similarly
confirmed, it is made so that the blessing will be greater and come more
quickly. Even Western science has been plagued by questions of this type,
and one may debate whether to follow the advice of one doctor or another,
or none at all. Like these other systems, Ifa divination depends upon an
underlying foundation of belief frequently reinforced by its successes,
while its failures are rationalized or forgotten. A number of sanctions reinforce this belief (Bascom, 1941: 43-54) and shift the blame for failures
from the system of divination to other causes, such as the ignorance or
dishonesty of the diviner. As in the case of a doctor whose patient dies, a
number of explanations are possible, and while the doctor's skill or knowledge may be questioned, the system of medicine itself is not. And as with
prayers and rituals, there can be other benefits aside from all questions
of actual efficacy.

For clients the immediate advantage of consulting Ifa is the resolution
of doubts about the course of action to be taken in any case where he cannot decide for himself between the known alternatives. Except to test the
ability of an individual diviner, clients do not ask Ifa a question the answer
to which is obvious, or a problem they can solve using their own reason
and knowledge of the circumstances. Thus in choosing a house site, only
those which seem suitable for the purpose would be proposed in terms of
specific alternatives. In effect, the specific choices presented to Ifa are
those for which a decision can be reached only with difficulty, because the
alternatives are relatively equal in merit and, accordingly, the consequences will be similar regardless of the choice. In this Ifa probably resembles all other systems of divination, or the advice sought of a doctor,
a priest, or any authority regarded as having greater wisdom. As a proverb says, "One is not wiser than the person who casts Ifa for him [A ki
igbọn ju ẹni-ti o ma d(a)-Ifa fun-(ẹ)ni lọ], implying, among other things,
that if the diviner did not know more than we do, we would not consult
him. Even the tossing of a coin can end indecision and lead to positive
action. But when decisions are left to divine guidance rather than chance,
the individual has far greater assurance that he is following the correct
course of action. He can proceed with greater confidence; and, accordingly, in some cases he probably has a greater chance of success.

In addition, as Park (1963: 196-197) has argued, this divine sanction
legitimizes the client's decision on a course of action and shifts the responsibility for its consequences from the client to the gods. If the choice
of a house site leads to a physical separation from the lineage and segmenta-
tion, this cannot be blamed on the client as an act of his free will, because
the choice was made by Ifa.

The cogency of Park's argument is readily apparent when one considers the manner in which the choice between two or more candidates for

office can be "fixed" without the connivance of the diviner, as described in the following chapter. This can be done for personal gain or other ulterior motives by those responsible for the choice, but it also permits them to make certain that the candidate they consider best qualified is selected. In either case they are absolved of personal responsibility and shielded from offending the rejected candidates. Unless the ruse is suspected, the blame is placed on Ifa, on the candidate's own destiny, on Qlǫrun the Sky God, who assigned it, or on the candidate's own behavior, which may have offended his ancestral guardian soul or one of the deities.

An answer that will satisfy the client is built into the system of divination. The diviner cannot fail to arrive at the client's problem, unless he has not learned an appropriate verse. If he knows enough verses for the figure that is cast, he can touch upon the major problems that confront any client in Yoruba society, and many other societies as well. The Yoruba themselves take a similar view, maintaining that answers to all problems are to be found in Ifa, and blaming the ignorance of the diviner rather than the system when he fails to recite a verse applicable to their needs. When this happens, the answer is that the diviner does not know enough, and the obvious solution is to consult another diviner who knows more. A proverb refers satirically to the diviner who hesitates and looks up helplessly because he has not learned enough verses or cannot remember what comes next: "One who doesn't know Ifa is looking up; but there is no Ifa in the attic." [Ai-gbǫ-(I)fa li a nwo-(o)ke, Ifa kan ko si ni para.]

The interpretation of the client's problem depends on the number and the kind of verses which a diviner has memorized for the figure which is cast. In Ifę it is maintained that a diviner must know at least four verses for every figure, or a minimum of 1024 verses, before he can begin to practice professionally on his own. A respected diviner of middle age said that he knew only four verses for most figures, but that more experienced diviners like Agbǫnbǫn knew about eight. More verses are learned for the paired figures than for the combinations.

In Igana a novice is expected to know at least two verses for each figure before he can divine on his own. The Araba of Igana said he knew about four verses for all figures except Eji Ogbe, for which he knew eighty. In Mękǫ a novitiate is tested by his seniors, but one verse for each figure is regarded as sufficient for him to pass. Two of the principal Mękǫ diviners admitted that for one figure (Oturupǫn-tewere) they knew only one verse, and for another (Edi Ika) only two, though they knew more for the other figures.

The more verses that a diviner knows for each figure, the more likely he is to be able to recite one that touches on the client's problem. A diviner does not stop studying once his apprenticeship is completed and he has begun to practice on his own. He continues to learn new verses and medicines from his instructor and from other diviners who are willing to teach him, usually for a fee. In effect the period of studying never ends, and a diviner keeps learning until he dies.

It must be stressed, however, that the diviner earns his reputation not by the number of verses he can recite, but by his success in securing favorable solutions to his client's problems. His reputation and his business depend on satisfied clients, who recommend him to their friends and relatives. An Ifẹ diviner explained that one who can recite a hundred verses for a figure may not be as successful as one who knows only four, because "some verses are better than others." This evaluation refers to the fact that while certain verses may refer specifically to a single problem, some of them have several specific interpretations, and others are very general, foretelling only unspecified good or bad fortune.

To take a specific example, seven verses were recorded from one Ifẹ diviner for the figure Iwori Meji. Of these, the first one recited, though referring to a journey, is the most general in its prediction, stating only that "Ifa says he will not allow us to see evil in the matter for which we have divined" (35-1). The second applies to several different problems, with any of which the client may be concerned, implying good fortune not only in it but in the others as well. "Ifa says he sees the blessing of visitors, the blessing of money, the blessing of children, and the blessing of a title" for the client (35-2). The third specifies two separate problems, referring to something that has been lost and to someone who is about to become a chief (35-3). The fourth is applicable only to someone who is contemplating a journey (35-4), and the fifth to someone who is having trouble with his relatives, who do not allow him to have a home, a farm, or peace (35-5). The sixth refers to three children of the same mother, of whom the youngest is ill or is causing trouble because he is argumentative (35-6); and the last refers to a group of six relatives, one of whom is ill or all but one of whom has died (35-7).

Some systems of divination appear to depend upon vague generalities that are left up to the client to interpret specifically in terms of his own situation. Like the ink blots of the Rorschach test, they are relatively unstructured, rather than structured, like T.A.T. cards. Without verses of the former type, which predict only evil or good fortune in vague terms, even the best babalawo would frequently be unable to answer their client's questions. Understandably, these verses are highly prized by the diviners. The first verse (35-1) cited above is an acceptable answer on ritual occasions such as an annual festival, when the question is whether things will go well during the coming year; and it could be accepted by a client who felt his case was not correctly stated in any of the other six verses.

However, some clients would expect the diviner to be able to mention his problem more specifically, and would be satisfied with this verse only if they were contemplating a journey. Even more highly regarded, for this reason, are the verses that mention several specific problems (e.g. 35-2), all of which may be derived from the precedent case and explanatory tale, as in verse 167-1. Ifa divination depends more upon multiple alternatives, stated in the several verses recited for a figure as well as within single verses, than on unstructured generalities. It is more of a shotgun than a blanket technique, but the blanket covers up when the shotgun misses.

The statements of the client's problems in the verses and the predictions about their outcome reveal not only the many reasons which cause a person to consult the diviners, but also a great deal about the goals and values underlying Yoruba behavior. In one sense they reflect universal problems faced by human beings the world over and values that are shared by many different systems of belief; in another, they mirror the way in which these common problems are viewed and these common values expressed in terms of Yoruba beliefs.

It should not be surprising that the greatest number of verses are concerned with death, either directly or by implication. These amount to thirty-six verses[1] or almost 20 per cent of the total recorded; but others are concerned with long life (1-1, 1-5, 2-3, 17-3, 183-1, 225-3) and abiku or children who wish to die (1-4, 19-3, 33-1). Illness is also a major concern, mentioned in 14 verses;[2] others deal with avoiding or overcoming bad medicine (19-1, 167-1, 243-4, 246-1, 247-2), witches (3-3, 34-1, 224-2, 239-2), and evil spirits (3-2, 6-2, 239-1, 244-2, 247-2). One verse predicts the death of anyone who invokes evil on the client's head (248-4); others warn against being confined to one spot (183-2), having a weak voice (181-3), and giving birth to a dumb mute (225-4). Death, illness, and physical disabilities are universal problems, but they were thought by the Yoruba to result from what we would consider to be supernatural causes, rather than germs, viruses, or genes.

The number of verses that express the desire for children reflect a widespread value, but one that is far stronger among the Yoruba and in other African societies with lineage systems than, for example, in the United States. The Yoruba belief in reincarnation gives added importance to the perpetuation of the lineage. In promising children, one verse adds, "Ifa says that the name of this person will not die out" (52-4); and, in all, twenty-eight verses promise children if the sacrifice is made.[3] Others are concerned with abiku, as noted above, with keeping the pregnancy from being spoiled (6-4, 19-2, 183-2, 225-4, by witches in the first and last case), and with impotence (9-1, 20-2, 34-1). To have children a man must have a wife, and the more wives he has, the more children he can hope to have. Wives are promised in twenty-four verses,[4] and two warn against the loss of a wife through death (7-5) and desertion (54-5). Three verses instruct

---

1. 1-4, 3-3, 7-2, 7-5, 17-2, 18-4, 18-7, 18-9, 18-10, 19-1, 19-3, 33-1, 33-6, 34-2, 35-6, 35-7, 54-7, 86-1, 101-1, 111-1, 123-1, 153-1, 167-1, 170-2, 175-2, 181-1, 181-3, 225-2, 239-1, 239-2, 241-2, 241-3, 243-3, 245-4, 248-1, 256-3. Underlining indicates that the problem is implied rather than stated specifically.

2. 6-6, 9-2, 18-2, 30-2, 33-6, 153-1, 154-1, 170-1, 175-1, 183-1, 241-1, 243-4, 247-2, 256-4.

3. 1-3, 1-9, 4-2, 4-3, 5-3, 6-5, 7-2, 9-1, 18-1, 18-6, 18-11, 19-3, 20-3, 33-4, 35-2, 52-4, 54-2, 54-3, 86-3, 103-1, 137-1, 181-1, 225-3, 246-2, 247-4, 248-2, 249-3, 255-2.

4. 1-9, 1-10, 1-11, 3-4, 7-4, 34-1, 35-2, 52-5, 54-3, 54-5, 101-1, 103-2, 123-1, 131-1, 137-1, 153-1, 175-1, 245-2, 246-2, 247-1, 247-3, 248-3, 249-3, 249-6.

women to become "wives of Ifa" (3-4, 7-2, 17-2), and one (4-3) predicts the
birth of a daughter who will marry a diviner. None of the other verses recorded promise husbands, which is not surprising in a polygynous society
where all women marry.

To get married, a man needs money to give as bridewealth to his wife's
family, and it is also important in his social advancement. Eleven of the
verses promise money;[5] and others promise wealth (3-1, 6-1, 18-3, 18-5,
246-3) or property (1-10, 14-3, 247-3). Several speak of the loss of the
money given as bridewealth (7-5, 123-1) or of avoiding debts incurred to
pay bridewealth (33-1, 33-2). Some verses promise profits (7-3, 256-2),
the repayment of losses (249-2), or that something lost will be found (35-3);
or they warn against losses (6-2, 54-4) or a spoiled business deal (241-4).

Money also enables a man to compete for a title or to increase his social status if he is not eligible for one. One verse says that the client will
not take a title but will be more important than a chief (245-3); another says
that even if he is not made a chief, he will have more honor than those who
are chiefs (225-3). Title-taking is mentioned in ten verses;[6] others simply
speak of attaining an important position (2-3, 54-7, 170-3, 222-1, 255-1,
256-1) or becoming important (2-1, 2-2). The loss of a title and the loss of
a position are mentioned in two verses (246-4, 255-1). Three verses say
that a man will build or own his own house (137-1, 243-1, 256-2), which is
a promise of status as lineage head (Bale) rather than of wealth, since
houses were lineage, not personal, property. The same promise is implied
in three verses which say that the client will take new land for a settlement
(33-5, 52-2, 167-1), since it also belonged to the lineage. An important
measure of a man's social status is the number of those who follow him
when he goes about town (Bascom, 1951: 496-497); and his influence depends
on the number of followers and relatives he can count upon for support.
Followers are mentioned or implied in nine verses, almost as often as titles.[7] Other verses promise honor, glory, or fame (1-8, 52-1, 52-3, 54-7,
111-2, 131-1, 243-4, 250-2), making a name (1-6), not being forgotten (1-2),
avoiding disgrace or shame (5-2, 168-1, 241-1, 250-3), and avoiding or ending ridicule or insults (20-1, 246-2, 255-3, 256-2).

The sequence of the steps to a successful male career are clearly
spelled out in several verses: money, wives, children, and title (35-2);
money, wives, children, house, and title (137-1); money, wives, children,
title, and long life (225-3). These steps also correspond to the ranking of
the five kinds of good in the world, but in it long life ranks first (see Chapter V).

Other verses are more varied in their predictions. The client should
become a diviner or an Ifa worshiper (6-3, 86-2); he will be able to take
a rest (1-8, 18-3); he will receive visitors (18-5, 35-2) or make a new
friend (1-9). He will avoid or overcome his enemies (35-5, 137-2, 247-2),

_____

5. 1-9, 5-1, 5-4, 9-3, 35-2, 52-3, 137-1, 225-3, 245-3, 249-3, 255-3.
6. 14-3, 17-4, 18-1, 18-3, 35-2, 54-2, 137-1, 181-1, 225-3; 246-2.
7. 7-4, 18-11, 18-12, 131-1, 225-3, 243-1, 249-1, 255-3, 256-2.

an evil wisher (4-1), a trouble-maker (166-1), a tale-bearer (225-2), or
an enemy (35-3, 52-2, 54-1, 54-5, 255-1, 256-1). A hunter may kill someone accidentally (167-1), or the client may be taken as a thief (3-4, 14-1,
246-4). He is warned against having to take an oath or trial by ordeal (166-
1), being lost on a trip (183-1), or being injured in a storm (33-1, 33-2).
His secrets may be revealed (153-1, 168-1), or his promises may become
empty (250-1). The client's children may become enemies (5-3), or he may
have no peace with his wife (245-2). Something is taking everything away
from him (247-5), or he may be left with no one to take care of him (7-1).
Several verses warn that the client may not be able to enjoy the fruits of
his own labor (120-1, 183-2, 243-2) or receive credit for his own accom-
plishments (183-2), or that others may destroy what he has achieved (52-
2).

Many verses are less specific. The clients will achieve their destiny
(14-2, 52-1, 52-3, 225-3, 244-1, 245-1, 255-3, 256-1) or receive a benefit
or blessing (18-5, 52-3, 170-1, 170-3, 250-1). They will be successful
(1-1, 1-2, 7-1, 14-2, 52-1, 55-1, 222-3, 243-2, 249-1, 250-3), avoid failure
(52-4), or not draw a blank in an undertaking (4-4, 18-8). Someone will assist them (120-2, 222-1); they will be provided for (54-8); things will be
easy for them (7-2, 250-2) or set right for them (17-1, 24-1). They will
find their way in life (247-5), sit down in peace (249-4), find peace of heart
(35-3) or contentment (225-3, 256-5). The client will be able to join forces
with others so as not to be worthless (181-2); others will not be able to
hinder him or have power over him (55-2); no one will outdo him (1-1).
Things may be spoiled for him (7-1, 14-2, 54-1), or his efforts may come
to an impasse (183-3). The client is troubled (3-1, 170-2, 246-3) or unlucky (255-3), or he is warned against a dire affliction (33-6) or an evil
(35-1, 35-4, 86-1, 166-1, 175-1).

In addition, several verses contain specific admonitions about the client's own conduct. A wife is advised to be very considerate of her husband (1-7), and other clients are warned against being overjoyed (170-1,
170-3) or overambitious (244-1), against spoiling something important
through a small detail (35-7), or against losing everything through adultery
(245-4). Others are warned not to break an oath (256-3), to avoid fights
(9-1, 48-1, 154-1), and to beware of someone who has a powerful supporter
who will come to his assistance (167-1, 245-4).

Among the occasions on which clients consult the diviners are undertaking a journey (3-2, 14-1, 14-3, 35-1, 35-4, 52-3, 120-1, 175-2, 183-4,
247-2, 256-5) or a business deal (241-4, 256-2), building a new house (137-
1), or taking new land (33-5, 52-2, 157-1). The client is troubled by his
relatives who will not let him have a house or a farm (35-5), or he is involved in a case in court (246-3, 249-6). Or he is acting as if he had lost
his way (247-5), or as if he were cursed (225-1) or insane (243-1).

VIII. PROFESSIONAL ETHICS

As indicated in Chapter VI, the sacrifice specified in the verse may be modified; but since the question whether the sacrifice should be altered is asked in terms of two specific alternatives, it can be assumed that there are no modifications in 50 per cent of the cases. The client may not suggest to the diviner how it should be modified, because "one does not bargain with Ifa as one does in the market place." The diviner has complete discretion in making these proposals, but they are subject to acceptance or rejection by Ifa; and once approval has been indicated, no further modifications may be suggested. If the prescribed sacrifice is large and expensive, it is likely that smaller amounts of money or goods will be proposed, and if it is inexpensive, they may be increased; but this decision also depends upon the diviner's estimate of his client's wealth. The diviners say that a goat or a sheep is the most expensive addition that would be suggested unless the client were a king, in which case a cow might be mentioned; a poor man would not be asked to sacrifice a cow, "because Ifa is no fool."

Within certain limits the principle of charging what the traffic will bear is admitted by the diviners and accepted as fair by their clients. In discussing this question, one diviner cited the proverb, "Whatever amount pleases one is what we sell Ifa for." [Oye ti o ba wu-(ẹ)ni ni a ta Ifa-(ẹ)ni pa.] Nevertheless, even if a client is rich, a diviner is expected to be reasonable in his suggestions and to be guided by the sacrifice mentioned in the verse which he has just recited to the client. The diviners say that it would be unfair to take advantage of a sick person or to charge strangers more than relatives. The clients say that Ifa teaches the diviners to be kind and that if they know a client is poor, they may suggest a hair in place of a horse, some wool in place of a ram, or a feather in place of a chicken; or they may suggest a calabash of water, or sixteen pebbles, or something else of no value. As noted earlier, one informant said that sacrifices are generally more expensive when they are not modified, suggesting that the diviners usually propose reductions. Should a diviner charge too much, he might lose some of his clientele, but the other diviners would do nothing about it. It is significant that none of the Ifẹ diviners had earned the reputation of overcharging.

However, that there are dishonest diviners who falsify their predictions is believed by both clients and diviners, and this belief is confirmed by the precautions that the clients take to conceal their problems (see pp. 68-69). A case in point is cited in one of the Ifa verses (247-2) in which a king's diviner, who was having an affair with the king's wife, heard that another diviner was coming; he instructed that the new diviner was to be killed as a human sacrifice because he feared that his guilt would be revealed, as indeed it was. In another verse (244-2) a false diviner pleased his clients by promising them blessings, whereas a truthful diviner correctly warned them against evil spirits. Wishing to believe the first prophecy, they bound the truthful diviner and left him in the forest until the evil

76

spirits arrived and they saw that he had been telling the truth. Eshu intervened to save the truthful diviner, who, in turn, saved the clients.

Any diviner who controls the figure that is cast or modifies its interpretation so as to falsify the message of Ifa must deliberately depart from the principles of divination in which he has been trained for many years. To do so defeats the entire purpose of divination by giving a message other than the one Ifa intends for the client to receive, and this is considered strictly unethical. Clients avoid diviners whom they suspect of such practices, while the diviners deny that they themselves engage in them, and both agree that few individuals are actually guilty of them. The diviner's ignorance rather than his dishonesty is the usual excuse for failures.

The clients themselves may control the outcome in some situations without the connivance or even the knowledge of the diviner. If candidates for an office are selected through two specific alternatives, naming them in succession until one is chosen, the one first named has twice the chance of being chosen as the one named second, and the one named tenth has less than one chance in a thousand (see Chapter V, Table 8). Moreover, as the diviners themselves acknowledge, the choice can be "fixed," rather than left to chance, by the individual who conceals the bone and the cowries in his hands. He simply announces that whichever object Ifa selects represents "No" in the case of candidates to be rejected, and that it represents "Yes" in the case of the one agreed upon beforehand. No one can challenge his statement, as he alone knows what he has whispered to the objects. The same deception can be practiced when Ifa is presented with a direct choice between two candidates, and it is probably common practice where a successor to the king or another important position has already been selected after long campaigning and careful consideration and Ifa is asked to confirm the wisdom of the choice.

It is important that the candidate who is to be rejected must not become suspicious, lest he ask that the alternatives be named aloud. He is usually prepared for the occasion by those who arrange this deception, by making him believe that everyone wants him to be selected, and great disappointment is expressed when another candidate is chosen. The conclusion is that it is much safer for a candidate to trust the diviner and insist that everything be done openly than to allow the alternatives to be concealed on the grounds that the diviner might be able to control the figures cast.

It might also be safer to insist that the divining chain, rather than the palm nuts, be used. There is little chance that the fall of the divining chain can be controlled if it is a good instrument that permits the free fall of the seeds, and it is significant that this is the type of chain preferred by diviners (see pp. 29-30), and that choices between specific alternatives are usually made with it.

It is possible that an unscrupulous diviner might achieve sufficient skill in manipulating the palm nuts to be able to control the figure he produces, and perhaps even escape detection by his colleagues. This would be difficult to do directly, as the palm nuts are not easy to handle. However, he might simply continue "beating" them until the desired number remained in his hand. For example, if it suited his purpose to produce the

figure Ogbe Meji, he could pick the nuts up again if two were left as he
normally does when three or more are left, and continue beating until only
one remained. The rapidity with which the nuts are beaten would make it
difficult for an observer to tell the number remaining, and even an expert
could not be certain that he had not felt some nuts slipping from his grasp
(see Chapter IV). The client's protection against such practices lies in
his ability to conceal his problem and in his choice of a diviner on the basis of his reputation for honesty.

It appears easiest for a diviner to falsify the results in the recitation
of the verses. Here he might select from all the verses he has learned,
regardless of the figures with which they are associated, in order to find
one that fits the problem with which he believed the client to be concerned,
or he might improvise one to fit it. It would be even easier for him simply
to keep on reciting verses memorized for other figures until he came to
one that touches on the client's problem; but any of these subterfuges might
be detected if his apprentices or another diviner were present. The diviner
is expected to recite the verses for the figure as he learned them, without
knowing which applies to the client's problem. He may alter their order if
he wishes; but if he is honest, he must recite only the verses belonging to
the figure that is cast.

An unscrupulous diviner must be subtle enough to avoid arousing the
suspicions of his clients, as well as to avoid detection. An informant explained that if the first verse recited for him by a diviner should pertain
to housebuilding (e.g. 167-1), he would be suspicious because it was common knowledge at the time that he was building a new house. Even if he
had come to ask about a completely different problem, he would distrust
the diviner and his advice, and would not make the prescribed sacrifice,
believing that the diviner was guessing or was "twisting" Ifa to fit the situation. If the message of Ifa is twisted in this way, neither the prediction nor
the sacrifice are relevant to what Ifa intended to convey. Similarly, if a
woman who is childless after several years of marriage were told in the
first verse that she was going to have a child (e.g. 20-3), she would suspect the diviner whether or not this was what she had come to inquire
about. The Araba of Igana said that a diviner may even avoid reciting
first a verse that touches on a problem which, he happens to know, concerns the client, because the client would suspect him of lying. Even an
honest diviner is not above suspicion. There is an Ifa saying to the effect
that "If we cast Ifa today, it must not come to pass today," because people
will suspect the diviner whose prediction was accurate.

An apparent contradiction is involved here, for a diviner's skill is
judged in part by his ability to recite the appropriate verse immediately
while others touch upon it later or not at all. Earlier I concluded that
"where a diviner's reputation for honesty is doubted, the fact that he answers the client's question immediately is held against him, whereas if
his reputation for honesty is beyond reproach, it is taken as evidence of
his skill" (Bascom, 1941: 51). This may be a partial explanation, but the
nature of the problem is probably the critical factor. When it is common
knowledge that the client is faced by the problem cited in the first verse,
he suspects the diviner's honesty; but when the problem is known only to a

few, and perhaps only to himself, he respects his skill. A clever diviner could, of course, also recite several verses before the one he improvises or takes from a different figure to suit the client's known problem.

Aside from his skepticism when the first verse recited refers to his problem, the client is protected in several other ways: by his choice of the diviner he consults, by his ability to conceal his problem, by whatever familiarity he may have gained through prior consultations, by the fact that the diviner's apprentices and colleagues who know the verses are often present, and by the fact that the reputation of a successful diviner could be ruined if he were detected in reciting verses from the wrong figure.

The main protection of the client, however, is that it is unnecessary for a diviner to falsify a prediction if he knows sufficient verses, although clients are not aware of this fact. Whether even the diviners themselves realize it is open to question, although they recognize the advantage of knowing more verses, and they prize some verses that "are better than others" (see Chapter VII).

There is no way of determining the proportion of unethical diviners. Though both clients and diviners believe that they exist, the former are hesitant to make accusations, and the latter are quick to affirm their own innocence. There is no question in my own mind, on the basis of my experience, that most of the babalawo are honest, as both diviners and clients assert. They operate in perfectly good faith, employing a system in which they believe implicitly and in terms of which they themselves offer sacrifices, make decisions, and in fact order their own lives. They believe that they can best serve both their clients' and their own interests by transmitting the message of their deity, Ifa, as accurately as possible.

It is possible for clients to test a diviner's accuracy through specific alternatives, and in two of the verses (35-3, 54-4) this is done by the mythological character. In the latter, when the cow of the Sea Goddess died, she had it covered with cloths like a human corpse, and told her followers to announce her own death. When they called the diviners to learn if any sacrifice was required, they all announced, because they were not skillful in the use of specific alternatives, that the kind of evil with which they were confronted was death. The followers of the Sea Goddess asked if there were not another diviner; and when he came, he announced that the evil involved a loss. The Sea Goddess then revealed herself, rewarded him, and chose him as her diviner.

The diviners themselves may test their divining chains in this way to see whether or not they are telling the truth. Before beginning to divine in the morning, they may find whether a particular chain is "talking" through specific alternatives, asking questions whose answers they already know — for example, whether "The sun will set tonight" or "The sun will not set tonight." Or they may send someone into another room to put one of his hands on the wall, out of sight, and ask whether "It is the right hand" or "It is the left hand." If the wrong answer is selected, they conclude that the chain is "not talking" that day, and test another in a similar fashion. It is for this reason that diviners have several chains. Not all diviners test their chains, one maintaining that "anyone is willing to talk when he wakes up in the morning," and it is considered unnecessary to test the palm nuts in this way because they are reliable, whereas the divining chains are not.

The reason for maintaining that the divining chain is an inferior and less reliable instrument may derive from the fact that it is more often used for the technique of specific alternatives. If many questions are asked, conflicting answers may be given, and occasionally the answers may contradict what is said in the verse. In the instance cited earlier, where the figure Otura Irosun was cast for a client who wished to learn about taking a trip, the verse selected (183-4) warned that he would lose his way if he did not sacrifice. However, in the inquiries through specific alternatives, good rather than evil was indicated, and the kind of good specified was children. In discussing this with the diviner, he indicated that such contradictions were not infrequent, but when either good or evil is confirmed, the prediction is more certain. Nevertheless a sacrifice would still be required. He was more puzzled by the reference to children in this context, though he showed little concern, pointing out that the correct answer had come out eventually through the verse, and citing the proverb "Like proverbs, like proverbs, is how Ifa speaks." [Bi owe, bi owe n(i)-Ifa sọrọ.]

IX. THE DIVINERS

The Ifa diviners are most commonly called babalawo or "father has secrets" (baba-li-awo) or simply awo, secrets or mysteries. They may also be distinguished from the others who worship Ifa as "fathers of those who have Ifa" (baba onifa). The term onifa or "those who have Ifa" (o-ni-Ifa) refers to all Ifa worshipers, including the babalawo, as does its synonym, Qlǫrunmila, or "those who have Qrunmila" (Q-li-Qrunmila). The worshipers of Ifa include men who inherit or are initiated into the worship of Ifa without becoming diviners, and women who are told to care for the palm nuts of their father but can never become babalawo. Only men can become babalawo. The babalawo are also the priests of Ifa, serving other Ifa worshipers as well as divining for those who worship other deities.

Some, but not all, of the worshipers of Ifa learn to "recite Ifa" (kifa, ki-Ifa) without becoming diviners. As a matter of individual choice they may memorize Ifa verses by studying with the babalawo, after which they may be referred to as "those who recite the deity" (akişa, a-ki-orişa). The full significance of this is not clear, or how it is related to those members of the other religious cults who recite the praise names of their deities. In one verse (6-3), however, the client is instructed either to practice divination or to recite Ifa. In Igana it was estimated that there were about three hundred who knew Ifa verses in 1938, as against twenty practicing babalawo. In Mękǫ in 1951 the estimate was twenty practicing diviners and perhaps two hundred Ifa worshipers. In Ifę the number of babalawo in 1937 was variously estimated by informants at from two to four hundred; an estimate in 1965 gave 120 babalawo and about one hundred other worshipers. According to the 1952 census, Ifę had a population of 110,000, Igana 9,000, and Mękǫ 5,000.

All babalawo undergo two expensive initiations, the details of which are too elaborate to be considered here (See Dennett, 1906: 251-253; Maupoil, 1943: 271-332), in the course of which they receive their two sets or "hands," each of sixteen palm nuts. Training in divination often begins before the first ceremony, and it continues afterward until the pupil is released by his teacher to practice divination on his own. Even after his release, a diviner continues to learn Ifa and has obligations to his teacher.

Four grades of babalawo are recognized in Ifę. The lowest grade of practicing Ifa diviners are known as ęlęgan or "those who have ęgan" (ę-li-ęgan), or as "secret of ęgan" (awo ęgan). The precise meaning of ęgan could not be determined, but Mękǫ diviners say it refers to a bag containing medicine prepared with leaves, medicine calabashes (ado), and other unspecified materials; most Mękǫ babalawo are said to prefer to have this rather than the odu, which marks the third grade in Ifę, because it is much less expensive. Unlike the other three grades, the ęlęgan shave their heads completely, and for this reason they are sometimes referred to as ajarimǫdi, meaning "those who shave their heads but do not tie (their hair)" (a-ja-ori-ma-di).

Diviners of the second grade undergo a third initiation ceremony, after which they are known as adoşu or "those who create a tuft of hair" (a-da-osu).

81

a general term for initiates into the cults for the Yoruba gods, or as "those who have a tuft of hair" (oloşu, o-li-oşu), or as "secret of tuft of hair" (awo oşu). They shave their heads, leaving a circular spot of hair (oşu) on the right side toward the back of the head, as explained in a myth in the following chapter. Formerly the tuft of hair was braided, but in recent times it has been clipped short. To be eligible to become an adoşu a diviner must belong to a compound that has an origi; this is a mound of earth built in front of the compound containing secret materials, which informants refused to discuss. Frobenius (1926: 171) illustrates one covered with potsherds with a stone projecting from the top, but potsherds are not always in evidence, and some are covered with cement (see Plate 21). The name "origi" was not explained, but Origi appears as the name of the father of Ẹla in an Ifa myth recorded at Ileşa (see Chapter XI). The number of origi in Ifẹ was estimated at more than fifty, all of which are said to have been constructed long, long ago, when Odua and the other deities lived on earth; no new ones have been added, although some have had to be repaired or rebuilt, as was the case about 1894 when the people of Ifẹ returned from Işọya, where they had taken refuge during the wars of the last century.

Diviners of the third grade have gone through a still more expensive initiation which few can afford; Ifẹ diviners said that it costs from £200 to £300. They are known as olodu or "those who have odu" (o-li-odu). Odu is interpreted as meaning something large or bulky, and its composition again is a carefully guarded secret. In Ifẹ it is kept in a special type of container, which is large, cylindrical in shape, fashioned of wood, and either painted red, white, and black with camwood, chalk, and charcoal (see Plate 21) or decorated in the same colors with beadwork. Other diviners may have similar containers, known as apẹrẹ or the apẹrẹ of Ifa (apẹrẹ Ifa), but theirs are unbeaded and unpainted. Both types may be used as stools to sit on, but they are normally kept with the other divining apparatus and materials in the shrine of Ifa, and they are carried out into the street during the Ifa festivals.

In Ifẹ the shrine or "house of Ifa" (ile Ifa) of an olodu is in an alcove (sasara) in the main chamber (akodi ọkankan) of the compound, with a raised mud floor and mud sides and ceiling; it can be closed off from the rest of the room by means of a curtain or mat. No woman is permitted to enter the alcove in which an odu is kept. Both the odu and the origi are important in the worship of Ifa rather than in divination and, as in Ifẹ, diviners believed that to reveal their contents would cause their death, this subject was not pressed; but some evidence from other sources is available.

J. Johnson (Dennett, 1906: 253) refers to the Igba Odu, or calabash of odu, which he describes as follows: "The Igbadu is a covered calabash, containing four small vessels made from coconut shells, cut, each into two pieces in the middle, and which hold besides something unknown to the uninitiated, one a little mud, another a little charcoal, and another a little chalk, and another some camwood,[1] all which are intended to represent

---

1. It may be this, rather than the divining bowl, to which Frobenius' remarks about these materials refer. See Chapter III.

certain Divine attributes, and which, with the vessels containing them, represent the four principal Odus—Eji Ogbè, Ọ̀yẹ̀kún Meji, Ibara Meji, and
Edí Meji—and this calabash is deposited in a specially and well-prepared
wooden box called Àpèrè. The box is regarded as very sacred and as an
emblem of Divinity, and is also worshipped. It is never opened, except on
very special and important occasions, as when perhaps a serious difference
is to be settled, and not without washed hands and often the offering of blood
to it . . . . the room where it is deposited is considered so sacred that no
woman nor any uninitiated man is ever permitted to enter into it, and the
door opening into it is generally beautified with chalk and charcoal colour-
ing, giving it a spotted appearance."

Epega (1931: 16) refers to the "Igba Odu (Odu Calabash) or, as it is also
called, Igba Iwa (the Calabash or Container of Existence) . . . . In this calabash wonder-working charms are stored by a great babalawo who gives
directions as to how it should be worshipped, with the strict warning, of
course, that it should never be opened except the devotee is exceedingly
grieved and therefore anxious to leave this world. Igba Iwa is so made as
not to be easily opened."

Mẹko diviners said that their odu is unlike that sketched and described
by Maupoil (1943: 168-170). They said it consists of a covered white calabash containing a crude clay figure like those which represent Eshu, and is
kept on a mud platform (itage) in a special room (iyara odu) which only Ifa
worshipers can enter. The calabash is opened each year during the annual
festival, when an animal is sacrificed to it; but it is very dangerous and
women and young men cannot enter the shrine where it is kept. Ileşa diviners also keep their odu in a calabash in a special room.

In Ifẹ the status of olodu is of less significance than elsewhere because
there is a still higher category, that of the diviners of the Ọni or King
(Awọni, Awo Ọni), all of whom must be olodu. This group, which is discussed in the following chapter, is headed by Araba, followed by Agbọnbọn
and fourteen other individual titles.

Diviners of any of the three highest grades are also referred to as
oluwo, meaning chief or master of secrets (olu awo); but this term has
several meanings. An ẹlẹgan may become recognized as an oluwo by vir-
tue of his knowledge of Ifa and his skill in divination; and the term is also
used to refer to the one who teaches Ifa to an apprentice, who is known as
a child of secrets (ọmọ awo). Epega (n.d.: III, 3) also notes that anyone
who teaches a person Ifa is called his oluwo, and this meaning was also recorded at Ileşa.

Oluwo is also the title of the head of all the babalawo of Ọyọ, followed
by the second oluwo, third oluwo, and so on. J. Johnson (Dennett, 1906:
264), followed by Frobenius (1913: I, 244, 251), Farrow (1926: 103), Lucas
(1948: 179-180), Abraham (1958: 80, 39), and Idowu (1962: 164), describes
the Oluwo as the chief babalawo, with Ajigbọna (or Adjigbona, Ajubọna) as
his chief assistant; however, J. Johnson and Frobenius note that one may
speak of the babalawo from whom he received his Ifa as his oluwo. In
Mẹko the diviner who teaches one how to divine is known as his ojugbọna,
a term which in Ifẹ refers to the subordinates who serve as assistants of
the King's diviners; the oluwo is a relative who is in charge of the initiation,

and if there is no diviner on either the father's or mother's side the relative is assisted by an unrelated diviner.

The babalawo are distinguished by a beaded bracelet worn on the left
wrist and known as ide or the beads of Ifa (ide Ifa), which generally are of
imported tan and light green beads, also known as etutu ǫpǫnyǫ. These are
called etutu ǫpǫyǫ in Ileşa and otutu ǫpun in Mękǫ, where the green beads
are distinguished as dark or "black" (dudu) and the tan ones as "red" (pupa).
One verse (256-3) refers to the use of these beads by Qrunmila worn around
his neck, and in another (35-3) they serve to identify Hyena as a babalawo.
In Ifę the bracelet may also include a palm nut or a light opal-colored glass
bead (emu) of European manufacture, as well as beads of other colors. The
tan and green beads are worn as medicine by others, although not around
the wrist, but the opal-colored bead is used only by babalawo.

The cow-tail switch (irukęrę, irukę, iru) or fly whisk is another insignia
of the babalawo, though similar whisks, made of horse tails, are used by
the chiefs. One of the verses (54-4) explains why these are always carried
by the babalawo when they go out to divine. A beadworker from Ęfǫn Alaye
spoke of making beaded whisks for diviners, but in Ifę and in Mękǫ these
are reserved to the King. The divining bell or tapper which the diviners
sometimes carry, also serves to identify them.

In addition, the diviners use an iron staff (ǫręrę, osun, osu), to which
are attached many small conical bells with iron clappers, which jingle each
time the staff is touched to the ground (see Plate 21). On ceremonial occasions it is used as a walking stick, and at other times it is stuck upright
into the ground in the patio of the diviner's house, where sacrifices are
periodically offered to it. In Ileşa it is known as the "staff of ǫręrę" (ǫpa
ǫręrę), and Epega (1931: 17) mentions it as osu. In Mękǫ the osun is a
smaller iron standard whose name was interpreted as meaning "not sleep"
(o sun). Each diviner has one stuck into the ground at his Ifa shrine, and it
is said to guard him while he sleeps. It must never be allowed to fall over,
lest the owner die; and at his death it is knocked down. In Mękǫ it is considered as a symbol of the God of Medicine (Qsanyin), who is described as
the owner of herbs and leaves and is venerated by the babalawo because
they so often use leaves in preparing medicines for their clients. Its
Dahomean counterpart (asen) is also regarded as representing Qsanyin
(Maupoil, 1943: 175, 218).

Most diviners in Ifę were trained through a system of apprenticeship
similar to that in the arts and crafts.[2] A father often prefers to have his
son learn Ifa (kǫ Ifa) from another diviner, so that he will not be treated
too leniently but will be given sufficient discipline to learn well; and if the
father is dead, there is no choice but to apprentice the child. No special
fees are required, but an apprentice must serve (sin) his master by fulfill-

------

2. A diviner at Mękǫ maintained that children were apprenticed only
when a woman who is troubled by abiku (successive deaths of her children)
is instructed in an Ifa verse to give her son as an apprentice to a diviner,
so that he may be protected by being close to Ifa. Apprenticeship is common in Ifę.

ing any tasks assigned to him, including running errands, purchasing materials in the market for a client's sacrifice, and carrying his master's divining bag on his shoulder when he goes out. Because of the latter function,
a diviner's apprentice is often spoken of as one who hangs a bag (akǫpo,
a-kǫ-apo). When he goes out with his master, he may be given a small
gift out of the payment his master receives, perhaps one penny out of six
pence. Some apprentices are fed and lodged by their masters; others sleep
and take their evening meal at home. Individuals who learn Ifa as adults
may pay a diviner to teach them rather than serving as apprentices; there
are no fixed rates for this, but in 1937 one man was giving his teacher food
and palm wine, plus a penny a day to teach him for as long a period each
day as he wanted.

Whether they learn as apprentices or are taught by their fathers, instruction may begin as early as five, six, or seven years of age. The pupil
learns by observing the divinations performed by the teacher for his clients
and by specific instruction in which the pupil is first taught to name the figures. The teacher prepares a divining chain, usually of pieces of calabash
joined by a simple cord, with which the pupil practices identifying the sixteen paired figures, followed by the combinations. Learning to choose between specific alternatives is followed by the far more tedious task of memorizing the verses, beginning again with Ogbe Meji and the other paired figures. The teacher recites a verse and asks the pupil to repeat it, correcting
him when he makes mistakes and prompting him when he forgets. Frequent
tests are given by marking a figure on the divining tray or forming it with
the divining chain, and asking the boy to give its name and to recite its
verses. Some figures like Ofun Ogunda require that an atonement be made
before its verses are recited, because they are considered powerful and
dangerous. One of the verses (249-1) of this figure says, "To find out if a
child is brave enough to recite Ifa, or if he is not brave enough to recite Ifa,
we use Ofun Eko (i.e. Ofun Ogunda) to test him."

The sacrifices and medicines or "leaves of Ifa" may be taught with the
verses with which they are associated or later when the verses have been
mastered. The pupil must be taught to find the required leaves in the forest, and an Ileṣa diviner said that he must learn to recognize and use over
four hundred leaves. Some of the medicines require atonements or "cool-
ings" (etutu) before their incantations can be recited, and with the medicines
not associated with verses they are usually learned late in the apprenticeship or after it has been completed.

In Mękǫ a novitiate is tested by his seniors before he can practice on
his own; they give him a divining tray, powder, and palm nuts and tell him
to divine. He marks the figures on the tray, names them, and recites the
verses, but one verse for each figure is sufficient for him to pass. A Mękǫ
diviner said that if a boy begins to study Ifa at six or seven years of age,
he may be able to learn enough to divine for others by the time he is twelve
or thirteen. A diviner from nearby Ilara said that he began to study with
his father at about the age of ten, and that he knew enough to divine by himself by the time he was about thirteen; nevertheless he had to stay with his
father working for him and learning from him until he was about twenty,

when he began to practice on his own, and he has continued to learn from others since his father died.

The duration of the period of training, mentioned by diviners in their own cases, varied from three, four, and five to nine and ten years; but none of them stopped learning when it was completed. The informant who dictated most of the verses had been studying Ifa thirty years, and most diviners continue to study Ifa as long as they live, either by associating with their colleagues while they are divining, or by paying other diviners to teach them specific verses or medicines. In some cases these have fixed prices; more often the teacher can ask any price he likes, and it can be reduced through bargaining. Once a diviner has agreed to teach a particular verse or medicine and payment has been received, he must teach it correctly without holding back any part of it. According to a Mẹkọ informant, however, one may pay for the medicines, but there is no charge for the verses.

Ataiyero (1934: 8) states that diviners should serve as apprentices for three to six years or more. Epega (1931: 12) says, "Before a man can become a Babalawo he has to learn Ifa for three to five or seven years. The primary 16 Odu Ifas and their branches are to be learnt in the first year. . . . In the second year the learner has to learn how to receive Ibo [i.e. to use specific alternatives] for Ifa in divination and the procedure in Ifa temple or groves. In the third year he has to learn the way of expressions [i.e. the verses] belonging to each Odu. This is the most difficult part of the Odu Ifas to master."

When the apprenticeship is ended and the new diviner begins to practice on his own, he must give his teacher part of whatever he receives as payment (eru) through divining, and this obligation continues as long as the teacher lives. It seems that the basis of sharing varies, and in Ifẹ the amount to be given is often left up to the pupil. An Ilẹṣa diviner said that for twenty years he took all his earnings to his teacher, who returned about a fifth to him; afterward he gave his teacher one shilling and some chickens each year until he died. In Ifẹ he is also expected to go to the assistance of his teacher whenever he is called upon and to stay with him several days if necessary.

In Igana every sixteen days, on the day of secrets (ọjọ awo) sacred to Ifa, Araba, the diviner of the town chief, feeds his apprentices and those who have studied under him. In 1938 there were five of these in his own compound and twenty-seven outside. Each brings two kola nuts and casts them to ask Ifa about their welfare. Before departing, one of them casts the divining chain for Araba, noting the figure, and then asks Ifa, "Do you accept this day and all that we have done?" using two specific alternatives. If the answer is negative, he will ask through a succession of questions what remains to be done. This is then done, the verses are recited, and Araba provides the materials for the sacrifice in the appropriate verse. After the sacrifice has been performed, the apprentices leave, clapping and singing Ifa's songs. Similar meetings with one's teacher are also held in Ifẹ between the meetings of the King's diviners.

One becomes a diviner in much the same way that he becomes a worshiper of any other deity: by following the worship (and profession) of his
father, by being told through divination that one should become a diviner,
or by a combination of these reasons. One of the verses recorded (6-3) indicates that the client should become a diviner: "Ifa says this is a boy who
is a diviner; he was serving Ifa when he came from heaven. The rising or
setting sun must not find him in the farm, and his feet must not brush the
dew from the farm road." It is understood to be tabu for this client to engage in farming, which involves spending nights in the far farms, and that
he should devote himself to divining. This is not a general tabu for diviners, however, and must be stated specifically in the verse.

The same tabu is imposed in another verse (86-2) on a client who is
instructed to worship Ifa: "Ifa says that this is someone who should not go
to farm, and who must not touch the dew with his feet. And we say that Ifa
is thinking of someone; he should be sacrificing to Ifa." In this case, because becoming a diviner is not specifically mentioned, it is understood
that the client may become a trader, weaver, or carver, or practice some
other craft. Some diviners farm on the side; some are so busy divining
that they have no time for farming; and some are prohibited from farming
by verses of this type (86-2, 6-3). If they break the tabu, their crops will
wither and they themselves will become ill. They are allowed to go to the
farms to gather the leaves required for medicines, but they must not so
much as pull a weed or enter a field of yams or corn.

One of the Ifa verses says that divination is to be preferred to farming and to the gathering of honey: "The fire is very hot on the face of one
who gathers honey; the sun is very, very hot on the buttocks of the farmer;
the one who gathers honey has losses; the honey bee swarms, and the honey
of the Ado bee spoils; but the house of a diviner is never empty" (18-8).
Another says, "An elder who learns Ifa does not have to eat stale kola nuts"
(131-1). Farrow (1926: 37) refers to a proverb that says, "The wisest
priest is he who adopts the worship of Ifa," but Akǫda, one of the King's diviners, said that this does not hold in Ifę, because divination is none too
lucrative.

Amosun, another of the Awǫni, has never engaged in farming, because
it was tabued for him, though his sons farm for him and give him some
of the yams and other produce from his land. Though he refused to go into
specific details,[3] he estimated that for every shilling's worth of farm produce he receives from his sons, he earns five shillings from divining.
"Look at my house" (which was large), he said. "Look at my people" (who

---

3. He refused even to say how many sons he had, asserting that this
knowledge could be used to bewitch them. He did explain that as long as a
son works for his father (sin baba), his produce goes entirely to the father,
whereas after sons have started working on their own, they may plant 2000
yam heaps for their fathers and 1000 for themselves, or only 200 for their
father and 2000 for themselves, just to help him.

were numerous). "I feed them, and what I have comes mostly from Ifa."

A diviner may wish to see his son follow his own profession, as a drummer may want his son to become a drummer, but neither this nor the fact that Ifa has been worshiped in the family is enough to make it attractive for young boys. The boys do not adopt divination as a career, like that of blacksmith or weaver, because the initiations are too expensive and the work of learning the figures and memorizing the verses, sacrifices, medicines, and other rituals associated with the worship of Ifa are too tedious. No one becomes a babalawo to make money, they say. It is usually through misfortune that one becomes a diviner: through illness, losses in trade, the lack of children, or the death of one's wives or children.[4]

Agbọnbọn, who was the second ranking of the King's diviners and the most respected babalawo in Ifẹ until his death about 1947, was told by his father when he was about four or five years old that he should study Ifa, but he refused. Later he was sent away from home four times as an indentured laborer or "pawn" (iwọfa). Before he left home the first time, his father told him that although he was a Christian, he had been born to become a babalawo, and explained that he should have been sent to a diviner to study Ifa, though this was no longer possible because it was necessary to pawn him to someone else. According to Agbọnbọn, this happened in 1854. When his father redeemed him, he returned to his father and worked his farm for him. While he was in the farm, a ghost appeared to him and commanded him to eat dust. When he did so, he swelled up and became ill, and this happened to him each time he returned home after having been redeemed.

About 1888, while they were at Isọya, about seven miles to the south, where the people of Ifẹ had been driven through war, Agbọnbọn's father called him and told him, "I will not return to Ifẹ with you, because I am about to die. You were not made to be a farmer; you were meant to be a babalawo. I have seen this many times during my dreams." He gave Agbọnbọn a divining chain. His father was a man "who had been to heaven and returned" (ayọrunbọ) to earth and who had powers to foresee future events, but Agbọnbọn was told that before he himself was born, his father had been a babalawo. When his father died, Agbọnbọn "inherited" one of his wives, and he acquired another when his brother died, making seven in all with the five he had previously married.

About 1894 the people returned from Isọya to Ifẹ, but after they arrived, all his wives and his children suddenly died. "What can I do?" he asked himself in despair. He wrapped up his set of palm nuts and £2-10-0 that he had, and started out of town to die by himself in the bush. When he had

---

4. According to the Araba of Lagos this is not the case in Lagos, where boys voluntarily adopt divination as a career. He suggested that Ifẹ may have differed because so many families were converted to Christianity, so that Ifa must "fight with" people to make them come to him. However, the pattern of refusing initiation into the cults until the deity fights with the person is widespread among the Yoruba and applies to many deities.

walked only about three hundred yards, he met chief Jagunoşin at the place where his house now stands. Jagunoşin asked him where he was going and, noting his despondency, asked him if he had been fighting with his wives. Agbọnbọn replied, "No. All my wives and my children are dead, and I am going into the bush to die." Jagunoşin said, "You are a coward and a lazy man. Do you know what you were made for?" Jagunoşin took him home, and at his suggestion Agbọnbọn consulted a diviner.

He was told that unless he became a babalawo himself, his family and his property would continue to be lost, so he became a diviner. This was about 1895, and since then he has become wealthy and respected. In 1937 he had so many wives that he said he had lost count of them, though there must have been about two hundred, of whom there were only twenty whom he really loved.

According to Agbọnbọn, a man becomes a babalawo through his destiny (iwa); afterward he tries to become an Awọni so that he will become important and one whom others cannot "cheat" (rẹjẹ) by taking things from him without payment or by calling on him for free labor (ọwẹ). In the old days, he said, there were forty-nine people in Ifẹ who could not be mulcted by anyone. At the top was the Qni, the King of Ifẹ, followed by his sixteen town and palace chiefs (Ijoye Qni), after whom came the sixteen Awọni, and finally the sixteen Otu priests who dispose of sacrifices made by the Awọni for the Qni in his palace. Nevertheless, he added, he would rather be wealthy than an Awọni, for with money one can do almost anything.

As another example, the case of an ordinary babalawo may be taken for comparison. Samuel Elufişoye's father had been a babalawo, but he and his family had left Ifa and become Christians when the missionaries came to Ifẹ. About 1913 Samuel's children began to die as soon as they were born, and all his wives died also. He went to Agbọnbọn, who divined for him and told him that his trouble would continue unless he returned to the worship of Ifa. He began to study divination; soon afterward a "wife of Ifa" was given to him, and later he was given another (see Plates 19-20). Both of them began to bear children for him, and he began to have money and to dress better. In 1937 he was of middle age, and fairly successful and respected. Both of these wives were still living, and none of his children had died "except those whom Qlọrun had not created to live long."[5] Two young boys, whose fathers had died, were studying Ifa as his apprentices. Samuel himself became Agbọnbọn about 1950 and held this title until his death on January 18, 1964.

A girl may be told through divination that she is a "wife of Ifa" (aya Ifa, iyawo Ifa), meaning that she should marry a diviner. The diviner gives no bridewealth for her, although he may give her presents before and at the time of marriage, and he is responsible for some of her expenses. This is considered as one of the diviner's "payments" (eru) which, even if relatively infrequent, is of considerable significance, as the cost of bridewealth in Ifẹ in 1937 was £13-0-0.

---

5. See the discussion of destiny in Chapter XI.

A wife of Ifa is "inherited" like other wives at her husband's death, even if he should die before she has reached the age of marriage. If she should elope with another man, either before or after marriage, it is believed that Ifa will "fight with her" and send her back to her husband through sickness or misfortunes, as it was with her own welfare in mind that she was told by Ifa to marry a babalawo. In Igana it was explained that if a wife of Ifa leaves her husband for another man, the diviner may not claim bridewealth in court, but he may claim recompense for presents given during the period of betrothal. It is believed that Ifa will bring her back to him by causing illness; when she consults another diviner about her trouble, she will be told that it is caused by the fact that she left her husband, because she was destined to be the wife of Ifa.

When, as may happen, the diviner Ifa selects as her husband is prohibited to her in marriage because of kinship and the rules governing incest, she is married to someone else, but not until after making an atonement to release her from Ifa. Her husband must provide a rat, a fish, a she-goat, a chicken, maize beer, and a length of firewood as gifts to Ifa, and her father pays the diviner £2-10-0, £5-0-0, or another amount of money less than the value of bridewealth, as determined through specific alternatives. Similar atonements are required if her father begs for her release because she is already betrothed to another man.

A girl may be told to become the wife of Ifa at her first divination or when she is ill during childhood, as in three of the verses recorded here (3-4, 7-2, 17-2); or it may be predicted before she is born when her mother consults the diviners because she has been unable to conceive or because of an illness during pregnancy, and is told that she will bear a daughter who should become a wife of Ifa. If either type of verse is selected as appropriate, the diviner whom she is to marry is determined through specific alternatives. In Igana, where there are no Awoni, the first question is whether or not the husband-to-be is in the lineage of the diviner consulted. If affirmative, the diviners in this lineage are mentioned in order of their age; if negative, other diviners in town are mentioned in order of their seniority and experience. In Ifẹ the first question is whether the husband-to-be is one of the Awoni or not, and then names of individual diviners in the category are suggested until one is selected. As the chances of the Awoni being indicated on the first choice is fifty-fifty, and as there are at most only sixteen of these against several hundred ordinary diviners, the King's diviners benefit more often in this way than the ordinary diviners.

X. THE KING'S DIVINERS

The sixteen babalawo of the King of Ifę, known as Awǫni or "secrets of the Qni" (Awo Qni), appear to be a special institution restricted to the Qni and the kingdom of Ifę. Other Yoruba kings have their special diviners, but organizations of comparable complexity are not mentioned in the literature, nor were they noted during field research in Qyǫ and Ileşa or on brief visits to the capitals of other Yoruba kingdoms. Nevertheless, this is consonant with the traditions that Ifę was formerly the dominant ritualistic and political center of the Yoruba, that Ifa himself once lived at Ifę, and that Ifa divination spread from Ifę to other parts of West Africa.

The Awǫni rank above all other diviners in Ifę. In the words of one of the latter, all other babalawo "count as nothing" no matter how much Ifa they may know or how skilled they may be in divination. In order to become an Awǫni a man must be a native of Ifę; he must be a practicing babalawo; and he must first have become an olodu. Two olodu (Eruda and Oyinnipępę) whom some informants named as Awǫni could not acquire this status, despite their skill as diviners, because they were foreigners (elu) in Ifę. Ifę men who acquire odu only because in divination they are told to do so in order to avoid illness or misfortune are also ineligible, because they do not practice divination.

In earlier times there were probably more eligible olodu than could be accommodated in these sixteen positions; but in 1937 the last five titles were unfilled because eligible candidates had been unable to afford the third and most expensive initiation. The son of the former Tędimǫle was a recognized oluwo and an old man, but had never been able to acquire the odu necessary for him to take his father's title. Also, although alien religious influences have had less effect on Ifa than on some Yoruba cults, there has still been considerable attrition, because men who would normally have filled these posts have given up Ifa in favor of Christianity and Islam. The Awǫni pointed out that formerly every male in the compound from which Araba is chosen (Oketaşę) would have become a babalawo; but in 1937 there were only five babalawo out of the sixty-seven adult males on the tax roles.

Each Awǫni has an individual title and, although a fifth outlay of money is required, becoming an Awǫni constitutes the taking of a title rather than a fourth form of religious initiation. The sixteen titles are listed below according to the order recognized in 1937:

1. Araba, a title whose meaning was explained as Silk Cotton Tree (Ceiba pentandra), which, because of its size, is spoken of as "Araba, father of trees" (araba baba igi), and refers to his importance. Araba is also the title of the head diviner in Igana and other Yoruba towns.

2. Agbǫnbǫn, said to mean the one who comes first, and to be the name of the first-born child of Qrunmila.

3. Agęşinyǫwa, first held by a man who was wealthy enough to own a horse which he mounted (a-gun-ęşin) and rode to the meetings of the diviners.

4. Aṣẹda, interpreted as meaning the one who makes creatures (a-ṣe-ẹda) because he "creates people in heaven."

5. Akọda, a title which usually means sword-bearer or "one who hangs a sword" (a-kọ-ida) but which was interpreted as a corruption of Akọde, meaning one who arrives first, because he is the one who calls the others at the annual festival and thus precedes them. This and the previous title are mentioned in a greeting to Ifa which Epega (1931: 17) translates "Akọda who taught Ifa to the whole world; and Aṣẹda who taught all the ancients (the) understanding" (Akọda ti nkọ gbogbo aiye ni Ifa, Aṣẹda ti nkọ gbogbo agba ni imọran).

6. Amosun, meaning the "one who takes osun," refers to the iron staff (osun, ọrẹrẹ) which the first Amosun carried for Ifa.

7. Afẹdigba, explained as meaning "owner of ẹdigba," refers to the large beads (ẹdigba) which each of the Awọni own. Afẹdigba arranges the beads of Araba while he dances, helping him to keep them in place.

8. Adifolu, said to mean one who divines all kinds of Ifa, mixing them together, though in practice he divines as others do.

9. Ọbakin, the "king ọkin" (Ọba ọkin), referring to a white bird (ọkin) identified by Abraham as an egret, which is spoken of as king of the birds and whose highly valued feathers are worn on the crowns of some Yoruba kings. He is described as the head of deposed kings, with the explanation that when they seek refuge with Araba and eventually leave to settle elsewhere, he serves as their representative or intermediary in Ifẹ.

10. Olori Iharefa, the "head of the Iharefa," who are the officials in charge of Ifa in the palace. Though the latter do not practice divination, they know a great deal about it, and often more than many diviners.

11. Lodagba, which was translated as "steward," is the one who serves food and drink for the other Awọni, and takes care of any that is not consumed.

12. Jọlọfinpẹ, meaning "allow the king to remain long (in office)" (jẹ-Ọlọfin-pẹ) or "Long live the King." His function is to treat the Ọni if he is ill. This and the following positions were vacant.

13. Mẹgbọn, said to mean "I am not wise" (ẹmi o gbọn), because the original holder of this title was respected for his rank rather than his skill.

14. Tẹdimọlẹ, meaning "press waist against ground (tẹ idi mọ ilẹ), because in the olden days he remained seated by the shrine of Ifa and could never leave it. In more recent times he had to remain by the shrine in Araba's house during Egbodo Erio, the second annual festival for Ifa.

15. Erinmi, not explained, but perhaps referring to a deity of the same name, whose meaning is "elephant of the water" (erin omi) or hippopotamus.

16. Elesi, also not explained, but perhaps meaning the "one who owns esi (e-li-esi), referring to a carved stone or wooden figurine prepared by the diviners in order to keep evil away from Ifẹ so that the townspeople will not die.

Effectively only two positions have fixed status, that of Araba and that of Agbọnbọn. The remaining titles are ranked on the basis of the seniority of the incumbents, and unless one of them becomes Araba or Agbọnbọn,

they keep their titles for life. In earlier times all titles were said to have
had fixed rankings, and an individual was promoted (reye, re-oye) upward
through them as those above him died. There was considerable disagreement among the Awǫni themselves about the earlier ranking, but it was
worked out and agreed upon by them (as was the order given above) at one
of their regular meetings as 1, 2, 5, 4, 3, 6, 8, 10, 9, 14, 15, 16, 13, 7, 11,
12.

Other evidence suggests that the title Lodagba (11) should have been
ranked last, as in effect he did in 1937, with five positions unfilled. Its
holder compared his position with the character after whom the figure Ǫṣẹ
Otura was named, who also served as "steward" of all the paired figures
(see Chapter IV). He also said that formerly there was one additional title,
and that Lodagba ranked seventeenth, with the seventeen titles equivalent
to the diviners' seventeen palm nuts, including the oduṣǫ. The diviners
claim that the original order of these titles is recorded in the Ifa verses,
with each being mentioned in a verse of the figure to which it corresponds
in rank. It should be noted, however, that Akǫda is named as a diviner for
verse Ǫṣẹ Meji (239-1) in the fifteenth position, and that Araba appears in
a verse for Ǫyẹku Ogbe (17-4) in the thirty-second position.

A number of informants maintained that the title of Araba was an Ǫyǫ
title introduced into Ifẹ in fairly recent times, and that formerly Agbǫnbǫn
had been head of the Awǫni; in support of this they quoted the saying,
"Agbǫnbǫn is the diviner of Ile-Ifẹ" (Agbǫnbǫn ni awo Ile-Ifẹ). One of the
Awǫni maintained that the first Araba, by the name of Agiri, was the son
of the Araba of Irẹsa by Mǫndẹ, a daughter of Arolu who was then the
Agbǫnbǫn. As the result of a quarrel Agiri left Irẹsa and came to Ifẹ to
live in the compound of his grandfather, Arolu. When Arolu died, Agiri
said that he wanted to become Agbǫnbǫn, but another candidate in the compound challenged his right to do so because he was related to the lineage
through a female. To avoid another quarrel, Agiri took the title of his father and settled at Oketaṣẹ near the grove of Ifa (igbo Ifa). According to this
informant there had been only eleven Araba in Ifẹ, and the title has not been
confined to Oketaṣẹ: (1) Agiri, who came from Irẹsa but was an Ifẹ on his
mother's side, (2) Gidiogbo of the Ile Araba Gidiogbo, (3) Kirǫsinla of Ile
Kirǫsinla, (4) Budugbu of Ile Olugbodo, (5) Lameloye of Oketaṣẹ, who was
driven out by Ǫni Abeweila and fled to Ifẹwara. He was succeeded by (6)
Kinfolarin of Ile Olugbodo, who was Agbǫnbǫn when this happened. After
King Abeweila died, most Ifẹ people were at Iṣǫya, where they had taken
refuge because of war. Lameloye went to Iṣǫya and Kinfolarin restored the
title of Araba to him, resuming his former title of Agbǫnbǫn. When Lameloye died, Kinfolarin again became Araba, and he was succeeded by (7)
Afala at Oketaṣẹ, (8) Jolugbo at Ile Atibi, (9) Fayẹmi at Irẹmǫ, (10) Ogbolu
at Ile Ṣeru, and (11) Ipẹti at Oketaṣẹ.

However, it is generally accepted that the title of Araba is restricted
to the lineage of Oketaṣẹ compound and to men who can claim descent from
it through their mother. The title of Amosun is similarly "owned" by the
lineage of Ile Araba Gidiogbo and its two subsidiary compounds (Ile Otutu
and Ile Ajagbukǫ), but Amosun himself said that it had rotated between this

lineage and two others (Ile Kirǫsinla and Ile Olugbodu) until the title of
Araba became more important. Mǫgbǫn "belongs" to Irǫmǫ quarter, Tǫdi-
mǫle to Ilare quarter, and Ǫbakin to the people of Ijugbǫ, one of five out-
lying villages that moved into Ifǫ during the wars of the last century and
perhaps even earlier. All other titles are open to any qualified candidate.

In former times those who were eligible to become Awǫni competed
for the position whenever there was a vacancy. If Araba died, the choice
of his successor would be made by Agbǫnbǫn, and vice versa; when a lower
title was vacant, they would decide together or leave the choice to Ifa in
case of doubt or disagreement. The installation of a candidate is marked
by a feast (ihaye, iha-oye; iwuye, iwu-oye), which he must provide for all
the Awǫni, the chiefs, and the Ǫni. He must also give the Awǫni money and
a case of Gordon's gin. The amount of money has varied, having been £ 3-
10-0 in earlier times, raised briefly to £ 5-0-0, and then reduced to £ 2-
10-0. One to five shillings out of this is given to the assistants (Ojugbǫna)
who serve as messengers of the Awǫni; five shillings six pence is sent to
the King's messengers or attendants (Ǫmǫsǫ) who are responsible for the
Ifa shrine (Ile Ǫmirin) in the palace; and the rest is divided into two parts.
One half is divided between Araba and Agbǫnbǫn, with Araba taking a shilling or two more than Agbǫnbǫn. The second half is divided among the other Awǫni according to their rank. Araba also takes home three bottles of
gin; Agbǫnbǫn, two; and the other seven bottles are drunk at the feast.

Except for the Araba and Agbǫnbǫn, each of the junior Awǫni in effect
move up one position at the death of an Awǫni who is senior to them. In
recognition of this, each of the junior Awǫni give £ 1-0-0 and five or six
bottles of gin to those above them. Thus if No. 5 dies, 1-4 share in all the
gifts without giving anything themselves; 5 shares in the gifts of 7-16; 7
shares in the gifts of 8-16; and so on. A man chosen to fill the position of
Araba must pay £ 20-0-0 and one case of Gordon's gin to the Awǫni, £ 10
to the Ǫni, and £ 10 to the attendants of the Ifa shrine in the palace.[1] In return he receives payments of £ 10-0-0 and £ 5-0-0 from the Ǫni during the
Ǫni's installation.

Formerly the Awǫni wore a red tail-feather from the African grey
parrot in the braided tuft of hair (oṣu) on their head, but now that the hair
is clipped short, the feather is worn in a large European felt hat (ikori).
This type of hat can be used by anyone, but if he presumed to wear a red
parrot feather in it, he would be asked scornfully, "What kind of a chief
are you?" Araba and Agbǫnbǫn, the two highest ranking Awǫni, wear finely plaited straw hats or "miters" (oro, ide oro) of the type that are worn
by the principal town chiefs and by Lǫwa, the head of the inner or palace
chiefs. Neither kind of hat may be worn until an Awǫni has made the feast
that marks his installation.

---

1. Agbǫnbǫn maintained that payment to the Ǫni was initiated during
the reign of the predecessor of Aderǫmi, who intervened in the selection
of Ogbolu as Araba, whereas formerly the Awǫni themselves had the final
say as to who would be chosen.

Only the Awǫni may wear white headties during their meetings. Other
diviners may wear them at other times, but when present at the meetings
of the Awǫni they remove them and tie them about their waists; and a diviner of lower rank must bare his head and prostrate himself in greeting
when he meets an Awǫni in the street. Formerly these headties were white
women's sashes (ǫja), locally woven by women, but in 1937 imported white
toweling was in common use. White headties were common, but the babalawo
were not restricted to the use of white cloth, as has been reported. Formerly they often wore light blue garments, because they did not look dirty as
quickly as white cloth, and in 1937 they wore whatever cloths they liked,
with the wealthier diviners using imported velvet or velveteen of varied
colors.

The Awǫni use a special type of whisk made of a ram's beard with a
handle an inch or more in diameter, whereas that of the ordinary diviner's
cow-tail switch is less than half an inch. When two Awǫni meet in the street,
they cross the handles of their whisks, with the handles pointing down, and
exchange the greetings "Ogbedu" and "Ogbǫmurin."[2] Only the two highest
ranking diviners, Araba and Agbǫnbǫn, are permitted to hold a whisk in each
hand when dancing. The Awǫni also have long strings of a special type of
large beads (ędigba, ogbara), which are worn during the annual festival
over one shoulder and across the chest (see Plate 21 A). According to
one informant the Awǫni and the Ǫni must use round divining trays only.

At any time of year the Ǫni may send for the Awǫni to divine for the
good of the town as a whole because there has been an accident or trouble,
or because of a dream or other omen. They go to a special chamber (Ile
Ǫmirin) in the palace (afin) that houses a shrine of Ifa and where Ifa is consulted, and use the Ǫni's divining apparatus. They ask, "What must be done
so that the Ǫni may live long, that the town may be in peace, that there will
not be trouble among us Awǫni, that the women of Ifę may not be barren,
that there may be no sickness or famine in town, and that there may be no
deaths among the young people." The Ǫni provides whatever is prescribed
as the sacrifice, which is made in the palace, with animals killed in the
open court in front of the council hall. The Ǫni's sacrifices are disposed
of by a special group of priests known as Otu, whose meaning is explained
in verse 181-4. Sacrifices for the town as a whole may also be made by
the Awǫni as a result of their own divinations, in which case they provide
the materials themselves.

The Awǫni are also responsible for the annual festivals for Ifa, which
are associated with eating the first new yams (egbodo) of the season. The
first festival is Egbodo Ǫni, or New Yams of the King, before which the
Ǫni and the palace retinue are not permitted to eat new yams. The festival

---

2. These greetings, which could not be translated, are said to be Ifa's
"passwords." "Ogbedu" is said to have been the first thing Ifa said when he
wanted to take kola nuts, and the passwords are repeated while casting kola
nuts for Ifa and on other ritual occasions.

takes place near the end of June. It is said that formerly the sixteen Awǫni
went to the Ifa grove near Oketaşę and built a house of Ifa (ile Ifa). They
killed a goat, divided it, and wrapped it in the leaves with which the house
was thatched, so that the house lasted only one day and had to be rebuilt
each year. This part of the festival is no longer observed.

On the first day all the Awǫni go to the grove and "break the leaves of
Ifa" (jawefa, ja-ewe-Ifa); they pick sixteen special kinds of leaves and bring
them back to the King's palace. They also bring the first new corn of the
season to the palace, with which they make cornstarch porridge (ori, ękǫ
tutu). In the evening they return to the palace to "bury the palm nuts in the
cornstarch porridge" (rifa lori, ri-Ifa li-ori). The palm nuts of the Qni are
left in the porridge in a large tub overnight, and the Awǫni remain all night
in the palace sleeping near them, except for Araba, who sleeps opposite
them on the verandah of the King's messengers (ǫdę Ęmęsę). Only Araba
is permitted to have a fire, and this night is known as "to sleep without making fire" (asundana, a-sun-i-da-ina).

On the morning of the second day the Awǫni go home, but toward evening they return to the palace again. They take the leaves they have gathered
and grind them together in water with the King's palm nuts, which have been
taken from the tub of cornstarch porridge. In this way they "wash the Ifa"
(węfa, wę-Ifa) or palm nuts of the Qni in the leaves of Ifa. The palm nuts
are then placed in the King's divining bowl (ǫpǫn igede), which is placed in
his Ifa shrine and covered with fine cloths. That evening many animals are
killed, including a cow, a she-goat, and a ram. Some of the blood and meat
is put on the palm nuts as a "sacrifice to Ifa" (bǫfa, bǫ-Ifa) and left in the
divining bowl overnight. A small new yam is split in two, palm oil is poured
on it, and it is taken to the shrine of Eshu. The rest of the meat is divided
among the Qni, his wives, his messengers (Ęmęsę), the town and palace
chiefs, and Araba and Agbǫnbǫn. The meat is taken home and some of it is
cooked and eaten with new yams, which are usually two types of yellow
yams (ǫlǫ and igangan), especially good for making yam loaf. Thereafter
the Qni and other participants may eat yams until the end of the season.
The Awǫni again remain all night in the palace.

On the third day the Awǫni "eat the top of Ifa" (ję irefa, ję ire-Ifa);
they take the food from the top of the palm nuts, cook it, and eat it. The
day is spent in eating and drinking, with gin supplied by the Qni, and Ifa's
drums (kęręgidi) are beaten all day.[3] On the fourth and fifth day they rest
at home.

On the sixth day the Awǫni, the town chiefs, and the palace chiefs assemble in front of the Ifa shrine in Araba's house, where they are served
yams, stew, and drinks. Late in the afternoon Araba—spotted red, white,
and black with camwood, chalk, and charcoal—leaves his house and goes

---

3. In Ifę, Ifa has a set of four drums, known as kęręgidi. The individual drums are named firigba, jǫngbondan or regeje, kęręgidi, and another jǫngbondan or regeje. Other kinds of drums are used for Ifa in other Yoruba towns.

with the others to the nearby market in front of the palace. There the
chiefs, followed by the Awǫni, dance individually in reverse order of their
ranking, and an hour or so after dark they return home.

On the seventh day they return to the palace, and Araba divines for the
Ǫni, the chiefs, the Ęmęsę, and all the people of the palace, using the palm
nuts and the divining tray of the Ǫni. Each person comes to him in turn,
saying, "What shall I do that I may live to make this festival again next
year?" The materials required as sacrifices are provided by the Ǫni. On
this day the Ęmęsę or the Ogungbę, who served as police in earlier times,
are free to catch sheep and goats wandering about town for the sacrifices
that are prescribed. If an owner sees his animal being taken and begs the
Ęmęsę or Ogungbę to leave it, they do so; but if not, the owner has no recourse. One woman came wailing to the palace with her husband, begging
to have her goat returned; but the Awǫni denied having it. They asked if
she knew which man had taken it, but she said she hadn't been there to see
him. She was told that she couldn't even be sure that the Ęmęsę or Ogungbę
had taken it, and that she should go home and look for it. Her husband
begged the Awǫni quietly to return the goat, but it did no good even though
he was a junior sibling of the Awǫni who was in charge of the animals to be
sacrificed.

The appearance of Araba spotted "like a leopard" on the afternoon of
the sixth day is in commemoration of an encounter with Odua, the deity
who created the earth, as given in the following Ifa myth, ascribed to the
figure Ogbe Ǫsę.

When Odua was King of Ifę, Olokun the Sea Goddess was his wife, and
Ǫrunmila was her lover. Ǫrunmila consulted the diviners to learn what he
should do so that Odua would not catch him with his wife. The diviner told
him to sacrifice a pigeon, a fowl, camwood, chalk, and charcoal. They
took a knife and cut three incisions in his skin, rubbing one of the three
powders into each of the cuts. Then they told him he could continue to
sleep with Olokun without fearing anything.

One day Ǫrunmila and Olokun overslept, and Odua came upon them at
dawn. But Eshu, to whom the sacrifice had been made, came to Ǫrunmila's
aid; he spoiled Odua's eyesight, so that Odua thought Ǫrunmila was a leopard. Odua ran away in fright, and Ǫrunmila returned home safely. Ǫrunmila began to praise the diviners who had protected them, saying that what
they had said had come true. After that, as long as he lived, he spotted
himself annually like a leopard; and since his time, Araba has done the
same.

Egbodo Erio, the festival of New Yams of the Oluwo, usually takes
place in July and generally follows the pattern of Egbodo Ǫni. The first
day is known as "Dawn will break good for the babalawo" (ojumǫ a mǫ awo
rire). Early in the morning they gather sixteen kinds of leaves[4] (jawefa).

---

4. The names of the sixteen leaves were given as mǫriwo (young
fronds of the oil palm, Elaeis guineensis), tętę (Amaranthus spp.) ewe
jęmijoko or ewe jęnjoko (Cissampelos spp.), ewe banabana (Albizzia spp.),
ewe alukerese (Ipomoea involucrata), ewe ita (Celtis Soyauxii), ewe ǫkika

Ifa's drums are beaten all day, and they are beaten every day during the
festival. The divining bowls are colored red, white, and black, with camwood, chalk, and charcoal. Toward evening all of the babalawo and other
Ifa worshipers in Ifẹ take their palm nuts, divining trays, and bowls and
their other apparatus and ritual paraphernalia to the house of an olodu.
Here each one puts his palm nuts in cornstarch porridge (rifa lori) made
of new corn and leaves them in it overnight; each diviner uses a separate
tub so that the sets of palm nuts do not become mixed. The diviners remain at the house of the Olodu for the nine days of the festival, sleeping on
the verandah near the alcove for Ifa.

On the morning of the second day, each diviner washes his palm nuts
(wẹfa) and puts them in his divining bowl, which is placed in the alcove that
serves as Ifa's shrine. In the evening he kills a she-goat or a fowl, whatever he wishes to sacrifice to Ifa (bọfa), and puts some of the blood and
meat on the palm nuts. Some meat is cooked and eaten with new yams, and
one new yam is split, sprinkled with palm oil, and taken to Eshu.

On the sixth day the blood is washed from the palm nuts, using a different set of "leaves of cleanliness" (ewe ifin), and the babalawo divine for
each other, using their own sets of palm nuts and making the sacrifices
that are prescribed. No babalawo can divine for himself; in support of
this they cite the proverb: "However sharp the knife, it cannot carve its
own handle." [Ọbẹ t(i)-o mu ki gbẹ kuku ara rẹ.] On the seventh day, each
babalawo divines for his wives, who come to the house of the olodu for this
purpose, and makes the sacrifices specified for them. Again the question
asked is what must be done in order to be able to live to celebrate the festival again next year, and the women may also pray to have children, money,
or other blessings. The eighth day is another day of rest.

On the afternoon of the ninth and final day, a she-goat is killed and
blood is allowed to flow on the origi in front of the house as a sacrifice.
The head of the goat is taken into the house and, after lengthy prayers, it
is touched to the foreheads of the babalawo, their wives, and their children.
Kola is cast to determine if the sacrifice is acceptable; a series of figures
are marked on the divining tray and recited briefly; and the olodu puts a
little of the divining powder in the mouths of those present.

The diviners retire to dress in their finest clothes and ornaments,
fastening their headties about their waists, and the Awọni wear their
strings of large beads over one shoulder and across the chest. Meanwhile,
each Ifa bowl is set on a divining tray and wrapped in fine cloths. When
the diviners return, no women must be present; they enter the room walking backward and touch their foreheads to the ground before the wrapped
bowls. Selected young people enter the room, and each diviner puts his
bowl on the head of his son or daughter, a young "wife of Ifa," or a young

---

(Spondias Monbin), ewe omu (Cyperus esculentes?), ewe ade (Myrianthus
arboreus?), ewe alugbinrin (Triclisia subcordata?), ewe ibaigbo (Mitragnya
stipulosa?), and rẹnrẹn, ewe orijin, ewe apese, ewe olojongbolu, and eti
ologbo (unidentified).

apprentice. This is the day when they "carry Ifa" (gbefa, gbe-Ifa). The children carry the bowls containing the palm nuts of Ifa out into the street in front of the house, where they line up with a child carrying the cylindrical container of odu in front (see Plate 21). They stand in place while the diviners dance about them to drumming and singing, which the olodu begins by calling "O-o-o Şoko," with the others responding "Bani." Afterward they go back into the olodu's house, where they sleep again that night, and the next morning they return home.

After Egbodo Erio the worshipers of Ifa and of the "white deities" can eat new yams, but many people cannot do so until other rituals have been performed. The worshipers of Qramfę are permitted to eat yellow yams but may not eat new white yams until the Edi festival, which comes in October or November. Before Egbodo Erio new yams are taboo to all except the participants in Egbodo Qni, the Christians and Muslims, and those who do not worship anything. All who worshiped Yoruba deities formerly observed this tabu.

Egbodo Ifę, the Festival of New Yams of Ifę, known also as the Ogido Festival (Qdun Ogido), follows in August when the worshipers of many other deities eat new yams for the first time; but the diviners have nothing to do with this ceremony. Their next ceremony is the Ęwunrin Festival (Qdun Ęwunrin), which comes in September or October. More sacrifices are offered to Ifa in thanks for having lived through the three new yam ceremonies, and the diviners shave their hair, which has been allowed to go unshaven since the beginning of Egbodo Erio.

The Awoni hold meetings (ajo, ajo Ifa) at Oketaşę, the home of Araba, every sixteenth day on Qjaifę, the day sacred to Ifa. At these meetings they discuss the affairs of Ifa, sharing their knowledge and teaching each other the verses; they discuss the conduct of their own members, and they eat and drink together. For these meetings each member in turn provides food (prepared at his own home) and drink. In discussing the conduct of their own members, they will decide whether they have obeyed the rules of the Awoni, and, if not, they will try those accused and impose fines on offenders. The rules are similar to those of other guilds in Ifę:

1. An Awoni must not seek another Awoni's wife. If the wife of Araba or Agbonbon is involved, the offender is handed over to the Qni for punishment. In any case he is dismissed from his position, but he may be reinstated later if he comes from a good family and they plead for him. In this case he will have to pay a fine, including forty kola nuts, a she-goat, a case of gin, and an amount of money to be determined. The fine varies depending on his wealth.

2. The Awoni must not "poison" (make bad medicine against) each other. If the person dies, the offender is dismissed and cannot be reinstated, and he is turned over to the Qni for punishment. The same thing happens if Araba or Agbonbon are poisoned, even if they recover. If another Awoni is poisoned but recovers, the offender is dismissed, but again may be reinstated if he comes from a good family and they plead for him. Again a fine, including gin and money, is imposed.

3. The Awoni must not conspire against one of their members. An

offender is dismissed for this, and if the conspiracy is against Araba or
Agbọnbọn, he is turned over to the Ọni for punishment. If several Awọni
are jointly guilty of conspiracy, they are not dismissed but fined a case of
gin each.

4. An Awọni must not speak against a fellow member behind his back.

5. One Awọni must not leave another when he is in trouble without seeing that things have been set right for him. If an Awọni does this to Araba,
it is reported to the Ọni; but the Awọni deal with the offender themselves.

6. No Awọni may divulge the discussions at their meetings to an out-
sider.

If a member is suspected of breaking any of these rules, someone is
appointed to watch him. When enough evidence has been gathered, he is
brought before the entire group and tried by them. Witnesses are called,
and the offender is given an opportunity to question them and to defend himself. If he can prove that he is innocent, then the fine that he was in jeop-
ardy of having to pay is imposed upon the person who falsely accused him.
The decision is reached solely on the basis of the evidence, and there is no
divination on such occasions. When the evidence has been heard, the Awọni
retire to discuss it, and when they have reached agreement, one of the group
is sent back to report the verdict.

If the offense is minor, a unanimous decision is not required; if two of
the Awọni disagree with the rest, including Araba and Agbọnbọn, they are
simply ignored. In a serious case no decision is reached until there is unanimous agreement; court is adjourned until new evidence is discovered.
If the minority is later proved wrong, however, they are each fined four
bottles of gin for having persisted in their opinion. If the Awọni are split
more or less evenly, even if Araba and Agbọnbọn are on the same side,
court is adjourned and outsiders will be asked to watch the accused and collect new evidence. If Araba and Agbọnbọn stand alone against the other
Awọni, the matter is serious. Court is adjourned and each side meets by
itself to reconsider its positions. Agbọnbọn and Araba will give serious
consideration to the fact that all the others disagree with them; and the
other Awọni will say to each other, "We must think deeply about this matter. Our elders disagree with us, and they must have a reason for doing
so." In the end one side or the other must change its mind, go to notify
the other, and beg its pardon.

At one of these meetings the Awọni discussed the past and present
ranking of their titles. Araba was seated in front of the alcove that served
as his Ifa shrine, facing away from it into the large room in which it was
situated. The curtain of the alcove was open, suggesting that some rituals
had been performed before I was admitted, at about 11:00 A.M. The Awọni
were seated against the wall to the right of Araba, with Agbọnbọn second
and the others in order of their seniority; they extended to the corner and
most of the way down the right side of the room. Along the wall opposite
Araba and Agbọnbọn were diviners who had studied under the Awọni, some
of whom were elderly oluwo, and young boys who were still apprenticed to
those present. Other diviners may come to the meetings, but they are not
invited, and all would know that they came only to share in the food. On

the left side of the room were women and children of Araba's compound,
many of whom had come to see the Whiteman. Divining bags were hung on
pegs in the wall, as were the large felt hats of the Awǫni. Araba and
Agbǫnbǫn wore their straw mitres, and the other Awǫni wore cloth headties; the other diviners had removed their headties and fastened them
around their waists. Following the discussion, I was invited to stay and
watch the proceedings.

The ordinary babalawo and apprentices moved toward Araba, gathering
in semicircles and occupying most of the floor. Araba gave a calabash containing water and ten kola nuts to Lodagba, the "steward" of the Awǫni, who
knelt at the entrance of the alcove, facing it. He led the singing, beginning
with the conventional call "O-o-oh şoko" and response "Bani" and a song
addressed to Igi, a slave of Ifa, "Igi, open your eyes and see your enemy"
(Igi, şi-oju ki o ri-odi rę). The other Awǫni remained silent, but the other
babalawo and the apprentices responded as the chorus and clapped their
hands in simple time to the music.

Lodagba held up the calabash and prayed to Ifa. He then took the kola
nuts out of the calabash, and poured a little water in front of Araba's odu.
He broke one of the kola nuts into its four sections and removed the small
bits (işęju obi, işę-oju obi) near the center and replaced them in the calabash. Holding the broken kola nut up to Ifa, he said, "Qrunmila, this is
yours. Eat it." He then divined by casting the four sections of kola nut on
the ground, determining on the first cast that the augury was good, and
then asking in turn about the five kinds of good on successive casts, and
finally if a sacrifice was required. Neither palm nuts nor the divining
chain were used on this occasion. When he finished, he replaced one section of the kola nut in the calabash and passed the others and the unbroken
nuts to the oluwo, who divided them into sections. One of the apprentices
took the calabash and touched it to the head of each of the Awǫni, starting
with Araba and Agbǫnbǫn, so that any ill luck would leave their heads and
could be thrown away with the water.

At this point, after seven songs had been sung, the rhythm picked up
and the hand-clapping took on a sophisticated syncopation. Lodagba sang,
"Child of the house, you take this to Eshu" (Qmǫde ile, ę gba yi a Eşu) and
the chorus responded, "Run quickly, Eshu accepts it" (Ire tete, Eşu gba).
The apprentice took the calabash with water and pieces of kola nuts outside and poured some at the shrine of Eshu and some at the iron walking
stick (ǫręrę, osun) that serves as a symbol of Ifa, while the ceremony continued.

The sections of kola and a small calabash of maize beer were placed
near a round altar with stones on it which symbolizes Qramfę, one of the
major deities of Ifę. Araba knelt by the altar, poured a little maize beer
on the altar, and took a sip of it himself. He said the password "Agbedu,"
and the others responded "Ogbǫmurin." He took a section of kola nut,
touched his forehead to the ground, and then returned to his seat. He was
followed by Agbǫnbǫn and the other Awǫni, and by the oluwo.

After this, the food was served by Lodagba and the assistants. The
men gathered in small groups to eat together, and later food was passed

to the women. When the dishes and the leaves in which the food was wrapped had been cleared away, the singing began again, and the syncopated clapping was louder and more precise than ever. One of the oluwo passed a calabash of maize beer to the Awọni, starting with Araba and Agbọnbọn; and as each drank in turn, he complimented them and called out their praise names, pausing while the chorus responded, "Very clean is what the oluwo[5] drink, very clean" (Toro ni erio mu, toro). When the calabash reached Olori Iharefa, the singing stopped; he drank in silence because he was so junior that "he is only a boy among the Awọni." Lodagba did not sit and drink with the Awọni, because his duties as steward kept him busy on the floor.

Finally, the man whose turn it was to feed the group at the next meeting came forward to receive the calabash of maize beer, which is spoken of as the "calabash of meeting" (igba ajọ). As he took it, he was told, "Your meeting is seventeen[6] days away," and he replied, touching it to his head and chest, "My head accepts it, my chest accepts it."[7] The meeting was adjourned.

---

5. The word erio, which appears also in the name of the second Ifa festival, Egbodo Erio, was said to mean the Awọni plus all the oluwo, i.e. all babalawo who wear the special hairdo. One diviner said it meant all the deities (ẹbura).

6. Actually sixteen days. The Yoruba, like the ancient Greeks, include both the initial and final days in reckoning time. Thus they speak of their four-day week as having five days (which in Ifẹ are named after the towns major markets): Ọjaifẹ, Irẹmọ, Aiyegbeju, Itakọgun, Ọjaifẹ. In Ọyọ these days are known by names of deities: Ọjọ Awo for Ifa, Ọjọ Ogun for the God of Iron, Ọjọ Jakuta for Ṣango the God of Thunder, and Ọjọ Oṣala for the God of Whiteness. Frobenius (1913: I, 256) erred in adding Ọjọ Ọsẹ as a fifth and holy day or Sunday. Ọjaifẹ or Ọjọ Awo is the holy day or Ọjọ Ọsẹ for Ifa, as the other days are for Ogun, Ṣango, and Oriṣala.

7. Ori mi gba, Aiya mi gba. This statement is also made during initiation of a babalawo when he first receives his second set of palm nuts, signifying he takes it with all his heart. See J. Johnson (Dennett, 1906: 252).

XI. THE SYSTEM OF BELIEF

Some elements of the complex world view of the Yoruba must be discussed at least briefly for readers to understand the many references to
them that appear in the Ifa verses, and the significance of Ifa divination itself. This section is primarily concerned with three deities, Ifa, Eshu, and
Qlǫrun, and with the concept of fate or destiny and its relationship to the
multiple souls of mankind. The importance of these two concepts and the
role of these three deities stands out clearly in the verses. Ifa or Qrunmila is the God of Divination who informs mortals of the wishes of Qlǫrun;
Eshu is the Divine Trickster and the Messenger of Qlǫrun, delivering sacrifices to him and seeing to it that clients who sacrifice attain their ends
while those who fail to do so are punished; Qlǫrun is the Sky God, who is revealed in the Ifa verses as the God of Destiny.

Since at least 1800 the Yoruba have been in direct contact with Islam,
although during the nineteenth century they were warring against their Muslim neighbors, and for more than a hundred years Christian missions have
been established within Yoruba territory. Yoruba beliefs have been influ-
enced by both these religions, but those discussed below are probably as
close to those of the pre-contact period as can be hoped for at this date,
since they were mainly recorded in 1937-38 from babalawo who had remained apart from both Islam and Christianity. Moreover, their interpretations were drawn from verses they had memorized in their youth, and
they were often able to cite verses in support of their statements. As Idowu
(1962: 7) observes, the verses "belong to the most fixed and reliable section
of the oral traditions." In some cases there are obvious evidences of acculturation, as in the myth below told by Agbǫnbǫn, the most respected and very
senior diviner of the Qni, which speaks of books, teachers, Whitemen, Christians, Muslims, turbans, airplanes, and chloroform; but these are obvious re-
interpretations that have been added to an ancient myth. Finally, much of
the following is based on a direct analysis of the verses recorded in Part
Two.

There are many deities (ębura, ebǫra, imǫlę, oriṣa) according to
Yoruba belief, the full number never having been recorded. Informants
frequently speak of 400 Deities, as do the Ifa verses (3-2, 34-2, 111-1,
168-1, 256-3), but this is a mystic number and can be taken only as meaning a great many. The verses also speak of Qrunmila, Eshu, the Sea Goddess, and the 400 Deities (1-11), of the 400 Deities and the Egungun (7-5),
and of the 400 Deities on the right and the 200 Deities on the left (249-1).
Each deity has special attributes and some have specific functions or powers, but all can give children, protection, and other blessings to their worshipers who are faithful.

The God of Whiteness or Big Deity (Oriṣala, Oriṣanla, Oṣala), also
known as the "King who has a white cloth" (Qbatala), who created the first
man and woman and who fashions the human form in the mother's womb, appears in a number of verses, as do unspecified members of his pantheon of
white deities (oriṣa funfun). The word orisha (oriṣa) has often been trans-

lated as deity, and it is sometimes used in Ifẹ as a synonym for ẹbura; but
in its more specific sense it means one of the more than fifty members of
the pantheon of the God of Whiteness. Many other deities also appear in the
verses, including the God of Thunder (Ṣango), the God of War and Iron (Ogun),
the God of Smallpox (Ṣọpọna), and the God of Medicine (Ọsanyin), but those
most often mentioned and those most directly associated with this system of
divination are Ifa or Ọrunmila, Eshu, and Ọlọrun.

Ọlọrun, the Sky God, is the "One who owns the sky" [Ọ-l(i)-ọrun] or
"King of the sky" (Ọba ọrun) and is commonly referred to as Olodumare.
The meaning of this name is explained in one of the verses (54-2) as "One
who has odu, child of Python" (Ere). However, an Ọyọ diviner maintained
that Ere is simply the name of the mother of the sixteen figures of Ifa, with
Ọlọrun being her seventeenth child. Before Ọlọrun was born, Ere went to
Ifa to report that she had had a sign that she would have another child. Ifa
told her that it would be a boy and that it would be an important child, more
powerful than anyone else in heaven or on earth. When Ọlọrun was born,
they called him "One who has figure (of Ifa), the child of Ere" (olodu ọmọ
Ere).

Some writers have offered different interpretations,[1] but in Ifẹ this
name is clearly understood to refer to Ọlọrun, and in the Ifa verses Olodumare is identified as "King of the Sky" (256-3).[2]

Although called child of Python, and although he appears in Ifa myths
cited in this chapter as a slave trader, a cuckold, and the brother of Ọrunmila, Ọlọrun has been syncretized with the Christian God and the Muslim
Allah. He is equivalent to Nyame among the Ashanti and to other West African "high gods," standing above and beyond all other deities. He has no
special worshipers, no cults, and no shrines; prayers are addressed to him,
but no sacrifices are offered directly to him. Yet he is neither so remote
nor so unconcerned that he does not intervene in affairs on earth.[3] In the
verses we see Ọlọrun giving food (241-1), property (14-3), money (255-3),
wives (54-3), children (54-2), titles (246-4), honor (243-4), and blessings
(250-1, 255-1, 256-1); repaying losses (249-2); and defeating enemies (248-
4). As the deity who assigns and controls the individual destinies of mankind, Ọlọrun has a prominent place in Ifa divination.

---

1. Lucas (1948: 74) gives Olodumare as a title of Ifa. Epega (1931:
10, 11, 22) identifies Olodumare as Odudua, as God, and as the one to whom
Eshu takes the sacrifices. Ṣowande (n.d.: 31, 33b, 41) regards Olodumare
as one element in the Holy Trinity along with Ọlọrun and Ẹlẹda (the ancestral guardian soul). Crowther, J. Johnson, and Farrow equate Olodumare
with Ọlọrun but give as its meaning "the Almighty One" or "the Ever-righ-
teous One." Various other interpretations of its meaning have been suggested.

2. See also the verse from Ogudabede (Ogunda-Ogbe) cited by Lijadu
(1923: 8).

3. Idowu (1962) has also argued that Ọlọrun is by no means as removed
from human affairs as he has sometimes been pictured to be.

Eshu (Eşu, Eşu Bara, Ẹlẹgbara, Ẹlẹgba) is the youngest and the clev-
erest of the deities. He is the divine messenger (iranşe), and one of his
roles is to deliver the sacrifices he receives to Qlọrun. Understandably,
the diviners consider this role important. He is also a trickster, the divine
counterpart of Tortoise in Yoruba folktales, who not only delights in trouble-
making but serves Qlọrun and the other deities by causing trouble for human
beings who offend or neglect them. He is notorious for starting fights (5-3,
48-1, 131-1), killing people by toppling walls and trees on them, and causing
calamities to deities and humans alike; but his role in delivering sacrifices
to God (see p. 60) is hardly consistent with his identification with Satan by
Christians and Muslims, which can only be understood as the result of the
failure to find the equivalent of the Devil in Yoruba belief. One verse does
speak of Eshu eating a sacrifice (123-1), but another tells how he carries
sacrifices to heaven and reports who made them (33-2). In another verse
he is identified as the one appointed by Qlọrun to watch the other deities
on earth (256-3).

Eshu's reputation for maliciousness is undoubtedly due to his important
role as the divine enforcer, punishing those who fail to make the sacrifice
prescribed for them and rewarding those who do. He forces a woman to be
killed by the 400 Deities because they thought she was spying on them (34-2),
leaves Sakeu to die in mid-air (244-1), and causes two friends to die on the
same day (18-10), all because of failures to sacrifice. Another pair of
friends die on the same day because they failed to appease Eshu, although
it is not specifically stated that he caused their death (18-9). Frog is also
injured and loses the crown after failing to appease Eshu, without Eshu's
intervention being specified (170-1). The King of the Termites sacrifices
and is made king, but when he refuses to make a second sacrifice against
death, Eshu gathers his band of rascals and they destroy his termite hill,
roast him, and eat him (54-1). Ojuro fails to sacrifice and Eshu causes her
to lose her way; but when her relatives sacrifice for her, she finds it again
(247-5). Another character makes a sacrifice to have children but not a
second sacrifice so that they will not become enemies; when her children
are born, Eshu causes them to fight, and both are killed (5-3). In only one
of the verses recorded does Eshu cause a fight without specific provocation,
and even here the implication may well be that one of the two friends failed
to sacrifice (48-1).

In as many instances, however, Eshu saves those who have sacrificed
or assists them in obtaining what they wanted. He calls a storm to destroy
Dove's nest and kill her children because she not only had failed to sacrifice but dared to brag about it; yet Pigeon, who did sacrifice, is spared (33-
1). Because Calico sacrificed, Eshu intervenes to save it when all the other
cloths, who had failed to sacrifice, are being taken away to heaven (18-4).
Only three trees sacrifice when all are told to do so; Eshu carries their sacrifices to heaven and reports their names; and when a storm destroys the
others, they are spared (33-2). Qrunmila himself postpones a sacrifice and
is taken as a thief; but when he makes the sacrifice, Eshu helps him not only
to escape the charge but to be handsomely rewarded for being falsely accused (14-1). Hyena makes a sacrifice and becomes king; and when he fails

to make a second sacrifice, Eshu causes him to be deposed; but when Hyena finally makes the sacrifice, Eshu helps to regain the crown (35-3). When the king's wife has her slave perform a sacrifice for her, Eshu gives the promised child to the slave (33-4). Ajaolele sacrifices, and Eshu causes him to fight with the chief's daughter; but through this he marries her and two other wives without having to give bridewealth (131-1). Eshu intervenes to save the people of Mọrẹ from Death (6-2), helps Cock win a hoeing contest and thus a bride (123-1), and helps Qrunmila marry Earth (1-10) and a daughter of the Sea Goddess (1-11), all because sacrifices had been made. Under somewhat different circumstances, he clears Qrunmila of the false accusations of the 400 Deities (246-3), captures a false diviner, and saves the one who is telling the truth (244-2).

Much of what Eshu does is done through magical transformations, which he accomplishes by clapping his hands (1-10), throwing dust and clapping his hands (244-2), blinking his eyes (1-11), and pointing his staff (247-5) or medicine (17-10). He also closes pits magically (1-11), transforms water and small pieces of meat into blood and goats' legs (35-3), and intervenes without the use of magic (14-1, 123-1, 131-1, 244-1, 256-3).

Eshu is a close associate of Ifa, and one verse (1-9) refers to the occasion when Ifa was going to befriend Eshu. An Ifa myth, told by a Yoruba informant from a Muslim family who was studying in England, accounts for the close relationship of Eshu and Ifa as follows:

Qrunmila was a very wealthy man. Once when he was entertaining his many companions who had come to eat and drink with him, he asked them, "I wonder, how many friends do I have?" They protested that they were all his friends, but he was not satisfied. He consulted the diviners, who told him to make any sacrifice that he wanted, and he gave them some money. They instructed him to go home, hide himself on top of the ceiling of his room, and have his wife announce that he had died.

When these instructions had been followed, his companions mourned for him, each coming in turn to console his wife, and each pretending to be more sorrowful than the other. After the first one had expressed his sympathy, he said, "Do you remember that large gown that we had made for our society a few years ago?" Qrunmila's wife said that she did, and asked him why he mentioned it. He replied, "Well, Qrunmila asked me to buy it for him, but he did not repay me." The wife asked how much it had cost, and he replied "Forty-five pounds." At this point she excused herself and went to talk to Qrunmila where he was hiding. She asked him if he had heard what his friend had said, and Qrunmila answered, "Yes. Take the money and pay him."

One by one each of his friends came to the house to express their sympathy; each claimed that Qrunmila owed them money, and each received payment. Finally Eshu came, with tears streaming down his cheeks. After he had offered his sympathy, Qrunmila's wife asked, "Isn't there anything more? Didn't Qrunmila owe you any money?" "What?" replied Eshu, "Indeed no! He was always my benefactor, and I owe what I have to him." When Qrunmila heard this, he came down from his hiding place and revealed that he was still alive. Since that time, Eshu and Ifa have been close friends.

The story that Eshu was the one who taught Ifa how to divine — reported by Baudin (1885: 34), Ellis (1894: 58-59), and Cole (1898; quoted in Dennett 1906: 270), Frobenius (1913: I, 229-232), Farrow (1926: 37), and Lucas (1948: 73-74) — was denied by diviners at Qyǫ and Igana as well as at Ifę. However, a Mękǫ diviner said that he had heard that Eshu had done so and that Eshu had given Ifa his divining tray, but he did not know the myth.

Like other Yoruba deities, Ifa has a number of different names, and dozens of longer praise-names. The name Ifa is interpreted as meaning scraping, because he "scrapes" (fa) sickness and other evils away from those who are afflicted, or because he scrapes the powder on the divining tray in marking the figures. In the verses Ifa is also referred to as Alumǫ, meaning "To beat and know" or that he beats palm nuts and knows the future (6-3, 18-9).

Most commonly he appears in the verses as Qrunmila, but of the various names only Ifa is used to refer to the system of divination. As a result it has sometimes been maintained that the name Ifa refers only to the system, whereas Qrunmila (or Qrunmla, Qrunla) refers to the deity who controls it.[4] However, in Ifę, Ifa is clearly recognized as one of the names of this deity, and both the morning invocation (Chapter III) and one Ifa verse (1-4, n. 2) make it clear that Ifa and Qrunmila are one and the same person. The name Qrunmila is derived by Ifę diviners from an earlier name for Ifa, namely Ęla, which they interpreted as based on the verb la, "to open." The name Ęla appears in the Ifa myths, including the following one recounted by Agbǫnbǫn which explains the origin of the name Qrunmila, and its meaning as "Sky God recognizes Ęla" (Qlǫrun mǫ Ęla):

Ęla was the younger brother of Qlǫrun, the Sky God, who was a trader who traveled widely and dealt largely in slaves. When Qlǫrun was away trading, Ęla had intercourse with Qlǫrun's wives, and the children of these affairs are the "wives of Ifa" who are given to diviners without bridewealth.

One time Ęla sent his children far away to trade in goods; and when they reached the boundary between heaven and earth, the slaves of Qlǫrun fell upon them and stole all their goods. When Ęla heard this, he asked, "Who can steal my property from my children?" He took his bow and arrow and set out with his other children, his servants, and his slaves; and when they met, they began to fight with Qlǫrun's followers. Everyone on earth came to help Ęla, but the battle continued. On the seventh day a heavy rain fell, beating on both sides, and they both withdrew.

On the following day, Ęla's followers spread their clothes to dry, and Qlǫrun's followers spread out their shirts and turbans. Qlǫrun sat in a chair looking at Ęla in the distance, and Ęla was looking at Qlǫrun, his elder brother. At first neither recognized the other, because Ęla had been young when Qlǫrun left home; but then Qlǫrun did recognize his brother,

---

4. Idowu (1962: 76-77) maintains this distinction, yet on the next page he cites a verse from Iwori Meji which says "Ifá, fix your eyes upon me and look at me well." See also Clarke (1939: 235-236) and Bascom (1942: 43).

and he went to him and embraced him. They ate and drank together, and
the next day they announced that there would be no more fighting. As Ẹla's
followers were returning to earth, they met people who were still coming
to help them and who asked them why they were returning so soon. They
replied, "Ọlọrun recognized Ẹla yesterday" [Ọlọrun mọ Ẹla l(i)-ana], and
since that time Ẹla has been called Ọrunmila.

This was discounted as folk etymology by an Ifẹ diviner in 1965 who offered the following explanation: When the deities first came to earth, they
had no special powers or duties, and they asked Olodumare to assign them
work for which they were gifted. Olodumare said that Ogun did not know
his work, and he gave him war (ogun). He said that Orişala did not know
his work, and he gave him art (ọna).[5] He said that Olokun should be a trader and that Aje, the Goddess of Money, should become a middleman (alarobọ),
buying from Olokun and reselling at a profit. All the deities were assigned
their specific duties. When they asked Ọrunmila what work had been assigned to him, he replied, "Only Ọlọrun knows the one the one who will prosper." And that is why they call him "Ọlọrun knows the person who will prosper" (Ọlọrun mọ ẹni ti o la).

However, informants in 1937-38 maintained that this was a misinterpretation and that the explanation that it means "Ọlọrun knows the one who will
be saved" (Ọlọrun mọ ẹni ti o la) was a Christian invention. In support of
Agbọnbọn's interpretation it was said that in earlier times diviners were
greeted by the people of Ifẹ "Pẹlẹ, ọmọ Ọlọrun mọ Ẹla" (Gently, child of
Ọlọrun recognized Ẹla), but that this has been contracted to "Pẹlẹ, ọmọ
Ọrunmila."

Ifa is also known as Agbọnniregun, a name that appears in several of
the verses (1-7, 6-1, 20-1) as well as in an abbreviated form, Agbọnnire (1-
2). Şowande (n.d.: 46-47) cites a verse from Ogbe Ofun which interprets
the meaning of this name as "This coconut must have a long life!" (Agbọn
yi ma ni iregun o!). An Igana diviner reported that its meaning is explained
in a verse from Irẹtẹ Ogbe as "Coconut that will never be forgotten" (Agbọn
ti o ni regun). Awodire, an Ifẹ diviner, cited the following myth, which gives
a third interpretation:

The God of Whiteness and his son Akala (one of his attendants) and
Ọrunmila and his son Amosun (one of the Awọni) left Olodumare and came
from heaven to earth, where they met two hundred people. They placed the
two hundred people in charge of Akala and gave him a drum. When they
reached Oketaşẹ, Ọrunmila planted vegetable seeds and yams for Amosun
to eat, and he and the God of Whiteness returned to heaven. Amosun's veg-
etables and yams grew well, but Akala and his people soon ate what food
they had. They were too hungry to dance; one of them tried to beat Akala's
drum, but he was so hungry he became dizzy and fell down. Then Akala
gave two of his followers to Amosun in return for food; and when that was
gone, he gave Amosun two more. Finally, when he had given all his people

---

5. The allusion here is to the role of the God of Whiteness in fashioning the child within the mother's womb, as a woodcarver fashions a figurine.

to Amosun, he traded his drum for food. Then Akala was left with nothing.

After two years had passed, Qrunmila and the God of Whiteness decided to visit the earth to see how their children were faring. When they reached Ita Yemo (the street of the wife of the God of Whiteness), they asked where they could find Akala, but no one knew him. They asked again at Qjaifẹ market and again at the house of the Goddess of Money (ile Aje), but no one knew him. Then Qrunmila said "Let us ask for my son, Amosun, to see if anyone knows him." They asked for Amosun and were told, "He stays at Oketaṣẹ beating his drum." When they reached Oketaṣẹ, they saw Amosun wearing a crown, with many people dancing before him. Amosun shook his cow-tail switch at Qrunmila and sent eight people to greet him, saying, "Amosun greets you; he who has food will give you food, those who are hungry for meat. He who feeds a friend with his followers, he greets you." Then Amosun's people took Qrunmila's bag and ate the six coconuts he had inside it.

In disgust Qrunmila reproached his son, "Amosun, I am your father! I looked for you but could not find you. Finally I came here and when I saw you, you would not get up and come to meet me. You only shook your cow-tail switch at me, and your followers took my coconuts and ate them. Ah!" Then the people were sorry and said "Oh, this is the father who brought us coconuts." That is why people say that they took the "coconuts of reproach" (agbọn oniregun).

Qrunmila said that Amosun should always sacrifice to him at that spot, and he left with him the boy whom he had bought to come with him and help carry his load. This boy they called "The one he bought to come" (A-ra-bọ), and he was the first Araba (the highest ranking Awọni). Then Qrunmila tied a cloth around his waist, sank into the ground, and turned into stone. That is why they still sacrifice to Qrunmila at that very spot at Oketaṣẹ until today.

Ifa is often spoken of as a scribe or clerk, "one who writes books" (akọwe, a-kọ-iwe). Like other clerks who serve as secretaries and book-keepers in modern business and government, Ifa "wrote" for the other deities, and he taught the babalawo to "write" the figures of Ifa on their divining trays. In Ileṣa he is also described as a learned man or scholar (amuye), because of all the knowledge and wisdom in the Ifa verses, and as the interpreter (agbonfọ) between the gods and humans. In Qyọ he is also spoken of as an interpreter (onitumọ), the one who translates, who explains, or "who loosens knowledge, who hears the Qyọ dialect" (onitumọ gbedegbẹyọ, o-ni-tu-imọ gbọ-ede-gbọ-Ẹyọ). Qlọrun gave him the power to speak for the gods and communicate with human beings through divination, and when Ṣango or Oriṣala or any other deity wishes a special sacrifice, he sends a message to the human beings on earth through Ifa. Although he serves all the deities in this way, Ifa is not their servant; rather he is the wisest of the deities according to the babalawo, and according to some the father of all the deities except Qlọrun.

The following myth, said to be based on a verse from Ofun Ogunda, tells that Ifa was the inventor of writing, how the Christians came to wear long trousers, and how the oluwo came to wear a tuft of hair on their heads.

Agbǫnbǫn, who told it, began by explaining that Qlǫrun is also called Aja-lǫrun (Aja-li-ǫrun) or "Ceiling at Heaven," because that is where he was born.

Qlǫrun was the eldest of the deities, and the first child of the King of the Air (Qba Orufi). Some forty years afterward the King of the Air had a second son, Ęla, who was the father of the diviners. In the morning all the Whitemen used to come to Ęla to learn how to read and write, and in the evening his African children, the babalawo, gathered around him to memorize the Ifa verses and learn divination. Ifa taught them to write on their divining trays, which the Muslims copied as their wooden writing boards (wala), and the Christians copied as the slates used by school children and as books.

At first he taught only people from his own town, Ifę, but later understudies were sent to him from the surrounding districts. They were known as "Ifa of Ęla accepts them" (Ifa Ęla gba), and sick children were also sent to him, and they studied with him while they were being cured. Those who did not learn from him became the deaf and the dumb.

After his pupils were trained, he placed them in the surrounding towns and called them Tişa (teacher, from English). One of these teachers was at Ipętęmodu, a town eight miles from Ifę, where one of Ęla's fiancées lived. She was to marry him in four days, but the teacher liked her and wanted to steal her from Ęla. Finding no other way to do so, before the wedding day he bought some medicine [di-(ę)mi-di-(ę)mi] to make her stop breathing; from it the Whitemen learned about chloroform. He gave it to the girl and told her she should put some of it into her nostrils when she reached Ęla's house. She did as she was instructed, and everyone thought that she had died. Since it was a tabu for Ęla to see a dead person, she was quickly wrapped in a cloth, carried away, and laid at the base of an iroko tree (Chlorophora excelsa).

The teacher and his helpers were waiting there, and they carried her to his house where she revived. She became his wife and began to sell palm oil in the market. One day, one of Ęla's sons recognized her in the market and told his father about it; but Ęla said that no one can see the dead, and that anyway he had no wish to see her again because she had been dead.

Later the same thing happened with another teacher at Ędunabǫn, about two miles away, and then at Moro and at Aşipa. When Ęla's fourth bride "died," he was suspicious. He had her body wrapped in a cloth, but instead of having it carried to an iroko tree, he had it placed inside a room in his house. When the girl revived, she began to weep and beg forgiveness. Ęla threatened to have her killed as a sacrifice to his head, but finally she revealed how the teacher at Ipętęmodu had first used medicine and how the others had learned the trick and obtained medicine from him.

Ęla sent for the four teachers and asked them why they had stolen his wives. They replied, "Are you the only person in the world who can have wives?" Ęla told them to leave and never come back to him again. They agreed to this, saying that they had been taught enough about divining, and

Ẹla gave them each a set of palm nuts and the sixteen figures to use on their
own. When they went, however, they stole all of Ẹla's fiancées in other
towns.

When Ẹla learned of this, he made Ifa against them so that their ankles
were covered with sores (elerinja), and these sores drew flies. As a result,
they made long trousers to cover them; formerly trousers had reached only
to the knees. When this did not stop them from stealing his fiancées, Ẹla
gathered his followers and went out to meet them in force. He defeated them
and drove them south until they reached the coast, and he stayed there seven-
ty years to prevent their return. There were no houses in those days, only
huts.

Finally his people at home began to sing to him, begging him to return:

Palm nuts come home, oh;	Ikin bọ wa-(i)le-o,
The annual festival is calling you, oh;	Qdun ma pe-o,
Erigiabọla.	Erigiabọla.
Palm tree come home, oh;	Qpẹ bọ wa-(i)le-o,
The annual festival is calling you, oh;	Qdun ma pe-o,
Erigiabọla.	Erigiabọla.
Palm nuts come home, oh;	Ikin bọ wa-(i)le-o,
The annual festival is dancing, oh;	Qdun ma jo-o,
Erigiabọla.	Erigiabọla.

When Ẹla heard this song, he used something[6] and flew back through the air;
it is what is now known as an airplane. When he landed, he called his wives
and asked how they had been treated by his other pupils, whom he had left behind with them. They said that the ones who had yams had shared them with
them, and those who had money had given them some.

Ẹla then called these teachers. He shaved their heads, leaving a spot of
hair as he wore his, and in it he put a red feather from the tail of the parrot.[7]
The last man he shaved had a bald spot in the middle of his head, so he left
the spot of hair off to one side, and that is the way the Awọni wear their hair
until this very day. He placed each of his faithful teachers in a quarter of
the town, and told the townspeople to go to the one in their quarter and learn
from him. Those whom he had driven to the coast, who wore long trousers,
returned their palm nuts and refused to serve him. They are the educated
Christians of Lagos; and when they return to Ifẹ, they try to get their revenge
by cheating the people Ẹla left there.

Idowu (1962: 101-102) considers Ẹla distinct from and older than Qrunmila, although he cites a saying that Ẹla is the child of Agbọnniregun. At one
point Agbọnbọn said that Qrunmila was the son of Ẹla, but he then told the

---

6. This probably refers to a magical charm known as "carrier medicine"
(ogun egbe). See verse 170-3.

7. Later Agbọnbọn explained that Ẹla created this hair style so that his
faithful teachers would be taken care of by others, and explained that all who
wear it receive free meals.

myth that gives Ẹla as an earlier name for Qrunmila. These differences of
opinion arise from the Ifa verses, which give contradictory accounts. The
following myth, ascribed to Ogunda Meji by the Ileṣa diviner who told it,
makes Qrunmila the predecessor of Ẹla:

One day Qlọfin, the king, sent for Qrunmila. Qrunmila was just about
to prepare a sacrifice with a chicken, and he could not leave it unfinished.
After the sacrifice he shared the chicken with his sons. He gave a wing to
Ibọru, a wing to Ibọyẹ, and a leg to Ibọṣiṣẹ (see Chapter III). He took his
iron walking stick (ọpa ọrẹrẹ) and stuck it in the ground at Qlọfin's palace.
When he had divined for the king, he returned home. Five days later Qlọfin
sent for him again.

Meanwhile, Qlọfin's three hunters (Arîsîtasî, Arîsîtasî, and Àtàmàtàsî)
went to the forest to hunt elephant. They shot an elephant together, but it
did not die. It came to the square in front of Qlọfin's palace and put its
trunk on the palace wall. When they saw this wonder, they called Ogunnipẹtẹ,
the diviner of the house of the Alara, and Qgbọntẹrẹ, the diviner of the Ajero,
and diviner Jewejimọ, and diviner Apaja Oji. They cut open the elephant
and in its bowels they found a bundle wrapped in white cloth. Inside it was a
covered calabash, and in the calabash they found a new-born babe with a
beard and with white hair on his head; in each fist were eight palm nuts
(ikin). Qlọfin exclaimed that he had never seen such a thing in his life, and
then he sent for Qrunmila. When Qrunmila arrived, Qlọfin reported what
had happened, and Qrunmila began to sing:

"What do we call the new-born babe?
"He is the one called Ẹla.
"How can we know the new-born babe?
"He is the one we call Ẹla, son of Origi."

In accounting for the reason why the worshipers of all other deities consult Ifa, an Qyọ diviner cited the following myth, attributed to Qṣẹ Ogunda:
Pa bi ọsanja, Dẹrẹdẹrẹ bi okun ole, and Onṣọkọṣọ ni ta Qba where the three
diviners who cast Ifa for Ifa when Death, Illness, Loss, Court Case, and
Fight were coming to attack the people on earth. They told him to offer one
he-goat, lots of money, five covered calabashes (igbademu), cudgels (kumọ,
olugbongbo), palm oil, indigo dye, blood, and cold water as an atonement
(etutu). He put the atonement outside his house and waited. Death came and
drank the dye. Illness came and drank the blood. Loss came and drank the
palm oil. Court Case came and drank the cold water. Fight came, but he
found nothing to drink, so he started to fight with the others. The five evils
took up the cudgels and began to beat each other, and the people on earth
were saved. Since then the ancestral guardian souls of all the people Ifa
saved belong to him, and everyone on earth relies on him. This is the reason why the worshipers of the God of Thunder, the God of Iron, the river god-
desses, and all other deities consult the diviners and make the sacrifices
that they prescribe.

Ifẹ diviners consistently name Ifẹ as the town where Ifa lived when he
came from heaven, and Oketaṣẹ as his compound. In recent years a large
concrete temple for Ifa has been erected at Oketaṣẹ compound, the home of

the Araba of Ifẹ, with funds contributed by babalawo from many parts of Nigeria. Ifẹ is acknowledged by the Fọn (Herskovits, 1938: II, 202; Maupoil, 1943: 32) and the Ewe (Spieth, 1911: 189) as the source from which Ifa divination was derived.

Sometimes Ifa is associated with Ifẹ or Ado or both, but there are several towns known as Ado. One Mẹkọ diviner named Ifẹ as his home. Another said that, although he came from Ifẹ, his proper town is Ado Ewi, which he said was near Ado Ekiti, east of Ilẹṣa; here one may see the first palm tree and the figures of Ifa marked on the stones. A diviner from nearby Ilara said Ifa came from the sea to Ifẹ and then went to Ado Ewi near Ado Ekiti, and that Ado Ewi is his proper town, where one can see his sacred palm tree with sixteen fronds. However, as an Ilẹṣa diviner pointed out, Ewi is the title of the king of Ado Ekiti, so that Ado Ewi is Ado Ekiti and not a separate town; he held that Ifa came from Ifẹ, but that he traveled around, staying at Ado Ekiti, Ilẹṣa, and other towns.

According to an Igana diviner the figures of Ifa are to be seen marked on stone not at Ado Ekiti but at Ado Awaiye, sixteen miles south of Isẹyin; Ado Awaiye is the father of all towns named Ado, and Ifa practiced as a diviner there for a long time; but his proper home is on Oke Gẹti[8] in Ifẹ, where he was born and where he finally became a deity. There is a very large granite outcropping near Ado Awaiye, on top of which I have seen bedrock mortars ground into the stone; perhaps these holes are referred to as the figures of Ifa, but they are also found in other parts of Yoruba territory, including Igana. Bowen (1858: xvi) says, "The head-quarters of Ifa are at Ado, a village on top of an immense rock near Awàye," which was still inhabited in 1884 (Chausse and Holley, 1885: 89-90). Burton (1863: I, 189) refers to "a mountain near Awaye, a gigantic cone of granite eight to ten miles in circumference, seen from the distance of several days' journey towering solitary above the landscape, and surmounted, it is said, by a palm-tree, bearing sixteen boughs" (see also Maupoil, 1943: 42).

An Ọyọ diviner said that Ifa stayed first in Ifẹ and then in many towns, including Ado Awaiye, where he became a deity and where his palm tree and the sixteen figures are to be seen; Ado Ekiti; and Irẹsa beyond Benin; and on Oke Igbeti in heaven. An Ifa verse from Ọkanran Edi states that at one point Ifa went to Ado Ayiwọ (unidentified) to live (Epega, n.d.: V, 11; Lijadu, 1923: 59). Benin City is also known as Ado, and there is still another Ado thirteen miles north of Badagry. Ifa is associated with Ado as well as Ifẹ, but there is disagreement as to which Ado is meant.

Aside from the deities, many other elements of the Yoruba system of belief appear in the verses, including twins (ibeji), children who are "born to die" (abiku), witches (ajẹ, ara aiye, iya mi), and a variety of evil spirits. Also mentioned are dreams (1-7, 7-1, 35-7, 101-1, 175-2) and omens (175-2), oaths (166-1, 256-3) and ordeals (166-1, 246-4), curses (225-1, 248-4, 246-3) and the evil eye (167-1), and various good and bad charms or medi-

---

8. An Ife diviner also mentions Oke Gẹti as the home of Ifa's father, without revealing its location except to deny that it is in heaven.

cines. Prominent in the verses, and more directly associated with the beliefs underlying Ifa divination, are the related concepts of destiny and the
ancestral guardian soul.[9]

The Yoruba believe in multiple souls, but beliefs about them vary from
place to place and from individual to individual. The breath (ẹmi) resides
in the lungs and chest and is man's vital force; the shadow (ojiji), which follows him about but has no function, is recognized as a second soul in Ọyọ
and in Mẹkọ but was not mentioned as such in Ifẹ; the ancestral guardian
soul (ẹlẹda, ipọnri, ipin), which has no sensible manifestation, is associated
with the head and is often referred to as the "owner of the head" (olori).

The importance of the ancestral guardian soul was repeatedly stressed
by informants. "The ipọnri is worshiped by everyone, by kings and by the
poor alike." "The head is more important to everyone than their own deity."
"It is greater than the deities that turned into stone." Its importance is due
in large part to its relationship with the individual's fate and his luck, which
is also associated with the head. Good things come to a lucky person with
little apparent effort, but an unlucky person is not only unfortunate in his
own affairs; he also brings bad luck to his relatives and associates. A lucky
person is called "one who has a good head" (olori rere) or "one who has a
good ancestral guardian soul" (ẹlẹda rere), whereas an unlucky person is
one who has a bad head or ancestral guardian (olori buruku, ẹlẹda buruku).
Calling someone olori buruku is likely to lead to a fight, because it is an insult to his ancestral guardian soul and thus almost a curse.

The ancestral guardian soul is specifically associated with the forehead
(iwaju), the crown (atari, awujẹ), and the occiput (ipakọ). Many Yoruba believe that all three parts of the head are controlled by a single soul,[10] that of
the ancestral guardian; but Ifẹ diviners maintain they are associated with
three distinct souls. According to one, these three souls remain in the head
until death, when all three go to heaven, where the ancestral guardian gives
an account of all the good and evil that the person did on earth. As in a court
trial on earth, a good person is released and then can be reborn, but bad
persons are held and punished. It is the ancestral guardian who is a member
of his "council in heaven" and who takes to heaven the sacrifices which the
person makes to his own head. The only way to sacrifice to the ancestral
guardian soul is to sacrifice to the head (bọ ori), and anything that is given
to the forehead or the occiput goes to the ancestral guardian soul in the
crown, but is shared with the other two. Another Ifẹ diviner said that the
ancestral guardian soul is the senior, followed by the forehead, with the occiput the youngest. He maintained that each individual has two ancestral
guardians, one residing in his head and the other in heaven. The one in heav-
en is his individual spiritual counterpart, or double, which is doing exactly

---

9. For further details see Bascom (1960: 401-410) and Idowu (1962:
169-185).

10. This is true in Mẹkọ, and would account for the fact that the diviners
there employ only four symbols when asking to whom adimu should be offered (see Chapter V).

the same things in heaven that he himself is doing on earth; it is always in adult form, even when the living individual is still a child.

One of the verses (248-1) mentions the character's spiritual double in heaven as "his second person of heaven" (ęnikeji rę ǫrun). Another tells how Ifa came to be the intermediary of the ancestral guardian soul, collecting for him whatever sacrifices he requires and carrying them to him (111-1). To retain the support and protection of the ancestral guardian soul it is necessary to offer sacrifices to the head as prescribed by the diviners, and in Ifę an additional annual sacrifice is also required.

Suicides never reach heaven and, having renounced earth, belong to neither; they become evil spirits and cling to the treetops like bats or butterflies. Criminals and other wicked persons are condemned to the bad heaven (ǫrun buburu), which is described as hot like pepper and is sometimes spoken of as the "heaven of potsherds" (ǫrun apadi), referring to something broken beyond repair, for they can never be restored to the living through reincarnation. Those who have been good on earth reach the good heaven (ǫrun rere), which is also called the heaven of contentment (ǫrun alafia) or the heaven of breezes (ǫrun afęfę). Here the air is fresh and everything is good, the wrongs of earth are righted, the multiple souls are reunited, and life is much as it is on earth. Here they remain until they are reborn, returning to earth in another generation, but usually in the same lineage so that they can rejoin their children. As in many other African societies the lineage is a self-perpetuating group that includes the departed ancestors, the living, and those yet to be born; the Yoruba belief in reincarnation gives this notion a cyclical and endless character. An ancestral guardian soul may be reborn again and again in succeeding generations.

One of the functions of Ifa divination is to determine which ancestral soul is reincarnated in a newborn child and what tabus he or she should observe. In Ifę it is necessary to identify the ancestral guardian soul in order to know the correct day to offer annual sacrifices to it. For this purpose a diviner, who must be an olodu, is consulted shortly after a child is born, and the verse selected may reveal which occupation he is most likely to be successful in and other elements of his destiny. The figure cast on this occasion is in some ways a chart of the child's future life, and it may be carved into a piece of calabash shell (Figure 3) so that it will not be forgotten; the "feet" at the bottom are so that the figure will not be misinterpreted by being read upside down. As soon as an individual is old enough to memorize the figure, the carving can be thrown away; but if his parents should die while he is still young, he can have the carving interpreted by a diviner when he grows up.

Before a child is born (or reborn), the ancestral guardian soul appears before Qlǫrun to receive a new body (shaped by the God of Whiteness), a new breath, and its fate or destiny (iwa) during its new life on earth. Kneeling before Qlǫrun, this soul is given the opportunity to choose its own destiny, and it is believed to be able to make any choice it wishes, although Qlǫrun may refuse if the requests are not made humbly or if they are unreasonable. Destiny involves the individual's character, occupation, and success, which can be modified by human acts and by superhuman beings and forces; and it

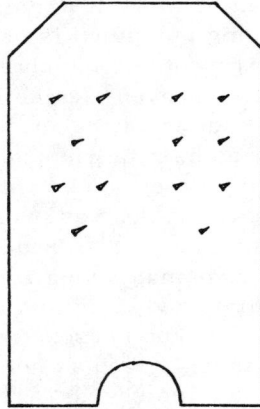

FIGURE 3. PIECE OF CALABASH SHELL
MARKED WITH QKANRAN OFUN

involves a fixed day upon which the souls must return to heaven. This day
cannot be altered except by suicide, as noted above. It cannot be postponed
by prayers, sacrifices, magic, or any other means. The allotted span of
life can never be extended, but it can be shortened by offended deities, by
evil spirits, by "witches," by the curses or evil magic of one's enemies, by
swearing falsely, at human hands as punishment for crimes, and in other
ways. If one has the full support and protection of his ancestral guardian
soul, of Qlǫrun, and of his personal deity, he will live out his allotted span
of life, but if not he will die before his time.

Those who are killed before their time is up become ghosts and remain on earth until their appointed day arrives. Those who die naturally because they are old and have lived out their allotted span of life go directly
to heaven. They are spoken of as "one who has (his) day" (ǫlǫjǫ), meaning
that he has reached the day assigned by Qlǫrun. A child who dies when only
a few years or even a few days old may also have done so. As one diviner
explained, if a child dies at an early age or is born dead, its breath and ancestral guardian soul report to heaven, and may be sent back to earth immediately to be reborn again, and this time the child may live to a ripe old
age. However, there are other children who are abiku, or "one born to die"
(a-bi-ku). If a woman has several children in succession who die at child-
birth or in infancy, or even when older, they may not be several sets of
souls who die early but one abiku being repeatedly reborn only to return
shortly to heaven. It has been granted a short life span by Qlǫrun because
it does not want to remain long on earth but prefers to go back and forth between earth and heaven.

A person's destiny determines, within limits, whether he will be lucky
or unlucky, rich or poor, kind or cruel, wise or foolish, popular or unpopu-
lar, and it determines the number of children he will have. It also prescribes for him the occupation he should follow. If an apprentice learns

quickly or can do better work than his teacher, people know that his skill
was given to him by Qlǫrun as part of his destiny. If he is insane, feeble-
minded, or sick, and if his affliction cannot be traced to evil-doers, they
say that it came from Qlǫrun.

A diviner explained that an individual cannot basically change his own
destiny, but he can spoil it by breaking a tabu (ewǫ) and others can spoil
it for him through the use of medicine (ogun) or witchcraft (aję). The role
of Ifa is to improve one's lot by advising what must be done to keep an evil
destiny from being as bad as it might otherwise be, and to ensure that one
receives all his blessings if his destiny is good. In one of the verses (225-
1) the client is told that "he has come from heaven with a bad head," but
that he should sacrifice so that "his luck may not be completely bad."

Destiny (iwa) is specifically mentioned in seventeen of the 186 verses
recorded, and there are also frequent references to the head and the ancestral guardian soul. "Head who had knelt and chosen his destiny" is being
prevented from achieving it by slanderers (4-1). A son "comes from heav-
en bearing his calabash of destiny" (52-1). Qlǫrun will "put the calabash of
destiny into his hands" (245-3), has sent someone a "pouch of destiny" (54-
8), will "open the road of destiny for him" (54-1), and "create a large market of destiny" for someone (256-1). "Qlǫrun wants to give the lamp of destiny to someone"(244-1), he will "kindle the fire of destiny for him (18-3),
and "there is a man to whom Qlǫrun will give destiny . . . the fire of his
destiny will continue to dance up high" (245-1). Someone's head will "bring
him to a place where he will achieve his destiny" (35-3, 52-3, 255-1), he
should go seek his destiny (181-4), and he is warned to sacrifice "so that
his destiny may not spoil" (225-3). Ifa is involved in a few instances. Qrunmila "gives someone his destiny" (9-1), "Ifa will set his destiny in order"
(14-2), and "An Ifa has taken all his destiny and hidden it" (255-3) but will
"open the road" if a sacrifice is made.

The verses also speak of someone in trouble "because he has come
from heaven with a bad head" (225-1), of "someone who was given an easy
lot by Qlǫrun when he came from heaven" (250-2), and of someone who cannot be harmed by sacrifices and charms because "from heaven Qlǫrun has
sent him" (246-1). One verse says, "Whatever Qlǫrun has made, he has not
left unfinished" (248-1), and another carries the meaning "As the Sky God
has ordained things, so they are destined to be forever" (35-6). Informants
noted that when destiny is mentioned in the Ifa verses, it almost always
means great good fortune: money, wives, children, a fine house, a title,
many followers, a good character, a good reputation, fame, long life, and
anything else that one might desire. However, it does not mean that one
may postpone the appointed day upon which his souls return to heaven.

Qlǫrun, the Sky God, rather than Ifa, clearly emerges as the God of
Destiny. He assigns each individual's destiny at birth and, if he so pleases,
helps him to achieve it. As noted above, he may also intervene in human
lives to give wives and children and to bestow other blessings which their
destinies have in store for them. An individual's destiny is chosen by the
ancestral guardian soul which is reincarnated in him, and which watches
over him throughout life and protects him unless it is offended. Except for

the appointed day upon which an individual's several souls must return to heaven, destiny is not fixed and unalterable. It sets a chart for one's life which can bring many blessings if it is followed, but in order to achieve his destiny and to live out his allotted span, one must offer the proper prayers and sacrifices, employ protective medicines, and behave correctly in other ways.

Eshu and Ifa are Qlǫrun's agents and intermediaries. Sacrifices are not offered directly to Qlǫrun, but rather through Eshu, who carries them to heaven. Eshu serves both Qlǫrun and Ifa by punishing those who fail to sacrifice and helping those who sacrifice to gain their rewards. When the God of Thunder is angered, he can kill a person with lightning, and the other deities also have specialized means of "fighting with" those who offend them, but they may also call upon Eshu to use the variety of punishments at his command. Qlǫrun, apparently, must rely solely on Eshu on such occasions. Despite his reputation as a trouble-maker and evil-doer, which is admitted freely by his own worshipers, in the verses Eshu is remarkably even-handed in his role as a divine enforcer.

Ifa is the one who transmits and interprets the wishes of Qlǫrun to mankind, and who prescribes the sacrifices that Eshu carries to him. The importance of Ifa divination may well be due to the fact that, except for prayers, it apparently provides the most direct access to Qlǫrun, who controls man's destinies. It provides a knowledge of what destiny lies ahead in life, what occupation should be followed, what special tabus are to be observed, which ancestral guardian soul is to receive annual sacrifices, and which deity an individual is to worship. It provides a means of determining what sacrifices are necessary to achieve one's destiny, to receive the blessings that have been promised, and to live out the full span of life that has been assigned. It also tells when special sacrifices are required by the ancestral guardian soul, by that of one's father or mother or by the many different deities, and when medicine should be prepared. It can give warning against witches, evil spirits, bad medicine, curses, ordeals, and broken oaths. Because the verses and predictions touch on such a wide range of religious beliefs and prescribe sacrifices to so many different "supernatural" beings and forces, Ifa divination is the focal point in Yoruba religion.

An individual had his own personal deity and sometimes worshiped that of his father and mother as well, but he did not give offerings to the hundreds of other Yoruba gods unless he was instructed to do so by a diviner. But all believers in the Yoruba religion turned to Ifa in time of trouble, and on the advice of the babalawo all sacrificed to Eshu and through him to Qlǫrun. This important trinity is public and available to all, and together Qlǫrun, Ifa, and Eshu grant and assist men to achieve the destiny which is assigned each individual before his ancestral soul is reborn.

The predictions of the babalawo also give practical advice for the client's own behavior, and give warning against slanderers, enemies, and other malefactors. Throughout life an individual consults Ifa in case of illness or trouble, when new ventures are to be undertaken, and when important decisions are to be made. When he cannot solve a problem through his own efforts, he may have first recourse to his personal deity or to charms and medicines, but if these fail or if he wishes to learn what lies ahead or which course to follow, he consults a diviner.

The ancestral guardian soul, the deities, evil spirits, witches, charms and medicines, curses, oaths, and ordeals were matters of serious belief, and religion in its various forms permeated all aspects of Yoruba life. Yet it would be wrong to conclude that the Yoruba were resigned to uncontrollable destinies, or that they were content to rely on divination and other religious practices to solve all their problems. Several Yoruba proverbs clearly convey the message that "God helps those who help themselves," and some show an almost skeptical attitude toward these religious beliefs: "Bravery by itself is as good as magic." "A Chief is calling you and you are casting Ifa; if Ifa speaks of blessing and the chief speaks of evil, what then?" "A charm for invisibility is no better than finding a big forest to hide in; a sacrifice is no better than many supporters; and a deity to lift me on to a platform is no better than having a horse to ride away on."[11]

------

11. "Aiya nini to ogun lǫtǫ." "Arę npe ǫ o nd(a)-Ifa, b(i)-Ifa rę fǫ ire, bi Arę fǫ ibi, nkǫ?" "Afęri kan ko ju bi ka ri igbo nla ba si lǫ; ębǫ kan ko ju ǫpǫ enia lǫ; orişa gbe mi le atete ko ju ori ęşin lǫ."

XII. THE DIVINATION VERSES

The verses, containing both the predictions and the sacrifices, constitute the core of Ifa divination. The choice of the correct verse from those
memorized by the diviner is the crucial point in any consultation, and it is
made by the client himself in full knowledge of his own problem. The figures themselves, which are shared with other widely distributed systems
of divination, and the mechanism by which the correct figure is selected,
are only means to the end of selecting the correct verse. The verses provide the key to the ultimate goal, that of determining the sacrifice required
to solve the client's problem. Once the sacrifice has been offered, matters
again rest in the hands of the gods.

The 186 verses published here represent fewer than a fifth of the number that an Ifẹ diviner is expected to have memorized before he begins to
practice, yet they constitute a sizable sample and can be regarded as ran-
domly chosen. Except for a test of the relationships between the verses
and myths and folktales, described below, the choice of the verses was left
up to the informants. It is worth noting that there was strong opposition by
some of the diviners to the recording of these verses, which they considered
as professional secrets whose publication might be to their economic dis-
advantage. As a result, nearly all were dictated by a single diviner. While
the number published here is insufficient to justify their anxieties, their attitude confirms the importance of the verses to the system of divination.

This study may take some of the mystery out of Ifa divination, but it
certainly does not permit the reader to divine for himself, since no verses
are presented for 203 of the 256 figures. Had I attempted to record one
verse for each figure, publication still would not have provided a satisfactory means of divination. More important, the fact that the client himself
selects the appropriate verse might again have been missed, and the mis-
take of concluding that there is a single prediction, sacrifice, or governing
deity for each figure might have been repeated.

Many other Yoruba and Fọn verses have been published in Yoruba,
French, and English, but usually in a less complete form. The three major
collections of Yoruba verses[1] are in Yoruba. In an attack on the teachings
of Ifa, first published in 1901, Lijadu (1923) includes 105 verses. In defend-
ing Ifa, Beyioku (1940) gives seventy-four verses, duplicating Lijadu's third
verse on page 5. The most important collection by Epega (n.d.), sold as

---

1. Two additional collections did not appear in time to be included in
the following analysis of duplication of verses. The first, by Şowande (1965),
contains eighty-nine verses in Yoruba for the first four paired figures and
is the first mimeographed publication in a projected series. The second,
by Abimbọla (forthcoming), contains sixty-four verses in Yoruba and English
for the sixteen paired verses; I do not recall any duplicate verses in this
manuscript in a hurried reading of it at Ibadan.

typewritten booklets, contains 621 verses and at least one verse for each of
the 256 figures; of these, twenty-five to thirty are clearly duplicates of
Lijadu's verses, but without evidence of plagiarism. Of the verses presented here, only three appear to duplicate those in these previous collections,
although two more may be variants.

A version of one verse (18-11) is given by Beyioku (1940: 5, 27), whose
first sentence is almost identical, letter for letter, but which varies somewhat toward the end. An abbreviated version of 33-1 is given by Epega (n.d.:
II, 93-94), with the name Ẹrukuku instead of Elemele. Epega (n.d.: III, 19)
has an abbreviated version of 18-10, but it is ascribed to a different figure,
and a variant of verse 181-1 (Epega, n.d.: VIII, 14-16). Lijadu (1923: 26)
gives a verse that is both reminiscent of and different from 239-1.

Beyioku (1940: 8) gives a verse that begins like 2-1, and another (1940:
32) whose introductory phrases resemble those of 86-1, but the remainder
of these two verses are quite different. Similar introductory phrases are
found in different verses (3-1, 3-2; 6-5, 6-6; 33-5, 33-6; 183-1, 183-2), even
when they are associated with different figures (1-7, 4-3; 153-1, 167-1; 6-3,
247-4), so that these two need not be considered as variants. In addition, a
truncated version of 256-3 is given by Idowu (1962: 52), although it is ascribed to a different figure. Except as noted, the verses are associated with
the same figures in these collections as they were by my informants.

It would take years to determine the number of Ifa verses; those which
are known vary not only from one diviner to another but also from one part
of Yoruba territory to another. It is often stated, both in print and by informants, that there are sixteen verses for each figure, giving a total of
4,096 verses; but as sixteen is a mystical number in Ifa divination, this is
only a conventionalized statement and perhaps even an underestimate. In
Ifẹ it is often maintained that while a diviner may begin to practice when he
knows four verses for each figure, he ought to know sixteen; but both clients
and diviners recognize that this is not the case, as diviners usually know
fewer than this for most figures and more than this for a few figures (see
Chapter VII). Individual diviners claimed to know fifty and eighty verses
for Ogbe Meji, and one informant estimated that for this figure the total
number might be in the neighborhood of two hundred, with considerably fewer for other figures. J. Johnson (Dennett, 1906: 247), followed by Dennett
(1910: 148), Frobenius (1926: 184), and Farrow (1926: 39), says that for
each figure there are 1680 verses, or a total of 430,080. This is completely unrealistic, but an estimate of 4,000 verses is probably conservative.

Because of the information these verses contain on theology, ritual,
and social and political status, and because the information is accepted as
truth rather than fiction, their importance extends beyond divination. As
indicated earlier, the verses constitute the unwritten scriptures of Yoruba
religion and have been aptly compared with the Bible by some literate
Yoruba. Beyioku (1940) has attempted to relate them to astrology, the sea-
sons, and modern science. A literate informant in Ifẹ maintained that they
contain four branches of knowledge: religion, history, medicine, and science, the latter referring to the explanations of characteristics of birds,
animals, plants, metals, and various other objects given in the verses.

Viewed as a form of folklore and verbal art, the verses incorporate praise-names, song texts, incantations, myths or "myth-legends" (Bascom, 1965: 4-12), folktales, proverbs whose meanings are sometimes explained in the narratives (18-9, 170-1, 170-3), and even a riddle, used as a proverb (249-6). Tortoise, the trickster in Yoruba folktales, appears as a character in some verses (166-1, 168-1, 222-1, 225-4, 249-6), though more frequently Eshu, his divine counterpart, appears in this role. In Yoruba folktales Tortoise often replaces the babalawo, serving as adviser to the other animals, and one Fọn myth tells how Tortoise was appointed by the Creator as the diviner for the birds and animals (Herskovits and Herskovits, 1958: 28).

The narratives in the Ifa verses resemble parables, and their function is similar to that of European exempla, tales used by priests during the Middle Ages as illustrations of their sermons. By providing exemplifications in the form of what happened to mythological characters under similar circumstances, they give added point and meaning to verses which otherwise would be curt or obscure. Frequently they serve to justify the prediction or some of the sacrificial materials, and they consistently suggest the importance of performing the sacrifices promptly and as directed.

Structurally the verses follow several different patterns, but one pattern predominates. Most verses may be considered to consist of three parts, (1) the statement of the mythological case which serves as a precedent, (2) the resolution or outcome of this case, and (3) its application to the client. This structure may be illustrated by one of the briefer verses (181-3):

(1) "One does not have truth in his belly and put wickedness in his stomach for nothing" was the one who cast Ifa for the God of Medicine. They said he should make a sacrifice lest something should stop the voice in his throat. Three cocks and one shilling seven pence eight oninis is the sacrifice.

(2) "When the God of Medicine made the sacrifice, he offered only one cock. From that time on his voice does not carry far, and he talks with a very tiny voice.

(3) "Ifa says that this person should sacrifice so that something will not take away his voice and so that people will not say, "Why is he talking this way with a tiny voice like that of the God of Medicine?"

(1) The first portion of the verse names the diviner or diviners (in quotation marks) and the mythological character (the God of Medicine) who came to consult them. It states his problem or, as in this case, the prediction made for him, and it usually names the items that he did or did not sacrifice. The case of the mythological character serves as a precedent for the client, if his problem is similar. (2) The second part explains what happened to the mythological character as a result of having made, or failed to make, the prescribed sacrifice. This may be stated briefly, or expanded at considerable length by introducing a Yoruba myth. Its purpose is to explain the first portion, which is often obscure. (3) The third portion is a statement made directly to the client, giving the prediction and in some cases stating the sacrifice that is required.

The diviners do not analyze the verses into the three sections above, but they do differentiate between the myth or "history" (itan) which some verses incorporate and the rest of the verse. The verses are known as rows (ẹsẹ), and are sometimes referred to as odu, the same word that is used for the figures of Ifa, or as the praise names (oriki, okiki, ekiki) of Ifa.

Occasionally one of the three portions may be omitted and the order of the second and third portions is sometimes reversed. Four verses omit the mythological case that usually serves as a precedent. One of these (18-8) begins with obscure phrases which resemble those identified as diviner's names, but there is no reference to a mythological client or his problem. Another (19-1) begins with phrases referring to attempts to kill someone by magic, which is the prediction made. Neither of these verses has a narrative, but two others (9-1, 247-2) begin simply by naming the two central figures in the tale without reference to their problems.

A different structure is found in nine of the verses (1-1, 1-2, 6-1, 18-5, 18-12, 35-2, 111-2, 137-1). This is illustrated in the first verse (1-1), which begins, "Qrunmila says it should be done bit by bit; I say it is bit by bit that we eat the head of the rat . . . ." In this instance neither the sacrifice nor the prediction is specified, though both are in other cases. The introductory "Qrunmila says" (or "He says") is repeated two, three, four, or five times, and in one instance (18-5) a tale about Qrunmila is incorporated.

In the more general pattern, the initial phrases are interpreted by the diviners as praise-names (oriki, okiki, ekiki) of diviners who were consulted by mythological characters in the remote past. Some are similar in form to the praise-names given to animals, plants, and various objects, as in "Smoke is the glory of the fire; lightning is the glory of rain; a big cloth is the glory of Egungun" (18-2). A number are adapted to divination in the following form, "Pouncing, the diviner of cat" (222-2), "Roots, the diviner of the base of the palm tree" (54-5), "Leaf sprouts, the diviner of the top of Eggplant" (166-1).

Like other praise-names, these initial phrases often resemble proverbs in their form of statement. Many also share the exaggerated overstatement characteristic of Yoruba proverbs, and some may well be proverbs that were once in current use: "Two people cannot sleep on a duiker hide" (54-4). "Mud does not float a boat" (183-4). "Eyelashes do not gather dew" (35-4). "An old cow does not speak" (86-2). "Fly does not display beads for sale" (204-1). "A hoe handle has a head, but it does not have brains" (35-1). "The back of Vulture's head resembles an axe handle, but it cannot split wood" (35-5). "A wall covers one's eyes, but does not close one's ears" (33-1). "The one who doesn't go to sleep knows where the sun rises" (55-1). "Thunder does not crash during the harmattan; lightning does not flash secretly . . ." (86-1). "The spittoon with a small mouth is drawn close to the cushion" (111-1). "One who does not build a house still does not have to sleep in the tree top; one who does not hoe yams still does not have to eat dirt; an elder who learns Ifa does not have to eat stale kola nuts" (131-1). Similar phrases are identified in the verses as praise-names of the mythological characters, as, for example, "Farm hut stands watch in the farm but does not catch thieves," a name for the Spotted Hyena (35-3).

The poetic imagery of some of these names is one of the aesthetic features of the Ifa verses. "Thin moon on the side of the sky, thin evening star
in the crescent of the moon" (1-6). "Night falls and we spread our sleeping
mats, day breaks and we roll them up; one who lays the warp threads must
walk back and forth . . ." (14-1). "Horse awakes in the morning; it takes the
bit in its mouth" (35-6). "Vulture's feathers reach to his thighs; for the rest
he wears trousers" (7-3). "Hips act indifferently but they get to sit on the
mat; nets act gently but they hold their loads firmly" (181-1).

On the other hand, these names often contain archaic words whose meanings are not known to the diviners themselves; they have been simply com-
mitted to rote memory without being understood. As a result they are sometimes impossible to translate, and there may be unavoidable errors in the
translations that have been attempted.

In many cases it is impossible to tell whether the names refer to one or
to several diviners, and the informants could not help in this matter. The
divisions that have been made in the interests of intelligibility are often pure-
ly subjective. A number of verses (e.g. 1-7, 1-11, 2-2, 3-4, 4-1) obviously
name only a single diviner, and three (1-4, 244-2, 247-2) clearly distinguish
two diviners. In these three cases, moreover, the initial phrases are clearly
identified as the names of diviners, supporting the interpretation of the Ifẹ diviners.

The names of the diviners are followed by an indefinite phrase "a da fun"
or "a d(a)-Ifa fun," which has been translated as "were the ones who cast Ifa
for" the mythological character, who is then named. This might also mean
"was cast for" and the initial passages have sometimes been interpreted as
the prediction stated in proverbial form (Bertho, 1936: 372; Alapini, 1950:
86-90). This interpretation is suggested by several verses in which the initial passages relate to the problem of the mythological character. ". . . If a
friend is exceedingly dear, he is like the child of one's own mother" a da fun
Qrunmila when he was going to befriend Eshu (1-9). "Death kindles a fire of
epin wood; disease kindles a fire of ita wood; Witches and Eshu kindle a fire
of munrun-munrun wood" a da fun Qrunmila when his child's health was not
good (256-4). Other examples (2-3, 241-4, 250-1, 250-3) are to be found, but
not in sufficient number to justify this interpretation. Generally, there is no
recognizable relation between the meaning of the initial phrases and the character's problem or its outcome.

The characters named as clients in the case which serves as a precedent
include well-known deities like Şango (243-1), Orişala (5-1, 103-2, 241-3),
Olokun (54-4), Qsanyin (181-3), Yewa (183-4), Qramfẹ, and Oluorogbo or Orişa
Alaşẹ (17-1), and Qrunmila or Ifa himself who appears in this role in twenty-
two of the verses recorded. Personifications of the figures of Ifa appear both
as central characters (18-7, 20-2, 35-1, 35-5, 247-1) and as diviners. The
400 Deities are clients in one verse (256-3), and the 400 Deities on the Right
and the 200 Deities on the Left in another (249-1). Among the other characters are Egungun (52-4); the Oluyare (247-5); Araba, the head priest of Ifa
(17-4); Ojugbẹdẹ, head of the blacksmiths and a priest of Ogun (7-3); the
mother of the priest of Qsara (18-1); Aganna, identified as the assistant rainmaker at Qyọ (250-1); Ojigigbogi, the diviner in heaven (33-2), and Witch (3-3).

Unidentified Yoruba kings (Qlǫfin) appear as clients in a number of verses (2-2, 35-7, 225-2, 225-4), as well as in other roles, and in two cases (1-1, 175-2) the reference is to the Qni of Ifę. Of all the kings mentioned specifically by title, the Alara of Ara appears most frequently (6-1, 33-4, 101-1, 225-3, 249-3), but the Ajero of Ijero (249-3), the Ewi of Ado Ekiti (247-2), the Qlǫfa of Qfa (2-3), and children of the Qni of Ifę (204-1) and of the Alafin of Qyǫ (18-3, 204-1) are also clients. Qna Işokun, an important chief at Qyǫ (18-6), and Lǫwa Ijaruwa, the important Ifę chief (249-5) are also named as central characters. In some verses the divination was for the people of Ilabesan (222-1), the people of Igbade (244-2), the people of Mǫrę, a quarter in Ifę (6-2, 6-5, 6-6), all the people of Ifę (24-1), and all the people of the world (236-1).

Other clients are Banana (1-3), Maize (248-2), Benniseed (86-3), Cactus (6-4), Kola (239-2), and the Qdan Tree (52-2); Vulture (1-5, 5-2, 241-1, 248-1), Vulturine Fish Eagle (248-1), Orange-Cheeked Waxbill (20-3), Pigeon (19-3, 33-1), Dove (33-1, 33-3), Cock (123-1), the Agbe vird (17-2) and the Olubutu bird (255-1); Lion (2-1), Leopard (167-1), Cat (1-12, 222-2), Hyena (35-3), Treebear (18-2), Grass Mouse (54-8), Porcupine (55-1), Sheep (Ewe) of Ipopo (18-11), Python (54-2), Lizard (54-5), Chameleon (225-1), two kinds of Frog (55-2, 170-1, 170-2, 170-3), Tortoise (168-1), Snail (20-1), a small shell like a periwinkle (54-7), King of the Termites (54-1), and Fly (245-2); Ereje, identified as the mother of Ram, Elephant, and Buffalo (86-1); and Olokunde, the mother of Horse and Breadfruit tree (5-3). He-goat, Ram, and Cock appear together as clients (18-6); as do Brass, Lead, and Iron (35-6), Maize Beer, Palm Wine, and Bamboo Wine (54-6); Urine, Spit, and Semen (241-2); and Month, Grindstone, and the mother of Waterside Garden (250-2). The 165 kinds of animals (166-1, 249-6), the 165 kinds of rats (246-4), the 165 kinds of trees (33-2, 183-1), the 165 kinds of leaves (250-3), and the 165 kinds of cloths plus Calico (18-4) appear jointly as clients. Other clients are Cloth (255-4), Dye and Mordant (183-2), Cutlass (243-2), Hook (4-4), Rod (2-1), Trumpet (246-2), Calabash of shea butter (241-4), Head (4-1), Eye (35-4, 256-1), Penis (4-2), Sun (1-6, 52-1), the Mother of Sun (103-1), the Mother of Rain (18-11), Earth (181-1, 181-4), Fire (222-3, 245-1), Road (17-3), Storehouse (243-4), Termite Hill (33-5, 33-6), Yam Heap (19-2), and Refuse Heap (247-3).

Characters of similar types appear in other roles in the verses, while those named as clients also include a number of whom the diviner may know nothing more than what is told in the verse itself, as, for example, Odogbo (3-1, 3-2), "Quavering Voice" (7-5), the "Seller of bean fritters at Eriwǫn" (243-3), and Şereke, the child of "Priest who kills eight hundred tortoises to eat" (255-2). In some of these instances the description of the client seems related to his problem, as in the case of Rascal (7-1), "Strong but stupid elder" (7-4), and it is clearly so in the case of Barren Woman (4-3).

It seems likely that there is more meaning in some of the verses than was understood by the diviners from whom they were recorded. The Qyǫ title, Qna Işokun (18-6), cited above, was not recognized, for example, but was interpreted as meaning the road to the town of Işokun. In another case (9-2) subsequent work with worshipers of Şǫpǫna and Boromun, the deities of smallpox and yaws, made it possible to identify the character Olugodo as the Lord of Yaws, and his parent Ẹkunlempe as the God of Smallpox. In a third verse (183-4) the name Yewa was interpreted as a contraction of "our mother" (yeye-wa), which makes sense in its context; but Yewa is also the Goddess of the River Yewa, near the Dahomean border, and is associated with raphia, which is mentioned in the verse. Finally, although the informant's interpretation may have some validity in Ifẹ, the narrative in one verse (153-1) is clearly related to a myth in Mẹkọ which explains why the worshipers of Qya, Goddess of the River Niger and principal wife of Şango, the God of Thunder, sacrifice to buffalo horns, and why Qya is also known as Iyansan or Yansan.

The second segment of the verse, stating what happened to the mythological character, may be expanded into a myth, as in this case, or it may be briefly stated as in the example given earlier. As in the earlier example, this may be simply a direct statement rather than a narrative: "from that time on his voice does not carry far, and he talks with a very tiny voice" (181-3), or "ever since she made the sacrifice, witches have had power over human beings" (3-3). Some simply state that the character did or did not make the prescribed sacrifice (e.g. 86-3), and even this may be left unsaid (1-6, 1-9, 5-2, 86-2); but in such cases what the character did and what the consequences were are generally clearly implied. Other verses relate a sequence of events so briefly that they hardly constitute a narrative: "He did not sacrifice. He took the woman as his wife. Afterward sores confined him to his house, and caused him to die" (1-12).

According to some diviners, each verse should have a narrative, even if they themselves do not know it. About fifty of the verses recorded include fairly long narratives, some of which are well-known myths and folktales; about twenty others have briefer tales associated with them. Some of the latter have barely the minimal requirements to be considered as prose narratives: "When these three children of the same mother were told to sacrifice against death, Brass sacrificed and Lead made an atonement, but Iron said that the diviners were telling lies. He said that as the Sky God had ordained things, so they are destined to be forever. The sacrifice that Iron refused to make is what is eating him away. Since that time if Iron has been buried in the ground for as long as four years, he begins to rust and spoil. But the sacrifice that Brass and Lead made is what prevents them from spoiling even if they stay in the ground for many years" (35-6). Only one of these minimal narratives (48-1) appears in the published collections of Yoruba folklore, but other tales of comparable simplicity do (Ogumefu, 1929: 2-3, 5-6, 6-7, 17-18).

Some of these "minimal narratives" are summaries of longer tales. The story of Eshu's two-colored hat (48-1) is given in a much longer version by Frobenius (1913: I, 240-243), while the tale of Pigeon and Dove (33-1) is reduced to the following in the version recorded by Epega (n.d.: II, 93-94):

"'Ẹrukuku of the house' sacrificed; 'Ẹrukuku of farm' did not sacrifice. 'Ẹrukuku of the farm' bore two children; 'Ẹrukuku of the house' bore two children. 'Ẹrukuku of the farm' said she did not sacrifice, but she had born children. She built her house in the top of a Silk Cotton tree. A thunderstorm came and the tree fell, and both children of 'Ẹrukuku of the farm' (Dove) died. She cried, 'The first or the second, she does not see (either). 'Ẹrukuku of the house' (Pigeon), she cried, 'It touches the pot with its back; it does not die.'"

One wonders in such cases whether the diviner learned only the abbreviated version or whether he simply did not recite the complete narrative.

Most of the myths appearing in the verses are aetiological or explanatory in nature. Malinowski (1954: 108-111) has argued that aetiological myths do not really "explain" anything; rather they state a precedent and provide a sanction for customs and institutions. The latter function is very important, but, as far as I can judge, these tales were accepted formerly as explanations of the characteristics of birds, animals, insects, plants, and other things, as well as of customs and details of rituals. These explanations are stated in terms of precedents, to be sure, as events that were believed to have happened, but this does not mean that they do not explain why something is as it is or should be done as it has been. There is a need to vouch for the antiquity of social and religious institutions, but hardly a need to justify the characteristics of brass, lead, and iron (35-6).

The verses account for the four "eyes" on the diviner's palm nuts (175-2); the fact that the diviners carry cow-tail switches (54-4); the role of Ifa in relation to the ancestral guardian soul (111-1); the use of she-goats instead of humans as sacrifices to Ifa (204-1); why Iwori Meji ranks third among the figures of Ifa (35-5); the "meaning" of the names of some of the Ifa figures (18-10, 20-2, 247-1, 249-2); the meaning of Olodumare, a praisename of the Sky God (54-2); the meaning of Otu, the name of a group of Ifẹ priests (181-4); and why certain songs are sung by these priests (181-4), for deities (6-5), and at funerals (183-4). They explain the origin of the tabu on the use of red cloths for burials (18-4); the use of the red parrot's tail feathers by the Oluyare, another group of Ifẹ priests (247-5); why some deities are worshiped and others are not (249-1); the tiny voice in which the God of Medicine speaks (181-3); the fact that tortoises are sacrificed to him (168-1); and the fact that witches have the power to harm humans (3-3). They explain why no one on earth or in heaven can face the God of Thunder (243-1) and why Ram, his favorite sacrificial animal, paws the ground when it thunders, and lightning flashes (86-1).

They also explain why some trees live longer than others (183-1); why some are not destroyed by storms (33-2); why some leaves are useful for medicine while others are not (250-3); why Euphorbia kamerunica has thorns and is poisonous (6-4); why some plants can be used for fish poison (245-4); and why horses are poisoned by breadfruit (5-3). They explain why Lion is king of the animals (2-1) and Ọkin is king of the birds, and why Olubutu, who was deposed, has red feathers (255-1); why Pigeon and Goat live in town and Dove and Leopard live in the forest (33-1, 167-1); how Cock got its long tail feather (123-1); how Vulture got its white head (1-5); why Vulture is not hungry when a catastrophe strikes a town (241-1); and why people kill the Vulturine Fish Eagle but not the Vulture (248-1). They explain why brass and lead do not rust like iron (35-6); why spit and urine do not produce children

like semen (241-2); why mordant drips, and the meaning of the sound of its
dripping (183-2). They explain the fly's buzzing (245-2), the dove's call
(33-3), the cock's crow (123-1), and the lion's roar (2-1). They account for
the lines on the palm of the hand (14-1), and the marks on the shell of the
tortoise (166-1, 168-1).

It is not always necessary for the explanations to be spelled out in detail. Thus it is understood that Maize (248-2) and Benniseed (86-3) have
many seeds and that the mother of Rain has many raindrops (18-11) because
they made the sacrifices prescribed for them in order to have children, as
is specifically stated in the case of Banana (1-3). Similarly, it is understood that things do not slip from the claws of Cat (222-2) and that Sun is
known "around the world" (1-6, 52-1, 103-1) because they both sacrificed.

In addition to their usual functions in myths and tales, these aetiological elements serve another purpose in the Ifa verses: by referring to the
features of plants, animals, objects, or rituals which are common knowledge or which the client can verify for himself, they substantiate the truth
of the verse, with its prediction and sacrifice, and the system of divination
as a whole.

Furthermore, the explanation of these well-known characteristics is in
terms of whether or not they made the sacrifices prescribed by the diviners,
reinforcing the belief that sacrifices should be made according to the instructions. An exception is to be found in one verse (1-7), where a different but
no less convincing logic is employed. In place of making a sacrifice a wife,
whose husband had made a charm against her because she had been insolent
to him and refused to prepare food for him, is instructed to wash his clothes,
clean his room, prepare yam loaves and palm wine for him, and be especially kind to him.

In almost a third of the verses recorded, the mythological character
fails to sacrifice or otherwise disregards the advice of the diviners. Almost
inevitably he suffers misfortune as a consequence, whereas the characters
who sacrifice as instructed generally prosper. The moral of the narratives
in the verses is clear. It is advisable to sacrifice and dangerous not to do
so; it is best to make the sacrifices exactly as instructed; it is desirable to
make them as soon as possible; and it is better to give something than nothing at all. There is no verse in Part Two in which the character prospers
without at least having appeased Eshu.

Some verses specifically state why the characters failed to sacrifice.
They did not have enough money (33-2); they suspect the diviners of lying
(250-1), of simply trying to increase their own wealth (35-7), or of naming
as the sacrifice something they happen to need at the moment (33-1). They
say that they will wait until they have seen the promised blessing (170-1),
or they postpone the sacrifice on other grounds (3-2, 14-1, 120-2, 183-4).
They consider the manner of making the sacrifice beneath their dignity (33-
4); they prefer to rely on their own resources to ward off evil (54-1, 167-1),
or they argue that the sacrifice is unnecessary because they have done the
same thing many times without making one (247-5). They maintain that
when the Sky God does something, he does not leave it unfinished (248-1);
that, as the Sky God has ordained things, so they are destined to be forever

(35-6); and that the same results will occur whether or not a sacrifice is made (33-1).

It is likely that every possible reason or excuse for not making the prescribed sacrifice is cited in the verses. By stating the possible objections openly, and by showing how failure to sacrifice leads consistently to misfortune, the verses recited for the client reinforce his belief in the system of divination, in which he is already indoctrinated by folktales he has heard from childhood (Bascom, 1943: 45-47).

In two of the above instances the characters actually offered the prescribed sacrifices but refused to offer them in the correct manner. Five of Qrunmila's own sons insisted that the diviners should kill their sacrificial goats when they should not have done so, and they themselves were killed (35-7). A king's wife refused to carry her sacrificial goat on her back like a baby, sending her slave to do so for her; the slave received the child for which the goat had been sacrificed (33-4).

In another verse (244-2) there is a clear warning against choosing the verse with an attractive prediction while disregarding warnings of danger through wishful thinking. One diviner promised blessings for the townspeople of Igbade, but another warned them of impending danger. Preferring the former prediction, they seized the second diviner and beat him; but when the evil he had foretold befell them, he intervened to save them.

Many of the verses have an internal consistency which gives them both an aesthetic unity and a sense of logic. This is achieved in various ways, including the relation of the names of the diviners of the clients to the remainder of the verse. More commonly it is done by relating the prediction for the client to the narrative about the mythological character. In one verse (167-1) this is done with great skill: three separate predictions derive from elements in a widespread African folktale.

In other verses the narrative shows how items included in the sacrifices were instrumental (and thus necessary) in bringing the character good fortune or in saving him from disaster. Thus the three hoes and the three pots which Cock sacrificed help him to win a hoeing contest and a bride (123-1). A pot which Pigeon sacrificed is given to her to use as a house, but Dove, who refused to sacrifice, has her nest destroyed by a storm (33-1). Qrunmila plants the peanuts he has sacrificed, as instructed, and takes as wives two girls who steal from his field (3-4). A knife which Qrunmila has sacrificed is used to keep him from being identified as a thief and to bring him wealth (14-1); and the razor sacrificed by Aja-olele gets him into a fight through which he takes three chief's daughters in marriage (131-1). In these and other verses (1-10, 1-11, 35-3, 120-2, 222-2, 222-3, 225-2, 245-1) the tales provide a justification for specific items being included in the sacrifice.

Conversely, in other cases a part of the sacrifice which the character fails to make is instrumental in bringing about his downfall (e.g. 53-2). One such verse (54-1) does not make the point as effectively as might have been done: the King of Termites made only a part of the prescribed sacrifice, although he did include the hoe and the digging stick which eventually brought about his destruction.

Another means by which internal consistency is achieved is punning or playing on words, which is also a characteristic feature of Yoruba proverbs and other forms of verbal art. Over a century ago Vidal noted that "the point of the proverb very often lies in the fact of two words having a very similar sound with a wholly different sense, making the proverb, in such cases, a play upon the word" (Crowther, 1852: 29). In addition to the numerous cases in which the diviner's names are derived from the name of the figure (e.g. 4-1, 17-3),[2] there are puns on thunderstorm (iji) and shelter (iji) (33-1), on the kind of yams (egun) sacrificed and a hunter's lookout platform (egun) (153-1); on concerning (nipa) and powerful (nipa) (103-2), on improve in health (san) and benefit (san) (52-3), and on improve in health (san) and clear (şan) (101-1). In one verse (246-4), in which rats are accused of stealing locust beans (ji iru), the prediction concerns someone waving a cow-tail switch (ji iru), which would more commonly be given as ju iru or ju irukẹrẹ.

A special type of pun which similarly contributes to internal consistency is that designated here as word magic, in which the name of an object sacrificed resembles the words expressing the result desired by the client. Thus the figure Iwori Meji, who has sacrificed a mortar and tẹtẹ and gbegbe leaves in order to find a place to live, recites the formula "The mortar (odo) will testify that I see room in which to settle (do), the tẹtẹ leaf will testify that I see room in which to stretch out (tẹ), the gbegbe leaf will testify that I see room in which to dwell (gbe)" (35-5). Water (omi) is sacrificed so that the client can breathe (imi), ochra (ila) so that he will gain honor (ọla), and salt, used to make food tasty or "sweet" (dun), so that his affairs will be sweet (dun) (1-8). Pigeon touches her child's head against a pot she has sacrificed while saying, "My child touches the pot (ikoko) with its head; it will not die (ko ku) any more" (19-3, 33-1). In making a charm or "medicine" associated with the figure Irosun Ọşẹ, divining powder (iyẹ-irosun) is mixed with soap (ọşẹ) (111-2). A woman who desires to conceive is instructed to sacrifice steamed beans (ọlẹ), the allusion being to an embryo (ọlẹ) (52-4). Twenty cowries (oko) are added to larger amounts of money for characters whose case involves a farm (oko) (3-4, 86-2, 86-3) and for a character identified as Penis (oko) (4-2), though in other verses (4-1, 4-3, 5-1, 6-1) neither word magic nor puns on this word are recognizable.

In Yoruba, myth-legends (itan) and folktales (alọ) are terms for distinct categories of prose narratives. The former are accepted as "history" that is believed to have happened; the latter are regarded as fiction. Diviners describe all Ifa narratives as itan, but some are told as folktales in other contexts than divination (e.g. 225-4). In some instances this may reflect the effects of acculturation on Yoruba beliefs, which have changed rapidly during the past century. Even myths about the deities are regarded as superstitious by Yoruba converts to Christianity and Islam, but formerly they were matters of faith and clearly myths by any definition. The early Yoruba dictionaries define itan as "narration of old traditions; recording of past events"

---

2. In some cases names of figures appear other than the one to which the verse pertains, as in verse 19-1.

(Crowther, 1852: 164) but give no term for folktales. They define alǫ as "riddle, enigma," a meaning which it retains today, with the folktale being distinguished when necessary as alǫ alapagbe, referring to the chorus (egbe) of the songs that occur in so many of the tales. It may be tempting to speculate that in Crowther's time there were no folktales, and that as individual myths lost their element of belief, they were classed with riddles as lacking serious content and meant only for children. However, the use of alǫ to refer to folktales can be traced back at least eighty years (Bouche, 1885: 222 ff.). Apparently the diviners were taught to respect all Ifa narratives, whereas in other contexts the majority of Yoruba have long considered some of them to be amusing fiction.

The diviners are recognized as knowing more folktales than other individuals, but they may not use this knowledge for secular purposes. In Ifę it is a professional tabu for diviners to tell folktales (pa alǫ) for amusement, or even to join in singing the songs in the tales when they are being told by someone else. Nevertheless, the fact that many of these tales, describing the successes and failures of characters who do or do not sacrifice, are heard repeatedly from childhood reinforces the faith in the system of divination. Conversely, the existence of a group of specialists who systematically memorize both myths and folktales, and who recite them daily to outsiders as part of their professional duties, must affect the continuity and perhaps even the quantity of Yoruba folklore. In addition, the appearance of folktales in the ritual context of divination gives them important functions, which go far beyond that of simple amusement (Bascom, 1941, 1943, 1954).

At least thirteen of the narratives in the 186 verses have been published in collections of Yoruba folklore. As an elementary test of this relationship, eleven of the tales published by Frobenius (1926, 233-243, 288-292), selected at random, were cited to one diviner in Ifę, who matched six with verses of Ifa as follows:

Frobenius (233-237)	Tale 17, Part A.	Ifa 175-1.
Frobenius (237-238)	Tale 17, Part B.	Ifa 225-4.
Frobenius (238-240)	Tale 18.	Ifa -----.
Frobenius (241-244)	Tale 19.	Ifa 123-1.
Frobenius (244-246)	Tale 20.	Ifa 54-5.
Frobenius (246-247)	Tale 21.	Ifa -----.
Frobenius (247-248)	Tale 22.	Ifa ----- (but cf. 86-1)
Frobenius (248-250)	Tale 23.	Ifa 167-1.
Frobenius (250)	Tale 24.	Ifa -----.
Frobenius (250-254)	Tale 25.	Ifa -----.
Frobenius (288-289)	Tale 44.	Ifa 168-1.
Frobenius (289-292)	Tale 45.	Ifa 222-1.

This informant said that he had heard an Ifa verse with Frobenius' Tale 25 in it, but that he himself had not learned it; and undoubtedly the percentage could have been increased by pursuing the matter with other diviners. In addition to these seven verses three others (48-1, 86-1, 153-1) and variants of three more (14-1, 170-3, 245-2) are found as tales in collections of Yoruba folklore. It is probably quite safe to assume that the fifteen Ifa myths[3] presented here in Part I, and that all Yoruba and Fǫn tales which mention Ifa divination or diviners, are to be found in the Ifa verses (e.g. Walker and Walker, 1961: 71-75; Herskovits and Herskovits, 1958: 173-214). Some diviners maintain that all Yoruba myths and folktales are derived from Ifa verses; one admitted that he had heard tales for which he did not know the associated verses himself, but he insisted that there are no folktales which do not have associated verses. It could as easily be argued, and it is more likely in most cases, that traditional myths and tales have been incorporated into the verses.

Many tales and motifs in the verses, in fact, are widely spread in Africa. Not only has the story about Lizard's bride (54-5) been recorded as a folktale by Frobenius, but Motif 2474.1, "Why lizard bobs his head up and down," appears in quite different tales told among the Ekoi (Talbot, 1912: 378-380), the Ibo (Basden, 1921: 278-279), the Fǫn (Herskovits and Herskovits, 1958: 324-326), the Ewe (Courlander, 1963: 41-44), and the Ashanti (Courlander and Prempeh, 1957: 70-76), in Togo (Cardinall, 1931: 170-173) and Ghana (Barker and Sinclair, 1917: 45-49; Itayemi and Gurrey, 1953: 99-100), and among the far distant Bemba of Zambia (Courlander, 1963: 98-100).

The narrative about Fly and Birdlime (245-2) may be a variant of the widespread Tale Type 175, "Tar Baby and the Rabbit," whose African analogues often substitute birdlime for tar, pitch, or other sticky substances (Klipple, n.d.: 213-233); more conventional tar baby stories have been reported for the Yoruba in several sources. If more were known about African tale types without foreign analogues, it would probably be possible to identify many of the narratives in the Ifa verses as tale types. In addition to the tale of Fly and Birdlime, it seems likely that the seven Ifa narratives recorded by Frobenius as Yoruba folktales, and seven others will prove to be tale types. Others, of course, may represent tale types also.

Only Yoruba versions have been found for some of these fifteen tales, but of these there are two versions for verses 14-1 and 54-5, three for 170-3, four for 86-1, five for 168-1 and 222-1, and six for 225-4. Some tales, however, are more widely known in West Africa, and can be taken as tale types even though an index of African tale types remains to be compiled.

The tale of Eshu's two- or four-colored cap which causes two friends to fight when they start arguing about what color it is (48-1) has been recorded in four Yoruba versions and in an analogue from the Mpongwe of Gabon which involves a two-colored coat—half red and half blue (Milligan, 1912: 57).

The narrative about the bird or animal who wins a farming contest and a bride (123-1) has been recorded in five Yoruba versions, and among the Ibo to the East (Thomas, 1918: 84-86) and the Fǫn of Dahomey to the West (Herskovits and Herskovits, 1958: 418-420). The victor is Cock in all five Yoruba versions, Eagle among the Ibo, and Pig in the Fǫn tale.

---

3. Pages 30, 36-37, 38-39, 39, 48-49, 66, 97, 104, 106, 107-108, 108, 108-109, 110-111, 112 (bis).

The tale of alternate housebuilding or farming (167-1) is known in two Yoruba versions and has been recorded in twelve other African versions: among the Ibo (Thomas, 1913-1914: VI, 90-91), at Porto Novo in Dahomey (Bouche, 1885: 32-33), among the Ewe of Togo (Ellis, 1890: 270-271) and the Ashanti of Ghana (Rattray, 1930: 38-41), in Ghana (Barker and Sinclair, 1917: 141-143), among the Limba of Sierra Leone (Finnegan, 1967: 330-332), the Lamba of Zambia (Doke, 1927: 179-181), and in five Congo versions from the Luba (Bouveignes, 1938: 107-116; Burton, 1961: 50-55, 183-186), the Lulua (Badibanga, 1931: 29-30), and the Lega (Meeussen, 1962: 83-84). (1) Two animals come to the same place on alternate days to build a house (or make a farm), each being surprised at the progress being made in his absence; (2) they live together for a while, and then the apparently weaker animal frightens the stronger away, usually through the evil eye or some other form of magical power. In the Limba tale the stronger animal frightens the weaker by killing six bush cows with the evil eye; the weaker frightens the stronger by being able to carry all of them; and both run away, leaving the house deserted. In one Yoruba version the weaker animal does all of the work in the first half of this story.

Since the first and second parts of this story can be told separately, it probably represents two separate tale types, making a total of sixteen in this selection of Yoruba Ifa verses. The first part, by itself or with a different ending, has been recorded among the Hausa of northern Nigeria (Skinner, n.d.: II, tale 1), in Swahili from Tanzania (Lademann et al., 1910: 84), where it is posed as a dilemma tale, and among the Kamba of Kenya (Augustiny, 1925: 219-223). The second portion has been recorded separately among the Tiv of northern Nigeria (Abraham, 1940: 69) and the Fọn of Dahomey (Trautmann, 1927: 35-37). The protagonists are as follows:

Leopard and Goat	Yoruba, two versions
Leopard and Goat	Ibo
Leopard and Ram	Ashanti
Leopard and Ram	Ghana
Leopard and Wolf	Porto Novo
Leopard and Mongoose	Lulua
Leopard and Palm-Rat	Luba (Bouveignes)
Leopard and Squirrel	Luba (Burton)
Leopard and Bushbuck	Luba (Burton)
Lion and Bushbuck	Swahili
Lion and Antelope	Lega
Lion and Hare	Tiv
Lion and Donkey	Limba
Lion and Man	Lamba
Panther and Hyena	Fọn
Bush Cat and Hyena	Ewe
Hyena and Monkey	Hausa
Man and Bird	Kamba

The tale of the hunter and his animal wife who resumes her original form when her secret is revealed (153-1) has been recorded in seven

Yoruba versions and in six others among the Popo or Gun (Trautmann, 1927: 45-46) and the Fǫn (Trautmann, 1927: 43-45; Quénum, 1938: 39; Herskovits and Herskovits, 1958: 232-235, 235-236), and in Bahia, Brazil (Verger, 1957: 403) where, as in the Yoruba variant from Mękǫ, it is associated with the goddess Ǫya. Verger, who says that this association does not seem to be known in Nigeria, asks whether the descendants of Yoruba in Brazil have preserved traditions which have been forgotten in Nigeria, or whether a folktale has been blended with a myth; the Mękǫ variant provides an answer (see n. 7, verse 183-1).

The animal changes into a beautiful woman by removing her hide, which the hunter steals; she marries him and later is called an animal, usually by a co-wife who has learned the secret by intoxicating their husband; the animal puts on her skin and returns to the forest. In the Yoruba tales she is an African buffalo, hind, deer, or duiker; in the Fǫn versions she is a buffalo, hind, or antelope; in the Brazilian version she is a hind; and in the Gun version she is an unidentified animal. Some of these variations may result from the difficulties of translating African animal names.

This tale is suggestive of the Melusine and Swan Maiden stories, but these versions do not involve a quest, and Klipple does not cite them under Tale Types 400 or 465A. The Hausa also tell tales about a gazelle wife who returns to the forest when her secret is revealed (Skinner, n.d.: I, tales 11 and 81; Tremearne, 1911: 458-459), as do the Bulu of Cameroons about a porcupine wife (Krug and Herskovits, 1949: 358-359). Similar stories are also told about fruit wives by the Ekoi (Talbot, 1912: 134-135), tree wives by the Fǫn (Herskovits and Herskovits, 1958: 275-284, 322-324), "Mammy Water" or mermaid wives by the Gun (Trautmann, 1927: 41-42), and fish wives by the Twi-speaking people of Ghana (Ellis, 1887: 207-211) and in Liberia (Camphor, 1909: 235-239). Clarke (n.d.: 158, 141) cites references to somewhat similar stories about vegetable children under Motif C963.3 and to quite different tales about animal husbands under Motifs B650-B659.

The tale of the hunter saved from a forest spirit by his dogs (175-1), known in four Yoruba versions, has twenty-two other African parallels, among the Gola of Liberia (Westermann, 1921: 486-492); the Temne (Thomas, 1916: III, 58-60) and the Limba of Sierra Leone (Finnegan, 1967: 117-124, 143-146); the Ashanti (Rattray, 1930: 164-169); the Fǫn (Herskovits and Herskovits, 1958: 186-190, 240-241, 271-272, 275-284, 284-287), the Ekoi (Dayrell, 1913: 11-13; Talbot, 1912: 247-254) and the Hausa of Nigeria (Tremearne, 1913: 298-299; Skinner, n.d.: II, tales 3 and 7); the Digo (Nyika) of Tanzania (Dammann, 1935-1936: 217-219); the Lia of eastern Congo Kinshasa (Mamet, 1960: 114-119); the Yao of Malawi (MacDonald, 1882: II, 365; Stannus, 1922: 335-336); the Sotho of northern Transvaal (Hoffman, 1915-1916: 305); and the Nama Hottentots (Schultze, 1907: 398-399) and the Xhosa of the Republic of South Africa (Theal, 1886: 122-126). It has also been reported in four versions from the Cape Verde Islands (Parsons, 1923: I, 121-125, 125-131, 131 n. 2, 131-132), in one Spanish version (Hernádez de Soto, 1886: 249-257), and in eight versions among Afro-American groups, including an Uncle Remus tale from Georgia (Harris, 1892: 91-100), a tale from North Carolina (Parsons, 1917: 189-190), two from British Guiana (Harris, 1892: v-vi), and four from the Bahamas (Parsons, 1918: 66, 66-67, 67-68, 69-70).

Usually a forest spirit or animal appears as a beautiful woman, marries a hunter, chases him up a tree in the forest, and tries to cut down the tree and kill him; but she is destroyed by his dogs, whom he calls from home by name. The hunter is replaced by two boys in the North Carolina tale, and by two girls in the Xhosa version. This tale type is distinct from other tales cited by Clarke (n.d.: 123) under Motif B421, "Helpful Dog," which deal with the origin of death from a falsified message (Motif A1335.1), the acquisition of fire (Motif A1414), or the discovery of palm wine (Motif A1428).

Even the names of the dogs, when these have been translated, often show striking similarities, a fact that was accepted as decisive in establishing the historical relationships between Little Red Riding Hood and its homologues in French; and where the names of the dogs are not translated or even recorded, their actions are sometimes indicative. My informants could not fully translate the names of the first two dogs which they interpreted as meaning "One who cuts child of kerewu" and "Osǫpaka takes the child and swallows it"; the name of the third dog was translated as "One who sweeps the ground and sweeps dry leaves (see n. 2, verse 175-1). Fuja (1962: 155) translates the three Yoruba names as Cut to Pieces, Swallow Up, and Clear the Remains. Frobenius (1926: 236) gives them as Abschneider, Zuschnappende und Verschlucker, and Reiniger des Platzes. Walker and Walker (1961: 17-19) do not give the Yoruba names but say that the first dog killed the woman, the second lapped the blood, and the third cleaned up the spot.

Westermann does not translate the Gola names but says that the first dog (Gobla) tore the forest devil in two and devoured the upper part, and the second dog (Kaba) devoured the lower part. Similarly, Thomas says that the two dogs (Kinkoyanduri and Kero) in the Temne tale divided the spirit in the middle. Finnegan gives the names of the dogs as Kondengmukure, Sosongpeng, and Salialoho in the first Limba tale and as Denifela, Sangsangoso, and Tungkangbai in the second. She translates only one name as meaning "jumping well," but she comments that "The recurrence of these unusual and attractive names seemed to be one of the effective points about the story for the audience," and that in the first tale the roles of the dogs were recounted "with great vigour and excitement which the audience found very effective." In the first Limba tale the dogs bit the monster open and tore out the flesh; they split him up; and they scattered the bits. In the second one they bit the spirit to pieces, chewed her up, and "scattered her all." It is significant, as Finnegan notes, that while the names of the dogs are often given, that of the hunter rarely is.

Rattray translates the Ashanti names as Sniff-sniff, Lick-lick, Tie-in-knots, and Gulp-down. Among the unnamed and unnumbered dogs in the second Fǫn tale "there were those who ate only blood; there were those who ate nothing but bones; there were those who ate nothing but flesh. One ate nothing but skin, one took what fell. One goes only for the rescue, and one eats only the eyes of animals." In the fourth Fǫn tale seven of the forty-one dogs are named (Loka, Loke, Loki, Wesi, Wesa, Gbwlo, and Gbwloke); they "caught the monsters, tore them in two, and swallowed them." In Talbot's Ekoi tale the wife is torn in pieces by the unnumbered dogs, only one of whom is named (Oro Njaw). In one Hausa tale translated by Skinner the names are Blood-Drinker, Squasher, and Sorcerer; in the other they are Slasher who slaughtered the woman, Blood-drinker who drank up her blood, and Cold Wind who blew away the rest of the blood.

Of the many dogs in the Digo tale only Mimina is named; "das Untier wurde gepackt, getötet und gänzlich aufgefressen." In the Lia tale only two of the twelve dogs are named (Bakolo and Ibenga); the dogs tore the spirit into bits. In the first Cape Verde tale the three dogs (Flower, Hour, and Moment) simply seized and killed the old lady; in the second, three lions (Hour, Wait, and Moment) took the old woman and her children after having been told, "I don't want to see a particle of them left"; for the third tale we have only the names of the three dogs (Caléjon, Seléjon, and Hetéjon); and in the fourth Cape Verde tale there is only one dog, named Little Lion, who is told, "Seize her, and don't let a drop of her blood fall on the ground."

Neither the roles nor the names of the dogs are very suggestive in the Spanish tale (Hierro, Plomo, and Acero; i.e. Iron, Lead, and Steel), the tale from Georgia (Minny-Minny-Morack and Follamalinska), the tale from North Carolina (King Kilus and King Lovus), the two tales from British Guiana (Yarmearoo and Gengamaroto; Ya-me-o-ro and Cen-ga-mo-ro-to), or in one of the tales from the Bahamas (Watchman, Tiger, and Lion). But in the three other Bahamian tales the names of the dogs are given as Cut-Throat, Chaw Fine, and Suck-Blood; as Cut-Throat, Chew-Fine, and Suck-Blood; and as Ring-Wood, Cut-Throat, Chew-Fine, Suck-Blood, and Stowit All.

Even the verse (1-7) that gives practical advice to a wife, suggesting that she cook for her husband, wash his clothes, clean his house, and take maize beer to his shrine in order to regain his favor, has a parallel in a Limba folktale from Sierra Leone (Finnegan, 1967: 177-179).

Finally, the tale of the talking skull (or animal) that refused to talk (181-1, 181-4, 249-5) is probably another tale type, or possibly two. In addition to five Yoruba variants (see n. 1, verse 181-4), there is a folktale (unidentified but possibly Yoruba) from Nigeria (Anonymous, 1930: 14-16) of a talking sheep, which resembles verse 249-5. The tale of the talking skull has been recorded for the Efik (Jablow, 1961: 213-214, source unidentified) and the Nupe of Nigeria (Frobenius, 1924b: 150-151; Frobenius and Fox, 1937: 161-162), the Tem of central Togo (Frobenius, 1924c: 234-235), in Swahili from Tanzania (Lademann et al., 1910: 83), among the Yao of Malawi (Stannus, 1922: 322), and the Lamba of Zambia (Doke, 1927: 177). It has been recorded with a singing tortoise in Ghana (Barker and Sinclair, 1917: 119-121) and with a talking leopard for the Bakongo of Congo (Courlander, 1963: 64-66). These tales are distinct from those involving Motif E632.1, "Speaking (singing) bones of murdered person reveal murder" (Clarke, n.d.: 226) and Motifs D1318 ff. "Magic object reveals guilt" (Clarke, n.d.: 192-193), but are related to Motif K1162.+, "Dupe tricked into reporting speaking skull, is executed for lying" (Clarke, n.d.: 392-393). The motif

of the speaking head (D1610.5) appears in a quite different Yoruba tale recorded by Frobenius (1926: 294-296).

Because the verses are recited only as a part of the ritual of divination,
and because they should be recited verbatim as they have been memorized,
it is to be expected that innovations will be uncommon; but for these very
reasons any innovations are of increased significance for the study of cultural change. The question of creativity arises not only with regard to the
ultimate origins of the verses, but also concerning the possibilities of their
modification and of the introduction of new ones. On the latter two points,
at least, some evidence can be presented.

Effects of European acculturation—and, accordingly, evidence of cultural change—are to be seen in the verses dealing with Calico (18-4) and
the King who owns a European chair (225-4), and those in which guns are
mentioned (153-1, 175-1). Peanuts, introduced from the Americas, figure
in two verses (3-4, 55-2), and maize and maize products in a number of
others (9-2, 54-6, 55-2, 167-1, 241-2, 241-3, 243-4, 248-2, 256-3). The city
of Ibadan, which was not founded until the nineteenth century, is also mentioned (170-3). The references to a deity of the neighboring Nupe (103-2)
and to sara (248-3) and the presence of other Hausa loan words are also
evidence of cultural borrowing, though in these instances possibly prior to
European penetration.

A Mękǫ diviner explained that new verses are learned when one dreams
that he is divining; when one awakes in the morning, he repeats what he did
in his dreams. This is confirmed by Epega, who says that new verses may
be derived from dreams, and also that some individuals are born with Ifa
verses "inside them," so that as soon as they are taught the figures and a
few verses of Ifa, they introduce new verses. Thus while no new figures
can ever be added, there is no end to the knowledge of Ifa (Epega, n.d.:
XVI, 6). If new verses can be introduced from dreams or through individual creativity, it is clear that all verses need not be derived from the corpus of African folklore.

Four "Ifa verses" recited in jest by Ifę diviners have been included
here under the heading of parodies. Railway (257-1, 257-2), Whiteman
(257-3), and the owner of a plantain tree (257-4) appear as central characters. Whether or not these parodies are ever accepted as proper verses,
they show not only effects of cultural change but also how skillfully Ifa
verses can be improvised. The first two may be compared with the following Fǫn tale which Alapini (1950: 109-112) records as associated with the
figure Oturupǫn Otura:

Before the train appeared on earth it came, as souls do, before God;
and it was told to sacrifice chickens, eggs, bananas, and seats in a com-
fortable, luxurious room. Wagon made the sacrifice, but Locomotive refused. When they reached earth, both white and black travelers seated
themselves pell-mell on the seats Wagon had set up in his beautiful compartment, singing and shouting, and eating the chickens, eggs, and bananas
he had prepared. Well fed, they got out and went to Locomotive. They
touched him with the tip of their finger but saw that it became dirty. Then,
shaking and grinding, Locomotive pulled, while Wagon followed, singing.

Part Two:

THE VERSES OF IFA

OGBE MEJI[1] - 1

    Qrunmila ni   o di   iherehere, m(o)-(n)i iherehere l(i)-a j(ę)-ori
    Qrunmila say it become bit:by:bit, I-say   bit:by:bit be-we eat-head (of)

eku, iherehere ni a   j(ę)-ori   ęja, a   t(i)-okun t(i)-ǫsa   la
rat, bit:by:bit be we eat-head (of) fish; one:who from-sea from-lagoon come

gb(a)-ori   ęrinla ki kere   n(i)-Ifę o d(e)-aiye,   a ki igba du-du
accept-head (of) cow   not be:small at-Ifę   it arrive-world; we not take big-big

t(o)-erin   a ki şe   yękętę t(o)-ęfǫn.   ǫja ki it(o)-ǫja i-gba-le,
equal-elephant; we not make stubby equal-buffalo; sash not equal-sash to-tie-upon;

elu-k(u)-elu   ki it(o)-Qni; okun ki it(o)-okun   Yemideregbe, Yemideregbe
king-any-king not equal-Qni; rope not equal-rope (of) Yemideregbe, Yemideregbe

l(i)-orukǫ a   p(e)-O-l(i)-okun.
be-name   we call-One:who-has-sea.

    Qrunmila ni k(i)-a   wǫn   n(i)-ibu k(i)-a   wǫn   n(i)-iro,
    Qrunmila say should-we measure at-breadth should-we measure at-height;

gbǫgbǫrǫgbǫ l(i)-ǫwǫ yǫ   j(u)-ori   gbǫgbǫrǫgbǫ ni mǫriwo
very:long   be-hand appear surpass-head, very:long   be young:fronds (of)

ǫpę   yǫ   j(u)-ǫgǫmǫ,   igbo ki-(i)di ki iroko   ki   o
palm:tree sprout surpass-palm:fronds; forest not-tie that iroko (tree) should it

ma yǫ,   a ki ik(o)-ere   jǫ   ki t(i)-agogo   ki   o ma yǫ,
not appear; we not gather-play be:together that that-(of)-gong should it not appear;

t(i)-emi   yǫ   t(i)-emi   yǫ,   l(i)-akǫ   ke.
'That-(of)-me appear, That-(of)-me appear,' be-Grey:Heron cry.

    Nję   ti   yesi ni o yǫ-(o)ri   ju?
    "Well:then, that (of) who be it appear-head surpass?

    Dedere ǫran   ǫpę   ni o yǫ-(o)ri   ju,   dedere.
    "Plainly affair (of) palm:tree be it appear-head surpass, plainly.

    B(i)-ǫkan yǫ   a ja-(ǫ)na;
    "If-ǫkan   sprout it reach-road;

    Dedere ǫran   ǫpę   ni o yǫ-(o)ri   ju,   dedere.
    "Plainly affair (of) palm:tree be it appear-head surpass, plainly.

    B(i)-ǫgan yǫ   a ja-(ǫ)na;
    "If-ǫgan   sprout it reach-road;

    Dedere ǫran   ǫpę   ni o yǫ-(o)ri   ju,   dedere.
    "Plainly affair (of) palm:tree be it appear-head surpass, plainly.

    T(i)-emi   yǫ   t(i)-emi   yǫ l(i)-akǫ   ke;
    "'That-(of)-me appear, that-(of)-me appear' be-Grey:Heron cry;

    Dedere ǫran   ǫpę   ni o yǫ-(o)ri   ju,   dedere.
    "Plainly affair (of) palm:tree be it appear-head surpass, plainly.

---

1. Also known as Eji Ogbe; both mean "two Ogbe," or "double Ogbe."

1 - 1

Qrunmila says it should be done bit by bit; I say it is bit by bit that we should eat the head of the rat; it is bit by bit that we should eat the head of the fish. The one who comes from the sea, who comes from the lagoon to receive the head of the cow was not unimportant at Ifẹ[1] long ago. We are not as large as the elephant nor as stout as the buffalo. The sash that is worn underneath is not as fine as the sash that is tied on top. No king is as great as the Qni. No string of cowries is as long as that of Yemideregbe; Yemideregbe is what we call the Sea Goddess.[2]

Qrunmila says that we should measure the length and measure the breadth. The hand reaches much higher than the head; young palm fronds reach much higher than old palm fronds.[3] No forest is so dense that the iroko tree[4] cannot be seen; no music is so loud that the gong cannot be heard. "Mine is important, mine is important" is the cry of the Grey Heron.

"Well then, whose affair is most important?

"Clearly Palm Tree's affair is most important, clearly.

"Qkan sprouts, it reaches the road;

"Clearly Palm Tree's affair is most important, clearly.

"Qgan sprouts,[5] it reaches the road;

"Clearly Palm Tree's affair is most important, clearly.

"'Mine is important, mine is important' is the cry of the Grey Heron;

"Clearly Palm Tree's affair is most important, clearly.

---

1. Ifẹ is the Yoruba city where these verses were recorded, and Qsa is the lagoon to the south along the Nigerian coast. The Qni, mentioned below, is the king (ọba) of Ifẹ. According to Yoruba mythology it was at Ifẹ that the earth was created by Odua (or Oduduwa), a deity from whom the Qni and other Yoruba kings claim descent.

According to Ifẹ diviners, this is the first verse of Ifa. It is also the first Ifa verse written in a santeria note book from Cuba. See Bascom, 1952: 174-176.

2. Olokun is considered to be masculine by some Yoruba groups, but feminine in Ifẹ. The reference here is to her reputed wealth (Cf. n. 2, verse 249-2). Note also the pun on sea (okun) and the cord (okun) on which cowries and beads are strung.

3. New palm fronds grow out at the top of the oil palm tree (Elaeis guineensis) and stand up, while the old fronds fall down at its side.

4. The iroko or African Oak or African Teak (Chlorophora excelsa) is one of the largest trees of the West African rain forest.

5. Both ọgan and ọkan were described by informants as vines or creeping plants, the former being thorny. Dalziel gives ọgan as a name for Combretum platypterum, C. bracteatum, and C. racemosum; and ọkan for C. mucronatum and C. micranthum. He describes the latter as a small tree which often forms thickets. In any event, from the context here and in verse 35-3, it would seem that they are noted for spreading quickly.

The word yọ is used in this verse with a number of different meanings: to appear above, or be higher than; to be heard above; to be more important than; to sprout; and as a part of the cry of the Grey Heron.

A   ki   ik(o)-ere   jǫ   ki   t(i)-agogo   ki   o   ma   yǫ;
"We   not   gather-play   be:together   that   that-(of)-gong   should   it   not   appear;

Dedere   ǫran   ǫpę   ni   o   yǫ-(o)ri   ju,   dedere.
"Plainly   affair   (of)   palm:tree   be   it   appear-head   surpass,   plainly.

OGBE MEJI - 2

Qrunmila ni   o di   ę-l(i)-ęsę   m(u)-ęsę, mo ni   o di
Qrunmila say it become one:who-have-row take-row; I   say it become

ę-l(i)-ęsę   m(u)-ęsę, o ni   oko   m(u)-ęsę ti-rę   ko
one:who-have-row take-row; he say twenty:cowries take-row that-(of)-his not

ba   ja.
join (it) reach.

Qrunmila ni   o di   ę-l(i)-ęsę   m(u)-ęsę, mo ni   o di
Qrunmila say it become one:who-have-row take-row; I   say it become

ę-l(i)-ęsę   m(u)-ęsę, o ni   ǫgbǫn-(o)wo   m(u)-ęsę ti-rę   ko
one:who-have-row take-row; he say thirty-cowries take-row that-(of)-his not

ba   ja.
join (it) reach.

Qrunmila ni   o di   ę-l(i)-ęsę   m(u)-ęsę, mo ni   o di
Qrunmila say it become one:who-have-row take-row; I   say it become

ę-l(i)-ęsę   m(u)-ęsę, o ni   ogoji   m(u)-ęsę ti-rę   ko
one:who-have-row take-row; he say forty (cowries) take-row that-(of)-his not

ba   ja.
join (it) reach.

Mo ni   nję   baba   mi Agbǫnnire ta-ni   i   ba   ęsę ti-rę
I   say well:then father   my Agbǫnnire, who-be he join row that-(of)-his

ja?   O   ni   ęwadǫta   ni-(ǫ)kan ni o   ba   ęsę ti-rę   ja;
reach? He say fifty   (cowries) at-one   be he join row that-(of)-his reach;

nitori-ti   a   ki   ka-(o)wo-ka-(o)wo   k(i)-a   gbagbe ęwadǫta.
because-that we not count-cowries-count-cowries that-we forget fifty (cowries).

Ifa ni   o   ko ni   ję-ki   a   gbagbe ęni-ti   o   da   Ifa yi,
Ifa say he not be consent-that they forget person-that he cast Ifa this,

oluwarę   si nfę   ęe ohun kan yio ba   ęsę ja   ni ohun ti   o
person:in:question and wanting do thing one will join row reach at thing that he

nfę   ęe na   yi.
wanting do the this.

"No music is so loud that the gong cannot be heard;
"Clearly Palm Tree's affair is most important, clearly."[6]

6. The importance of the affairs of Palm Tree refers to the use of palm nuts in Ifa divination. Otherwise the meaning of this entire verse is obscure, probably because no story accompanies it. It consists solely of phrases comparable to the names of diviners which introduce other verses (Cf. n. 1, verse 35-3); but no divination is cited as a precedent, no sacrifice is specifically stated, and there is no specific prediction. However, the implication is that the client will live for a long time, that no one will excell him, that he will be prominent among his associates, and that he will succeed in whatever he undertakes. The rat and fish mentioned in the verse are the sacrifice, to which snail, kola nut, and cold water are usually added.

1 - 2

Qrunmila says each should take his own row;[1] I say each should take his own row; he says that Twenty Cowries takes his row but cannot finish it.
Qrunmila says each should take his own row; I say each should take his own row; he says that Thirty Cowries takes his row but cannot finish it.
Qrunmila says each should take his own row; I say each should take his own row; he says that Forty Cowries takes his row but cannot finish it.
I say, "Well then, my father Agbǫnnire,[2] who can complete his row?" He says Fifty Cowries alone can complete his row, because we cannot count money and forget Fifty Cowries.
Ifa says he will not allow the person for whom this figure was cast to be forgotten. This person wants to do something; he will "complete his row" in the thing he wants to do.

1. The row (ǫsǫ) refers to a row in the fields to be hoed or weeded. Here, and elsewhere in these verses, it is often used in a broader sense to mean any undertaking, so that "completing one's row" means being successful in a given venture.
2. Agbǫnnire is a shortened form of Agbǫnniregun, another name for Qrunmila or Ifa.

OGBE MEJI - 3

Ebiti   pa-(i)lẹ   n(i)-(i)gbe   wọ-(i)lẹ   n(i)-(i)gbe   tu-(e)rutu
"Deadfall kill-ground at-punishment drag-ground at-punishment loosen-dust"

a   da   fun Qlọmọagbiti ti   o   tori   ọmọ d(a)-Ifa, nwọn ni ki
(be) who cast for Qlọmọagbiti that she because (of) child cast-Ifa, they say should

o   ru-(ẹ)bọ   kojo mẹrin, eku mẹrin, ati ẹja mẹrin. Qlọmọagbiti ni
she offer-sacrifice (of) pot four,   rat four,   and fish four.   Qlọmọagbiti be

orukọ ti   a   pe   ọgẹdẹ. O   gbọ o   si ru-(ẹ)bọ.
name that we call Banana. She hear she and offer-sacrifice.

Qlọmọagbiti wa   ọmọ titi   ko ri,   o   mu eji k(an)-ẹta
Qlọmọagbiti seek child until (she) not see (it), she take two against-three

o   lọ s(i)-ọdọ   babalawo o   si bere bi on (yi)o ti   ṣe ni
(cowries) she go to-presence (of) diviner   she and ask if she will that do have

ọmọ? Nwọn ni ki   o   ru-(ẹ)bọ,   o   si ru-(ẹ)bọ;   o   fi
child? They say should she offer-sacrifice, she and offer-sacrifice; she take

awọn (ohu)n-kan ti   a   da-(o)rukọ nwọn-yi ru-(ẹ)bọ;   o   si wa
those thing-one   that we break-voice those-this offer-sacrifice; she and come

di   ọ-l(i)-ọmọ   pupọ. Lati igba-na ni a ko ti   fẹ   ọmọ
become one-who-have-child many. From time-the be we not have miss child

wẹrẹ ku ni-(i)di   ọgẹdẹ. Qmọ ki itan   ọwọ   yeye,   ọmọ wẹrẹ
young (1) at-waist (of) banana. Child not finish hand (of) mother, child tiny

ko ni tan   l(i)-ẹsẹ   ọgẹdẹ.
not be finish at-foot (of) banana.

Ifa ni   nitori   ọmọ ni e-l(i)-eyi   ṣe d(a)-Ifa bi o   ba
Ifa say because (of) child be one:who-be-this make cast-Ifa; if she should

ru-(ẹ)bọ   ọmọ ko ni tan   ni ọdẹdẹ   e-l(i)-eyi   lai-lai.
offer-sacrifice child not be finish at verandah (of) one:who-be-this ever-ever.

_____

1. Fẹ . . . ku means "to miss," or "to fail to find."

_____

OGBE MEJI - 4

Igbo   ni-(i)gbo-(i)na   Qdan   l(i)-ọdan   orun"   a   da
"Forest be-forest-(of)-fire" "Grassland be-grassland (of) sun" (be) who cast

fun Qrunmila ni-(ọ)jọ t(i)-Ifa nlọ ki   ọwọ   a-bi-ku   bọ-(i)lẹ
for Qrunmila at-day   that-Ifa going push hand (of) one:who-born-die enter-ground

ni koto   atitan.   Ni-(i)gba-ti Qrunmila nṣe   a-bi-ku,   o
at hole (of) refuse:heap. At-time-that Qrunmila making one:who-born-die, he

tọ   awọn babalawo Igbo-ni-(i)gbo-(i)na   ati Qdan-l(i)-ọdan-
approach those diviner   "Forest-be-forest-(of)-fire" and "Grassland-be-grass:

1 - 3

"The deadfall punishes the ground by striking it and then dragging the game along it, raising dust" was the one who cast Ifa for Qlǫmǫagbiti[1] when she cast Ifa because she wanted children. They said she should sacrifice four pots,[2] four rats, and four fish. Qlǫmǫagbiti is what we call the Banana. She heard and offered the sacrifice.

Qlǫmǫagbiti had been trying and trying to have children but had not had any; she took five cowries and went to the diviners, and asked what she had to do in order to have children. They said she should sacrifice, and she did sacrifice. She sacrificed those things we have mentioned, and she became the mother of many children. From that time on, one always finds young children on the banana plant. Children will not be wanting at the hand of the mother, young children will not be wanting at the foot of the banana.[3]

Ifa says it is for the sake of children that this person has cast Ifa; if she makes a sacrifice, children will never be wanting on her verandah.[4]

---

1. Analyzed as Q-l(i)-ǫmǫ-agbiti or One:who-has-child-agbiti. The meaning of agbiti was not known to informants.
2. A small narrow-mouthed pot, holding about a cup. These are generally used as containers for the oil applied to the hands and arms.
3. The fruit and the new sprouts are spoken of as the children of the banana plant. This verse thus explains why banana bears so much fruit, and why so many new plants spring up around it.
4. Note the pun here on verandah (ǫdędę) and banana (ǫgędę).

---

1 - 4

"Forest is the forest of fire" and "Grassland[1] is the grassland of the sun" were the ones who cast Ifa for Qrunmila on the day that he[2] went to bury medicine against abiku[3] in a hole in a refuse heap. When Qrunmila was troubled by abiku, he went to the diviners "Forest is the forest of fire" and "Grassland is the grass-

---

1. Qdan is the open grassland north of the rain forests (igbo) of the coast of West Africa.
2. From the literal translation it is obvious that in this verse Qrunmila and Ifa are the same individual. See also n. 1, verse 18-5.
3. Children who are destined to die, or "born to die." See Chapter XI, Farrow (1926: 84), and Ellis (1894: 111-114). Another diviner explained that Qrunmila was told to put leaves of Ifa in a pot of water, have his wife pour it over a he-goat, and bury the goat in a refuse heap.

orun   lọ, nwọn si sọ   fun   pe ki   o ru-(ẹ)bọ,   o si
land-(of)-sun" go; they and speak for (him) that should he offer-sacrifice, he and

ru-(ẹ)bọ,   lati igba-na ni a-bi-ku   ti da-(ọ)wọ-duro   ni ara
offer-sacrifice; from time-the be one:who-born-die have cause-hand-stand at body

      awọn obinrin rẹ.
(of) those woman his.

      Ifa ni a-bi-ku   nba   e-l(i)-eyi   ja, bi o ba   si le
      Ifa say one:who-born-die joining one:who-be-this fight, if he should and be:able

ru-(ẹ)bọ   yio da-(ọ)wọ-duro.
offer-sacrifice will cause-hand-stand.

OGBE MEJI - 5

      Orogbo   Oṣugbo Aja-ni-mọrọ-tipẹ-tipẹ   a   da fun-
      "Bitter:kola (of) Ogboni; Ceiling-at-smithy-tightly-tightly"(be) who cast for-

(I)gun, ọmọ   Olojongboloro a-l(u)-afin   ba wọn gb(e)-ode
Vulture, child (of) Olojongboloro one:who-beats-afin join them dwell:at-outside

      Qra; a ki r(i)-opepe   Igun   l(i)-a(ti)tan,   orogbo   kangẹ kangẹrẹ
      (of) Qra; we not see-young (of) Vulture at-refuse:heap; bitter:kola feeble feeble,

kangẹrẹ n(i)-Ifẹ, orogbo   kangẹrẹ. Ifa ni e-l(i)-eyi   yio di   arugbo,
feeble at-Ife; bitter:kola feeble.   Ifa say one:who-be-this will become old:per-

      o ni bi a ki iti   ri ọmọde   Igun,   bẹ-ni   e-l(i)-eyi
son; he say as we not have see young:child (of) Vulture, thus-be-(it) one:who-be-

      yio di   arugbo.
this will become old:person.

      Igun   ni kin-ni on yio ṣe ti   on yio fi   di   arugbo?   O lọ si
      Vulture say what-be he will do that he will take become old:person? He go to

ọdọ   awọn babalawo, nwọn ni ki   o ru-(ẹ)bọ,   ki   o si
presence (of) those diviner,   they say should he offer-sacrifice, should he and

bu iyẹ   rẹ le   ori, ni-(i)gba-ti Igun   ru-(ẹ)bọ   ti o si bu
dip wood:dust its upon head; at-time-that Vulture offer-sacrifice that he and dip

iyẹ   rẹ le   ori, ori rẹ si bẹrẹ si fun-fun   bi ẹni-pe
wood:dust its upon head, head his and begin to be:white-be:white like person-that

o wu   iwu   ati igba-na ni ori   Igun   ti ma
he become:grey grey:hair, from time-the be head (of) Vulture have (continuative)

nfun-fun   ti o si dabi   iwu;   a ki si mọ ọmọde
being:white-be:white that it and resemble grey:hair; we not and know young:child

      Igun   ati agba yatọ   nitori-ti   ori   gbogbo wọn ni o pa.
(of) Vulture and elder different because-that head (of) all   them be it be:bald.

land of the sun."[4] They told him that he should make a sacrifice, and he sacrificed. From that time on, his wives stopped bearing abiku.

Ifa says that abiku are "fighting with" this person; if he is able to sacrifice,
they will stop.

---

4. In this verse it is clear that two diviners are referred to, because of the
use of "awǫn babalawo" and "ati."

---

1 - 5

"Bitter-kola[1] of the Ogboni society;[2] very tight ceiling of the smithy" was
the one who cast Ifa for Vulture, the child of "Olojongboloro who beats the afin
drum[3] with those who live at the town of Qra." Vulture's children are never seen
on the refuse heap.[4] Feeble, feeble bitter-kola,[5] feeble at the town of Ifę, feeble
bitter-kola. Ifa says this person will live to be very old. He says that as we
never see young vultures, even so this person will become very old.

Vulture asked what he had to do in order to live to old age. He went to the
diviners, and they said he should make a sacrifice and sprinkle divining powder
on his head.[6] When Vulture sacrificed and sprinkled the divining powder on his
head, it became white, like a person whose hair is turning grey. From that time
on, Vulture's head has always been white, and it looks like he has grey hair. We
cannot tell the difference between young and old vultures, because the heads of
both are bald.[7]

---

1. Garcinia kola.

2. Oṣugbo is often an alternate name for the Ogboni society, but in Ifę it is
said to be the name of a particular status within the society. Cf. n. 3, verse 181-
1.

3. Informants could not describe this type of drum.

4. This is not literally true. The statement refers to the fact, elaborated
later, that all vultures appear to be old.

5. Note the pun here on bitter-kola (orogbo), and old person (arugbo) which
appears later. This pun is emphasized by applying the adjective "feeble" to the
bitter-kola, instead of to the old person.

6. In making a sacrifice, the figure (odu) is usually marked in the divining
powder on the tray. Then some is given to the client to eat, or to put in a line
down the center of his head. See Plate 20.

7. This verse explains how Vulture's head came to be white, and why one
cannot tell old and young Vultures apart.

OGBE MEJI - 6

Ina tin l(i)-ęgbę   ǫrun, Agunmǫla tin l(i)-ęhin   oşu   a   da
"Fire thin at-side   (of) sky; Venus   thin at-back (of) month" (be) who cast

f(un)-A-mǫ-ka   orukǫ ti   a   pe   ǫjǫ. Ifa ni e-l(i)-eyi   yio
for-One:who-known-around, name that we call day. Ifa say one:who-be-this will

ni   orukǫ ni ohun ti   o da Ifa si yi, yio si ni   orukǫ şugbǫn ki   o
have name at thing that he cast Ifa to this, will and have name but   should he

ru-(ę)bǫ   eku kan ęja kan, akikǫ ti   o ni   ogbe l(i)-ori kan ati
offer-sacrifice (of) rat one, fish one, cock that he have comb at-head one, and

ędęgbęta   ati epo.   A-(yi)o mu ori   eku ati ęja na, a-(yi)o
500   (cowries) and palm:oil. We-will take head (of) rat and fish the; we-will

ge dię ni-(i)nu   ogbe   akikǫ na a-(yi)o ko   si-(i)nu   ewe
cut small at-belly (of) comb (of) cock the we-will gather (them) to-belly (of) leaf

ęla kan; A-(yi)o lǫ   wǫn pǫ;   a-(yi)o fi   sin gbęrę ejilelogun
ęla one. We-will grind them be:together; we-will take (them) cut incision 22

si ori   ęni-ti   o wa   da   Ifa yi.
to head (of) person-that he come cast Ifa this.

OGBE MEJI - 7

Irǫ-(I)fa   a b(i)-ęnu   ginginni   a   da f(un)-Ore ti   işe
"Tapper-(of)-Ifa it bear-mouth pointed" (be) who cast for-Ore   that make

obinrin   Agbǫnniregun. Ifa ni obinrin kan wa ti   o nya-(o)ju   si
woman (of) Agbǫnniregun. Ifa say woman one exist that she insulting-eye to

ǫkǫ   rę, ki   o   ma   tǫ-(o)ju   ǫkǫ   rę gidi-
husband her, should she (continuative) care:for-eye (of) husband her completely-

gidi   nitori-ti   ori   ǫkǫ   na nfę   ba   ja   nitori-
completely because-that head (of) husband the wanting join (her) fight, because-

na ki   o ni   igba iyan   męfa, ki   o fǫ aşǫ   ǫkǫ
the should she have loaf (of) pounded:yam six, should she wash cloth (of) husband

rę, ki   o si ma   pa-(i)le   ǫkǫ   rę ki   o si
her, should she and (continuative) rub-house (of) husband her, should she and

ni amu   ǫti şękętę   kan ki   o gbe   si idi   Ifa
have jar (of) liquor maize:beer one, should she carry (it) to base (of) Ifa (of)

ǫkǫ   rę l(i)-oni.
husband her at-today.

Ore ni-(ǫ)kan şoşo ni aya   Agbǫnniregun ni akoko yi,   ko si fęran
Ore at-one   only be wife (of) Agbǫnniregun at time this, not and love

Agbǫnniregun rara, bi o ba   lǫ si ode,   Ore a   ma   bu
Agbǫnniregun at:all; if he should go to outside, Ore will (continuative) insult (him)

1 - 6

"Thin fire on the side of the sky, thin evening star[1] in the crescent of the moon"[2] was the one who cast Ifa for "One who is widely known," the name that we use for Sun.[3] Ifa says this person will make a name for himself[4] in the matter for which he has cast Ifa, but that he should sacrifice one rat, one fish, one cock with a comb[5] on its head, one penny five oninis,[6] and palm oil. We will take the head of the rat and the fish, and a small piece cut from the comb of the cock. We will put these in an ęla leaf,[7] and grind them together. We will cut twenty-two small incisions[8] on the head of the person for whom this figure was cast, and rub this mixture into them.

---

1. Venus, the planet which is seen near the new moon.
2. Literally "month"; the moon is usually referred to as oşupa.
3. Literally "day"; the usual word for sun is orun.
4. It is not necessary to add that the Sun made the sacrifice, and therefore became known round the world. This is referred to in the title given to him, "One who is widely known," and is brought out more specifically in verses 52-1 and 103-1.
5. Note that a cock with a comb (ogbe) is required as sacrifice for the figure Ogbe Meji.
6. The onini is a Nigerian coin worth one-tenth of a penny.
7. Epiphytic Orchidaceae.
8. Medicines are frequently administered by rubbing them into small incisions (gbęrę) on the body.

---

1 - 7

"Ifa's bell has a pointed mouth"[1] was the one who cast Ifa for Ore, the wife of Agbǫnniregun.[2] Ifa says there is a woman who is insolent to her husband. She should be very considerate of her husband, because he is planning to punish her. Therefore she should make six loaves[3] of pounded yams; she should wash her husband's clothes; she should rub the walls and floor of his house; and she should take a pot of maize beer today to the place where he keeps his Ifa.

Ore was Agbǫnniregun's only wife at this time, but she did not love him at all. When he went out in public Ore would insult him,

---

1. Ifa's bell is the instrument with which the diviner taps the tray before he begins to divine (see Chapter III and Plate 13). Its tusklike end is referred to here as a "pointed mouth." See also verse 4-3.
2. Qrunmila, Ifa.
3. Pounded yams (iyan or dǫmbai) are made into lumps referred to as loaves (igba or araba).

ko si jẹ   wa onjẹ de.   Ni-(i)gba-ti Agbọnniregun ri iwa
not and consent seek food wait:for (him). At-time-that Agbọnniregun see charac-

        aya rẹ yi, o mu-(a)ra o fi   ta iku, arun, ofun, işẹ
ter (of) wife his this, he take-body he take (her) sell death, disease, loss, poverty,

ati iya   l(i)-ọrẹ. Ni ọjọ na gan   ni Ore sun ti o si la
and punishment at-gift.   At day the identical be Ore sleep that she and dream

ala;   ni-(i)gba-ti ilẹ   mọ ti o si ji,   o fi eji-k(an)-ẹta
dream; at-time-that earth clear that she and awake, she take two-against-three

        o lọ s(i)-ọdọ   babalawo pe k(i)-o   yẹ   on wo,
(cowries) she go to-presence (of) diviner   that should-they examine her look;

nwọn ni orun ti o sun ko dara nitori-pe   ọkọ   rẹ ti fi
they say sleep that she sleep not be:good because-that husband her have take (her)

ta iku, arun, ofun, işẹ   ati iya   l(i)-ọrẹ, nitori-na ki   o
sell death, disease, loss, poverty, and punishment at-gift, because-the should she,

Ore lọ mu aşọ   ọkọ   rẹ ki   o fọ,   ki   o pa ile
Ore, go take cloth (of) husband her should she wash (it), should she rub house (of)

ọkọ   rẹ ni ẹmeji ki   o si gun iyan   araba mẹfa si idi
husband her at twice, should she and pound pounded:yam loaf six to base (of)

Ifa   ọkọ   rẹ.
Ifa (of) husband her.

    Ni-(i)gba-ti Ore şe ohun gbogbo nwọn-yi tan, ti Agbọnniregun de
    At-time-that Ore do thing all   those-this finish, that Agbọnniregun arrive

ti o si ri aşọ ti o fi   ibo-(a)ra ti aya rẹ ti fọ,   ti
that he and see cloth that he take (it) cover-body that wife his have wash (it), that

o ri ile ti o pa,   bi o si ti wọ-(i)le ti o de   idi
he see house that she rub (it), as he and have enter-house that he arrive base (of)

Ifa rẹ ti o ba   araba   iyan   mẹfa ni idi   Ifa, Agbọnniregun
Ifa his that he meet loaf (of) pounded:yam six   at base (of) Ifa, Agbọnniregun

wa   da-(o)hun   o ni:
come break-voice he say:

    O şoko, nwọn ni   bani
    "Oh shoko"; they say "Bani"

    Iku   ma ma   p(a)-Ore mọ, o
    "Death not (continuative) kill-Ore again, oh;

    Ore n(i)-iyan,   Ore l(i)-ọbẹ, Ore
    "Ore has-pounded:yam, Ore has-stew, Ore.

    Arun   ma ma   ş(e)-Ore mọ, o
    "Disease not (continuative) make-Ore again, oh;

    Ore n(i)-iyan,   Ore l(i)-ọbẹ, Ore
    "Ore has-pounded:yam, Ore has-stew, Ore.

    Ofun ma ma   ş(e)-Ore mọ, o
    "Loss not (continuative) make-Ore again, oh;

and she refused to prepare food for him. When Agbọnniregun saw his wife's true character, he got ready and gave her away to death, disease, loss, poverty, and punishment.[4] On that very day Ore went to sleep and had a dream; when dawn came and she awoke, she took five cowries and went to the diviners to be examined. They said she had had a bad dream because her husband had given her away to death, disease, loss, poverty, and punishment. Therefore she should take her husband's clothes and wash them; she should rub his house twice; and she should prepare six loaves of pounded yams and take them to the place where her husband kept his Ifa.

When Ore had done all these things, Agbọnniregun came home. When he saw that his wife had washed his clothes and had rubbed the walls and floor of the house, and as he entered the house and found the six loaves of pounded yams where he kept his Ifa, Agbọnniregun said:

"Oooooh shoko"; they answered "Bani."[5]
"Death do not trouble Ore any more, oh;
"Ore has made pounded yams; Ore has made stew, Ore.
"Disease do not trouble Ore any more, oh;
"Ore has made pounded yams; Ore has made stew, Ore.
"Loss, do not trouble Ore any more, oh;

---

4. He made bad "medicine" so that she would suffer all of these evils.

5. These words, which could not be translated and were not understood by informants, are the introduction to many of the songs and recitations which appear in the Ifa verses. Even where it is not stated as explicitly as it is here, they always follow the traditional leader-chorus pattern, with the diviner saying "Oooooh shoko" and his students and assistants and others who have gathered to watch the divination responding "Bani."

Ore n(i)-iyan,   Ore l(i)-ǫbę,   Ore
"Ore has-pounded:yam, Ore has-stew, Ore.

Iya   ma ma   j(ę)-Ore mǫ,   o
"Punishment not (continuative) eat-Ore again, oh;

Ore n(i)-iyan,   Ore l(i)-ǫbę,   Ore.
"Ore has-pounded:yam, Ore has-stew, Ore."

Bayi ni Ore bǫ l(i)-ǫwǫ   awǫn ohun ti Agbǫnniregun ti   fi le
Thus be Ore slip at-hand (of) those thing that Agbǫnniregun have put upon (her)

l(i)-ǫwǫ pe ki   nwǫn ba on ję   ni iya.
at-hand that should they join him eat (her) at punishment.

OGBE MEJI - 8

Qrunmila ni o di   hin; mo ni o di   imi   sin-sin,   o ni
Qrunmila say it become 'hin'; I   say it become breath (of) rest-rest; he say

ęni-ti   o ba   fi omi ru-(ę)bǫ   işe   ni sin-(i)mi.
person-that he should take water offer-sacrifice make (who) have rest-breath.

Qrunmila ni o di   hin, mo ni o di   imi   sin-sin,   o ni
Qrunmila say it become 'hin'; I   say it become breath (of) rest-rest; he say

ęni-ti   o ba   fi ila ru-(ę)bǫ   işe   ni ini ǫla.
person-that he should take ochra offer-sacrifice make (who) have have honor.

Qrunmila ni o di   hin, mo ni o di   imi   sin-sin,   o ni
Qrunmila say it become 'hin'; I   say it become breath rest-rest; he say

ęni-ti   o ba   fi iyǫ ru-(ę)bǫ   işe   ni ǫran rę dun.
person-that he should take salt offer-sacrifice make (who) have affair his be:sweet.

Igba   omi tutu kan, a-(yi)o da   iyǫ s(i)-inu rę, a-(yi)o rę ila
Calabash (of) water cool one; we-will pour salt to-belly its; we-will cut ochra

s(i)-inu   omi na pęlu,   a-(yi)o fi iyę-(i)rosun
to-belly (of) water the together:with (it); we-will take wood:dust-(of)-irosun (tree)

tę Eji Ogbe, a-(yi)o da   s(i)-inu rę, ęni-ti   o da Ifa na yio mu
press Eji Ogbe; we-will pour (it) to-belly its; person-that he cast Ifa the will drink

n(i)-inu   omi na, ęni-k(u)-ęni   ti o ba   fę   le   mu n(i)-
at-belly (of) water the; person-any-person that he should want, be:able drink at-

inu   omi na pęlu   l(i)-ęhin   na a-(yi)o da eyi-ti   o
belly (of) water the together:with (him); at-back (of) the we-will pour this-that it

ba   şiku si idi   Eşu. Ifa ni ęni-ti   a da on   fun yi
should remain to base (of) Eshu. Ifa say person-that we cast him (Ifa) for this

nfę   i-sin-(i)mi yio si ni i-sin-(i)mi   yio si ni ǫla pęlu.
wanting to-rest-breath will and have to-rest-breath, will and have honor together:

with (it).

"Ore has made pounded yams; Ore has made stew, Ore.
"Punishment, do not trouble Ore any more, oh;
"Ore has made pounded yams; Ore has made stew, Ore."

It was in this way that Ore escaped from the things which Agbọnniregun had set against her in order to punish her.

---

1 - 8

Qrunmila says we should sigh 'hin';[1] I say we should take a breath and rest; he says that the one who sacrifices water will have a breathing spell.
Qrunmila says we should sigh 'hin'; I say we should take a breath and rest; he says that the one who sacrifices ochra will have honor.
Qrunmila says we should sigh 'hin'; I say we should take a breath and rest; he says that the one who sacrifices salt will find satisfaction in his affairs.[2]
One calabash of cold water is required. We will pour salt into it; we will slice ochra into it also. We will mark Eji Ogbe[3] in the divining powder; we will add the divining powder to the water also. The person for whom this figure was cast will drink of the water, and anyone else who wishes may drink of it also. Afterward we will pour whatever is left at the base of Eshu. Ifa says that the person for whom we cast this figure wants a breathing spell; he will get a breathing spell, and will gain honor also.[4]

---

1. "Hin" represents the sound of exhaling air as in sighing.
2. Note the word magic in this verse. Water (omi) is sacrificed so as to get a chance to breathe (imi); Ochra (ila) is sacrificed to gain honor (ọla). The play on words with reference to salt is once removed. Salt is added to food to season it properly, to make it "sweet" (dun), and is sacrificed here so that one's affairs will go well, so they will be "sweet" (dun).
3. An alternate form of Ogbe Meji, the name of the figure.
4. There is also the clear implication that he will also find satisfaction in the way things are going for him.

OGBE MEJI - 9

Pǫnripǫn şigidi   ni   işe   awo   inu   igbo,   Ogogoro l(i)-
"Pǫnripǫn shigidi" be (who) make secret (of) belly (of) forest; "Ogogoro" be-

awo   Ijamǫ, b(i)-ǫrę ba   dun   l(i)-a-dun-ju   a dabi
secret (of) Ijamǫ, "If-friend should be:sweet at-to-be:sweet-surpass he resemble

iye-kan   a   da   fun Qrunmila t(i)-o   nlǫ   ba   Eşu d(i)-
(those) (of) mother-one" (be) who cast for Qrunmila that-he going join Eshu be-

oluku.
come-friend.

A ki ba   Eşu d(i)-oluku   k(i)-oju   owo   pǫn-(ę)ni
"We not join Eshu become-friend that-eye (of) cowries be:red-(of)-person;

Eşu şe   ni   mo wa   ba   ǫ   d(i)-oluku
"Eshu make be (who) I   come join you become-friend.

A ki ba   Eşu d(i)-oluku   k(i)-oju   aya pǫn-(ę)ni
"We not join Eshu become-friend that-eye (of) wife be:red-(of)-person;

Eşu şe   ni   mo wa   ba   ǫ   d(i)-oluku
"Eshu make be (who) I   come join you become-friend.

A ki ba   Eşu d(i)-oluku   k(i)-oju   ǫmǫ pǫn-(ę)ni
"We not join Eshu become-friend that-eye (of) child be:red-(of)-person;

Eşu şe   ni   mo wa   ba   ǫ   d(i)-oluku.
"Eshu make be (who) I   come join you become-friend."

A-(yi)o pa akikǫ ni a-pa-l(a)-aiya   a-(yi)o fǫ   igbin kan si   a-(yi)o
We-will kill cock at to-kill-split-chest; we-will break snail one to (it); we-will

bu epo   si   a-(yi)o gbe   lǫ si idi   Eşu. Ifa ni e-l(i)-
dip palm:oil to (it); we-will carry (it) go to base (of) Eshu. Ifa say one:who-be-

eyi nfę   ni   ǫrę   titun kan, ǫrę   na yio şe   ni anfani.
this wanting have friend new one; friend the will make (him) at benefit.

OGBE MEJI - 10

Qmǫ-(ǫ)wǫ   tori   iyan   o yǫ-(i)ke,   ataparako şe
"Child-(of)-hand because:of pounded:yam it sprout-hump; thumb   make

ęhin kokoko pa-(o)bi   a   da   fun Qrunmila ti   o   ma   fę
back stiff   kill-kola" (be) who cast for Qrunmila that he (continuative) love

Aiye ǫmǫ   E-l(i)-ewu   emure,   nwǫn ni ki   Qrunmila ru-
Earth, child (of) "One:who-has-gown pleasing"; they say should Qrunmila offer-

(ę)bo   ki o ba   ri aya na fę,   eku kan, ęgbędǫgbǫn,   ati ayebǫ
sacrifice that he should see wife the love, rat one, 5000 (cowries), and hen

adię   meji. A-(yi)o so ilękę-k(u)-ilękę mǫ   eku na ni idi   a-(yi)o lǫ
chicken two. We-will tie bead-any-bead against rat the at waist; we-will go

1 - 9

"Ponripon shigidi"[1] the diviner inside the forest, "Ogogoro" the diviner of Ijamo,[2] and "If a friend is exceedingly dear, he is like the child of one's own mother" were the ones who cast Ifa for Qrunmila when he was going to befriend Eshu.

"Those who befriend Eshu are not troubled by want of money;
"Eshu, you are the one I am going to befriend.
"Those who befriend Eshu are not troubled by want of wives;
"Eshu, you are the one I am going to befriend.
"Those who befriend Eshu are not troubled by want of children;
"Eshu, you are the one I am going to befriend."

We will kill a cock by tearing it open at the breast. We will break open a snail and pour it and palm oil into the cock. We will carry it to the base of Eshu. Ifa says this person desires to make a new friendship; the new friend will be of benefit to him.[3]

---

1. This phrase could not be translated by informants. Shigidi here is something very dangerous, but is not the image (shigidi) used by the Yoruba in sorcery. Ponripon in another connection means thick; but pon describes the degree of redness of anything, and redness is associated with things which are dangerous or powerful.
2. This could be the name of a town, or of a person.
3. There is also the implication of a blessing of money, wives, and children in this verse.

---

1 - 10

"Because of pounded yams the fingers develop humps;[1] the thumb stiffens its back to split kola nuts"[2] was the one who cast Ifa for Qrunmila when he was in love with Earth, child of "The one with the pleasing gown." They said Qrunmila should sacrifice one rat, one shilling three pence, and two hens so that he might marry her. We will tie any kind of beads about the waist of the rat; we will

---

1. Pounded yam is served in large loaves. Since it is tough, the knuckles of the fingers appear as humps when small pieces are broken off to eat.
2. Kola nuts are broken into sections before eating. For this the thumbnail is used, and the thumb is held rigid, with the thumb making a right angle.

fi   gun-(i)lẹ   si-(i)nu   igbẹ,   Ọrunmila ru-(ẹ)bọ.
take (it) stab-ground to-belly (of) forest; Ọrunmila offer-sacrifice.

Aiye jẹ ọmọ   ọba obinrin, igba aṣọ ni Aiye ro,   o si sọ   pe
Earth eat child (of) king woman, 200 cloth be Earth wrap, she and speak that

ẹni-k(u)-ẹni   ti o ba   ri idi   on ni on yio fẹ.   Ni-
person-any-person that he should see waist (of) her be she will love (him).   At-

(i)gba-ti Ọrunmila fi   eku yi gun-(i)lẹ   si inu   igbo ni-(i)gba-ti o
time-that Ọrunmila take rat this stab-ground to belly (of) forest, at-time-that it

di   owurọ   ọjọ-(e)keji ti Aiye lọ ya-(i)gbẹ   ni-(i)nu   igbo, Eṣu
become morning day-second that Earth go split-forest at-belly (of) forest, Eshu

pa-(a)tẹ mọ   eku na, o di   aye, ilẹkẹ ti Ọrunmila so mọ   ni
clap-palm against rat the, it become alive, bead that Ọrunmila tie against (it) at

idi   di   sẹgi, ni-(i)gba-ti Aiye ri eku yi . pẹlu   sẹgi ni idi   rẹ,
waist become sẹgi, at-time-that Earth see rat this together:with sẹgi at waist its,

o   bẹrẹ si ile   kiri, ni-(i)bi-ti o gbe ti nle   kiri gbogbo
she begin to chase (it) about, at-place-that she take have chasing (it) about all

igba aṣọ   idi rẹ tu,   o si wa ni ihoho, ni-(i)bi-ti o gbe
200 cloth (of) waist hers loosen, she and exist at naked; at-place-that she take

ti nsa-re   kiri ni ihoho, ni akoko na ni Ọrunmila wa   bẹ   ẹbọ
have running-go about at naked, at time the be Ọrunmila come peep:at sacrifice

ti o ru wo,   ti o si ba   Aiye ni ihoho. Ni-(i)gba-ti Aiye ri
that he offer look:at (it), that he and meet Earth at naked. At-time-that Earth see

Ọrunmila, o ni o pa-(o)ri, o ni o ti sọ   pe ẹni-k(u)-ẹni
Ọrunmila, she say it kill-head, she say she have speak that person-any-person

ti o ba   ri idi   on ni on yio fẹ; bayi ni Aiye di   aya
that he should see waist (of) her be she will love; thus be Earth become wife (of)

Ọrunmila, Ọrunmila si lọ ko   gbogbo ẹru   Aiye wa   si ile   ara-
Ọrunmila, Ọrunmila and go gather all   load (of) Earth come to house (of) people-

rẹ. Aiye si joko   ti.   Ni-(i)gba-ti Ọrunmila fẹ Aiye tan   ni
his. Earth and sit:down against (him).   At-time-that Ọrunmila love Earth finish be

o bẹrẹ si kọ-(o)rin ti o njo   ti o nyọ   pe:
he begin to sing-song that he dancing that he rejoicing that:

        A gb(a)-Aiye ka-(i)lẹ,
        "We take-Earth against-ground,

        Awa o   lọ mọ,   o, e, e.
        "We not go again, oh, ay, ay."

Ifa ni a-(yi)o ri aya kan fẹ,   ti ire   yio wa   l(i)-ẹhin   obinrin
Ifa say we-will see wife one love, that goodness will exist at-back (of) woman

na, a-(yi)o si ni   igba-(o)hun-igba-(o)hun lati ẹsẹ   obinrin na wa.
the; we-will and have 200-thing-200-thing   from foot (of) woman the come.

---

take the rat and stick it into the ground[3] inside the forest. Qrunmila sacrificed.

Earth was the daughter of the king. She wore two hundred cloths about her waist, and she said that she would marry anyone who saw her bare buttocks. On the morning of the day after Qrunmila had stuck the rat into the ground, Earth went into the forest to defecate. Eshu clapped his hands[4] and the rat came to life, and the beads that Qrunmila had tied about its waist became sẹgi beads.[5] When Earth saw the rat with sẹgi beads on its waist, she began to chase it about. As she chased it, all two hundred of the cloths fell from her waist, and she was naked. At the same time Qrunmila came to examine his sacrifice, and he met Earth running around naked. When Earth saw Qrunmila, she said, "That does it!" She said she had agreed to marry anyone who saw her bare buttocks. So Earth became Qrunmila's wife; Qrunmila brought all her possessions to his house, and Earth settled down with him. When Qrunmila had married Earth, he began to sing and dance, rejoicing:

> "We captured Earth;
> "We will never leave her, oh, ay, ay."[6]

Ifa says we will find a woman to marry, and that through her we will receive a blessing. The woman will bring us two hundred of every kind of goods.[7]

---

3. The dried rats used in sacrifices are impaled on sticks. In this case it is the stick itself which is stuck into the ground, so that the rat stands up.

4. By clapping his hands, Eshu accomplished this magical transformation. Cf. verse 244-2.

5. Sẹgi are very valuable beads which are found buried in the ground.

6. There is a double meaning to this song. The obvious meaning is that we love Earth, our wife, so much that we never want to leave her. The second is that we enjoy life on this earth so much that we never want to die.

7. The number 200 is derived from the number of cloths worn by Earth, and is not to be taken literally. It simply means that we will come to have a great many possessions. Cf. verse 14-1.

OGBE MEJI - 11

Ejinrin fa   gburu-gburu   wọ-(i)lu   a   da   fun Ọrunmila ti   o
"Ejinrin crawl widely-widely enter-town" (be) who cast for Ọrunmila that he

nlọ   fẹ   eyi   Toro   ọmọ   O-l(i)-okun.   Nwọn ni   ki   Ọrunmila
going love this "Narrow," child (of) One:who-has-sea. They say should Ọrunmila

ru-(ẹ)bọ   ki   o   ba   le   fẹ,   akikọ meji, ayebọ kan, eku, ẹja,
offer-sacrifice that he should be:able love (her), cock two, hen one, rat, fish,

ọkẹ meji, ati ẹgbafa;   o ru-(ẹ)bọ.   N(i)-igba-ti Ọrunmila nlọ
bag two, and 12,000 (cowries); he offer-sacrifice. At-time-that Ọrunmila going

si ile   O-l(i)-okun,   o ko   ọkẹ meji dani, ni-(i)gba-ti Ọrunmila
to house (of) One:who-has-sea, he gather bag two hold, at-time-that Ọrunmila

fi   ma   de   ile   O-l(i)-okun,   Eṣu ṣẹ-(o)ju
take (them) (continuative) reach house (of) One:who-has-sea, Eshu squeeze-eye

mọ   l(i)-ara, ni-(i)gba-ti Toro   ri Ọrunmila, o ni on ni
against (him) at-body; at-time-that "Narrow" see Ọrunmila, she say he be (who)

on (yi)o fẹ.   O-l(i)-okun   ni gbogbo Irun-(i)mọlẹ ti   o   ti   nfẹ
she will love. One:who-has-sea say all   400-Deity   that they have wanting

Toro   ti   ko gba.   Nibo ni Ọrunmila mu   Toro   gba?
"Narrow" that (she) not accept (them). Where be Ọrunmila take "Narrow" take?

Ọrunmila ni on yio mu   lọ, bayi ni O-l(i)-okun   bẹrẹ si kẹ
Ọrunmila say he will take (her) go, thus be One:who-has-sea begin to indulge

Ọrunmila; o ni lati ọjọ ti gbogbo Irun-(i)mọlẹ ti nfẹ   Toro,   o
Ọrunmila; she say from day that all   400-Deity   have wanting "Narrow," she

jaja ri ẹni-ti   yio fẹ.
finally see person-that (she) will love.

Ni-(i)gba-ti awọn Irun-(i)mọlẹ ri pe   Toro   fẹ   Ọrunmila, inu   bi
At-time-that those 400-Deity   see that "Narrow" love Ọrunmila, belly vex

wọn, nwọn mu-(a)ra, nwọn fi   ọtun   ṣe   ayẹ, nwọn fi   osi
them, they take-body, they take right (hand) make pit, they take left (hand)

ṣe   iran, nwọn fi okorokoro ṣe   a-jin-jin-d(e)-ọrun.
make abyss, they take front   make to-be:deep-be:deep-arrive-sky.

Ni-(i)gba-ti Eṣu ri eyi, o mu ọkan n(i)-inu   akikọ meji ti   Ọrun-
At-time-that Eshu see this, he take one at-belly (of) cock two that Ọrun-

mila fi   ru-(ẹ)bọ,   o sọ   si-(i)nu   ayẹ   ọtun, o di,
mila take (them) offer-sacrifice, he throw (it) to-belly (of) pit (of) right, it tie;

o sọ   ọkan si-(i)nu   iran   osi, o di, o sọ   ayebọ si-(i)nu a-jin-
he throw one to-belly (of) abyss (of) left, it tie; he throw hen   to-belly to-be:

jin-d(e)-ọrun   okorokoro, o di; awọn Irun-(i)mọlẹ si   ti   sọ
deep-be:deep-arrive-sky (of) front,   it tie; those 400-Deity   and have speak

fun o-l(i)-odo   ti yio tu   nwọn pe bi nwọn ba   ri   babalawo
for one:who-have-river that will paddle them that if they should see diviner

1 - 11

"Ejinrin[1] spreads and spreads until it enters the town" was the one who cast Ifa for Qrunmila when he was going to marry Narrow, child of the Sea Goddess. They said Qrunmila should sacrifice two cocks, one hen, a rat, a fish, two bags,[2] and three shillings so that he might be able to marry her. He made the sacrifice. When Qrunmila went to the Sea Goddess' house, he took two bags with him. When he arrived, Eshu blinked his eyes[3] at him, making him very handsome. When Narrow saw Qrunmila, she said he was the one she would marry. The Sea Goddess said all the Four Hundred Deities had wanted Narrow, but she had refused them; where then could Qrunmila take Narrow to escape their anger? Qrunmila said he would take her away. Then the Sea Goddess began to be hospitable to Qrunmila. She said that all the Four Hundred Deities had wanted to marry Narrow; but finally she had found someone she was willing to marry.

When the Four Hundred Deities saw that Narrow loved Qrunmila, they were angry; they got ready and dug a pit on the right side; they dug an abyss on the left side; and in front they dug a hole as deep as heaven is high.

When Eshu saw this, he took the two cocks that Qrunmila had sacrificed. He threw one into the pit on the right, and it closed; he threw the other into the abyss on the left, and it closed; he threw the hen[4] into the hole in front, which was as deep as heaven is high, and it closed. The Four Hundred Deities had already told the ferrymen at the river Qrunmila had to cross that if a diviner

---

1. A creeping vine (<u>Momordica</u> <u>Balsamina</u>, <u>M</u>. <u>Charantia</u>, or <u>M</u>. <u>foetida</u>).
2. Two empty matlike bags used in carrying and storing money and clothing.
3. This is different from our wink; both eyes are flicked lightly shut at the same time. By doing this, Eshu has the power to transform a person by making them very ugly or, as in this case, very beautiful.
4. The two cocks, the hen, and the two bags included in the sacrifice are instrumental in making it possible for Qrunmila to attain his goal.

kan ti   o   ba   mu obinrin kan l(i)-ęhin, ko gbǫdǫ tu   wǫn; ni-(i)gba-ti
one that he should take woman one at-back, not must paddle them; at-time-that

Qrunmila fi   ma   de   ǫdǫ   o-1(i)-odo   o di
Qrunmila take (continuative) reach presence (of) one:who-have-river, he tie

obinrin rę Toro   si-(i)nu   ǫkę kan o da   ǫkan de l(i)-ori, o di
woman his, "Narrow," to-belly (of) bag one, he cover one (1) at-head; he tie (her)

o gbe   ru,   ni-(i)gba-ti o de   ǫdǫ   o-1(i)-odo,
he take (her) carry; at-time-that he arrive presence (of) one:who-have-river,

o-1(i)-odo   ko mǫ pe babalawo na ti   awǫn Irun-(i)mǫlę wi
one:who-have-river not know that diviner the that those 400-Deity   speak (of)

ni,   o si tu   wǫn gun oke, ni-(i)gba-ti Qrunmila de   ǫja
be (this); he and paddle them climb hill; at-time-that Qrunmila arrive market (of)

Ifę, o sǫ   ka-(i)lę,   o tu   ǫkę l(i)-ori   obinrin, obinrin na
Ifę, he throw (her) against-ground, he loosen bag at-head (of) woman, woman the

si yǫ   ja-(o)de   ara ta gbogbo awǫn Irun-(i)mǫlę inu si bi wǫn.
and appear reach-outside, body kick all   those 400-Deity   belly and vex them.

Qrunmila njo,   o nyǫ,   o ni:
Qrunmila dancing, he rejoicing, he say:

    O şoko   Bani
    "O shoko." "Bani."

    Ejinrin fa   gburu-gburu wǫ-(i)lu,   o
    "'Ejinrin crawl widely-widely enter-town,' oh,

        a   da fun emi Qrunmila
    "(Be) who cast for me, Qrunmila,

    Ti   nlǫ fę   Toro,   ǫmǫ   O-1(i)-okun.
    "That (I) going love 'Narrow,' child (of) One:who-has-sea.

    Awǫn Irun-(i)mǫlę f(i)-ǫtun   ş(e)-ayę o,
    "Those 400-Deity   take-right make-pit, oh;

    Awǫn Irun-(i)mǫlę f(i)-osi şe-(i)ran;
    "Those 400-Deity   take-left make-abyss;

    Nwǫn fi   okorokoro ş(e)-a-jin-jin-d(e)-ǫrun;
    "They take front   make-to-be:deep-be:deep-reach-sky.

    Nwǫn le   f(i)-ǫtun ş(e)-ayę, o;
    "They be:able take-right make-pit, oh;

    Ki   nwǫn f(i)-osi şe-(i)ran;
    "That they take-left make-abyss;

    Ki   nwǫn f(i)-okorokoro ş(e)-a-jin-jin-d(e)-ǫrun;
    "That they take-front   make-to-be:deep-be:deep-reach-sky;

    K(o)-(ni)-o-n(i)-ile   ma re-(i)le   gbain.
    "Not-(say)-one:who-have-house not go-house, 'gbain.'

---

1. Da . . . de means "cover."

traveling with a woman should come to them, they must not ferry them across.
When Qrunmila was approaching the ferrymen, he put his wife, Narrow, inside
of one bag and he put the other bag over her head. He tied her up, and carried
her. When he came to the river, the ferryman did not know that this was the
diviner of whom the Four Hundred Deities had spoken, and he paddled them
across the river. When Qrunmila arrived at the market in Ifẹ, he put the bags
down and untied them; and his wife stepped out. All of the Four Hundred Deities
were disappointed and they were angry; but Qrunmila was dancing and rejoicing.
He said:

"Oooooh Shoko." "Bani."[5]
"Ejinrin spreads and spreads until it enters the town; oh,
"Was the one who cast Ifa for me, Qrunmila,
"When I was going to marry Narrow, the child of the Sea Goddess.
"The Four Hundred Deities dug a pit on the right side;
"The Four Hundred Deities dug an abyss on the left side;
"In front they dug a hole as deep as heaven is high.
"They can dig a pit on the right side, oh;
"They can dig an abyss on the left side;
"They can dig a hole in front, as deep as heaven is high;
"They didn't say one can't go to his own house, 'gbain.'[6]

---

5. The traditional introduction to Ifa songs and recitations. See n. 4, verse
1-7.

6. An exclamation, the meaning of which is not clear.

Qrunmila gbe   mi s(i)-ǫkę gbe   mi s(i)-ǫrǫrǫ rę
"Qrunmila carry me to-bag   carry me to-purse yours;

K(i)-a jǫ   ma   lǫ gbęrę-gbęrę;
"That-we be:together (continuative) go slowly-slowly;

Ni-(i)bi o da   l(i)-o da   k(i)-a jǫ   ma
"At-place it where:be (it) be-it where:be (it) that-we be:together (continuative)

    lǫ.
    go."

Ifa ni a-(yi)o fę   obinrin kan, gbogbo enia   ni yio ma   doyi
Ifa say we-will love woman one, all   person be will (continuative) spin

yi-(ę)ni   ka,   ti nwǫn yio si   ma   di rikişi si-(ę)ni   ki
turn-person around, that they will and (continuative) tie plot   to-person, should

a   ma foya, a-(yi)o fę   obinrin na.
we not fear, we-will love   woman the.

OGBE MEJI - 12

O ku gbe   ohun   oro, (e)m(i)-a rin dodo   ohun ǫjingbin;
"He die be:lost voice (of) pain, I-will   walk deep:sound (of) voice very:deep;

ologbo ni   fi   ǫdun   şe   ara   a   da fun ǫmǫ   a-
cat   be (he) take raphia:cloth make style" (be) who cast for child (of) "One:who-

r(i)-ęsę şanşa   tu-(ę)rupę nwǫn ni aya şanşa kan l(i)-o gba? Nwǫn ni
see-foot very:long loosen-dirt" they say wife slender one be-he take? They say

afi-bi   o ba   ru   obi męrindinlogun, abo   adię   męta, awo dudu
unless-if he should offer kola sixteen,   female chicken three, plate black

tun-tun   igba-(a)-de-mu   tun-tun ęgbęta;   ko ru-(ę)bǫ.
new-new, calabash-to-cover-drink new-new, 600   (cowries); not offer-sacrifice.

O si gba aya na, l(i)-ęhin   eyi egbo da   si ile,   eyi si
He and take wife the, at-back (of) this sore cause (him) to house, this and

mu ki   ǫkunrin na ku. Ifa ni ęni-ti   a ba   da Ifa yi fun
take that man   the die. Ifa say person-that we should cast Ifa this for (him)

ti   ko ba   ru,   ara-(a)iye   yio ma   ba (ohu)n-kan
that (he) not should offer (it), people-(of)-earth will (continuative) spoil thing-one

rę ję.
his (1).

---

1. Ba . . . ję means "to spoil."

"Qrunmila, carry me in your bag; carry me in your purse,
"So that we may go together slowly;
"So that wherever we may be going, we may go together."

Ifa says we will marry a woman. Everyone will try to twist us and turn us, and they will conspire against us; but we should not be afraid. We will marry the woman.

---

1 - 12

"He is lost to us through death, is a cry full of pain; I will walk, talking to myself in a very low voice;[1] Cat is the one that dresses in style with raphia cloth"[2] was the one who cast Ifa for "He scatters dirt with very long feet."[3] They asked, "Is he going to take a slender woman as his wife?" They said it would be bad for him unless he sacrificed sixteen kola nuts, three hens, a new black plate,[4] a new calabash for covering drinks, and one penny eight oninis. He did not sacrifice.

He took the woman as his wife. Afterward sores confined him to his house, and he died. Ifa says that if the person for whom this figure was cast does not make a sacrifice, witches[5] will spoil something he has.

---

1. These two phrases are recited in mourning the death of a relative.
2. Qdun is a cloth woven of both cotton and raphia.
3. The "long" feet referred to here are those of the cat.
4. A plate of locally made black ware.
5. Ara-(a)iye is a euphemism for witches.

OGBE - (Q)YĘKU - 1

Ogbe-(ọ)yęku, baba   amulu,   O-gbo-a-tọ,   awo
Ogbe-Qyęku, father (of) combination. To-grow:old-to-live:long, secret (of)

ędan   a   da f(un)-ędan, k(i)-ędan   işe   ku, agba   Iworo a   ku
Rod, (be) who cast for-Rod;   before-Rod make die, elder (of) Iworo will remain

kata-kata.
scattered-scattered.

O-l(i)-owo-(i)la   ti   ik(ọ)-awun ko gbọdọ kọ-(i)gbin   a
"One:who-has-money-(of)-cut that cut-Miser not must cut-Snail" (be) who

da   fun kiniun ọmọ   a-ri-(i)tọ   gba-(i)ju   ti mbę   ni
cast for Lion, child (of) "One:who-see-urine take-dense:forest" that existing at

a-pe-yanję   ọmọ   ęranko.
to-assemble-mulct child (of) animal.

Ifa ni o ri ęni-kan   ti ko ni   igba   ti ko ni awo ti
Ifa say he see person-one that not have calabash that not have plate that

gbogbo enia   ati awọn ara   ile   rę npe   ni o-l(i)-ori   bu(ru)-
all   people and those people (of) house his calling at one:who-have-head be:bad-

buru ti   nwọn si nfi   şe   ę-l(i)-ęya;   Ifa ni oluwarę
be:bad that they and taking make that:which-be-ridicule; Ifa say person:in:question

yio di   enia nla l(i)-ęhin   ọla   ati pe   yio si ma
will become person big at-back (of) tomorrow and that (he) will and (continuative)

ran oro.
send spite.

Ni akoko lai-lai   gbogbo awọn ęranko ni ima   rę   kiniun ję, bi
At time ever-ever all   those animal be (continuative) mulct Lion (1); if

o ba   sun s(i)-ilę, nwọn a   ma   gun   l(i)-ori nwọn ko
he should sleep to-ground, they will (continuative) climb (him) at-head, they not

si bikita   fun;   kiniun wa   mu-(a)ra o tọ   awọn babalawo lọ,
and show:respect for (him); Lion   come take-body he approach those diviner go,

o si bere pe kin-ni   ohun ti on le şe ti on fi le ni iyi ati ọwọ
he and ask that what-be thing that he can do that he take can have glory and honor

l(i)-oju   awọn ęgbę   on? Awọn babalawo ni ki   o ru-(ę)bọ
at-eye (of) those companion (of) him? Those diviner   say should he offer-sacri-

keregbe   omi kan, eru, kumọ męta, ewe   Ifa—ewe   ọwọ—
fice (of) calabash (of) water one, ashes, club three, leaf (of) Ifa—leaf (of) honor—

nwọn ni ki   o gbo ewe   Ifa na si-(i)nu   omi, ki   o da   eru
they say should he crush leaf (of) Ifa the to-belly (of) water, should he pour ashes

na si,   ki   o si gbe   mu, ati-pe bi o ba   dubu-(i)lę
the to (it), should he and take (it) drink; and-that if he should lie:across-ground

_____

1. Rę . . . ję means "to mulct."

2 - 1

Ogbe Qyẹku, father of combinations.[1] "He lives to a ripe old age," the diviner of Rod,[2] was the one who cast Ifa for Rod. Before Rod dies, the elders of Iworo will nearly all be dead.

"The one who circumcises the tortoise must not circumcise the snail" was the one who cast Ifa for Lion, the child of "His urine captures the dense forest,"[3] when the other animals were taking advantage of him.

Ifa says he sees someone who owns neither a plate nor a calabash;[4] everyone, including his own relatives, say he has a "bad head"[5] and are making fun of him. Ifa says this person will become important in the near future and that he will have his revenge.

From the beginning of time all the animals took advantage of Lion. If he lay asleep on the ground, they climbed on top of him; they never showed him proper respect. Lion got ready and went to the diviners; he asked them what he could do to gain honor and glory among his associates. The diviners said that he should sacrifice one calabash of water, ashes, three clubs, and Ifa's leaves (the "leaf of honor").[6] They said he should crush the leaves of Ifa in the water, add the ashes to it, and then drink it. And they told him that when he lay down

---

1. Ogbe Qyẹku is regarded as the "oldest" and most powerful of these figures in which both halves are different. It ranks immediately after the "pairs" or double (meji) figures, and is therefore at the head of all the "mixtures" or combinations (amulu). See Chapter IV.

2. A rod of brass or iron, such as is used by the Ogboni society and the worshipers of Qshun. A piece of metal, of course, can "outlive" even the elders of Iworo, who seem to epitomize long life and old age.

3. The meaning of this name is explained later in the verse. One informant included "when the other animals were taking advantage of him" as part of the name.

4. A common idiom indicating poverty.

5. That is, that he has bad luck, and that he is therefore worthless.

6. Brillantaisia patula. Note that in order to gain honor, a leaf known as "leaf of honor" is added to the concoction to be drunk.

si ibi-k(u)-ibi   ki   o   ma   tǫ   yi   ara   ka.   Ni-(i)gba-
to place-any-place, should he (continuative) urinate turn body around. At-time-

ti   kiniun si ti   şe eyi tan,   bi o   ba   ma   sun, yio si tǫ
that Lion   and have do this finish, if he should (continuative) sleep, will and uri-

    yi   ara rę ka;   bi awǫn ęranko ba   si   fę   lati ma   gun
nate turn body his around; if those animal should and want to (continuative) climb

    l(i)-ori bi ti   at(i)-ęhin wa, bi nwǫn ba   ti   da   itǫ
(him) at-head like that (of) from-back come, if they should have go:across urine

rę kǫja nwǫn a   şubu lu-(i)lę   nwǫn a   si di   oku,   bayi ni
his pass, they will fall strike-ground they will and become corpse; thus be

kiniun di   ęni   ęru l(i)-arin   awǫn ęranko, bi nwǫn ba   si gbǫ
Lion   become person (of) fear at-middle (of) those animal; if they should and hear

ohun rę, ęru a   ba   wǫn, nwǫn a   si ma   gbǫn riri. Lati
voice his, fear will meet them, they will and (continuative) shake 'riri.' From

igba-na ni kiniun ti ma   nke pe afi enia, afi emi,
time-the be Lion have (continuative) crying that "Unless person, unless me,

afi   Q-l(i)-ǫrun.
unless One:who-has-sky."

OGBE - (Q)YĘKU - 2

    Ogbe-(ǫ)yęku-yękętę   a   da   f(un)-Q-l(i)-ǫfin   t(i)-opo yę
    "Ogbe-Qyęku-Stubby" (be) who cast for-One:who-has-palace that-dais avoid

    l(i)-ori rę. Ifa ni   ęni-kan   ni o   wa   l(i)-ori   oye yi   ti
(him) at-head his. Ifa say person-one be who exist at-head (of) title this, that

a-(yi)o pa   n(i)-ipo   da ti a-(yi)o fi ęni-ti   wa ni ikǫkǫ
we-will change (him) at-position (1); that we-will take person-that exist at corner

d(i)-ipo   rę. Ęni   ikǫkǫ na ni gbogbo ara-(a)iye   yio ma
close-position his. Person (of) corner the be all   people-(of)-earth will (con-

        ra ǫwǫ si   ti   nwǫn yio si ma   juba   fun.
tinuative) rub hand to (him) that they will and (continuative) pay:homage for (him).

Orişa kan si ni yi ti   gbogbo ile   ti nsin   ti nwǫn ko si sin
Orisha one and be this that all   house have serving that they not and serve

mǫ; igbo si kun bo   oju-(ę)bǫ   rę; ki a tunşe ki   a
again; forest and fill cover eye-(of)-sacrifice its; should we repair (it) should we

si ta   mǫriwo   si ęnu   ǫna rę. Ęni   ikǫkǫ ti
and suspend young:palm:fronds to mouth (of) road its. Person (of) corner that

t(i)-ǫmǫde   t(i)-agba   ti nfi   oju tinrin rę yio si di
that-(of)-young:child that-(of)-elder have taking eye sneer his will and become

---

1. Pa . . . da means "change."

anywhere, he should first make a circle of urine about the spot. After Lion had made this sacrifice, when he wanted to sleep, he urinated around the place where he was going to lie down. When the other animals wanted to climb on top of him, as in times past, if they stepped over his urine, they fell dead upon the ground. Thus Lion came to be feared by the other animals; when they hear his voice, they are frightened and tremble 'riri.'[7] And since then, when Lion roars, he says, "Aside from man, aside from myself, aside from the Sky God, who else is there?"[8]

---

7. "Riri" describes the way in which a person trembles in fright.

8. This verse explains why the Lion is the king of the animals and why all other animals fear him, and also what Lion says when he roars.

---

2 - 2

"Stout Ogbe Qyẹku"[1] was the one who cast Ifa for a king who had been dethroned. Ifa says there is someone who has a title; he will be removed from office and a person who stays in the corner will be chosen to fill his position. All people will rub their hands[2] to the person of the corner, and pay homage to him. There is also a deity that was once worshiped by all the people of a house; but they do not worship him any more and the forest has overgrown his altar. We should renovate the altar and tie young palm fronds at its entrance. The person of the corner is someone at whom young children and old people alike are sneering; but he will leave his corner and come

---

1. The name of the diviner is derived from the name of the figure.

2. The palms of the hands are rubbed together as in a supplication, when asking to be excused from expressing an opinion during a trial or a discussion. The gesture is made to those of higher rank to show that the matter is too difficult for you to decide, or that you have nothing significant to add to what has already been said. The implication here is that everyone will defer to the client and look to him to make the important decisions, because of the position he will occupy.

ẹni-(i)gbangba.   Adiẹ   kan wa   ni ile   ẹni-ti   o da   Ifa
person-(of)-open:place. Chicken one exist at house (of) person-that he cast Ifa

yi, adiẹ   na ni   ọmọ 1(i)-ẹhin, ki   a   ko   adiẹ   na ti   on
this, chicken the have child at-back; should we gather chicken the that (of) it

ti   ọmọ rẹ ki   a fi   ru-(ẹ)bọ.
that (of) child its should we take (them) offer-sacrifice.

OGBE - (Q)YẸKU - 3

  Ori ti ko ba   ni rin ihoho yio ri a-1(i)-aṣọ   ni-(i)gba-ti
  "Head that not should be walk naked will see one:who-has-cloth at-time-that

ọja   ba   to   a   da f(un)-Q-1(i)-ọfa   a   ta-(a)poti
market should equal" (be) who cast for-One:who-has-Qfa who sell-box (of)

aran ọmọ   a-wukọ   gbinrin bi erin   fọn   ọmọ   a-
velvet, child (of) "One:who-cough 'gbinrin' like elephant blows," child (of) "One:

fi-(i)koko   wọn-(i)lẹkẹ   f(un)-ale   rẹ ọmọ   a-
who-take-top:of:calabash measure-bead for-concubine his," child (of) "One:who-

j(ẹ)-aiye gbẹdẹ-gbẹdẹ bi ẹni   nla-(o)yin.   Ifa ni ẹni   ikọkọ kan
eat-world wet-wet   like person licking-honey." Ifa say person (of) corner one

yio di   ẹni-(i)gbangba   yio si de   ipo   nla kan ti yio si
will become person-(of)-open:place, will and arrive position big one that will and

pẹ   pupọ ni ipo   na.
be:long much at position the.

  Q—1(i)-ọfa   a ta apoti   aran jẹ arugbo   ko si ni   igba
  "One:who-has-Qfa who sell box (of) velvet" eat old:person not and have cala-

        tabi awo, ṣugbọn o ni   aṣọ nla kan ni-(i)nu   odidi   ti on papa
bash or plate, but   he have cloth big one at-belly (of) hiding:place that he him-

        ko-jẹ   lo, ṣugbọn awọn enia ni ima   tọrọ   rẹ lọ si ode;
self not-consent use, but   those people be (continuative) request his go to out-

        Q-1(i)-ọfa   mu-(a)ra o tọ   awọn babalawo lọ, o bere pe
side; One:who-has-Qfa take-body he approach those diviner go, he ask that

bawo ni on yio ti   ṣe ni lari?   Nwọn ni ki   o ru-(ẹ)bọ
how be he will have do have importance? They say should he offer-sacrifice (of)

obukọ dudu kan, ẹgbarun   ati aṣọ nla kan ti o wa   ni odidi
he:goat black one, 10,000   (cowries) and cloth big one that it exist at hiding:place

rẹ. O gbọ o si ru-(ẹ)bọ.   Ko 1(i)-ọjọ ko 1(i)-oṣu ọba Qfa ku,
his. He hear he and offer-sacrifice. Not at-day not at-month, king (of) Qfa die,

awọn ara   Qfa mu Q-1(i)-Qfa   a ta apoti   aran nwọn fi
those people (of) Qfa take "One:who-have-Qfa who sell box (of) velvet" they take

out into the open. There is a hen at the house of the person for whom this figure was cast. This hen has chicks; we should take both the hen and its young to make the sacrifice.

---

2 - 3

"The head that should not go naked will find a cloth seller when the market opens"[1] was the one who cast Ifa for "The King of Qfa who sells a box full of velvet,"[2] child of "One who coughs 'gbinrin'[3] like the trumpeting of an elephant," child of "One who uses the top of a calabash to measure out beads for his mistresses,"[4] child of "One who enjoys the world wet and soggy, like someone licking honey."[5] Ifa says that a person who stays in the corner will come out into the open; he will occupy an important position, and he will remain in office a long time.

"The King of Qfa who sells a box full of velvet" was an old man who owned neither a plate nor a calabash; but he had a large cloth hidden away. He never used this cloth himself, but others borrowed it from him to dress up to go out in. The King of Qfa got ready, and he went to the diviners; he asked them what he must do in order to gain importance. They said he should sacrifice one black he-goat, two shillings six pence, and one large cloth which he had hidden away. He heard and he sacrificed. Soon afterward the King of Qfa[6] died, and the people of Qfa took "The King of Qfa who sells a box full of velvet" and

---

1. The implication of this name, like that of a proverb, is much broader than its literal meaning. In this case the meaning is that class or nobility will be recognized; and that each person will get his due. The allusion is to the fact that the legendary character, though at first poor and of no importance, was made King of Qfa.

2. The legendary character is referred to as the King of Qfa even before he assumed that title. The name itself is an allusion to the large cloth mentioned later in the verse, which he had hidden away. The velvet refers to the large cloth and the box (apoti) to the hiding place (odidi).

3. This word is said to be the sound of a cough, or the sound made by iron striking a stone anvil. The reference to elephant, which is associated with royalty, indicates that this is the name of an important person.

4. The lid of a calabash is used in measuring small things of little value. It is not a standardized measure. And while it is appropriate for measuring something like kernels of corn, it would never be used for anything as valuable as beads except by a person who did not have to worry about money. Thus the name implies that the individual is very rich and generous, since he doesn't stop to count out the beads one by one.

5. These are all names of individuals from whom the King of Qfa is descended.

6. That is, the one who was king at the time of the divination; not the legendary client, but his predecessor.

ję ǫba ni ireti   pe ko ni pę   ki   o to   ku, şugbǫn ni-
(him) eat king at expectation that not be be:long before he equal die; but   at-

(i)gba-ti o de   ori   oye tan, kaka ti   iba fi ku işe
time-that he arrive head (of) title finish, instead that (he) should take die, make

ni ara rę tubǫ   nle   si; aiye   awǫn ara   Qfa si wa
be body his continue being:strong to; world (of) those people (of) Qfa and exist

dun   o si dę   wǫn l(i)-ǫrun nwǫn ko si tun fę   pe ki   o
be:sweet it and be:soft (for) them at-neck, they not and then want that should he

ku mǫ.
die again.

Ifa ni ęni   ikǫkǫ kan yio di   ęni   igbangba yio si
Ifa say person (of) corner one will become person (of) open:place, will and

de   ipo   nla kan ti yio si pę   pupǫ ni-(i)nu   ipo   na ki
arrive position big one, that will and be:long much at-belly (of) position the before

o   to   ku.
he equal die.

OGBE - (I)WORI[1] - 1

Ęhin   l(i)-a k(un)-erin;   ęhin   l(i)-a k(un)-
"Back (of its death) be-we divide-elephant; back (of its death) be-we divide-

ęfǫn; ęhin   l(i)-a k(un)-araba iyan   ǫmǫ
buffalo; back (of its preparation) be-we divide-loaf (of) pounded:yam," child (of)

Ologogololo l(i)-o   d(a)-Ifa k(o)-Odogbo ni-(ǫ)jǫ ti   o wa   ni-(i)nu
Stark:naked be-who cast-Ifa for-Odogbo at-day that he exist at-belly (of)

oyikiti   ipǫn-(o)ju.   Ifa ni ęni-kan   wa   n(i)-isisiyi ni-(i)nu
surrounded redness-(of)-eye. Ifa say person-one exist at-right:now at-belly (of)

ipǫn-(o)ju   nla, bi o ba   ni iya   ti o wa   ni aiye ki   o
redness-(of)-eye big; if he should have mother that she exist at earth should he

bǫ   ori   iya   na, bi o ba   si ku ki   o bǫ   ǫ.
sacrifice:to head (of) mother the; if she should and die, should he sacrifice:to her.

Nwǫn ni ni ǫdun yi ni ǫrǫ   rę pe.   Nwǫn ni ki   o ru-
They say at year this be riches his be:complete. They say should he offer-

(ę)bǫ;   o ru-(ę)bǫ   ęiyę-(i)le   męrin, Iwǫwǫ —akun-k(u)-akun—
sacrifice; he offer-sacrifice bird-(of)-house four,   bead —bead-any-bead —

męrin, ęgbarin o le   ǫgǫrin.   O ru-(ę)bǫ,   nwǫn ni bi o ba
four,   8000   it upon 80 (cowries). He offer-sacrifice, they say if he should

---

1. Also known as Ogbe-w(o)-ęhin (Ogbe-look:at-back). Cf. n. 1, verse 3-4.

made him king, expecting that it would not be long until he would die. But after he took office, instead of dying, he continued in good health; and everything went well for the people of Qfa and everything was easy for them. Then they did not want him to die any more.

Ifa says that a person in the corner will come out into the open and will attain an important position, and he will stay in that position a long time before he dies.

---

3 - 1

"After it is dead, we cut up an elephant; after it is dead, we cut up a buffalo; after it is prepared, we cut up a loaf of pounded yams," child of Stark Naked,[1] was the one who cast Ifa for Odogbo when he was living in the midst of trouble.[2] Ifa says that right now someone is in great trouble. If his mother is still alive on earth, he should sacrifice to her head; if she is dead, he should sacrifice to her at her grave.

They said that Odogbo's riches would be complete during that year. They said he should make a sacrifice; he sacrificed four pigeons, four beads (any kind of beads), two shillings, and 80 cowries. He made the sacrifice. They said when he had

---

1. This refers to the yam loaf, which is completely naked in the sense that its surface is plain, undecorated, and uncovered.

2. As explained later, Odogbo's trouble was poverty.

ru-(ẹ)bọ   tan   ki   o   lọ bọ   iya   rẹ, nwọn ni ile   ni
offer-sacrifice finish, should he go sacrifice:to mother his; they say house be

ire   rẹ wa   ko gbọdọ lọ si ibi-kan.
goodness his exist; not must go to place-one.

    Ni-(i)gba-ti Odogbo ru-(ẹ)bọ   tan   ti   o si bọ   iya
    At-time-that Odogbo offer-sacrifice finish that he and sacrifice:to mother

rẹ, o joko   si ile titi   di   ọjọ kẹrin, ṣugbọn ko ri ohun-k(u)-
his, he sit:down to house until (it) become day fourth, but   not see thing-any-

ohun bi ire;   ni-(i)gba-ti o di   ijọ karun Odogbo mu-(a)ra o lọ si
thing like goodness; at-time-that it become day fifth   Odogbo take-body he go to

oko   igi, o ni o ko ni jẹ-ki   ebi   ki   o pa on ku; ni-
farm (of) tree, he say he not be consent-that hunger should it kill him die; at-

(i)gba-ti o de   oko   o ṣẹ-(i)gi   dara-dara, o si ru   ni a-ru-
time-that he arrive farm, he break-wood good-good, he and carry (it) at to-carry-

t(o)-ẹru   bi o ti   gb(e)-ẹru ti o mbọ,   iya   rẹ di   ẹiyẹ o
equal-load, as he have carry-load that he coming, mother his become bird she

si bẹrẹ si wi-pe:
and begin to speak-that:

        Odogbo da-(i)gi   nu
        "Odogbo throw-wood be:lost,

        Ire   ti   de-(i)le   l(i)-ẹhin rẹ.
        "Goodness have arrive-home at-back yours."

    Ni-(i)gba-ti Odogbo gbọ, o ni o yio ru   eyi de-(i)le   bi o ti
    At-time-that Odogbo hear, he say he will carry this arrive-house, as he have

de-(i)le   ti o fi idi   igi sọ-(i)lẹ   bẹ-ni o jin   si-
arrive-house that he take waist (of) wood strike-ground, so-be it fall:down to-

(i)lẹ   akun, bayi ni owo   de,   ti ọla   de ti o si di
ground (of) bead, thus be cowries arrive, that wealth arrive that he and become

ọ-l(i)-ọrọ.   Odogbo wa   bẹrẹ, o ni bẹ-ni awọn babalawo wi,
one:who-has-riches. Odogbo come begin; he say so-be those diviner   speak,

nwọn ni:
they say:

      Ẹhin   l(i)-a k(un)-erin,
    "'Back (of its death) be-we divide-elephant;

      Ẹhin   l(i)-a k(un)-ẹfọn,
    "Back (of its death) be-we divide-buffalo;

      Ẹhin   l(i)-a k(un)-araba
    "Back (of its preparation) be-we divide-loaf (of)

        iyan   ọmọ   Ologogololo
        pounded:yam,' child (of) Stark:naked;

finished this sacrifice, he should sacrifice also to his mother.[3] They said that
his blessing was to be found at home and that he must not go anywhere.

When Odogbo had made the sacrifice and had sacrificed also to his mother,
he stayed at home for three days;[4] but he did not see anything like a blessing.
On the fourth day he got ready and went to the farm to fetch wood, saying that he
was not going to starve to death. When he reached the farm, he chopped a good
pile of firewood and started back with as much as he could carry. As he was returning, carrying his load, his mother appeared as a bird, and she began to sing:

> "Odogbo, throw away your wood;
> "The blessing came to your house while you were gone."

When Odogbo heard this, he said that he would carry the wood home anyway.
When he reached home and dumped the load of wood to the ground, its end broke
through the ground into a pit of beads.[5] In this way money and wealth came to
Odogbo, and he became a rich man.[6] Odogbo began to sing; he said it was just
as the diviners had predicted when they said:

> "'After it is dead we cut up an elephant;
> "After it is dead we cut up a buffalo;
> "After it is prepared we cut up a loaf of pounded yams,'
>   child of Stark Naked;

---

3. The first sacrifice goes to Eshu for the Sky God.

4. Note that there is a difference between English and Yoruba in counting
days. The Yoruba count both the first and the last days, so that what we would
call three days they call four.

5. Beads, especially valuable ones of the kind known as ṣẹgi, are often
found in pits in the ground in this way. See n. 5, verse 1-10, and n. 2, verse
249-2.

6. In this case the outcome was successful even though Odogbo did not observe the diviner's instruction that he must not leave his house or his mother's
command to throw away his wood. He made the sacrifice, however.

Ni ǫjǫ ti   on, Odogbo wa   ni-(i)nu
"At day that he, Odogbo, exist at-belly (of)

    oyikiti   ipǫn-(o)ju.
    surrounded redness-(of)-eye.

Odogbo da-(i)gi   nu,
"Odogbo throw-wood be:lost,

    Ire   ti   de-(i)le   l(i)-ęhin rę.
    "Goodness have arrive-house at-back his."

OGBE - (I)WORI - 2

Ęhin   l(i)-a k(un)-erin,   ęhin   l(i)-a k(un)-
"Back (of its death) be-we divide-elephant; back (of its death) be-we divide-

ęfǫn, ęhin   l(i)-a k(un)-araba   iyan,   ǫmǫ
buffalo; back (of its preparation) be-we divide-loaf (of) pounded:yam," child (of)

Ologogololo l(i)-a da-Ifa   k(o)-Odogbo ni-(ǫ)jǫ ti   o nlǫ   mu-(i)lę-
Stark:naked be-who cast-Ifa for-Odogbo at-day   that he going take-ground-(of)-

(i)bu-(i)do   l(i)-oko. Nwǫn ni ibi kan pa-(i)bu-(i)do   de
place-(of)-settling at-farm. They say evil one pitch-place-(of)-settling wait:for

    si ibę   nwǫn ni ki   o ma-şe lǫ. Nwǫn ni ki   o ru-(ę)bǫ
(him) to there; they say should he not-do go. They say should he offer-sacrifice

    obukǫ kan, ati ęgbafa.   O ni on nlǫ, o ni o yio wa   ru
(of) he:goat one, and 12,000 (cowries). He say he going, he say he will come offer

bi on ba   de.   N(i)-igba-ti o de   oko o ba   awǫn Irun-(i)mǫlę,
if he should arrive. At-time-that he arrive farm, he meet those 400-Deity,

nwǫn ki i   mǫ-(i)lę   nwǫn bę   l(i)-ori, nwǫn si gbe   ori rę
they push him against-ground, they cut (him) at-head, they and carry head his

ha   iwawa ǫpę;   n(i)-igba-ti awǫn ara   ile   reti rę titi
stick:in young palm:tree; at-time-that those people (of) house expect his until

ti   nwǫn ko ri,   nwǫn wa   lǫ si oko.
that they not see (him), they seek (him) go to farm.

    N(i)-igba-ti nwǫn de   oko, nwǫn ba   ori rę n(i)-ibi-ti   ęiyę gbe
At-time-that they arrive farm, they meet head his at-place-that bird take

nsę   ę. N(i)-igba-ti nwǫn ri i, nwǫn pada   nwǫn nbǫ   wa   si ile;
chirping (at) it. At-time-that they see it, they return they coming come to house;

nwǫn wa   bi   ara   wǫn lere pe bawo ni awǫn yio ti   şe   ro   bi
they come asking people their (1)   that how be they will have make report if

---

1. Bi . . . lere means "to ask."

"On the day that I, Odogbo, was living in the midst of trouble.
"Odogbo, throw away your wood;
"The blessing came to your house while you were gone."

_____

3 - 2

"After it is dead, we cut up an elephant; after it is dead we cut up a buffalo; after it is prepared, we cut up a loaf of pounded yams," child of Stark Naked, was the one who cast Ifa for Odogbo[1] on the day that he was going to take land and settle in the farm. They said evil was waiting there for him; they said he must not go. They said he should sacrifice one goat and three shillings. He said he would go anyway, and that he would make the sacrifice when he came back. When he reached the farm, he met the Four Hundred Deities. They shoved him to the ground and cut off his head. They took his head and stuck it in a young palm tree. The people of his house waited for him, but he did not return; so they went to the farm to look for him.

When they got to the farm, they found his head where birds were chirping at it. When they saw it, they started back home, asking each other what they would report when

_____

1. The names of the diviner and of the legendary character are the same here as in verse 3-1, but the circumstances are different.

awǫn ba   de   ile;   n(i)-igba-ti nwǫn ko mǫ   eyi-ti   nwǫn yio ṣe ni
they should arrive home; at-time-that they not know this-that they will do be

wǫn ba   bẹrẹ si k(ǫ)-orin wi-pe:
they should begin to sing-song say-that:

>   Ẹiyẹ nsẹ-(o)ku   oge
>   "Bird chirping-(at)-corpse (of) neat:person"

>   Ẹiyẹ nsẹ   o   ǫṣẹrẹṣẹrẹ
>   "Bird chirping, oh 'ǫshẹrẹshẹrẹ.'"

Ifa ni   ibi kan p(a)-agǫ de   ẹni-kan   ni oko tabi ẹni-kan   nfẹ
Ifa say evil one pitch-tent wait:for person-one at farm or   person-one want-

lǫ si ibi-kan   iba-ṣe   idalẹ,   ibi duro de   ni ibi-ti   o
ing go to place-one should-make distance, evil stand wait:for at place-that he

nlǫ   na ki   o ru-(ẹ)bǫ   ki   o to   lǫ.
going the, should he offer-sacrifice before he equal go.

OGBE - (I)WORI - 3

A-joko   i-f(i)-ẹhin-ti   agba bi ẹni-ti-o   naro   n(i)-
"To-sit:down (not) to-take-back-lean elder like person-that-who stand:up be-

iri   l(i)-o   d(a)-Ifa fun (Q)la-(y)i-l(u)-okun   ǫmǫ   A-
appearance" be-who cast-Ifa for Honor-turns-strikes-rope child (of) One:who-

ṣ(e)-Oro ṣ(e)-Qbalufǫn ti o ni ipa   on ko ni ka   aiye. Nwǫn
does-Oro does-Qbalufǫn that she say strength (of) her not be match earth. They

ni ipa   rẹ yio k(a)-aiye.   Nwǫn ni ki   o ru-(ẹ)bǫ.   O
say strength hers will match-earth. They say should she offer-sacrifice. She

ru   akika   meji, oruka   ǫwǫ rẹ ati ẹgbẹtalelǫgbǫn. (Q)la-(y)i-l(u)-
offer pangolin two, ring   (of) hand hers and 6600 (cowries). Honor-turns-strikes-

okun ni orukǫ ti a ipe ajẹ ati igba-na ni ajẹ ti   ni   agbara l(i)-
rope be name that we call witch; from time-the be witch have have power at-

ori   ẹda.
head (of) creature.

Ifa ni   ajẹ   mu ẹni-kan   n(i)-isisiyi afi-bi o ba   le   fi
Ifa say witch take person-one at-right:now unless-if he should be:able take

ẹbẹ   ti,   boya   wǫn ko ni mu a   lǫ.
request push (them), perhaps they not be take him go.

---

they reached home. Not knowing what to do, they began to sing:

> "The birds are chirping at the corpse of a 'dandy,'
> "The birds are chirping, oh, 'ọshẹrẹshẹrẹ.'"[2]

Ifa says an evil has pitched its tent in the farm and is waiting for someone. Or else someone wants to go somewhere, perhaps at a distance; evil awaits him where he is going. He should sacrifice before he goes.

---

2. The sound of birds chirping.

---

3 - 3

"An elder who sits without leaning back gives the appearance of a person standing" was the one who cast Ifa for "Wherever honor turns, it finds wealth,"[1] the child of "One who worships Oro and Ọbalufọn."[2] She said that her strength was no match for this world. They said her strength would be a match for this world. They said she should sacrifice. She sacrificed two pangolins,[3] the ring from her finger, and one shilling seven pence eight oninis. "Wherever honor turns, it finds wealth" is what we call witches; ever since she made the sacrifice, witches have had power over human beings.[4]

Ifa says witches will seize someone right now unless he can beg them to change their mind by sacrificing; then perhaps they will not take him away.

---

1. Wealth here is referred to as the cord or rope (okun) upon which cowries are strung.
2. Oro and Ọbalufọn are deities.
3. Scaly anteaters (<u>Uromanis</u> <u>longicaudata</u> <u>Briss</u>). See Maupoil (1943: 280).
4. This verse thus explains why witches can harm humans.

OGBE - (I)WORI - 4

Ogbe-w(o)-ẹhin   wo   b(i)-aja rẹ   yio ba   pa-(i)kun   l(i)-o
"Ogbe-look:at-back look:at if-dog   yours will meet kill-squirrel" be-who

d(a)-Ifa k(o)-Qrunmila ti   o nsọ-(ẹ)kun   a-l(i)-ai-l(i)-obinrin;
cast-Ifa for-Qrunmila that he shedding-tears (of) one:who-be-not-have-woman;

nwọn ni ki   o ru-(ẹ)bọ   pe ni ọdun yi ni   yio ri ire
they say should he offer-sacrifice that at year this be (he) will see goodness (of)

aya. O si ru   agbọn   ẹpa   kan, ayebọ adiẹ   meji ati ẹgbaji o le
wife. He and offer basket (of) peanut one, hen   chicken two, and 4000   it upon

oko.
20 (cowries).

N(i)-igba-ti o ru-(ẹ)bọ   tan, nwọn bu   fun   n(i)-inu
At-time-that he offer-sacrifice finish, they share (it) for (him) at-belly (of)

ẹpa   na pe ki   o lọ ma   gbin; n(i)-igba-ti ẹpa   yi gbo
peanut the that should he go (continuative) plant; at-time-that peanut this grow:old

ti o si to   wa, Qrunmila bẹrẹ si ri ọwọ n(i)-inu rẹ o si ro   pe
that it and equal dig, Qrunmila begin to see hand at-belly its he and think that

ikun   ni o nwa   jẹ, o si bẹrẹ si şọ   oko   ẹpa   rẹ.
squirrel be who digging eat, he and begin to watch farm (of) peanut his.

Ni ọjọ kan bi o ti   nşọ   ẹpa   rẹ o ri awọn wundia meji, bi nwọn
At day one as he have watching peanut his, he see those maiden two; as they

ti wọ inu   oko   ẹpa   Qrunmila, nwọn bẹrẹ si wu, bẹ-ni
have enter belly (of) farm (of) peanut (of) Qrunmila, they begin to dig; so-be

Qrunmila ja-(o)de   si wọn o si mu awọn ni ole, awọn wundia yi si
Qrunmila reach-outside to them he and take them at thief; those maiden this and

bẹrẹ si bẹ   ẹ pe ki   o jọwọ   ki   o ma-şe mu awọn ni ole.
begin to request him that should he grant:favor should he not-do take them at thief.

Qrunmila da-(o)hun   o ni nitori-ti   ki   on ba   ni   aya ni nwọn
Qrunmila break-voice he say because-that should he should have wife be they

şe sọ   fun on pe ki   on ki   o gbẹ ẹpa   yi, şugbọn bi ẹ   ti
do speak for him that should he should he plant peanut this, but   if you have

wa   nji   wu yi, bawo ni on yio ti   şe le   fi fẹ   obinrin mọ.
come stealing dig this how be he will have do be:able take love woman again?

Nwọn ni ki   o jọwọ   awọn yio kuku fẹ ẹ;   bayi ni Qrunmila fẹ
They say should he grant:favor they will rather love him; thus be Qrunmila love

awọn mej(i)-(m)eji.
those two-two.

Awọn wundia meji kan wa,   aya   Ifa ni wọn, ki   a mu wọn fun
Those maiden two one exist; wife (of) Ifa be they; should we take them give

Ifa ki nwọn ma ba   ko   abuku   ba awọn ara   ile   wọn.
Ifa that they not should gather disgrace meet those people (of) house theirs.

3 - 4

"Ogbe, look back[1] and see if your dog will kill a squirrel"[2] was the one who cast Ifa for Qrunmila when he was weeping because he had no wife. They said that he should sacrifice that he might find a wife during that year. He sacrificed a basket of peanuts, two hens, and one shilling, plus twenty cowries.[3]

When he had finished sacrificing, the diviners put aside some of the peanuts for him to plant. When these peanuts were ripe enough to harvest, Qrunmila noticed that someone was stealing them. He thought that a squirrel was digging and eating them, and he began to keep watch over his peanut field.

One day as he was watching his peanuts, he saw two maidens. As they entered his peanut field and began to dig, Qrunmila came out from where he had been hiding and caught them in the act of stealing his peanuts. The maidens began to beg him to spare them and not to take them as thieves.

Qrunmila replied that it was in order for him to get a wife that the diviners had told him to plant these peanuts;[4] but if they came and stole them, how would he ever be able to get married? They said that he should spare them; they would rather marry him than be taken as thieves. So Qrunmila married them both.

There are two maidens together; they are wives of Ifa;[5] we should give them to Ifa so that they may not bring disgrace upon their family.

---

1. Ogbe-w(o)-ẹhin, an alternative name of the figure Ogbe-(I)wori, is incorporated into the diviner's name.

2. A squirrel is later suspected of digging up Qrunmila's peanuts.

3. Though in itself this is not a very convincing example, the sacrifice of twenty cowries (oko) in a verse which involves a farm (oko) of peanuts follows the pattern of word magic. See Chapter XII.

4. It is implied that Qrunmila was to use the profit from the peanuts for bridewealth. Although this did not happen, Qrunmila nevertheless got two wives, without having to give bridewealth, through planting the peanuts.

5. A woman who is told by a diviner that she is destined to be a "wife of Ifa" must be given in marriage to a diviner without bridewealth being given for her (see Chapter IX).

Qkọnrin kan si wa   ti   o nfẹ   fẹ   aya kan yio ri aya na fẹ bi ọfẹ
Man   one and exist that he wanting love wife one, will see wife the love as free,

ni obinrin na yio tẹ   l(i)-ọwọ bi o ba   le   ru-(ẹ)bọ.
be woman the will reach (him) at-hand if he should be:able offer-sacrifice.

Ki   o-l(i)-obinrin   kan şọ-(a)ra ki a   ma ba   mu   ni ole
Should one:who-be-woman one watch-body that they not should take (her) at thief

ni ọdun yi.
at year this.

OGBE - (E)DI - 1 A

   Ogbe di   pẹ(rẹ)-pẹrẹ   l(i)-o d(a)-Ifa k(o)-ori ti   o kun-(i)lẹ
   "Ogbe close generous-generous" be-who cast-Ifa for-Head that he kneel-ground

ti o yan-(i)wa   ti e-l(i)-enini   ko jẹ-ki   o şe e. Ifa ni
that he choose-destiny that one:who-has-enmity not consent-that he do it. Ifa say

on ri alaromọ kan ti ko fẹ ki a şe (ohu)n-kan   ẹni.   Ifa ni on
he see evil:wisher one that not want that we do thing-one (of) person. Ifa say he

yio ba-(ẹ)ni   şe-(o)gun   alaromọ   na. O ni ki   a ru-(ẹ)bọ
will join-person make-war (of) evil:wisher the. He say should we offer-sacrifice

    akikọ-(a)diẹ mẹta ati ẹgbata o le   oko.
(of) cock-chicken three and 6000   it upon twenty:cowries.

OGBE - (E)DI - 1 B

   Ogbe di   pẹ(rẹ)-pẹrẹ   l(i)-o d(a)-Ifa k(o)-ori ti   o kun-(i)lẹ
   "Ogbe close generous-generous" be-who cast-Ifa for-Head that he kneel-ground

ti o yan iwa   ti e-l(i)-enini   ko jẹ-ki   o şe.   Ifa
that he choose destiny that one:who-has-enmity not consent-that he do (it). Ifa

ni alaromọ kan ni yi ti ko fẹ ki a şe (ohu)n-kan   ẹni.   Ifa
say evil:wisher one be this that not want that we do thing-one (of) person. Ifa

ni on yio ba-(ẹ)ni   şe-(o)gun   alaromọ   na. N(i)-igba-ti ori to
say he will join-person make-war (of) evil:wisher the. At-time-that Head equal

ru-(ẹ)bọ   ni ohun gbogbo ti o nşe to   gun   ti o si
offer-sacrifice be thing all   that he doing be:in:order be:orderly that they and

ni ọna. Akukọ adiẹ   mẹta ati ẹgbata o le   oko   owo   ẹyọ.
have road. Cock   chicken three and 6000   it upon twenty cowries (of) ẹyọ.

And there is a man who wants to take a wife; he will marry her without giving bridewealth if he is able to sacrifice. And a woman should be careful lest she be taken as a thief this year.

---

4 - 1 A

"Ogbe closes very generously"[1] was the one who cast Ifa for Head, who had knelt and chosen his destiny,[2] and enemies prevented him from achieving it. Ifa says he sees an evil-wisher who does not want us to succeed in what we are doing. Ifa says he will aid us in conquering the evil-wisher. He says that we should sacrifice three cocks and one shilling six pence, plus twenty cowries.

---

1. This name implies that whatever the client wishes will be granted. Note the pun on the name of the figure, Ogbe-(E)di.
2. Each soul, before leaving heaven to be born, is believed to kneel before the Sky God to choose its destiny on earth (see Chapter XI).

---

4 - 1 B

"Ogbe closes very generously" was the one who cast Ifa for Head, who had knelt and chosen his destiny, and enemies prevented him from achieving it. Ifa says there is an evil-wisher who does not want us to succeed in what we are doing. Ifa says he will aid us in conquering the evil-wisher. After Head had made the sacrifice, everything that he was doing straightened out, and the way was clear to success.[1] Three cocks and one shilling six pence, plus twenty cowries,[2] is the sacrifice.

---

1. The Yoruba idiom is "to have a road." Aside from the addition of this sentence and minor differences in wording, this is the same as verse 4-1 A.
2. Owo ęyǫ are the large cowries used as money.

OGBE - (E)DI - 2

Oni   wiri-wiri   ija   Ogbe- (E)di; ọla   wiri-wiri   ija
"Today hazily-hazily fight (of) Ogbe-Edi;   tomorrow hazily-hazily fight (of)

Ogbe-(E)di, akọ ẹiyẹ ni   f(i)-apa ş(e)-ọgan, Ogbo-l(i)-ogbo ọpẹ   ni
Ogbe-Edi; male bird be (it) take-wing make-????, Old-be-old   palm:tree be

w(u)-omu   l(i)-ẹhin l(i)-o d(a)-Ifa fun Lukoun ti   o ngb(e)-ogun lọ si
(it) sprout-omu at-back" be-who cast-Ifa for Lukoun that he carrying-war go to

Il(u)-ẹjẹ.   Nwọn ni odidi enia   ni nwọn yio mu ti   ibẹ bọ.
Town-(of)-blood. They say entire person be they will take from there come.

Nwọn ni ki   o ru-(ẹ)bọ   ayebọ adiẹ   meji, ẹgbaji o le   oko
They say should he offer-sacrifice (of) hen   chicken two, 4000 it upon twenty

owo   ẹyọ.
cowries ẹyọ.

Lukoun ni orukọ ti   oko jẹ.   Il(u)-ẹjẹ   ni orukọ   obo.   Ẹni-
Lukoun be name that penis eat. Town-(of)-blood be name (of) vagina. Person-

kan ni o nşe   (ohu)n-kan   oşu rẹ l(i)-ọwọ yi ki   o ru-(ẹ)bọ
one be she making thing-one   (of) month her at-hand this should she offer-sacri-

ki o ba   le   di   ọmọ. Ọkọnrin kan si nfẹ   ba ẹni-ti
fice that it should be:able become child. Man   one and wanting join person-that

o   nri (ohu)n-kan   oşu rẹ ni ọrọ pọ   ki nwọn ru-
who seeing thing-one (of) month her have word be:together should they offer-

(ẹ)bọ   ki odidi enia   le   ti   ibẹ ja-(o)de.
sacrifice that entire person be:able from there reach-outside.

OGBE - (E)DI - 3

Irọ-(I)fa   a b(i)-ẹnu   ginginni l(i)-o d(a)-Ifa fun agan
"Tapper-(of)-Ifa it bear-mouth pointed" be-who cast-Ifa for barren:woman

ai-bi   ti o tori t(i)-ọmọ   d(a)-Ifa. Nwọn ni yio bi
not-bear (child) that she because that-(of)-child cast-Ifa. They say will bear

ọmọ. Eku meji, ẹja meji, agbebọ adiẹ   meji, ati ẹgbaji o le   oko.
child. Rat two, fish two, hen   chicken two, and 4000 it upon twenty:

Ifa ni   obinrin kan nwa   ọmọ. Yio si bi   ọmọ-(o)binrin kan a
cowries. Ifa say woman one seeking child. Will and bear child-woman   one we

ko si gbọdọ pa   orukọ rẹ da. Dada ni ọmọ na yio ma   jẹ
not and must change name her (1). Dada be child the will (continuative) eat.

Ki   e-l(i)-eyi   ti a d(a)-Ifa yi fun   ki o ru-(ẹ)bọ
Should one:who-be-this that we cast-Ifa this for (her) should she offer-sacrifice

---

1. Pa . . . da means "to change."

4 - 2

"Today Ogbe Edi's fight, very hazily,[1] tomorrow Ogbe Edi's fight, very hazi-ly; the male bird is the one that does . . .[2] with its wings; an old palm tree is the one that has the omu plant[3] in back" was the one who cast Ifa for Lukoun when he was making war on the Town of Blood. They said one whole person would be brought from there.[4] They said he should sacrifice two hens and one shilling, plus twenty cowries.[5]

Lukoun is the name that penis is called. Town of Blood is the name of vagina. Someone is menstruating at this very moment; she should sacrifice that the dis-charge may become a child.[6] And a man wants to have an affair with a woman who is menstruating; they should sacrifice so that a complete person may emerge from it.

---

1. Described as being like fog or smoke; or as things appear when the eyes are opened and shut very rapidly. Ogbe Edi is the name of the figure.
2. Informants could not translate the word ogan in this context.
3. An unidentified plant that is said to sprout out of the base of old palm trees.
4. The reference here is to the birth of a child.
5. Cf. n. 2, verse 4-1 B. Here twenty cowries (oko) are included in a verse involving penis (oko).
6. The Yoruba believe that the menstrual fluid develops into the embryo and later the child. Cf. verses 14-1, 86-3.

---

4 - 3

"Ifa's bell has a pointed mouth"[1] was the one who cast Ifa for the barren woman who divined because she had no children. They said she would give birth to a child. Two rats, two fish, two hens, and one shilling, plus twenty cowries, was the sacrifice. Ifa says a woman is seeking a child; she will give birth to a girl whose name must not be changed. Dada[2] is what the child will be called. The one for whom this figure was cast should complete the sacrifice

---

1. Cf. n. 1, verse 1-7.
2. The name "Dada" is given to children born with prominent tufts of hair. Such children are especially sacred to the God of Thunder. Note that the mother is told to sacrifice to the God of Thunder in addition to her sacrifice to the Sky God.

tan   ki   o   si   tun   lọ bọ   Şọngo pẹlu.   Ifa ni   on
finish should she and then go sacrifice:to Shango together:with (him). Ifa say he

ri   ire   ọmọ-(o)binrin kan babalawo ni   yio si şe   ọkọ   rẹ.
see goodness (of) child-woman   one, diviner   be (who) will and make husband her.

OGBE - (E)DI - 4

Jẹ   (e)mi-lọ, sẹ   (e)m(i)-bọ l(i)-o   d(a)-Ifa f(un)-ariwọwọ ti   o ngb(e)-
"Quiet I-go,   smooth I-come" be-who cast-Ifa for-Hook   that he taking-

ogun lọ si i-n(i)-iti,   nwọn ni   ko ni şan-(ọ)wọ   bọ.   Ẹiyẹ-
war go to that:which-have-bunch; they say not be be:empty-hand come. Bird-(of)-

(i)le meji, akikọ meji, ati ẹgbaji.   O ru-(ẹ)bọ.   Lati   igba-na
house two,   cock two, and 4000 (cowries). He offer-sacrifice. From time-the

ni ariwọwọ ki iti şan-(ọ)wọ   bi o ba   na   si oke fa ohun-k(u)-ohun.
be Hook   not have be:empty-hand if he should stretch to hill pull thing-any-thing.

Ifa ni   a nna-(ọ)wọ   si ohun kan. Ifa ni ki   a ru-(ẹ)bọ   ki
Ifa say we stretching-hand to thing one. Ifa say should we offer-sacrifice that

a ma ba   p(a)-ofo   n(i)-inu   (ohu)n-kan ti a nna-(ọ)wọ   si
we not should crack-emptiness at-belly (of) thing-one that we stretching-hand to

na iba   şe   işẹ   tabi (ohu)n-kan miran.
the, should make work or   thing-one another.

OGBE - (Q)BARA[1] - 1

Didun   ni-(i)şẹ   ẹiyẹ gbigbọn ni t(i)-ọkunrun,   ọkunrun l(i)-o   mọ
"Sounding be-work (of) bird, shaking be that-(of)-invalid; invalid be-who know-

(i)şẹ   ajẹ le   şe l(i)-oru, (ẹ)-ku   abọ   ma   re-
work (of) witch be:able do at-night; (you)-be:greeted (of) arrival, (continuative) go-

wa   l(i)-o d(a)-Ifa k(o)-Orişala Qşẹrẹgbo ti   yio ba wọn na-(ọ)ja
come" be-who cast-Ifa for-Orishala Qshẹrẹgbo that will join them spend-goods

f(i)-ọgbọ na   ti o ma   şe gẹgẹ   ire   aje.   Nwọn
take-flax spend that he (continuative) make just (like) goodness (of) money. They

ni ki   o ru   eku meji, ẹja meji, igbin meji, ahun meji, adiẹ   meji, akikọ
say should he offer rat two, fish two, snail two, Miser two, chicken two, cock

ati ayebọ ati egbejilelogun.   Orişala Qşẹrẹgbo ru-(ẹ)bọ.
and hen,   and 4400   (cowries). Orishala Qshẹrẹgbo offer-sacrifice.

---

1. Also known as Ogbe Oniwara.

and then go and sacrifice to the God of Thunder also. Ifa says he sees the blessing of a daughter; a diviner will be her husband.

<h2 style="text-align:center">4 - 4</h2>

"Quietly I go, smoothly I return"[1] was the one who cast Ifa for Hook[2] when it
was waging war against a tangled snarl.[3] They said it would not return empty-
handed. Two pigeons, two cocks, and one shilling was the sacrifice. He made the
sacrifice. Since then, Hook does not return empty-handed when it reaches up to
pull anything down.[4]

Ifa says we are stretching out our hands toward something.[5] Ifa says we should
sacrifice lest we draw a blank in that for which we are reaching, whether it is some
work or something else.

---

    1. This seems to refer to the motions of the hook when it is used to pull some-
thing down.

    2. A hook, also known as Ariwǫ or Arigǫgǫ, which is made from a forked stick
and is shaped like a Yoruba hoe handle.

    3. As when someone uses a hook to pull down something snarled from a tree.

    4. The verse thus explains why hooks are useful implements for plucking fruit
or pulling down things which are out of reach.

    5. Like Hook.

<h2 style="text-align:center">5 - 1</h2>

"Noise-making is the task of birds, trembling is that of invalids;[1] an invalid
is the one who knows what witches can do at night; welcome, goodbye"[2] was the one
who cast Ifa for the God of Whiteness[3] when he was about to trade in the flax market[4] and do just as well as if he were to receive a blessing of money. They said he
should sacrifice two rats, two fish, two snails, two tortoises,[5] two chickens—one a
cock and the other a hen—and one shilling one pence two oninis. The God of Whiteness made the sacrifice.

---

    1. The reference is to a person shivering with chills and fever.

    2. Ma re-wa is a salutation used when a person is going away for a short time.
It means "come back soon," or "until you return," and should be compared with o-d(i)-
abǫ (it-become-arrival) and e-rin-wa-o (you-walk-come-oh).

    3. Orishala, or Orishanla the "big deity," or Qbatala the "King that has a white
cloth" heads a pantheon of "white deities" (orisha funfun) associated with snails, shea
butter, white beads, white cloths, and other white things (see Chapter XI). Informants
could not translate "Qshęręgbo," but presumably it is a praise-name of Orishala, because in verse 241-3 Orishala Qshęręgbo states that he was the one who "created
both slaves and freeborn" (cf. n. 3, verse 9-1). Epega (n.d.: XIII, 2) and Lijadu (1923:
9) cite verses mentioning Qbatala Qshęrę-Igbo, and Beyioku (1940: 5) gives Qbatala
Qshęrę Majigbo in the same verse cited by Lijadu.

    4. Qgbǫ is the name for both European flax and linen and for a local plant
(<u>Omphalogonus</u> <u>nigritanus</u>) whose fibers are used in making cord.

    5. Referred to here by his title, "Miser."

Ifa ni   a   nlǫ   ṣe   owo   kan tabi a   fǫ   ṣe iṣǫ   kan ki   a
Ifa say we going make transaction one or   we want do work one should we

ru-(ǫ)bǫ   ki   Q-l(i)-ǫrun   ki   mu-(ǫ)ni   pade aje   n(i)-ibǫ.
offer-sacrifice that One:who-has-sky should take-person meet money at-there.

OGBE - (Q)BARA - 2

Imǫnamǫna san kan-(i)lǫ   san kan-(ǫ)run l(i)-o   d(a)-Ifa ko-(I)gun
"Lightning   flash touch-earth flash touch-sky" be-who cast-Ifa for-Vulture

otuyǫ   awo   Ilode ni-(ǫ)jǫ ti o mbǫ   l(i)-ode   aiye. Nwǫn ni
feathery secret (of) Ilode at-day that he coming at-outside (of) earth. They say

oju ko ni ti   nwǫn ni ni akoko ti   oju ba   ma   ti
eye not be push (him); they say at time that eye should (continuative) push (him)

ti ebi   ba   ma   pa   ni-(i)sǫlǫ yio ṣǫ.   Nwǫn ni
that hunger should (continuative) kill (him) be-disaster will happen. They say

ki   o ru-(ǫ)bǫ   obukǫ kan, ǫgbǫdǫgbǫn,   oru   epo
should he offer-sacrifice (of) he:goat one, 5000   (cowries), pot (of) palm:oil

ati aṣǫ   ara rǫ. Nwǫn ni ǫjǫ ti o ba   w(a)-aiye ni a-(yi)o gbǫ
and cloth (of) body his. They say day that he should come-earth be we-will hear,

a ko ni gbǫ iku rǫ ati pe ǫjǫ ti ebi   ba   ma   pa
we not be hear death his and that day that hunger should (continuative) kill (him)

ni isǫlǫ   yio ṣǫ.
be disaster will happen.

Ifa ni   ǫni-kan   ni,   o ni on ko ni jǫ-ki   oju ki o ti.
Ifa says person-one be (it); he say he not be consent-that eye that it push

O ni bi oju ba   ma   ti   ǫni-(e)keji rǫ ǫrun
(him). He say, if eye should (continuative) push (him), person-second his sky

yio ran l(i)-ǫwǫ aṣiri rǫ yio si   ma   bo   lati ǫdǫ
will send at-hand, secret his will and (continuative) be:covered from presence

Q-l(i)-ǫrun   wa.
One:who-has-sky come.

OGBE - (Q)BARA - 3

Tǫmutǫmu o b(i)-aiya   pi   l(i)-o   d(a)-Ifa f(un)-O-l(i)-okun-
"Hassock   it bear-chest hard" be-who cast-Ifa for-One:who-has-endurance-

de ni-(ǫ)jǫ ti o nfi   ǫkun   oju nṣe   irahun   ǫmǫ. Nwǫn ni
arrive at-day that she taking tears (of) eye making moaning (of) child. They say

ki   o ru-(ǫ)bǫ   ko ru-(ǫ)bǫ   yio bi-(ǫ)mǫ ṣugbǫn ki
should she offer-sacrifice, (if) not offer-sacrifice will bear-child but   that

Ifa says that we are going to do some business or that we want to do some work; we should sacrifice that the Sky God may lead us to money.

---

5 - 2

"Lightning flashes; it touches earth; it touches heaven"[1] was the one who cast Ifa for Feathered Vulture, the diviner of Ilode ward[2] on the day that he was coming to earth. They said that he would not be disgraced; they said that when he was in disgrace and dying of hunger there would be a disaster.[3] They said he should sacrifice one he-goat, one shilling three pence, a pot of palm oil, and the cloth from his body. They said that we will hear of the day that Vulture came to the earth, but we will never hear of his death,[4] and that on the day when he is dying of hunger a disaster will occur.

Ifa says there is someone; he says he will not allow him to be disgraced. He says that if he should be disgraced, his spiritual double[5] in heaven will aid him, and the secret which he has brought from the presence of Sky God will remain covered.

---

1. This appears to be an adaptation of a Yoruba riddle, "A slender staff touches earth; it touches heaven" [Qpa tẹrẹ kan-(i)lẹ; o kan-(ọ)run], the answer to which is "Rain." See Bascom, 1949: 10.
2. One of the five major divisions of the city of Ifẹ.
3. Since Vulture feeds off the sacrifices that are made and the animals that die, any disaster is to Vulture's advantage. Cf. verses 241-1, 248-1. It is understood that Vulture made the sacrifice.
4. Informants explained that the bodies of dead vultures are never found. Cf. verse 248-1.
5. The ancestral guardian soul. See also verses 241-1, 241-4, 248-1.

---

5 - 3

"A hassock has a hard chest"[1] was the only one who cast Ifa for "The one with endurance arrives" when she was weeping and moaning because she had no children. They said she should sacrifice. They said that if she did not sacrifice, she would bear children; but that lest

---

1. Yoruba hassocks are similar to those made by the Hausa; they are thought of as sticking out their chests as if they were very brave.

awǫn ǫmǫ rę   ma ba   ma   ba ara şe   ǫta   ni ki   o
those child hers not should (continuative) with body make enemy be should she

ru-(ę)bǫ   fun ewurę   dudu kan, aşǫ i-tę-(i)lę-(i)di
offer-sacrifice for she:goat black one, cloth to-spread-(on)-ground-(of)-waist

rę,   ejielogun,   ati akikǫ męta. O   ru   ewurę   kan, aşǫ i-tę-
hers, 44,000   (cowries), and cock three. She offer she:goat one, cloth to-spread-

(i)lę-(i)di   rę,   ejielogun   şugbǫn ko ru   akikǫ-(a)dię
(on)-ground-(of)-waist hers, 44,000   (cowries) but   not offer cock-chicken

męta; o ni ki   on şa bi-(ǫ)mǫ. N(i)-igba-ti o   ma   bi,
three; she say that she only bear-child. At-time-that she (continuative) bear,

o bi   ęşin o si bi   afǫn.
she bear Horse she and bear Breadfruit.

    Oju   ǫmǫ tun npǫn   ęşin o si npǫn   afǫn   na gęgę bi
    Eye (of) child then being:red Horse, it and being:red Breadfruit also just as

ti-rę.   Awǫn mej(i)-(m)eji tun tǫ   awǫn babalawo lǫ, babalawo
that-(of)-hers. Those two-two   then approach those diviner   go, diviner

si tun ka   ębǫ   fun wǫn gęgę bi ti   iya   wǫn na, awǫn na
and then count sacrifice for them just like that (of) mother their also, they also

si tun ru   oye   ębǫ   ti iya   wǫn na ru.
and then offer amount (of) sacrifice that mother their also offer.

    N(i)-igba-ti ęşin l(i)-oyun,   afǫn   bi-(ǫ)mǫ, bę-ni   Eşu
    At-time-that Horse have-pregnancy, Breadfruit bear-child; so-be-(it) Eshu

wa   da-(o)hun   o ni Awǫn ǫmǫ   O-l(i)-okun-de
come break-voice he say, "Those children (of) One:who-has-endurance-arrive

ti   a ni ki   iya   wǫn ru-(ę)bǫ   ti ko ru-(ę)bǫ   ni-(e)yi.
that we say should mother their offer-sacrifice that not offer-sacrifice be-this."

O wa   da ija si-(i)lę ni arin wǫn; ni-(i)bi-ti   nwǫn gbe nja,
He come cast fight to-ground at middle their; at-place-that they take fighting,

ęşin tę   ǫmǫ   afǫn   pa.   Inu bi afǫn   pupǫ. Ni-(i)gba-
Horse press child (of) Breadfruit kill (him). Belly vex Breadfruit much. At-time-

ti ęşin bi, afǫn   lǫ bu omi fun   n(i)-igba-ti ǫmǫ   ęşin mu
that Horse bear, Breadfruit go dip water for (it), at-time-that child (of) Horse drink

tan, ǫmǫ   ęşin ku, ati ǫjǫ na ni ęşin ati afǫn   ti di
finish, child (of) Horse die; from day the be Horse and Breadfruit have become

ǫta.
enemy.

    Ifa ni ęni-kan   ni   yio bi-(ǫ)mǫ yi şugbǫn ki   o ru-(ę)bǫ
    Ifa say person-one be (who) will bear-child this but   should she offer-sacri-

    ki awǫn ǫmǫ na ma ba   di   ǫta l(i)-ęhin   ǫla.
fice that those child the not should become enemy at-back (of) tomorrow.

her children become enemies, she should sacrifice one black she-goat, the under-garment[2] from her waist, eleven shillings,[3] and three cocks. She sacrificed the she-goat, the undergarment from her waist, and the eleven shillings, but not the three cocks; she said she just wanted to bear children. When she gave birth, she gave birth to Horse and Breadfruit.

The desire for children troubled Horse, and it troubled Breadfruit just as it had their mother. They both consulted the diviners. The diviners named for them the same sacrifice that had been prescribed for their mother, and they offered the same part of it that their mother had sacrificed before them.[4]

While Horse was pregnant, Breadfruit gave birth to her child. Eshu said, "These are the children of 'The one with endurance arrives' whose mother was told to make a sacrifice but did not do so." He caused a fight between them, and while they were fighting Horse trampled on the child of Breadfruit and killed him. Breadfruit was very angry. When Horse gave birth to her child, Breadfruit brought water for it, and when Horse's child had drunk the poisoned water, it died.[5] Ever since that day Horse and Breadfruit have been enemies.

Ifa says this is someone who will bear a child, but she should sacrifice lest her children become enemies soon afterwards.

------

2. This is the general term for the garments worn by women under their clothing; it includes both the tobi of the old women, and the yẹri or ilaburu of the maidens.

3. Ejielogun is a shortened form of ejilelogun.

4. They did not sacrifice the three cocks so that their children would not be enemies.

5. This refers to the belief that the African Breadfruit (Treculia africana) is poisonous to horses. See Dalziel (1937: 286). The verse thus explains why this is true.

OGBE - (Q)BARA - 4

Ogbe-(Q)bara da   t(i)-ẹ-l(i)-ẹgan   l(i)-o   ku   Ifa şe
"Ogbe-(Q)bara cast that-(of)-one:who-has-contempt be-who remain, Ifa make

gbogbo ohun nihun-nihun   a   da   k(o)-Qrunmila ti   o nlọ
all   things everything-everything" (be) who cast for-Qrunmila that he going

si apa   okun ilaji   ọsa,   n(i)-Iwọnran n(i)-ibi-ti   ẹja gbe nşe
to arm (of) sea   middle (of) lagoon, at-Iwọnran at-place-that fish take doing

bẹbẹ l(i)-oju   omi.   Nwọn ni k(i)-o   ru   eku mẹrin, ẹja mẹrin, ẹyọ
feat at-face (of) water. They say should-he offer rat four, fish four, loose

ere, ẹiyẹ-(i)le   fun-fun   mẹrin, ẹgbasan.
bean, bird-(of)-house be:white-be:white four,   18,000 (cowries).

A-(yi)o mu ewe   ẹla (efunlẹ); a-(yi)o lọ   pẹlu   imọ
We-will take leaf (of) ẹla (efunlẹ); we-will grind (it) together:with palm:leaf

ọpẹ   diẹ;   a-(yi)o pa ẹiyẹ-(i)le   kan a-(yi)o fi   ẹjẹ   rẹ po
(of) palm:tree small; we-will kill bird-(of)-house one; we-will take blood its turn;

a-(yi)o fi   sin gbẹrẹ [oye-k(u)-oye]   si ori.
we-will take (it) cut incision (amount-any-amount) to head.

Ifa ni   on ri   ire   l(i)-ẹhin   odi   fun ẹni-kan,   o ni yio
Ifa say he see goodness at-back (of) town:wall for person-one, he say will

l(i)-owo   pupọ ti   ibẹ bọ, nitori-ti   bi igi ba   wọ-(e)we, okun
have- cowry much from there come, because-that if tree should shed-leaf, rope

a si wọ-(e)we, şugbọn ati wọ-(e)we   ọpẹ   a ma   şoro.
it and shed-leaf, but   to shed-leaf (of) palm:tree it (continuative) be:difficult.

OGBE - (Q)KANRAN - 1

Agbọnniregun ni o di   Ogbe-kan, mo ni o di   Ogbe-kan, o
Agbọnniregun say it become Ogbe-touch; I   say it become Ogbe-touch; he

ni ẹsẹ kan ti on kan s(i)-ile   A-l(i)-ara   ni o fi   nla
say foot one that it touch to-house (of) One:who-has-Ara be he take being:wealthy

ti o ntu   yẹbẹ-yẹbẹ   s(i)-ode; o ni eyi-ti   o kan s(i)-ile
that he loosening lavish-lavish to-outside; he say this-that it touch to-house (of)

a-k(ọ)-apo   t(i)-on   na, t(i)-ọla   ni.
one:who-hang-bag that-(of)-him the, that-(of)-wealth be.

Ifa ni   o ri ire   ọla. Ẹiyẹ-(i)le   meji ayebọ adiẹ   meji
Ifa say he see goodness (of) wealth. Bird-(of)-house two, hen   chicken two,

ati ẹgbaji o le oko.   Ifa ni ọla   de.
and 4000 it plus twenty:cowries. Ifa say wealth arrives.

---

5 - 4

"Ogbe Ọbara[1] cast Ifa that the critic[2] remains; Ifa does all things everywhere" was the one who cast Ifa for Ọrunmila when he was going to the shore of the ocean, to the middle of the lagoon, at Iwọnran where fish perform tricks on the surface of the water. They said he should sacrifice four rats, four fish, some loose beans, four white pigeons, and four shillings six pence.

We will take some ẹla (efunlẹ) leaf.[3] We will grind it with a small piece of palm leaf. We will kill one of the pigeons. We will mix its blood with this. We will cut any number of incisions on the head, and rub this mixture into them.

Ifa says he sees a blessing for someone from beyond the town wall. He says lots of money will come to this person from there. Because while the tree may shed its leaves, and the liana may shed its leaves, for the palm tree to shed its leaves is very difficult.[4]

---

1. Note the reference to the name of the figure.

2. One who criticises everything and has contempt for everything.

3. Efunlẹ may refer to one of the many kinds of epiphytic Orchidaceae which are known as ẹla.

4. Note that a piece of a palm leaf is included as one of the ingredients of the medicine that is to be made.

---

6 - 1

Agbọnniregun[1] says Ogbe should touch[2] you; I say Ogbe should touch you; he says that when Ogbe stopped at the house of the King of Ara for just a moment, he became wealthy and began to spend money lavishly[3] in the streets; he says that that which stops at the house of his apprentice[4] is wealth.

Ifa says he sees the blessing of wealth. Two pigeons, two hens, and one shilling plus 20 cowries is the sacrifice. Ifa says wealth is coming.

---

1. Ọrunmila or Ifa.

2. Note the pun on the name of the figure, Ogbe-(Ọ)kanran.

3. The figure of speech used here is "to burst open like a bud."

4. An apprentice carries his master's bag and runs errands for him (see Chapter IX).

OGBE - (Q)KANRAN - 2

Ẹkikun ki-pẹ   d(i)-ẹkikun   erin,   Abata ki pẹ   d(i)-
"Ẹkikun not-be:long become-ẹkikun (of) elephant," "Mud   not be:long become-

abata   ẹfọn,   Orere ki pẹ   d(i)-orere   ọmọ-(o)binrin   Ilaun
mud   (of) buffalo," "Street not be:long become-street (of) child-woman   (of) Ilaun"

awọn l(i)-o   d(a)-Ifa fun wọn   ni Mọrẹ Agbada ni-(ọ)jọ ti   e-bi-bi
they be-who cast-Ifa for those at Mọrẹ Agbada at-day   that that:which-push-push

nbi   wọn s(i)-ọrun.   Nwọn ni   ki   nwọn ru   ikoko   ẹwa, ayebọ adiẹ,
pushing them to-sky.   They say should they offer pot   (of) ẹwa, hen   chicken,

ati ẹgbarun   ẹni-(ọ)k(an)-ọkan ni yio se   ti-rẹ.
and 10,000   (cowries); person-one-one be will cook that-(of)-his.

   Ifa ni   ohun kan ti   nṣe-(ẹ)ni   ni ofun ṣugbọn Q-l(i)-ọrun   ṣe tan
   Ifa say thing one have doing-person at loss, but   One:who-has-sky do finish

ti   yio da-(ọ)wọ   rẹ duro fun-(ẹ)ni.   Ki   ẹni-kan   ru-(ẹ)bọ   ki
that will cause-hand his stand for-person. Should person-one offer-sacrifice that

ohun-kan ma ba   ma   wa   ti   ode   ọrun ko   wọn lọ.
thing-one not should (continuative) come from outside (of) sky gather them go.

Ki   awọn ara   kan ru-(ẹ)bọ   nitori   eburu.
Should those people one offer-sacrifice because (of) evil:spirit.

   Ni akoko kan awọn eburu   a   ma   ti   ode   ọrun wa
   At time one those evil:spirit they (continuative) from outside (of) sky   come

ko   awọn ara   Mọrẹ lọ si ọrun. Nwọn tọ   awọn babalawo lọ; nwọn
gather those people (of) Mọrẹ go to sky.   They approach those diviner go; they

ni ki   nwọn ru-(ẹ)bọ.   Nwọn si   ru-(ẹ)bọ.   Nwọn mu   adiẹ
say should they offer-sacrifice. They and offer-sacrifice. They take chicken

nwọn-yi, nwọn pa wọn.   Nwọn se   wọn, nwọn ko   gbogbo rẹ le   ori
those-this they kill them. They cook them, they gather all   its upon head (of)

ẹwa na n(i)-inu   apadi,   nwọn ni ki   nwọn gbe   e lọ si inu   igbo
ẹwa the at-belly (of) potsherd, they say should they carry it go to belly (of) forest

ti o kọ-(o)ju   si ile   wọn, ti   a npe   ni igbo   Qlọṣẹ.   N(i)-
that it turn:toward-face to house their; that we calling at forest (of) Qlọshẹ. At-

igba-ti awọn eburu   de   ibẹ   ti   nwọn ri   onjẹ, nwọn bẹrẹ si jẹ-(oh)un.
time-that those evil:spirit arrive there that they see food, they begin to eat-thing.

N(i)-igba-ti nwọn jẹ-(oh)un tan,   ni Eṣu sọ   fun wọn pe awọn ara
At-time-that they eat-thing finish, be Eshu speak for them that those people (of)

Mọrẹ ni o   se   onjẹ na bayi ni awọn eburu   na ba   pada.   Nwọn ni
Mọrẹ be who cook food the thus be those evil:spirit the should return. They say

   iku ki jẹ-(oh)un   ẹni   ki o pa-(ẹ)ni.
"Death not eat-thing (of) person that he kill-person."

   Ifa ni ki   a p(a)-ese   fun eburu.   Lati igba-na ni iku   ko
   Ifa say should we kill-provision for evil:spirit. From time-the be death not

6 - 2

"It is not long before the ẹkikun leaf[1] belongs to the elephant,"[2] "It is not long before mud belongs to the buffalo,"[3] and "It is not long before the street belongs to the girl from the town of Ilaun"[4] they were the ones who cast Ifa for the people of Mọrẹ Agbada ward[5] on the day that something evil was forcing them to heaven[6] against their will. They said they should sacrifice a pot of boiled corn and beans,[7] a hen, and two shillings six pence. They said each person should cook his own corn and beans.

Ifa says something is causing someone a loss, but that the Sky God will put a stop to it. Someone should make a sacrifice lest something come from heaven and carry him and his family away. A group of people should sacrifice because of evil spirits.

Once upon a time evil spirits were coming from heaven and carrying the people of Mọrẹ ward back with them. They consulted the diviners. The diviners said they should sacrifice, and they sacrificed. They took the chickens they had sacrificed and killed them. They cooked them and placed everything on the boiled corn and beans in a potsherd. They said they should take the sacrifice into the grove of trees that faced their house and which we call the grove of Ọlọshẹ.[8] When the evil spirits arrived at the grove and saw the food, they began to eat it. When they had finished eating it, Eshu told them that the people of Mọrẹ were the ones who had cooked it, and that they should go back to heaven. They replied, "Death does not eat a person's food and then kill him."

Ifa says we should prepare food for evil spirits. Since that time death has not

----

1. The leaf of a tall tree, like a palm tree, which is used in weaving atinrin mats.

2. It is not long after they have appeared before elephants eat them.

3. It is not long before "bushcows" or African buffalos are wallowing in the mud.

4. Cf. verses 6-5, 6-6. Because these names are followed by the plural awọn it is clear that several diviners are mentioned. Ilaun could not be identified.

5. Mọrẹ is the name of a ward of the town of Ifẹ, one of its five major divisions. Agbada is a title of that quarter, the meaning of which could not be given by informants.

6. That is, causing them to die.

7. A dish of food made of boiled corn or boiled corn and beans.

8. The name of a deity worshiped particularly by the people of Mọrẹ ward in Ifẹ.

ti   nmu   awọn ara   Mọrẹ mọ.   Qd(un)-ọdun ni awọn ara   Mọrẹ
have taking those people (of) Mọrẹ again.   Year-year   be those people (of) Mọrẹ

si   ma   nse   iru   onjẹ yi   lọ si igbo   Qlọsẹ.   Ifa ni awọn
and (continuative) cooking kind (of) food this go to forest (of) Qlọshẹ. Ifa say those

ara   kan ni o   wa   l(i)-agbo yi, ki   nwọn ru-(ẹ)bọ   ki   eburu
people one be who exist at-flock this, should they offer-sacrifice that evil:spirit

ma ba   wọ   inu rẹ.
not should enter belly its.

OGBE - (Q)KANRAN - 3

Omi-(i)gbo   ni   f(i)-oju   j(ọ)-aro,   omi   eluju   ọdan
"Water-(of)-forest be (it) take-eye resemble-dye; water (of) field (of) grass:

ni   f(i)-oju j(ọ)-ero   adin, ekurọ   oju   ọna o
land be (it) take-eye resemble-drippings (of) adi; palm:nut (of) eye (of) road it

fi   ara jọ   ikin ko ri ẹjẹ mu   bi ikin   a   da   fun A-lu-
take body resemble ikin not see blood drink like ikin" (be) who cast for To-beat-

mọ   ti   o nlọ   ra ẹda   l(i)-ẹru. Nwọn ni afi   bi o ba   le
know that he going buy creature at-slave. They say unless if he should be:able

sin   ẹda   rẹ. O ni on yio sin.   Ẹda   ni a ipe ikin, A-lu-
serve creature his. He say he will serve (it). Creature be we call ikin, To-beat-

mọ   ni a-i-pe   Qrunmila.
know be we-to-call Qrunmila.

Ifa ni   ọmọ-(ọ)kunrin kan ni-yi,   babalawo ni,   Ifa ni ọmọ na i-sin
Ifa say child-man   one be-this, diviner   be (he); Ifa be child the to-serve

lati ọrun wa.   Orun ko gbọdọ ba   n(i)-inu   oko. Ko si gbọdọ
from sky come. Sun not must meet (him) at-belly (of) farm. Not and must

fi   ẹsẹ gbọn enini ni ọna   oko.
take foot shake dew   at road (of) farm.

Ifa ni a si tun nfẹ   ra ohun kan ki   oluwarẹ   ki   o
Ifa say we and then wanting buy thing one should person:in:question should he

ma-ṣe r(o)-oju   ohun ti   yio ra na, bi owo   ko ba   to   ki
not-do spoil-eye (of) thing that (he) will buy the, if cowries not should equal should

o fi owo   si   ohun ti yio ṣe   ni anfani ni o fẹ   ra yi.
he put cowries to (them), thing that will make (him) at benefit be he want buy this.

Qjọ ti enia nfi   owo   gba ikin ni yi.
Day that person taking cowries take ikin be this.

Njẹ   oko me   le   yun,
"Well:then, farm I   (not) be:able go,

A-lu-mọ
"To-beat-know;

taken the people of Mǫrę away any more. And every year the people of Mǫrę
cook this kind of food and take it to the grove of Qlǫshę.[9] Ifa says that this is a
group of people who live together in a compound;[10] they should sacrifice lest evil
spirits enter their compound.

---

9. This verse thus explains why the people of Mǫrę ward carry boiled corn
and beans to the grove of Qlǫshę during the Coconut Festival (ǫdun agbǫn).

10. A compound is known as a "flock of houses" (agbo ile).

---

6 - 3

"The water of the forest is like indigo dye;[1] the water of the grassland is
like palm kernel oil;[2] palm nuts embedded in the path are like the palm nuts of
Ifa, but they do not drink blood like Ifa's palm nuts"[3] was the one who cast Ifa
for "He beats palm nuts and knows the future" when he was going to buy Ęda[4]
as his slave. They said he must serve his Ęda. He said he would serve it. Ęda
is what we call the palm nuts of Ifa. "He beats palm nuts and knows the future"
is what we call Qrunmila.

Ifa says this is a boy; he is a diviner; he was serving Ifa when he came from
heaven. The rising or setting sun must not find him in the farm, and his feet
must not brush the dew from the farm road.[5]

And Ifa says we want to buy something. The person in question should not
be deterred from buying it. If there is not enough money, he should add to it.
This thing he wants to buy will benefit him. This is the day he is buying his set
of palm nuts.

> "Well then, I cannot go to the farm,
> "He beats palm nuts and knows the future;

---

1. The water which gathers in the forest is colored by the rotting leaves so
that it resembles the very dark blue of indigo.

2. The oil (adi or adin) made from the white palm kernels is to be distinguished from the orange palm oil (epo) made from the pericarp. Palm kernel
oil is used in making soap and in rubbing the body after bathing.

3. Palm nuts embedded in the road and the sixteen palm nuts (ikin) used in
divining are both polished through use, but only the ones used in divining receive
the blood of sacrifices. Cf. verse 247-4.

4. Ęda is usually translated as "creature" or "that which has been created,"
and refers to the ancestral guardian soul. Here, however, it is specifically
equated with the set of palm nuts used in divining.

5. He is supposed to devote himself to divining, as is spelled out below.

Ẹ   wa   wo   iṣẹ   ẹda   nṣe
"You (not) come look:at work creature doing,

A-lu-mọ
"To-beat-know.

Odo   me   le   yun,
"River I   (not) be:able go,

A-lu-mọ
"To-beat-know;

Ẹ   wa   wo   iṣẹ   ẹda   nṣe,
"You (not) come look:at work creature doing,

A-lu-mọ
"To-beat-know.

Qja   me   le   yun,
"Market I   (not) be:able go,

A-lu-mọ
"To-beat-know;

Ẹ   wa   wo   iṣẹ   ẹda   nṣe,
"You (not) come look:at work creature doing,

A-lu-mọ
"To-beat-know.

Idalẹ   me   le   yun
"Distance I   (not) be:able go,

A-lu-mọ
"To-beat-know;

Ẹ   wa   wo   iṣẹ   ẹda   nṣe,
"You (not) come look:at work creature doing,

A-lu-mọ
"To-beat-know."

Ifa ni   ẹda   ẹni-kan   ki iṣe iṣẹ kan ju   Ifa lọ, iṣẹ
Ifa say creature (of) person-one not do work one surpass Ifa go, work (of)

ẹni-kan   ko si ni oko bi ko ṣe   ni arin   ilu, ki   oluwarẹ
person-one not be at farm if not make at middle (of) town, should person:in:ques-

pada   si ẹhin ki   o   ma   ṣ(e)-awo tabi ki   o   ma
tion return to back should he (continuative) do-secret or   should he (continuative)

ki   Ifa. Ewurẹ   kan, ẹgbawa   ai-din   ki   o ru-(ẹ)bọ
recite Ifa. She:goat one, 20,000 (cowries) not-lessen should he offer-sacrifice

tan   ki   o lọ ma   bọ   Ifa rẹ pẹlu   ewurẹ   kan.
finish should he go (continuative) sacrifice:to Ifa his together:with she:goat one.

"Won't you come and see what Ẹda is doing for me?[6]
"He beats palm nuts and knows the future.
"I cannot go to the river,
"He beats palm nuts and knows the future;
"Won't you come and see what Ẹda is doing for me?
"He beats palm nuts and knows the future.
"I cannot go to market,
"He beats palm nuts and knows the future;
"Won't you come and see what Ẹda is doing for me?
"He beats palm nuts and knows the future.
"I cannot go to distant places,
"He beats palm nuts and knows the future;
"Won't you come and see what Ẹda is doing for me?
"He beats palm nuts and knows the future."

Ifa says the destiny of someone is to do nothing more than Ifa. He must not work in the farm but inside the town. This person should return to what he had been doing,[7] and either divine or recite the verses of Ifa. He should sacrifice one she-goat and five shillings, no less, and then he should go and sacrifice one she-goat to his own Ifa also.

---

6. Since Ẹda here means the palm nuts of Ifa, the request is for people to come and see how he is prospering through divining.

7. It is explained earlier in the verse that he was worshiping Ifa before he was born.

OGBE - (Q)KANRAN - 4

Ita-(i)gbangba   n(i)-t(i)-elu   a   da   f(un)-ǫrǫ   ti
"Square-(of)-open:place be-that-(of)-stranger" (be) who cast for-Cactus that

o   nlǫ si eluju   Igango ti   o   nlǫ   mu-(i)lę-(i)bu-do   nitori-
she going to field (of) Igango, that she going take-ground-(of)-place-settle because-

ti   ǫmǫ.   Nwǫn ni ewurę   kan ni ębǫ   ati ęgbawa   ai-din.
that (of) child. They say she:goat one be sacrifice and 20,000 (cowries) not-lessen.

Nwǫn ni ki   ar(a)-aiye   ma ba   ma   tǫ iję   rę wo
They say should people-(of)-earth not should (continuative) taste blood her look:at

ni oş(u)-oşu.   Qrǫ   ru-(ę)bǫ   ewurę   kan ęgbawa   ewe
at month-month. Cactus offer-sacrifice (of) she:goat one, 20,000 (cowries), leaf

   Ifa.
(of) Ifa.

   A sin   ni-gbęrę; oju   gbęrę   na ni ęgun   ara   ǫrǫ
   We cut (her) at-incision; eye (of) incision the be thorn (of) body (of) Cactus

titi di   oni yi.   Lati ǫjǫ na ni iję   ara   ǫrǫ   ko şe
until become today this. From day the be blood (of) body (of) Cactus not make

mu   mǫ.
drink again.

   Ifa ni ki   obinrin kan ru-(ę)bǫ   ki   ar(a)-aiye   ma ba
   Ifa say should woman one offer-sacrifice that people-(of)-earth not should

ma   ki-(ǫ)wǫ bǫ   inu rę, ki o   ma ba   ma   ri
(continuative) push-hand enter belly her, that she not should (continuative) see

inu   ni oş(u)-oşu.
belly at month-month.

OGBE - (Q)KANRAN - 5

Ęri ki pę   di   ęri   ękikun Eluju ki ipę   di   eluju
"River not be:long become river (of) ękikun," "Field not be:long become field

ękun,   Ode-(i)gbangba   ki ipę   di   ode   ǫmǫde
(of) leopard," "Outside-(of)-open:place not be:long become outside (of) young:child

ode   Ilaun   a   da   fun wǫn ni Mǫrę Agbada n(i)-ibi-ti   nwǫn
(of) outside (of) Ilaun" (be) who cast for those at Mǫrę Agbada at-place-that they

gbe tori   t(i)-ǫmǫ   da Ifa, nwǫn ni nwǫn a   bi ǫmǫ. Igba
take because that-(of)-child cast Ifa; they say they will bear child. Calabash (of)

ęwa męwa, ayebǫ adię   męwa, ati ęgbawa   ni ębǫ.
ęwa ten, hen chicken ten,   and 20,000 (cowries) be sacrifice.

   Nwǫn ni ǫmǫ yio ka   wǫn l(i)-ori. N(i)-igba-ti ǫdun fi   ma
   They say child will go:around them at-head. At-time-that year take (continu-

6 - 4

"The open square belongs to foreigners"[1] was the one who cast Ifa for Cactus[2] when she was going to move to the field of Igango because she had no children.[3] They said that one she-goat and five shillings, no less, was the sacrifice. They said that witches would not drink her menstrual blood to keep her from having children. Cactus sacrificed one she-goat, five shillings, and Ifa's leaf.

Small incisions were made on the body of Cactus and medicine was rubbed into them. The scars of these cuts are the thorns that Cactus has until this very day. From that time on, the blood of Cactus cannot be drunk.[4]

Ifa says a woman should sacrifice so that witches will not reach into her womb to destroy the embryo, and so that she will not menstruate every month.[5]

———————

1. That is, it is public property. The word "foreigner" or "stranger" (elu) refers to Yoruba who are not native to a given town.

2. Euphorbia kamerunica.

3. Cactus was going to leave her compound and build her own house in hopes that she might bear children.

4. This verse explains how cactus came to have thorns, why it has so many children, and why the "blood" or sap (oje) of cactus is bitter, and can be used as fish poison. Dalziel reports that it is highly purgative and is used as an ordeal and in arrow poison.

5. That is, so that she may conceive.

———————

6 - 5

"It is not long before the river belongs to the ẹkikun leaf," "It is not long before the field belongs to the leopard," and "It is not long before the open street belongs to the child from the town of Ilaun"[1] were the ones who cast Ifa for the people of Mọrẹ Agbada ward where they had cast Ifa because they had no children. They said they would bear children. Ten calabashes of boiled corn and beans, ten hens, and five shillings[2] was the sacrifice.

They said each of them would have a child. When the year had

———————

1. Because these names are so similar to those in verse 6-2, they have also been interpreted as referring to several individuals. Note that this verse and 6-2 and 6-6 all have several points of similarity. Aside from the names of the diviners, they all refer to Mọrẹ ward and to the worship of Qsara and Qlọshẹ.

2. Since cowries are counted by the two thousand, there are ten units of cowries required, as there are ten hens and ten calabashes of boiled corn and beans.

　　　　　yi-po　　gbogbo　　wǫn ni o　　bi　　ǫmǫ si ǫwǫ.　Lati ǫjǫ yi　ni
ative) turn-turn all　　(of) them be they bear child to hand.　From day this be

nwǫn ko ti　npa　　ǫdun　　ęwa ję ni Mǫrę, ti　nwǫn ma　　　　nşe ni
they　not have killing year (of) ęwa eat at Mǫrę, that they (continuative) doing at

ǫd(un)-ǫdun.　N(i)-igba-ti　o di　　　ǫdun-(e)keji ni nwǫn bęrę si ima
year-year.　At-time-that it become year-second be they　begin to (continuative)

jo　ti　nwǫn kǫ-(o)rin　　pe:
dance that they　singing-song that:

　　　　　　　　Qsara ma　　　　　　k(o)-ǫmǫ　　　de　　　o
　　　　　　　　"Qsara (continuative) gather-child arrive, oh,

　　　　　　　　Hin, hin, hin, hin.
　　　　　　　　"Hin, Hin, Hin, Hin!

　　　　　　　　Qmǫ ni (e)m(i)-a ba　　wǫn bi　　　o
　　　　　　　　"Child be I-will　　join them bear, oh,

　　　　　　　　Hin, hin, hin, hin!
　　　　　　　　"Hin, hin, hin, hin!

　　　　　　　　Q-1(i)-ǫmǫ　　　　　　ma　　　　　ku　　　　　　ǫmǫ o
　　　　　　　　"One:who-has-child (continuative) be:greeted (of) child, oh,

　　　　　　　　Hin, hin, hin, hin.
　　　　　　　　"Hin, hin, hin, hin!"

　　Ifa ni　ǫmǫ npǫn　　　obinrin kan l(i)-oju ki　　o　ru-(ę)bǫ
　　Ifa say child being:red woman one at-eye　should she offer-sacrifice (of)

igba　　　　ęwa męwa, ayębǫ adię　　męwa, ati ęgbawa.　　　　Bi o
calabash (of) ęwa ten,　hen　chicken ten,　and 20,000 (cowries). If she

ba　le　　ru-(ę)bǫ,　　　ni ida-yi　ęmirin　ǫmǫ ni obinrin na yio
should be:able offer-sacrifice, at time-this next:year child be woman the will

ma　　　pǫn.
(continuative) carry:on:back.

OGBE - (Q)KANRAN - 6

　　Ęri　ki ipę　di　　ęri　　ękikun, Eluju ki ipę　di　　eluju
　　"River not be:long become river (of) ękikun," "Field not be:long become field

　　ękun,　　Ode-(i)gbangba　　ki ipę　di　　ode　　　ǫmǫde
(of) leopard," "Outside-(of)-open:place not be:long become outside (of) young:child (c

ode　　　Ilaun　　a　da　fun wǫn ni Mǫrę Agbada n(i)-ibi-ti　nwǫn gbe
outside (of) Ilaun" (be) who cast for those at Mǫrę Agbada at-place-that they　take

njo　egemǫpati nitori-ti　　　ǫmǫ. Ifa ni ęni-kan　　nşe　ai-san,
dancing egemǫpati because-that (of) child.　Ifa say person-one making not-be:better,

ki　o ru-(ę)bǫ　　ki o ba　le　ję-(oh)un, tabi ǫmǫ　　ǫwǫ kan
should he offer-sacrifice that he should be:able eat-thing, or　child (of) hand one

run its course, they all bore children. From that day on they have not missed eating boiled corn and beans at Mọrẹ ward; they have done it every year.[3] The next year they began to dance, and to sing:

> "Qsara,[4] brings us children, oh,
> "Hin, hin, hin, hin![5]
> "I will bear children with the others, oh,
> "Hin, hin, hin, hin!
> "Greetings of children, you who have children, oh,
> "Hin, hin, hin, hin!"

Ifa says a woman is troubled by the desire for children. She should sacrifice ten calabashes of boiled corn and beans, ten hens, and five shillings. If she is able to make this sacrifice, by this time next year she will be carrying a child on her back.[6]

---

3. This verse, like 6-2, explains why the dish of boiled corn and beans is sacrificed every year by the people of Mọrẹ ward.

4. Qsara is a deity who was the husband of Qlọshẹ (see verse 6-2). He is identified with a body of water in Qlọshẹ's grove, opposite Mọrẹ ward along the Ilesha road in Ifẹ.

5. These sounds have no meaning, but are added to the song simply to make it "sound sweet."

6. Note the pun on "carry on back" (pọn) and "be red" (pọn).

---

6 - 6

"It is not long before the river belongs to the ẹkikun leaf," "It is not long before the field belongs to the leopard," and "It is not long before the open street belongs to the child from the town of Ilaun"[1] were the ones who cast Ifa for the people of Mọrẹ Agbada ward where they were dancing the egemọpati[2] because they had no children. Ifa says someone is not well; he should make a sacrifice so that he may be able to eat. Or a babe in arms

---

1. Cf. n. 1, verse 6-5, and nn. 1 to 3, verse 6-2.

2. A drum rhythm used at the Coconut Festival (ọdun agbọn), which is performed by the people of Mọrẹ ward in honor of Qsara and Qlọshẹ.

nṣe   amodi,   ko jẹ-(oh)un, ki   a   ru-(ẹ)bọ   ki   o ba   le
making sickness, not eat-thing, should we offer-sacrifice that it should be:able

jẹ-(oh)un. Obukọ   kan,   ọgọfa ori,   ẹgbafa.
eat-thing. He:goat one, 120   cornstarch:porridge, 12,000 (cowries).

      N(i)-igba-ti nwọn ru-(ẹ)bọ   yi ti   nwọn gbe   si ẹhin-(ẹ)kun-
      At-time-that they offer-sacrifice this that they carry (it) to back-door-(of)-

(i)le ibi-ti   ọmọ na gbe nṣe   ai-san,   awọn ẹgbẹ   rẹ jẹ-
house place-that child the take making not-be:better, those companion his eat-

(oh)un tan,   ni nwọn wa   nk(ọ)-orin   pe:
thing finish, be they come singing-song that:

                    Jẹ o   egemọpati.
                    "Eat, oh, egemọpati."

Bi awọn ẹgbẹ   ọmọ na ba   ti   jẹ onjẹ nwọn-yi   tan   a-
As those companion (of) child the should have eat food those-this finish one:who-

l(i)-ai-san   na yio jẹ-(oh)un.
be-not-be:better the will eat-thing.

OGBE - (I)ROSUN[1] - 1

      Ogbe r(i)-Osun,   Osun   ri A-w(o)-oro   a da
      "Ogbe sees-Camwood; Camwood sees One:who-look:at-ritual" (be) who cast

fun Nwọnmile ti   o nlọ   ri baba rẹ ni oju   ala.
for Rascal   that he going see father his at eye (of) dream.

                    Mo ri   baba mi l(i)-oni,
                    "I see father my at-today,

                    Iba   ẹkun
                    "Father (of) leopard,

                    Iba   ese,
                    "Father (of) cat,

                    Iba   amọkiṣitẹkun,
                    "Father (of) panther,

                    Ababa ti   ọrun wa   gɔe   mi,
                    "Father from sky come assist me,

                    Iba   ọmọ ko ṣ(e)-ai gbe   ọmọ rẹ,
                    "Father (of) child not do-not assist child his,

                    Iba   ọmọ.
                    "Father (of) child."

----

      1. Also known as Ogbe t(ẹ)-ọwọ bo osun (Ogbe stretch-hand dip camwood),
"Ogbe dips out camwood."

is ill and cannot eat anything; we should sacrifice so it will be able to eat. One he-goat, 120 lumps of cornstarch porridge, and three shillings is the sacrifice.

When they had made the sacrifice and carried it out behind the house where the child was lying ill, his companions finished eating it and they came back singing:

"Eat, oh, egemọpati."

As his companions finish eating the food, the child who is not well will eat something.

---

7 - 1

"Ogbe sees Camwood;[1] Camwood sees the priest" was the one who cast Ifa for Rascal when he was dreaming about his father.

"I saw my father today;
"Father of leopard,
"Father of cat,
"Father of panther,[2]
"Father come from heaven to help me;
"The child's father does not refuse to help his child,
"The child's father."

---

1. Ogbe and Camwood appear here as names of people. Note the pun on the name of the figure, Ogbe-(I)rosun.

2. Amọkiṣitẹkun is a title of a feline identified as a panther by informants and described as about the size of a dog. Its meaning could not be analyzed, but it is also known as a-mọ-t(o)-ẹkun (one:who-know-equal-leopard), meaning "The one who knows as much as leopard." Note that all the animals mentioned are felines.

Ifa ni   ęni-kan   gbagbe baba rę ti   ko ba   tǫ-(o)ju   baba
Ifa say person-one forget father his that not should care:for-eye (of) father

rę, ko ni ri   ęni   tǫ-(o)ju   on na ni aiye. Agbo kan ati ęgbaje
his, not be see person care:for-eye his also at earth. Ram one and 14,000 (cow-

         ni ębǫ.   Ki   a   ru-(ę)bo   tan ki   e-l(i)-eyi   lǫ
ries) be sacrifice. Should we offer-sacrifice finish should one:who-be-this go

fi agbo na bǫ   baba rę, şugbǫn bi o ba   wa ni aiye ki   o
take ram the sacrifice:to father his, but   if he should exist at earth should he

lǫ fi   bǫ   o ni ori ki ǫran rę ba   le   ni ǫna; (ohu)n-
go take (it) sacrifice:to him at head that affair his should be:able have road; thing-

kan   e-l(i)-eyi   yio baję pata-pata   bi ko ba   tǫ-
one (of) one:who-be-this will spoil completely-completely if not should care:for-

(o)ju   baba rę; yala bi o wa   ni ǫrun tabi ni aiye.
eye (of) father his; either if he exist at sky or   at earth.

OGBE - (I)ROSUN - 2

Tara o b(i)-oju węrę   a   da   fun Qrunmila ti o nlǫ gbe A-
"Pebble it bear-eye tiny" (be) who cast for Qrunmila that he going take One:who

ri-(i)ye-wę   ni iyawo.   Ifa ni aya   Ifa kan ni-(e)yi, bi a ko ba
see-mother-be:coy at junior:wife. Ifa say wife (of) Ifa one be-this, if we not should

mu   fun Ifa oku   ni.   Obinrin kan si tun ni-(e)yi bi o   ba
take (her) give Ifa corpse be (she). Woman one and then be-this if she should

le   ru-(ę)bǫ   yio bi-(ǫ)mǫ pupǫ.
be:able offer-sacrifice will bear-child many.

    A-ri-(i)ye-wę   a   b(i)-ǫmǫ węrę
    "One:who-see-mother-be:coy will bear-child tiny;

    A-ri-(i)ye-wę   a   b(i)-ǫmǫ węrę
    "One:who-see-mother-be:coy will bear-child tiny;

    Qrunmila l(i)-o gbe A-ri-(i)ye-wę   n(i)-iyawo
    "Qrunmila be-who take One:who-see-mother-be:coy at-junior:wife;

    A-ri-(i)ye-wę   a   b(i)-ǫmǫ węrę.
    "One:who-see-mother-be:coy will bear-child tiny."

Obinrin aya   Ifa kan ni-(e)yi, yio bi-(ǫ)mǫ bi o ba   le   ru-
Woman wife (of) Ifa one be-this, will bear-child if she should be:able offer-

(ę)bǫ   ayebǫ adię   marun, ęgbarun.   Ki   o   ru-(ę)bǫ
sacrifice (of) hen chicken five, 10,000 (cowries). Should she offer-sacrifice

tan ki   obinrin na si ma   pa ile   Ifa, ni (ohu)n-kan rę
finish should woman the and (continuative) rub house (of) Ifa, be thing-one her

fi le   dę   l(i)-ǫrun.
make be:able be:soft (for) (her) at-neck.

Ifa says someone has forgotten his father and that if he does not take care of his father there will be no one on earth to take care of him. One ram and three shillings six pence is the sacrifice. When this sacrifice has been made, this person should go and sacrifice the ram to his father; but if the father is still alive, he should sacrifice the ram to his father's head so that the way to success may be clear for him. Something of the person concerned will spoil completely if he does not take care of his father, whether he is on earth or in heaven.

---

7 - 2

"Pebbles have tiny eyes"[1] was the one who cast Ifa for Qrunmila when he was going to take "She is coy when she sees her mother"[2] as his wife. Ifa says this is a wife of Ifa;[3] if she is not given to Ifa, she will die. And then there is a woman who will bear many children if she is able to sacrifice.

"She is coy when she sees her mother will bear tiny children;
"She is coy when she sees her mother will bear tiny children;
"Qrunmila is the one who took She is coy when she sees her mother
      as his wife;
"She is coy when she sees her mother will bear tiny children."

This is a woman who is a wife of Ifa; she will bear children if she is able to sacrifice five hens and two shillings six pence. When she has completed the sacrifice, she should begin to rub the house of Ifa;[4] then things will be easy for her.

---

1. Informants said that this meant only that they "come in small pieces," but tara refers to pebbles of laterite (yangi), which has a pitted surface.
2. This name carries the meaning that as a girl she turns and shuffles shyly, trying to get her mother to do something or to give her something that she has been denied.
3. See n. 5, verse 3-4.
4. The walls and floor of the room in which the Ifa paraphernalia are kept are rubbed regularly with dung by the women worshipers of Ifa and those who come to Ifa for children.

OGBE - (I)ROSUN - 3

Gunnugun hu-(i)run   de   gbọgbọrọ   itan, o fi   (i)y(i)-o-ku
"Vulture   sprout-hair arrive length   (of) thigh, he take this-which-remain

bọ ṣokoto   a   da   fun Ojugbẹdẹ ni-(ọ)jọ ti Ogun ma   fi
wear trousers" (be) who cast for Ojugbẹdẹ at-day that Ogun (continuative) take

ọna   ọwọ rẹ han.   Nwọn ni ki   o ru   ẹiyẹ-(i)le   meji ati
art (of) hand his appear. They say should he offer bird-(of)-house two and

egbejila.
2400   (cowries).

Ifa ni ohun ti   a   tori   rẹ da-(i)fa yi a-(yi)o ri ire   n(i)-
Ifa say thing that we because (of) its cast-Ifa this, we-will see goodness at-

inu rẹ, Ifa ni ni ọdun yi ni Ogun yio fi   ọna   ere rẹ han.   Ila
belly its; Ifa say at year this be Ogun will take road (of) gain his appear. Ochra

ni Ojugbẹdẹ gbin ni ọdun na o si ri ere pupọ l(i)-ori   ila   na.
be Ojugbẹdẹ plant at year the he and see gain much at-head (of) ochra the.

OGBE - (I)ROSUN - 4

Adepeju ni awo   A-l(i)-aran,   Okoromu ni awo   Ẹsa,
"Adepeju" be secret (of) One:who-has-velvet, "Okoromu" be secret (of) Ẹsa,

Itamọjẹ awo   Itamọpo   a   da   fun agba gọlọtọ ti o nfọ   ori
"Itamọjẹ" secret (of) Itamọpo (be) who cast for Elder Stupid that he grinding corn:

            l(i)-odo ni ai-n(i)-igba;   nwọn ni kin-ni o ṣe   ti o
starch:porridge at-river at not-have-calabash; they say what-be it make that he

nfọ-(o)ri   l(i)-odo ni ai-n(i)-igba?   O ni iya
grinding-cornstarch:porridge at-river at not-have-calabash? He say punishment

    ai-ni   enia   ni o njẹ   on.
(of) not-have persons be it eating him.

Ifa ni on ri ire   enia ati ire   aya fun ẹni-ti
Ifa say he see goodness (of) people and goodness (of) wife for person-that

o da on yi. Ayebọ adiẹ   meji, obi mẹwa, ati ẹgbẹrindilogun ni
who cast him[1] this. Hen   chicken two, kola ten,   and 3200   (cowries) be

ẹbọ.   A-(yi)o fi   ewe   ọkọ di obi na; a-(yi)o ma   fi
sacrifice. We-will take leaf (of) hoe tie kola the; we-will (continuative) take

    bọ   ori rẹ ni-(ọ)k(an)-ọkan l(i)-oj(umọ)-ojumọ.
(them) sacrifice:to head his at-one-one   at-dawn-dawn.

---

1. That is, Ifa.

---

7 - 3

"Vulture's feathers reach to his thighs; for the rest[1] he wears trousers" was the one who cast Ifa for Ojugbẹdẹ[2] on the day that the God of Iron taught him his handicraft. They said he should sacrifice two pigeons and seven pence two oninis.

Ifa says that we will find a blessing in the thing for which we cast this figure. Ifa says that during this year the God of Iron will show us the way to make a profit. That year Ojugbẹdẹ planted ochra, and he made a big profit on the ochra.

---

1. That is, for the rest of his leg, which is not covered with feathers.
2. Ojugbẹdẹ is the head of the Ifẹ blacksmiths and the God of Iron is their patron.

---

7 - 4

Adepeju leaf, the diviner of "The one who owns velvet"; Okoromu, the diviner of the town of Ẹsa; and Itamọjẹ, the diviner of Itamọpo were the ones who cast Ifa for "Strong but stupid elder"[1] who was so poor that he ground cornstarch porridge at the river without a calabash. They said, "Why are you grinding cornstarch porridge at the river without a calabash?" He said he was suffering because he had nobody.[2]

Ifa says he sees the blessing of people and the blessing of wives for the person who cast this figure. Two hens, ten kola nuts, and nine pence six oninis[3] is the sacrifice. We will wrap the kola nuts in "hoe" leaves; we will sacrifice one each day, at dawn, to his head.

---

1. An old person who has brawn, but not brains.
2. That is, because he had no relatives or friends to help him financially, even in buying a calabash. Not having a calabash or a plate is a euphemism for poverty. Cf. n. 4, verse 2-1; and n. 4, verse 18-11.
3. Ẹgbẹrindilogun is a shortened form of Ẹgbẹrindinlogun.

OGBE - (I)ROSUN - 5

A-pa-(o)ri   awo   Ẹgba, Ọṣọṣọ-n(i)-irun-agbọn   awo
"One:who-be:bald-head" secret (of) Ẹgba, "Pointed-at-hair-(of)-chin" secret

Ẹsa Abaṣoṣo   ori rari-rari   awo   ode-(I)jẹbu
(of) Ẹsa, "Tuft:of:hair (of) head too:big-too:big" secret (of) outside-(of)-Ijẹbu (be)

a   da   fun Ololo-l(i)-ohun   ti   i-ṣ(e)-ọkọ   ọbuntun. Nwọn ni
who cast for Quavering-at-voice that to-make-husband (of) bride.   They say

ki   Ololo-l(i)-ohun   ru-(ẹ)bọ   ki   aya rẹ wundia   ita   ma
should Quavering-at-voice offer-sacrifice that wife his maiden (of) square not

ba   ku, ki   gbogbo iṣẹ   ati   wahala   e-l(i)-eyi   l(i)-ori
should die, that all   work and difficulty (of) one:who-be-this at-head (of)

obinrin na ma ba   gbe.   Igiripa   obukọ kan ẹgbafa   ada
woman the not should be:lost. Full:grown he-goat one, 12,000 (cowries), cutlass

ọwọ rẹ, ati aṣọ   ara rẹ ni ẹbọ.   Ifa ni ki   e-l(i)-eyi
(of) hand his, and cloth (of) body his be sacrifice. Ifa say should one:who-be-this

ru-(ẹ)bọ   nitori   aya rẹ a-fẹ-s(i)-ọna   kan ki   o   ma ba
offer-sacrifice because (of) wife his to-love-to-road one that she not should

di   ati gbe n(i)-iyawo   ki   iku   ma de   ki   owo   ọkọ
become to take at-junior:wife, that death not arrive that cowries (of) husband

si   di   egbe.
and become loss.

N(i)-igba-ti Ololo-l(i)-ohun   gbọ ẹbọ   ko ru-(ẹ)bọ,   ko l(i)-
At-time-that Quavering-at-voice hear sacrifice not offer-sacrifice, not at-

ọjọ ko l(i)-oṣu   aya   Ololo-l(i)-ohun,   a-fẹ-s(i)-ọna   ko   igba
day not at-month, wife (of) Quavering-at-voice, to-love-to-road, gather calabash

o   da   ori kọ   odo lọ fọ   ko si mọ   pe   ni ọjọ na gan
she turn head turn:toward river go wash (them) not and know that at day the iden-

ni awọn Irun-(i)mọlẹ ati awọn Egun   nti   ọrun bọ   wa   si aiye.
tical be those 400-Deity   and those Egungun leaving sky   come come to earth.

N(i)-igba-ti awọn ba   ni odo   nwọn bẹrẹ si ki   bayi pe:
At-time-that they meet (her) at river they begin to greet (her) thus that:

Ọbuntun, o   ma   ku   odo yi,
"Bride,   you (continuative) be:greeted (of) river this,

Ṣ(e)-ọmu   lẹ-lẹ,   ṣ(e)-ọmu   lẹ-lẹ-lẹ;
"Make-breast sway-sway, make-breat sway-sway-sway;

O   ba   f(i)-igba   ṣ(e)-omi   ko mi,
"You should take-calabash make-water for me,

Ṣ(e)-ọmu   lẹ-lẹ,   ṣ(e)-ọmu   lẹ-lẹ-lẹ;
"Make-breast sway-sway, make-breast sway-sway-sway;

T(i)-igba   t(i)-igba   gbunrun ngundun,
"That-(of)-calabash that-(of)-calabash, gbunrun ngundun,

7 - 5

"Bald headed one," the diviner of the Ẹgba;[1] "Pointed beard," the diviner of the town of Ẹsa; and "Too big a tuft of hair[2] on the head," the diviner of the town of Ijẹbu Ode were the ones who cast Ifa for "Quavering voice,"[3] who was engaged to be married.[4] They said that "Quavering voice" should sacrifice lest his bride-to-be should die and all the work and the difficulties he had been through because of her[5] be lost. One full-grown he-goat, three shillings, the cutlass from his hand, and the cloth from his body was the sacrifice. Ifa says this person should make a sacrifice because of his bride-to-be, that death should not come to her just as she is about to become his wife, and the money he has given as bridewealth be lost.

When "Quavering voice" heard the sacrifice, he did not make it. Shortly afterward his bride-to-be took her calabashes and went to the river to wash them; she did not know that on that very day the Four Hundred Deities and the Egungun[6] were coming to the earth from heaven. When they met her at the river, they began to greet her thus:

"Bride, greetings of the river,[7]
"Make your breasts quiver, make your breasts quiver;
"Dip me some water with your calabash,
"Make your breasts quiver, make your breasts quiver;
"With your calabash, with your calabash, 'gbunrun ngundun,'[8]

---

1. A Yoruba subgroup.

2. A type of hairdress in which the hair is tied into a tuft or knot. The messengers (Ilari) of the chief of the town of Igana, for example, dress their hair in this fashion.

3. Ololo is the sound that this man made when he tried to talk.

4. After an agreement of marriage has been made, and until the groom has fulfilled his obligations to the prospective father-in-law and the bride comes to live with him, the bride is known commonly as iyaw(o)-ọna, or junior:wife-(of)-road, indicating that she does not yet live with her husband. In this verse the terms ọbuntun, wundia ita, and aya a-fẹ-s(i)-ọna appear, all of which mean the same thing.

5. This refers primarily to the work done by a man for his prospective father-in-law, and his difficulties in raising the bridewealth.

6. The Egungun are a group of deities represented by costumes which completely conceal the body of the wearer. Often referred to as "masquerades," some types of Egungun costumes have masks; others do not. One type of Egungun (alagọ) is made in honor of a relative who has recently died. (See Bascom, 1944: 48-59). Like other deities, the Egungun receive sacrifices and they can grant children. Cf. verse 52-4.

7. The Yoruba have a large number of similar greetings: greetings of the house, greetings of the farm, greetings of work. These mean, I greet you at the river, at home, at the farm, at your work, etc.

8. This represents the sound made when swallowing the water.

Ṣ(e)-ọmu   lẹ-lẹ   ṣ(e)-ọmu   lẹ-lẹ-lẹ.
"Make-breast sway-sway, make-breast sway-sway-sway."

Bayi ni o   bẹrẹ si fi   igba   bu omi   fun ẹni-(ọ)k(an)-ọkan n(i)-inu
Thus be she begin to take calabash dip water for person-one-one   at-belly

awọn Egun   nwọn-yi ti Egun   na si nmu   omi ti o   si
(of) those Egungun those-this that Egungun the and drinking water that they and

ngbe igba   mi   pẹlu   titi gbogbo igba   ti   ọmọ-(o)binrin
taking calabash swallow together:with until all   calabash that child-woman

yi ko   wa   si odo wa fọ   fi tan.   N(i)-igba-ti o kan
this gather come to river come wash (them) take finish. At-time-that it touch

o-l(i)-ori   awọn Egun   nwọn-yi ori rẹ si fẹrẹ   to   igba,
one:who-be-head (of) those Egungun those-this, head his and almost equal 200,

o bẹrẹ si wi-pe:
he begin to say-that:

Ọbuntun o   ma   ku   odo yi,
"Bride   you (continuative) be:greeted (of) river this,

Ṣ(e)-ọmu   lẹ-lẹ,   ṣ(e)-ọmu   lẹ-lẹ-lẹ;
"Make-breast sway-sway, make-breast sway-sway-sway;

O   ba   f(i)-igba   ṣ(e)-omi   ko mi,
"You should take-calabash make-water for me,

Ṣ(e)-ọmu   lẹ-lẹ,   ṣ(e)-ọmu   lẹ-lẹ-lẹ;
"Make-breast sway-sway, make-breast sway-sway-sway;

T(i)-igba   t(i)-igba   gbunrun ngundun,
"That-(of)-calabash that-(of)-calabash 'gbunrun ngundun,'

Ṣ(e)-ọmu   lẹ-lẹ,   ṣ(e)-ọmu   lẹ-lẹ-lẹ.
"Make-breast sway-sway, make-breast sway-sway-sway."

Ọmọ-(o)binrin yi ni igba   tan, Egun yi da-(o)hun o ni:
Child-woman this say calabash finish; Egungun this break-voice he say:

O   ba   f(i)-ọwọ ṣ(e)-omi   ko mi,
"You should take-hand make-water for me,

Ṣ(e)-ọmu   lẹ-lẹ,   ṣ(e)-ọmu   lẹ-lẹ-lẹ;
"Make-breast sway-sway, make-breast sway-sway-sway;

T(i)-ọwọ   t(i)-ọwọ   gbunrun ngundun,
"That-(of)-hand that-(of)-hand 'gbunrun ngundun,'

Ṣ(e)-ọmu   lẹ-lẹ,   ṣ(e)-ọmu   lẹ-lẹ-lẹ.
"Make-breast sway-sway, make-breast sway-sway-sway."

Bi ọmọ-(o)binrin yi ti   fi   ọwọ bu omi fun Egun   yi o si gbe-
As child-woman this have take hand dip water for Egungun this he and take-

mi,   nwọn si nba   ọna ti-wọn   lọ. N(i)-igba-ti iya
swallow (her), they and joining road that-(of)-their go. At-time-that mother (of)

ọmọ-(o)binrin yi gbọ ni ile   o   yọ   apasa   o si gbati awọn
child-woman this hear at house she pull:out sword (of loom) she and follow those

"Make your breasts quiver, make your breasts quiver."

So she began to dip water with her calabashes for each one of the Egungun, and the Egungun were drinking the water and swallowing the calabashes with it until all the calabashes that the girl had brought to the river to wash were gone. When it became the turn of the chief of the Egungun, whose heads numbered almost two hundred, he began to say:

"Bride, greetings of the river,
"Make your breasts quiver, make your breasts quiver;
"Dip me some water with your calabash,
"Make your breasts quiver, make your breasts quiver;
"With your calabash, with your calabash, 'gbunrun ngundun,'
"Make your breasts quiver, make your breasts quiver."

The girl said that the calabashes were gone; the Egungun answered:

"Dip me some water with your hands,
"Make your breasts quiver, make your breasts quiver;
"With your hands, with your hands, 'gbunrun ngundun,"
"Make your breasts quiver, make your breasts quiver."

As the girl dipped water for the Egungun with her hands, he swallowed her, and the Egungun went on their way. When the girl's mother at home heard what had happened, she took the sword[9] from her loom and set out after the

---

9. The wooden piece used to beat up the weft threads on the vertical looms on which women weave.

Egungun na n(i)-igba-ti o   ba   wǫn o   bęrę si kǫ-(o)rin pe:
Egungun the; at-time-that she meet them she begin to sing-song that:

           Ęyin l(i)-ę   gb(e)-ǫmǫ mi j(ę)-ǫmǫ,
           "You be-who take-child my eat-child,

           Ij(ę)-ǫmǫ, ij(ę)-ǫmǫ   ǫrangun,
           "Eat-child, eat-child (of) Qrangun";

awǫn ti   ǫ   ba   kan   a   si da-(o)hun   pe:
those that she should touch they and break-voice that:

           Awa ko l(i)-a   gb(e)-ǫmǫ rę,
           "We not be-who take-child your,

           Ij(ę)-ǫmǫ   ǫrangun
           "Eat-child (of) Qrangun."

Bayi ni o   nbere ti   o   si npa   gbogbo awǫn Egun   ti   o ba   kan
Thus be she asking that she and killing all   those Egungun that it should touch

titi o fi ba   o-l(i)-ori   wǫn; n(i)-igba-ti o ba   o si
until she take meet one:who-be-head their; at-time-that she meet (him) she and

bere b(i)-akan-na l(i)-ǫwǫ rę; o-l(i)-ori   wǫn si da-(o)hun   pe:
ask like-one-the at-hand his; one:who-be-head their and break-voice that:

           Emi l(i)-o   gb(e)-ǫmǫ rę,
           "I   be-who take-child your,

           Ij(ę)-ǫmǫ   ǫrangun.
           "Eat-child (of) Qrangun."

     Nwǫn si fi   ija p(e)-ęta   titi obinrin yi fi   bę gbogbo ori
     They and take fight call-three until woman this take cut all   head (of)

o-l(i)-ori   wǫn yi   tan   ti   o si şubu lu-(i)lę   şugbǫn n(i)-igba-
one:who-be-head their this finish that he and fall strike-ground, but   at-time-

ti a   la   inu   Egun yi wo   ti nwǫn ma   ba   ǫmǫ
that they open belly (of) Egungun this look:at that they (continuative) meet child

yi o   ti   ku.
this she have die.

     Ifa ni ki   ǫkunrin kan ru-(ę)bǫ   ki iyawo   rę a-fę-s(i)-ǫna
     Ifa say should man   one offer-sacrifice that junior:wife his to-love-to-road

ma ba   ku ki owo   ti o şe le   l(i)-ori ma ba   di   egbe.
not should die that cowries that he do upon (her) at-head not should become loss.

Ki   a   si tun ru-(ę)bǫ   fun ǫmǫ-(o)binrin kan ki o   ma ba   ku
Should we and then offer-sacrifice for child-woman one that she not should die

ni ǫjǫ   ǫdun gan.
at day (of) year identical.

Egungun. When she caught up with them she began to sing:

> "You are the ones who took my child and ate her,
> "And ate her, who ate the child of Qrangun.[10]

Each one that she came to answered:

> "We are not the ones who took your child,
> "Who ate the child of Qrangun."

Thus she questioned all the Egungun that she came to and killed them one by one, until she came to their chief. When she met him, she asked him the same question; the chief of the Egungun answered:

> "I am the one who took your child,
> "Who ate the child of Qrangun."

They fought and fought until the woman had cut off all the heads of the chief Egungun, and he fell to the ground. But when·this Egungun was cut open, they found that the child was already dead.[11]

Ifa says a man should sacrifice that his bride-to-be should not die and the money that he has spent upon her become a loss. And then we should sacrifice for a girl lest she die during this very year.

----

10. The title of the king of the town of Ila, which is about 60 miles northeast of Ifę.

11. This is reminiscent of many African tales in which a monster is cut open, and the persons he has swallowed are released. While in this case his victim is dead, it is significant that they looked to see. With the tale ending in this way, the prediction of the diviners is fulfilled.

OGBE - (O)GUNDA[1] - 1

Akin ǫmǫ   ǫ-1(i)-ǫfin,   Awurẹ   ǫmǫ   ǫ-1(i)-
Hero child (of) one:who-has-palace; Unassuming child (of) one:who-has-

ǫfin.   Akin mba   Awurẹ   ja   o si fa   ni oko tu,   1(i)-ẹhin-
palace. Hero joining Unassuming fight he and pull (him) at penis loosen, at-back-

na o le   Awurẹ   si oko n(i)-igba-ti nwǫn fi   jẹ ǫba; n(i)-igba-
the he chase Unassuming to farm at-time-that they take (Hero) eat king; at-time-

ti o le   lǫ si oko o fi   obinrin akiriboto kan ran-(i)ṣẹ   si
that he chase (him) go to farm he take woman akiriboto one send-message to (him)

ni oko   awǫn mej(i)-(m)eji si ngbe   inu   igbo, nwǫn nṣe iṣẹ wǫn,
at farm; those two-two   and dwelling:at belly (of) forest, they doing work their,

nwǫn si jẹ-(oh)un   ni oko.
they and eating-thing at farm.

   Ni ǫjǫ kan oriṣa nti   iranje   ile   lǫ si iranje   oko, ebi   n-
   At day one Orisha leaving iranje (of) house go to iranje (of) farm, hunger it-

si npa,   bi o ti   nlǫ o ngbǫ   ohun   awǫn mej(i)-(m)eji ti
and killing (him); as he have going he hearing voice (of) those two-two   that

nwǫn nṣ(ǫ)-ǫrǫ   n(i)-ibi-ti   nwǫn gbe fẹ gun iyan.   Oriṣa
they speaking-word at-place-that they take want pound pounded:yam. Orisha

si pa-(a)tẹ   si wǫn popo. N(i)-igba-ti nwǫn p(o)-oju w(o)-ẹhin   ti nwǫn
and clap-palm to them 'popo.' At-time-that they turn-eye look:at-back that they

ri oriṣa nwǫn ni pa-(ẹ)nu   mǫ   titi ti nwǫn fi   gun   iyan
see Orisha they and kill-mouth against until that they take pound pounded:yam

tan,   bẹ-ni iyan   ai-fǫ   ni oriṣa jẹ.
finish, so-be pounded:yam not-speak be Orisha eat.

   N(i)-igba-ti nwǫn gun iyan   tan,   nwǫn ko   fun oriṣa;
   At-time-that they pound pounded:yam finish, they gather (them) give Orisha;

o jẹ o yo;   n(i)-igba-ti o yo   tan,   o bi nwǫn lere ohun
he eat he be:satisfied; at-time-that he be:satisfied finish, he ask them (2) thing

ti nwǫn nṣe ni arin   igbo. Awurẹ   si da-(o)hun   pe, n(i)-igba-
that they doing at middle (of) forest. Unassuming and break-voice that at-time-

ti o pẹlu   aburo   on nja   ni o fa   1(i)-oko tu
that he together:with younger:sibling his fighting be he pull (him) at-penis loosen

ti o si le   on si oko ti on si fi   obinrin akiriboto ran-(i)ṣẹ
that he and chase him to farm that he and take woman akiriboto send-message

---

   1. Also known as Ogbe yǫ-(i)nu (Ogbe melt-belly), "Ogbe calms our anger."
The implication is that the prediction in store for one for whom this figure is
cast will put him at ease and calm him down.
   2. Bi . . . lere means "ask."

9 - 1

Hero, child of the king; Unassuming,[1] child of the king. Hero was fighting with Unassuming, and he pulled off his penis. Afterward when they made Hero king, he chased Unassuming to the farm. When he drove him away, he sent a woman with a constricted vagina[2] to him. They both lived in the forest, working and eating in the farm.

One day the God of Whiteness was going from Iranje of the house to Iranje[3] of the farm, and he was hungry. As he walked along, he heard these two talking where they were getting ready to pound yams. The God of Whiteness clapped his hands 'popo.'[4] When they looked behind them and saw the God of Whiteness, they kept their mouths closed until they had finished pounding the yams. In this way the God of Whiteness had 'speechless yams'[5] to eat.

When they had finished pounding the yams, they gave them to the God of Whiteness and he ate until he was satisfied. When he had eaten his fill, he asked them what they were doing in the middle of the forest. Unassuming explained that when they were fighting, his younger brother had pulled off his penis and had driven him to the forest and had sent him this woman with the constricted vagina.

---

1. Awurę is an abbreviation of Awurętętę, which appears later in the verse. It means a man who goes about his work quietly without making a fuss and without boasting about what he is doing, but who nevertheless does his work surely and well. Others may call him a lazy man, a fool, or 'a farmer,' but he is really the wisest and most competent of them all.

Note that the form of this verse is unusual in that it starts directly by naming the characters of the tale. There is no dialogue with Qrunmila, and no citing of a precedent divination.

2. A woman described as being able to urinate, but not to have sexual intercourse, possibly because of excessive scar tissue forming after clitoridectomy.

3. The meaning of Iranje could not be explained by informants, but it is named in another verse as the place Qbatala Qshęrę-Igbo came from (Epega, n.d.: XIII, 2). Although identified only as Orisha, it is to be understood that this deity is Orishala or Qbatala, the God of Whiteness, who fashions the human form within the mother's womb by opening the eyes, mouth, nose, and ears, and by separating the arms, legs, toes, and fingers much as a woodcarver does when making a figurine. He is also credited with fashioning the first humans, male and female, in a similar manner. Albinos, hunchbacks, cripples, children with six toes or six fingers, and individuals with other deformities are sacred to him. Cf. Chapter XI and n. 3, verse 5-1. Snails and one of his tabus are mentioned in this verse.

4. Popo is the sound made when the hands are clapped.

5. It is a tabu for Orishala to eat yams which have not been prepared in silence.

si on.   Oriṣa ṣọ   fun wọn pe o nlọ,   ki   nwọn ki   o   wa   igbin
to him. Orisha speak for them that he going, should they should they seek snail

(ọ)k(an)-ọkan de   on.
one-one   wait:for him.

     N(i)-igba-ti oriṣa de,   o mu igbin kan, o ni ki   ọkunrin bọ
     At-time-that Orisha arrive, he take snail one, he say should man   take:off

aṣọ rẹ s(i)-ilẹ   ki   o si la-(i)tan   rẹ. N(i)-igba-ti o ṣe bẹ tan,
cloth his to-ground should he and open-thigh his. At-time-that he do so finish,

oriṣa ṣe   ha si igbin na. O si yọ.   O si mu   o ju   mọ
Orisha make 'ha' to snail the. It and appear. He and take (it) he throw (it) against

          ni abẹ.   O tun sẹ bẹ na   fun obinrin pẹlu,   ti-rẹ   na
(him) at bottom. He then do so also for woman together:with, that-(of)-hers the

si duro mọ   ni abẹ.   O si sọ   fun wọn pe ki   wọn ki
and stand against (her) at bottom. He and speak for them that should they should

o   lọ ma   sun ti   ara wọn bi ti   at(i)-ẹhin wa.
they go (continuative) sleep against body their as that (of) from-back come.

     N(i)-igba-ti o di   oru bi nwọn ti   sun, ni igbin ti   abẹ
     At-time-that it become night as they have sleep, be snail that (of) bottom

ọkunrin ran   mọ   ti   obinrin ti o ti la-(ẹ)nu   o si bọ
(of) man   fasten against that (of) woman that it have open-mouth, it and enter

s(i)-inu rẹ.   Ko l(i)-ọjọ ko l(i)-oṣu inu   obinrin bẹrẹ si ga,   oyun
to-belly hers. Not at-day not at-month belly (of) woman begin to be:high; preg-

      de.   Awọn enia ti o ri wọn wa   nsọ   fun ọba na pe
nancy arrive. Those people that they see them come speaking for king the that

obinrin yi   l(i)-oyun   ṣugbọn o j(ẹ)-iyan   o ni ko le   ri bẹ. N(i)-
woman this have-pregnancy but   he eat-dispute he say not be:able see so. At-

igba-ti o si bi,   nwọn tun wa   sọ   fun   ṣugbọn ko gba   wọn
time-that she and bear, they then come speak for (him) but   not accept them

gbọ. N(i)-igba-ti o tun l(i)-oyun   l(i)-ẹkeji nwọn tun wa   sọ
hear. At-time-that she then have-pregnancy at-second, they then come speak

fun.   O wa da-(o)hun o ni bi o ba   ri bẹ iṣe ni ki   nwọn
for (him). He come break-voice he say if he should see so make be should they

wọ   on lu-(i)lẹ   lati ori   opo ti on joko   le   yi, ki
drag him strike-ground from head (of) dais that he sit:down upon (it) this, should

nwọn ki   o   si bẹ on l(i)-ori. Awọn ara   ilu ran-(i)ṣẹ   pe
they should they and cut him at-head. Those people (of) town send-message call

obinrin yi ati Awurẹ.   N(i)-igba-ti o de   gbogbo ilu pe
woman this and Unassuming. At-time-that they arrive all   town assemble

o si joko.   Bi Akin, ọba ọ-l(i)-ọfin,   ti ri ti obinrin yi
they and sit:down. As Hero, king one:who-has-palace, have see that woman this

dide ti o fẹ lọ tọ,   o dide o fẹ sa wọ ile.   Awọn ara
arise that she want go urinate, he arise he want run enter house. Those people

The God of Whiteness told them that he was going away, but that they should each find a snail and keep it until he returned.

When the God of Whiteness came back, he took one of the snails. He told the man to take off his clothes and spread his legs. When the man had done this, the God of Whiteness said "Ha!" to the snail. It came out of its shell, and he threw it against the man's groin. Then he did the same for the woman, and her snail stuck to her groin. He told them to go and sleep together as they had done before.

When night fell and they were asleep, the snail from the man's groin fastened itself against the woman's snail, which had opened its mouth, and it entered the woman's belly. Soon afterward the woman's belly began to swell; she became pregnant. The people who saw these two came and told the king that this woman was pregnant, but he contradicted them, saying it could not be so. When she gave birth to her child, they came and told him again, but he would not believe them. When she became pregnant for a second time, they again came to tell him. He replied that if he should ever see this happen, they should drag him from the throne[6] upon which he was sitting and cut off his head. The townspeople sent word to this woman and to Unassuming to come. When they arrived, the whole town assembled and sat down before the king. When Hero, the king, saw this woman get up to go to urinate, he saw that she was pregnant; he got up, too, and tried to run into the house. But the people

---

6. A raised platform of mud, or dais, upon which a chief or a king sits. The raised mud sleeping platforms are the same in construction, and are known by the same name.

ilu   rę fa   lu-(i)lę   nwǫn si bę   l(i)-ori.
(of) town his pull (him) strike-ground they and cut (him) at-head.

Para-para gbi n(i)-ilę   l(i)-a gbǫ;
"Loud-loud gbi at-ground be-we hear;

A-ki   igbǫ pęlę-pęlę gbi;
"We-not hear soft-soft gbi;

Ęhin-(ę)kun-(i)le   Awurętętę l(i)-a ti   wǫ para-para lǫ;
"Back-door-(of)-house (of) Unassuming be-we have drag loud-loud go;

Ǫrunmila ni o ni a   şe pęlę-pęlę fi iwa   jin-(ę)ni;
"Ǫrunmila say he be who do soft-soft take destiny give-person";

Ifa ni ki   a ma-şe ja   ki   ǫkunrin-kan ru-(ę)bǫ   ki ara
Ifa say should we not-do fight, should man-one   offer-sacrifice that people

ile   rę ma ba   şe   ni ijamba ni ibi   ija.   Oko   nda
(of) house his not should do (him) at injury at evil (of) fight. Penis causing

ęni-kan   ni-(ǫ)jǫ ǫmǫ si nda   ęni-kan   ni amu.   Ki   o ru-
person-one at-day, child and causing person-one at trouble. Should he offer-

(ę)bǫ   si orişa kan ki   orişa na ki   fi ǫmǫ ta l(i)-ǫrę. Igiripa
sacrifice to orisha one that orisha the should take child sell at-gift.   Full:grown

obukǫ ati akikǫ-(a)dię (ti   ǫkunrin); ewurę kan ati ęrindilogun
he:goat and cock-chicken [that (of) man];   she:goat one and 32,000   (cowries)

(ti   obinrin).
[that (of) woman].

OGBE - (O)GUNDA - 2

Kukunduku, pętęnlęki, igbado   ęgbęrin,   ęgbęrin igbado   a
"Yam;   pętęnlęki; corn   (of) 800   (cowries); 800   corn" (be) who

da   fun Oluogodo ǫmǫ   Ękunlempe a   le   Elu   w(ǫ)-ǫya   ǫmǫ
cast for Oluogodo child (of) "Ękunlempe who chase Stranger enter-Niger," child

a   f(i)-odi   ǫkǫ tę-(i)lę   mǫraganniganni. Nwǫn
(of) "One:who take-wrong:side (of) spear press-ground 'mǫraganniganni.'" They

ni ki   o wa   ru-(ę)bǫ   nwǫn ni ara rę ko ya, nwǫn ni ni ǫdun
say should he come offer-sacrifice they say body his not heal, they say at year

yi   ni ara rę (yi)o ya. Akikǫ-(a)dię męfa ati ęgbafa.   Oluogodo
this be body his will heal. Cock-chicken six   and 12,000 (cowries). Oluogodo

ru-(ę)bǫ.
offer-sacrifice.

Oluogodo ma   de   ǫmǫ   Ękunlempe o,
"Oluogodo indeed arrive, child (of) Ękunlempe, oh,

of his town pulled him to the ground and cut off his head.

"What we hear is the sound of people doing things loudly;[7]
"We do not hear the sound of people who do things quietly;
"We drag the one who does things loudly to Unassuming's door;[8]
"Orunmila says he does things quietly when he gives someone his destiny."[9]

Ifa says we must not fight. A man should sacrifice so that his relatives will not injure him during a fight. And someone's penis is setting his dates for him,[10] and he is troubled because he has no children. He should sacrifice to a deity so that the deity may give him a child. The sacrifice is a full-grown he-goat and a cock (for a man); and a she-goat and eight shillings[11] (for a woman).

---

7. The word "gbi" was said to mean the sound of someone doing something.

8. To have him pronounce judgment on his offense. The meaning of this, like that of a proverb, is extended far beyond the literal meaning of the words themselves. The implication is that the unassuming man may be committing the same offense as the man whose case he is called upon to judge; but that since he does it quietly without boasting and publicity, others do not know about it and do not attempt to interfere.

9. That is, a person may receive aid from Orunmila without even knowing what has happened.

10. He cannot have sexual relations regularly. Cf. verse 20-2.

11. Erindilogun is a shortened form of erindinlogun.

---

9 - 2

"Yam; petenleki;[1] two pence four oninis worth of corn; 800 kernels of corn" was the one who cast Ifa for Oluogodo, the child of "Ekunlempe[2] who chased the foreigner into the Niger River," child of "He uses the other end of his spear as a walking stick 'moraganniganni.'"[3] They said he should come and make a sacrifice. They said his body was not healing; they said it would heal during that year. The sacrifice was six cocks and three shillings; Oluogodo made the sacrifice.

"Oluogodo did arrive, child of Ekunlempe, oh,

---

1. Informants suggested that this may be the name or title of a type of yam.

2. The informant could not explain or identify Oluogodo or Ekunlempe. However, later work with worshipers of Boromun and Sopona made it clear that Olu Ogodo means "Lord of Yaws" and refers to Boromun, the Goddess of Yaws. Ekunl(i)-Empe, meaning "Leopard at Empe" refers to Sopona, the God of Smallpox, whose town is said to be Empe.

3. Moraganniganni describes the motion of a person using a walking stick.

Igi   nda   gba   ara   nya.
"Tree breaking 'gba,' body healing."

Ifa ni   ara   ęni-kan   ko ya.   Ifa ni   ara oluwarę   yio
Ifa say body (of) person-one not heal. Ifa say body person:in:question will

ya   bi o   ba   le   ru-(ę)bǫ.
heal if   he should be:able offer-sacrifice.

OGBE - (O)GUNDA - 3

Mo y(i)-aiye   ka   l(i)-awo   Ęgba, Ǫna ni mo rin   rin   rin   titi
"I   turn-earth around" be-secret (of) Ęgba; "Road be I   walk walk walk until

ti   mo de-(I)jębu   mura,   ogborogan n(i)-(i)da, n(i)-ibi-ti   nwǫn gbe nfi
that I   arrive-Ijębu remote, broad   at-sword," at-place-that they take taking

oj(umǫ)-ojumǫ sun-(ę)kun   aje.   Nwǫn ni nwǫn yio ni   aje   l(i)-ǫwǫ;
dawn-dawn   shed-tears (of) money. They say they will have money at-hand;

ęiyę-(i)le   męrin,   ęfun   ado   lǫpǫ-lǫpǫ,   ęgbarin.   Nwǫn
bird-(of)-house four,   chalk (of) Benin much-much,   8000   (cowries). They

ru-(ę)bǫ.   Nwǫn bęrę si ni   aje.
offer-sacrifice. They begin to have money.

Ifa ni   e-l(i)-eyi   yio ni   aje   l(i)-ǫwǫ pupǫ. Owo   de
Ifa say one:who-be-this will have money at-hand much.   Cowries arrive

şugbǫn ki   o   ru-(ę)bǫ.
but   should he offer-sacrifice.

OGBE - (I)KA - 1

Ailę   lę   a tę-(ę)ni,   ojumǫ mǫ a ka-(ę)ni, a-
"Evening become:dark we spread-mat, dawn   clear we roll-mat; one:who-

da-(o)wu ni   po-yi   ręrę   ka-(i)lę,   oku   l(i)-o ku ni
cast-cotton be (he) turn-turn back:and:forth around-ground; corpse be-he die be

a   gbę-(i)lę   l(i)-o jin   gbun-gbun l(i)-oju   ojo   a   da   fun
we dig-ground be-it be:deep down-down at-eye (of) coward" (be) who cast for

Ǫrunmila n(i)-ǫjǫ ti   o   nş(e)-awo   r(e)-ode   Ika. Nwǫn ni ki   o
Ǫrunmila at-day   that he making-secret go-outside (of) Ika. They say should he

ru-(ę)bǫ   ǫbę-gbaguda kan ti   o   wa   n(i)-inu   akǫ,   iwǫ
offer-sacrifice (of) knife-gbaguda one that it exist at-belly (of) sheath, fallen

obi ai-la,   ayebǫ adię   meji, eku meji, ęja meji, ati egbejilelogun
kola not-open, hen   chicken two, rat two, fish two, and 4400   (cowries)

"Wood breaks 'gba,'[4] his body is healing."

Ifa says someone's body will heal if he can make a sacrifice.

---

4. Gba is the sound made when wood breaks. This is said to mean that the person will get well as quickly as wood breaks.

---

9 - 3

"I go around the world," the diviner of the Ẹgba, and "I walk and walk and walk along the road until I come to remote Ijẹbu,[1] broad at sword" (were the ones who cast Ifa for them)[2] where they were weeping every day because they did not have money. They said they would have money. Four pigeons, lots of chalk from Benin, and two shillings was the sacrifice. They made the sacrifice; and they began to have money.

Ifa says this person will have lots of money. Money is coming, but he should make a sacrifice.

---

1. The Ẹgba and Ijẹbu are Yoruba subgroups.
2. This is omitted from the Yoruba text, and the people are not identified. This would seem to indicate that the verse is incomplete.

---

14 - 1

"Night falls and we spread our sleeping mats, day breaks and we roll them up; one who lays the warp threads must walk back and forth;[1] when someone dies, we dig a hole that is very, very deep in the eyes of a coward" was the one who cast Ifa for Ọrunmila when he was going to Ika[2] to divine. They said he should sacrifice one gbaguda knife[3] with its sheath, some fallen kola[4] still in the pod, two hens, two rats, two fish, and one shilling one penny two oninis

---

1. The warp threads for the men's horizontal looms are laid out by running them around stakes stuck into the ground in two parallel lines in a manner that makes it possible to lay a warp several hundred yards long in a fairly small area. The weaver must walk back and forth between the lines of stakes, winding the warp thread about two adjacent stakes in each line each time.
2. Ika here is the name of a town; note the reference to the name of the figure, Ogbe Ika.
3. A small knife with a straight blade.
4. Kola nuts which had not been picked from the tree, but which had become ripe enough to fall to the ground by themselves.

nitori   ki   nwǫn ma ba   mu   ni ole ni ibi-ti   o nlǫ.   Qrunmila
because that they not should take(him) at thief at place-that he going. Qrunmila

ni o di   abǫ   ki   o to   wa   ru   ębǫ   na. Ifa ni ęni-
say it become arrival before he equal come offer sacrifice the. Ifa say person-

kan nlǫ si idalę   kan ki   o ru-(ę)bǫ   ki   a   ma ba   mu
one going to distance one should he offer-sacrifice that they not should take (him)

ni ole ni idalę   ti o nlǫ na.
at thief at distance that he going the.

   N(i)-igba-ti Qrunmila nlǫ   si ode-(I)ka,   o si tǫ   awǫn ba-
   At-time-that Qrunmila going to outside-(of)-Ika, he and approach those di-

balawo lǫ nwǫn ni ki   o ru-(ę)bǫ,   şugbǫn o ni o di   igba-ti
viner go they say should he offer-sacrifice, but   he say it become time-that

on ba   de   ki   on to   wa   ru   ębǫ   na; bi o ti nlǫ ti
he should arrive before he equal come offer sacrifice the; as he have going that

o si de   ęnu   ibode   ilu na o ri obi ti o so
he and arrive mouth (of) town:gate (of) town the he see kola that it bear:fruit

oju rę si wǫ,   o si yǫ   ǫbę gbaguda ti o wa   ni ǫwǫ rę n(i)-
eye his and enter (it), he and pull:out knife gbaguda that it exist at hand his at-

inu   akǫ,   o si fi   ka   ǫkan n(i)-inu   awǫn eso   obi
belly (of) sheath, he and take (it) pluck one at-belly (of) those fruit (of) kola

nwǫn-yi bi o ti ka tan, bę-ni ęni-ti   o ni obi de   o
those-this, as he have pluck finish, so-be person-that he have kola arrive he

si fę   mu Qrunmila ni ole, şugbǫn n(i)-ibi-ti   nwǫn gbe nja   ija-
and want take Qrunmila at thief, but   at-place-that they take fighting fight-

ka-(i)di,   ti Qrunmila nfę   sa lǫ, ǫbę ti o mu dani bu
go:around-waist, that Qrunmila wanting run go, knife that he take hold cut (him)

ni atęlę-l(i)-ǫwǫ, Qrunmila si sa-lǫ.   N(i)-igba-ti Qrunmila sa-lǫ tan,
at palm-at-hand, Qrunmila and run-go. At-time-that Qrunmila run-go finish

ęni-ti   o ni obi wa s(i)-ile o si tǫ   ǫba   ilu   Ika
person-that he have kola come to-house he and approach king (of) town (of) Ika

lǫ o si sǫ   fun   pe ęni-kan   ji   on ni obi ka   şugbǫn n(i)-
go he and speak for (him) that person-one steal him at kola pluck but   at-

igba-ti o nfę   mu u o sa lǫ; nitori-na   ki   ǫba jǫwǫ   ki
time-that he wanting take him he run go; because-the should king grant:favor that

o ba   on pe awǫn ara   ilu jǫ   ati alejo ati o-n(i)-
he should he call those people (of) town be:together and visitor and one:who-has-

ile   nitori-pe   ole na wa l(i)-arin   ilu.
house because-that thief the exist at-middle (of) town.

   N(i)-igba-ti Qrunmila gbǫ eyi, ęru ba   o si tun tǫ   awǫn
   At-time-that Qrunmila hear this, fear meet (him) he and then approach those

babalawo lǫ nwǫn si sǫ   fun   pe ki   o tun wa   ru   ębǫ
diviner go they and speak for (him) that should he then come offer sacrifice

so that he would not be taken as a thief at the place to which he was going. Qrunmila said he would not make the sacrifice until he returned. Ifa says someone is
going to a distant place; he should sacrifice lest he be taken as a thief at the
place to which he is going.

When Qrunmila was going to the town of Ika, he consulted the diviners. They
said that he should make a sacrifice, but he said that he would not make the sacrifice until he came back. On his way, when he approached the town gate, he saw a
kola tree that bore fruit, and he longed to have some. He pulled the gbaguda knife
he had in his hand out of its sheath and with it cut off one of the pods of kola.[5]
Just as he had cut it down, the owner of the kola came along, and he tried to catch
Qrunmila as a thief; but while they were wrestling with each other, and Qrunmila
was trying to run away, the knife that he held cut Qrunmila on the palm of his
hand, and he escaped. After Qrunmila had run away, the owner of the kola came
home from the farm. He went to the king of Ika and told him that someone had
stolen his kola, but that when he tried to catch him, he had run away; therefore,
the king should please summon the people of the town, including both the foreigners and the townspeople, because the thief was somewhere in town.

When Qrunmila heard about this, he was frightened, and he again consulted
the diviners. They told him that he should make the sacrifice

---

5. Note that Qrunmila, who was told to sacrifice a gbaguda knife in its
sheath and fallen kola lest he be caught in the act of stealing, gets into trouble
when cutting kola from the tree (before it was ripe enough to fall) with a gbaguda
knife that had a sheath.

ti   ko ru   ki   on to   lọ ṣugbọn o ni lati   ru   ẹbọ   na ni
that not offer before he equal go but   he be in:order:to offer sacrifice the at

ilọ-po   meji-meji; Qrunmila si   ru   ẹbọ   na gẹgẹ-bi awọn babalawo
twist-turn two-two;   Qrunmila and offer sacrifice the just-as those diviner

ti   sọ   fun;   n(i)-igba-ti o ru   ẹbọ   tan,   nwọn ni ki   o
have speak for (him); at-time-that he offer sacrifice finish, they say should he

lọ fi   ọbẹ   gbaguda na gun idi   Eṣu o si   ṣe bẹ.
go take knife gbaguda the stab base (of) Eshu he and do so.

     Ki   ilẹ   to   mọ,   Eṣu ti   mu ọbẹ o si ti   fi   la
     Before ground equal clear, Eshu have take knife he and have take (it) cut

ọwọ   gbogbo awọn enia ti   o   wa   ni ilu ati oyun   inu ati
hand (of) all   those people that they exist at town and pregnancy (of) belly and

aṣẹ   idi; n(i)-igba-ti ilẹ   mọ,   ti   gbogbo ilu   pe,
menstruation (of) waist; at-time-that ground clear, that all   town assemble,

ọba   Ika sọ   fun wọn pe   ọkunrin kan ji   obi ka,   o-l(i)-obi
king (of) Ika speak for them that man   one steal kola pluck, one:who-has-kola

si ni on mọ   nitori-ti   ọbẹ bu oluwarẹ   ni ọwọ, ọba si
and say he know (him) because-that knife cut person:in:question at hand, king and

ni ki   o   ma   wa   oluwarẹ   na li arin   nwọn, bi o
say should he (continuative) seek person:in:question the at middle (of) them, as he

si ti   nrin   arin   awọn enia   ka,   o ri Qrunmila ni arin
and have walking middle (of) those people go:around, he see Qrunmila at middle

wọn o si tọ-(i)ka-si   pe   ọkunrin na ni-(e)yi; n(i)-igba-ti Qrun-
their he and point-finger-to (him) that man   the be-this; at-time-that Qrun-

mila gbọ bayi, o bere pe   kin-ni o ṣe   mọ on? O ni nitori-ti
mila hear thus, he ask   that what-be it make know him? He say because-that

ọbẹ kọ ọ   l(i)-ọwọ ni.   Qrunmila ni njẹ   ki   gbogbo enia   ki
knife cut him at-hand be (it).   Qrunmila say well:then should all   people should

o   ma   la   ọwọ wọn ati ọba ati o-l(i)-obi   pẹlu;
they (continuative) open hand their and king and one:who-has-kola together:with

     n(i)-igba-ti gbogbo   wọn la   ọwọ wọn, ila wa   ni ọwọ   gbogbo
(them); at-time-that all   (of) them open hand their, cut exist at hand (of) all

wọn pata-pata.
them completely-completely.

     N(i)-igba-ti o-l(i)-obi   ri   eyi, ẹru ba,   Qrunmila si bẹrẹ
     At-time-that one:who-have-kola see this, fear meet (him), Qrunmila and begin

si sọ-(ẹ)kun pe   nwọn d(a)-ole   mọ   on nwọn si pu-(i)rọ mọ   on; n(i)-
to shed-tears that they cause-thief against him they and tell-lie against him; at-

igba-ti Qrunmila nsọ-(ẹ)kun   Eṣu sọ   fun ọba   Ika pe Qrunmila ko
time-that Qrunmila shedding-tears Eshu speak for king (of) Ika that Qrunmila not

ma   gbọdọ sọ-(ẹ)kun, nitori-na   ki   o tete   ya-(a)ra
(continuative) must shed-tears, because-the should he quickly be:quick-body

that he had not made before he left home; but that this time he must make it two-fold. Qrunmila made the sacrifice just as the diviners had told him. When he had finished, they said that he should stick the gbaguda knife[6] into the base of Eshu; and he did so.

Before daybreak Eshu had taken the knife[7] and with it cut the hands of all the people who were in the town, including even the unborn embryos and the children still unconceived.[8] When dawn came and all the people of the town had assembled, the King of Ika told them that a man had been stealing kola; and that the owner of the kola said he would recognize him because his hand had been cut by a knife. The king told the owner of the kola to look for the thief among the people who were gathered there. As he walked about through the people, he saw Qrunmila among them and pointed his finger at him, saying, "This is the man." When Qrunmila heard this, he asked how the owner of the kola could identify him. He answered that he could identify him because the knife had cut his hand. Qrunmila said, "Well then, let everyone open his hands, including the king and the owner of the owner of the kola as well." When they opened their hands, there were scars on the hands of each and every one of them.[9]

When the owner of the kola saw this, he was frightened,[10] and Qrunmila began to cry that they had accused him of being a thief and had been telling lies about him. While Qrunmila was weeping, Eshu told the King of Ika that he must not let Qrunmila weep; therefore, he should hasten

---

6. There is an inconsistency here. Since the sacrifice was doubled by the diviners because of the postponement, there should be two gbaguda knives; but only one is mentioned.

7. The knife which Qrunmila sacrificed is thus instrumental in extricating him from his difficulties.

8. To ensure that all the people to be born in the future will have lines on their palms. Note the reference in the text to the Yoruba belief that the menstrual fluid develops into the embryo.

9. This verse thus explains how people came to have lines on the palms of their hands.

10. Because he could be charged with having accused someone falsely.

ma   bę;   gbogbo ilu bę   Qrunmila titi   şugbǫn ko fę
(continuative) request (him); all   town request Qrunmila until, but   not want

gbǫ, n(i)-igba-na ni nwǫn bere l(i)-ǫwǫ   Qrunmila pe kin-ni   yio
hear; at-time-the be they ask at-hand (of) Qrunmila that what-be (he) will

gba?   Qrunmila ni   igba-(o)hun-(i)gba-(o)hun ati ǫmǫ-(ǫ)kunrin męwa ati
accept? Qrunmila say 200-thing-200-thing   and child-man   ten   and

ǫmǫ-(o)binrin męwa ni on yio gba   l(i)-ǫwǫ wǫn, ǫba   Ika si ko   gbo-
child-woman ten   be he will accept at-hand their; king (of) Ika and gather all

gbo nwǫn fun.   N(i)-igba-ti o gba   wǫn tan ti o ko   wǫn
        them give (him). At-time-that he accept them finish that he gather them

de   ile   ni o ba   bęrę si jo   ti o nyǫ   o si nkǫ-(o)rin
arrive house be he should begin to dance that he rejoicing he and singing-song

pe:
that:

> O şoko;   bani!
> "Oh shoko." "Bani!"

> Ojumǫ a   m(ǫ)-awo   rire o!
> "Dawn will clear-secret good, oh!

> Ojumǫ a   m(ǫ)-awo   rire,
> "Dawn will clear-secret good;

> A-ji-bǫ-wa-ba   l(i)-a ba-(i)la l(i)-ǫwǫ o!
> "To-awake-come-come-meet be-we meet-cut at-hand, oh!

> Ojumǫ a   m(ǫ)-awo   rire.
> "Dawn will clear-secret good."

OGBE - (I)KA - 2

Ęşin gb(e)-ori ga   l(i)-ogun   a   da f(un)-Awo-şa-
"Horse carry-head be:high at-war" (be) who cast for-Secret-pick:up:one:by:

(i)le-ka   ǫmǫ   Qrunmila ti o nro-(o)ko   ti o nş(e)-
one-house-go:around, child (of) Qrunmila that he hoeing-farm, that he making-

ǫdę ti o si nşe   owo   çja   tita.
hunter that he and making transaction (of) goods to:sell.

Ifa ni ęni-kan   wa ti o ję-pe   bi o ba   na-(ǫ)wǫ le işę
Ifa say person-one exist that he eat-that if he should stretch-hand upon work

kan, Ifa ko nję-ki   işę na ni   çju; Ifa nba   oluwarę   ja,
one, Ifa not consenting-that work the have eye; Ifa joining person:in:question fight,

nitori-na ki o lǫ bǫ   Ifa na ki o tǫ-(o)ju   ikin kan
because-the should he go sacrifice:to Ifa the, should he care:for-eye (of) ikin one

pęlu;   Ifa ni gbogbo ohun ti e-l(i)-eyi   ba   nfi   ǫwǫ
together:with (it); Ifa say all   things that one:who-be-this should putting hand

to beg him to stop. All the townspeople begged and begged him to stop, but he would not listen. Then they asked Qrunmila what he would take to forget what had happened. Qrunmila said he would take two hundred of every kind of goods[11] from them, and in addition ten boys and ten girls. The King of Ika gathered all these things together and gave them to Qrunmila.[12] When he had received them all, and had carried them home, he began to dance, rejoicing and singing:

"Oooooh shoko." "Bani."
"The dawn will break good for the diviner, oh!
"The dawn will break good for the diviner;
"When we wake up and come to find something, we find scars on the hand, oh!
"The dawn will break good for the diviner."

---

11. Cf. n. 7, verse 1-10.

12. Cf. the similar tale recorded by Frobenius (1926: 287-288) in which Tortoise, who replaces Qrunmila, is caught and killed.

---

14 - 2

"A horse carries his head high in battle" was the one who cast Ifa for "Diviner chooses his houses carefully," the child of Qrunmila, when he was farming, hunting, and trading in merchandise.

Ifa says there is someone whom, when he stretches his hands to do something,[1] Ifa does not allow to see his work come to a successful conclusion. Ifa is fighting with this person, therefore he should sacrifice to the Ifa and also take care of a set of palm nuts. Ifa says that he will spoil everything that this person puts his hand

---

1. That is, when he tries to do anything. Cf. verse 4-4.

le   ni on yio ma   ba   jẹ on yio si   ma   ja okun
upon be he will (continuative) spoil (it) (1), he will and (continuative) cut rope

di   l(i)-oju; afi   bi e-l(i)-eyi   ba   tọ-(o)ju   Ifa na n(i)-igba-
close at-eye; unless if one:who-be-this should care:for-eye (of) Ifa the, at-time-

na ni ọran rẹ yio to   ma   yan ori; n(i)-igba-ti gbogbo awọn
the be affair his will be:in:order (continuative) get head; at-time-that all   those

ọmọ ti   a   bi   l(i)-oju rẹ ba   ku tan   ni Ifa yio to   ma
child that they bear at-eye his should die finish be Ifa will equal (continuative)

gbe iwa   rẹ gun   bi o ba   le   tọ-(o)ju   Ifa na ki
take destiny his be:orderly if he should be:able care:for-eye (of) Ifa the should

o   ma   bọ.
he (continuative) sacrifice:to (it).

───────────────

    1. Ba . . . jẹ means "spoil."

──────────────────────────────

OGBE - (I)KA - 3

    Ogbe k(i)-a-re-(i)le   ọmọ   ọṣin ọmọ   ọrun, ọmọ   O-
    "Ogbe that-we-go-house," child (of) king, child (of) altar; child (of) "One:who-

l(i)-Ogun   rẹrẹ   alede   a   da   fun Qrunmila n(i)-ọjọ ti   o
has-God:of:iron low   (of) outside" (be) who cast for Qrunmila at-day that he

nre-(i)le   Ijero   Qlọmọ Qfẹ. Ifa ni ẹni-kan   nfẹ   lọ si idalẹ
going-house (of) Ijero (of) Qlọmọ Qfẹ. Ifa say person-one wanting go to distance

kan n(i)-ibẹ ni Q-l(i)-ọrun   ma   fi   alubarika rẹ si;   yio
one, at-there be One:who-has-sky (continuative) take property his to (him); will

si di   ọba le   wọn l(i)-ọwọ; t(i)-ẹru   t(i)-ọmọ   ilu
and become king upon them at-hand; that-(of)-slave that-(of)-child (of) town

na bi yio ma   fi   ori ba-(i)lẹ   fun   ti nwọn yio si fi
the be will (continuative) take head touch-ground for (him) that they will and take

ori s(i)-abẹ rẹ; ṣugbọn ki   o ru-(ẹ)bọ   ẹiyẹ-(i)le   mẹrin
head to-bottom his; but   should he offer-sacrifice (of) bird-(of)-house four

ati ẹgbarin.
and 8000   (cowries).

──────────────────────────────

QYẸKU OGBE[1] - 1

    Qdẹ   ṣ(i)-apo   yọ-(o)ro,   arọnimọja tu   apo   yọ   ogun,
    "Hunter open-pouch pull:out-poison; Arọnimọja loosen pouch pull:out medicine;

agbẹ   wa ibi   rirọ-rirọ kọ iṣu si   a   da   fun Oluorogbo ti   iṣe
farmer seek place soft-soft hoe yam to" (be) who cast for Oluorogbo that make

i-kọ   aja-l(i)-aiye, a   lu-(i)kin fun Oluṣonṣo ti   iṣe i-kọ
to-hang (of) king-at-earth, who beat-ikin for Olushonsho that make to-hang (of)

to; he will break the string and clog up the beads[2] unless this person takes care of the Ifa. If he does so, then his affairs will be set in order and will reach a successful conclusion. After all the children born to him have died, Ifa will set his destiny in order, if he is able to take care of the Ifa and to sacrifice to it.

2. A metaphor for spoiling everything, based on the way in which beads are spoiled when their string breaks and sticks in the openings so that they cannot be restrung, or a pipe is spoiled when a match breaks in cleaning it, clogging up the hole so that it cannot be smoked. Cf. n. 4, verse 244-1.

14 - 3

"Ogbe that we go home,"[1] King's child, Altar's child, the child of "He worships the God of Iron beneath a low, wide-spreading tree" was the one who cast Ifa for Qrunmila on the day that he was going home to Qlǫmǫ Qfę ward in the town of Ijero.[2] Ifa says someone wants to go to a distant place; at that place the Sky God will give him many possessions and he will be king over the people there. Both the slaves and the townspeople will prostrate themselves before him and bow down before him. But he should sacrifice four pigeons and two shillings.[3]

1. It is possible that this is an alternative name for the figure Ogbe-(I)ka. Note that it is a pun on the name of this figure, and also that it implies that the client, like Qrunmila, is about to go home.
2. Informants were not certain of the meaning of either Qlǫmǫ Qfę or Ijero, but pointed out that the former is the name of a ward in the town of Ilesha, about twenty miles away. Ijero is a town east of Ilesha.
3. Since cowries are counted by the two thousand, there are four units of cowries as well as four pigeons.

17 - 1

"The hunter opens his pouch and takes out poison;[1] Arǫnimǫja loosens his pouch and takes out medicine;[2] the farmer seeks a soft piece of ground in which to plant his yams" was the one who cast Ifa for Oluorogbo, the apprentice[3] of "King on earth"[4] and who beat palm nuts for Olushonsho, the apprentice of

1. Oro (poison) is used by hunters, both as an ingredient in charms and on the tips of arrows.
2. Arǫnimǫja (or Arǫni) is a spirit living in the forest; he frequently abducts humans and either kills them or sends them back with a vast knowledge of charms and medicines. It is to this that the phrase refers. Cf. Farrow (1926: 65).
3. An apprentice carries his master's bag and runs errands for him. Cf. n. 4, verse 6-1.
4. Oluorogbo is a title of Orisha Alashę, one of the white deities. Aja is said to be a contraction of ǫ-l(i)-ǫja (one:who-has-market), the "owner of the market," and to refer to the ruler of a town; and some informants identify the "King on earth" with such rulers as the Qni of Ifę and the Alafin of Qyǫ. However

aja-1(i)-ọrun, nwọn ni bi o ba   da   ki   aiye bajẹ, Oluorogbo a   tun
king-at-sky, they say if it should cause that earth spoil, Oluorogbo will repair

aiye ṣe, bi o ba   da   ki   ọrun bajẹ Oluṣonṣo a   tun   ọrun ṣe,
earth (2), if it should cause that sky spoil, Olushonsho will repair sky (2);

Oluṣonṣo   ni orukọ ti   a   pe Ọramifẹ.
Olushonsho be name that we call Ọramfẹ.

    Ifa ni Oriṣa yio tun   aiye   ẹni   ṣe ni ọran ti   a   da   Ifa si
    Ifa say Orisha will repair earth (of) person (2) at affair that he cast Ifa to

yi.   Eku mẹrin, ẹja mẹrin, igbin mẹrin ni ẹbọ;   a-(yi)o ru-(ẹ)bọ
this. Rat four, fish four, snail four be sacrifice; we-will offer-sacrifice

tan   a-(yi)o lọ di ibo   fun Oriṣa.
finish; we-will go tie covered for Orisha.

---

    1. This figure is commonly known as Qyẹku-1(u)-Ogbe, meaning Qyẹku-
against-Ogbe. Cf. n. 1, verse 17-3.
    2. Tun . . . ṣe means "repair."

QYẸKU OGBE - 2

    Aṣedere awo   agbe   a   da fun agbe ti o nlọ gbe Olukori
    "Ashedere secret (of) Agbe" (be) who cast for Agbe that he going take Olukori

ni iyawo,   o ni bi eji nṣu   fẹrẹ bi ojo nku   giri o ni on ko
at junior:wife; he say if rain darkening 'fẹrẹ' if rain sounding 'giri' he say he not

ni ṣ(e)-ai-gbe   Olukori aya on de   ile   koko.
be make-not-take Olukori wife his arrive house entirely.

    Ifa ni aya on kan wa bi a ko ba   mu   fun on aya na yio
    Ifa say wife his one exist, if we not should take (her) give him, wife the will

ku. Ayebọ adiẹ   meji, eku meji, ẹja meji, ati ẹgbaji   ni ẹbọ;
die. Hen   chicken two, rat two, fish two, and 4000 (cowries) be sacrifice;

n(i)-igba-ti a ba   ru-(ẹ)bọ   tan   a-(yi)o lọ mu obinrin na fun
at-time-that we should offer-sacrifice finish, we-will go take woman the give

babalawo ti ibo ba   mu   pe ki   a mu obinrin na fun.
diviner   that ibo should take (him) that should we take woman the give (him).

"King in the sky."[5] They said that if it should happen that the earth should spoil, Oluorogbo will set it right again; if it should happen that heaven should spoil, Olushonsho will set it right again. Olushonsho is the name that we call Qramfẹ.

Ifa says that a deity[6] will set the world of this person right again in the matter for which he cast this figure. Four rats, four fish, and four snails is the sacrifice. We will finish making this sacrifice; then we will carry a covered offering[7] to this deity.

---

4. (Cont.) here it seems to refer to a deity, the counterpart of the Sky God, who is ruler over the earth; but no details concerning such a deity could be obtained. His association with Orisha Alashe makes it unlikely that the reference is to Ogboni, the Earth God and son of Odua.

5. Olushonsho, as this verse explains, is a title of Qramfẹ (or Qramifẹ), a God of Thunder and the Ifẹ counterpart of Shango. His name is said to mean Qra-has-Ifẹ [Qra-n(i)-Ifẹ] or "Qra owns the town of Ifẹ. "The King in the sky" was interpreted as being Q-l(i)-ọrun, the Sky God. Although some informants equate Qramfẹ with the Sky God, he is specifically described here as his messenger or apprentice.

6. Orisha does not seem to refer to Orishala here, but rather to one of his followers, Orisha Alashẹ, who is mentioned in this verse by his title Oluorogbo.

7. An ibo here is a covered offering, usually of little monetary value (cold water, kola nuts, etc.) which is carried to the deity either enclosed in a calabash with a lid (such as igbademu), or wrapped in a bag or leaf.

---

17 - 2

"Ashedere," the diviner of the Agbe bird,[1] was the one who cast Ifa for the Agbe bird when he was going to take Olukori as his wife. He said that the storm clouds might grow dark "fẹrẹ," and the rain might beat down "giri,"[2] but he still would not fail to bring home his wife.

Ifa says that this is his wife;[3] if we do not give this woman to him, she will die. Two hens, two rats, two fish, and one shilling is the sacrifice.[4] When we have completed the sacrifice, we will give the woman to a diviner who is indicated through the use of specific alternatives[5] as the one to whom the woman should be given.

---

1. Agbe is identified as "a kind of woodcock" in the CMS Dictionary, as a cockatoo by Bowen (1858), and as "the bird Blue Touraco Musophagidae, i.e. Cuckoo Family" by Abraham (1958).

2. Giri represents the sound made by rain falling heavily; fẹrẹ describes the way in which rain clouds gather.

3. That is, a "wife of Ifa." See n. 5, verse 3-4.

4. Since cowries are counted by the two thousand, there are two units of cowries, as there are two hens, rats, and fish.

5. See Chapter V.

QYẸKU OGBE - 3

Qyẹku-l(u)-ogbe   Qyẹku-l(u)-ogbe   a   da fun ọmọ ti   ko
"Qyẹku-against-Ogbe, Qyẹku-against-Ogbe" (be) who cast for "Child that not

ku ti o nya   l(i)-aye; nwọn ni ibi   ti-rẹ   ni a-(yi)o fi   agba
die that he turning at-alive"; they say if (not) that-(of)-his be we-will take elder

dida   ti   si, nwọn ni aguntan kan ati ẹgbawa   ni ẹbọ.   Q-
caused lean to, they say ewe   one and 20,000 (cowries) be sacrifice. "One:who-

l(i)-ọmọ o fi ai-ku ya l(i)-aye ni orukọ ti   a   pe ọna. Ifa ni ki
be-child he take not-die turn at-alive" be name that we call road. Ifa say should

ẹni-kan   ru-(ẹ)bọ   ki o ba   le   di   agba.
person-one offer-sacrifice that he should be:able become elder.

QYẸKU OGBE - 4

Qpa   irin ba-(i)lẹ   ha nana   a   da fun Araba ti   a   nlọ
"Staff (of) iron strike-ground 'ha nana'" (be) who cast for Araba that they going

fi   jẹ oye   oju-(i)le;   nwọn ni iṣe ni a-(yi)o ma
take (him) eat title (of) eye-(of)-house; they say make be we-will (continuative)

pe   sin.   Ifa ni ki   ẹni-kan   ru-(ẹ)bọ   nitori
assemble serve (him). Ifa say should person-one offer-sacrifice because (of)

oye ti   a   njẹ ni idile   rẹ; o ni ẹni-kan   ti iṣe ọmọ   oye
title that they eating at lineage his; he say person-one that make child (of) title

yio jẹ oye na. Agbo kan, ibo-(a)ra   aṣọ fun-fun   kan, ati ẹgbajọ
will eat title the. Ram one, cover-body cloth be:white-be:white one, and 16,000

        ni ẹbọ.
(cowries) be sacrifice.

QYẸKU MEJI[1] - 1

Agada   a b(i)-aiya   koto   a   da fun (Q)lasumogbe ti
"Wooden:sword it bear-chest (of) hole" (be) who cast for Qlasumogbe   that

o nf(i)-ẹkun   oju ṣe irahun   ọmọ. Nwọn ni ewurẹ kan, iru
she taking-tears (of) eye make moaning (of) child. They say she:goat one, tail

    ẹṣin, aṣọ kijipa   itẹ-(i)lẹ-(i)di   rẹ, ati ejielogun.
(of) horse, cloth homespun spread:on-ground-(of)-waist her, and 44,000 (cowries).

---

1. Also known as Eji Qyẹ.

17 - 3

"Qyẹku next to Ogbe, Qyẹku next to Ogbe"[1] was the one who cast Ifa for "The child that does not die but returns to life."[2] They said no one would be as old as he. They said one ewe and five shillings is the sacrifice. "The child who does not die but returns to life" is the name of Road.[3] Ifa says someone should make a sacrifice that he may be able to grow old.

_____

1. Qyẹku-l(u)-Ogbe is a commonly used alternative name for Qyẹku Ogbe.
2. Is reincarnated in another child. Cf. Bascom (1960).
3. This verse thus explains why a road "lives" for such a long time, and why it is older than human beings. Road is identified as the character for whom the precedent divination was made, and it is implied that he made the sacrifice.

_____

17 - 4

"An iron staff strikes the ground 'ha nana'"[1] was the one who cast Ifa for Araba[2] when he was going to take a title belonging to his house. They said we must assemble to serve him. Ifa says someone should make a sacrifice because of a title that is to be taken in his lineage; he says that someone who is descended from the chief will be made chief. One ram, one white cloth to cover the body, and four shillings is the sacrifice.

_____

1. The sound made by an iron staff, vibrating after its end has been struck against the ground. Cf. n. 5, verse 19-1.
2. The title of the chief priest of Ifa and highest ranking diviner.

_____

18 - 1

"Toy swords have hollow chests"[1] was the one who cast Ifa for Qlasumogbe when she was weeping and moaning because she had no child. They said she should sacrifice one she-goat, the tail of a horse, her homespun[2] underclothing, and eleven shillings.

_____

1. Agada is a toy wooden sword made for children. It is shaped like a short cutlass, and has a groove running along the length of the blade. It is to this groove that the "hollow chest" refers.
2. A type of cloth made locally of coarse, unevenly spun cotton thread, which in Lagos is looked down upon as "back-woods" or "up-country cloth," aṣọ oke (cloth of the hill).

(Ọ)lasumogbe gbọ   ẹbọ   o   ru-(ẹ)bọ.   Nwọn ni   yio bi   ọmọ-
Ọlasumogbe hear sacrifice she offer-sacrifice. They say will bear child-

(ọ)kunrin kan ati pe   ni oju rẹ   ni ọmọ na yio ṣe   jẹ oye. Ifa ni obinrin
man   one and that at eye her be child the will make eat title. Ifa say woman

kan ni-(e)yi ti   o   nwa   ọmọ bi o   ba   le   ru-(ẹ)bọ   yio bi
one be-this that she seeking child, if she should be:able offer-sacrifice will bear

ọmọ-(ọ)kunrin kan, ni oju   obinrin na ni ọmọ na yio ṣe   jẹ oye kan.
child-man   one, at eye (of) woman the be child the will make eat title one.

    N(i)-igba-ti (Ọ)lasumogbe nwa   ọmọ ti   ko ri   o   tọ
    At-time-that Ọlasumogbe   seeking child that (she) not see (it), she approach

awọn babalawo lọ nwọn sọ   fun   yio bi ọmọ ṣugbọn ki   o   ru-
those diviner go; they speak for (her) will bear child but   should she offer-

(ẹ)bọ   ati-pẹlu   pe ni oju rẹ ni ọmọ na yio ṣe   jẹ oye;
sacrifice to-together:with (this) that at eye hers be child the will make eat title;

ko l(i)-ọjọ   l(i)-oṣu (Ọ)lasumogbe l(i)-oyun   o si bi ọmọ-
not at-day (not) at-month Ọlasumogbe   have-pregnancy she and bear child-

(ọ)kunrin kan; n(i)-igba-ti o d(i)-agba   nwọn si fi   jẹ oye
man   one; at-time-that he become-elder they and take (him) eat title (of)

Ọ-l(i)-Ọsara;   ni ọjọ ti   o nlọ gb(a)-oye, ojo bẹrẹ si rọ, o fẹ
One:who-has-Ọsara; at day that he going accept-title, rain begin to fall, he want

ya   ki   iya   rẹ ṣugbọn ojo ko jẹ-ki   o ya   o si bẹrẹ si rọ o
turn greet mother his but   rain not consent-that he turn, it and begin to fall it

si nku   giri o si bẹrẹ si kọ-(o)rin pe:
and sounding 'giri,' he and begin to sing-song that:

        Ọlasumogbe mẹ mọ le   ya,
        "Ọlasumogbe I   not be:able turn;

        A-gbe-(i)ji   mọ-(ọ)ba ojo de.
        "One:who-dwell:at-thunderstorm" know-king, rain arrive."

Lati ọjọ na ni awọn ara   Mọrẹ ti   ma   nkọ-(o)rin yi n(i)-
From day the be those people (of) Mọrẹ have (continuative) singing-song this at-

igba-ti nwọn ba   lọ di agbọn   ti   nwọn ba   si njo.
time-that they should go tie coconut that they should and dancing.

ỌYẸKU MEJI - 2

    Efi   ni-(i)yi   ina, imọnamọna ni-(i)yi   ojo, aṣọ nla ni-(i)yi
    "Smoke be-glory (of) fire; lightning   be-glory (of) rain; cloth big be-glory

    Egun   a   da fun ọfafa   ti iṣe ọmọ   ọ-l(i)-ọla
(of) Egungun" (be) who cast for Tree-bear that make child (of) One:who-has-wealth

Qlasumogbe listened and she made the sacrifice. They said she would bear a son
and that she would live to see her child take a title. Ifa says that this is a woman
who is seeking children; if she is able to make a sacrifice, she will bear a son.
She will live to see her child take a title.

When Qlasumogbe was seeking children and could not find any, she consulted
the diviners. They told her that she would give birth to a child, but that she
should make a second sacrifice so that she might also live to see her child take
a title. Soon afterward Qlasumogbe became pregnant and gave birth to a boy.
When he grew up, he was made the chief priest of Qsara.[3] On the day that he was
going to receive his title, rain began to fall. He wanted to stop to greet his mother,[4] but the rain would not let him. The rain began to fall and to beat down "giri,"[5]
and he began to sing:

> "Qlasumogbe, I cannot stop to see you;
> "'He lives in the rain' knows the king, rain comes."[6]

From that day on, the people of Mǫrę ward have sung this song whenever they
"tie the coconut"[7] and dance.

---

3. A deity. See n. 4, verse 6-5.

4. When a chief or priest is installed, he goes about town accompanied by
his friends and followers, visiting and greeting his relatives and the town officials.

5. The sound made by rain falling heavily. Cf. n. 2, verse 17-2.

6. Informants, with considerable uncertainty, interpreted this as meaning
that someone by this name saw the king for the first time when it was raining.

7. During the Coconut Festival (ǫdun agbǫn), which is performed by the
people of Mǫrę ward in the city of Ifę in honor of the deities Qsara and Qlǫshę
(cf. verses 6-2, 6-5, 6-6), the dancers tie to their ankles rattles made of pebbles enclosed in dried coconut leaves. This verse explains the origin of one of
the songs used in this festival.

---

18 - 2

"Smoke is the glory of fire;[1] lightning is the glory of rain; a big cloth is the
glory of Egungun"[2] was the one who cast Ifa for Tree Bear,[3] the child of "One who
has had wealth

---

1. In the same sense that we speak of hair as a woman's crowning glory,
but also with the meaning "Where there's smoke there's fire."

2. This refers, of course, to the costumes beneath which the Egungun dancers conceal their bodies. Cf. n. 6, verse 7-5.

3. The ǫfafa or ǫwawa (Tree Hyrax) is an herbivorous animal that lives in
trees. It is said to eat the leaves of the trees, but only those leaves which do
not have holes. Its call, "wa wa wa wa," can be clearly heard at night.

kan igba   owurọ   ti   a   ni   ki   o   ru-(ẹ)bọ   ojojo,   obukọ
one time (of) morning that they say should he offer-sacrifice (of) sickness, he:goat

kan, ẹgbafa,   ati aṣọ dudu kan.
one, 12,000 (cowries), and cloth black one.

N(i)-igba-ti ọfafa   tọ   awọn babalawo lọ ti   nwọn si sọ   fun
At-time-that Tree:bear approach those diviner   go that they and speak for

pe ki   o ru-(ẹ)bọ   nitori   ai-san   nla kan, ọfafa
(him) that should he offer-sacrifice because (of) not-be:better big one, Tree:bear

gbọ ẹbọ   ko si ru-(ẹ)bọ   na ṣugbọn ko pẹ   l(i)-ẹhin na ai-
hear sacrifice not and offer-sacrifice the; but   not be:long at-back the not-

san   bẹrẹ si ṣe   ọfafa   o fẹrẹ   ku; n(i)-igba-na ni o tun lọ
be:better begin to make Tree:bear, he almost die; at-time-the be he then approach

awọn babalawo lọ nwọn si tun sọ   fun   pe afi   bi o ba   le
those diviner   go they and then speak for (him) that unless if he should be:able

ṣe   ẹbọ   ti awọn ti sọ   fun   pe ki   o ṣe   ni ilọ-
make sacrifice that they have speak for (him) that should he make (it) at twist-

po meji-meji. Ọfafa   ṣẹṣẹ wa ru-(ẹ)bọ   yi, nwọn si sọ   fun
turn two-two.   Tree:bear just come offer-sacrifice this, they and speak for

pe bi ai-san   na ti ṣe   to   yi, nwọn ni yio ni   ohun ati-
(him) that as not-be:better the have make equal this, they say will have voice and-

pe ko si igi ti   yio fi ọwọ rẹ le   ti ko ni le-gun   de   ori.
that not be tree that will put hand his upon that not be be:able-climb arrive head.

Ifa ni ẹni-kan   gbajumọ ni-(e)yi, ki   o ru-(ẹ)bọ   ti ai-
Ifa say person-one gentleman be-this, should he offer-sacrifice that not-

san   ma ba   ṣe   to-bẹ   ti   yio fi ta ile   ati ọna rẹ tan
be:better not should make equal-so that will take sell house and road his finish

ki   ai-san   na to   san   ati-pe ki ai-san   na ma ba
before not-be:better the equal be:better and-that that not-be:better the not should

ti   si ẹhin   odi.
push (him) to back (of) town:wall.

QYẸKU MEJI - 3

O-l(i)-owo   wi-(ẹ)jọ   omi   ile   Alake, O-l(i)-
"One:who-has-cowries speak-case water (of) house (of) Alake, One:who-has-

owo   ko jẹ-(e)bi omi   ọna   Ijero, Ko si omi kan ti   a ipa
cowries not eat-guilt water (of) road (of) Ijero, Not be water one that we kill

otoṣi   si omi   Ijero, omi   Ojugbe   a   da   fun Awo-
destitute:person to water (of) Ijero, water (of) Ojugbe" (be) who cast for Secret-

bọ   ọmọ   ọba l(i)-Ẹyọ a   j(ẹ)-ori   l(i)-oko   iṣẹ   igbanraye;
come child (of) king at-Qyọ who eat-shea:butter at-farm (of) poverty long:ago;

since the morning of his youth." They said he should make a sacrifice against sickness, of one he-goat, three shillings, and one black cloth.

When Tree Bear consulted the diviners and they told him that he should sacrifice because of a serious illness, Tree Bear heard the sacrifice, but did not make it. Not long afterward, Tree Bear fell ill; he nearly died. Then he again consulted the diviners, and they told him that things would be bad unless he could make the sacrifice they had prescribed for him, and that now he must make it two-fold. Tree Bear made the sacrifice as soon as he could. They told him that since his illness had been so great, he would make himself heard, and that there would be no tree within his reach that he would not be able to climb to the very top.[4]

Ifa says that this is a gentleman.[5] He should make a sacrifice lest he become so ill that his house and home must be sold[6] before the illness is cured, and lest the illness drive him out of town.[7]

---

4. This verse explains why the tree bear can be heard so clearly at night, and why it can climb so well. The idiom "to have a voice" means also "to be listened to" and thus implies that the client will become a person whose opinions are respected.

5. A person of moderate means, but good reputation.

6. To pay the doctor's fees. "House and road" is an idiom for all the property that one owns.

7. That is, so that he may not contract a contagious disease like leprosy, because of which he would have to be isolated, and leave town.

---

18 - 3

"'The rich man states his case in court,' water near the house of the Alake;[1] 'The rich man is not judged guilty,' water on the road to Ijero;[2] 'There is no water in which we kill a poor man,'[3] water of Ijero, water of Ojugbe" was the one who cast Ifa for "Diviner comes," the child of the King of Qyǫ, the one who ate shea butter in the farm because of poverty long, long ago.

---

1. The king of Abęokuta.

2. A town in Ekiti, east of Ifę.

3. The names of these three bodies of water, taken together, have the following meaning: A creditor, or the "one who owns the money" is always given a chance to present his side of the case in a trial, and he is never judged guilty in a suit to collect money, since loaning of money is not a crime. However, in spite of the fact that the courts may operate in favor of the rich, a person cannot be condemned to death simply because he is poor and cannot pay his debts.

nwọn ni   ni ọdun-ni   ni Ọ-l(i)-ọrun   tan   ina   iwa   fun.   Ẹiyẹ-
they say at year-this be One:who-has-sky kindle fire (of) destiny for (him). Bird-

(i)le   mẹrin, ẹgbarun,   ati şokoto   idi   rẹ.
(of)-house four,   10,000 (cowries), and trousers (of) waist his.

       N(i)-igba-ti Awo-bọ   ti işe ọmọ   ọba   ode   Ẹyọ şe
    At-time-that Secret-come that make child (of) king (of) outside (of) Qyọ make

yi tan   ko l(i)-ọjọ ko l(i)-oşu ọba   ode   Qyọ ku nwọn lọ mu
this finish not at-day not at-month king (of) outside (of) Qyọ die they go take (him)

jẹ ọba l(i)-ode   Qyọ. Ifa ni ẹni-kan   wa   ti işẹ nşẹ   ti
eat king at-outside (of) Qyọ. Ifa say person-one exist that poverty being:poor that

amu   si nda.   Ifa ni   yio si tun pada di   o-l(i)-
trouble and driving (him). Ifa say (he) will and then return become one:who-has-

owo   ti gbogbo enia   yio ma   pe   sin   yio si j(ẹ)-
cowries that all   persons will (continuative) assemble serve (him) will and eat-

oye   ile   baba rẹ.
title (of) house (of) father his.

QYẸKU MEJI - 4

       Qpa gbongbo ni   ş(i)-(w)aju a-gbọn-(e)nini, atẹlẹ-(ẹ)sẹ   mej(i)-(m)eji
    "Staff short   be (it) move-front it-shake-dew; sole-(of)-foot two-two

a   jija-du   ọna gborogan-gborogan, apasa   a b(i)-ẹnu
they to:fight-compete:for road hard-hard;   sword (of loom) it bear-mouth

bọmbọ,   a   da fun ẹrunlọjọ aşọ a   bu   fun kẹlẹku. Nwọn ni ki
dull" (be) who cast for 165   cloth who share for Calico. They say should

ẹrunlọjọ aşọ ru-(ẹ)bọ   ki   kẹlẹku na ru-(ẹ)bọ   ki wọn ki
165   cloth offer-sacrifice should Calico also offer-sacrifice that they should

o   ma ba   ri iku   a-jọ-ku   Ẹrunlọjọ aşọ   ko ru-
they not should see death (of) to-be:together-die. 165   cloth not offer-

(ẹ)bọ   şugbọn kẹlẹku ni-(ọ)kan ni o ru-(ẹ)bọ.
sacrifice but   Calico at-one   be he offer-sacrifice.

       Ko l(i)-ọjọ ko l(i)-oşu ni oluwa   awọn aşọ nwọn-yi   ku, awọn
    Not at-day not at-month be master (of) those cloth those-this die, those

ara-(i)le   si pe gbogbo wọn pe ki   nwọn ma   mu-(a)ra
people-(of)-house and call all   them that should they (continuative) take-body

lati ba   ba o-l(i)-owo   wọn lọ si ọrun; nwọn ko   gbogbo awọn
to   meet join one:who-has-cowries their go to sky; they gather all   those

aşọ nwọn-yi ka-(i)lẹ   nwọn si mu kẹlẹku na pẹlu   wọn
cloth those-this around-ground they and take Calico the together:with them,

şugbọn Eşu da-(o)hun   o ni:
but   Eshu break-voice he say:

They said that the Sky God would kindle the fire of destiny for him during that year. Four pigeons, two shillings six pence, and the trousers from his waist was the sacrifice.

When "Diviner comes," the child of the King of Ǫyǫ, had made this sacrifice, the King of Ǫyǫ died soon afterward, and they took "Diviner comes" and made him King of Ǫyǫ. Ifa says someone is living in poverty and is being driven here and there by troubles. Ifa says he will return a rich man; everyone will gather to serve him, and he will take a title in the house of his father.

---

18 - 4

"When it is held in front, even a short staff brushes the dew from the path; the soles of both feet strive hard with one another to win the road;[1] the sword[2] of the women's loom has a dull edge" was the one who cast Ifa for the 165 kinds of cloths,[3] and who shared it[4] with Calico. They said the 165 kinds of cloths should make a sacrifice, and that Calico should also sacrifice lest they all meet death at the same time. The 165 kinds of cloths did not sacrifice, but Calico alone sacrificed.

Soon afterward the owner of these cloths died, and the people of his house called all the cloths together to get ready to accompany their owner to heaven. They laid out all the cloths on the ground, putting Calico among them. But Eshu said:

---

1. That is, to get ahead of one another, to compete as in a race.

2. Cf. n. 9, verse 7-5.

3. Many things are spoken of as having 165 varieties. There are said also to be 165 kinds of trees (verses 33-2, 183-1); 165 kinds of animals (166-1, 249-6); 165 kinds of rats (246-4); and 165 kinds of leaves (250-3).

4. This means that the prediction also applies to a person other than the actual client, as where, later in this verse, a prediction is made about the head of the client's lineage. The word "bu" is also used with reference to the sharing of food.

       O ṣoho;
       "Oh shoko";

awọn enia   ni:
those people say:

       Bani.
       "Bani."

O ni:
He say:

       Kẹlẹ   ru   o,
       "Calico offer, oh;

       Kẹlẹ   tu,
       "Calico atone;

       A-fin-(o)ju   aṣọ   ki iy(un)-ọrun.
       "One:who-decorate-eye (of) cloths not go-sky."

N(i)-igba-ti Eṣu wi   bayi tan   ni awọn enia   mu kẹlẹku kuro l(i)-arin
At-time-that Eshu speak thus finish be those people take Calico depart at-middle

    awọn aṣọ (e)y(i)-o-ku   ti nwọn ma   fi   sin
(of) those cloth this-which-remain that they (continuative) take (them) bury

oku;   lati igba-na ni a ko ti gbọdọ fi aṣọ ti o ba   ni   pupa
corpse; from time-the be we not have must take cloth that it should have red

tabi ti o ba   jẹ aṣọ pupa sin oku.   Ẹbọ: aṣọ pupa kan, obukọ
or   that it should eat cloth red bury corpse. Sacrifice: cloth red   one, he:goat

kan, ati ẹgbafa.
one, and 12,000 (cowries).

    Ifa ni ki   ẹni-ti   o da Ifa yi ki   o ru-(ẹ)bọ   ki o
    Ifa say should person-that he cast Ifa this should he offer-sacrifice that he

ma ba   ri iku a-jọ-ku.   Ki (ba)ba-(i)le   ile
not should see death to-be:together-die. That father-(of)-house (of) house (of)

e-(l)i-eyi   papa   na ki   o ru-(ẹ)bọ   pẹlu   ki
one:who-be-this especially the should he offer-sacrifice together:with (him) that

o ma ba   ri iku ni ọdun yi.
he not should see death at year this.

QYẸKU MEJI - 5

    Qrunmila ni o yio bi   yibi-yibi,   nwọn ni ki   Ifa ki
    Qrunmila say he will bear greatness-greatness; they say should Ifa should

o ma   bi yibi-yibi,   n(i)-igba-ti o ma   bi
he (continuative) bear greatness-greatness; at-time-that he (continuative) bear

o bi Oko.
he bear Farm.

"Oh shoko";[5]

and the people answered:

"Bani."

He said:

"Calico sacrificed, oh;
"Calico propitiated;
"The fashionable cloth[6] should not be taken to heaven."

When Eshu finished speaking, the people set Calico apart from the other cloths in which the corpse was to be buried. From that time on, we have been forbidden to bury the dead in a red cloth or any cloth which has red in it.[7] The sacrifice is one red cloth, one he-goat, and three shillings.

Ifa says that the person for whom this figure was cast should make a sacrifice in order that he and his relatives should not meet death at the same time, and especially that the Bale[8] of this person's house should sacrifice with him, that he should not meet death during this year.

-----

5. Cf. n. 4, verse 1-7.

6. Calico is compared here to humans who are neat, well-dressed, and careful about their appearance; to a man of fashion.

7. This verse thus explains why no cloths that have any red coloring may be used by the Yoruba in burials, but the usual reason given is that if cloth with red in it were used, the deceased would be reborn as a leper.

8. The lineage head; eldest male member of the lineage of the compound.

-----

18 - 5

Qrunmila said he would beget something great; they said Ifa should beget something great; when he begat, he begat Farm.[1]

-----

1. In this verse also it is clear that Qrunmila and Ifa are the same person. See also n. 2, verse 1-4.

Qrunmila ni o yio bi   yibi-yibi,   nwọn ni ki   Ifa ki
Qrunmila say he will bear greatness-greatness; they say should Ifa should

o   ma   bi   yibi-yibi,   n(i)-igba-ti o   ma   bi
he (continuative) bear greatness-greatness; at-time-that he (continuative) bear

o bi   Qja.
he bear Market.

Qrunmila ni o yio bi   yibi-yibi,   nwọn ni ki   Ifa ki
Qrunmila say he will bear greatness-greatness; they say should Ifa should

o   ma   bi   yibi-yibi,   n(i)-igba-ti o   ma   bi
he (continuative) bear greatness-greatness; at-time-that he (continuative) bear

o bi   Ogun.
he bear War.

Qrunmila ni o yio bi   yibi-yibi,   nwọn ni ki   Ifa ki
Qrunmila say he will bear greatness-greatness; they say should Ifa should

o   ma   bi   yibi-yibi,   n(i)-igba-ti o   ma   bi
he (continuative) bear greatness-greatness; at-time-that he (continuative) bear

o bi   Qna.
he bear Road.

Qrunmila ni o yio bi   yibi-yibi,   nwọn ni ki   Ifa ki
Qrunmila say he will bear greatness-greatness; they say should Ifa should

o   ma   bi   yibi-yibi,   n(i)-igba-ti o   ma   bi
he (continuative) bear greatness-greatness; at-time-that he (continuative) bear

o bi   Ile   n(i)-ik(an)-ẹhin   wọn.
he bear House at-stand-back   (of) them.

L(i)-ẹhin   eyi Qrunmila şe   awo   lọ si ile   O-l(i)-okun
At-back   (of) this Qrunmila make secret go to house (of) One:who-has-sea

o si gbe   ọdun mẹrindilogun l(i)-ọhun, ki   o   to   de;   n(i)-igba-ti
he and dwell:at year sixteen   at-there, before he equal arrive; at-time-that

o mbọ   ile   Ogun ni o kọkọ ya ti o de   si;   Ogun ki   baba
he coming house, War be he first turn that he arrive to (him). War greet father

rẹ titi   o si fun   ni onjẹ pupọ n(i)-igba-ti o jẹ ti   o mu   tan,
his until, he and give (him) at food much, at-time-that he eat that he drink finish,

o sọ   fun Ogun ọmọ rẹ ti   o nfẹ   gbọn-(ẹ)sẹ Ogun si sọ   fun
he speak for War child his that he wanting shake-foot, War and speak for (him)

pe ẹni-kan   ki gbọn-(ẹ)sẹ nihin; Qrunmila si tun mu-(a)ra o lọ si
that person-one not shake-foot here; Qrunmila and then take-body he go to

ọdọ   Qja   ọmọ rẹ na   b(i)-akan na pẹlu   ni o si
presence (of) Market child his also; like-one the together:with (him) be he and

şe ti   o jẹ ti   o mu   ti   o si bere pe on nfẹ   gbọn-(ẹ)sẹ ti
do, that he eat that he drink that he and ask that he wanting shake-foot that

Qja   si sọ   fun   pe ko le   ri aye   gbọn-(ẹ)sẹ; o si tun
Market and speak for (him) that not be:able see chance shake-foot; he and then

Qrunmila said he would beget something great; they said Ifa should beget
something great; when he begat, he begat Market.

Qrunmila said he would beget something great; they said Ifa should beget
something great; when he begat, he begat War.

Qrunmila said he would beget something great; they said Ifa should beget
something great; when he begat, he begat Road.

Qrunmila said he would beget something great; they said Ifa should beget
something great; when he begat, he begat House last of all.

After this Qrunmila went to the house of the Sea Goddess to divine, and he
lived there sixteen years before he returned. When he was coming home, War
was the first one he stopped to visit. War greeted his father at great length,
and gave him lots of food. When Qrunmila had finished eating and drinking, he
told his child, War, that he wanted to defecate.[2] War told him that no one could
defecate in his house. Qrunmila then got ready and went to visit Market, who also was his child. He did the same things at the house of Market: he ate and drank
and then said he wanted to defecate, and Market told him that there was no place
to defecate. Then he

---

2. To "shake your feet" is a Yoruba euphemism for defecation.

lọ si ọdọ   Oko   bẹ gẹgẹ ni o si tun ṣe, b(i)-akan-na ni o si tun
go to presence (of) Farm, so just be he and then do, like-one-the be he and then

sọ   fun   pẹlu;   o tun lọ s(i)-ọdọ   Qna o si
speak for (him) together:with (the others): he then go to-presence (of) Road he and

tun ri bẹ gẹgẹ fun   ni ile   Qna, l(i)-ẹhin na ni Qrunmila mu-(a)ra
then see so just for (him) at house (of) Road; at-back the be Qrunmila take-body

o lọ s(i)-ọdọ   Ile.
he go to-presence (of) House.

     N(i)-igba-ti o de   ọdọ   rẹ ti Ile   ri baba rẹ, o pa ewurẹ
     At-time-that he arrive presence his that House see father his, he kill she:goat

kan, o na si ṣe   onjẹ pupọ, o gun iyan   o si pe awọn ọrẹ
one, he also and make food much, he pound pounded:yam he and call those friend

rẹ pe ki   nwọn wa ba on ṣe ikẹ   baba rẹ; n(i)-igba-ti
his that should they come with him make indulgence (of) father his; at-time-that

Qrunmila jẹ ti o mu   tan o ni on nfẹ   gbọn-(ẹ)sẹ, Ile   sa-re, o
Qrunmila eat that he drink finish he say he wanting shake-foot, House run-go, he

ṣi   yara fun baba rẹ o ni iwọ ni o ni ile on ki   baba rẹ lọ
open room for father his he say you be who have house his should father his go

gbọn-(ẹ)sẹ si ibi-k(u)-ibi   ti o ba   wu   ni inu   yara na.
shake-foot to place-any-place that it should please (him) at belly (of) room the.

N(i)-igba-ti Qrunmila wọ   yara o ti il(e)-ẹkun mọ   ori o si gbọn-
At-time-that Qrunmila enter room he push house-door against head he and shake-

(ẹ)sẹ s(i)-inu   yara na. N(i)-igba-ti o ja-(o)de   o si tun ti
foot to-belly (of) room the. At-time-that he reach-outside he and then push

il(e)-ẹkun. Ko pẹ   o tun sọ   fun Ile   pe on tun nfẹ   ṣu
house-door. Not be:long he then speak for House that he then wanting defecate

o si tun ṣi yara miran fun   pe ki   o lọ ṣu   n(i)-inu rẹ.
he and then open room another for (him) that should he go defecate at-belly its.

N(i)-igba-ti Qrunmila wọ-(i)le   o tun ti il(e)-ẹkun mọ   ori o tun
At-time-that Qrunmila enter-house he then push house-door against head he then

gbọn-(ẹ)sẹ bi ti   akọkọ.
shake-foot like that (of) first.

     N(i)-igba-ti Qrunmila ṣu   tan o ni ki   Ile   ki   o lọ ṣi
     At-time-that Qrunmila defecate finish he say should House should he go open

il(e)-ẹkun   yara-(e)kini o ni ki   o lọ ko   imi   ti on ṣu,
house-door (of) room-first he say should he go gather excrement that he defecate;

n(i)-igba-ti o wọ-(i)le   o ba owo   o kun inu   yara na gigirọrọ,
at-time-that he enter-house he meet cowries it fill belly (of) room the very:high;

n(i)-igba-ti o ṣi il(e)-ẹkun   iyara-(e)keji o ba   orişi-(o)rişi
at-time-that he open house-door (of) room-second he meet different-different

ilẹkẹ; n(i)-igba-na ni Qrunmila wa   sọ   pe lati oni   lọ gbogbo iṣẹ ti
bead; at-time-the be Qrunmila come speak that from today go all   work that

went to visit Farm, and did likewise; and Farm told him the same thing that the others had. Then he went to visit Road and exactly the same things happened to him at Road's house. Finally Qrunmila got ready and went to visit House.

When he arrived and House saw his father, he killed a she-goat and cooked lots of food; he pounded yams and he told his friends to come and help him entertain his father. When Qrunmila had finished eating and drinking, he said he wanted to defecate. House ran and opened a room for his father. He said, "You are the owner of my house. My father can defecate anywhere that he pleases in this room." When Qrunmila entered the room, he closed the door after him and he defecated in the room. When he came out, he shut the door again. Not long afterwards he told House that he wanted to defecate again, and House opened another room for him, so that he might go to defecate in it. When Qrunmila went in, he again closed the door after him and again he defecated as he had the first time.

When Qrunmila finished defecating, he said that House should go and open the door of the first room. He said House should go and clean up the excrement that he had left there. When he went in, he found that the room was piled high with money. When he opened the door of the second room, he found many different kinds of beads. Then Qrunmila said that from that day henceforth, the profits of everything that

Oko, Qna, Qja   ati Ogun ba   ṣe, Ile   ni ki   o   ma   jẹ
Farm, Road, Market and War   should do, House be should he (continuative) eat

ere wọn.
gain their.

Ifa ni   alejo   kan nbọ   ki   a   tọ-(o)ju   rẹ ki   ore   ati ire
Ifa say visitor one coming should we care:for-eye his that kindness and good-

rẹ   ma ba   kọja ẹni   nitori-ti   anfani wa   l(i)-ara   alejo na.
ness his not should pass person because-that benefit exist at-body (of) visitor the.

QYẸKU MEJI - 6

Biri-biri   l(i)-ọkọ da   bẹ-na   ni ọmọ   ar(a)-aiye   ṣe
"Turn-turn be-boat cause so-also be children (of) people-(of)-earth do" (be)

a   da   f(un)-Qna-(I)ṣokun ti   iṣe   ọmọ   ọba   l(i)-ode   Qyọ.
who cast for-Qna-Ishokun   that make child (of) king at-outside (of) Qyọ.

Iku   dudu ni   k(un)-osun   dudu, iku   pupa ni   k(un)-osu   pupa,
"Death black be (it) rub-camwood black; death red   be (it) rub-camwood red;

ai-mọ-kun   a   kun ilẹ-pa   ọrun do-do-do,   ọrọ   bi   eyi bi
not-know-rub (be) who rub ground-be:red (of) sky   far-far-far, word like this like

eyi   a   da   fun Itu ti   iṣ(e)-ọkọ   ewurẹ   a   bu   f(un)-agbo
this" (be) who cast for Itu that make-husband (of) She:goat who share for-Ram

ṣagi-ṣagi ti   iṣ(e)-ọkọ   I-la-(i)yẹfun, a   da   fun akikọ   Qta
solid-solid that make-husband (of) To-lick-flour, who cast for Cock (of) Qta

galaja   ti   iṣ(e)-ọkọ   agbebọ yanran-yanran.
very:tall that make-husband (of) Hen   good-good.

Ẹni-ti   o   ba   nṣ(e)-ojo   ki   o   ma m(u)-ohun ṣ(e)-akin,
"Person-that he should making-coward should he not take-voice make-hero;

ẹni-ti   o   ba   nṣ(e)-akin   ki   o   ma m(u)-ohun ṣ(e)-ojo   ọba
person-that he should making-hero should he not take-voice make-coward; king

ko jẹ-ki   a   ṣ(i)-ogun   il(u)-obinrin   ki   n-ba   wọn   lọ, k(i)-
not consent-that we open-war (of) town-(of)-woman that I-join them go; should-

ẹni   huwa   gbẹdẹ-gbẹdẹ k(i)-ẹni   ku   pẹlẹ-pẹlẹ   k(i)-ọmọ   ẹni
person behave gently-gently that-person die softly-softly, that-child (of) person

le   na   ọwọ gbọ-gbọ-gbọ   le-(ẹ)ni   sin   a   da   f(un)-A-
be:able stretch hand long-long-long upon-person bury" (be) who cast for-One:who-

l(i)-Apa-Moru ọmọ   a   ji   ni oj(umọ)-ojumọ f(i)-ẹja   ti   o ni
has-Apa-Moru, child (of) "One:who awake at dawn-dawn   take-fish that it be

nla ru-(ẹ)bọ   nitori   ọmọ.
big offer-sacrifice because (of) child."

Farm, Road, Market, and War should do would be enjoyed by House.[3]

Ifa says that a visitor is coming; we should take good care of him lest his kindness and goodness pass us by, because the visitor brings something that can benefit us.

---

3. The verse thus explains why the produce of the farm, the profit of trading in the market and in other towns, and the spoils of war are all brought back to the house to be consumed.

---

18 - 6

"Unsteady is the boat; so also are human beings"[1] was the one who cast Ifa for Qna Ishokun[2] who was the child of the king of Qyǫ.

"Black death rubs his body with black camwood;[3] red death rubs his body with red camwood; one who doesn't know how, rubs his body with the red earth of the far distant sky;[4] words like this, like this" was the one who cast Ifa for Itu, the husband of She-goat and who shared it[5] with Husky Ram, the husband of "The one who licks flour,"[6] and who cast Ifa for "Very tall cock of the town of Qta," the husband of "Very good[7] hen."

"One who is a coward should not talk like a hero; one who is a hero should not talk like a coward; the king does not allow us to make war upon a town of women,[8] that I go with them; one should behave gently so that he may die quietly, and his children be able to come to bury him"[9] was the one who cast Ifa for the chief of Apa-Moru, the child of "The one who wakes every dawn to sacrifice a big fish because she does not have children."

---

1. A fickle person who denies tomorrow what he says today is as unreliable and unsteady as a canoe being tossed upon the waves.

2. Translated by the informants as "Road to Iṣokun," this was later identified as the title of an important chief and a member of the royal family at the town of Qyǫ. Cf. S. Johnson (1921: 42).

3. According to the informant, "black camwood" means charcoal. However Dalziel (1937: 357-358) gives osun dudu as a name for Pterocarpus erinaceus and osun pupa, "red camwood" (or, better, barwood), for Pterocarpus osun.

4. The meaning of this entire passage is obscure. Neither charcoal nor camwood are used to rub the body of the dead before burial in Ifę, though camwood is used by living people to decorate themselves. The red earth and the far distant sky, however, are said to refer to interment after death, and the passage of the soul to heaven. The only meaning that informants could read into this passage is: "Anyone who doesn't know how to behave correctly must die."

5. See n. 4, verse 18-4.

6. "The one who licks flour" is a praise name of a female sheep; "Husky Ram" is that of a male sheep; and Itu, that of a male goat.

7. Yanran-yanran represents the sound made by a brick which has been correctly baked when it is tested by tapping; it means "good" or "up to the required standard."

8. That is, he will not let us attack a town composed only of women, or take the women of our own town as slaves.

9. This means that a person who lives a good life and treats others considerately will die quietly at home; but a person who behaves badly is apt to die in jail or far from home, so that his children cannot bury him.

N(i)-igba-na l(i)-o wa   di   o-ni-ṣẹ-(i)gba   ekinni, mo
"At-time-the be-it come become one:who-be-make-time first;   I

      de   ode   Aro.
      arrive outside (of) Aro.

Mo ni   kin-ni   nwọn nṣe   l(i)-ode   Aro?
"I   say, what-be they doing at-outside (of) Aro?

Nwọn ni   nwọn nj(ẹ)-oye   titun l(i)-ode   Aro ni.
"They say, they eating-title new at-outside (of) Aro be (it).

Mo ni   O-l(i)-oye   yio gbo   bi Oluyẹyẹ ti   gbo,
"I   say, One:who-has-title will grow:old like Oluyẹyẹ have grow:old;

Mo ni   O-l(i)-oye   yio gbo   bi Oluyẹyẹtuyẹ;
"I   say, One:who-has-title will grow:old like Oluyẹyẹtuyẹ;

Yio gbo   igbo   Oluaso ọgbọgbọ iyawo
"Will grow:old grow:old Oluaso young   junior:wife

O   ṣ(e)-arẹwa   ṣ(e)-akin,
"Who make-beauty make-hero,

Ti o fi ọmọ   owu   ṣe   ilẹkẹ s(i)-ọrun,
"That she take child (of) hammer make bead to-neck,

Ti ọmọ   owu   jẹ jẹ jẹ ti o d(i)-ọkinni.
"That child (of) hammer eat eat eat that it become-needle.

Ẹ   pẹlẹ, ara   ode   Apa,
"You softly, people (of) outside (of) Apa,

Ọmọ   a-f(i)-oj(umọ)-ojumọ   bi-(ọ)mọ bi ẹiyẹ,
"Child (of) one:who-take-dawn-dawn bear-child like bird,

A-l(i)-Apa   ọmọ   ẹja,
"One:who-has-Apa child (of) fish,

(Ọ)mọ-(ẹ)ja-(ọ)mọ-(ẹ)ja   l(i)-a-ipe A-l(i)-Apa,
"Child-(of)-fish-child-(of)-fish be-we-call One:who-has-Apa,

A-l(i)-Apa   ọmọ   ẹja.
"One:who-has-Apa, child (of) fish."

Ẹja nla kan, ewurẹ   kan, ati agbebọ adiẹ   kan ni ẹbọ.
Fish big one, she:goat one, and hen   chicken one be sacrifice.

Ifa ni e-l(i)-eyi   yio bi-(ọ)mọ pupọ.
Ifa say one:who-be-this will bear-child many.

QYẸKU MEJI - 7

K(i)-ẹni   ma f(i)-inu   han   tan   f(un)-obinrin, obinrin l(i)-eke,
"Should-person not take-belly appear spread for-woman;   woman be-liar,

obinrin l(i)-ọ-da-(i)lẹ,   Olojongbodu l(i)-obinrin   iku jẹ,
woman be-one:who-break-ground; Olojongbodu be-woman   (of) death eat;

"Then for the first time I come to the town of Aro.

"I say, What are they doing at Aro?

"They say they are taking a new title at Aro.

"I say, The chief will grow old like Oluyẹyẹ[10] has grown old;

"I say, The chief will grow old like Oluyẹyẹtuyẹ.

"He will grow as old as Oluaso, the young wife,

"Who was both beautiful and brave,

"Who used blacksmith's hammers[11] as beads for her neck,

"And the hammers wore down and down and down until they were as
     thin as needles.[12]

"Go softly,[13] people of the town of Apa,

"Child of One who every morning begets children like birds,

"Chief of Apa, child of fish,

"Child of fish, child of fish is what we call the Chief of Apa,

"Chief of Apa, child of fish."

One big fish, one she-goat, and one hen[14] is the sacrifice. Ifa says that this person will bear many children.

---

10. The names Oluyẹyẹ and Oluyẹyẹtuyẹ, whose tones are different, have no meaning, but they apparently stand for someone who lived to a ripe old age.

11. The blacksmith's large hammer is known as owu; the smaller one is known as the "child" of owu.

12. That is, Oluaso lived so long that her beads, even though they were made of blacksmith's hammers, almost wore away.

13. This phrase is used as a salutation in much the same way as the English "hello."

14. Note that all these appear in the names of the legendary characters.

---

18 - 7

"One should not reveal secrets to women, women are liars, women are the ones who break oaths; Olojongbodu is what the wife of Death is called;[1]

---

1. Note that this identification is repeated in the verse.

ọpẹ   tẹrẹ   eti ẹba   odo akunnu yẹ-(o)ri bẹsẹ,   oku
palm:tree slender (of) ear side (of) river fruitful avoid-head at:once, corpse (of)

iku   gbirimu ni ilẹ   a   da   f(un)-Eji Qyẹ ti   nlọ yẹ-(i)ku
death 'gbirimu' at ground" (be) who cast for-Eji Qyẹ that (he) going avoid-death

l(i)-ori   Alayunrẹ.
at-head (of) Alayunrẹ.

    Njẹ   ta-ni yẹ-(i)ku   oni l(i)-ori   awo?
    "Well:then who-be avoid-death today at-head (of) secret?

    Kiki iyẹ   l(i)-o yẹ-(i)ku   oni l(i)-ori   awo.
    "Only wood:dust be-who avoid-death today at-head (of) secret."

    A-(yi)o fi   iyẹ-(i)rosun   tẹ   Qyẹku Meji s(i)-ori   ọpọn
    We-will take wood:dust-(of)-irosun (tree) press Qyẹku Meji to-head (of) tray;

a-(yi)o ma   bu   le   ori tabi ki   a   ma   fi   fọ
we-will (continuative) share upon head or should we (continuative) take (it) grind

ẹkọ   tutu mu, tabi a-(yi)o mu ewe arọ a-(yi)o lọ   a-
cornstarch:porridge cool drink, or we-will take leaf arọ we-will grind (it); we-

(yi)o fi   tẹ   Qyẹku Meji a-(yi)o ma   fi   mu ẹkọ.
will take (it) press Qyẹku Meji; we-will (continuative) take (it) drink cornstarch:

gruel.

    Nwọn p(a)-ero   pọ,   nwọn pe Olojongbodu ti işe   obinrin
    They kill-thought together, they call Olojongbodu that make woman (of)

iku, nwọn bere l(i)-ọwọ rẹ pe kin-ni iku jẹ? O ni iku a   ma
death; they ask at-hand hers that what-be death eat? She say death he (continu-

    jẹ eku, ẹja, ati ẹran; nwọn mu eku, ẹja, ati ẹran fun iku   n(i)-igba-
ative) eat rat, fish, and meat; they take rat fish, and meat for death; at-time-

ti iku jẹ tan t(i)-ọwọ   t(i)-ẹsẹ   rẹ nwa-riri,   oku
that death eat finish that-(of)-hand that-(of)-foot his trembling-'riri,' corpse (of)

iku wa   şe   gbirimu.
death come make 'gbirimu.'

    A-(yi)o fi   eku, ẹja, ati ẹran ru-(ẹ)bọ   a-(yi)o gbe   lọ si idi
    We-will take rat, fish, and meat offer-sacrifice we-will carry (it) go to base

    Eşu.
(of) Eshu.

QYẸKU MEJI - 8

    Ina kan-kan   ni-(i)waju   a-rẹ-(o)yin;   orun kan-kan-
    "Fire fierce-fierce at-front (of) one:who-gather-honey; sun fierce-fierce-

kan ni-(ẹ)ba-(i)di   agbẹ; t(i)-a-rẹ-(o)-yin   a di
fierce at-side-(of)-waist (of) farmer; that-(of)-one:who-gather-honey it become

the slender, fruitful palm tree beside a river ducks its head suddenly so that the body[2] of Death falls to the ground 'gbirimu'"[3] was the one who cast Ifa for the Eji Qyę[4] when he was going to avoid Death on the head of Alayunrę.

"Well then, who avoids Death today on the head of the diviner?
"Only divining powder avoids Death today on the head of the diviner."

We will mark Qyęku Meji in the divining powder on the tray; we will put some on the client's head; or we will take some of it, grind it with cornstarch porridge, and drink it.[5] Or we will take an arǫ leaf[6] and grind it; we will mark Qyęku Meji in it; we will drink it with cornstarch gruel.[7]

They consulted together. They called Olojongbodu, who was the wife of Death. They asked her what Death ate. She said that Death ate rats, fish, and meat. They gave Death rats, fish, and meat, and when Death had finished eating, his hands and feet began to tremble "riri," and Death's body fell down "gbirimu."[8]

We will sacrifice rats, fish, and meat; we will carry the sacrifice to the base of Eshu.

---

2. Even when a living person falls down, it is said that his "corpse" (oku) falls.

3. The sound of a body falling to the ground. Cf. n. 2, verse 19-1.

4. Eji Qyę is an alternative name for the figure Qyęku Meji and here it appears as the name of the character. There is an involved pun on these two names for the figure, "he avoids death" [o yę-(i)ku], and divining powder (iyę).

5. Cf. n. 6, verse 1-5.

6. Crossopteryx febrifuga.

7. Cornstarch gruel (ękǫ mimu) is a hot liquid which frequently serves as breakfast. Cornstarch porridge (ękǫ tutu), mentioned earlier, is a solid which in this case is mixed with cold water so that it may be drunk. Cf. Bascom (1951: 128-129).

8. Gbirimu refers to the sound made by the fall of Death's body; riri describes his trembling. The implication is that Death, having eaten their food, is afraid to kill them. Cf. "Death cannot eat a person's food and then kill him" (verse 6-2). It is further implied that the client, like Eji Qyę, can escape death if he makes the prescribed sacrifice.

---

18 - 8

"The fire is very hot on the face of the one who gathers honey;[1] the sun is very, very hot on the buttocks of the farmer;[2] the one who gathers honey has

---

1. The fire used to smoke out the bees. The one who gathers honey is always in danger of being burned.

2. As he bends over, hoeing or weeding in the farm.

egbe, oyin   o şi,   ado   o rę,   ile   awo   ko ni gb(e)-
loss, honey:bee it move, Ado (bee) it wither, house (of) secret not be dwell:at-

ofo.
emptiness."

    Ifa ni   on ko ni ję-ki   a p(a)-ofo   ni ohun ti   a   da   Ifa
    Ifa say he not be consent-that we crack-emptiness at thing that we cast Ifa

si yi.   Ayebǫ adię   meji ati ęgbęrindilogun   ni ębǫ.
to this. Hen   chicken two and 3200   (cowries) be sacrifice.

QYĘKU MEJI - 9

    Qkunrin yakata l(i)-ori   igba,   igba   ku, ǫkunrin yakata ko lǫ
    "Man   straddle at-head (of) eggplant, eggplant die, man   straddle not go"

    a   da   f(un)-Aro   ile   a   lu-(i)kin f(un)-Aro   oko.   Ifa ni
    (be) who cast for-Aro   (of) house who beat-ikin for-Aro   (of) farm. Ifa say

ki   awǫn mej(i)-(m)eji tabi awǫn ǫrę meji ru-(ę)bǫ   ki nwǫn ki
should those two-two   or   those friend two offer-sacrifice that they should

o   ma ba   ri iku a-jǫ-ku,   igiripa obukǫ kan, ęgbafa,
they not should see death to-be:together-die, (of) full:grown he:goat one, 12,000

       ati aşǫ i-bo-(a)ra   (ǫ)k(an)-ǫkan.
(cowries), and cloth to-cover-body one-one.

    Aro   ile   ati Aro   oko ję ǫrę   meji, nwǫn ni ki   nwǫn ru-
    Aro (of) house and Aro (of) farm eat friend two,   they say should they offer-

(ę)bǫ   ki nwǫn ki   o   ma ba   ri iku   a-jǫ-ku,   Aro
sacrifice that they should they not should see death to-be:together-die; Aro (of)

ile   kǫ   ko ru-(ę)bǫ   bę-ni Aro   oko ko pa   Eşu; Aro
house refuse not offer-sacrifice so-be Aro (of) farm not appease Eshu; Aro (of)

ile   ku si ile   ti   oko ku si oko. Nwǫn ni ki   nwǫn ma
house die to house that (of) farm die to farm. They say should they (continuative)

gbe Aro   oko lǫ si ile; n(i)-igba-ti nwǫn gbe Aro   oko de
carry Aro (of) farm go to house; at-time-that they carry Aro (of) farm arrive

ile nwǫn ni ki   awǫn ǫmǫ   rę wa   şe   ere   oku   fun baba
house they say should those children his come make play (of) corpse for father

wǫn, nwǫn ni awǫn pę   l(i)-oko awǫn ko tun mǫ   ilu   lilu,
their, they say they be:long at-farm they not then know drum to:be:beaten,

nitori   eyi ni awǫn Ifę şe   ma   nwi-pe   Aro pę   l(i)-
because (of) this be those Ifę make (continuative) speaking-that "Aro be:long at-

oko ko tun mǫ   ilu lilu   on na ni o   si mu ki awǫn ǫmǫ
farm not then know drum to:be:beaten," they also be who and take that those child

tabi isǫgan   ile   ma   k(ǫ)-orin bi oku   ba   ku pe:
or   male:relatives (of) house (continuative) sing-song if corpse should die that:

losses; the honey bee swarms, and the honey of the Ado bee[3] spoils; but the house of a diviner is never empty."[4]

Ifa says he will not allow us to draw a blank in the thing for which we are divining. Two hens and nine pence six oninis is the sacrifice.

---

3. There are two types of bees: (1) the igan or oyin, which lives in trees or hives and whose honey is known simply as oyin or oyin igan; and (2) the Ado bee, which lives underground and whose honey is known as oyin ado. The honey bee moves to a new hive when its honey has been taken.

4. This passage as a whole points out that the life of a diviner is to be preferred to that of the farmer and to that of the person who gathers honey. Note that though these phrases resemble those usually interpreted as diviners' names, no divination for a legendary character is cited.

---

18 - 9

"The man stands guard[1] over eggplant,[2] the eggplant dies, but the man still stands over it" was the one who cast Ifa for Aro of the house and beat the palm nuts for Aro of the farm. Ifa says that two people or two friends should sacrifice one full-grown he-goat, three shillings, and one cloth to cover the body each, lest they both meet death at the same time.[3]

Aro of the house and Aro of the farm were two friends. The diviner said that they should make a sacrifice, lest they both meet death at the same time. Aro of the house refused to sacrifice, and Aro of the farm also failed to appease Eshu. Aro of the house died in the house, and Aro of the farm died in the farm. They said that Aro of the farm should be carried to the house. When they had carried Aro of the farm to the house, they said that his children should come and begin the entertainment for the dead[4] for their father. But they said that they had been so long in the farm that they no longer knew how the drums should be beaten. Because of this the people of Ifẹ still say that "Aro stayed in the farm so long that he no longer knew how the drums should be beaten."[5] And they also are the ones whose children or the male relatives in the house[6] sing, when anyone dies,

---

1. To stand astride something to keep it from escaping.

2. Solanum incanum.

3. Müller (1902: 280) cites a similar prediction, also from Ọyẹku Meji, recorded at Atakpame, Togo. Cf. verse 18-10.

4. A part of the funeral ceremonies, spoken of as the "play of the dead," is performed to amuse the deceased; on the surface, at least, it is jolly.

5. This verse thus explains the origin of this Ifẹ proverb, which is used to chide anyone who has forgotten the traditional rituals. It may also be used to ridicule those who live most of the time in the farm and who are despised as ignorant.

6. In terms of age the male clan members of a compound are divided into three groups: the elders (agba ile), the adult males (isọgan) who have achieved economic independence from their fathers, and the "children of the house" (ọmọ ile)—the young men and boys who are still dependent on their fathers. The isọgan are responsible for funerals of clan members.

Jorojorojo a-lu-mọ
"Jorojorojo to-beat-know;

Jo jo a-lu-mọ
"Jo jo to-beat-know."

titi   di   oni   yi   ni ilu   Ile-Ifẹ.
until become today this at town (of) Ile-Ifẹ.

QYẸKU MEJI - 10

Iku   te   ori   igba,   igba   gbiria ilẹ,   alukunrin f(i)-
"Death alight:on head (of) eggplant, eggplant 'gbiria' ground; alukunrin make-

ai-wẹ   o f(i)-ai-kun   o ndan   rojo-rojo   bi ọmọ   a-
not-wash he take-not-rub he shining brightly-brightly like child (of) one:who-

l(i)-adi"   a   da   fun Alapa   ile   o si lu   ikin fun Alapa   oko.
have-adin" (be) who cast for Alapa (of) house he and beat ikin for Alapa (of) farm.

Ifa ni ki   awọn ọrẹ   meji ru-(ẹ)bọ   ki nwọn ki o   ma ba   ri
Ifa say should those friend two offer-sacrifice that they that they not should see

iku   a-jọ-ku   pọ.   Igiripa   obukọ (ọ)k(an)-ọkan, ẹgbafa,
death (of) to-be:together-die together. Full:grown he:goat one-one,   12,000

        ati aṣọ pupa ti   nwọn k(o)-ẹgbẹ   ra ni ẹbọ   na.
(cowries), and cloth red that they gather-companion buy be sacrifice the.

Alapa   ile   ati Alapa   oko jẹ ọrẹ   meji, nwọn si jumọ   ra
Alapa (of) house and Alapa (of) farm eat friend two, they and together buy

aṣọ   pupa (ọ)k(an)-ọkan ni i-bo-(a)ra,   ẹbọ   ya ba   awọn ọrẹ   meji
cloth red one-one   at to-cover-body; sacrifice turn meet those friend two

yi pe ki   nwọn ru-(ẹ)bọ   nwọn gbọ ẹbọ   nwọn ko ru.
this that should they offer-sacrifice; they hear sacrifice they not offer (it).

Eṣu si na   ẹbọn (ogun   tabi i-ṣa-si)   si wọn, nwọn si bẹrẹ si ṣe
Eshu and stretch ẹbọn (medicine or to-send-to) to them, they and begin to make

ai-san   ni ọjọ kan na.
not-be:better at day one the.

N(i)-igba-ti Alapa   ile   ri pe ai-san   na pọ   o sọ
At-time-that Alapa (of) house see that not-be:better the be:great, he speak

fun awọn ara   ile   rẹ pe bi o ba   ku ki nwọn ki   o   gbe
for those people (of) house his that if he should die that they should they carry

on tọ   Alapa   oko lọ nitori-ti   on ni   yio mọ etutu
him approach Alapa (of) farm go because-that he be (who) will know atonement

on ni ṣiṣe.   N(i)-igba-ti Alapa   oko na ri pe ai-san   on
his be to:be:done. At-time-that Alapa (of) farm also see that not-be:better his

npọ   o ni bi o ba   ku ki   awọn ara   ile   on ma
being:great, he say if he should die should those people (of) house his (continuative)

"Jorojorojo,[7] 'He beats palm nuts and knows the future';
"Jo, Jo, 'He beats palm nuts and knows the future'"[8]

until this very day, in the town of Ifẹ.

---

7. "Jorojorojo" and "Jo, Jo" in the following line have no meaning but are
said to be included simply to "make the song sweet."

8. "He beats palm nuts and knows the future" is one of the praise names of
Qrunmila (see verse 6-3). This verse also explains the origin of a song associated with funerals in Ifẹ.

---

18 - 10

"Death alights on top of the eggplant, the eggplant falls to the ground "gbiria";[1]
the alukunrin bird does not bathe, it does not rub its body, but it shines very brightly like the child of one who makes palm kernel oil"[2] was the one who cast Ifa for
Alapa of the house and beat palm nuts for Alapa of the farm. Ifa says that two
friends should make a sacrifice lest they both meet death at the same time. A full-
grown he-goat each, three shillings, and the red cloths which they had bought together as comrades[3] is the sacrifice.

Alapa of the house and Alapa of the farm were two friends each of whom had
bought a red cloth to cover his body at the same time. A sacrifice involved these
two friends; they were told that they should sacrifice. They listened, but did not
make the sacrifice. Eshu pointed ẹbọn (medicine or "send to someone"[4]) at them,
and they became ill on the same day.

When Alapa of the house saw that his illness was serious, he told his family
that if he should die, they should carry his body to Alapa of the farm, because he
was the one that knew the atonement that was to be made at his death. When
Alapa of the farm also saw that his illness was serious, he said that if he should
die, his family should

---

1. The sound of falling to the ground. Cf. n. 2, verse 19-1, and n. 8, verse
18-7.

2. The oil (adi or adin) made from the kernels of the palm nut is used in rubbing the body (cf. n. 2, verse 6-3). The members of the adin maker's family are
kept very shiny, since they have all the oil they wish to use.

3. Friends, or the members of a club, frequently wear identical garments as
a symbol of their comradeship.

4. A type or category of charm which, as its name indicates, works on the
victim at a distance.

gbe   on   tọ   Alapa   ile   lọ nitori   ti   on ni   yio mọ   etutu
carry him approach Alapa (of) house go because that he be (who) will know atone-

    on ni   şişe.
ment his be to:be:done.

    Ko pẹ   l(i)-ẹhin na awọn mej(i-m)eji ku, ọjọ kan na ni nwọn si ku,
    Not be:long at-back the those two-two   die, day one the be they and die,

awọn enia   Alapa   ile   di i   nwọn ngbe   lọ si oko, nwọn
those people (of) Alapa (of) house tie him they carrying (him) go to farm; they

si fi   aşọ pupa ti   on pẹlu   ọrẹ   rẹ jọ   ra bo,
and take cloth red   that he together:with friend his be:together buy cover (him);

awọn enia   Alapa   oko na si di i   n(i)-igba-ti o ku nwọn si
those people (of) Alapa (of) farm also and tie him at-time-that he die, they and

fi   aşọ pupa ti   on pẹlu   ọrẹ   rẹ jọ   ra bo,   nwọn
take cloth red   that he together:with friend his be:together buy cover (him); they

si ngbe   lọ si ile; şugbọn ki   nwọn to   le   gbe   ọkan
and carrying (him) go to house; but   before they equal be:able carry one

de   ọdọ   ekeji rẹ nwọn ni lati   kọja ni arin   ọja
arrive presence (of) second his they be in:order:to pass at middle (of) market

    Ejigbomẹkun; bi nwọn ti   o   ru   awọn oku   nwọn-yi ti   yọ,
(of) Ejigbomẹkun; as they that they carry those corpse those-this have appear,

ọkan ni apa eyi ati ekeji ni apa ọhun ti   nwọn si fi   aşọ pupa b(i)-akan-
one   at arm this and second at arm there that they and take cloth red   like-one-

na bo   awọn oku   mej(i)-(m)eji, awọn ara   ọja   si wi-pe   o
the cover those corpse two-two,   those people (of) market and speak-that "It

ma   yẹ awọn oku   meji yi o; awọn oku   meji ti o yẹ ni
(continuative) suit those corpse two this, oh"; those corpse two   that it suit be

a npe   ni Qyẹku-Meji.
we calling at Qyẹku-Meji.

QYẸKU MEJI - 11

    Qyẹ   şẹşẹ nla   ọmọ   ar(a)-aiye   şebi   ojumọ l(i)-o
    "Light:of:dawn just opening, child (of) people-(of)-earth suppose dawn be-it

nmọ   a   da   fun Aguntan-(I)popo ti ko l(i)-okun l(i)-ọrun ti   ọmọ
clearing" (be) who cast for Ewe-(of)-Ipopo that not have-rope at-neck   that child

    ar(a)-aiye   ni ko l(i)-okun   ọmọ bibi n(i)-inu ti   o şe
(of) people-(of)-earth say not have-endurance (of) child born at-belly, that it make

tan   ti   o nbi-(ọ)mọ   ni yindin-yindin.
finish that she bearing-child at many-many.

carry his body to Alapa of the house, because he was the one who knew the atonement that was to be made at his death.[5]

Not long afterward both of them died; it was on the same day that they died.
The family of Alapa of the house wrapped him and set out carrying him to the
farm; to cover him they used the red cloth[6] that he had bought with his friend.
And the family of Alapa of the farm also wrapped him when he died, and to cover
him they also used the red cloth that he had bought with his friend. They set out,
carrying him to the house. But before they could carry one to the other, they had
to pass each other in the center of Ejigbomękun market. As they came out into
the market carrying the two dead bodies, one on this side and the other on that,
and with both bodies covered with the same kind of red cloth, the people in the
market said, "This is fitting for these two dead bodies, oh." The two dead bodies
for which it is fitting is what we call Qyęku-meji.[7]

---

5. In accordance with the Yoruba institution of "best friends" (korikosun),
these two had confided in each other what rituals and sacrifices had to be made
at their death. The refusal to sacrifice thus not only brought about their deaths,
but also caused them to be buried without the proper atonements.

6. Red cloths are tabu for burial. Cf. verse 18-4.

7. Note the pun on the name of the figure (Qyęku Meji), which takes the form
of giving an etymological interpretation of its meaning: o-yę-(o)ku-meji (it-suits-
corpse-two). Cf. the similar verse recorded by Epega (n.d.: III, 19) for Qyęku
Iwori.

---

18 - 11

"The first signs of dawn[1] are just appearing; people think that day is breaking" was the one who cast Ifa for Ewe of the town of Ipopo who did not have a rope
about her neck, of whom people said that she was no longer able to bear children.[2]
Time passed, and she bore a great many children.

---

1. Note the pun on the alternative name of the figure, Eji Qyę.

2. Believing that she would never again be in heat, people felt that it was no
longer necessary for her to be tethered by a rope. Note the pun on "rope" (okun)
and "endurance" (okun). Ewe is given as aguntan or agutan.

Ni Şopo-Agada o bi   Eyinkoto   a   da fun Şopere ti işe yeye
"At Shopo-Agada he bear Eyinkoto" (be) who cast for Shopere that make mother

Ojo.
(of) Rain.

Qwọ   l(i)-a b(a)-eji
"Flock be-we meet-rain,

Eji ki ni-(ọ)kan rin.
"Rain not at-one   walk."

Ifa ni e-l(i)-eyi   yio bi-(ọ)mọ yio si di   ẹ-l(i)-ẹni.
Ifa say one:who-be-this will bear-child will and become one:who-has-person.

QYẸKU MEJI - 12

Qrunmila ni o di   igbo, mo ni igbo ni,   igbo ni ai ba   ẹhan,
Qrunmila say it become crowd; I   say crowd be (it); crowd be we meet ẹhan,

igbo ni ai ba   esi, a ki ri a-ni-(ọ)kan-rin   nadu-nadu, a ki ri
crowd be we meet boar; we not see one:who-at-one-walk mum-mum; we not see

a-ni-(ọ)kan-rin   yunrẹ nadu-nadu ni orukọ ti ai pe aguntan; yunrẹ ni
one:who-at-one-walk greedy; mum-mum be name that we call ewe;   greedy be

orukọ ti ai pe ọya.
name that we call Cane:rat

Ifa ni e-l(i)-eyi   yio di   igbo   ko si n(i)-ọkan rin. Eku
Ifa say one:who-be-this will become crowd, not and at-one   walk. Rat

mẹwa, ẹja mẹwa, ati agbebọ adiẹ   mẹwa.
ten, fish ten, and hen   chicken ten.

QYẸKU - (I)WORI - 1

E-l(i)-eku   nmu eku pe mi l(i)-aiya, aiya mi ko ni   gba   eku,
"One:who-has-rat taking rat call me at-chest, chest my not be (it) accept rat,

aiya   Qyẹku-gbiri l(i)-agba, ẹ-l(i)-ẹja   nmu ẹja pe mi l(i)-aiya,
chest (of) Qyẹku-'gbiri' be-elder, one:who-has-fish taking fish call me at-chest,

aiya mi ko ni   gba ẹja aiya   Qyẹku-gbiri l(i)-agba, edi pọnripọn,
chest my not be (it) accept fish, chest (of) Qyẹku-'gbiri' be-elder, Edi thick,

omi di   edi nana   il(u)-oro,   owo   ati ọmọ ni aiya mi
water become Edi vibrating town-(of)-ritual, cowries and child be chest my

nwa   o.
seeking, oh."

"At Shopo-Agada she gave birth to Eyinkoto" was the one who cast Ifa for Shopere, who was the mother of Rain.

> "It is in flocks that we meet rain,
> "Rain does not walk alone."[3]

Ifa says that this person will have children and will have many followers.[4]

---

3. Rain drops do not come singly.

4. A person's followers includes both his friends and the members of his family—all those upon whom he can count for support in legal, financial, or social matters. Cf. n. 2, verse 7-4. A large personal following is one of the main personal goals of the Yoruba. (See Chapter VII.) Though there are two divinations cited as precedent in this verse, both imply the same prediction. Both rain drops and the children of Ewe of the town of Ipopo are numberless (yindin-yindin). Cf. the versions of this verse recorded by Beyioku (1940: 5, 27).

---

18 - 12

Qrunmila says there will be a crowd; I say there is a crowd. In crowds we find ehan;[1] in crowds we find wild boars. We don't find "One who keeps silent"[2] walking alone; we don't find "Greedy" walking alone. "One who keeps silent" is the name that we call Ewe; "Greedy" is the name that we call Cane Rat.[3]

Ifa says that this person will form a crowd[4] and will not walk alone. Ten rats, ten fish, and ten hens is the sacrifice.

---

1. An unidentified wild animal living in the forest.

2. One who can talk, but doesn't want to. Cf. verse, 249-5.

3. Thryonomys swinderianus, popularly called "Cutting Grass." See Abraham (1958: 533).

4. That is, he will have many followers. Cf. n. 4, verse 18-11.

---

19 - 1

"Someone who owns rats sends rats at my chest to call me;[1] my chest will not accept them; the chest of Reverberating[2] Qyeku is the elder;[3] Someone who owns fish sends fish at my chest to call me; my chest will not accept them; the chest of Reverberating Qyeku is the elder; Thick Edi,[4] the water becomes Vibrating[5] Edi of the town where rituals are held; my chest is seeking money and children, oh."[6]

---

1. That is, someone is using rats (and fish) to make medicine to cause my death.

2. Gbiri is the sound of something big and heavy falling to the ground, or of the shot of a cannon reverberating. It may appear as gbiri-gbiri-gbiri, pronounced with decreasing volume, like an echo gradually dying away. Qyeku Gbiri may be an alternative name for Qyeku Iwori. Cf. verses 19-2 and 19-3.

3. Notes 3—6 appear on p. 261.

Ifa ni ki   ẹni-kan   ru-(ẹ)bọ   ki   a   ma ba   fi   ogun
Ifa say should person-one offer-sacrifice that they not should take medicine

pa   tabi a-pe-ta   pa: Obukọ kan, ẹgbafa.   Ifa ni on
kill (him) or to-call-shoot kill (him): He:goat one, 12,000 (cowries). Ifa say he

ko ni   jẹ-ki   a ku.
not be (he) consent-that we die.

QYẸKU - (I)WORI - 2

Qyẹku-gbiri   a   da   fun ebe   n(i)-igba-ti o   ma
"Qyẹku-'gbiri'" (be) who cast for yam:heap at-time-that she (continuative)

ni oyun   ij(ẹ)-(oh)un si inu, nwọn ni ki   o   ru-(ẹ)bọ   ki
have pregnancy (of) eating-thing to belly; they say should she offer-sacrifice that

ọmọ   inu rẹ le   gbo: obukọ kan, aṣọ ẹlẹpa   kan, ẹgbata
child (of) belly hers be:able grow:old: he:goat one, cloth lightly:dyed one, 6000

              ọna marun ki   o jẹ owo   ti   iya   ati ẹgba owo
(cowries) (of) road five   should it eat cowries that (of) mother and 2000 cowries

     ọmọ   inu rẹ.
(of) child (of) belly hers.

Ifa ni on ko ni   jẹ-ki   a bi ọmọ ni ọjọ   ai-pe;
Ifa say he not be (he) consent-that we bear child at day (of) not-complete.

Ifa ni ki   a-b(i)-oyun   ru-(ẹ)bọ   ki o ma ba   bi-
Ifa say should one:who-bear-pregnancy offer-sacrifice that she not should bear-

(ọ)mọ ni ọjọ   ai-pe.   A ko gbọdọ ki   Ifa yi ni oju   a-
child at day (of) not-complete. We not must greet Ifa this at eye (of) one:who-

b(i)-oyun.
bear-pregnancy.

Babalawo ko gbọdọ ki Ifa yi ni oju   a-b(i)-oyun,   bi o
Diviner   not must greet Ifa this at eye (of) one:who-bear-pregnancy; if he

ba   ki Ifa yi ni oju   a-b(i)-oyun,   oyun   na ni
should greet Ifa this at eye (of) one:who-bear-pregnancy, pregnancy the be

lati   bajẹ.
in:order:to spoil.

QYẸKU - (I)WORI - 3

Qyẹku-gbiri   a   da   fun ẹiyẹ-(i)le   ọmọ   a-tẹ-
"Qyẹku-'gbiri'" (be) who cast for bird-(of)-house, child (of) "One:who-spread-

itẹ-sun-orun-ọmọ   ni Ekiti Ẹfọn ti o   da Ifa nitori   ọmọ.
nest-sleep-sleep-(of)-child at Ekiti Ẹfọn" that she cast Ifa because (of) child.

Ifa says that someone should make a sacrifice lest he be killed with medicine or "call and shoot."[7] One he-goat and three shillings is the sacrifice. Ifa says that he will not allow us to die.

---

3. That is, my chest, which is very strong like that of "Reverberating Qyẹku," will resist the bad medicine; Qyẹku will protect me.

4. Edi is the name of one of the sixteen basic Ifa figures, but it appears here in a figure whose name does not involve Edi.

5. Nana describes the way something sways or vibrates, like a clock spring held at one end. Cf. n. 1, verse 17-4.

6. These phrases resemble those interpreted as diviner's names, but no divination for a legendary character is cited.

7. A type or category of charm which can cause death at a distance.

---

19 - 2

"Reverberating Qyẹku"[1] was the one who cast Ifa for Yam Heap when she was pregnant with food. They said that so that the child in her belly would be able to mature, she should sacrifice one he-goat, one lightly dyed cloth,[2] five piles of money of one shilling and six pence each for the mother, and six pence for her unborn child.

Ifa says that he will not let us bear our child prematurely. Ifa says that a pregnant woman should make a sacrifice so that she will not give birth to her child prematurely. We must not recite this verse in the presence of a pregnant woman.[3]

(The diviner must not recite this verse in the presence of a pregnant woman; if he should recite this verse in the presence of a pregnant woman, the pregnancy is certain to spoil.[4])

---

1. Cf. n. 2, verse 19-1.

2. A cloth which has been dipped only once in indigo, and is therefore light blue in color.

3. The diviner must make certain that no pregnant women are present before he recites this verse. If the client herself is present, arrangements will be made for the sacrifice without reciting the verse to her as is usually done.

4. This is not recited as a part of the verse itself, but it is a part of the instructions given to the diviners when they are learning the verse.

---

19 - 3

"Reverberating Qyẹku"[1] was the one who cast Ifa for Pigeon, child of "The one who makes her nest and sleeps like a child at Ekiti Ẹfọn"[2] when she cast Ifa because she had no children.

---

1. See n. 2, verse 19-1.

2. The town of Ẹfọn-Alaye, east of Ilesha, which was the capital of Ẹfọn, one of the Ekiti Yoruba kingdoms.

Nwọn ni   yio bi   ọmọ, şugbọn ki   o   ru-(ẹ)bọ.   Ikoko titun
They say (she) will bear child, but   should she offer-sacrifice. Pot   new

meji, ayebọ adiẹ   meji, ati ẹgbaji   ni ẹbọ.
two, hen   chicken two,   and 4000 (cowries) be sacrifice.

N(i)-igba-ti ẹiyẹ-(i)le   ru   ẹbọ   yi tan   nwọn gbe ọkan fun
At-time-that bird-(of)-house offer sacrifice this finish, they take one   give

u n(i)-inu   awọn ikoko meji na, nwọn ni bi ọmọ rẹ ba   ti fi
her at-belly (of) those pot   two the, they say if child hers should have take

ori kan   ikoko yi   ko ni   ku mọ.   N(i)-igba-ti ẹiyẹ-(i)le   ba
head touch pot   this, not be (it) die again. At-time-that bird-(of)-house should

bi-(ọ)mọ ti ọmọ rẹ ba   si fi   ori kan ikoko o   bẹrẹ si wi-
bear-child that child hers should and take head touch pot   she begin to speak-

pe:
that:

Mo ş(e)-ẹbọ   Ọyẹku-gbiri, Ọyẹku-gbiri,
"I   make-sacrifice (of) Ọyẹku-'gbiri,' Ọyẹku-'gbiri,'

Ọmọ mi f(i)-ori   kan-(i)koko ko ku mọ.
"Child my take-head touch-pot   not die again."

Ifa ni e-l(i)-eyi   nwa   ọmọ, yio bi-(ọ)mọ şugbọn ki   o   ru-
Ifa say one:who-be-this seeking child; will bear-child but   should she offer-

(ẹ)bọ   ki   awọn ọmọ rẹ ma ba   ma   ku n(i)-igba-ti o
sacrifice that those child hers not should (continuative) die at-time-that she

ba   bi   wọn.
should bear them.

QYẸKU - (E)DI - 1

Ọyẹku-(E)di   a   da   fun igbin, nwọn ni ki   o   ru-(ẹ)bọ
"Ọyẹku-Edi" (be) who cast for Snail; they say should he offer-sacrifice (of)

a-l(i)-a-ş(e)-ire: akikọ adiẹ   mẹta ati ẹgbata.   Igbin ko
one:who-be-he-make-play: cock chicken three and 6000 (cowries). Snail not

ru-(ẹ)bọ.   Lati igba-na ni gbogbo aiye ti   ma   nfi   igbin
offer-sacrifice. From time-the be all   earth have (continuative) taking Snail

şe   a-l(i)-a-ş(e)-ire.   Agbọnniregun ni   rin-(ọ)wọ-rin-(ọ)wọ
make one:who-be-he-make-play. Agbọnniregun say squeeze-hand-squeeze-hand

ni a (yi)o ma   he   igbin. Ifa ni ki   ẹni-kan   ru-(ẹ)bọ
be we will (continuative) pick:up snail. Ifa say should person-one offer-sacrifice

a-l(i)-a-ş(e)-ire.   A-l(i)-a-ş(e)-ire   de.
(of) one:who-be-he-make-play. One:who-be-he-make-play arrive.

They said she would bear children, but that she should make a sacrifice. Two new pots, two hens, and one shilling[3] was the sacrifice.

When Pigeon had completed this sacrifice, they took one of the two pots and gave it to her. They said if her child should touch this pot with its head, it would not die. When Pigeon gave birth to her child, she touched its head against the pot and began to recite:

"I made the sacrifice of Reverberating Qyẹku, Reverberating Qyẹku,
"My child touches the pot with its head; it will not die any more."[4]

Ifa says that this person is seeking children; she will have children but she should make a sacrifice lest her children die as soon as they are born.

---

3. As cowries are counted by the two thousand, there are two units of cowries as there are two pots and two hens.

4. There is a play on words and word magic in the use of a pot (ikoko) so that the child will not die (ko ku) again. The belief is that several children who die very young in succession, as abiku, are in reality one child who fails to live in its successive rebirths. (Cf. n. 3, verse 1-4). This verse is to be compared with verse 33-1, where Pigeon begins to live in a pot.

---

20 - 1

Qyẹku Edi"[1] was the one who cast Ifa for Snail. They said he should sacrifice three cocks and one shilling six pence[2] against one who showed contempt for him. Snail did not make the sacrifice. From that time, the whole world has been showing contempt for Snail.[3] Agbọnniregun says, "Bare handed, bare handed we will catch[4] snail." Ifa says someone should make a sacrifice against one who shows contempt for him. One who shows contempt for him is coming.

---

1. The name of the diviner is identical with that of the figure.

2. Since cowries are counted by the two thousand, there are three units of cowries as well as three cocks.

3. No one is afraid of snail since "it has no teeth."

4. The Yoruba word "he" is even more insulting; it is applied to the gathering of fruit. This verse thus explains why no one is afraid of snails, and why people can catch snails without weapons and without any protection on the hands.

QYẸKU - (E)DI - 2

Qna tọ   tara   ma ya   a   da   fun Qyẹ n(i)-igba-ti o
"Road be:straight straight not turn" (be) who cast for Qyẹ at-time-that he

nlọ gbe ọbuntun   adugbo wa   ile,   nwọn ni ki   o ru-(ẹ)bọ
going take bride   (of) ward   come house; they say should he offer-sacrifice

ki oko rẹ ma ba   d(a)-oju ti: obukọ kan, ẹgba   meje.
that penis his not should break-eye push (him): he:goat one, 2000 (cowries) seven.

Qyẹ ko ru-(ẹ)bọ.
Qyẹ not offer-sacrifice.

N(i)-igba-ti Qyẹ mu iyawo   de   ile   ko le   ba   sun,
At-time-that Qyẹ take junior:wife arrive house not be:able join (her) sleep,

nwọn ni Qyẹ ni?   Nwọn ni Qyẹ ti o ti ku ni idi ni;   lati igba
they say Qyẹ be (he)? They say Qyẹ that he have die at waist be (he); from time

na ni a ti npe   ni Qyẹku-(E)di.
the be we have calling (him) at Qyẹku-(E)di.

Ifa ni ki   ẹni-kan   ru-(ẹ)bọ   arun   a fi aṣọ bo
Ifa say should person-one offer-sacrifice (of) disease we take cloth cover

mọ-(a)ra;   tabi oko nda   ẹni-kan ni-(ọ)jọ, ki   o ru-(ẹ)bọ
against-body; or   penis causing person-one at-day,   should he offer-sacrifice

ki o le   ri oko do   iyawo   rẹ ti o nfẹ   gbe.
that he be:able see penis copulate:with junior:wife his that he wanting take.

QYẸKU - (E)DI - 3

Pẹkubẹ, awo   Olongo l(i)-o da   fun Olongo n(i)-igba-ti o r(un)-
Pẹkubẹ, secret (of) Waxbill be-who cast for Waxbill at-time-that she grieving-

agan   ai-bi-(ọ)mọ   nwọn ni yio bi ọmọ, nwọn ni ki   o
(of)-barren:woman not-bear-child, they say will bear child, they say should she

ru   ayebọ adiẹ meji, ewurẹ kan, ati ẹgbawa,   o ru. O bi
offer hen chicken two, she:goat one, and 20,000 (cowries), she offer. She bear

ọmọ o si bẹrẹ si yọ   o nwi-pe:
child she and begin to rejoice she speaking-that:

          Ifa   Pẹkubẹ ṣẹ,   Pẹkubẹ,
          "Ifa (of) Pẹkubẹ happen, Pẹkubẹ;

          Mo l(i)-oyun   mo bi-(ọ)mọ, Pẹkubẹ.
          "I   have-pregnancy, I bear-child, Pẹkubẹ."

Ifa ni ki   a sọ   fun e-l(i)-eyi   pe o nwa   ọmọ ki   o
Ifa say should we speak for one:who-be-this that she seeking child should she

ru-(ẹ)bọ   yio si bi-(ọ)mọ.
offer-sacrifice will and bear-child.

---

20 - 2

"The road is very straight, it does not turn" was the one who cast Ifa for Qyẹ when he was going to bring home a bride from his ward.[1] They said he should sacrifice one he-goat and three shillings six pence[2] so that his penis should not disgrace him. Qyẹ did not make the sacrifice.

When Qyẹ brought his bride home, he was not able to sleep with her. They said, "What kind of an Qyẹ is he?" They said "He is Qyẹ who has died at his waist." From that time on we have been calling him Qyẹku-(e)di.[3]

Ifa says someone should make a sacrifice against a disease which can be concealed under his clothing,[4] or that someone's penis is setting his dates for him;[5] he should make a sacrifice so that he can have intercourse with the wife he wants to marry.

---

1. A neighbor, a girl living in the same ward of the town.
2. Seven units of 2000 cowries, or 14,000 cowries.
3. This verse thus explains how this figure got its name. Note the pun which is the basis of the etymology: Qyẹku-(E)di, the name of the figure, and Qyẹ-ku-(i)di, Qyẹ-die-waist.
4. This refers to social diseases.
5. That is, he cannot have sexual relations regularly. Cf. verse 9-1.

---

20 - 3

"Pẹkubẹ, the diviner of Waxbill"[1] was the one who cast Ifa for Waxbill when she was grieving because she was barren and had no children. They said she would bear children; they said she should sacrifice two hens, one she-goat, and five shillings. She sacrificed. She bore children and she began to rejoice, singing:

> "The Ifa of Pẹkubẹ came true, Pẹkubẹ;
> "I am pregnant, I bear children, Pẹkubẹ."

Ifa says we should tell this person who is seeking children that she should make a sacrifice and she will bear a child.

---

1. The Orange-cheeked Waxbill (Estrilda Melpoda M.). The meaning of Pẹkubẹ is unknown.

QYẸKU - (Q)WỌNRIN - 1

Qka   gbe-(i)nu   itẹ ga-(o)ju   Ere   gbe pa-(a)kurọ
"Snake stay-belly (of) nest stretch-eye, Python stay beside-waterside:garden

ga-(ọ)run   oye Oṣumare-ẹgọ gbe ọju   Q-l(i)-ọrun   kẹ
stretch-neck (of) title, Rainbow-fool stay face (of) One:who-has-sky spread

yanran-yanran"   a   da   fun wọn ni agbaigbo   Ifẹ kiribiti   n(i)-igba-ti
bright-bright" (be) who cast for them at whole   (of) Ifẹ all:around at-time-that

aiye wọn d(a)-oju   de bi igba.
world their cover-face (1) like calabash.

Ifa ni   ohun ti   a   d(a)-ẹbọ   si (ohu)n-kan na ti   bajẹ, ṣugbọn ohun
Ifa say thing that we cast-sacrifice to thing-one the have spoil, but   thing

ti   a   le   ṣe ti   o le   dara   ni ki   a   ru-(ẹ)bọ   si.
that we be:able do that it be:able be:good be should we offer-sacrifice to (it).

Ohun mẹfa-mẹfa: iti   eku mẹfa, ẹja mẹfa, aṣọ mẹfa, ọkẹ   owo
Thing six-six: bunch (of) rat six,   fish six,   cloth six,   bag (of) cowries

mẹfa, aguntan mẹfa, gbogbo ohun mẹfa-mẹfa, ati ilu   mẹfa. Nwọn ru   ẹbọ
six,   ewe   six,   all   thing six-six,   and drum six.   They offer sacri-

yi   tan,   nwọn gbe   si Mesi Alukunrin, bi nwọn ti   gbe   si Mesi
fice this finish, they carry to Mesi Alukunrin, as they have carry to Mesi

Alukunrin tan,   ni ojo bẹrẹ si rọ, nwọn ba   ko   ilu   mẹfa na si ita,
Alukunrin finish, be rain begin to fall, they meet gather drum six   the to square,

nwọn bẹrẹ si kọ-(o)rin pe:
they begin to sing-song that:

>   Ẹbọ   l(i)-a ṣe
>   "Sacrifice be-we make,
>
>   Ojo ko rọ a ngbẹ-(ọ)ka
>   "Rain not fall, we planting-guinea:corn,
>
>   Ẹbo   l(i)-a ṣe
>   "Sacrifice be-we make.
>
>   Ẹbọ   l(i)-a ṣe
>   "Sacrifice be-we make,
>
>   O-n(i)-Igbo-(ọ)m(ọ)-ẹkun
>   "One:who-has-Igbo-child-(of)-leopard,
>
>   Ẹbo   l(i)-a ṣe
>   "Sacrifice be-we make,
>
>   Ojo ko rọ a ngbẹ-(ọ)ka.
>   "Rain not fall, we planting-guinea:corn.

---

1. Da . . . de means "to cover."

24 - 1

"The Qka snake stays in its nest stretching out its face;[1] Python stays by the waterside stretching out its neck like one who wants to become a chief; Rainbow, the foolish one, stays in the heavens, spreading very brightly"[2] was the one who cast Ifa for all the people of Ifẹ when things were going badly for them, when their world was covered like a calabash.

Ifa says that the affair for which we are divining has spoiled, but that we can set it right by sacrificing. Six of everything must be sacrificed: six bunches of dried rats, six bunches of dried fish, six cloths, six bags of money (thirty shillings), six ewes—six of everything—and six drums. The people of Ifẹ completed the sacrifice, and when they carried these things to Mesi Alukunrin,[3] rain began to fall.[4] They brought the six drums to the square and began to sing:

> "We are making a sacrifice;
> "Rain does not fall, we are planting guinea corn;
> "We are making a sacrifice.
> "We are making a sacrifice;
> "Oh King of the Igbo, Children of Leopard,[5]
> "We are making a sacrifice;
> "Rain does not fall, we are planting guinea corn."

---

1. This kind of snake does not run away when hunters come to kill it, but rises up and peers out at them to see what is happening. The CMS Dictionary lists ọka as "a species of boa constrictor. See 'Ẹlẹbu' = cobra," and for "cobra" gives ọka. Abrahams suggests that it may be the Gaboon viper. It is also called "Nana Buruku's snake" (ejo Buku), and is described in Mẹkọ as small, about a foot long, with black and red markings.

2. As the rainbow is thought of as a python (ere), all three statements contain a reference to snakes. Cf. the last with verse 35-6.

3. A place in the square before the palace at Ifẹ (formerly a building within the palace walls) where humans were formerly executed.

4. The implication of this verse, made clear in Yoruba mythology, is that it rains nowadays when planting time comes only because the very early inhabitants of Ifẹ made the sacrifice described here. It is said that at this time there were no yams or maize, and that guinea corn was the only food.

5. The names Igbomẹkun and Ejigbomẹkun (cf. verse 18-10) appear in a number of Yoruba myths and are commonly interpreted by informants as referring to an ancient town with the word used here (Onigbomẹkun) as the title of its ruler. However, an Ifẹ diviner explained Onigbomẹkun as meaning O-n(i)-Igbo-(ọ)m(ọ)-ẹkun or "Owner of Igbo, Child (or Children) of Leopard"; he identified him as Qsangangan Qbamakin and "Igbo" as his subjects—the people from whom Mọrẹmi saved the people of Ifẹ. This interpretation, which is followed here, was confirmed by a priest of Qsangangan Qbamakin, who added that Qsangangan Qbamakin is a deity (ẹbura) who once ruled as an early king of Ifẹ and that the Igbomẹkun were the original inhabitants of Ifẹ. Cf. n. 6, verse 247-5.

Ifa ni (ohu)n-kan ti   a   d(a)-ẹbọ   si yi ti   bajẹ, afi-bi   a   ba
Ifa say thing-one that we cast-sacrifice to this have spoil, unless-if we should

ru   ẹbọ   ni ohun na le fi   dara.
offer sacrifice be thing the can take be:good.

IWORI OGBE[1] - 1

Iwori a-bọ-gbe.
"Iwori to-sacrifice-aid."

Ọrọ bo-(ẹ)ni   l(i)-oju ma di-(ẹ)ni   l(i)-eti   a   da   fun Elemele
"Wall cover-person at-eye not tie-person at-ear" (be) who cast for Elemele

ile   a   lu-(i)kin fun Elemele   oko ni-(ọ)jọ ti nwọn nfi   ọmọ ṣe
(of) house who beat-ikin for Elemele (of) farm at-day that they taking child make

a-bi-ku.
one:who-born-die.

N(i)-igba-ti Elemele   ile   ati ti   oko nlọ da Ifa l(i)-ọwọ
At-time-that Elemele (of) house and that (of) farm going cast Ifa at-hand (of)

Ọrunmila, ni-(i)gba-ti nwọn de   ẹhin-(ẹ)ku(n)-(i)le   Ọrunmila, nwọn
Ọrunmila, at-time-that they arrive back-door-(of)-house (of) Ọrunmila, they

gbọ ti Oṣu   aya rẹ da-(o)hun   o ni ko si ikoko ni ile,   o ni ẹni-
hear that Oshu, wife his, break-voice she say not be pot   at house, she say person-

ti o ba   wa   d(a)-ẹbọ   l(i)-oni ki   Ọrunmila ki   o yan
that he should come cast-sacrifice at-today should Ọrunmila should he choose

ikoko meji, ọpa-(a)tori   (ọ)k(an)-ọkan, iṣu marun, ọbẹ ṣilo   kan,
pot   two, branch-(of)-atori one-one,   yam five,   knife for:cutting:food one,

ati ọgọrun-o-le-marun igbado fun   ni ẹbọ.
and 105   corn   for (them) at sacrifice.

N(i)-igba-ti Elemele   ile   ati ti   oko wọ-(i)le   nwọn da
At-time-that Elemele (of) house and that (of) farm enter-house they cast

arun   si-(i)lẹ nwọn da Iwori a-bọ-gbe;   n(i)-igba-na ni Ọrun-
five (cowries) to-ground they cast Iwori to-sacrifice-aid; at-time-the be Ọrun-

mila da-(o)hun   o ni: Ọrọ bo-(ẹ)ni   l(i)-oju ma di-(ẹ)ni   l(i)-eti ni-
mila break-voice he say: "Wall cover-person at-eye not tie-person at-ear" be-

yi o ni ẹ ngbọ bi aya   on ti nwi jọ-(oh)un?   Nwọn ni
this; he say you hearing as wife (of) him have saying resemble-things? They say

awọn ko gbọ; o ni nitori   a-bi-ku   ọmọ ni ẹ   ṣe   wa
they not hear; he say because (of) one:who-born-die child be you make come

---

1. Also known as Iwori a-bọ-gbe, meaning Iwori that brings help through a
sacrifice. See n. 1, verse 33-1.

Ifa says that the affair for which we are divining has spoiled, and that it cannot be put right again unless we make a sacrifice.

---

33 - 1

"Iwori which brings help through a sacrifice."[1]

"A wall covers one's eyes but does not close one's ears"[2] was the one who cast Ifa for "Elemele of the house" and who beat palm nuts for "Elemele of the farm" when their children were dying like abiku.[3]

When "Elemele of the house" and "Elemele of the farm" were going to have Qrunmila cast Ifa for them, and when they reached the back door of his house, they heard Oshu, Qrunmila's wife, say that there was not a pot in the house. She said that if anyone came to sacrifice that day, Qrunmila should name as their offering two pots, one switch[4] each, five yams, one knife for cutting food,[5] and 105 ears of corn.

When "Elemele of the house" and "Elemele of the farm" entered the house, they dropped five cowries on the ground and "Iwori which brings help through a sacrifice" was cast for them. Then Qrunmila said, "A wall covers one's eyes but does not close one's ears." He said, "Did you hear what my wife was just saying?" They said they had not heard. He said "You have come to divine because of abiku."

---

1. Iwori abogbe is an alternative name for the figure Iwori Ogbe.

2. Meaning that one can hear but not see what is happening on the other side side of a wall. The reference is to overhearing what Qrunmila's wife said.

3. Children destined to die; see n. 3, verse 1-4.

4. The twig of the atori bush (Glyphaea lateriflora) is used as a switch or whip.

5. Any knife for cutting food, regardless of its shape; generally the names of different kinds of knives are based on their shape.

d(a)-Ifa; nwǫn ni bę-ni   nitotǫ. O ni ki   nwǫn şe   ikoko meji, işu
cast-Ifa; they say so-be-(it) truly. He say should they make pot   two, yam

marun, ǫpa-(a)tori   (ǫ)k(an)-ǫkan, ǫbę-şilo   kan, ati ǫrunlǫrun
five,   branch-(of)-atori one-one,   knife-for:cutting:food one, and 105

igbado.
corn.

      N(i)-igba-ti nwǫn de   ǫna, Elemele   oko da-(o)hun o ni on
      At-time-that they arrive road, Elemele (of) farm break-voice she say she

ko ni   ru   eyi-ti on fi eti   on gbǫ ti aya rę nkǫ
not be (she) offer this-that she take ear (of) her hear that wife his teaching (him)

yi; o ni adamǫ b(i)-o mǫ Ifa to yi aya rę ni o nkǫ   ni
this; she say how   if-he know Ifa equal this, wife his be she teaching (him) at

ębǫ   ti   yio yan?   Ati papa nitori   iji   ti o wi
sacrifice that (he) will choose? And especially because (of) shelter that he say

gan,   ni on ko fi   ni ru-(ę)bǫ   na, ati pe ni ori   iji
identical, be she not take (it) be offer-sacrifice the, and that at head (of) shelter

na gan   ni on yio lo kǫ ile   si. Elemele   ile   ni ori   on
the identical be she will use build house to. Elemele (of) house say head (of) her

ko dara to-bę; o ni on yio lǫ ru-(ę)bǫ   ti   on; o ru
not be:good equal-so; she say she will go offer-sacrifice that (of) her; she offer

işu marun, ǫrunlǫrun igbado, ikoko meji, atori kan, ati ǫbę-şilo
yam five,   105   corn, pot two, atori one, and knife-for:cutting:food

kan. Qrunmila gbe ǫkan fun   ni-(i)nu   ikoko meji yi, o ja ewe
one. Qrunmila take one give (her) at-belly (of) pot   two this, he cut leaf (of)

Ifa si,   o ni n(i)-igba-ti o ba   ma   bi,   inu   ikoko ni
Ifa to (it), he say at-time-that she should (continuative) bear, belly (of) pot be

ki o ma   bi awǫn ǫmǫ rę si,   ati pe bi o ba   bi
should she (continuative) bear those child hers to (it), and that if she should bear

     tan, ki o ma   wi-pe   "Qmǫ mi f(i)-ori   kan
(them) finish, should she (continuative) speak-that "Child my take-head touch

ikoko ko ku mǫ." O ni ǫmǫ na ko si ni ku.
pot   not die again." He say child the not and be die.

      N(i)-igba-ti Elemele   oko nlǫ   ɔ lǫ kǫ-(i)le   rę s(i)-ori
      At-time-that Elemele (of) farm going, she go build-house hers to-head (of)

egungun   o si bi ǫmǫ meji si ori rę; n(i)-igba-ti ǫmǫ rę
silk:cotton:tree she and bear child two to head its; at-time-that child hers

nd(i)-agba,   o ni on nlǫ ki Elemele   ile.   N(i)-igba-ti o
becoming-elder, she say she going greet Elemele (of) house. At-time-that she

de   ile   o bilere pe o ti bi? O ni o ti bi; o ni
arrive house, she ask   that she have bear? She say she have bear; she say

ǫmǫ melo   ni o bi? Elemele   ile   ni ǫmǫ meji ni o bi. O
child how:many be she bear? Elemele (of) house say child two be she bear. She

They said "So it is, truly." He said that they should sacrifice two pots, five yams, one switch apiece, one knife for cutting food, and 105 ears of corn.

When they got outside, "Elemele of the farm" said that she would not make the sacrifice which with her own ears she had heard Qrunmila's wife teaching him. She said, "How is it that if Qrunmila knows so much about Ifa, his wife is teaching him what sacrifice to prescribe?"[6] And in particular she would not sacrifice because of her shelter, which he had mentioned specifically, but she would build her house in the top of that very shelter.[7] "Elemele of the house" said that her luck was not that good; and that she would make the sacrifice. She sacrificed five yams, 105 ears of corn, two pots, one switch, and one knife for cutting food. Qrunmila took one of the two pots and put Ifa's leaves into it. He said that she should give birth to her children in this pot, and that when they were born, she should say, "My child touches the pot with its head, it will not die any more."[8] Qrunmila said that the child would not die.

"Elemele of the farm" built her house in the top of a silk cotton tree, and there she gave birth to two children. When these children were growing up, she said she was going to visit "Elemele of the house." When she reached her house, she asked, "Have you given birth?" and "Elemele of the house" replied that she had. She asked, "How many children have you?" and "Elemele of the house" said she had two children. "Elemele of the farm"

---

6. Qrunmila is, of course, supposed to know more than anyone else about Ifa divination, and certainly more than a woman.

7. This shelter is the silk cotton tree, araba or egungun (Ceiba pentandra), in which she builds her nest. It is implied here that Qrunmila warned her that this was dangerous, and that she should sacrifice so that evil would not befall her.

8. Cf. n. 4, verse 19-3. It is understood that, as in verse 19-3, she should touch her children's heads to the pot while saying this.

ni   o   ti   ko ru-(ẹ)bọ   meji ni on na bi.   O ni şe   on ti
say she have not offer-sacrifice two be she also bear. She say make she have

sọ   pe ki   o   ma ru-(ẹ)bọ   n(i)-igba-na? O ni bẹ-ni bi awọn ko
speak that should she not offer-sacrifice at-time-the? She say so-be if they not

ba   ru-(ẹ)bọ,   bi awọn ti bi yi na ni awọn iba   bi.   Eşu
should offer-sacrifice, as they have bear this also be they should bear. Eshu

wa   da-(o)hun o ni n(i)-igba-ti Elemele   oko ko ru-(ẹ)bọ   tan
come break-voice he say at-time-that Elemele (of) farm not offer-sacrifice finish

o   tun nfi   on şe   fa-(o)ri?   O wa ran-(i)şẹ,   si ojo pe ki
she then taking him make shave-head? He come send-message to rain that should

iji   ki   o lọ ba Elemele   oko ja.
thunderstorm should it go join Elemele (of) farm fight.

    N(i)-igba-ti Elemele   oko ri pe ojo şu,   o ni on nlọ   si
    At-time-that Elemele (of) farm see that rain darken, she say she going to

ile   on; n(i)-igba-ti o nlọ ẹfufu gbe   lọ jina si ọna   ile
house (of) her; at-time-that she going wind carry (her) go far to road (of) house

rẹ,   ko si mọ ọna mọ; ni ọjọ keji ni o to de   ile   ni-
hers, (she) not and know road again; at day second be she equal arrive house at-

(i)bi-ti   o   bi ọmọ si. Ki   o to de   ibẹ, ẹfufu ti wo igi
place-that she bear child to. Before she equal arrive there, wind have break tree

lu   ọmọ rẹ mọ   ibi-ti   o gbe bi ọmọ si l(i)-ori   igi; awọn
strike child hers against place-that she take bear child to at-head (of) tree; those

ọmọ na si ti ku. O ri kukute ti o   ma   nba   le   ki
child the and have die. She see stump that she (continuative) alighting upon before

o   to fo gun ori   egungun;   awọn ọmọde   meji si ko
she equal fly climb head (of) silk:cotton:tree those young:child two and gather

awọn ọmọ rẹ mej(i)-(m)eji nwọn nfi   wọn şe-(i)re.   Elemele   oko
those child hers two-two   they taking them make-play. Elemele (of) farm

tun pada wa   s(i)-ọdọ   Elemele   ile   o ni iji   ti
then return come to-presence (of) Elemele (of) house she say thunderstorm that

o ja   ti   şe on ni ibi; o ni kukute ti on fi   ş(e)-ami ibẹ
it fight (her) have do her at evil; she say stump that she take (it) make-sign there

on ko ri, ati awọn ọmọ   on pẹlu.   N(i)-igba-na ni Elemele
she not see, and those child (of) her together:with (it). At-time-the be Elemele

    ile   dide o bọ si idi   ikoko, o gbe ọmọ rẹ o ni ọmọ
(of) house arise she drop to bottom (of) pot,   she take child hers she say "child

    on f(i)-ori   kan   ikoko ko ku."
(of) her take-head touch pot   not die."

    Elemele   ile   ni orukọ ti a pe ẹiyẹ-(i)le;   Elemele   oko
    Elemele (of) house be name that we call bird-(of)-house; Elemele (of) farm

ni orukọ ti   a   pe adaba.
be name that we call dove.

said that she had not offered a sacrifice, but that she had two children also. She said, "Didn't I tell you at the time that I needn't sacrifice?" She said it would have been the same if they hadn't sacrificed, as their children would have been born anyway. Eshu protested, saying, "First 'Elemele of the farm' refused to sacrifice, and now is she going to brag about it?" He sent word to the rain to send a thunderstorm to fight "Elemele of the farm."

When "Elemele of the farm" saw the clouds growing dark, she said she had to be going home. While she was going, the wind carried her far out of her way, so that she no longer knew her way home, and it was not until the next day that she reached her nest. Before she arrived, the storm had broken down the tree and thrown her children to the ground, and her children were dead. She saw the stump upon which she used to alight before flying to the top of the silk cotton tree, and that two human children had picked up her own two children and were playing with them. "Elemele of the farm" returned to "Elemele of the house" and told how the thunderstorm had fought with her and brought evil upon her. She said that she had not seen either the stump that marked her way home or her children.[9] Then "Elemele of the house" flew into her pot and, taking her children, said, "My child touches the pot with its head; it will not die." "Elemele of the house" is what we call Pigeon; "Elemele of the farm" is what we call Dove.[10]

---

9. There is an inconsistency here which is left unexplained. First it is said that she saw the stump, and found that her children had been killed; while here it says that she had not seen either. The stump was used as a landmark, by which she recognized the tree in which her nest was.

10. Without stating it explicitly, this verse explains why the dove continues to live in the treetops in the forest, while the pigeon lives in the house in pots set out for her by men. An alternate explanation of this is offered in verse 33-3. Cf. the version of this verse recorded by Epega (n.d.: II, 93-94) and quoted in Chapter XII.

Ifa ni ki   ęni-ti   a   da Ifa yi fun,   ki   o   ru-(ę)bǫ
Ifa say should person-that we cast Ifa this for (him), should she offer-sacri-

nitori   i-b(i)-eji   kan ki nwǫn ma ba   ku, ati ki iji
fice because one:who-born-two one that they not should die; and that thunder-

ki   o ma ba   gbe   o-ni-(i)ji   kan lǫ; ati-pe ki
storm should it not should carry one:who-be-shelter one go; and-that should

ęni-ti   a   da Ifa yi fun,   ki   o   ma-şe rin ni-(i)nu   ęfufu
person-that we cast Ifa this for (him), should he not-do walk at-belly (of) wind

ni ǫdun yi ki igi ki   o ma ba   da pa.
at year this that tree should it not should break kill (him).

IWORI OGBE - 2

Alukerese fi   irakoro d(i)-agba   a   da k(o)-Ojigigbogi ti
"Alukerese take crawling become-elder" (be) who cast for-Ojigigbogi that

işe Oluwo   ode   ǫrun. Nwǫn ni ki   o   lǫ j(ę)-işę
make Oluwo (of) outside (of) sky.   They say should he go eat-message (of)

ębǫ   fun awǫn ara   rę ni ile;   nwǫn ni gba-(e)ruku-gba-(i)lę   kan
sacrifice for those people his at house; they say sweep-dust-sweep-ground one

nbǫ   ki o ma ba   le   pa gbogbo ęrunlǫjǫ igi   oko; nwǫn ni
coming that it not should be:able kill all   165   tree (of) farm; they say

ki   nwǫn ma   şe   ęgb(ęwa)-ęgbęwa   o-l(i)-ori-
should they (continuative) make 2000-2000   (cowries) one:who-has-head-

du-(o)ri,   akikǫ (ǫ)k(an)-ǫkan.
strive:for-head, cock one-one.

Gbogbo   nwǫn ni awǫn ko ni   ęgb(ęwa)-ęgbęwa   ti awǫn yio
All   (of) them say they not have 2000-2000   (cowries) that they will

fi   ru-(ę)bǫ.   N(i)-igba-ti o de   ǫdǫ   atori o şe
take (them) offer-sacrifice. At-time-that he reach presence (of) Atori, he make

ęgbęwa   ati akikǫ kan; ariran şe   irinwo,   esun şe   irinwo
2000   (cowries) and cock one; Ariran make 400   (cowries), Esun make 400

ti-rę.   N(i)-igba-ti nwǫn ru   ębǫ   yi tan,   Eşu gbe
(cowries) that-(of)-his. At-time-that they offer sacrifice this finish, Eshu carry

ębǫ   na o di   ode   ǫrun; nwǫn bere pe awǫn melo   ni o
sacrifice the it become outside (of) sky; they ask that they how:many be who

ru-(ę)bǫ?   O ni awǫn męta ni o   ru-(ę)bǫ,   o ni ariran, atori
offer-sacrifice? He say those three be who offer-sacrifice, he say Ariran, Atori

ati esun; nwǫn ni ki   iji   lǫ ba awǫn ęrunlǫjǫ igi   oko
and Esun; they say should thunderstorm go join those 165   tree (of) farm

ja,   n(i)-igba-ti o de   ǫdǫ   wǫn o bęrę si lǫ   ori wǫn pǫ
fight; at-time-that it reach presence their, it begin to twist head their together

Ifa says that the person for whom we have cast this figure should sacrifice that her twins may not die, and that a thunderstorm may not carry away her shelter, [11] and that the person for whom this figure was cast should not walk outside in the wind this year lest he be killed by a falling tree.

---

11. This can be either a thing, as in the case of "Elemele of the farm," or a person, or a guardian spirit. Note the play on the words "shelter" (iji) and "thunderstorm" (iji).

---

33 - 2

"The Alukerese vine[1] creeps to old age" was the one who cast Ifa for Ojigigbogi who was the Oluwo[2] in heaven. They said he should take word to the people of his house that they should sacrifice, lest a heavy storm should sweep the ground clean[3] and kill all the 165 kinds of trees of the farm. They said they should offer six pence each, and one cock apiece.

The trees all said they did not have the six pence with which to sacrifice. However, the Atori bush[4] sacrificed the six pence and the cock; and the Ariran grass[5] and the Esun grass[6] each gave one penny two oninis. When they had finished, Eshu carried their sacrifices to heaven, where they asked him how many had sacrificed. He said that three had sacrificed, and they were Ariran, Atori, and Esun. They said that a thunderstorm should go to fight with the 165 trees of the farm. When the storm came, it began to twist their heads together

---

1. A creeping plant (Ipomoea involucrata), which grows very slowly. Cf. verse 181-1.

2. Oluwo is one of the titles among babalawo; see Chapter IX.

3. "Sweep-dust-sweep-ground" may refer to a storm or to a supernatural force that comes to earth from heaven and kills people.

4. A bush (Glyphaea lateriflora) with flexible twigs that are used in making switches.

5. An unidentified grass standing a foot or two high.

6. Elephant grass (Pennisetum purpureum) or perhaps Saccharum spontaneum. Described as wild grass resembling sugar cane, used for feeding horses, it stands six feet high and has a blade an inch or two wide.

o si   nfa   wǫn tu;   n(i)-igba-ti o de   ǫdǫ   esun, esun ni on
it and pulling them loosen. At-time-that it reach presence (of) Esun, Esun say he

ru   irinwo, o dǫbalę;   n(i)-igba-ti o de   ǫdǫ   ariran
offer 400,   he prostrate (himself); at-time-that it reach presence (of) Ariran,

o bęrę si kǫ-(o)rin pe:
he begin to sing-song that:

> Tę-(o)ri   wǫn o tę-(o)ri   wǫn
> "Press-head their, oh, press-head their

> Igba ariran ęfufu lę-lę
> "200 Ariran wind sway-sway

> Tę-(o)ri   wǫn ba-(i)lę   igba ariran
> "Press-head their touch-ground, 200 Ariran"

O tę-(o)ri   ariran ba-(i)lę.   N(i)-igba-ti o de   ǫdǫ   atori,
It press-head (of) Ariran touch-ground. At-time-that it reach presence (of) Atori,

atori ni:
Atori say:

> O-şoko   bani
> "O-shoko." "Bani."

O ni:
He say:

   Alukerese o l(i)-o fi   irakoro rakoro d(i)-agba   a   da   fun iwǫ
"'Alukerese, oh, be-who take crawling crawl become-elder' they cast for you

Ojigigbogi ti işe Oluwo   ode   ǫrun, nwǫn ni ki   o lǫ j(ę)-
Ojigigbogi that make Oluwo (of) outside (of) sky; they say should he go eat-

işę   ębǫ   fun awǫn ara   rę ni-(i)le.
message (of) sacrifice for those people his at-house."

O ni:
He say:

   Ęfufu-lęgę-lęgę   o,
   "Wind-sway-sway, Oh,

   O   ma   ranti   ę-1(i)-ęgbęwa,
   "You (imperative) remember one:who-has-2000 (cowries),

   O   ma ş(e)-si ranti   ę-1(i)-ęgbęwa
   "You not do-not remember one:who-has-2000 (cowries)."

O ni:
He say:

   Atori ni-(i)gi   orişa   o,
   "Atori be-tree (of) orisha, oh;

   Iji   p(a)-ori p(a)-okun mǫ   mǫ pa-(a)tori o,
   "Thunderstorm kill-head kill-rope (imperative) not kill-Atori, oh;

   Atori ni-(i)gi   orişa
   Atori be-tree (of) orisha"

and to pull them up by the roots. But when it reached Esun, he said that he had
offered one penny two oninis, and he prostrated himself and the storm passed
over him. When it came to Ariran, he began to sing:

> "Bend down their heads, oh, bend down their heads.
> "The 200 Ariran are swaying in the wind,
> "Bend down their heads to the ground, 200 Ariran."

The storm bent the heads of the Ariran to the ground, and passed over them.
When it reached Atori, Atori said:

> "O shoko." "Bani."

He said:

> "'The Alukerese vine creeps to old age' was the one who cast Ifa for Ojigig-
bogi who was the Oluwo in heaven. They said he should take word to the people
of his house that they should sacrifice."

He said:

> "Swaying in the wind, oh.
> "Remember the one who sacrificed sixpence;
> "Do not forget to remember the one who sacrificed sixpence."

He said:

> "Atori is the tree of the gods[7] oh;
> "Let the thunderstorm break down trees and pull down vines, but do not kill
>   Atori, oh.
> "Atori is the tree of the gods."

---

7. Switches made from the atori bush are used in the festivals of certain
deities.

O ni:
He say:

        Ma   şe   bẹlẹjẹ, atori
      "(Imperative) make slender, Atori

        Ma   şe   bẹlẹjẹ, o, atori
      (Imperative) make slender, oh, Atori"

    Ifa ni ki   ẹni-ti   a da Ifa yi fun   ki   o bẹrẹ
    Ifa say should person-that we cast Ifa this for (him) should he bend:down

fun iji   ki iji   ki   o le   foda.
for thunderstorm that thunderstorm should it be:able jump:over (him).

IWORI OGBE - 3

    Ọkanjuwa agbẹ ni   gbẹ owu akurọ   ki o ba   le
    "Greedy   farmer be (he) plant cotton waterside:garden that it should be:able

şe   ọmọ kurubu-kurubu   a   da fun Adaba ti o nlọ nfẹ Otegbe.
make child huge-huge"   (be) who cast for Dove that he going loving Otegbe.

    Ifa ni ẹni-kan   nfẹ   fẹ obinrin kan pẹpẹrẹ bayi bi ko ba   ru-
    Ifa say person-one wanting love woman one slender, thus if not should offer-

(ẹ)bọ,   gbese   rẹ ni   yio le   wọ   inu   igbo lọ.
sacrifice, debt (of) her be (it) will chase (him) enter belly (of) forest go.

    Adaba fẹ Otegbe ko ru-(ẹ)bọ,   gbese   rẹ si le   wọ
    Dove love Otegbe not offer-sacrifice, debt (of) her and chase (him) enter

inu   igbo lọ, n(i)-igba-ti o de   igbo o bẹrẹ si ke pe Gbese
belly (of) forest go; at-time-that he arrive forest he begin to cry that "Debt (of)

Otegbe sun mi; igbe na ni i ma   ke titi   di   oni yi.
Otegbe tire me"; cry the be he (continuative) cry until (it) become today this.

Akikọ-(a)diẹ marun ati ẹgbarun   ni ẹbọ.
Cock-chicken five   and 10,000 (cowries) be sacrifice.

IWORI OGBE - 4

Agbo-ti-(i)ku-tọ   a   da f(un)-A-l(i)-ara   ti aya rẹ
  "Ram-from-belly-urinate" (be) who cast for-One:who-has-Ara that wife his

tori   ọmọ da Ifa; nwọn ni ki   o ru-(ẹ)bọ   igiripa
because (of) child cast Ifa; they say should she offer-sacrifice (of) full:grown

obukọ kan, akikọ-(a)diẹ kan, ati ẹgbẹtalelọgbọn.   Nwọn ni aya rẹ
he:goat one, cock-chicken one, and 6600   (cowries). They say wife his

He said:

> "Be slender, Atori;
> "Be slender, oh, Atori."[8]

Ifa says that the person for whom this figure was cast should bend down during thunderstorms so that they may pass over without harming him.

---

8. This verse explains why the Esun, Ariran, and Atori plants are flexible and can survive the heavy thunderstorms, while the larger trees of the forest are broken down or torn up by the roots.

---

33 - 3

"The greedy farmer plants cotton in the waterside garden so it may have very large bolls" was the one who cast Ifa for Dove when he wanted to marry Otegbe.

Ifa says someone wants to marry a slender woman; if he does not sacrifice, he will have to hide in the forest because of the debt he owes on her bridewealth.

Dove married Otegbe, but did not sacrifice, and his debt on her bridewealth drove him into the forest. There he began to cry, "Otegbe's debt has tired me out"; this is the cry of the Dove until this very day.[1] Five cocks and two shillings six pence[2] is the sacrifice.

---

1. This verse explains why the dove lives in the forest, and also the origin of his cry. For another explanation of why the dove lives in the forest, see verse 33-1.

2. There are five cocks and five units of 2000 cowries.

---

33 - 4

"Ram urinates from the belly" was the one who cast Ifa for the King of Ara, whose wife cast Ifa because she wanted a child. They said she should sacrifice one full-grown he-goat, one cock, and one shilling seven pence eight oninis. They said his wife

yio şe   ki   o   to   ri   ǫmǫ bi.   Bi o   ba   ru-(ę)bǫ   yi
will do (this) before she equal see child bear. If she should offer-sacrifice this

tan,   yio gbe   obukǫ na pǫn   lǫ si idi   Eşu.
finish, (she) will carry he:goat the carry:on:back go to base (of) Eshu.

    Nwǫn ni nitori-ti   Eşu ni   yio fun   ni ǫmǫ. O ni on ko
    They say because-that Eshu be (who) will give (her) at child. She say she not

le   tori   ǫmǫ gbe obukǫ pǫn   lǫ si-(i)di   Eşu; o
be:able because (of) child carry he:goat carry:on:back go to-base (of) Eshu; she

ni ki Gbǫndin ęru   on ki   o gbe   obukǫ na pǫn   lǫ si
say that Gbǫndin slave (of) her should she carry he:goat the carry:on:back go to

idi   Eşu. N(i)-igba-ti Gbǫndin gbe   obukǫ pǫn   de idi
base (of) Eshu. At-time-that Gbǫndin carry he:goat carry:on:back arrive base

    Eşu ti o nbǫ   ni ile l(i)-ęhin igba-ti nwǫn ti fi   obukǫ
(of) Eshu that she coming at house, at-back (of) time-that they have take he:goat

bǫ   Eşu tan, Eşu gbe ǫmǫ pǫn   Gbǫndin wa   si ile;
sacrifice (to) Eshu finish, Eshu carry child carry:on:back Gbǫndin come to house

n(i)-igba-ti o di   o-ri-ka-ş(e)-k(un)-ęwa   Gbǫndin bi   ǫmǫ, nwǫn si
at-time-that it become it-not-count-make-add-ten Gbǫndin bear child; they and

mu ilękę pupa nwǫn se   mǫ   ǫmǫ   Gbǫndin l(i)-ǫrun, nwǫn ni
take bead red they string (them) against child (of) Gbǫndin at-neck; they say

ki aya Alara   wa wo   ǫmǫ   Gbǫndin, o ni oju
should wife (of) One:who-has-Ara come look:at child (of) Gbǫndin; she say eye (of)

on ti nri   pipǫn   ina, oju   on ti nri   rębęrębę   orun, ki on
her have seeing redness (of) fire, eye (of) her have seeing redness (of) sun, that she

şęşę wa   ma   wo   akun pupa   ǫrun ǫmǫ   Gbǫndin? O
just come (continuative) look:at bead red (of) neck (of) child (of) Gbǫndin? She

ni iku ya   ju   ęsin.
say death be:quick surpass shame.

    Ifa ni ki   ęni-ti   a da on fun   yi ma şe da   ęja,
    Ifa say should person-that we cast him for (him) this not make suspect lie;

o ni bi o ba fę bi-(ǫ)mǫ ki   o ma d(a)-ęja;   igiripa
he say if she should want bear-child should she not suspect-lie. Full:grown

obukǫ kan ni ki   obinrin kan gbe pǫn   lǫ si idi   Eşu ki
he:goat one be should woman one carry carry:on:back go to base (of) Eshu, should

o lǫ fi   ru-(ę)bǫ.
she go take (it) offer-sacrifice.

_____

should do this before she could bear a child. If she completed this sacrifice, then she must carry the he-goat on her back[1] to the shrine of Eshu.

They said this was because Eshu was the one who would give her the child. She said she could not carry a he-goat on her back to Eshu for the sake of a child. She said that her slave, Gbọndin, would carry the goat for her. When Gbọndin had carried the he-goat on her back to Eshu and was returning home after they had finished sacrificing it to Eshu, Eshu carried a child on his back to the house of Gbọndin. After less than ten months' time Gbọndin bore a child, and they tied red beads about its neck. They said the King of Ara's wife should come to look at Gbọndin's child. She replied that her eyes had seen the redness of fire, and her eyes had seen the redness of the sun, so why should she come just to look at red beads on the neck of the child of her slave? She said, "Death is better than shame."

Ifa says that the person for whom this figure was cast should not doubt the truth of Ifa; he says that if she wants to bear a child, she must have no doubts. A woman should carry a full-grown he-goat on her back to the shrine of Eshu and offer it as a sacrifice.

----

1. As Yoruba women carry their children.

IWORI OGBE - 5

Iwori-a-bǫ-gbe   jijẹ   Iwori-a-bǫ-gbe   mimu   Iwori b(o)-
"Iwori-to-sacrifice-aid to:eat," "Iwori-to-sacrifice-aid to:drink," "Iwori cover-

ǫmǫ   Ogbe mǫ-(i)lẹ   ki   ǫmǫ   Ogbe ma ba   ku   a   da
child (of) Ogbe against-ground that child (of) Ogbe not should die" (be) who cast

fun Baba-(i)ka(ra)   ti   o nlǫ   ko   awǫn ǫmǫ rẹ mu ilẹ
for Father-(of)-household that he going gather those child his take ground (of)

(i)bu-(i)do   ni oko,   nwǫn ni ki   o ru-(ẹ)bǫ   igiripa
place-(to)-settle at farm.   They say should he offer-sacrifice (of) full:grown

obukǫ kan, ẹgbafa   pipe,   ati aşǫ a-bi-rǫrǫ.
he:goat one, 12,000 (cowries) complete, and cloth that:which-bear-fringe.

Baba-(i)ka(ra)   ni orukǫ ti   a pe ǫgan.   Nwǫn ni ibi-
Father-(of)-household be name that we call termite:hill. They say place-

ti o gbe nlǫ   mu ilẹ   yio gba;   n(i)-igba-ti o ru-(ẹ)bǫ
that he carry going take ground will accept (him); at-time-that he offer-sacrifice

tan   nwǫn bo   ẹbǫ   na mǫ-(i)lẹ;   nwǫn ni ki   o joko   le.
finish they cover sacrifice the against-ground; they say should he sit:down upon

O bẹrẹ si bi-(ǫ)mǫ;   gbogbo awǫn ǫmǫ rẹ nyǫ.   Nwǫn ni ǫgan
(it). He begin to bear-child; all   those child his rejoicing. They say termite:

bi-(i)wo ni o di   t(i)-eku t(i)-ẹiyẹ   ni   yio ma
hill bear-hole be it become that-(of)-rat that-(of)-bird be (they) will (continuative)

sa wǫ.
run enter.

Ifa ni ẹni-kan   nlǫ   mu-(i)lẹ,   ki   o ru-(ẹ)bǫ   ki ibẹ
Ifa say person-one going take-ground, should he offer-sacrifice that there

le   gba.
can accept (him).

IWORI OGBE - 6

Iwori-a-bǫ-gbe   jijẹ   Iwori-a-bǫ-gbe   mimu   Iwori b(o)-
"Iwori-to-sacrifice-aid to:eat," "Iwori-to-sacrifice-aid to:drink," "Iwori cover-

ǫmǫ   Ogbe mǫ-(i)lẹ   ki   ǫmǫ   Ogbe ma ba   ku   a   da
child (of) Ogbe against-ground that child (of) Ogbe not should die" (be) who cast

fun Baba-(i)ka(ra)   ti   a ni ki   o ru-(ẹ)bǫ   nitori
for Father-(of)-household that they say should he offer-sacrifice because (of)

arun   ori. Igiripa   ewurẹ kan ati ẹgbawa   pipe   ni
disease (of) head. Full:grown she:goat one and 20,000 (cowries) complete be

ẹbǫ.   Baba-(i)ka(ra)   ni orukǫ ti   a pe ǫgan;   o kǫ   ko
sacrifice. Father-(of)-household be name that we call termite:hill; he refuse not

33 - 5

"Iwori which brings help through a sacrifice,[1] is to be eaten," "Iwori which brings help through a sacrifice, is to be drunk"[2] and "Iwori shields Ogbe's child so that it will not die" were the ones who cast Ifa for "Father of Household" when he was gathering his children together to take land to settle in the farm. They said he should sacrifice one full-grown he-goat and three shillings, complete, and a fringed cloth.

"Father of Household" is what we call Termite Hill. They said that the place to which he was going to take land would be large enough to accommodate him. When he had completed the sacrifice, they buried it in the ground and told him to settle there. He began to have many children and all his children were rejoicing. They said that a termite hill which has a hole will have rats and birds entering it.

Ifa says that someone who is going to take new land should sacrifice so that he may find a place to accommodate him.

---

1. An alternative name for the figure Iwori Ogbe. See n. 1, verse 33-1.
2. This probably refers to the medicine prepared with this verse, which then is eaten or drunk.

---

33 - 6

"Iwori which brings help through a sacrifice, is to be eaten," "Iwori which brings help through a sacrifice, is to be drunk" and "Iwori shields Ogbe's child so that it will not die" were the ones who cast Ifa for "Father of Household."[1] They said he should sacrifice against a disease of the head. One full-grown she-goat and five shillings, complete, was the sacrifice. "Father of Household" is what we call Termite Hill. He refused

---

1. The names of the diviners and of the main character here are identical to those in verse 33-5, but the circumstances are different.

si ru-(ẹ)bọ;   arun   ori bẹrẹ si mu ọgan   o si bẹrẹ si
and offer-sacrifice; disease (of) head begin to take termite:hill he and begin to

ti   ori jin.
from head fall:down.

Ifa ni ẹni-kan   jẹ o-l(i)-roi   ni-(i)nu   ile   kan, ki
Ifa say person-one eat one:who-be-head at-belly (of) house one, should

ẹni   na ru-(ẹ)bọ   ki arun   ori ki   o ma ba   ma
person the offer-sacrifice that disease (of) head should it not should (continuative)

ba   ja   ki   o si ti   ibẹ   ma ku nitori-ti   bi ẹni   na ba
join (him) fight should he and from there not die; because-that if person the should

ku, iya   nla ni yio ma   jẹ awọn ara   ile   rẹ ti o
die, punishment big be will (continuative) eat those people (of) house his, that they

wa   ni ile   na; arun   ori ni yio si pa ẹni   na.
exist at house the; disease (of) head be will and kill person the.

IWORI - (Ọ)YẸKU - 1

Ijatijati   awo   ọrun   ọpẹ   a   da fun
"Dead:fruit:of:palm:tree secret (of) neck (of) palm:tree" (be) who cast for

Olukoun l(i)-ọgbọn   Ijiwo ti a   ni ki   o ru-(ẹ)bọ   nitori
Olukoun at-precinct (of) Ijiwo that they say should he offer-sacrifice because (of)

oko   idi   rẹ: ṣokoto   idi   rẹ, obukọ kan, aike kan, ati
penis (of) waist his: trousers (of) waist his, he:goat one, axe one, and

ẹgbẹtalelọgbọn.   Olukoun ko ru-(ẹ)bọ;   n(i)-igba-ti nwọn ngbe iyawo
6600   (cowries). Olukoun no offer-sacrifice; at-time-that they taking junior:

bọ   Olukoun sa wọ   inu   igbo lọ; Olukoun ni a-i-pe   do-
wife come, Olukoun run enter belly (of) bush go; Olukoun be we-to-call copulate:

(i)gi-do-(i)gi.
with-tree-copulate:with-tree.

Ifa ni ki   e-l(i)-yi   ru-(ẹ)bọ   nitori   oko   idi
Ifa say should one:who-be-this offer-sacrifice because (of) penis (of) waist

rẹ ki ara-(a)iye   ma ba   fi   oko   idi   rẹ da   ni
his, that people-(of)-world not should take penis (of) waist his cause (him) at

idagiri   nitori-ti   nwọn ngbe   iyawo   kan bọ   wa   ba.
catastrophy because-that they carrying junior:wife one come come meet (him).

---

to sacrifice, and a head disease began to afflict him, so that he began to crumble at the top.[2]

Ifa says someone who is head of a house should sacrifice, lest a disease of the head afflict him and lest he should die from it; because if he should die, a dire affliction will fall upon his relatives who live in his house. A disease of the head will kill him.

---

2. The comparison of the crumbling of the top of the termite hill and the head disease is clearer in Yoruba, since the word "ori" indicates both "head" and "top."

---

34 - 1

"Dead fruit and dead leaves of the palm tree,"[1] diviner of the palm tree's neck, was the one who cast Ifa for Olukoun of Ijiwo precinct.[2] They said Olukoun should sacrifice the trousers he was wearing, one goat, one axe, and one shilling seven pence eight oninis on account of his penis.[3] Olukoun did not sacrifice. When they were bringing his bride to him he ran into the forest.[4] Olukoun is what we call the bird "Copulate with tree."[5]

Ifa says that this person should sacrifice because of his penis, lest witches injure it, because a wife will soon be brought to him.

---

1. The dead fruit and dead leaves at the head of the palm tree, near the region from which the palm wine is tapped.

2. Ijiwo is a precinct in the ward or "quarter" (adugbo) of Mọrẹ in Ifẹ.

3. Note that the "trousers of his waist" are sacrificed for "the penis of his waist." In verse 4-2 Lukoun is identified as Penis.

4. Because he could not have intercourse, having failed to make the sacrifice.

5. This unidentified bird gets its name from the motions it makes when alighting on a tree. This verse explains why it lives in the forest, and why it goes through its characteristic motions.

IWORI - (Q)YẸKU - 2

Egungun   eluju duro l(i)-oko nwo   işe   ilu   roro
"Silk:cotton:tree (of) field stand at-farm looking:at doings (of) town intensely"

a   da   fun Şe-(i)wọ-mọ   ti   o   nlọ   şe   ọkọ   Biri-biri; nwọn
(be) who cast for Make-you-know that he going make husband (of) Turn-turn; they

ni   ki   o   ru-(ẹ)bọ   ki   o   ma ba   şe   agbako   iku   ni ọdun
say should he offer-sacrifice that he not should make misfortune (of) death at year

yi.   Şe-(i)wọ-mọ   ko   ru-(ẹ)bọ   agutan kan, aşọ, ibo-(a)ra   kan, ati
this. Make-you-know not offer-sacrifice (of) ewe   one, cloth cover-body one, and

ẹtala.
26,000 (cowries).

N(i)-igba-ti Şe-(i)wọ-mọ   ti   işe   ọkọ   Biri-biri kọ   ko
At-time-that Make-you-know that make husband (of) Turn-turn refuse not

ru-(ẹ)bọ,   ni-(ọ)jọ-kan ti   awọn Irun-(I)mọlẹ nfọ   aşọ   ni Eşu ta
offer-sacrifice, at-day-one that those 400-Deity   washing cloth be Eshu kick

Biri-biri ni idi,   o   si   lọ   ba   wọn n(i)-ibi-ti   nwọn ti   gbe nfọ
Turn-turn at waist; she and go meet them at-place-that they have take washing

aşọ.   N(i)-igba-ti nwọn ri   nwọn ko   ọfa   bo   o,   nwọn si   bẹrẹ
cloth. At-time-that they see (her) they gather arrow cover her, they and begin

si kọ-(o)rin nwọn nle   lọ pe:
to sing-song they chasing (her) go that:

Biri-biri bẹ   a   wo n(i)-ibi a   gbe nfọ-(a)şọ
"Turn-turn peep:at us look at-place we take washing-cloth;

Biri-biri bẹ   a   wo n(i)-ibi a   gbe nfọ-(a)şọ
"Turn-turn peep:at us look at-place we take washing-cloth."

Nwọn nwa   nwọn si le   de   ẹhin-(ẹ)kun-(i)le   Şe-
They seeking (her) they and chase (her) arrive back-door-(of)-house (of) Make-

(i)wọ-mọ; n(i)-igba-ti Şe-(i)wọ-mọ   ngbọ   igbe   iyawo   rẹ   o   bọ
you-know; at-time-that Make-you-know hearing cry (of) junior:wife his, he come

s(i)-ode,   n(i)-igba-ti   nwọn ri-i   nwọn bẹ   l(i)-ori, nwọn si   pa
to-outside; at-time-that they see-him, they cut (him) at-head, they and kill

Biri-biri aya rẹ pẹlu   n(i)-igba-na ni nwọn nkọ-(o)rin   pe:
Turn-turn wife his together:with (him); at-time-the be they singing-song that:

Şe   iwọ mọ   o   şe şe
"Make you know you do do?

Şe   iwọ mọ   o   şe şe
"Make you know you do do?"

Ifa ni   ki   obinrin kan ma fi   ẹsẹ ko   ọran wọ-(i)le   lai!
Ifa say should woman one not take foot gather affair enter-house, alas!

Ki   ọran   na   ma ba   pa   ọkọ   pa aya pẹlu.
That affair the not should kill husband kill wife together:with (him).

---

34 - 2

"The silk cotton tree in the field stands in the farm watching closely what is happening in town"[1] was the one who cast Ifa for "Didn't you know?" when he was going to become the husband of Whirler.[2] They said he should sacrifice lest he should meet his death during that year. "Didn't you know?" did not make the sacrifice of one ewe, one cloth to cover the body, and six shillings six pence.

"Didn't you know?" the husband of Whirler refused to sacrifice. One day when the Four Hundred Deities were washing their clothes, Eshu forced Whirler to go where they were washing. When they saw her they shot arrows at her, and they began to sing as they chased her:

"Whirler has spied on us where we were washing our clothes;
"Whirler has spied on us where we were washing our clothes."

They followed her chasing her until she came to the back door of her husband's house; and when "Didn't you know?" heard the cries of his wife, he came out. When they saw him, the deities cut off his head and killed his wife Whirler with him. Then they began to sing:

"Didn't you know, you shouldn't have done it?
"Didn't you know, you shouldn't have done it?"

Ifa says that a woman should sacrifice lest trouble follow her footsteps home; and lest it kill both her husband and herself.

---

1. Cf. the proverb "The bat suspends itself upside down but watches the doings of all the birds": "Adan dorikodo o nwo işe ęiyę gbogbo."

2. One who whirls, spins, or turns about.

IWORI MEJI[1] - 1

Eru-(ǫ)kǫ   l(i)-ori   ko ni   mundunmundun a   da   k(o)-Eji-koko
"Handle-(of)-hoe have-head not have brain"   who cast for-Two-Knot

Eji-(I)wori ti   o nlǫ   s(i)-ode   Ǫyǫ; nwǫn ni   ki   o   ru   ęiyę-
Eji-Iwori   that he going to-outside (of) Ǫyǫ; they say should he offer bird-(of)-

(i)le meji, ęyin   adię   meji, ati   ęgbędǫgbǫn.   Nwǫn ni   ko ni
house two, egg (of) chicken two, and 5000   (cowries). They say not be (he)

ri   ibi n(i)-ibę, nwǫn ni   ire   ni   yio ri.   Ifa ni on ko ni ję-
see evil at-there, they say goodness be (he) will see. Ifa say he not be consent-

ki   a   ri ibi ni ohun ti   a   da Ifa si yi.
that we see evil at thing that we cast Ifa to this.

Oju   awo   ki ri-(i)bi, Eji-(I)wori
"Eye (of) secret not see-evil, Eji-Iwori;

Oju   awo   ki ri-(i)bi, Eji-(I)wori
"Eye (of) secret not see-evil, Eji-Iwori."

IWORI MEJI - 2

Ǫrunmila ni   o di   si   mo ni k(i)-o-ro   yę-(ę)ba   o ni
Ǫrunmila say it become 'sssi'; I   say that-who-stands avoid-side; he say

k(i)-a   şǫ   omi da, k(i)-a ma ba   da   omi si alejo l(i)-ara,
should-we watch water cast, that-we not should cast water to visitor at-body,

mo ni alejo wo   ni?   O ni   alejo   aje   ni.
I   say visitor which be (it)? He say visitor (of) money be (it).

Ǫrunmila ni   o di   si;   mo ni k(i)-o-ro   yę-(ę)ba   o ni
Ǫrunmila say it become 'sssi'; I   say that-who-stands avoid-side; he say

ki   a şǫ   omi da ki a ma ba   da   omi si alejo l(i)-ara, mo
should we watch water cast, that we not should cast water to visitor at-body, I

ni alejo wo   ni?   O ni   alejo   aya ni.
say visitor which be (it)? He say visitor (of) wife be (it).

Ǫrunmila ni   o di   si;   mo ni ki o-ro   yę-(ę)ba   o ni
Ǫrunmila say it become 'sssi'; I   say that who-stands avoid-side; he say

ki   a şǫ   omi da, ki a ma ba   da   omi si alejo l(i)-ara, mo
should we watch water cast, that we not should cast water to visitor at-body, I

ni alejo wo   ni?   O ni   alejo   ǫmǫ ni.
say visitor which be (it)? He say visitor (of) child be (it).

------

1. Also known as Eji-(I)wori and as Eji Koko (two knots). See n. 2, verse
35-1.

35 - 1

"A hoe handle has a head, but it does not have brains"[1] was the one who cast Ifa for "Two-Knots,[2] Eji Iwori," when he was going to Qyọ. They said he should sacrifice two pigeons, two chicken eggs, and one shilling three pence. They said he would not see evil where he was going; they said that a blessing was what he would see. Ifa says he will not allow us to see evil in the matter for which we have divined.

"The diviner's eye will not see evil, Eji Iwori;
"The diviner's eye will not see evil, Eji Iwori."[3]

---

1. The "head" of the hoe handle is the knot in the piece of wood into which the blade is fastened. Though it looks like a head, it has no brains inside it. The reference here is to the marrow or meat inside the head, and not to intelligence or sense.
2. "Two-Knots" is an alternative name of the figure, Iwori Meji or Eji Iwori. It appears here as a character for whom a divination was performed. Koko is a knot in a piece of wood and the allusion here is to the "head" of the hoe-handle. The word "koko" is onomatopoetic, and really refers to anything which makes the sound "koko" when tapped.
3. This is used as a song, repeated by children when going home to expected punishment. It is believed that if it is repeated, their parents will not punish them.

---

35 - 2

Qrunmila says we should cry "Sssi."[1] I say that whoever is in the way should duck. He says that we should look before we throw water into the street, lest we throw water upon a visitor. I say, "What visitor?" He says, "A visitor who will bring money."

Qrunmila says we should cry "Sssi." I say that whoever is in the way should duck. He says that we should look before we throw water into the street, lest we throw water upon a visitor. I say, "What visitor?" He says, "A visitor who will bring wives."

Qrunmila says we should cry "Sssi." I say that whoever is in the way should duck. He says that we should look before we throw water into the street, lest we throw water upon a visitor. I say, "What visitor?" He says, "A visitor who will bring children."

---

1. Sssi is a warning cried at night before throwing water or refuse into the street.

Ǫrunmila ni o di   si;   mo ni ki o-ro   yẹ-(ẹ)ba   o ni
Ǫrunmila say it become 'sssi'; I   say that who-stands avoid-side; he say

ki   a   ṣǫ   omi da   ki a ma ba   da   omi si alejo l(i)-ara, mo
should we watch water cast, that we not should cast water to visitor at-body, I

ni alejo wo   ni?   O ni alejo   oye ni.
say visitor which be (it)? He say visitor (of) title be (it).

Ifa ni on ri ire   alejo, ire   aje,   ire   aya,
Ifa say he see goodness (of) visitor, goodness (of) money, goodness (of) wife,

ire   ǫmǫ, ati ire   oye. O ni   ki   a ni   ẹiyẹ-
goodness (of) child, and goodness (of) title. He says should we have bird-(of)-

(i)le kan ati agbebǫ adiẹ   kan.
house one and hen   chicken one.

IWORI MEJI - 3

Ǫkan yǫ   ṣinṣin, ǫkan wǫ   inu   igbo Ǫgan yǫ   lǫlǫ,
"Ǫkan sprout firm, ǫkan enter belly (of) forest; Ǫgan sprout long:and:slender

ja-(ǫ)na   Ati g(un)-oke nṣ(e)-ǫmǫ   n(i)-idi biripe yunyun   a   da
reach-road" "To climb-hill making-child at-waist biripe yunyun" (be) who cast

k(o)-Ahere   ṣǫ-(o)ko   ma m(u)-ole ti iṣ(e)-ǫmǫ   O-ni-
for-"Farm:hut watch-farm not take-thief" that make-child (of) "One:who-have-

suru   awo   Akin-(ẹ)ja.   Nwǫn ni ǫdun yi ni ori rẹ yio ti
patience," secret (of) "Hero-(of)-fish." They say year this be head his will push

de   ibi-ti   yio gbe   ma   ṣe iwa.   Nwǫn ni   ki
(him) arrive place-that will carry (continuative) make destiny. They say should

o ru-(ẹ)bǫ: eku meji, ẹja meji, ati adiẹ   meji. O gbǫ ẹbǫ   o
he offer-sacrifice: rat two, fish two, and chicken two. He hear sacrifice, he

ru-(ẹ)bǫ.
offer-sacrifice.

N(i)-igba-ti o ṣe,   ǫba   awǫn ara   Igbodo ku, nwǫn mu ẹja
At-time-that it make, king (of) those people (of) Igbodo die, they take fish

nwǫn de   s(i)-inu   igba.   Nwǫn ni ẹni-k(u)-ẹni   ti   o
they cover (it) to-belly (of) calabash. They say person-any-person that he

ba   le   ki   Ifa kan ohun ti awǫn de   si-(i)nu   igba   na
should be:able recite Ifa touch thing that they cover to-belly (of) calabash the

ti o ba   si le   da-(o)rukǫ   ẹja ni   awǫn yio fi   j(ẹ)-
that he should and be:able break-name (of) fish be (who) they will take (him) eat-

ǫba   ilu awǫn.
king (of) town their.

Qrunmila says we should cry "Sssi." I say that whoever is in the way should duck. He says that we should look before we throw water into the street, lest we throw water upon a visitor. I say, "What visitor?" He says, "A visitor who will bring a title."

Ifa says that he sees the blessing of visitors, the blessing of money, the blessing of wives, the blessing of children, and the blessing of a title. He says we should sacrifice one pigeon and one hen.

---

35 - 3

"Qkan sprouts firm; it enters the forest; Qgan[1] sprouts long and slender; it reaches the road," and "In climbing a hill, one's hips move biripe-yunyun"[2] were the ones who cast Ifa for "Farm hut stands watch in the farm but does not catch thieves," who was a child of "Patient One," the diviner of "Hero of fish." They said that that year his head would bring him to a place where he would achieve his destiny. They said he should sacrifice two rats, two fish, and two chickens. He heard and offered the sacrifice.

After a while, the King of the people of Igbodo died. They took a fish and put it in a covered calabash. They said that anyone who could recite Ifa verses which touched upon the thing they had put inside the calabash, that is, who mentioned the word "fish," would be made king of their town.

---

1. Cf. nn. 5 and 6, verse 1-1.
2. A phrase describing the motion of a person's hips when taking high steps in climbing.

Gbogbo awǫn babalawo   ilu   ki   Ifa titi nwǫn ko da-(o)rukǫ
All   those diviner   (of) town recite Ifa until they not break-name (of)

ęja nitori-na   nwǫn ko fun-(i)bo. L(i)-ęhin-na ni Ahere   şǫ-(o)ko   ma
fish, because-the they not know-ibo. At-after-the be "Farm:hut watch-farm not

m(u)-ole   nkǫja lǫ, nwǫn si pe   pe ki   on na wa   ki Ifa,
taking-thief" passing go, they and call (him) that should he also come recite Ifa,

nitori-ti   nwǫn ri ide   Ifa ni ǫrun   ǫwǫ rę. Şugbǫn o da   wǫn
because-that they see bead (of) Ifa at neck (of) hand his. But   he break them

l(i)-ohun pe   on ko mǫ Ifa, o si wi-pe:
at-voice that he not know Ifa, he and say-that:

Awǫn Qkan yǫ   şinşin, ǫkan wǫ   inu   igbo Qgan yǫ   lǫlǫ
"Those Qkan sprout firm,   ǫkan enter belly (of) forest; Qgan sprout long:and:

ja-(ǫ)na   Ati-g(un)-oke nş(e)-ǫmǫ   n(i)-idi biripe yunyun   a
slender reach-road; To-climb-hill making-child at-waist biripe yunyun (be) who

da fun on Ahere   şǫ-(o)ko   ma m(u)-ole ti iş(e)-ǫmǫ   O-
cast for him Farm:hut watch-farm not take-thief that make-child (of) One:who-

ni-suru,   awo   Alapa Akin-(ę)ja.
have-patience, secret (of) Alapa Hero-(of)-fish."

N(i)-igba-ti awǫn ara   ode   Igbodo gbǫ bayi, nwǫn ni o fun-
At-time-that those people (of) outside (of) Igbodo hear thus, they say he know-

(i)bo nitori-ti   o ki   Ifa o da-(o)rukǫ   ęja; nwǫn si mu   nwǫn
(i)bo because-that he recite Ifa he break-name (of) fish; they and take (him) they

fi   ję ǫba   ilu wǫn.   Ahere   şǫ-(o)ko   ma m(u)-ole ni orukǫ
take (him) eat king (of) town their. "Farm:hut watch-farm not take-thief" be name

ti   a-i-pe   ikoriko.
that we-to-call Hyena.

N(i)-igba-ti o to   iwǫn   ǫdun męta ni ikoriko di   ǫ-l(i)-
At-time-that it equal period (of) year three be Hyena   become one:who-have-

ǫla gbogbo ewurę ati aguntan   ilu bęrę si inu;   Eşu l(i)-o si ngbe
honor all   she:goat and ewe   (of) town begin to be:lost; Eshu be-he and taking

wǫn pa-mǫ   nitori-ti   ębǫ   oye nikan ni Ahere   şǫ-(o)ko
them kill-against because-that sacrifice (of) title alone be "Farm-hut watch-farm

ma m(u)-ole ru,   ko ru ębǫ   pe ki   on ki   o ma ri e-
not take-thief" offer, not offer sacrifice that should he should he not see one:who

l(i)-enini;   nitori-na   ni Eşu şe   ngbe awǫn ewurę   ati aguntan
be-slanderer; because-the be Eshu make taking those she:goat and ewe   (of)

ilu pa-mǫ.   Eşu si tun tǫ   awǫn ara   ilu lǫ, o sǫ   fun
town kill-against. Eshu and then approach those people (of) town go, he speak for

wǫn pe, Enyin ko mǫ pe ęni-ti   ę fi   şe   ǫba ni o npa
them that, "You   not know that person-that you take (him) make king be he killing

All the diviners of the town recited Ifa without mentioning the word "fish," because they did not know enough about specific alternatives.[3] Afterward as "Farm hut stands watch in the farm but does not catch thieves" was passing by, they called him to come and recite Ifa, because they saw the beads of Ifa on his wrist. But he replied that he did not know Ifa, and he said:

"'Qkan sprout firm, they enter the forest; Qgan sprouts long and slender, it reaches the road' and 'When one climbs a hill, his hips move biripe-yunyun' were the ones who cast Ifa for me, 'Farmhut stands watch in the farm but does not catch thieves' who am the child of 'Patient One,' diviner of Alapa, 'Hero of Fish.'"

When the people of Igbodo heard this, they said he did know about specific alternatives because when he recited Ifa, he mentioned "fish"; so they took him and made him king of their town. "Farm hut stands watch in the farm but does not catch thieves" is what we call Spotted Hyena.

After two years had passed, when Hyena had become a highly honored person, all the ewes and she-goats began to disappear from town. It was Eshu who was taking and hiding them because "Farm hut stands watch in the farm but does not catch thieves" had made only the sacrifice for a title, but had not sacrificed against a slanderer. Therefore Eshu was taking the ewes and she-goats in town and hiding them. Then Eshu went to the townspeople and said to them, "Don't you know that the person you have made king is the one who is killing

---

3. See Chapter V.

nyin ni ewurę   ati aguntan ję?   Awǫn ara   ilu   wa   pa   ero
you at she:goat and ewe   eat?" Those people (of) town come kill thought

pǫ   nwǫn yǫ   ikoriko ni oye.
together, they pull:out Hyena   at title.

    N(i)-igba-ti ikoriko ri   pe   nwǫn yǫ   on kuro   l(i)-ori   oye, o tun
    At-time-that Hyena   see that they pull him depart at-head (of) title, he then

tǫ   awǫn babalawo   ijǫsi   lǫ o si bi wǫn lere pe kin ni
approach those diviner   (of) the:other:day go, he and ask them (1)   that what be

on le   şe ti   on fi   tun le   padа s(i)-ori   oye on? Nwǫn ni
he be:able do that he take then be:able return to-head (of) title his? They say

ki   o ru   ekiri   ęran męfa, ęgbafa,   ati amu   epo   kan.
should he offer piece (of) meat six,   12,000 (cowries), and jar (of) palm:oil one.

Nwǫn ni ki   o gbe   lǫ si eti   odo   ni akikǫ   ki   ilę
They say should he carry (it) go to ear (of) river at cock (crow) before earth

ki   o to   mǫ, ki   o si joko   ti   ki   o ma
should it equal clear, should he and sit:down against (it) should he (continuative)

şǫ.   N(i)-igba-ti ilę   mǫ, ti awǫn obinrin   ara   ode
watch (it). At-time-that earth clear, that those woman (of) people (of) outside

    Igbodo si wa   pǫn omi ni ibi   odo ti ikoriko gbe ębǫ
(of) Igbodo and come draw water at place (of) river that Hyena   carry sacrifice

si, Eşu nmu ekiri   ęran (ǫ)k(an)-ǫkan o si nfi   s(i)-inu
to, Eshu taking piece (of) meat one-one   he and putting (them) to-belly (of)

amu wǫn. Bi o ti   nsǫ   ęran na si inu   amu wǫn, ni ęran na si
jar their. As he have throwing meat the to belly (to) jar their, be meat the and

ndi   itan tabi apa   ewurę, omi ti nwǫn pǫn s(i)-inu   amu
becoming thigh or arm (of) she:goat, water that they draw to-belly (of) jars

di   ęję. Eşu si sǫ   fun ikoriko pe ki   o tęle wǫn ki o
become blood. Eshu and speak for Hyena   that should he follow them should he

lǫ ko   wǫn. N(i)-igba-ti ǫran na si di   ęjǫ, Eşu wa   sǫ   fun
go gather them. At-time-that affair the and become case, Eshu come speak for

awǫn ara   ode   Igbodo pe ęni-ti   ę yǫ   l(i)-oye ti ę
those people (of) outside (of) Igbodo that person-that you pull:out at-title that you

ni o npa   nyin ni ęran ję, ni ęnyin na papa   si tun ran awǫn obinrin
say he killing you at meat eat, be you   also yourself and then send those woman

nyin pe ki   o lǫ ma   ko   awǫn ęran na wa?   O ni (it)
yours that should they go (continuative) gather those meat the come? He say (it)

ko ni şişe,   ko ni aişe afi-bi   ę ba   tun le   gba
not be to:be:done, not be not-do unless-if you should then be:able accept (him)

pada, ki ę si tun fi   j(ę)-oye.
return, that you and then take (him) eat-title.

―――――――

   1. Bi . . . lere means "to ask."

your ewes and she-goats and eating them?" The people of the town conferred together, and they took Hyena from the throne.

When Hyena saw they had removed him from his position, he went to the
diviners he had visited before, and he asked them what he could do to be able to
return to his post. They said he should sacrifice six pieces of meat,[4] three
shillings, and one pot of palm oil. They said he should take his sacrifice to the
bank of the river at cock's crow, before dawn, and sit down beside it and watch
it. When day broke, and the women of Igbodo came to draw water at the place at
the river where Hyena had brought his sacrifice, Eshu took the pieces of meat
and put one in each of their jars. As he put the meat into their jars, it turned
into front or hind legs of a she-goat, and the water that the women dipped into
their pots became blood. Eshu told Hyena to follow them and arrest them. When
this affair came to court, Eshu said to the people of Igbodo, "Have you taken your
king from the throne because he was killing your animals and eating them, while
you yourselves have been sending your wives to bring the same meat home?" He
said, "Whether you like it or not, you must find a way to take him back and make
him king again."

---

4. Lumps of meat of the size that are served in Yoruba stews, each of which
is about a mouthful. This part of the sacrifice is instrumental in restoring Hyena
to the throne.

Ifa ni   ohun kan ti   sǫ-(i)nu   ni ǫwǫ   ęni   (ohu)n-kan na tun
Ifa say thing one have throw-be:lost at hand (of) person, thing-one the then

npada   bǫ   ati pe bi ęni-kan   tabi ęni-ti   o da Ifa yi ba
returning come; and that if person-one or person-that he cast Ifa this should

de   ipo   oye kan, ki   o ru-(ę)bǫ   ki o ma ba   ri
arrive position (of) title one, should he offer-sacrifice that he not should see

e-1(i)-enini   ti yio mu ki nwǫn yǫ   l(i)-ori   oye na.
one:who-be-slanderer that will take that they pull:out (him) at-head (of) title the.

IWORI MEJI - 4

Ipenpe-(o)ju   nwǫn ko ni   enini, agba-1(i)-agba irun-(a)gbǫn nwǫn ko
"Lashes-(of)-eye they not have dew,   elder-be-elder hair-(of)-chin they not

şe   lǫlǫ   a   da fun oju ni-(i)gba-ti o nlǫ   s(i)-ode   Apere;
make fine:color" (be) who cast for Eye at-time-that he going to-outside (of) Apere;

Apere ni orukǫ ti   aiye ję. Nwǫn ni ki   o ru-(ę)bǫ: ęiyę-
Apere be name that earth eat. They say should he offer-sacrifice: bird-(of)-

(i)le meji ati ǫgbǫkanla.   Nwǫn ni ki   o ma ri ibi.
house two and 2200   (cowries). They say should he not see evil.

N(i)-igba-ti oju nbǫ   ni ode   Apere, o tǫ   awǫn babalawo
At-time-that Eye coming at outside (of) Apere, he approach those diviner

lǫ, nwǫn ni ki   o ru-(ę)bǫ   ki oju rę ma ba   ri bu(ru)-buru
go, they say should he offer-sacrifice that eye his not should see be:bad-be:bad

ni ode   aiye, ki   o mu ęiyę-(i)le   kan ki   o fi   kan
at outside (of) earth; should he take bird-(of)-house one should he take (it) touch

oju osi ki   o mu ekeji ki   o fi   kan oju ǫtun. A-(yi)o wa
eye left, should he take second should he take (it) touch eye right. We-will come

mu ǫkan ni-(i)nu   awǫn ęiyę-(i)le   nwǫn-yi a-(yi)o fi   ru-
take one at-belly (of) those bird-(of)-house those-this, we-will take (it) offer-

(ę)bǫ   pęlu ęwa   ni-(i)nu   owo   na; a-(yi)o mu ęiyę-
sacrifice with ten (cowries) at-belly (of) cowries the; we-will take bird-(of)-

(i)le keji lǫ si ile,   tabi babalawo yio mu   lǫ si ile.
house second go to house, or   diviner   will take (it) go to house.

Ifa ni ęni-ti   a da Ifa yi fun   nfę   lǫ si ęhin-
Ifa say person-that we cast Ifa this for (him) wanting go to back-(of)-

(o)di   tabi ajo   kan ki   o ru-(ę)bǫ   ki oju rę ma ba   ri
town:wall or   journey one; should he offer-sacrifice that eye his not should see

ibi l(i)-ǫhun.
evil at-there.

Ifa says that someone has lost something, but it will come back again; and that if someone, or if the person for whom this figure was cast, should achieve a position or a title, he should sacrifice that he will not encounter a slanderer who will cause him to be removed from it.

---

35 - 4

"Eyelashes[1] do not gather dew; old beards do not have good color" was the one who cast Ifa for Eye when he was going to Apere. Apere is what we call the earth. They said he should sacrifice two pigeons and six pence six oninis. They said he would not see evil.

When Eye was coming to Apere, he went to the diviners. They said he should sacrifice so that his eyes should not see anything bad on earth; he should take one pigeon and touch it to his left eye, and take the other and touch it to his right eye. We will take one of these two pigeons and sacrifice it with ten of the cowries. We will take the second pigeon home, or the diviner will take it home with him.

Ifa says that the person for whom this figure was cast wants to go out of town or on a journey. He should sacrifice that his eyes should not see evil where he is going.

---

1. Ipenpe includes the eyelashes, the eyelid, the eyebrow.

IWORI MEJI - 5

Palakungọ palakungọ, ipakọ   igun   jọ   eru   ake, bẹ-ni
"Not:round, not:round; occiput (of) Vulture resemble handle (of) axe, so-be

ko şe   la-(i)gi   a   da fun Eji-koko Eji-(I)wori ti   o   ma
not make split-wood" (be) who cast for Two-Knot Eji-Iwori that he (continuative)

kẹta odu   w(a)-aiye.
third figure come-earth.

Ifa ni ẹni-kan   ni-yi ti awọn ara   ile   rẹ nda   l(i)-
Ifa say person-one be-this that those people (of) house his causing (him) at-

amu   ti nwọn ko jẹ-ki   o ri ile   ati oko gbe yi,   şugbọn ti
trouble, that they not consent-that he see house and farm dwell this, but   that

o ba   ni ẹbọ,   yio ri iba-(i)lẹ   ọkan, yio ati bo-(o)ri
he should have sacrifice, will see touch-ground (of) heart, will and cover-head

gbogbo awọn ọta   rẹ.
(of) all   those enemy his.

N(i)-igba-ti awọn odu   mẹrindilogun nbọ-wa   si aiye Eji-koko
At-time-that those Figure sixteen   coming-come to earth, Two-Knot

Eji-(I)wori si fẹ   şe   ẹkẹta wọn wa   si ode   aiye şugbọn awọn
Eji-Iwori and want make third their come to outside (of) earth, but   those

odu   mẹrindilogun di ọtẹ   mọ,   nwọn ni ko ni ri aye gbe
Figure sixteen   tie conspiracy against (him), they say not be see room dwell

ni-(i)nu   aiye. N(i)-igba-na ni Eji-koko Eji-(I)wori mu-(a)ra o lọ si
at-belly (of) earth. At-time-that be Two-Knot Eji-Iwori   take-body he go to

ọdọ   awọn babalawo pe ki   nwọn ki o yẹ   on wo pe
presence (of) those diviner   that should they should they examine him look that

bawo ni on yio ti şe le   ri aye gbe ni-(i)nu   aiye. Nwọn ni
how be he will have make be:able see room dwell at-belly (of) earth. They say

ewurẹ kan, odo,   tẹtẹ, gbegbe, ati ejielogun   ni ẹbọ.
she:goat one, mortar, tẹtẹ, gbegbe, and 44,000   (cowries) be sacrifice.

Eji-koko Eji-(I)wori gbọ ẹbọ   o ru-(ẹ)bọ.   Nwọn ni ki
Two-Knot Eji-Iwori   hear sacrifice he offer-sacrifice. They say should

o tun ma   pada lọ si ode   aiye; n(i)-igba-ti o tun pada
he then (continuative) return go to outside (of) earth; at-time-that he then return

de   ode   aiye o sọ   fun awọn odu   mẹdogun na pe on de;
arrive outside (of) earth he speak for those Figure fifteen   the that he arrive;

nwọn ni şe awọn ti sọ   fun   pe ko si aye fun   lati
they say make they have speak for (him) that not be room for (him) in:order:to

gbe   joko   ni aiye? N(i)-igba-na ni Eji-koko Eji-(I)wori wa   da-(o)hun
dwell sit:down at earth? At-time-the be Two-Knot Eji-Iwori   come break-voice

o sọ   fun wọn bi awọn babalawo rẹ ti   kọ   pe:
he speak for them as those diviner   his have teach that:

35 - 5

"Not round, not round;[1] the back of Vulture's head resembles an axe handle, but it cannot split wood" was the one who cast Ifa for "Two-Knots, Eji Iwori"[2] when he was coming to earth as the third[3] figure of Ifa.

Ifa says this is someone whose relatives are causing him trouble; they do not allow him to find a house or a farm. But if he sacrifices, he will find peace of heart and will overcome all his enemies.

When the sixteen Figures of Ifa were coming to the earth, "Two-Knots, Eji Iwori" wanted to be third among them on earth; but the other Figures conspired against him. They told him that there was no room for him to live on earth. Then "Two-Knots, Eji Iwori" got ready and went to the diviners, that they might examine his case and tell him how he might be able to find a place to live on earth. They said that one she-goat, a mortar, the tẹtẹ leaf, the gbegbe leaf,[4] and eleven shillings were required as sacrifice.

"Two-Knots, Eji Iwori" heard and he offered the sacrifice. They said he should return to earth again. When he reached the earth he told the other fifteen Figures that he had come. They said, hadn't they told him that there wasn't room on earth for him to live? Then "Two-Knots, Eji Iwori" replied as his diviners had taught him:

-----

1. Something flattened, or oval-shaped like a vulture's head.
2. See n. 2, verse 35-1. Here the allusion is to the knot into which the axe blade is inserted.
3. In rank order. See Chapters IV and V.
4. Tẹtẹ is <u>Amaranthus</u> <u>caudatus</u>; gbegbe is <u>Icacina</u> <u>trichantha</u>.

Odo   yio ni ki   n-ri ibi   do
"Mortar will say that I-see place (to) settle;

Tẹtẹ yio ni ki   n-ri ibi   tẹ
"Tẹtẹ will say that I-see place (to) stretch;

Gbegbe yio ni   ki   n-ri ibi   gbe.
"Gbegbe will say that I-see place (to) dwell."

N(i)-igba-ti awọn odu   (i)y(i)-o-ku   gbọ iru   i-da-(o)hun   bayi,
At-time-that those Figure this-which-remain hear kind (of) to-break-voice thus,

nwọn ni (Ohu)n-kan a a eyi-yi   ma   kuku le   o.   Nwọn ni
they say "Thing-one Ah ah this-this (continuative) indeed strong, oh." They say

ki   o   ma   joko rẹ; n(i)-igba-na ni Eji-koko Eji-(I)wori t(i)-o
should he (continuative) sit his; at-time-the be Two-Knot Eji-Iwori have-he

ri aye joko   ni ipo   ẹkẹta   awọn odu   iy(i)-o-ku.
see room sit:down at position third (of) those Figure this-which-remain.

IWORI MEJI - 6

Ẹṣin ji   ni owurọ   o ko   gbinringbinrin s(i)-ẹnu   Orun ko-
"Horse awake at morning, he gather bit   to-mouth" "Sun enter-

(i)bi   ṣẹrẹṣẹrẹ wọ-(i)le   Q-l(i)-ọrun   yi oṣu l(i)-atete
place (of) chinks   enter-house" "One:who-has-sky turn month at-high:place"

Oṣumare ẹgọ gb(e)-oju   Q-l(i)-ọrun   tan yanran-yanran   a
"Rainbow fool dwell-face (of) One:who-has-sky shine bright-bright" (be) who

da fun idẹ   a lu-(i)kin fun oje   a   bu   fun irin ti iṣe ọmọ ik(an)-
cast for Brass, who beat-ikin for Lead, who share for Iron that make child stand-

ẹhin   wọn.
back (of) them.

Ifa ni awọn ọmọ   iya   mẹta ni-yi,   ki   wọn ru-(ẹ)bọ   ki
Ifa say those child (of) mother three be-this. Should they offer-sacrifice that

eyi a-bi-k(an)-ẹhin   wọn ki   o ma ba   ku; ki awọn meji
this one:who-born-stand-back (of) them should he not should die; that those two

(i)y(i)-o-ku   ma ba   fi oju wọn sun-(ẹ)kun eyi   ọmọ kekere   (of)
this-who-remain not should take eye their shed-tears this (of) child small (of)

inu wọn; bẹ-ni eyi a-bi-k(an)-ẹhin   yi ẹnu rẹ mu ju
belly their; so-be this one:who-born-stand-back this mouth his sharp surpass

ẹnu   abẹ lọ o si le   j(ẹ)-iyan pupọ. Nitori-na ki   nwọn
mouth (of) razor go, he and be:able eat-dispute much. Because-the should they

ni ọbọtọ ori,   obukọ kan, ẹiyẹ-(i)le   kan, ati ẹgbafa.
have lump (of) shea:butter, he:goat one, bird-(of)-house one, and 12,000 (cowries).

"The mortar will testify that I see room in which to settle,
"The tẹtẹ leaf will testify that I see room in which to stretch out,
"The gbegbe leaf will testify that I see room in which to dwell."[5]

When the other Figures heard this kind of a reply, they said, "Ah! ah! this is a very powerful thing indeed, oh!" They said he should take his seat; then "Two-Knots, Eji Iwori" found his place to sit down in the third position among the other Figures.

---

5. There is a play on words here, and the efficacy of the sacrifice depends in part on the sound of the names of the ingredients. The mortar (odo) insures room in which to settle (do), the tẹtẹ leaf insures room in which to stretch out (tẹ), and the gbegbe leaf insures room in which to dwell (gbe).

---

35 - 6

"Horse awakes in the morning; it takes the bit[1] in its mouth," "Sun enters the house through chinks in the wall," "Sky God turns the moon high up above," and "Rainbow, the foolish one, stays in the heavens, shining very brightly"[2] were the ones who cast Ifa for Brass, beat palm nuts for Lead, and shared[3] it with Iron, the last-born of these three children.

Ifa says that these are three children of the same mother. They should sacrifice so that the last-born among them will not die, and so that the two others will not have to weep for this small child in their midst. The tongue of the last-born is sharper than the edge of a razor,[4] and he argues a great deal. Therefore they should sacrifice a lump of shea butter, one he-goat, one pigeon, and three shillings.

---

1. This is an onomatopoetic word which refers to anything that makes the sound "gbinringbinrin."
2. Cf. verse 24-1.
3. See n. 4, verse 18-4.
4. The reference here is to Iron.

N(i)-igba-ti nwǫn ni ki   awǫn ǫmǫ   iya   mẹta nwǫn-yi   ru-
At-time-that they say should those child (of) mother three those-this offer-

(ẹ)bǫ   ai-ku   idẹ   ru-(ẹ)bǫ,   oje tu,   ṣugbǫn irin ni irǫ ni
sacrifice (of) not-die, Brass offer-sacrifice, Lead atone, but   Iron say lie be

awǫn npa,   o ni ohun ti   Ǫ-l(i)-ǫrun   ba   ti   ṣe   o ti   ṣe
they killing, he say thing that One:who-has-sky should have make he have make

tan.   Ẹbǫ   ti   irin ko ru   ni o ṣe   ma   njẹ.   L(i)-
finish. Sacrifice that Iron not offer be it make (continuative) eating (him). At-

ẹhin n(i)-igba-ti o ba   to   iwǫn   ǫdun marun ti ilẹ   ba   ti
back at-time-that it should equal period (of) year five   that ground should have

bo   a bẹrẹ si imu ipata a si fẹ bajẹ; ṣugbǫn ẹbǫ   ti   idẹ
cover (him) he begin to take rusty he and want spoil; but   sacrifice that Brass

ati oje ru   ni   ki jẹ-ki   wǫn bajẹ bi nwǫn tilẹ wa ni-(i)nu
and Lead offer be (it) not consent-that they spoil if they even exist at-belly (of)

ilẹ   fun iwǫn   ǫdun pupǫ.
ground for period (of) year many.

IWORI MEJI - 7

Ǫṣan   awo   Itori Polo   awo   Ilugun
Horse:whip secret (of) Itori, A:thing:with:a:big:base secret (of) Ilugun (be)

a   da   f(un)-ǫlǫfin l(i)-ode   awǫfin. Nwǫn ni ohun kan ribiti yio ti
who cast for-king   at-outside (of) palace. They say thing one round will from

oju   ǫrun ba-(i)lẹ   da   kelekele meje; nwǫn ni ki apa ki   o
eye (of) sky strike-ground break into:bits seven; they say that arm should it

ba   le   ka.   Nwǫn ko ru-(ẹ)bǫ   bẹ-ni nwǫn ko si pa
should be:able go:ground (it). They not offer-sacrifice so-be they not and appease

Eṣu.
Eshu.

He! agbajǫ   ile   kan ni ẹkun wǫ   yi.   Ifa ni awǫn mẹfa kan ni-
He! crowd (of) house one be tears enter this. Ifa say those six   one be-

yi   ki   a   ru-(ẹ)bǫ   ki nwǫn ma ba   ku tẹle-(a)ra-tẹle-(a)ra,
this, should they offer-sacrifice that they not should die follow-body-follow-body,

ki   o si ku   eyi a-bi-k(an)-ẹhin   wǫn; bi awǫn ara
should it and remain this one:who-born-stand-back (of) them; as those people (of)

ile   oku   nwǫn-yi ba   si nsǫ-(ẹ)kun   ti nwǫn ko si tete
house (of) corpse those-this should and shedding-tears, that they not and quickly

gbǫ ẹbẹ   ki   nwǫn si dakẹ   Eṣu ati awǫn Irun-(i)mǫlẹ yio ba
hear request should they and be:silent, Eshu and those 400-Deity   will meet

When these three children of the same mother were told to sacrifice against death, Brass sacrificed and Lead made an atonement, but Iron said that the diviners were telling lies. He said that as the Sky God has ordained things, so they are destined to be forever. The sacrifice that Iron refused to make is what is eating him away. Since that time if Iron has been buried in the ground for as long as four years,[5] he begins to rust and to spoil. But the sacrifice that Brass and Lead made is what prevents them from spoiling even if they stay in the ground for many years.

---

5. In the fifth year according to the Yoruba system of counting.

---

35 - 7

"Horse-whip," the diviner of the town of Itori,[1] and "Something with a big base,"[2] the diviner of the town of Ilugun, were the ones who cast Ifa for the king at his palace. They said something round would fall from heaven and break into seven pieces on the ground. They said he should sacrifice so that he might keep it under control. They did not sacrifice, and they did not appease Eshu.[3]

Hey! This is a compound which tears will enter. Ifa says there is a group of six people who should sacrifice so that they may not die one after another until only the last-born among them remains; and so that when their family is mourning and does not heed promptly the pleas to stop weeping, Eshu and the Four Hundred Deities may not

---

1. A pun on atori, a bush from which switches [ọpa-(a)tori] are made.
2. Something "like a palm tree."
3. To give a part of a sacrifice when one cannot afford to give it all, as Ariran and Esun did in verse 33-2.

wǫn tę-(ǫ)wǫ-gba   ękun na, eyi-ti   o ku   ni-(i)nu awǫn ǫmǫ na
them stretch-hand-accept tears the, this-that he remain at-belly their, child the

yio si tun ku pęlu.
will and then die together:with (them).

     N(i)-igba-ti Qrunmila lǫ si ęhin-odi   o fi awǫn ǫmǫ rę
     At-time-that Qrunmila go to back-(of)-townwall, he put those child his

ǫkunrin si-(i)lę   lǫ. N(i)-igba-ti   Qrunmila wa   l(i)-ǫhun a-ja-
man   to-ground go. At-time-that Qrunmila come at-there that:which-fight-

ka-(i)lę   arun   wǫ ilu. Nitori-ti   ko si Qrunmila ni ile   lati
about-earth (of) disease enter town. Because-that not be Qrunmila at house to

da Ifa, awǫn ǫmǫ rę ǫkunrin nwǫn-yi   tǫ   awǫn babalawo lǫ pe
cast Ifa, those child his man   those-this approach those diviner   go that

ki   nwǫn ki   o   yę   awǫn wo pe ·ohun ti   a-ja-ka-
should they should they examine them look that thing that that:which-fight-about-

(i)lę   arun   yi ko fi ni le   mu awǫn lǫ titi baba awǫn yio fi
earth (of) disease this not take be be:able take them go until father their will take

de.   Awǫn babalawo si sǫ   fun awǫn [Apo-oro,   Apo-le-ja,
arrive. Those diviner   and speak for those [Pouch-(of)-poison, Pouch-can-fight,

Ejemǫoluwǫnran, F(i)-eyi-ş(e)-e-l(i)-gbe,   Atęginnidękun,   Wo-
Ejemǫoluwǫnran, Take-this-make-one:who-be-assist, Atęginnidękun, and Look-

(ę)mi-l(i)-oju] ǫmǫ   Qrunmila pe ki   nwǫn ki   o   ru   ewurę
me-at-eye]   child (of) Qrunmila that should they should they offer she:goat

(ǫ)k(an)-ǫkan, itan   ekiri   (ǫ)k(an)-ǫkan, eku meji-meji, ęgb(afa)-ęgbafa.
one-one,   thigh (of) bush:goat one-one,   rat two-two   12,000-12,000

(cowries).

     N(i)-igba-ti nwǫn ko   gbogbo (ohu)n-kan nwǫn-yi   si-(i)lę   tan,   nwǫn
     At-time-that they gather all   thing-one those-this to-ground finish, they

ni afi-bi   awǫn babalawo nwǫn-yi   ba   pa awǫn ewurę nwǫn-yi   bę-
say unless-if those diviner   those-this should kill those she:goat those-this, so-

ni a ko gbǫdǫ pa wǫn. Ifa ni ęni-kan   ni-yi   ti o ti   nşe ohun nla
be we not must kill them. Ifa say person-one be-this that he have doing thing big

kan, ti o si ti   şe   tan; şugbǫn ki   o şǫ-(a)ra   gidigidi   ki
one, that he and have do (it) finish; but   should he watch-body completely that

o ma ba   fi ohun ke(re)-kere   kan baję.   Awǫn babalawo nwǫn-
he not should take thing be:small-be:small one spoil (it). Those diviner   those-

yi pa awǫn ewurę nwǫn-yi   nwǫn mu awǫn ǫrun   awǫn ewurę na
this kill those she:goat those-this, they take those neck (of) those she:goat the,

nwǫn fi wǫn le   ori   ębǫ,   şugbǫn eyi a-bi-k(an)-ęhin
they put them upon head (of) sacrifice, but   this one:who-born-stand-back (of)

wǫn, Wo-(ę)mi-l(i)-oju, sǫ   fun awǫn babalawo pe bi nwǫn ba   ti işe
them, Look-me-at-eye, speak for those diviner   that as they should have make

add to their tears by causing the one remaining child to die like the others.

When Qrunmila went on a journey, he left his six sons behind. When he had gone, an epidemic entered the town. Since Qrunmila was not at home to cast Ifa for them, his sons went to the diviners that they might examine their case and tell them what to do so that this epidemic could not kill them before their father returned. The diviners told Qrunmila's children—"Pouch of Poison," "Pouch can fight,"[4] "Ejemǫoluwǫnran," "This one can be of assistance," "Atęginnidękun,"[5] and "Look me in the eye" —that they should sacrifice one she-goat each, one thigh of bush goat each, two rats each, and three shillings apiece.

When they had finished gathering all these things together, they insisted that the diviners should kill the she-goats,[6] although they ought not to have killed them. Ifa says this is someone who has been doing something important and who has already accomplished it, but that he should watch himself carefully, lest it be spoiled through a small detail.[7] The diviners killed the she-goats as they were told and put their heads on top of the sacrifice; but the last-born, "Look me in the eye," told the diviners that they should make

---

4. A pouch or sheath made from telescoping tubes of bamboo or leather in which poison is kept.

5. The informant could not translate two of these names.

6. It is implied here, that they did not trust the diviners, suspecting that they would simply add them to their possessions.

7. As Qrunmila's children brought an expensive sacrifice to naught, by quibbling about a small point.

ru-(ẹ)bọ,   ni ki   nwọn ki   o   ṣe   ba   on ṣe   ti   on.
offer-sacrifice, be should they should they make take him make that (of) him.

Nwọn ko si   pa   ewurẹ ti-rẹ   ṣugbọn ti   awọn iy(i)-o-ku   ti
They not and kill she:goat that-(of)-his, but   that those this-which-remain that

nwọn pa ni nwọn ko   si-(i)nu   apadi   ti   nwọn si gbe   lọ si
they kill be they gather to-belly (of) potsherd that they and take (them) go to

idi   Eṣu. Bi nwọn ti   gbe   de   idi   Eṣu, eṣinṣin ṣu
base (of) Eshu. As they have carry (them) arrive base (of) Eshu, fly   gather

bo.   Awọn ẹburu   (iwin)[1] ri, nwọn si rọ   wọ   inu
cover (sacrifice). Those evil:spirit (iwin) see, they and gush enter belly (of)

ile;   awọn eburu   nwọn-yi si pa awọn marun ti   awọn babalawo pa
house; those evil:spirit those-this and kill those five   that those diviners kill

ewurẹ wọn, nwọn si fi eyi a-bi-k(an)-ẹhin   si-(i)lẹ.
she:goat their, they and put this one:who-born-stand-back to-ground.

     Ni oru   ọjọ na gan   ni Ọrunmila sun ti o si la   ala,
     At night (of) day the identical be Ọrunmila sleep that he and dream dream,

ala   na ko si dara.   O wa   da   Ifa, o da Iwori Meji, nwọn ni
dream the not and be:good. He come cast Ifa, he cast Iwori Meji, they say

ki   o   ma   pada lọ si ẹhin ile   rẹ. O si mu-(a)ra o wa
should he (continuative) return go to back house his. He and take-body he come

si ile,   ṣugbọn n(i)-igba-ti o fi   ma   de   ile   ko ba   awọn
to house, but   at-time-that he take (continuative) arrive house not meet those

ọmọ marun (i)y(i)-o-ku   ni ile; o ba   a-bi-k(an)-ẹhin
child five   this-which-remain at house; he meet one:who-born-stand-back (of)

wọn. N(i)-igba-ti o si bere   awọn marun (i)y(i)-o-ku,   nwọn pu-
their. At-time-that he and ask (of) those five   this-which-remain, they tell-

(i)rọ fun   pe nwọn lọ si oko. N(i)-igba-ti o to   iwọn   ọjọ marun
lie   for (him) that they go to farm. At-time-that it equal period (of) day five

ni eyi a-bi-k(an)-ẹhin   tọ   awọn ọrẹ   baba rẹ lọ, o ni
be this one:who-born-stand-back approach those friend (of) father his go, he say

ki   nwọn wa   tu   Ọrunmila ni-(i)nu ki   nwọn si tu   l(i)-
should they come ease Ọrunmila at-belly should they and loosen (him) at-

ọfọ   awọn ẹgbọn   on. N(i)-igba-ti nwọn si de   ọdọ
mourning (of) those elder:sibling (of) him. At-time-that they and arrive presence

     Ọrunmila ti nwọn tu   l(i)-ọfọ   tan,   o bẹrẹ si sọ-(ẹ)kun;
     (of) Ọrunmila that they loosen (him) at-mourning finish, he begin to shed-tears;

nwọn si bẹ   titi ko fẹ gbọ.   Ọrunmila wa   ka   ọwọ le-
they and request until not want hear (them). Ọrunmila come encircle hand upon-

(o)ri o bẹrẹ si sọ-(ẹ)kun wi-pe:
head he begin to shed-tears speak-that:

_____

     1. Iwin is another name for eburu.

his sacrifice as it ought to be made. They did not kill his she-goat, but the others they killed and put in broken pots and placed at the bottom of Eshu's shrine. When they had taken them to the base of Eshu, flies gathered, covering the sacrifice. The evil spirits saw this and rushed[8] into the house and killed the five children whose goats had been killed by the diviners, but they left the last-born alone.

On the night of that very day Qrunmila dreamed a dream, and his dream was not good. He cast Ifa, and he cast Iwori Meji. They said he should return to his home. He got ready and came home, but when he arrived at his house he did not find the five other children; he met only the last-born. When he asked about the other five, they lied to him saying they had gone to farm. When four days had passed, the last-born child went to his father's friends and asked them to come and comfort Qrunmila and let him begin to mourn for the elder brothers. When they had told Qrunmila, he began to weep; they pleaded and pleaded with him, but he would not listen. Qrunmila put his hands over his ears and began to cry:

---

8. Literally "gushed," like water.

Apo-oro   ọmọ mi o
"Pouch-(of)-poison, child my, oh,

Ọmọ   ẹni   wo-(ẹ)ni   l(i)-oju
"Child (of) person look-person at-eye,

K(i)-ẹni   rina ọmọ   ẹni
"Should-person see child (of) person.

Apo-le-ja   ọmọ mi o
"Pouch-can-fight, child my, oh,

Ọmọ   ẹni   wo-(ẹ)ni   l(i)-oju
"Child (of) person look-person at-eye,

K(i)-ẹni   rina ọmọ   ẹni
"Should-person see child (of) person.

Ejemọoluwọnran, ọmọ mi o
"Ejemọoluwọnran, child my, oh,

Ọmọ   ẹni   wo-(ẹ)ni   l(i)-oju
"Child (of) person look-person at-eye,

K(i)-ẹni   rina ọmọ   ẹni
"Should-person see child (of) person.

F(i)-eyi-ṣ(e)-e-l(i)-gbe,   ọmọ mi o
"With-this-make-one:who-be-assist, child my, oh,

Ọmọ   ẹni   wo-(ẹ)ni   l(i)-oju
"Child (of) person look-person at-eye,

K(i)-ẹni   rina ọmọ   ẹni
"Should-person see child (of) person.

Atẹginnidẹkun, ọmọ mi o
"Atẹginnidẹkun, child my, oh,

Ọmọ   ẹni   wo-(ẹ)ni   l(i)-oju
"Child (of) person look-person at-eye,

K(i)-ẹni   rina ọmọ   ẹni
"Should-person see child (of) person."

N(i)-igba-ti Ọrunmila sọ-(ẹ)kun titi ti ko gbọ ẹbẹ   ni Eṣu wa ba
At-time-that Ọrunmila shed-tears until that not hear request be Eshu come meet

     ti o si sọ   fun   pe bi ko ba   dakẹ   awọn ẹgbẹ   rẹ
(him) that he and speak for (him) that if not should be:silent those companion his

gbogbo yio ba   tẹ-(ọ)wọ-gba   ẹkun na, ọmọ rẹ a-bi-
all   will join (him) stretch-hand-accept tears the, child his one:who-born-

k(an)-ẹhin kan-na ti o ku   si-(i)lẹ yio si tun ku pẹlu.
stand-back one-the that he remain to-ground will and then die together:with (them).

"Pouch of Poison, my child, oh,
"When one's child looks him in the eye,
"One should see his child.
"Pouch can fight, my child, oh,
"When one's child looks him in the eye,
"One should see his child.
"Ejemǫoluwǫnran, my child, oh,
"When one's child looks him in the eye,
"One should see his child.
"This one can be of assistance, my child, oh,
"When one's child looks him in the eye,
"One should see his child.
"Atęginnidękun, my child, oh,
"When one's child looks him in the eye,
"One should see his child."

While Ǫrunmila was weeping, refusing to listen to the pleading of his friends, Eshu came to him and told him that if he did not keep quiet, he and all his comrades would add to Ǫrunmila's tears, by causing his last-born child who was still left to die also.

IWORI OFUN - 1

Qwọn sọ   ibi di   ire   agba l(i)-o d(a)-Ifa fun ogejan,
"Thorn change evil become goodness, rope" be-who cast-ifa for Ogejan,

ẹ-l(i)-ẹgbẹ   Ifa. Qwọn sọ   ibi di   ire   on li o
one:who-be-companion (of) Ifa. "Thorn change evil become blessing," he be who

da   inu   aiye   on li o   ko   gbogbo ire   wa   inu   aiye,
create belly (of) earth, he be who gather all   goodness come belly (of) earth.

ọran ti   ko ba   dara   ẹhin ni   da   si.
Affair that not should be:good back be (he) cast (Ifa) to.

N(i)-igba-ti Eṣu gbọ pe awọn ọrẹ   meji sọ   pe awọn ko ni
At-time-that Eshu hear that those friend two speak that they no be (they)

ja   lai-lai   n(i)-igba-na ni Eṣu lọ da   fila a-l(i)-awọ   meji;
fight ever-ever, at-time-the be Eshu go create cap that:which-has-color two;

apa kan fun-fun,   apa kan si dudu; o si lọ kọja l(i)-arin   l(i)-arin (of)
arm one be:white-be:white, arm one and black; he and go pass at-middle (of)

awọn mej(i)-(m)eji, o si da ija s(i)-ilẹ l(i)-arin   awọn.
those two-two,   he and cast fight to-ground at-middle (of) them.

Ẹbọ: abo adiẹ   fun-fun   kan, ẹiyẹ-(i)le   fun-
Sacrifice: female chicken be:white-be:white one, bird-(of)-house be:white-

fun   kan, adiẹ   dudu kan, ẹiyẹ-(i)le   dudu kan.
be:white one, chicken black one, bird-(of)-house black one.

Ewe   Ifa: Ewe a-lu-pa-yi-da,   ewe ọwọn sọ   idi
Leaves (of) Ifa: Leaf that:which-beat-change-this, leaf "thorn change evil

di   ire   ati ẹgbafa.
become blessing," and 12,000 (cowries).

EDI MEJI - 1

Ẹṣẹ-(i)dẹ   ni f(i)-oju tan-(i)na   Q-l(i)-ọbọunbọun   ni
"Breaking-(of)-brass be take-eye shine-fire" "One:who-has-buzzing be (who)

f(i)-apa mej(i)-(m)eji lu gbẹdu Ajija   gogoro awo   A-
take-arm two-two   beat gbẹdu" "Whirlwind very:tall" secret (of) One:who-

ji-gunwa   a da k(o)-A-ji-gunwa   ti o
awake-sit:in:splendor (be) who cast for-One:who-awake-sit:in:splendor that he

nti ode   ọrun bọ wa si i-kọ-(i)le   aiye.
leaving outside (of) sky come come to to-build-house (of) earth.

Ifa ni ọmọ-(ọ)kunrin kan ni a-(yi)o bi   yi ode   ọrun ni o
Ifa say child-man   one be we-will bear (be) this, outside (of) sky be he

ti gbe igba   iwa rẹ wa   ko ni si ẹni-ti   yio le
have carry calabash (of) destiny his come, not be and person-that will be:able

48 - 1

"Thorns turn evil into good, rope"[1] was the one who cast Ifa for Ogejan, companion of Ifa. "Thorns turn evil into good" was the one who created the earth and brought everything good to the earth. Afterward when his affairs did not go well, he divined.

When Eshu heard these two friends (Ifa and Ogejan) say that they never quarreled, he made a two-colored cap, one side of which was white and the other black. He passed between these two friends and caused them to fight.[2]

Sacrifice: one white hen, one white pigeon, one black chicken, and one black pigeon.[3]

Leaves of Ifa: the leaf "which transforms things when beaten"[4] and the leaf of "Thorns turn evil into good," and three shillings.

1. Informants explained that "thorns" (ọwọn) refers to a thorny plant more commonly known as ẹwọn. Ẹwọn is a name for several kinds of prickly bushes, but probably refers here to Acacia ataxacantha or A. pennata, from both of which rope is made. "Thorns turn evil into good, rope" refers to the use of this plant in making rope, despite its thorns, and to the fact that it is planted by diviners in their back yards, where it is readily available for making medicines.

2. It is understood that they began to fight about the color of Eshu's cap. This verse was recorded from the Araba of Modakẹkẹ, a suburb of Ifẹ settled during the wars of the last century; Araba afterward explained that the left side of the cap was black and the right was white. This verse was not known to four good Ifẹ diviners, but one informant had heard similar tales in which black, white, red, and green were used interchangeably. An Eshu worshiper at Ọyọ described Eshu as making best friends (korikosun) fight by wearing a cap which is black on one side and white on the other; and a more complete version of this tale, with a red and black cap, was recorded from an Eshu worshiper at Mẹkọ who concluded with the comment, "This is the real story. The babalawo tell it in Ifa so that people will make sacrifices." Compare also the tale as recorded by Frobenius (1913: I, 240-243), in which the cap has four colors: green, black, red, and white; and as recorded by Herskovits and Herskovits (1931: 455) from an Itsẹkiri Yoruba informant in which the cap is red and white.

3. Note the parallels in the colors of the birds to be sacrificed and the colors of Eshu's cap.

4. Uraria picta.

52 - 1

"The fractured surface of brass shines like fire," "'Buzzing One'[1] beats the gbẹdu drum with both hands," and "Very tall whirlwind," the diviner of "One who awakes and sits in royal splendor"[2] were the ones who cast Ifa for "One who awakes and sits in royal splendor" when he was coming from heaven to the dwelling places on earth.[3]

Ifa says that we will bear a son who comes from heaven carrying his "calabash of destiny."[4] There is no one who will be able

1. A large beetle with a black shell and red under-wings, whose name refers to the buzzing (bọunbọun) he makes when flying.

2. Notes 2-4 appear on page 313.

ko   l(i)-oju tabi ki   o   da-duro   n(i)-inu   ohun-k(u)-ohun;
meet (him) at-eye or   should he cause-(him)-stand at-belly (of) thing-any-thing.

iyi   rҽ yio pҿ   pupҿ l(i)-aiye, gbogbo enia   ni yio mҿ   ka-
Glory his will be:much much at-earth, all   persons be will know (him) go:around-

kiri agb(o)-aiye;   yio si ba ҽsҽ ja-(o)ri;   kijikiji   ҿmҿ na yio
about crowd-(of)-earth; will and with row reach-head; shaking (of) child the will

si mu-(i)lҽ   ka-(a)iye;   a-ji-gunwa   ni orukҿ ti a
and take-ground go:around-earth; one:who-awake-sit:in:splendor be name that we

pe ҿjҿ. Igba abҽrҽ, aguntan kan, aşҿ fun-fun   kan, epo   ati
call day. 200 needle, ewe   one, cloth be:white-be:white one, palm:oil and

egbejilelogun   ni ҽbҿ.   A-ji-gunwa   gbҿ ҽbҿ   o
4400   (cowries) be sacrifice. One:who-awake-sit:in:splendor hear sacrifice he

ru-(ҽ)bҿ.
offer-sacrifice.

EDI MEJI - 2

Koto-koto   ni a-ipilҽ   aran bi o ba   d(e)-oke   a di   gburudu
"Hollow-hollow be we-found aran, if it should arrive-hill it become huge

bi o ba   d(e)-oke a di   gbarada   a   da fun Ipҽsan ti işe
if it should arrive-hill it become immense" (be) who cast for Ipҽsan that make

(ba)ba-(i)lҽ   ҿja.   Ipҽsan ma   de   o (ba)ba-
father-(of)-ground (of) market. Ipҽsan (continuative) arrive, oh, Father-(of)-

(i)lҽ   ҿja,   ti o nlҿ mu ilҽ   ibu-(i)joko.   Ipҽsan ni orukҿ
ground (of) market, that he going take ground (of) place-sit:down. Ipҽsan be name

ti a pe ҿdan. O-l(i)-ori   rere ma   d(e)-ҿja   o.
that we call ҿdan. One:who-has-head good (continuative) arrive-market, oh.

Ifa ni ҽni-kan   ni-yi ti yio ni ibu-(i)joko   ati ipo pupҿ
Ifa say person-one be-this that will have place-sit:down and room much,

şugbҿn ki   o ru-(ҽ)bҿ   ki o ma ba   ri e-l(i)-enini   ati
but   should he offer-sacrifice that he not should see one:who-has-enmity and

ohun ti yio din   ibu-(i)joko   rҽ ku.
thing that will lessen place-sit:down his (1).

Nwҿn ni ki   ҿdan ru-(ҽ)bҿ   k(i)-o ma ba   ri e-l(i)-
They say should ҿdan offer-sacrifice that-he not should see one:who-be-

enini   ni ibu-(i)joko   rҽ obukҿ kan, akikҿ kan, ada   kan, ati
slanderer at place-sit:down his he:goat one, cock one, cutlass one, and

---

1. Din . . . ku means "to lessen," "to decrease."

to oppose him or to stop him in anything he undertakes. His glory will be great on earth; everyone will know him all around the world; and he will complete whatever he undertakes. The mention of the name of this child will cause the ground to tremble[5] around the world. "One who awakes and sits in royal splendor" is what we call Sun.[6] Two hundred needles, one ewe, one white cloth, palm oil, and one shilling two pence is the sacrifice. "One who awakes and sits in royal splendor" heard and made the sacrifice.

---

2. A king is said to gunwa when his chairs, carpets, and cushions are set out for him and he comes out in all his royal finery and sits with arms and legs spread out pompously. Possibly it is derived from gun-(i)wa, meaning to mount-destiny.

3. Not only in Nigeria, but all over the world, wherever houses are built.

4. Cf. n. 2, verse 4-1 A.

5. "Kijikiji" describes the way it vibrates at the mention of his name.

6. As in verses 1-6 and 103-1, Day (ǫjǫ) was interpreted as meaning Sun (orun). This verse explains why the sun is known and respected the world over, and predicts great fame for the child that is to be born. The rising of the sun in all its glory is compared here with a king sitting in royal splendor. In both this case and in verse 103-1 the rather unusual sacrifice of 200 needles is required; perhaps these symbolize the rays of the sun.

---

52 - 2

"Hollowing is the foundation of the aran drum;[1] if it goes up, it becomes huge; if it goes up, it becomes immense" was the one who cast Ifa for Ipǫsan, Chief of the Market. Ipǫsan arrives, oh, Chief of the Market; he is going to take new land on which to settle. Ipǫsan is what we call the Qdan tree.[2] A lucky person arrives at the market,[3] oh!

Ifa says this is someone who will have a settlement[4] of his own and lots of room, but he should sacrifice lest he encounter an enemy and a thing which will decrease the size of his settlement.

They said that Qdan tree should sacrifice one he-goat, one cock, one cutlass, and one shilling seven pence eight oninis, so that he would not encounter a slanderer at his settlement.

---

1. Kotokoto is said also to represent the scraping sound in hollowing out a log to make a drum. Aran is one of the types of drums used in the worship of Ifa.

2. The ǫdan tree (Ficus spp.) is called Chief of the Market here because it is commonly planted in Yoruba market places as a shade tree.

3. This phrase implies that he finds good fortune, that he "arrives at the market of destiny" (cf. verse 256-1), and, more specifically, that he will have a large family (cf. verse 225-3).

4. That is, a place to live. It is implied that he will also have a large number of people living with him.

ẹgbẹtalelọgbọn.   Nwọn ni   bi   yio ti   ni ibu-(i)joko   to   yio
6600   (cowries). They say if (he) will have that place-sit:down equal will

na   apa yio na   ẹsẹ,   ọdan gbọ ẹbọ   o   ru   obukọ kan,
stretch arm will stretch foot. Ọdan hear sacrifice, he offer he:goat one,

ẹgbẹtalelọgbọn   ti   işe   ti   ibu-(i)joko,   şugbọn ko ru   akikọ ati
6600   (cowries) that make that (of) place-sit:down, but   not offer cock and

ada   kan eyi-ti   o jẹ pe ki   o le   pẹ   ni ibu-(i)joko   na.
cutlass one this-that it eat that should he be:able be:long at place-sit:down the.

N(i)-igba-ti   ọdan de   ibu-(i)joko,   o   na   apa o na   ẹsẹ şugbọn
At-time-that ọdan arrive place-sit:down, he stretch arm he stretch foot, but

n(i)-igba-ti   o na   apa na   ẹsẹ tan,   awọn ọmọ   ara-(a)iye
at-time-that he stretch arm stretch foot finish, those child (of) people-(of)-earth

de,   nwọn mu ada   nwọn si bẹrẹ si fi   ada   wọn   l(i)-apa ati
arrive, they take cutlass they and begin to take cutlass (him) at-arm and

l(i)-ẹsẹ.
at-foot.

    Nitori-na   ki   e-l(i)-eyi   ru-(ẹ)bọ   ki o ma ba   fi
    Because-the should one:who-be-this offer-sacrifice that he not should take

ọwọ rẹ ş(e)-işẹ ni arọ   ki ara-(a)iye   ma ba   yi   da-nu
hand his do-work at morning that people-(of)-earth not should turn throw-be:lost

ni oju   alẹ   rẹ.
at face (of) evening his.

EDI MEJI - 3

    O   de   rere, o rin rere, o mọ irin   aseko[1] rin l(i)-ẹsẹ
    "You arrive good, you walk good, you know walking (of) time   walk at-foot

mej(i)-(m)eji, a şẹşẹ ko   ohun   ọrọ s(i)-ilẹ o de   gẹgẹ bi
two-two,   we just gather thing (of) riches to-ground, you arrive just like

ọmọ   o-ni-(ohu)n-kan   a da f(un)-ajeji   godogbo ti o
child (of) one:who-has-thing-one" (be) who cast for-Foreigner stout   that he

nlọ si ode   Ibini. Nwọn ni ori   ẹni-kan   yio mu   de
going to outside (of) Benin. They say head (of) person-one will take (him) arrive

ibi-ti   yio gbe şe iwa   kan, nwọn ni ọgangan ire   ni yio
place-that (he) will take make destiny one; they say inevitable goodness be will

     ma   şe.   Nwọn ni ki   ajeji-godogbo ti o nlọ si ode
(he) (continuative) make. They say should Foreigner-stout that he going to outside

---

1. Often written "asiko."

They said he would find a large enough place in which to settle, and that he would stretch out his arms and stretch out his legs.[5] Qdan tree heard the sacrifice, and he offered one he-goat and one shilling seven pence eight oninis for a place in which to settle, but he did not offer the cock and the cutlass that he might be able to stay there for a long time. When Qdan tree reached his settlement, he stretched out his arms and he streched out his legs; but when he had finished stretching them out, people came and took a cutlass[6] and began to cut off his arms and legs.

Therefore this person should sacrifice in order that what he has achieved in the morning of his life shall not be destroyed by others in the evening of his life.

---

5. The branches and roots of the tree.

6. This verse explains why the qdan tree grows in the market, and why people pass time by hacking at its roots and branches. It is understood that it met this fate through the cutlass which it refused to sacrifice.

---

52 - 3

"You arrive here excellently, you walk excellently; you know how to walk on time[1] with both feet; no sooner are riches spread on the ground than you arrive just like the child of their owner," was the one who cast Ifa for Stout Foreigner when he was going to Benin City. They said that someone's head will bring him to a place where he will achieve his destiny; they said a blessing is certain to reach him. They said that Stout Foreigner, who was going to

---

1. That is, arriving punctually.

Ibini   ru   eku meji, ęja meji, igbin meji, adię   meji, ati ejilelogun.
(of) Benin offer rat two, fish two, snail two, chicken two, and 44,000 (cowries).

O gbǫ ębǫ   o si ru-(ę)bǫ.
He hear sacrifice he and offer-sacrifice.

   N(i)-igba-ti o de   ode   Ibini ohun-k(u)-ohun ti o ba   fi
   At-time-that he arrive outside (of) Benin, thing-any-thing that he should take

ǫwǫ rę kan ni o ndi   rere; bi obinrin ko ba   ni oyun   ti o
hand his touch be it becoming good; if woman not should have pregnancy that she

ba   de   ǫdǫ   rę yio si l(i)-oyun,   bi nwǫn ba   gbe ǫmǫ
should arrive presence his will and have-pregnancy; if they should carry child

ke(re)-kere   ti ai-san   nşe de ǫdǫ   rę yio   san
be:small-be:small that not-be:better making arrive presence his will (it) be:better

fun u   Bayi ni ajeji-godogbo di   ǫ-l(i)-ǫrǫ   ati o-n(i)-
for him. Thus be Foreigner-stout become one:who-has-riches and one:who-has-

ile ni ode   Ibini.
house at outside (of) Benin.

   Ifa ni ęni-kan   ni-yi ti o nfę   lǫ si idalę,   ki   o mu-(a)ra
   Ifa say person-one be-this that he wanting go to distance, should he take-body

ki   o ru-(ę)bǫ   ki o ba   le   ri owo, iyi ati ǫla ni
should he offer-sacrifice that he should be:able see cowries, glory, and honor at

ibi-ti   o nlǫ na, ati pe ki   ibę ki   o le   san   dara-
place-that he going the, and that should there should it be:able benefit (him) be:good-

dara.
be:good.

EDI MEJI - 4

   Wa   nihin, ara   ǫrun ki idu   ara   wǫn ni-(i)le l(i)-o da
   "Come here, people (of) sky not refuse people their at-house" be-who cast

Ifa k(o)-Eji-ǫ-kǫ-mi   ti a   bi ni on ni-(ǫ)kan ti o ma
Ifa for-Second-no-refuse-me that they bear at him at-one,   that he (continuative)

fi   gbogbo inu   aiye şe ogun   ję. Eji-ǫ-kǫ-mi   ni
take all   (of) belly (of) earth make inheritance eat. Second-no-refuse-me be

orukǫ ti a-ipe   Egun.
name that we-to:call Egungun.

   Ifa ni ki   a bǫ   Egun kan, o ni Egun   na yio ş(i)-
   Ifa say should we sacrifice:to Egungun one; he say Egungun the will open-

il(e)-ękun ǫmǫ fun-(ę)ni obinrin kan yio bi ǫmǫ pupǫ.
house-door (of) child for-person; woman one will bear child many.

Benin, should sacrifice two rats, two fish, two snails, two chickens, and eleven shillings. He heard and he made the sacrifice.

When he reached Benin, everything he turned his hand to became good. If a woman who could not conceive came to him, she became pregnant; if they brought an ill child to him, it became well. Thus Stout Foreigner became a rich person and the owner of a house in Benin.

Ifa says this is someone who wants to go on a journey. He should sacrifice that he may be able to gain money, glory, and honor where he is going, and that his journey may be of great benefit[2] to him.

---

2. Note the pun on san (cure or heal) and san (benefit).

---

52 - 4

"Come here, people in heaven do not refuse their relatives a home"[1] was the one who cast Ifa for "My partner[2] does not refuse my requests," an only child who was about to inherit everything on earth. "My partner doesn't refuse my requests" is what we call the Egungun.[3]

Ifa says we should sacrifice to an Egungun. He says the Egungun will open the door of children for someone; a woman will bear many children.

---

1. This translation is open to question. One informant interpreted it as "people in heaven do not refuse themselves a house," but the diviner himself justified the interpretation given by stating, "No one has ever heard of anyone being refused admission to heaven."

2. Literally, "My Second," with reference to the guardian spirit in heaven.

3. See n. 6, verse 7-5. The dead "inherit everything on earth" in the sense that all living things must die.

Ki   a fi   ǫlę,   agbǫn   ękǫ,   paşan, ati
Should we take steamed:beans, basket (of) cornstarch:porridge, whip, and

obukǫ kan bǫ   Egun   na. Ifa ni orukǫ   ęni   ko ni parę
he:goat one sacrifice:to Egungun the. Ifa say name (of) person not be obliterated

ko si ni run   ni ohun ti   a d(a)-Ifa si. Şugbǫn ki   a   wa   ǫran
not and be perish at thing that we cast-Ifa to. But   should we seek affair (of)

ęni   si ǫdǫ   Egun.
person to presence (of) Egungun.

EDI MEJI - 5

L(i)-oni nkǫ?   apa   aja jagada ni-(i)mu-(i)na   ǫla
"At-today what:about? arm (of) dog broad at-place-(of)-fire; tomorrow

nkǫ?   apa   aja jagada ni-(i)mu-(i)na   Olokoşę fun-fun,
what:about? arm (of) dog broad at-place-(of)-fire; Whydah be:white-be:white,

irere   idi rę fun-fun   a d(a)-Ifa k(o)-Ogbegbe ranyin-
tail:feather (of) waist his be:white-be:white" (be) who cast-Ifa for-Ogbegbe ranyin-

ranyin ti o nlǫ fi ęsę   ǫrǫ   ba   ile.
ranyin that he going take foot (of) riches touch house.

Idu wa   f(i)-ęsę   ǫrǫ   ba   ilе mi;
"Idu come take-foot (of) riches touch house my;

Ogbegbe ranyinranyin wa   f(i)-ęsę   ǫrǫ ba ile mi.
"Ogbegbe ranyinranyin come take-foot (of) riches touch house my."

Ifa ni o ri ire   aya kan, a-(yi)o fę,   n(i)-ibi-ti   o
Ifa say he see goodness (of) wife one, we-will love (her), at-place-that she

kun-(i)lę   ti ę-l(i)-ęda   ęni   si ni o wa nisisiyi.
kneel-ground take one:who-be-creature (of) person to be she exist right:now.

Akikǫ kan, agbebǫ adię   kan, ati ęgbęrindinlogun ni ębǫ   ti Idu ru
Cock one, hen   chicken one, and 3200 (cowries) be sacrifice that Idu offered

n(i)-igba-na pęlu   ęiyę-(i)le   męrin.
at-time-the together:with bird-(of)-house four.

EDI - (Ǫ)KANRAN - 1

O şa   wǫn pa bi ęya   kutukutu   ko mu-(i)lę
"He pick:up:one:by:one them kill like yam:stick; early-early not take-ground

şe   bişa-bişa   a   da fun A-ri-(i)le-w(a)-ǫla   ǫmǫ
make stagger-stagger" (be) who cast for One:who-see-house-seek-honor, child

We should sacrifice red steamed beans,[4] a basket of cornstarch porridge, a whip, and a he-goat to the Egungun. Ifa says that the name of this person will not die out, and he will not fail in the thing concerning which we have cast Ifa, but that he should go to Egungun about the matter.

---

4. Word magic is implied here, as red steamed beans (ọlẹ) are sacrificed to produce pregnancy, and ọlẹ is the word for embryo.

---

52 - 5

"How about today? broad foreleg of a dog beside the fire; how about tomorrow? broad foreleg of a dog beside the fire; White Pin Tailed Whydah, its tail feather[1] is white" was the one who cast Ifa for Ogbegbe Ranyinranyin,[2] when he was bringing riches to whatever house he visited.

> "Idu,[3] bring riches and visit my house;
> "Ogbegbe ranyinranyin, bring riches and visit my house"

Ifa says he sees the blessing of a wife[4] whom someone will marry. At this very moment she is kneeling beside his ancestral guardian soul in heaven. One cock, one hen, and nine pence six oninis is the sacrifice that Idu offered at that time, along with four pigeons.

---

1. The Olokoṣẹ (or Ologoṣẹ) bird is the Pin Tailed Whydah (Vidua macroura). Males of this species have tail feathers (irere) which are two to three times the length of their bodies. See Fairburn (1933: 98), Abraham (1958: 756).

2. The meaning of this name could not be explained, except for saying that Ranyinranyin is the noise that Ogbegbe makes. In verse 54-7 ranyin means spinning or oscillating.

3. Idu, also unexplained, appears to be another name for Ogbegbe Ranyinranyin, for whom this figure was cast, as Idu is later named as the one who made the sacrifice.

4. There is no relation here between the prediction of taking a wife and the precedent case which refers to wealth.

---

54 - 1

"He picks them up one by one and cuts them like yam sticks;[1] early in the morning one does not dance bisha-bisha"[2] was the one who cast Ifa for "He has a house, but goes on to seek honor," the child

---

1. The sticks to which the yam vines are trained.
2. Bisha-bisha describes the motion of a person in dancing.

Ę-l(i)-ęgbęrin   a-mǫ-ka-(a)ra,   Nwǫn ni   ni oṣu   męta l(i)-oni
(of) One:who-has-800 to-build-go:around-self. They say at month three at-today

ni Q-l(i)-ǫrun   yio la   ǫna   iwa   fun,   ṣugbǫn ki   o ru-
be One:who-has-sky will open road (of) destiny for (him), but   should he offer-

(ę)bǫ   ǫdun męrin nitori   iku, n(i)-igba-ti aye ba   ma
sacrifice (of) year four   because (of) death, at-time-that room should (continu-

       gba   tan   ki o ma ba   ku ni akoko ti   ori rę yio dara.
ative) accept (him) finish, that he not should die at time   that head his will be:good.

Nwǫn ni ki   o ru obukǫ kan, ęgbafa,   ǫkǫ kan, agaro tabi ogigi
They say should he offer he-goat one, 12,000 (cowries), hoe one, agaro or   ogigi

meji, ęiyę-(i)le   meji, ati akikǫ meji. A-ri-(i)le-w(a)-ǫla   ru-
two, bird-(of)-house two, and cock two.   One:who-see-house-seek-honor offer-

(ę)bǫ   ṣugbǫn ko ru   akikǫ mǫ.
sacrifice but   not offer cock against (it)

    N(i)-igba-ti o di   oṣu kęta, ni nwǫn fi A-ri-(i)le-w(a)-
    At-time-that it become month third, be they take One:who-see-house-seek-

ǫla   j(ę)-ǫba n(i)-igba-ti o de   ori   oye, awǫn ǫmǫ rę pe;
honor eat-king, at-time-that he arrive head (of) title, those child his call (him);

nwǫn ni baba, nwǫn ni ki   o ru-(ę)bǫ   nitori   iku ti awǫn
they say father, they say should you offer-sacrifice because (of) death that those

babalawo wi,   o ni kaka   ki   iku pa on, on (yi)o fi   igba ęru
diviner   speak; he say instead:of should death kill him, he will take 200 slave

węrę-węrę de-(i)le,   o ni on yio fi   ęgbęrin enia   korokoro   di-
tiny-tiny   watch-house, he say he will take 800   persons sound-sound tie-

(ǫ)na, o ni on yio lǫ si aja   ilę   on yio ṣe   mini-mini si.
road, he say he will go to ceiling (of) ground he will make quiet-quiet to.

    N(i)-igba-ti o di   ǫdun kęrin ti Ęṣu si ri pe A-ri-(i)le-
    At-time-that it become year fourth that Eshu and see that One:who-see-house-

w(a)-ǫla   ko ru-(ę)bǫ,   o ko   awǫn iganniganni janmǫ l(i)-ęhin, o
seek-honor not offer-sacrifice, he gather those rascal   band   at-back, he

ko   ǫkǫ ati agaro tabi ogigi le   wǫn l(i)-ǫwǫ, o ni ki   nwǫn ma
gather hoe and agaro or   ogigi upon them at-hand; he say should they (continua-

    niṣo   ni ile   A-ri-(i)le-w(a)-ǫla,   o ni ki   nwǫn
tive) proceed at house (of) One:who-see-house-seek-honor, he say should they

   ma   wo   ile rę. Bayi ni nwǫn bęrę si wo   ile   A-
(continuative) break house his. Thus be they begin to break house (of) One:who-

ri-(i)le-w(a)-ǫla,   nwǫn si wa   ba   ni aja   ilę,   nwǫn
see-house-seek-honor, they and come meet (him) at ceiling (of) ground, they

si mu,   nwǫn si wa sun   ję. A-ri-(i)le-w(a)-ǫla
and take (him) they and come roast (him) eat. One:who-see-house-seek-honor

ni orukǫ ti a npe   olu   ǫgan   tabi ǫba   ikan   lati
be name that we calling Chief (of) Termite:hill or King (of) Termites; from

of "He has 800 people with whom to surround himself." They said that within the
third month from that day the Sky God would "open the road of destiny" for him,
but that before the fourth year he should sacrifice against death lest, when he had
found his destiny, he should die at the very time that his luck was good. They
said he should offer one he-goat, three shillings, one hoe, two digging sticks (either agaro or ogigi),[3] two pigeons, and two cocks. "He has a house but goes on to
seek honor" made a sacrifice, but he did not include the cocks.

In the third month, "He has a house but goes on to seek honor" was made king,
and when he had been crowned his children called on him. They said, "Father,
you should make the sacrifice against death that the diviners spoke of." He said
that rather than being killed by death, he would set 200 tiny slaves to watch his
house, and he would set 800 sturdy men to guard the road;[4] he said he would go
to his underground chamber and keep absolutely quiet.

When the fourth year came and Eshu saw that "He has a house but goes on to
seek honor" had not sacrificed, he called his band of rascals together behind him,
and gave them hoes and digging sticks. He said that they should go to the house
of "He has a house but goes on to seek honor"; he said that they should break down
his house. And so they began to wreck the house of "He has a house but goes on to
seek honor," and when they came upon him in his underground chamber, they seized
him, roasted him in the fire, and ate him. "He has a house but goes on to seek hon-
or" is what we call the "Chief of the Termite Hill," or the "King of Termites." And
from

---

3. The agaro, also known as ganmiro, is a digging stick with an iron head;
while the ogigi is made entirely of hard wood. These are used on hard soil, and
in breaking down termite hills.

4. The reference is to the different kinds of termites which inhabit the termite hill. Note that "He has a house but goes on to seek honor" is called the
child of "He has 800 people with whom to surround himself."

igba-na   ni   ǫmǫ   ara-(a)iye   ti   ma   ko   ǫkǫ, ogigi tabi
time-the be child (of) people-(of)-earth have (continuative) gather hoe, ogigi or

agaro ti   ǫgan   ti   nwǫn ma   nwo   ti   nwǫn si
agaro against termite:hill, that they (continuative) breaking (it), that they and

ma   nmu   olu   ǫgan   inu   rę sun   ję.
(continuative) taking Chief (of) Termite:hill (of) belly its roast (him) eat.

Ifa ni ki   a   ru-(ę)bǫ   nitori   e-l(i)-enini   ki   o
Ifa say should we offer-sacrifice because (of) one:who-has-enmity that he

ma ba   le   ba   isę   ǫwǫ   ęni   ję n(i)-igba-ti o ba
not should be:able spoil work (of) hand (of) person (1) at-time-that it should

ndara   fun-(ę)ni.
being:fine for-person.

EDI - (Q)KANRAN - 2

Ahere   oko sisun   ni mu ǫpǫlǫ tǫ   lu-(ę)ni   ni oru
"Farm:hut (of) farm sleeping be take frog jump strike-person at night" (be)

a   da fun ere   ti   o   nfi   ękun şe   irahun   ǫmǫ. Nwǫn ni
who cast for Python that she taking tears make moaning (of) child. They say

ki   o   ru-(ę)bǫ   ki o   le   bi   ǫmǫ ewurę kan, aşǫ
should she offer-sacrifice that she be:able bear child she:goat one, cloth

kijipa   ara rę   ejielogun.   O   gbǫ o   ru.
homespun (of) body hers, 44,000   (cowries). She hear she offer.

Ere   si l(i)-oyun   o   si bi   ǫmǫ; awǫn enia   si bęrę si
Python and have-pregnancy she and bear child; those people and begin to

wi-pe   O-l(i)-odu   ni ǫmǫ ti Ere   bi yi. N(i)-igba-ti ǫmǫ
speak-that One:who-has-odu be child that Python bear this. At-time-that child

na si d(i)-agba,   o   si j(ę)-ǫba ni oju   iya   rę, on ni gbogbo enia
the and become-elder, he and eat-king at eye (of) mother his, he be all   people

si npe   ni O-l(i)-odu-(ǫ)ma-(e)re[2]   titi   di   oni.
and calling at One:who-has-odu-child-(of)-Python until (it) become today.

Ifa ni ogbo-l(i)-ogbo obinrin kan ni-(e)yi-ti awǫn enia   ti   nro
Ifa say old-be-old   woman   one be-this-that those people have thinking

pe   ko le   bi   ǫmǫ mǫ, şugbǫn Q-l(i)-ǫrun   yio fun
that (she) not be:able bear child again, but   One:who-has-sky will give (her)

ni ǫmǫ kan, ǫmǫ na yio si j(ę)-ǫba ni oju   iya   rę, gbogbo enia   ni
at child one, child the will and eat-king at eye (of) mother his; all   people be

yio si ma   pe   sin   ni oju   iya   rę.
will and (continuative) assemble serve (him) at eye (of) mother his.

---

1. Ba . . . ję means "to spoil."
2. The usual form for "child" is ǫmǫ rather than ǫma.

that time on, humans have taken their hoes and their digging sticks to break down
termite hills, and, taking the "Chief of the Termite Hill" from the inside, have
roasted and eaten him.[5]

Ifa says we should sacrifice lest an enemy should be able to spoil a person's
work at the time when things are going well for him.

———————————

5. This verse explains why people roast and eat the "King of Termites," using
hoes and digging sticks to break down the termite hills. In this case hoes and digging sticks are used in bringing about the character's downfall, even though he included them in the sacrifice which he made.

———————————————————

54 - 2

"When we sleep in the farm hut, frogs jump on us in the night" was the one
who cast Ifa for Python when she was weeping and moaning for a child. They said
she should sacrifice one she-goat, the homespun cloth she was wearing, and eleven
shillings so that she might be able to have a child. She heard and she made the
sacrifice.

And Python became pregnant, and she gave birth to a child; and people began
to say that "One who has odu"[1] was this child that Python bore. And when the
child grew up, she lived to see him become king. He is the one whom all people
are calling "One who has odu, child of Python" (Olodumare)[2] until this very day.

Ifa says this is a very old woman whom everyone thinks is too old to bear
children any more, but the Sky God will give her a child, and she will live to see
him become king and to see everyone gather to serve him.

———————————

1. Odu in this context was variously interpreted as meaning "something big,"
"a large pot," and the ritual object diviners of high rank acquire, but not the figure
of Ifa.

2. Olodumare is an alternative name for Qlǫrun, the Sky God. This verse explains its meaning according to a commonly accepted folk etymology, and how the
name came to be used.

———————————————————

EDI - (Q)KANRAN - 3

Oko   Edi ko ni   ina,   ępǫn   Qkanran ko ni   ilęwu
"Penis (of) Edi not have lice; testicle (of) Qkanran not have downy:hair" (be)

a   da   fun Amure a-mi-titi   ti   ja-(o)gun l(i)-ęgbę   ǫrun, ti
who cast for "Sash   that:which-shake-titi that fight-war at-side   (of) sky," that

o lǫ fę   Qmǫ-l(i)-okun ati Qmǫ-n(i)-idę.   Nwǫn ni ki   o ru-
he go love "Child-be-bead" and "Child-be-brass." They say should he offer-

(ę)bǫ   ayebǫ adię   męrin, ęgbętalelǫgbǫn. Amure a-mi-titi
sacrifice (of) hen   chicken four,   6600 (cowries). "Sash   that:which-shake-titi

ti ja-(o)gun l(i)-ęgbę   ǫrun gbǫ o ru,   o si gbe Qmǫ-l(i)-okun ati
that fight-war at-side   (of) sky" hear, he offer, he and take "Child-be-bead" and

Qmǫ-n(i)-idę   ni iyawo   lǫ si ile   rę, nwǫn si bi   ǫmǫ fun
"Child-be-brass" at junior:wife go to house his; they and bear child for (him)

pupǫ-pupǫ.
many-many.

Ifa ni   ǫkunrin kan ni-(e)yi ti   Q-l(i)-ǫrun   yio fun   ni aya
Ifa say man   one be-this that One-who-has-sky will give (him) at wife

meji ni-(i)nu   ǫdun yi, awǫn aya na yio si bi   ǫmǫ fun   pupǫ.
two at-belly (of) year this, those wife the will and bear child for (him) many.

N(i)-igba-ti nwǫn bi   ǫmǫ awǫn enia si bęrę si kǫ-(o)rin wi-pe
At-time-that they bear child those people and begin to sing-song speak-that:

Ta-ni   l(i)-ǫmǫ yi   o,
"Who-be has-child this, oh;

Qmǫ-l(i)-okun
"Child-be-bead,

Qmǫ-n(i)-idę
"Child-be-brass."

EDI - (Q)KANRAN - 4

Qpę   atana   l(i)-o ję ebi   ada   Awǫ   ętu   ki
"Palm:tree (of) crossroad be-who eat guilt (of) cutlass" "Hide (of) Duiker not

gba enia-meji sun   a da fun O-l(i)-okun,   nwǫn ni ki ofun
accept persons-two sleep" (be) who cast for One:who-has-sea; they say that loss

kan ma   şe-(ę)ni   ǫdun yi. Ębǫ: eiyę-(i)le   meji, ęgba
one (continuative) make-person year this. Sacrifice: bird-(of)-house two, 2,000

marun. O-l(i)-okun   ko ru-(ę)bǫ.
(cowries) five.   One:who-has-sea not offer-sacrifice.

54 - 3

"Edi's penis does not have lice; Qkanran's[1] testicles do not have down" was the one who cast Ifa for "Sash[2] which sounds 'titi'[3] when it fights on the side of the sky," when he was going to marry "A child is better than beads" and "A child is better than brass."[4] They said he should sacrifice four hens and one shilling seven pence eight oninis. "Sash which sounds 'titi' when it fights on the side of the sky" heard and made the sacrifice. He married "A child is better than beads" and "A child is better than brass" and brought them home to his house; and they bore many children for him.

Ifa says this is a man to whom the Sky God will give two wives during this year, and that these wives will bear many children for him. When "A child is better than beads" and "A child is better than brass" gave birth to their children, people began to sing:

> "Whose child is this, oh?
> "A child is better than beads
> "A child is better than brass."[5]

---

1. Note the appearance of Edi and Qkanran, derived from the name of the figure, in the name of the diviner.
2. Amure is a sash or a girdle formerly worn by men.
3. "Titi" is the sound caused by shaking: in illustration the informant jiggled a table, causing the bottle on it to rock back and forth.
4. See verse 54-5, where these two names are applied to a single character.
5. The answer is that these two are the mothers.

---

54 - 4

"The palm tree at the crossroads is the one which feels the cutlass"[1] and "Two people cannot sleep on a duiker hide"[2] were the ones who cast Ifa for the Sea Goddess. They said someone would suffer a loss during that year.[3] The sacrifice is two pigeons and two shillings six pence. The Sea Goddess did not sacrifice.

---

1. People hack at any tree at the crossroad when passing by or when waiting for someone, as they do at trees in the market. Cf. verse 52-2.
2. The skin of the duiker is only about one and a half by two feet in size, not large enough for even one adult to sleep on.
3. It is understood that the same prediction applies to the client for whom this verse is recited.

N(i)-igba-ti o şe   malu   O-1(i)-okun   si ku, o si
At-time-that it make (later), cow   (of) One:who-has-sea and die, she and

mu malu na o si tan   si-(i)lę gęgę bi oku,   o ni ki awǫn
take cow the, she and spread (it) to-ground just like corpse, she say that those

enia   on sǫ   pe on ku, o si sǫ   fun awǫn enia rę ki
people (of) her speak that she die, she and speak for those people hers should

nwǫn lǫ pe awǫn babalawo wa,   pe ki   nwǫn wa   sǫ   gęgę bi ęhin
they go call those diviner   come, that should they come speak just like back

oku   on yio ti   ri. N(i)-igba-ti awǫn babalawo de   ti nwǫn si da
corpse her will have see. At-time-that those diviner   arrive that they and cast

Ifa titi, ko si ęni-ti   o mu ibo na rara, gbogbo awǫn babalawo si
Ifa until, not be person-that he take ibo the at:all, all   those diviner   and

bęrę si wi-pe   ęhin   oku   na yio dara.   L(i)-ęhin eyi ni awǫn
begin to speak-that back (of) corpse the will be:good. At-back this be those

enia   O-1(i)-okun   bi awǫn babalawo lere pe,   ta-ni   babalawo
people (of) One:who-has-sea ask those diviner   (1)   that, which-be diviner

ti o ku   s(i)-ęhin? Nwǫn ni o ku   Iru s(i)-ęhin, nwǫn si lǫ ran-
that he remain to-back? They say it remain Tail to-back   they and go send-

(i)şę   pe Iru n(i)-igba-ti Iru si de,   o da Ifa ti-rę   o si
message call Tail; at-time-that Tail and arrive, he cast Ifa that-(of)-his he and

sǫ   pe O-1(i)-okun   ko ku şugbǫn ofun li o şe.
speak that One:who-has-sea not die, but   loss be it make (her).

N(i)-igba-na ni O-1(i)-okun   ja-(o)de   n(i)-ibi-ti o ti sa-
At-time-the be One:who-has-sea reach-outside at-place-that she have run-

pa-mǫ   si, o si wi-pe   on gba   fun Iru nitori-pe   o mu ibo
kill-against to, she and speak-that she accept for Tail because-that he take ibo

na. Iru si yan ębǫ   ti-rę   ni ęsę-k(u)-ęsę fun O-1(i)-okun
the. Tail and choose sacrifice that-(of)-his at foot-any-foot for One:who-has-sea,

ewurę   meji, aşǫ kan, erundinlǫgbǫn   ki ofun ma ba   şe   O-
she-goat two, cloth one, 50,000   (cowries) that loss not should make One:who-

l(i)-okun mǫ.   O-1(i)-okun   gbǫ o si ru,   l(i)-ęhin eyi o sǫ
has-sea again. One:who-has-sea hear she and offer; at-back this she speak

fun awǫn babalawo pe   n(i)-igba-k(u)-igba ti   nwǫn ba   ti   nlǫ   si ode
for those diviner   that at-time-any-time that they should have going to outside

    awo   nwǫn nilati ma   mu Iru dani pęlu   wǫn lǫ si
(of) secret they must (continuative) take Tail hold together:with them go to

ode   awo. Lati igba-na ni awǫn babalawo ti   ma   mu
outside (of) secret. From time-the be those diviner   have (continuative) take

Iru dani. Gbogbo   awǫn si bęrę si kǫ-(o)rin wi-pe:
Tail hold. All   (of) them and begin to sing-song speak-that:

---

1. Bi . . . lere means "to ask."

After a while the Sea Goddess' cow died, and she took the cow and laid it out just like a human corpse. She told her family to say that she had died, and she told them to call the diviners to come and divine, just as if she had really died. When the diviners came, they all cast Ifa, but not one of them chose the correct specific alternative;[4] all the diviners said that following her death things would go well. Then the family of the Sea Goddess asked them if there was another diviner. They said that there was Tail. And they sent word to Tail that he should come. When Tail arrived, he cast his Ifa and declared that the Sea Goddess had not died, but that she had suffered a loss.

Then the Sea Goddess came out from where she had hidden herself; and she said that she would take Tail as her diviner because he had chosen the correct specific alternative. Tail named his sacrifice at once for the Sea Goddess: two she-goats, one cloth, and twelve shillings six pence, so that she would not suffer another loss. The Sea Goddess heard and made the sacrifice. Then she told the diviners that whenever they were going out to divine, they must bring Tail along with them. Since that time diviners always carry Tail with them. And they all began to sing:

---

4. See Chapter V.

Mo mire-(i)le   a-mu-(I)ru
"I   going-house to-take-Tail,

Iru l(i)-O-ni-(I)fę   lo
"Tail be-One:who-has-Ifę use."

EDI - (Q)KANRAN - 5

Işanşan awo   Idi   ǫpę   a   da fun alangba ni-(ǫ)jǫ
Root   secret (of) "Base (of) palm:tree" (be) who cast for Lizard at-day

ti   o   ma   ni   obinrin kan; nwǫn ni ki   o   ru-(ę)bǫ
that he (continuative) have woman one; they say should he offer-sacrifice (of)

akikǫ meji, ęiyę-(i)le   meji. Nwǫn ni yio fę   obinrin kan, nwǫn ni   bi o
cock two, bird-(of)-house two.   They say will love woman one, they say if he

ba   fę   obinrin na tan   ki   o ma ba   ri ęni-ti   yio ba
should love woman the finish that he not should see person-that will meet (him)

ti   obinrin na si igbo, nitori-na   ki   o ru   ębǫ   e-l(i)-
push woman   the to forest, because-the should he offer sacrifice (of) one:who-be-

enini   ile.   Alangba ru   ęiyę-(i)le   meji ki on ba   le
slanderer (of) house. Lizard offer bird-(of)-house two that he should be:able

ri obinrin fę, şugbǫn ko ru   akikǫ meji ki obinrin na ba   le   pę
see woman love, but   not offer cock two that woman the should be:able be:long

l(i)-ǫdǫ   rę.
at-presence his.

    Obinrin kan si wa   orukǫ rę a   ma   ję Qmǫ-l(i)-okun Qmǫ-
    Woman one and exist name her she (continuative) eat Child-be-bead Child-

n(i)-idę, gbogbo awǫn ęranko   igbo ni o si nfę   obinrin yi; şugbǫn
be-brass, all   those animal (of) forest be they and wanting woman this; but

ko gba fun ęni-kan   ni-(i)nu wǫn nitori-ti   o wi-pe   ęni-ti
not accept for person-one at-belly theirs because-that she speak-that person-that

yio ba   fę   on ni lati le   ka   ǫsan agba-lu-(i)mǫ   fun on
will should love her be to be:able pluck ǫsan elder-gather-knowledge for her

mu, ęni-ti   o ba si le   ka ǫsan yi fun on ni on yio fę;
drink, person-that he should and be:able pluck ǫsan this for her be she will love.

gbogbo awǫn ęranko   igbo şe   ti nwǫn ko le   ka   ǫsan fun Qmǫ-
All   those animal (of) forest make that they not be:able pluck ǫsan for Child-

l(i)-okun Qmǫ-n(i)-idę, şugbǫn alangba ni-(ǫ)kan ni o gb(e)-iyanju   ti   o
be-bead Child-be-brass, but   Lizard be-one   be he take-persevere that he

si ka   ǫsan fun Qmǫ-l(i)-okun Qmǫ-n(i)-idę o si di   aya rę.
and pluck ǫsan for Child-be-bead Child-be-brass she and become wife his.

"I am going home to get my Tail,
"Tail is what the King of Ifẹ uses."[5]

_____

5. This verse explains why diviners carry a cow-tail switch (irukẹrẹ), resembling that used by the King of Ifẹ.

_____

54 - 5

Roots,[1] the diviner of "The base of the palm tree" was the one who cast Ifa
for Lizard when he was going to take a wife; they said he should sacrifice two
cocks and two pigeons. They said he would love a woman and that he would marry
her, but that lest someone should drive her away into the forest, he should sacrifice because of a slanderer in his house. Lizard offered two pigeons that he might
take a wife, but did not sacrifice two cocks that she would be able to stay with him.
    And there was a woman whose name was "A child is better than beads, a child
is better than brass,"[2] who was desired by all the animals of the forest. But she
would not accept any of them because she said that the person who would marry
her must be able to pick star apples, "The elder who gathers knowledge,"[3] for her
to suck, and that anyone who picked these star apples for her she would marry.
All the animals of the forest tried but were unable to pick star apples for "A child
is better than beads, a child is better than brass." Lizard alone persevered, and
he picked star apples for "A child is better than beads, a child is better than brass,"
and she became his wife.

_____

1. Ishanshan is said to describe anything which resembles the way in which
the roots of a tree protrude from the trunk into the ground.
    2. These names, which refer here to a single individual, are used to refer to
two individuals in verse 54-3.
    3. Ọsan agbalumọ refers both to the African star apple (Chrysophyllum
africanum) and the White star apple (Chrysophyllum albidum). The qualifying
phrase was said, without further explanation, to refer to the man who stole the
true ọsan.

N(i)-igba-ti   o   fẹ   tan   ni gbogbo awọn ẹranko   igbo   wa   di
At-time-that he love (her) finish be all   those animal (of) forest come tie

rikişi mọ   alangba, nwọn si p(a)-ero   pọ,   nwọn si sọ   fun Qmọ-
plot   against Lizard, they and kill-thought together, they and speak for Child-

l(i)-okun Qmọ-n(i)-idẹ   pe   alangba ti   o   lọ fẹ   ko ni-(i)le,   bẹ-ni
be-bead Child-be-brass that Lizard that she go love not have-house; so-be (it)

nitotọ alangba ko ni-(i)le   ti   gbe, gbọnran   ogiri ni i   ma
truly Lizard not have-house that (he) dwell, crack   (of) wall be he (continua-

         sun kiri,   n(i)-igba-ti Qmọ-l(i)-okun Qmọ-n(i)-idẹ gbọ bayi ti   o
tive) sleep about. At-time-that Child-be-bead Child-be-brass hear thus that she

si   ri   pe alangba ko ni-(i)le   nitotọ, o   si lọ kuro ni ọdọ   rẹ n(i)-
and see that Lizard not have-house truly, she and go depart at presence his at-

igba-ti   alangba wa ile   ti   yio gbe lọ. N(i)-igba-ti alangba de
time-that Lizard seek house that (they) will dwell go. At-time-that Lizard arrive,

o bẹrẹ si wa   Qmọ-l(i)-okun Qmọ-n(i)-idẹ   şugbọn ko ri   ko si mọ
he begin to seek Child-be-bead Child-be-brass but   not see (her) not and know

ibi-ti   o   wa;   n(i)-igba-na ni alangba bẹrẹ si wa   kiri ti   o   si
place-that she exist; at-time-the be Lizard begin to seek (her) about that he and

nkọ-(o)rin   bayi pe:
singing-song thus that:

                Talo r(i)-ọmọ yi   o
                "Who see-child this, oh?

                Qmọ-l(i)-okun
                "Child-be-bead,

                Qmọ-n(i)-idẹ
                "Child-be-brass."

Bayi ni alangba bẹrẹ si kọ-(o)rin kiri ti   o   si nwa   obinrin rẹ yi   kiri
Thus be Lizard begin to sing-song about that he and seeking woman his this about

ti   o   si nwo   gbogbo ori   igi   igbo kiri ko si ri Qmọ-l(i)-
that he and looking:at all   head (of) tree (of) forest about not and see Child-be-

okun Qmọ-n(i)-idẹ   aya rẹ. Bayi ni alangba nwa   a kiri ti   o si
bead Child-be-brass, wife his. Thus be Lizard seeking her about that he and

nwo   ori   igi titi di   oni yi; on na   ni o nwa   kiri ti
looking:at head (of) tree until become today this; she also be he seeking about that

o si ma   nwo   ori   igi.
he and (continuative) looking:at head (of) tree.

      Ifa ni ẹni-ti   o wa   da Ifa yi yio ri obinrin kan fẹ   şugbọn
      Ifa say person-that he come cast Ifa this will see woman one love, but

ki   o ru   ẹbọ   e-l(i)-enini   ti yio ba   ọran
should he offer sacrifice (of) one:who-has-enmity that will spoil affair (of)

After he had married her, all the animals of the forest plotted against Lizard. They consulted together, and they told "A child is better than beads, a child is better than brass" that Lizard whom she had married did not own a house. Thus it was in truth, Lizard had no house in which to live; he slept about town in cracks in the wall. When "A child is better than beads, a child is better than brass" heard this, and when she saw that Lizard really had no house, she ran away from him while he was out looking for a house in which they could live. When Lizard returned, he looked for "A child is better than beads, a child is better than brass," but he did not see her, and he did not know where she was. Then Lizard began to go about looking for her, singing this song:

> "Who has seen this child, oh?
> "A child is better than beads,
> "A child is better than brass?"[4]

Thus Lizard began to sing as he went around looking for his wife and peering into the tops of all the trees of the forest, but he did not find "A child is better than beads, a child is better than brass." Thus Lizard has continued to go about searching for her and to look at the treetops until this very day; it is his wife that he is seeking for everywhere and for whom he is looking in the treetops.[5]

Ifa says that the person for whom this figure was cast will find a woman to marry, but that he should offer a sacrifice lest an enemy spoil his

---

4. Cf. the song in verse 54-3.

5. It is understood that this verse explains how the lizard came to have the characteristic motion of raising himself on his front legs and peering about. Cf. the version of this tale as recorded by Frobenius (1926: 244-246).

obinrin na jẹ mọ   ni l(i)-ọwọ to-bẹ   ti   obinrin na yio fi   nu
woman the (1) against (him) be at-hand equal-so that woman the will make be:lost

mọ   ni l(i)-ọwọ ti   a-(yi)o si fi   ma   wa   ka.
against (him) be at-hand, that we-will and take (continuative) seeking go:around.

Gbogbo enia   ni yio ti   fẹ   obinrin na ti   ṣugbọn e-l(i)-eyi   ni
All   people be will have want woman the that, but   one:who-be-this be (he)

yio fẹ,   ṣugbọn ki   a   ru   ẹbọ   e-l(i)-enini.
will love (her), but   should he offer sacrifice (of) one:who-be-slanderer.

Ẹni-kan   si   nfẹ   ṣe ohun kan ti   gbogbo enia   ti   sẹ ti   ohun na
Person-one and wanting do thing one that all   people have do that thing the

yio bọ   si-(ẹ)ni   l(i)-ọwọ ṣugbọn ki   a   ru   ẹbọ   e-l(i)-
will come to-person at-hand but   should he offer sacrifice (of) one:who-be-

enini   bi ohun na ba   tẹ-(ẹ)ni   l(i)-ọwọ tan   ki   o ma ba   tun
slanderer if thing the should reach-person at-hand finish, that it not should then

bọ   l(i)-ọwọ   ẹni.
slip at-hand (of) person.

EDI - (Q)KANRAN - 6

Jingbun jingbun finfin   a   da   fun ọtin   a   bu   fun
"Jingbun jingbun finfin" (be) who cast for Maize:Beer, they share for

ẹmu   a   lu-(i)kin fun ogurọ   ọmọ   iya   rẹ nwọn ni
Palm:Wine, they beat-ikin for Bamboo:Wine, child (of) mother his; they say

ki   awọn mẹt(a)-(m)ẹta ru-(ẹ)bọ   akikọ mẹta-mẹta, ki   nwọn ma
should they three-three   offer-sacrifice (of) cock three-three, that they not

ba   mu a-mu-bọ   mọ; Ọtin   ko ru-(ẹ)bọ,   ọgọrọ   ko
should take to-take-slip again; Maize:Beer not offer-sacrifice; Bamboo:Wine not

ru   bẹ-ni   Ẹmu   ọmọ   iya   wọn na   ko pa-(E)ṣu.   Lati
offer, so-be (it) Palm:Wine child (of) mother their also not appease-Eshu. From

igba-na bi ọtin,   ẹmu   tabi ọgọrọ   ba   npa   enia   ti
time-the if Maize:Beer, Palm:Wine, or Bamboo:Wine should killing person, that

o si mu u ti   o yo,   ti   o ba   si ti   le   sun,   ọtin,
he and drink it that he satisfied, that he should and have be:able sleep, Maize:Beer,

ẹmu   tabi ọgọrọ   ti   o mu   na yio fo   l(i)-oju rẹ. Ni ọjọ
Palm:Wine, or Bamboo:Wine that he drink the will clear at-eye his. At day

ti   ọtin,   ẹmu   ọgọrọ   ti   nmu   a-mu-bọ   ni-yi.
that Maize:Beer, Palm:Wine, Bamboo:Wine have taking to-take-slip be-this.

---

1. Ba . . . jẹ means "to spoil."

marriage so that he will lose his wife, and he will have to go around looking for her. Everyone will desire this woman, but this person is the one who will marry her; still he should offer a sacrifice against a slanderer. And someone wants to do something that everyone is attempting; it will come within his grasp, but he should sacrifice against a slanderer lest, when it is within his grasp, it should not slip away from him.

---

54 - 6

"Jingbun jingbun finfin"[1] was the one who cast Ifa for Maize Beer, shared[2] it with Palm Wine, and beat palm nuts for Bamboo Wine, three children of the same mother. They said that these three should sacrifice three cocks each, so that things would not slip from their grasp. Maize Beer did not sacrifice; Bamboo Wine did not sacrifice; nor did Palm Wine, child of the same mother, appease[3] Eshu. Since that time if Maize Beer, Palm Wine, or Bamboo Wine intoxicate[4] someone and he has drunk his fill, when he has had a chance to sleep, his head will clear again. This was the day that Maize Beer, Palm Wine, and Bamboo Wine let things slip from their grasp.

---

1. Jingbun jingbun finfin is an onomatopoeic name for one of the drum rhythms, but here it refers to the sound of drinking; jingbun jingbun represents the sound made in swallowing or gulping, and finfin the sucking sound made when drinking.

2. See n. 4, verse 18-4.

3. See n. 3, verse 35-7.

4. Literally, "to kill." It is implied that if these three alcoholic drinks had sacrificed, the people whom they appear to kill would not recover in the morning. Bamboo wine or raphia wine is made by tapping the Bamboo or Wine Palm (Raphia spp.). Palm wine is made by tapping the Oil Palm (Elaeis guineensis).

Ifa ni ki   e-l(i)-eyi   ru-(ę)bǫ   ki ohun rere ti o ti
Ifa say should one:who-be-this offer-sacrifice that thing good that he have

nmu   ma ba   le   ma   bǫ l(i)-ǫwǫ rę mǫ.
taking not should be:able (continuative) slip at-hand his again.

EDI - (Q)KANRAN - 7

Edi ranyin   ni o da fun okoto   nwǫn ni awǫn enia   yio gbe
"Edi spinning" be who cast for Periwinkle; they say those people will carry

de   ipo   rere ni-(i)nu   ǫdun yi   şugbǫn ki   o ru-(ę)bǫ
(him) arrive position good at-belly (of) year this, but   should he offer-sacrifice

akikǫ adię   męta ati ęgbędogun.   Ikoto   ko ru-(ę)bǫ.
(of) cock chicken three and 3000   (cowries). Periwinkle not offer-sacrifice.

N(i)-igba-ti o şe   awǫn enia bęrę si gbe ikoto   ga,
At-time-that it make (later), those people begin to carry Periwinkle be:high,

nwǫn si nta   a   n(i)-igba-ti ijo   ba   si wǫ   ikoto   l(i)-ara,
they and spinning him, at-time-that dance should and enter Periwinkle at-body,

a si ku l(i)-ęsę-k(u)-ęsę nitori-ti   ko ru-(ę)bǫ.
he and die at-foot-any-foot because-that (he) not offer-sacrifice.

Ifa ni awǫn enia yio gbe e-l(i)-eyi   si ipo   ǫla   kan
Ifa say those people will carry one:who-be-this to position (of) honor one,

şugbǫn ki   o ru-(ę)bǫ   ai-ku ki o ba   le   ję igba-dun
but   should he offer-sacrifice (of) not-die that he should be:able eat time-sweet

ipo   na.
(of) position the.

EDI - (Q)KANRAN - 8

Ogiri gba aşǫ   ilę-du   bo-(a)ra a la-(ę)nu   fǫ ni
"Wall accept cloth (of) earth-black cover-body; to open-mouth (not) speak be

ti   amǫ   a da fun afe   ti işe ǫmǫ   Olodumare
that (of) Lizard" (be) who cast for Grass:Mouse that make child (of) Olodumare;

nwǫn ni ki   o ru   agbo kan, aja kan, ati akikǫ adię   kan nitori-pe
they say should he offer ram one, dog one, and cock chicken one because-that

ori rę yio dara   ni ai-ro-tęlę   ni-(i)nu   ǫdun yi.
head his will be:good at no-think-beforehand at-belly (of) year this.

N(i)-igba-ti o şe   Olodumare ran-(i)şę   si aręmǫ   ǫmǫ
At-time-that it make (later), Olodumare send-message to first:born child

Ifa says that this person should sacrifice so that a good thing which he has within his grasp should not be able to slip out of his hands again.

---

54 - 7

"Edi spinning"[1] was the one who cast Ifa for Periwinkle.[2] They said he would be placed in a good position during that year, but that he should sacrifice three cocks and nine pence. Periwinkle did not sacrifice.

After a while people raised Periwinkle high, and they were spinning him like a top; but as soon as dancing had entered his body,[3] he suddenly fell dead[4] because he had not sacrificed.

Ifa says that people will place this person in a position of honor, but he should sacrifice against death, so that he will be able to enjoy the position.

---

1. The word "ranyin" does not describe spinning itself, but the secondary weaving or oscillating motion of the axis of a top.

2. Perhaps not correctly a periwinkle, but a spiral univalve shell about three quarters of an inch in diameter at the large end, and about an inch long, which is spun as a top by children.

3. That is, when the shell began to spin.

4. This verse thus explains why the okoto or ikoto shell is used as a top, and why it stops suddenly after spinning for only a short time.

---

54 - 8

"Wall uses a cloth of manure to cover itself;[1] Lizard[2] opens his mouth but does not speak" was the one who cast Ifa for Grass Mouse,[3] who was a child of the Sky God. They said he should sacrifice one ram, one dog, and one cock so that his luck would unexpectedly be good during that year.

After a while the Sky God send word to his own first-born[4] child

---

1. The layer of manure ("black dirt") rubbed on the walls of a house is compared here with the clothes worn by humans.

2. Amǫ (or alamu) lizard is a synonym for alangba. Cf. verse 54-5.

3. Spotted Grass Mouse (Lemniscomys striatus).

4. Presumably Grass Mouse.

Olodumare papa   pe   ki   o fi   agbo, aja, ati akikọ adię   ran-
(of) Olodumare himself that should he take ram, dog, and cock chicken send-

(i)ṣę   si on   ṣugbọn aręmọ   Olodumare ran-(i)ṣę   pada   pe on
message to him, but   first:born (of) Olodumare send-message return that he

ko ni   owo   ti   on yio fi   ra awọn (ohu)n-kan męta nwọn-yi   awọn
not have cowries that he will take (it) buy those thing-one three those-this; those

o-n(i)-iṣę   na si npada   lọ l(i)-ọwọ   ofo   n(i)-igba-na
one:who-have-message the and returning go at-hand (of) emptiness, at-time-the

ni afe   si pe wọn pada   o si fi   agbo, aja, ati akikọ adię ti
be Grass:Mouse and call them return he and take ram, dog, and cock fowl that

on papa   ti fę fi   ṣe ębọ   fun ara rę ran-(i)ṣę   si
he himself have want take (them) make sacrifice for body his send-message to

Olodumare; n(i)-igba-ti Olodumare ri   inu rę si dun   o si gbe
Olodumare; at-time-that Olodumare see (this) belly his and sweet he and carry

apo   iwa   ran-(i)ṣę   si afe.
pouch (of) destiny send-message to Grass:Mouse.

Afe   si bęrę si di   o-l(i)-okiki   enia   ni-(i)nu
Grass:Mouse and begin to become one:who-have-praise (of) people at-belly

aiye; Olodumare si wi-pe   ko si ęni-ti   yio ni   ori rere gęgę
(of) earth. Olodumare and speak-that not be person-that will have head good just

bi ti   afe   l(i)-aiye, o ni afe   ni yio ju   gbogbo
like that (of) Grass:Mouse at-earth, he say Grass:Mouse be will surpass all

awọn ọmọ   on lọ ni aiye, awọn enia si bęrę si wi-pe   o yę afe,
those child (of) him go at earth, those people and begin to say-that "It suit Grass:

nwọn ni o ra aja   ita   o fi   agbo bọ   baba rę,
Mouse," they say he buy dog (of) third:day, he take ram sacrifice:to father his,

nwọn si nkọ-(o)rin   wi-pe:
they and singing-song speak-that:

Ęni   ṣe oju ko ṣe o
"Person do eye not do, oh,

Ęni   ṣe-(ę)hin l(i)-o ṣe o
"Person do-back be-he do, oh,

Afe   ra-(a)ja   ita   o
"Grass:Mouse buy-dog (of) third:day, oh,

Afe   f(i)-agbo bọ   baba rę.
"Grass:Mouse take-ram sacrifice:to father his."

Ifa ni ęni-kan   wa ti baba rę   ọrun yio p(a)-ese   fun
Ifa say person-one exist that father his (in) sky will kill-provision for (him)

ni-(i)nu   ọdun yi ṣugbọn ki   o fi   agbo, aja, ati akikọ bọ
at-belly (of) year this, but   should he take ram, dog, and cock sacrifice:to

baba na.
father the.

————————————————————

to send him a ram, a dog, and a cock; but his first-born sent back word that he did not have money with which to buy these three things. The messengers were returning empty-handed, and then Grass Mouse called them back and gave them the ram, dog, and cock which he had wanted to sacrifice for himself for them to take to the Sky God.[5] When the Sky God saw what Grass Mouse had done, he was pleased, and he sent a "pouch of destiny" to Grass Mouse.

And Grass Mouse began to gain fame[6] on earth. The Sky God said that no one on earth would have good luck like that of Grass Mouse; he said that Grass Mouse would be more important than any of his other children on earth. And people began to say, "Grass Mouse deserves it";[7] they said "He bought a dog of the third day,[8] and he sacrificed a ram to his father"; and they sang:

> "Those who do things for you before your eyes don't count, oh;
> "Those who do things for you behind your back are the ones that
>   count, oh.
> "Grass Mouse bought a dog of the third day, oh;
> "Grass Mouse sacrificed a ram to his father, oh."

Ifa says there is someone whose father in heaven[9] will provide for him during this year, but he should sacrifice a ram, a dog, and a cock to his father.

---

5. After at first refusing, Grass Mouse changed his mind and gave these three things, which he had purchased to make the sacrifice prescribed by the diviners, to the Sky God. When a character fails to make a prescribed sacrifice, he usually meets with misfortune, but Grass Mouse gave the sacrifice directly to the Sky God, and as a result he was rewarded.

6. He became a person who has praise names (okiki or oriki).

7. The fame and good fortune of Grass Mouse (Afe) may refer to the use of the tail of a rat known as Afe-imojo instead of a cow-tail switch by the King of Qyǫ, according to Crowther, who cites a proverb, "Whoever kills afe-imojo must take it to Qyǫ; ęda only is due to the people of the province to eat" (ęda is a kind of rat remarkable for its fast breeding).

8. This may refer to Grass Mouse's hesitation in giving it to the Sky God.

9. That is, his own father who has died, not the Sky God.

EDI - (I)ROSUN - 1

Edi rusurusu, Edi o   sun,   Edi o   wo   ẹni-ti   ko sun ni
"Edi very:red, Edi who sleep, Edi who relax, person-that not sleep be (he)

mọ ibi ilẹ   gbe mọ"   a   da fun iwowo   ti   nlọ si-(i)nu
know place ground take clear" (be) who cast for Porcupine that going to-belly (of)

ọgan   nwọn ni ki   o fi ẹiyẹ-(i)le   meji, akikọ adiẹ   meji,
termite:hill; they say should he take bird-(of)-house two, cock chicken two,

ati egbejilelogun   ru-(ẹ)bọ.   Ṣugbọn babalawo na yio mu akikọ
and 4400   (cowries) offer-sacrifice. But   diviner the will take cock

adiẹ   kan fun ẹni-ti   o ru-(ẹ)bọ   na ni-(i)nu   awọn ohun ti
chicken one for person-that he offer-sacrifice the at-belly (of) those thing that

a yan   nwọn-yi pe ki   o lọ fi   bọ   ori rẹ. Iwowo
he choose those-this that should he go take (it) sacrifice:to head his. Porcupine

ru-(ẹ)bọ,   awọn enia si bẹrẹ si wi-pe   ori   iwowo   la-
offer-sacrifice, those people and begin to speak-that "Head (of) Porcupine open-

(ọ)na fun u   nitori-ti   o ru-(ẹ)bọ.
road for him because-that he offer-sacrifice."

Ifa ni ori   ẹni-ti   o da-(I)fa yi yio la-(ọ)na   fun   bi o
Ifa say head (of) person-that he cast-Ifa this will open-road for (him) if he

ba   ru-(ẹ)bọ.
should offer-sacrifice.

EDI - (I)ROSUN - 2

A ki i-di   a-l(i)-agẹmọ   mọ ori   owu   a
"We not to-catch:unaware one:who-be-chameleon (1) (at) head (of) cotton; we

ki i-di   odẹ fẹrẹfẹ   mọ epo   ẹpa   a   da fun
not to-catch:unaware bat quick-quick (1) (at) shell (of) peanut" (be) who cast for

Qlọramuole ọmọ   A-yi-bo-l(i)-ori-ohun-gbogbo,   Ojo ko
Qlọramuole child (of) "One:who-turn-cover-at-head-(of)-things-all," "Rain not

mu-(ọ)kọ-l(i)-ọra   ni ọjọ ti mu-(ẹ)ni-mu-(ẹ)ni   ọrun
drink-cornstarch:gruel-at-morning" at day that take-person-take-person (of) sky

de   n(i)-igba-ti ẹnimọ   ọrun nhan   nwọn ni ki   o ru igba
arrive at-time-that evil:thing (of) sky appearing; they say should he offer calabash

ogi   meji, ẹiyẹ-(i)le   meji, ati egbejila   nwọn ni e-
(of) cornstarch two, bird-(of)-house two, and 2400   (cowries); they say one:who-

l(i)-e-mu   ọrun ko ni   le   mu   lọ. Qlọramuole ni orukọ ti
be-who-take (of) sky not be (he) be:able take (him) go. Qlọramuole be name that

---

1. Di . . . mọ means "to catch unawares."

55 - 1

"Very red[1] Edi, Edi who sleeps,[2] Edi who relaxes; the one who doesn't go to sleep knows where the sun rises" was the one who cast Ifa for Porcupine[3] when he was going to break into a termite hill. They said he should sacrifice two pigeons, two cocks, and one shilling one pence two oninis. But the diviner will set aside one of the two cocks for the person to take and sacrifice to his head.[4] Porcupine sacrificed, and the people began to say, "Porcupine's head opened the way for him because he sacrificed."[5]

Ifa says that the head of the person for whom this figure is cast will "open the way" for him if he sacrifices.

---

1. "Rusurusu" is usually an adverb that qualifies verbs meaning only "to be red" (pipa, pipọn). The color indicated is a yellowish, red such as is seen only in the sky at sunset.

2. Note the pun here on Edi-(i)rosun and Edi o sun.

3. Iwowo (or egudu) was said to be the porcupine, more commonly known as orẹ.

4. To the soul which controls his luck.

5. The verse thus explains why the iwowo is successful in breaking into termite hills and eating the termites.

---

55 - 2

"One does not catch chameleons unaware on cotton plants; one does not catch nimble bats unaware on peanut shells"[1] was the one who cast Ifa for Qlọramuole,[2] child of "One who turns and covers over everything," "Rain prevents us from buying cornstarch gruel to drink in the morning"[3] on the day that something which takes people away arrived from heaven, when an evil thing from heaven was appearing. They said he should sacrifice two calabashes of cornstarch, two pigeons, and seven pence two oninis. They said that the thing from heaven which takes people away will not be able to take him. Qlọramuole is the name

---

1. These truisms are typical of the overstatements of proverbs, since chameleons are never found on cotton plants, nor bats on peanut shells.

2. This title could not be analyzed or its meaning explained.

3. These are two praise names for the parent of Qlọramuole. The latter, it was explained, implies that because it was raining, he was inside the house when the evil thing came, and thus escaped. Ẹkọ is a drink made of cornstarch (ogi) in warm water, which can be bought in the market and which commonly serves as the first meal of the day.

ọpọlọ jẹ, n(i)-igba-ti a ba   ba   ọpọlọ bi   ko jọ   eku işe   ni
frog eat, at-time-that we should meet frog, if (it) not resemble rat; make be

ai-fi   si-(i)lẹ.
not-put to-ground.

    Ifa ni ohun ti a da on si yi on ko ni jẹ-ki   apa   ara-
    Ifa say thing that we cast him to this he not be consent-that arm (of) people-

(a)iye   ka-(ẹ)ni   tabi on ko ni fi aye   fun ibi   lati ni
(of)-earth go:around-person or he not be take chance give place to have

agbara l(i)-ori   ẹni.
strength at-head (of) person.

QKANRAN MEJI - 1

    Qyẹ   ko san ara   imọnamọna ko jirẹrẹ bu   akọ aparo
    "Harmattan not crash thunder; lightning   not secretly flash; male partridge

ati abo   aparo   ko la ogbe l(i)-ori şanşan   a   da fun Ereje dudu
and female partridge not open comb at-head upright" (be) who cast for Ereje black,

yeye   agbo, on ni o bi erin   ati ẹfọn   o si bi agbo şe
mother (of) Ram, she be who bore Elephant and Buffalo, she and bore Ram make

ẹkẹta; awọn mẹt(a)-(m)ẹta gbẹ ila,   Şọngo si nwa   ti   ọrun ji   ila
third; those three-three   plant ochra, Shango and coming from sky steal ochra

nwọn ka,   n(i)-igba-ti iya   wọn ri pe a   nji   ila na ka,   o
their pluck, at-time-that mother their see that they stealing ochra the pluck, she

ni on ko ma   mọ ohun ti o nka   ila.   Erin   wa   bẹrẹ
say she not (continuative) know thing that it plucking ochra. Elephant come begin

si şọ,   ni-(ọ)jọ-kan Şọngo wa   ka   ila yi, n(i)-igba-ti o ri
to watch (it), at-day-one Shango come pluck ochra this, at-time-that he see

erin,   o bu mọ,   erin bẹ lu   igbo, ẹfọn na lọ
Elephant, he roar against (him), Elephant jump against forest; Buffalo also go

şọ-(o)ko   na, n(i)-igba-ti Şọngo ri ẹfọn,   o bu mọ,   on na
watch-farm the, at-time-that Shango see Buffalo, he roar against (him) he also

si bẹ lu   igbo pẹlu;   n(i)-igba-ti o kan agbo, n(i)-
and jump against forest together:with (Elephant). At-time-that it touch Ram, at-

igba-ti o nlọ o mu ewurẹ dani nitori-ti   ọmọ-ọdọ   agbo
time-that he going he take She:goat hold because-that child-young:animal (of) Ram

ni ewurẹ şe, n(i)-igba-ti Şọngo na nbọ   on na mu aja dani, n(i)-igba-
be She:goat make, at-time-that Shango also coming he also take Dog hold, at-time-

ti Şọngo yọ   si oko ti o ri agbo, o bu mọ   ọ, agbo na si
that Shango appear to farm that he see Ram, he roar against him, Ram also and

of Frog. When we see Frog, if it does not resemble a rat, we do not leave him alone.[4]

Ifa says he will not allow other people to hinder this person in the matter for which he has cast Ifa, nor will he give them a chance to have power over him.

----

4. The meaning of this is obscure, and could not be clarified by the inform-ant.

----

86 - 1

"Thunder does not crash during the harmattan;[1] lightning does not flash se-cretly; male and female partridges do not have upright combs on their heads" was the one who cast Ifa for black Ereje, mother of Ram, she who gave birth to Ele-phant and Buffalo, and whose third child was Ram. These three children planted ochra, and the God of Thunder came from the sky to steal it; when their mother saw that ochra was being stolen, she said she did not know what was picking it. Elephant began to watch the field, and one day the God of Thunder came back to pick ochra; when he saw Elephant, he roared at him, and Elephant fled into the forest. Buffalo also went to watch the farm; when the God of Thunder saw Buf-falo, he roared at him, and he, too, fled into the forest. When it came Ram's turn, he took She-goat along with him because she was his servant; and when the God of Thunder was coming, he brought Dog along. When the God of Thunder reached the Farm and saw Ram, he roared at him, but Ram

----

1. During the dry season, from about December through February, the dry, dust-laden harmattan wind blows down from the Sahara. Thunderstorms are associated with the rainy season, particularly during June and July.

bu   mǫ   bi o ti   ngun   agbo ni ǫbę,   bę-ni agbo na   nkan,
roar against (him), as he have stabbing Ram at knife, so-be Ram also butting

        N(i)-igba-ti o pę   ti nwǫn ti   nja,   ǫbę   Şǫngo da   owo
(him). At-time-that it stay that they have fighting, knife (of) Shango break, horn

        agbo na   si   da   pęlu;   Şǫngo ran aja pe ki   o lǫ mu
(of) Ram also and break together:with (it); Shango send Dog that should he go take

ǫbę   miran   wa   fun on, n(i)-igba-ti aja de   ǫna o ba   egungun, o
knife another come for him, at-time-that Dog arrive road he meet bone,   he

dubu-(i)lę   ti   i o nję,   agbo si ran ewurę lǫ mu owo
lie:across-ground against it he eating (it), Ram and send She:goat go take horn

miran, n(i)-igba-ti ara-(a)iye   na   ǫwǫ epo   işu si ewurę,
another, at-time-that people-(of)-world stretch hand husk (of) yam to She:goat,

o ni Oni ki işe ǫjǫ   epo bękękę bękękęrikę, bayi ni ewurę
she say "Today not make day (of) husk, bękękę, bękękęrikę," thus be She:goat

ko   owo miran wa   fun agbo, n(i)-igba-ti agbo ran owo mǫ-(o)ri
gather horn another come give Ram, at-time-that Ram fasten horn against-head

tan o le Şǫngo lu   igbę, lati igba-na ni Şǫngo ti wa l(i)-
finish he chase Shango against forest, from time-the be Shango have exist at-

ǫrun; ti apara ba   san,   ti imǫnamǫna ba   kǫ,   agbo a fi   ęsę
sky; that thunder should crash, that lightning   should flash, Ram he with feet

wa   ilę   a ni ija   on pęlu   rę tun ku   ękan.
scratch ground, he say fight (of) him together:with yours then remain once.

    Ifa ni ki   (ohu)n-kan bi ibi ma ti oko şe, ki   awǫn ǫmǫ
    Ifa say should thing-one like evil not from farm make, should those child

    iya   męta ma ba   fi   ori ki,   ki   iya   wǫn na   ma ba
(of) mother three not should take head perish, should mother their also not should

fi   ori gba   ni-(i)nu   ibi na. Ębǫ: obukǫ kan, ęgbędǫgbǫn,
take head strike at-belly (of) evil the. Sacrifice: he:goat one, 5000   (cowries),

ati işu męfa ni ębǫ   ki   a si ma   gbe ębǫ   na lǫ si
and yam six be sacrifice, should we and (continuative) carry sacrifice the go to

ǫna   oko.
road (of) farm.

ǪKANRAN MEJI - 2

    Ogbo ęrinla ki isǫ-(ǫ)rǫ   ę w(o)-ęyę   jingbinni l(i)-ǫrun
    "Old   cow   not speak-word, you look:at-decoration gorgeous at-neck (of)

ęşin   l(i)-o d(a)-Ifa fun Bilǫpę ti iş(e)-ǫmǫ bibi   Ǫrunmila. Nwǫn ni
horse" be-who cast-Ifa for Bilǫpę that make-child born (of) Ǫrunmila. They say

roared back; and when he began stabbing Ram with his knife, Ram began butting him. When they had been fighting a while, the God of Thunder's knife broke, and Ram's horn broke also. The God of Thunder sent Dog to bring him another knife, but when Dog reached the road, he found a bone and lay down to eat it. Ram likewise sent She-goat to bring him another horn; and when humans held out yam rinds to her, She-goat replied, "Today is no day for rinds, 'bẹkẹkẹ bẹkẹkẹrikẹ.'"[2] So She-goat brought another horn to Ram; and when Ram had fastened the horn to his head, he chased the God of Thunder away. Since that time the God of Thunder has remained in the sky, and when thunder crashes and lightning flashes,[3] Ram paws the ground with his feet, saying, "Our fight is not yet finished."[4]

Ifa says we should sacrifice, lest something evil come from the farm and lest three children of the same mother should perish, and their mother should also become affected by the evil. One he-goat, one shilling three pence, and six yams is the sacrifice; we should take it to the farm road.

---

2. The sound that a goat makes when it bleats.

3. Note the relationship here between the tale and the names of the diviners.

4. This verse explains why the God of Thunder lives in the sky, and explains the behavior of rams during thunderstorms. It differs somewhat from the explanation sometimes offered that the sound of thunder is caused by the God of Thunder's ram pawing the ground in the heavens. Rams are the main sacrificial animals for the God of Thunder, ochra is another of his favorite foods, and dogs, though not used as sacrifices, are sacred to him. Compare the versions of this tale recorded by Parkinson (1909: 166-169) and Itayemi and Gurry (1953: 53-55) and the variant recorded by Frobenius (1926: 247-248).

---

86 - 2

"An old cow does not speak; look at the gorgeous decoration on the neck of the horse" was the one who cast Ifa for Bilọpẹ, the child of Ọrunmila. They said

ki   o   wa   ru-(ę)bǫ   nitori   ki lǫ si oko: eku meji, ęja meji, ati
should he come offer-sacrifice because not go to farm, rat two, fish two, and

ayebǫ adię   meji, oko   ti   on ti   ęgbaji.
hen   chicken two, twenty:cowries against it against 4,000 (cowries).

    A-ru-lǫ-(I)fa: ki   a   pa ǫkan ki   a la   l(i)-aiya ki   a
    To-carry-go-Ifa: should we kill one should we split (it) at-chest, should we

bu epo   si   yio gbe   tǫ   Ęşu lǫ, a-(yi)o wa   mu ǫkan
dip palm:oil to (it); (we) will carry (it) approach Eshu go; we-will come take one

(i)y(i)-o-ku   fun ęni-ti   a   d(a)-Ifa na fun   pe ki   o lǫ
this-which-remain for person-that we cast-Ifa the for (him), that should he go

fi   bǫ   Ifa.
take (it) sacrifice:to Ifa.

    Ifa ni   ęni-kan   ni-yi ki lǫ si oko, ko si gbǫdǫ fi   ęsę rę kan
    Ifa say person-one be-this not go to farm, not and must take foot his touch

enini, ki a ni Ifa nro   ęni-kan;   ki   o lǫ ma   bǫ
dew, that we say Ifa thinking (of) person-one; should he go (continuative) sacrifice:

   Ifa.
to Ifa.

QKANRAN MEJI - 3

    Ikan winrin ikan winrin l(i)-o d(a)-Ifa ko Yanmǫti ti   o   nlǫ   si oko
    "One winrin one winrin" be-who cast-Ifa for Sesame that she going to farm

a-l(i)-oro   ǫdun ti o   nlǫ mu-(i)lę   (i)bu-do   nitori
that:which-has-ritual (of) year that she going take-ground place-settle because

ti   ǫmǫ, nwǫn ni yio bi-(ǫ)mǫ;   eku meji, ęja meji, oko
that (of) child, they say will bear-child. Rat two, fish two, twenty:cowries

ti   on ti   ęgbaji.   Ifa ni ęni-kan   nşe   (ohu)n-kan
against it against 4000 (cowries). Ifa say person-one making thing-one (of)

oşu   rę   l(i)-ǫwǫ, bi o ba   le   ru-(ę)bǫ   ǫmǫ ni   yio fi
month hers at-hand; if she should be:able offer-sacrifice child be (she) will take

   bi.   Yanmǫti ru-(ę)bǫ.
(it) bear. Sesame offer-sacrifice.

---

he should sacrifice two rats, two fish, two hens, and twenty cowries[1] in addition to one shilling, because he should not go to farm.

Instructions for making the sacrifice: One chicken will be killed and split open at the breast, and palm oil will be dipped inside it; we will take it to Eshu. We will give the other chicken to the person for whom this figure was cast, so he may take it to sacrifice to Ifa.

Ifa says that this is someone who should not go to farm, and who must not touch the dew with his feet.[2] And we say Ifa is thinking of someone; he should be sacrificing to Ifa.

---

1. This is another example of punning and word magic. Twenty cowries (oko) are added to the sacrifice of someone who must not go to farm (oko).

2. As one does when he goes to the farm early in the morning. The client here is instructed to give up farm work and to devote himself to the worship of Ifa. Cf. verse 6-3.

---

86 - 3

"One 'winrin,' one 'winrin'"[1] was the one who cast Ifa for Benniseed when she was going to the farm of ritual[2] to take land to settle so that she might bear children. They said that she would bear children if she sacrificed two rats, two fish, and twenty cowries[3] in addition to one shilling. Ifa says someone is menstruating at this moment; if she is able to make the sacrifice, she will bear a child. Benniseed sacrificed.[4]

---

1. Winrin winrin was explained as a tinkling sound such as is made by rattling a small chain.

2. Because benniseed is the principal tabu of the God of Smallpox, it is prohibited to plant benniseed near Yoruba towns. It is also used in "medicine" to cause an enemy to have smallpox.

3. Cf. n. 2, verse 86-2.

4. The implication of this verse is that it is because Benniseed or Sesame (Sesamum indicum) made the sacrifice that she bears so many "children," or seeds.

IROSUN QBARA - 1

Qpę   ku f(i)-ǫriwo   l(u)-adǫ   l(i)-o   d(a)-Ifa k(o)-a-
"Palm:tree die take-young:palm:frond beat-body" be-who cast-Ifa for-One:who-

l(i)-ara Işa.   Nwǫn ni aya kan ni o ma   fę ni ǫdun-ni yi, ki
has-Ara Isha.   They say wife one be he (continuative) love at year-be this, should

aya na ma ba   ş(e)-iku   pa   nwǫn ni ki   o ru ewurę kan,
wife the not should make-death kill (him); they say should he offer she:goat one,

ejielogun.   A-l(i)-ara   ko ru-(ę)bǫ.
44,000   (cowries). One:who-has-Ara not offer-sacrifice.

N(i)-igba-ti nwǫn bi A-l(i)-ara,   i-b(i)-eji ni nwǫn bi,   şugbǫn
At-time-that they bear One:who-has-Ara, to-bear-two be they bear, but

nwǫn fi   ǫkan pa-mǫ   nwǫn pa ǫkan ni-(i)nu   wǫn nwǫn si lǫ sin
they take one kill:against they kill one at-belly (of) them they and go bury (it)

si-(i)nu   igbo kan, n(i)-igba-ti A-l(i)-ara   wa ni ǫmǫde,   bi o
to-belly (of) forest one, at-time-that One:who-has-Ara come at young:child, if he

ba   nş(e)-ai-san,   ti nwǫn ba   lǫ wo   işę, awǫn babalawo a
should making-not-be:better that they should go look:at work, those diviner   will

sǫ   fun iya   rę pe   nibo ni a-ku-i-sin   kan wa?   Ki
speak for mother his that "Where be one:who-die-not-bury one exist?" Should

nwǫn lǫ bǫ   a-ku-i-sin   na, bi iya   rę ba   si bǫ
they go sacrifice:to one:who-die-not-bury the; if mother his should and sacrifice:

ara rę a   si le.
to (it), body his will and be:strong.

N(i)-igba-ti A-l(i)-ara   d(i)-agba   ti o to işę i-şe, bi o
At-time-that One:who-has-Ara become-elder that he equal work to-do, if he

ba   şe işę ko ni ri ori rę, n(i)-igba-ti o ri ti on ko nri   ori
should do work not be see head its, at-time-that he see that he not seeing head (of)

işę ti on nşe, o lǫ da Ifa, nwǫn sǫ   fun   pe ki   o tǫ-
work that he doing, he go cast Ifa, they speak for (him) that should he care:for-

(o)ju   a-ku-i-sin   kan, şugbǫn bi o ti ję-pe   ko mǫ
eye (of) one:who-die-not-bury one, but   as he have consent-that not know

ohun-k(u)-ohun nipa   a-ku-i-sin   na, n(i)-igba-ti o de
thing-any-thing concerning one:who-die-not-bury the, at-time-that he arrive

ile   o bi iya   rę lere, o si sǫ   bi o ti ri fun,   A-
house he ask mother his (1), she and speak as she have see for (him). One:who-

l(i)-ara si lǫ bǫ   ekeji rę ti o wa ni-(i)nu igbo ni-(i)bi-ti
has-Ara and go sacrifice:to second his that he be at-belly (of) forest at-place-that

---

1. Bi . . . lere means "to ask."

101 - 1

"The palm tree dies, the young fronds fall to its side" was the one who cast Ifa for the King of Ara Isha.[1] They said he would take a wife that year; but lest his wife cause his death, they said he should sacrifice one she-goat and eleven shillings. The King of Ara did not sacrifice.

When the King of Ara[2] was born, his mother gave birth to twins, but they hid one—they killed it and buried it in the forest.[3] When the King of Ara was a young child and he was ill and they examined him, the diviners asked his mother "Where is the one who died but was not given a funeral?" They said they should go to him and sacrifice to him; if his mother would do this, his body would become strong.

When the King of Ara grew old enough to work for himself,[4] he was unable to complete anything he tried to do. When he saw that he could not complete the work he was doing, he went and cast Ifa, and the diviners told him that he should care for one who had died but had not been given a funeral. But since he knew nothing about such a person, he asked his mother when he reached home, and she told him what she knew. The King of Ara went into the forest and sacrificed to his twin, where

---

1. This town, referred to afterward in the verse simply as Ara, is probably the Ara located about ten miles northeast of Ẹfọn-Alaye in Ekiti.

2. The character is referred to as the King of Ara even before he is crowned.

3. It was formerly customary to allow one twin to die. No funeral ceremonies were held for it, or for anyone dying in childhood. It was buried in the forest, but the parents and the surviving twin were obligated to sacrifice to it throughout their lifetimes, as this verse indicates.

4. That is, when he became independent of his father.

nwǫn sin   si.   Bayi ni A-l(i)-ara   bęrę si işę i-şe ti o
they bury (him) to (it).   Thus be One:who-has-Ara begin to work to-do that he

si bęrę si ni   l(i)-ǫwǫ.
and begin to have at-hand.

     N(i)-igba-ti o tun şe,   o fę fę obinrin, bi o ba   fę eyi,
     At-time-that it then make (later), he want love woman, if he should love this

          ko ni ni   ori, bi o ba   fę t(i)-ǫhun ko ni ni   idi, o si lǫ
(one), not be have head, if o ba love that-there not be have base, he and go

da Ifa, nwǫn ni afi-bi   o ba   le   bǫ   a-ku-i-sin
cast Ifa, they say unless-if he should be:able sacrifice:to one:who-die-not-bury

kan, o si lǫ bǫ,   o bęrę si ni   aya o si bi   ǫmǫ.
one, he and go sacrifice:to (it), he begin to have wife he and bear child.

     N(i)-igba-ti o şe   nwǫn fę ję oye   A-l(i)-ara,   o si
     At-time-that it make (later) they want eat title (of) One:who-has-Ara, he and

du   oye na, nwǫn ko si fę   fi   ję,   o si tun tǫ
compete:for title the, they not and want take (him) eat (it), he and then approach

awǫn babalawo lǫ, nwǫn si sǫ   fun   pe afi-bi   o ba   lǫ bǫ
those diviner   go, they and speak for (him) that unless-if he should go sacrifice:

  a-ku-i-sin   kan, o si lǫ bǫ   ekeji rę, l(i)-ęhin   na
to one:who-die-not-bury one, he and go sacrifice:to second his; at-back (of) the

ni nwǫn ba fi   ję A-l(i)-ara.
be they did take (him) eat One:who-has-Ara.

     N(i)-igba-ti o de   ori   oye, o wa   fę   obinrin kan, obinrin na
     At-time-that he arrive head (of) title, he come love woman one, woman the

si dara   pupǫ, o si fęran rę n(i)-igba-na ni o bęrę si gbagbe ekeji
and be:good much, she and love his, at-time-the be he begin to forget second

rę, bi o ba   la   ǫla   ri,   ko tun bikita   fun   mǫ
his, if he should dream dream see (him), not then show:respect for (him) again

nitori-ti   obinrin yi ti   gba ǫkan rę ko si ję-ki   o ranti
because-that woman this have take heart his not and consent-that he remember

ohun-k(u)-ohun mǫ.   N(i)-igba-ti ekeji rę ri pe ko ranti   on mǫ,
thing-any-thing again. At-time-that second his see that not remember him again,

o di   okete   o si gbę iho lati inu   igbo o si gbę wǫ ibi-
he become Giant:Rat he and dig hole from belly (of) forest he and dig enter place-

ti nwǫn nko   ohun ti nwǫn yio fi   se ǫbę si, o si fi
that they gathering thing that they will take (them) cook stew to, he and take

gbogbo rę ję. N(i)-igba-ti ilę   mǫ ti   obinrin yi ri eyi, o bęrę si
all   its eat. At-time-that ground clear that woman this see this, she begin to

sǫ-(ę)kun. A-l(i)-ara   wa sǫ   fun   pe ki   o ma sǫ-(ę)kun.
shed-tears. One:who-has-Ara come speak for (her) that should she not shed-tears

mǫ, o ni on yio fun   ni owo   lati   lǫ fi   ra omiran
again, he say he will give (her) at cowries in:order:to go take (them) buy another,

he had been buried. Thus the King of Ara began to accomplish things, and he began to accumulate property.

After a while he wanted to take a wife, but one woman after another that he
loved refused him.[5] So he went and cast Ifa again, and they told him that he must
sacrifice to one who had died but had not been given a funeral. And he went and
sacrificed again, and he began to have wives and to beget children.

After a while the people of Ara were choosing a new king, and he competed
for the title, but they did not want him. Again he visited the diviners and they
told him that he must go and sacrifice to one who had died but had not been given
a funeral. He sacrificed again to his twin, and afterward they crowned him King
of Ara.

When he had become king, he fell in love with a woman who was very beautiful and who returned his love. Then he began to neglect his twin. If he saw his
twin in a dream, he paid no attention to him because this woman had stolen his
heart and did not let him remember anything any more. When his twin saw that
the King of Ara no longer remembered him, he turned into a Pouched Rat[6] and
dug a hole from the forest to the place where they stored the things with which
to cook stew, and he ate all the food. When day broke, and this woman saw what
had happened, she began to cry. The King of Ara came to her and told her that
she should not weep; he said he would give her money so that she could buy more,

---

5. Idiomatically, "if he wanted to love this one, it didn't have a top; if he
wanted to love that one, it didn't have a bottom."

6. Giant Rat or Pouched Rat (Cricetomys gambianus), a large rat that
lives in the forest.

şugbọn obinrin yi   kọ.   N(i)-igba-na ni A-l(i)-ara   wa   pa-(i)şẹ
but   woman this refuse. At-time-the be One:who-has-Ara come kill-word

pe   ki   nwọn gbẹ ilẹ   ki   nwọn si lọ pa eku ti   fi   (ohu)n-kan ti
that should they dig ground should they and go kill rat that take thing-one that

aya   on ra jẹ.
wife (of) him buy eat.

   N(i)-igba-ti nwọn si bẹrẹ si gbẹ ilẹ,   nwọn gbẹ ilẹ   na kọja si ẹhin
   At-time-that they and begin to dig ground, they dig ground the pass to back

   odi,   nwọn si gbẹ de   ibi   igbo ti nwọn sin ekeji rẹ si,
(of) town:wall, they and dig arrive place (of) forest that they bury second his to,

o si pa-(i)şẹ pe ki   nwọn şan igbo na ki   nwọn ma   gbẹ
he and kill-word that should they clear forest the should they (continuative) dig

ilẹ   na lọ, n(i)-igba-ti nwọn ti   şan igbo yi, gbogbo awọn ẹranko
ground the go, at-time-that they have clear forest this, all   those animal (of)

igbo na fi   oju le   ode,   ibi-ti   ko yẹ ki   orun pa ni-(i)nu
forest the take eye appear outside, place-that (it) not suit that sun kill at-belly

   igbo na, orun npa;   ibi-ti   ko yẹ ki   ojo rọ si, ojo nrọ   si
(of) forest the, sun killing; place-that (it) not suit that rain fall to, rain falling to

ibẹ   bayi ni A-l(i)-ara   bẹrẹ si şe ai-san,   o wa   mu-(a)ra
there; thus be One:who-has-Ara begin to make not-be:better, he come take-body

o mu igba eku, igba ẹja, ọmọ-(o)binrin ai-gun-(ọ)mu   ọmọ-(ọ)kunrin ai-
he take 200 rat, 200 fish, child-woman not-come:out-breast, child-man   not-

rọ-(ẹ)pọn,   o ni ki   nwọn lọ fi   bọ   ekeji   on,
sprout-testicle; he say should they go take (them) sacrifice:to second (of) him,

ekeji rẹ ni o ko fẹ   mọ, o ni afi   A-l(i)-ara   gan   ni on
second his say he not want again, he say unless One:who-has-Ara identical be he

fẹ,   bayi ni A-l(i)-ara   ba-(i)ku.
want; thus be One:who-has-Ara meet-death.

   Ifa ni ẹni-kan   yio ri aya kan fẹ, şugbọn ki   tọ-(o)ju
   Ifa say person-one will see wife one love, but   should care:for-eye (of)

a-ku-i-sin   kan, ki obinrin na ma ba   şe iku pa-(ẹ)ni
one:who-die-not-bury one, that woman the not should make death kill-person

nipa   pe   yio mu-(ẹ)ni   gbagbe a-ku-i-sin   na.
concerning that (she) will take-person forget one:who-die-not-bury the.

IROSUN MEJI - 1

   Ebiti   ja-(ọ)wọ f(i)-aiya lu-(i)lẹ   l(i)-o d(a)-Ifa k(o)-Oye-ni-
   "Deadfall cut-hand take-chest strike-ground" be-who cast-Ifa for-Title-has-

(i)ran   ti o nsọ-(ẹ)kun   a-l(i)-ai-l(i)-oyun,   ti o
descendants that she shedding-tears (of) one:who-be-not-have-pregnancy that she

but she would not stop crying. Then the King of Ara commanded that the ground
should be dug up, and the rat which had eaten his wife's food should be killed.

When they began to dig, they dug past the town wall, and they dug until they
reached the spot in the forest where the King's twin had been buried. The King
of Ara commanded that they should clear away the forest, and keep on digging.
As they cleared the forest, all the wild animals ran out. Where it was not right
for the sun to shine in the forest, the sun was now shining; where it was not right
for rain to fall, rain was now falling. Thus the King of Ara became ill.[7] He got
ready and took two hundred rats, two hundred fish, a girl whose breasts had not
yet appeared, and a boy whose testicles had not yet developed; he said they should
take these and sacrifice them to his twin. But his twin said he did not want them;
he said he wanted only the King of Ara himself. And thus the King of Ara died.

Ifa says that someone will find a wife to marry, but that he should care for
one who has died but has not been given a funeral, lest the woman cause his death
by making him forget the one who has died but has not been given a funeral.

---

7. Note the pun here on san (to cure) and san (to clear).

---

103 - 1

"The deadfall is sprung, it strikes the ground with its chest" was the one who
cast Ifa for "Title has descendants" when she was weeping because she had not become pregnant and when she

si ngba-(a)wę   a-l(i)-ai-ri-pǫn.   Nwǫn ni ki   o
and taking-fast (of) one:who-be-not-see-carry:on:back. They say should she

ru-(ę)bǫ,   nwǫn ni ǫmǫ kan ni   yio bi yi, nwǫn ni gbogbo aiye
offer-sacrifice, they say child one be (she) will bear this, they say all   earth

ni yio mǫ,   kijikiji rę yio si gba aiye ka.   O ru   igba abęrę,
be will know (him), shaking his will and take earth go:around. She offer 200 needle,

agutan kan, ǫkanla,   amu   epo   kan. N(i)-igba-ti Oye-ni-
ewe   one, 22,000 (cowries), pot (of) palm:oil one. At-time-that Title-has-

(i)ran   ma   bi o bi ǫjǫ.
descendants (continuative) bear she bear day.

        Ifa ni ęni-kan   nsǫ-(ę)kun   ǫmǫ, yio si bi   ǫmǫ kan, ǫmǫ-
        Ifa say person-one shedding-tears (of) child, will and bear child one, child-

(ǫ)kunrin ni ǫmǫ na yio ję.
man   be child the will eat.

IROSUN MEJI - 2

        Igunnukun f(i)-oju s(i)-eyi, Igunnukun f(i)-oju s(i)-ǫhun l(i)-o d(a)-Ifa fun
        "Igunnukun put-eye to-this, Igunnukun put-eye to-there" be-who cast-Ifa for

Orişa ti o nlǫ gba Ida   Apara. Ifa ni ęni-kan   nfę   gba
Orisha that he going take Sword (of) Thunder. Ifa say person-one wanting take

obinrin kan, okiki yio pǫ   nipa   obinrin na, yio si n(i)-ipa
woman one; praise will be:much concerning woman the, will and have:strength

dię,   şugbǫn ki   a mu-(a)ra o ni   yio şe işe. Orişa ru
small, but   should we take-body; he say (we) will do work. Orisha offer

obukǫ kan, ęgbętalelǫgbǫn,   ati aşǫ dudu   ara rę l(i)-ębǫ.   N(i)-
he:goat one, 6600   (cowries), and cloth black (of) body his be-sacrifice. At-

igba-ti   Orişa gba obinrin yi tan   ęru nba   a   nitori-ti   o
time-that Orisha take woman this finish, fear meeting him because-that they

wi-pe   ęlomiran   yio gba   ni ǫwǫ   on, nitori-na o lǫ
speak-that another:person will take (her) at hand (of) him, because-the he go

kǫ   ile   rę si ǫna   agbala   ni-(i)gba-ku-(i)gba ti enia ba   ti
build house his to road (of) back:yard at-time-any-time   that people should have

nfę   kǫja ni-(i)bę ara a   bęrę si fun   Orişa pe boya   ęni-
wanting pass at-there, body will begin to squeeze[1] Orisha that perhaps person-

kan yio tun gba   ni ǫwǫ   on   N(i)-igba-na ni nwǫn wa   fi
one will then take (her) at hand (of) him be (it). At-time-the be they come take

da-(o)rin pe:
break-song that:

---

1. "Fun" means to wring out, or to squeeze dry.

was fasting because she had no child to carry on her back. They said she should sacrifice; they said she would give birth to a child who would be known to all the world and that the mention of his name would cause the whole world to tremble. She offered 200 needles, one ewe, five shilling six pence, and a pot of palm oil. When "Title who has descendants" gave birth, she gave birth to Sun.[1]

Ifa says that someone is weeping for a child, and that she will bear a child, and this child will be a boy.

––––––––––––––

1. Again this verse explains why the sun is known all over the world. Cf. verses 1-6 and 52-1, and n. 6, verse 52-1.

––––––––––––––––––––––––––––––

103 - 2

"Igunnukun[1] looks here, Igunnukun looks there" was the one who cast Ifa for Orisha when he was going to marry Sword of Thunder. Ifa says that someone is wanting to take a wife. There will be much gossip about the woman and it will be somewhat difficult, but we should go ahead; he says we shall succeed.[2] Orisha sacrificed one he-goat, one shilling seven pence eight oninis, and the black cloth he was wearing. When Orisha had married this woman, he was afraid because they said that someone else would take her away from him; so he built his house in the back yard, and whenever people passed by, he shrank with fear, lest someone should take her from him. Then they began to sing:

––––––––––––––

1. A Nupe deity (ẹbura Tapa) which, like the Egungun, is masked. It is described as a tall cylinder that can grow tall and grow short. See Nadel (1954: 189-190). Its worship was introduced to Ifẹ by a Nupe woman.

2. This interpretation, given by informants, is somewhat different from the literal translation, which is also uncertain. The whole verse, in fact, is obscure and apparently not understood by the diviner himself. Sword seems to have been the former wife, or perhaps the daughter, of Thunder, but the relationship is not specified in the text. Orisha here probably refers to Orisha of the Back Yard (Orişa Agbala), one of the "white deities" (orişa funfun), but it is not clear how he happened to be wearing a black cloth. See n. 4, verse 249-1.

Ǫsan   pǫn   werewere
"Midday be:ripe shimmering

Ẹni   o   fin-(i)dan   a   ri-(i)dan
"Person who want-consequences will see-consequences."

ĪROSUN ǪṢẸ[1] - 1

Akoto   itǫ a b(i)-ẹnu   boro   a   fa   m(ǫ)-ǫdǫ
"Calabash (of) spit it bear-mouth narrow we pull against-presence (of)

tẹmutẹmu   a   da   fun enia   ti   iṣe   ẹru   ipin;   nwǫn ni ki
hassock" (be) who cast for Person that make slave(of) Guardian; they say should

o   ru-(ẹ)bǫ   ki   o-l(i)-owo   rẹ   ǫrun ma ba   wa   mu
he offer-sacrifice that one:who-has-cowries his (of) sky not should come take

lǫ ni ǫdun yi: eku, ẹja, igbin, ẹiyẹ-(i)le,   ayebǫ adiẹ,   ati obukǫ
(him) go at year this: rat, fish, snail, bird-(of)-house, hen   chicken, and he:goat

pẹlu   ẹgbasan.   Enia   ko   ru-(ẹ)bǫ.
together:with 18,000 (cowries). Person not offer-sacrifice.

Awǫn irun-(i)mǫlẹ ran ipin   pe ki   o   lǫ mu enia   wa   si
Those 400-Deity   send Guardian that should he go take Person come to

ǫrun nitori-ti   enia   ko   sin   wǫn; n(i)-igba-ti ipin   de   aiye
sky because-that Person not serve them; at-time-that Guardian arrive earth

ti   o   mu enia   ti   o   si   nfa   lǫ ni ẹhin-(ẹ)ku(n)-(i)le   Ogun,
that he take Person that he and pulling (him) go at back-door-(of)-house (of) Ogun,

enia   ke   wi-pe   Ogun gba mi o,   ipin   nwǫ   mi l(i)-ẹsẹ lǫ; n(i)-
Person cry speak-that "Ogun take me, oh. Guardian dragging me at-foot go." At-

igba-ti   Ogun ja-(o)de   o ri ipin,   o si   bere pe   ki(n)-ni o de?
time-that Ogun reach-outside he see Guardian, he and ask   what-be it arrive?

Ipin   si   ro   ẹjǫ fun,   n(i)-igba-na ni Ogun ra-(ǫ)wǫ si wǫn, ipin
Guardian and state case for (him), at-time-the be Ogun rub-hand to them, Guardian

si   nmu enia   lǫ; bẹ-ni o   nmu   de   gbogbo ojude   awǫn Oriṣa
and taking Person go; so-be he taking (him) arrive all   outside (of) those Orisha

ti   o   wa   l(i)-aiye ti   nwǫn si   nja-(o)de   si wǫn, ti   ipin
that they exist at-earth that they and reaching-outside to them, that Guardian

nro-(ẹ)jǫ   fun wǫn, ti   awǫn na   si   ṣe gẹgẹ-bi Ogun ti   ṣe, nikẹhin ni
stating-case for them, that they also and do just-like Ogun have do, finally be

nwǫn nkǫja   ni ojude   Ǫrunmila, enia   si   kigbe   pe: Ǫrunmila o
they passing at outside (of) Ǫrunmila, Person and cry:out that "Ǫrunmila you

ma   gba mi ipin   nwǫ   mi l(i)-ẹsẹ lǫ.
(continuative) take me, Guardian dragging me at-foot go."

---

1. This figure is also known as Irosun ẹpẹrẹ. Cf. n. 1, verse 111-2.

"Shimmering[3] high noon,
"One who asks for trouble[4] will find trouble."

---

3. "Werewere" was described as referring to the shimmering of heat waves on a road during the heat of the day.

4. That is, one who wants to do something that is forbidden.

---

111 - 1

"The spittoon with a small mouth is drawn close to the cushion"[1] was the one who cast Ifa for Person[2] who was the slave of his Ancestral Guardian Soul.[3] They said he should sacrifice a rat, a fish, a snail, a pigeon, a hen, and a he-goat, together with four shillings six pence, lest his master in heaven carry him away during that year. Person did not sacrifice.

The Four Hundred Deities sent Guardian Soul to go and bring Person to heaven, because Person did not serve them.[4] When Guardian Soul arrived on earth, he seized Person and was dragging him past the back door of the God of Iron's house when Person cried out, "God of Iron! Help me, oh! Guardian Soul is dragging me away by my feet!" When the God of Iron came out, he saw Guardian Soul and he asked, "What is happening?" and Guardian Soul explained the case to him. Then the God of Iron rubbed his hands to them,[5] and Guardian Soul went on with Person. Thus they passed the houses of all the deities that are on earth, with the deities coming out to them, with Guardian Soul explaining the situation to them, and with all of them doing just what God of Iron had done. Finally, as they were passing Qrunmila's house, Person cried out, "Qrunmila! Help me! Guardian Soul is dragging me away by my feet."

---

1. This is another case of overstatement typical of proverbial expression, as the akoto is one of the largest calabashes, with a very broad mouth.

2. This is an unusual personification of a generalized individual.

3. The ancestral guardian soul is known also as ipǫnri, olori, ęlęda. It is the individual's counterpart in heaven, and controls his luck. See Chapter X.

4. That is, he failed to sacrifice to them.

5. This is a common gesture, meaning here that one wishes to be excused from passing judgment or intervening in a dispute. It is also a gesture of supplication, and it is made when paying homage to a person of high rank. Cf. n. 2, verse 2-2.

N(i)-igba-ti Qrunmila ja-(o)de   si wǫn, ipin   ro-(ẹ)jǫ   fun u,
At-time-that Qrunmila reach-outside to them, Guardian state-case for him,

Qrunmila si da-(o)hun   pe ki   ipin   fi enia   si-(i)lẹ, on yio
Qrunmila and break-voice that should Guardian put Person to-ground, he will

ma   wa   gba ohun ti nwǫn iba   ma   fi   sin
(continuative) come take thing that they should (continuative) take (them) serve

ipin   fun   ni ǫd(un)-ǫdun; ipin   si fi enia   si-(i)lẹ, lati ǫjǫ
Guardian give (him) at year-year.   Guardian and put Person to-ground, from day

na ni Qrunmila ti   ma   ngba ohun-k(u)-ohun ti   ori ẹni-(ǫ)k(an)-
the be Qrunmila have (continuative) taking thing-any-thing that head person-one-

ǫkan ba   gba, ti o ba   si fi   bǫ   ni ǫd(un)-ǫdun, ti
one   should take, that he should and take (it) sacrifice:to (it) at year-year,   that

o si lǫ ma   nko   fun ipin,   bi Qrunmila ba
he and go (continuative) gathering (them) give Guardian. If Qrunmila should

ko   de   ǫdǫ   ipin,   ipin   yio fun   ni ẹbun
gather (them) arrive presence (of) Guardian, Guardian will give (him) at gift

ti-rẹ,   ki   Qrunmila to   lǫ pẹlu   awǫn enia yio fun
that-(of)-his, before Qrunmila equal go together:with (Ipin) those people will give

    ni ẹbun ki   o ba   le   sǫ   ti-wǫn   ni rere ni ǫdo
(him) at gift should he should be:able speak that-(of)-them at good at presence

     awǫn irun-(i)mǫlẹ ati ipin.
(of) those 400-Deity   and Guardian.

     Lati igba-na ni a ti   ma   nsǫ   pe Qrunmila
     From time-the be we have (continuative) speaking that "Qrunmila (be)

ẹlẹri   ipin."   Ifa ni ki   ẹni-kan   ru-(ẹ)bǫ   ki
intermediary (of) Guardian." Ifa say should person-one offer-sacrifice should

awǫn o-l(i)-owo   rẹ   ǫrun ma ba   mu   lǫ. Ki   o si
those one:who-have-cowries his (of) sky not should take (him) go. Should he and

tǫ-(o)ju   orişa rẹ kan bi ko ba   tǫ-(o)ju   rẹ, orişa na yio mu
care:for-eye orisha his one; if not should care:for-eye its, orisha the will take

     lǫ.
(him) go.

IROSUN QṢẸ - 2

Qrunmila ni o ş(e)-ẹpẹrẹ; mo ni o ş(e)-ẹpẹrẹ; o ni şe   ni o
Qrunmila say it make-better; I   say it make-better; he say make (it) be it

ş(e)-ẹpẹrẹ fun işu ti o fi   ta.
make-better for yam that it take grow.

When Qrunmila came out to them, Guardian Soul explained the case to him, and Qrunmila replied that Guardian Soul should release Person. Qrunmila said that he would come and collect the things that people sacrificed to Guardian Soul each year. Guardian Soul released Person, and since that day Qrunmila has been collecting whatever the head of each person should require as its annual sacrifice and taking them to Guardian Soul.[6] When Qrunmila brings them to Guardian Soul, Guardian Soul gives Qrunmila some as his share; and before he goes, people also give Qrunmila something so that he will speak well of them in the presence of the Four Hundred Deities and of their Ancestral Guardian Souls.

Since that time we say, "Qrunmila is the intermediary of Guardian Soul."[7] Ifa says that someone should sacrifice, lest his masters in heaven should carry him away. And he should care for a deity of his; if he does not do so, the deity will carry him away.

---

6. The annual sacrifices that each individual makes to his own head or "luck" go to the ancestral guardian soul, who shares them among the deities. In Ifẹ these sacrifices are made at the individual's own festival (ọdun mi). If an individual is a worshiper of Ifa, he puts some food on his set of palm nuts; if not, he puts some food in the corner of the room for Qrunmila. This verse explains the ritual, and how Qrunmila came to have the role of collecting the sacrifices which the ancestral guardian soul requires.

7. Cf. Epega (1931: 14): "Qrunmila, Ẹlẹri ipin, Ibikeji Olodumare (Witness of Fate, Second Being to the Olodumare)."

---

111 - 2

Qrunmila says, "It is getting better";[1] I say, "It is getting better"; he says, "It is getting better for the yam that is growing."

---

1. This phrase has many applications, meaning always, "things are getting better." It can be used in reply to an inquiry about the health of a person who is ill, or about the progress of a person's studies, or in answer to a creditor's inquiry of a debtor about the chances of receiving further payments on the debt. Irosun ẹpẹrẹ is an alternative name for Irosun Qsẹ.

O ni   ṣ(e)-ẹpẹrẹ;   mo ni   o ṣ(e)-ẹpẹrẹ;   o ni   ṣe   ni o ṣ(e)-
He say (it) make-better; I   say it make-better; he say make (it) be it make-

ẹpẹrẹ fun igbado ti   o fi   y(ọ)-ọmọ.
better for corn   that it take sprout-child.

Qrunmila ni   o ṣ(e)-ẹpẹrẹ;   mo ni   o ṣ(e)-ẹpẹrẹ;   o ni   ṣe   ni o
Qrunmila say it make-better; I   say it make-better; he say make (it) be it

ṣ(e)-ẹpẹrẹ   fun ilẹ   ti   o fi   fi   ọgan   ṣ(e)-owo.
make-better for ground that it take take termite-hill make-horn.

Qrunmila ni   o ṣ(e)-ẹpẹrẹ;   mo ni   o ṣ(e)-ẹpẹrẹ;   o ni   o ṣ(e)-ẹpẹrẹ
Qrunmila say it make-better; I   say it make-better; he say it make-better

fun agan   ai-bi   Ile-Ifẹ ti   o   fi   di   ọ-l(i)-ọmọ.
for barren:woman not-bear (of) Ile-Ifẹ that she take become one:who-have-children.

Ẹiyẹ-(i)le   meji, akikọ meji, igbin meji, eku meji, ati ẹja meji pẹlu
Bird-(of)-house two, cock two, snail two, rat two, and fish two together:

egbejila   ni ẹbọ.   Ifa ni   a   nlọ   ṣe ohun kan, a-(yi)o ni
with 2400   (cowries) be sacrifice. Ifa say we going do thing one, we-will have

iyi   ni ibẹ,   a-(yi)o si   di   ẹni   iyi   ni ibẹ,   bi o ba   ṣe
glory at there, we-will and become person (of) glory at there; if it should make

owo   ni,   a-(yi)o di   ẹni   iyi   ni idi   owo   na,
transaction be (it), we-will become person (of) glory at bottom (of) transaction the,

     yio si   ṣ(e)-ẹpẹrẹ   fun-(ẹ)ni.
(it) will and make-better for-person.

Ewe   Ifa rẹ: Ewe ṣẹ-fun-ṣẹ-fun   —ẹfunlẹ—ewe   irẹ,
Leaf (of) Ifa its: Leaf make-be:white-make-be:white—ẹfunlẹ—leaf (of) irẹ,

ọṣẹ,   A-(yi)o gun   ori   eku ati ori   ẹja meji-meji yi   mọ,
soap. We-will pound head (of) rat and head (of) fish two-two   this against (these);

a-(yi)o pa   ọkan ni-(i)nu   awọn ẹiyẹ-(i)le   meji yi, a-(yi)o tẹ   ori
we-will kill one at-belly (of) those bird-(of)-house two this, we-will press head

rẹ mọ   ọṣẹ na l(i)-ori ni-(i)nu   igba,   a-(yi)o fi   iyẹ-
its against soap the at-head at-belly (of) calabash; we-will with wood:dust-(of)-

(i)rosun tẹ   Irosun Qṣẹ; a-(yi)o da   si   a-(yi)o   ma
irosun   mark Irosun Qṣẹ; we-will throw (it) to (the rest); we-will (continuative)

fi   wẹ.
take (it) wash.

He says, "It is getting better"; I say, "It is getting better"; he says, "It is getting better for the corn that is sprouting ears."[2]

Qrunmila says, "It is getting better"; I say, "It is getting better"; he says, "It is getting better for the ground on which a termite hill is growing like a horn."

Qrunmila says, "It is getting better"; I say, "It is getting better"; he says, "It is getting better for the barren woman of Ifę, who is becoming the mother of children."

Two pigeons, two cocks, two snails, two rats, and two fish, with seven pence two oninis, is the sacrifice. Ifa says we are going to do something through which we will gain glory; we will become a person with glory through it. If it is a business deal that we are about to engage in, we will become a person with glory through it, and things will be getting better for us.

Leaves of Ifa for this verse: The leaf of "Make-white-make-white"—that is, ęfunlę[3]—the leaves of the irę[4] tree, and soap. With these we will grind up the heads of both rats and both fish; we will kill one of the two pigeons and press its head into the soap on top of all this in the calabash. We will mark the figure Irosun Qşę[5] in the divining powder and pour the powder into the calabash. We will use this mixture to wash ourselves.

---

2. Spoken of here as the children of corn.

3. This plant, described as a vine, is identified by Dalziel as Evolvus alsinoides.

4. The West African rubber tree or Lagos silk-rubber tree (Funtumia elastica).

5. Note the two cases of word magic here. For the figure Irosun Qşę, divining powder from the irosun tree and soap (ǫşę) are used as ingredients in the medicine.

QWǪNRIN MEJI - 1

Ǫla-na-(ǫ)wǫ   ni   ş(e)-awo   wǫn l(i)-ode   Ido Ǫla-
"Wealth-stretch-hand" be (who) make-secret their at-outside (of) Ido, "Wealth-

na-(ę)sę   ni   ş(e)-awo   wǫn l(i)-ode   Ǫtun, Oto, Ǫya ni
stretch-foot" be (who) make-secret their at-outside (of) Ǫtun, Oto, Ǫya be (who)

ş(e)-awo   wǫn l(i)-ode   Koro Ewe   ǫla-jengetiele   Ibi ti o
make-secret their at-outside (of) Koro, "Leaf (of) honor-swaying," "Evil that it

ba   wa   l(i)-ori   awo   l(i)-oni ki   o   ma   di   ki
should exist at-head (of) secret at-today, should it (continuative) clear:out should

o   ma   re ilę   omi   a   da   fun Ǫrunmila n(i)-igba-ti o
it (continuative) go ground (of) water" (be) who cast for Ǫrunmila at-time-that he

nş(e)-awo   re ode   Ǫyǫ, nwǫn ni ki   o   ru-(ę)bǫ   akikǫ
making-secret go outside (of) Ǫyǫ they say should he offer-sacrifice (of) cock

adię   meji, ęiyę-(i)le   kan, obi męta, epo   pupa, nitori-pe   ki
chicken two, bird-(of)-house one, kola three, palm:oil red, because-that should

ǫna   ajo   rę ba   dara,   Ǫrunmila ru-(ę)bǫ,   o si   gbe
road (of) journey his should be:good, Ǫrunmila offer-sacrifice, he and carry

ębǫ   na si eti   odo.
sacrifice the to ear (of) river.

Ifa ni ki   a   ru-(ę)bǫ   nitori   ǫna   ajo,   ti a   nlǫ
Ifa say should we offer-sacrifice because (of) road (of) journey that we going

ki   a   ba   le   ko   işę   ęni   de-(i)le.
should we should be:able gather deed (of) person arrive-house.

QWǪNRIN MEJI - 2

A-de-olu-kę   nşe   awo   re ode   A-ji-
"To-arrive-(for)-family-indulge" making secret go outside (of) "To-wake-

kę-olu   A-de-tutu   nş(e)-awo   re ode   A-ji-f(o)-
indulge-family," "To-arrive-cool" making-secret go outside (of) "To-wake-jump-

ǫran-rere-lǫ   a   da   fun Ǫrunmila ni ǫjǫ ti   o   nşe   awo   rę
affair-good-show" (be) who cast for Ǫrunmila at day that he making secret go

ode   A-ji-kę-olu   ti nwǫn sǫ   fun   pe ki   o
outside (of) "To-wake-indulge-family" that they speak for (him) that should he

fi   ewurę   bǫ   oke   ipǫnri   rę pe ki   ǫna   ajo   rę
take she:goat sacrifice:to hill (of) guardian his that should road (of) journey his

ba   le   dara   fun,   Ǫrunmila ko bǫ   oke   ipǫnri   rę
should be:able be:good for (him); Ǫrunmila not sacrifice:to hill (of) guardian his

titi o fi   lǫ si ǫna   ajo   na, n(i)-igba-ti o de   ibi-ti   o nlǫ
until he take go to road (of) journey the; at-time-that he arrive place-that he going

120 - 1

"Wealth stretches out its hand," the diviner at Ido;[1] "Wealth stretches out its foot," the diviner at Qtun;[2] "Oto" and "Qya," the diviners at Koro;[3] "The leaf called 'Honor swaying'";[4] "The evil that exists on the diviner's head today will go away to the bottom of the water" were the ones who cast Ifa for Qrunmila when he was going to divine at Qyọ. They said he should sacrifice two cocks, one pigeon, three kola nuts, and red palm oil so that his journey would be good. Qrunmila sacrificed,[5] and he carried the sacrifice to the bank of a river.[6]

Ifa says that we should sacrifice because of a journey we are going to take, so that we may bring home the fruits of our labor.

---

1. A town about twenty-five miles southeast of Ila.
2. A town about fifteen miles east of Ila.
3. There are several towns by the name of Koro, but this was identified by informants as one about four miles from Imẹsi, which is twenty miles northeast of Ilesha.
4. Swaying like a supple plant upon which a bird has alighted.
5. Since Qrunmila is noted for his success in divining, it is not necessary to state that the sacrifice accomplished its purpose.
6. There seems to be some correlation between the names of the diviners and the instructions to the client. The last name describes evil leaving the head of the diviner and going to the bottom of the water, and Qrunmila carries his sacrifice to the edge of the river.

---

120 - 2

"He arrives for his family to indulge," the diviner of "He awakes to indulge his family," "He is cool when he arrives," the diviner of "He awakes to give good advice" were the ones who cast Ifa for Qrunmila on the day he was going to "He awakes to indulge his family" to divine. They told Qrunmila to sacrifice a she-goat to his ancestral guardian soul so that his journey would be good. Qrunmila did not sacrifice to his guardian soul until he had made the journey. When he arrived at the place where he was going

ş(e)-awo,   ko si ęni-ti   o wa   si ǫdǫ   rę lati   şe   awo,
make-secret, not be person-that he come to presence his in:order:to make secret;

n(i)-igba-ti o ri pe ebi   npa   on, n(i)-igba-na ni o pada wa   si-
at-time-that he see that hunger killing him, at-time-the be he return come to-

(i)le lati   wa bǫ   oke   ipǫnri rę, n(i)-igba-ti o pa
house in:order:to come sacrifice:to hill (of) guardian his. At-time-that he kill

ewurę na, o pin   fun awǫn agb(a)-agba   ilu, nwǫn si bęrę si
she:goat the, he divide (it) give those old-old   (of) town, they and begin to

fun   ni ęgbę(wa)-(ę)gbęwa,   Qrunmila di   o-l(i)-owo   ni ǫjǫ
give (him) at 2000-2000-(cowries), Qrunmila become one:who-has-cowries at day

na, o si bęrę si kǫ-(o)rin wi-pe:
the, he and begin to sing-song say-that:

> Kabi owo   mǫ   wa   o?
> "Where cowries (continuative) exist, oh?

> Ara   enia ni owo   ma   wa   o
> "People (of) person be cowries (continuative) exist, oh;

> Ara   enia l(i)-owo   ma   wa   o
> "People (of) person be-cowries (continuative) exist, oh."

Ifa ni ęni-ti   a da Ifa yi fun   yio ri olu-ran-l(i)-ǫwǫ
Ifa say person-that we cast Ifa this for (him) will see one:who-send-at-hand

ni-(i)nu   ohun-k(u)-ohun ti o ba   da   ǫwǫ le lati   şe bi ko
at-belly (of) thing-any-thing that he should throw hand upon in:order:to do, if not

tilę si owo   l(i)-ǫwǫ rę.
even be cowries at-hand his.

QWǪNRIN - (I)RĘTĘ - 1

Adan a b(i)-ara   dudu ękun   fi-(i)bi   kurumu-kurumu   tę-
"Bat   it bear-body black; leopard take-place spherical-spherical press-

(i)lę   i-jo   şęwę, i-rin   şęwę   a   da   fun akukǫ mǫgalaja ni-(ǫ)jǫ
ground; to-dance soft, to-walk soft" (be) who cast for Cock tall   at-day

ti o nlǫ fę Are-ęgę, ǫmǫ   O-l(i)-okun.   Nwǫn ni ki   o ru
that he going love Are-ęgę, child (of) One:who-has-sea. They say should he offer

ikoko męta, ǫkǫ męta, ęiyę-(i)le   męfa; akikǫ ru-(ę)bǫ.
pot   three, hoe three, bird-(of)-house six; Cock offer-sacrifice.

Gbogbo awǫn ęranko ati ęiyę   igbo ni nwǫn nfę   Are-ęgę, ǫmǫ
All   those animal and bird (of) forest be they loving Are-ęgę, child (of)

O-l(i)-okun,   şugbǫn O-l(i)-okun   wi-pe   ęni-k(u)-ęni   ti
One:who-has-sea, but   One:who-has-sea speak-that person-any-person that

to divine, no one came to him to divine; and when he saw that he would die of hunger, he returned to his house to make the sacrifice to his ancestral guardian soul. When he killed the she-goat, he divided it with the elders of the town, and in return they each gave him six pence. Qrunmila became a rich man that day and he began to sing:

> "Where is money to be found, oh?
> "Money is to be found among one's own followers,[1] oh;
> "Money is to be found among one's own followers, oh."

Ifa says that the person for whom this figure was cast will see someone who will aid him in anything he turns his hand to, even if he has no money at hand.

---

1. "Ara" refers to both a person's friends and relatives; the latter are generally distinguished as ara ile.

---

123 - 1

"Bat has a black body; the pads of leopard's paws are rounded; dance softly, walk softly" was the one who cast Ifa for Tall Cock when he was going to marry Are-ęgę, child of the Sea Goddess. They said he should offer three pots, three hoes, and six pigeons. Cock sacrificed.

All the animals and birds of the forest were in love with Are-ęgę, child of the Sea Goddess, but the Sea Goddess said that whoever

o ba   ba on kǫ ęran ni-(i)nu   oko on, ti o ba   si kǫkǫ ja-
he should for her hoe heap at-belly (of) farm hers, that he should and first reach-

(ę)sę ni on yio fi   ǫmǫ on fun   ni iyawo.   N(i)-igba-ti akikǫ
row   be she will take child her give (him) at junior:wife. At-time-that Cock

ru-(ę)bǫ,   ti Eşu si gba   ębǫ   ję tan   Eşu lǫ bo   awǫn
offer-sacrifice, that Eshu and accept sacrifice eat finish Eshu go cover those

ikoko męta na ti   akikǫ fi   ru-(ę)bǫ   ni-(i)nu   oko ti   nwǫn
pot   three the that Cock take (them) offer-sacrifice at-belly (of) farm that they

yio gbe kǫ-(ę)ran ni origun męt(a)-(m)ęta ti   oko na ni.
will take hoe-heap at corner three-three   that farm the have.

     Ki   ilę   to   mǫ   gbogbo awǫn ęranko ati awǫn ęiyę ti   lǫ bęrę
     Before ground equal clear, all   those animal and those bird have go begin

si kǫ-(ę)ran ni-(i)nu   oko yi ki   akikǫ to   ji,   nwǫn si ti
to hoe-heap at-belly (of) farm this before Cock equal awake, they and have

fęrę   kǫ-(ę)ran tan   ki   o to   de;   n(i)-igba-ti akikǫ de   ti
almost hoe-heap finish before he equal arrive. At-time-that Cock arrive that

o ri pe awǫn ęgbę   on ti   fęrę   kǫ-(ę)ran tan   o bęrę si
he see that those companion (of) him have almost hoe-heap finish, he begin to

nwi-pe: Ş(e)-ǫkǫ   şę, ş(e)-ęran gan.
speaking-that: "Make-hoe 'şę,' make-heap stand-up."

     Bayi ni akikǫ nkǫ-(ę)ran ti o si ya   ju   ti awǫn ti o
     Thus be Cock hoeing-heap that he and be:quick surpass that those that he

ti ba   ni-(i)nu   oko lǫ; n(i)-igba-ti odidę ri pe akikǫ fęrę   ba
have meet at-belly (of) farm go; at-time-that Parrot see that Cock almost meet

awǫn o ni Ho! aluko   ni Ę ya, ǫkǫ   akikǫ si ya; akikǫ si
them he say, "Ho!"; Woodcock say "You split," hoe (of) Cock and split; Cock and

tun mu ǫkǫ miran, o si tun bęrę si fi   k(ǫ)-ęran o nkǫ-(o)rin   pe:
then take hoe another, he and then begin to take (it) hoe-heap he singing-song that:

          Akikǫ, akikǫ, gęrę gba-(i)lę   gęrę
          "Cock, Cock, trail sweep-ground trail,

          Akikǫ, gęrę gba-(i)lę   gęrę
          "Cock, trail sweep-ground trail."

     N(i)-igba-ti nwǫn si tun ri pe akikǫ tun nş(e)-(iw)aju   wǫn odidę
     At-time-that they and then see that Cock then making-front (of) them Parrot

ni Ho! aluko   ni Ę ya   ǫkǫ   akikǫ si tun ya o si mu ǫkǫ
say, "Ho!" Woodcock say, "You split," hoe (of) Cock and then split he and take hoe

kęta, Eşu ti o si fę   ran akikǫ l(i)-ǫwǫ lǫ si ibi   ikoko kan o si
third, Eshu that he and want send Cock at-hand go to place (of) pot   one he and

lu,   ikoko yi si fǫ   ęsisun   si bęrę si fo ja-(o)de ni-(i)nu
strike (it), pot   this and break, queen:ant and begin to fly reach-out at-belly (of)

ikoko yi; awǫn (i)y(i)-o-ku   si bęrę si pa ęsisun   titi akikǫ fi
pot   this; those this-who-remain and begin to kill queen:ant until Cock take

would be the first to finish his row of yam heaps in hoeing her farm would be the one to whom she would give her child as wife. When Cock had made his sacrifice and Eshu had taken it and finished eating, Eshu took the three pots Cock had sacrificed[1] and buried one in each of the three corners of the farm where they were going to hoe yam heaps.

Before dawn, all the animals and birds had begun to hoe yam heaps in this farm before Cock awoke, and they had almost finished hoeing before he arrived. When Cock arrived and saw that his companions had almost finished hoeing, he began to repeat: "Make the hoe go 'shẹ,'[2] make the heaps rise up."

Thus Cock began to hoe quicker than anyone else at the farm. When Parrot saw that Cock had almost caught up to them, he said "Ho!"[3] and Woodcock said "You break"; and Cock's hoe broke. Then Cock took another hoe and again began to hoe, singing:

> "Cock, Cock spread your feathers so they sweep the ground;[4]
> "Cock, spread your feathers so they sweep the ground"

When they saw that Cock was again passing them, Parrot said "Ho!" and Woodcock said, "You break"; and Cock's hoe again broke; he took the third hoe[5] and Eshu, wanting to help Cock, went to one of the pots and struck it. It broke and queen-ants began to fly out of the pot; and the others began to kill the queen-ants and eat them, while Cock

---

1. Part of the sacrifice is instrumental to Cock's success.
2. The sound that a hoe makes when cutting the ground; note the word magic.
3. The sound that iron makes in breaking; note the word magic.
4. Gẹrẹ describes the way in which a cock spreads its wings when fighting, or how a gown that is too big drags along the ground.
5. The three hoes included in the sacrifice are also instrumental to Cock's success. Cf. n. 1.

kǫ-(ẹ)ran kǫja wǫn, n(i)-igba-ti nwǫn tun ri   pe akikǫ tun fẹ   kǫja wǫn
hoe-heap pass them; at-time-that they then see that Cock then want pass them

ti odidẹ ni Ho! ti aluko   ni   Ẹ   ya,   akikǫ na ni   Tipẹ-tipẹ
that Parrot say "Ho!" that Woodcock say, "You split," Cock also say, "Tight-tight

ni ikun   imu   arugbo   rǫ,   bayi ni akikǫ gbǫn gbogbo wǫn lǫ
be mucus (of) nose (of) old-person be:tough," thus be Cock pass all   them go

ti inu   obinrin si dun ti o   nkǫ-(o)rin pe:
that belly (of) woman and sweet that she singing-song that:

              Are-ẹgẹ m(o)-(n)i Are-ẹgẹ o, Are-ẹgẹ
              "Are-ẹgẹ I-say   Are-ẹgẹ, oh, Are-ẹgẹ;

              Erin   ma   ja-(ẹ)sẹ, Are-ẹgẹ
              "Elephant (continuative) reach-row, Are-ẹgẹ;

              Ẹfǫn   ma   ja-(o)ke, Are-ẹgẹ
              "Buffalo (continuative) reach-hill, Are-ẹgẹ;

              Akikǫ ǫkǫ   mi ma   ma   de   o, Are-ẹgẹ.
              "Cock husband my indeed (continuative) arrive, oh, Are-ẹgẹ."

       N(i)-igba-ti Are-ẹgẹ ri pe akikǫ ja   ẹsẹ ş(e)-(iw)aju gbogbo awǫn
       At-time-that Are-ẹgẹ see that Cock reach row make-front all   those

(i)y(i)-o-ku,   o   fo   mǫ   l(i)-ǫrun, O-l(i)-okun   si fi
this-who-remain, she jump against (him) at-neck, One:who-has-sea and take

Are-ẹgẹ fun akikǫ, gbogbo awǫn ẹranko ti   o   ku   si bi-(i)nu fi wǫn
Are-ẹgẹ give Cock, all   those animal that who remain and vex-belly put them

si-(i)bẹ lǫ.
to-there go.

       N(i)-igba-ti nwǫn nlǫ   l(i)-ǫna nwǫn bẹrẹ si di rikişi   ǫna ti   nwǫn
       At-time-that they going at-road they begin to tie plot   (of) road that they

yio fi   pa akikǫ ki nwǫn si gba Are-ẹgẹ l(i)-ǫwǫ rẹ. N(i)-igba-ti
will take (it) kill Cock that they and take Are-ẹgẹ at-hand his. At-time-that

nwǫn si de   ibi   odo kan, bi nwǫn ti   nwẹ   l(i)-ǫwǫ ni akikǫ ti
they and reach place (of) river one, as they have washing at-hand be Cock that

on ti   Are-ẹgẹ de,   nwǫn si ni ki   o wa wẹ   şugbǫn o ni on
he against Are-ẹgẹ arrive, they and say should he come wash but   he say he

ko wẹ, n(i)-igba-ti nwǫn si bẹrẹ si yǫ   l(i)-ẹnu o gbe Are-ẹgẹ
not wash, at-time-that they and begin to pull (him) at-mouth he take Are-ẹgẹ

ha   ẹnu,   n(i)-igba-ti nwǫn si ri pe o fẹ   ma   lǫ, nwǫn
stick:in mouth, at-time-that they and see that he want (continuative) go, they

ti   lu   omi bi o ti   bǫ   lu   omi o gbe Are-ẹgẹ mi.
push (him) strike water, as he have come strike water he take Are-ẹgẹ swallow.

N(i)-igba-ti akikǫ de   ile o fẹ pe ki   Are-ẹgẹ ja-(o)de   o
At-time-that Cock arrive house he want that should Are-ẹgẹ reach-outside, he

si f(i)-apa-l(u)-apa   o ni "Are-ẹgẹ ja-(o)de"   şugbǫn Are-ẹgẹ ko
and take-arm-beat-arm, he say "Are-ẹgẹ reach-outside" but   Are-ẹgẹ not

went on hoeing and almost passed them. When they saw that Cock again was about to pass them, Parrot said, "Ho!" and Woodcock said, "You break"; Cock said "Very tight, the mucus of an old person's nose is tough."[6] Thus Cock passed them all, and the girl was happy and she was singing:

> "Are-ẹgẹ; I say Are-ẹgẹ, oh, Are-ẹgẹ;
> "Elephant is finishing his row, Are-ẹgẹ;
> "Buffalo is reaching the end, Are-ẹgẹ;
> "Cock, my husband, is really getting there,
>   oh, Are-ẹgẹ."

When Are-ẹgẹ saw that Cock finished his row ahead of all the others, she threw herself about his neck; and the Sea Goddess gave Are-ẹgẹ to Cock in marriage. All the other animals were angry and left them there.

As they were walking along the road, they began to plot to kill Cock and to take Are-ẹgẹ from him. They came to a river, and as they were washing their hands, Cock and Are-ẹgẹ arrived. They told Cock to come and wash, but he said he did not wash. When they began to tease him, he put Are-ẹgẹ into his mouth. When the others saw that he wanted to go on, they pushed him into the water, and as he struck the water he swallowed Are-ẹgẹ. When Cock reached home, and wanted Are-ẹgẹ to come out, he flapped his wings and said, "Are-ẹgẹ, come out,"[7] but Are-ẹgẹ did not

---

6. A counter incantation to prevent the hoe from breaking.

7. This verse thus explains the meaning of Cock's crow and the origin of the longest of its tail feathers. Cf. this tale with the versions given by Bouche (1884-1885: 122-123), Lomax (1913: 3-4), Frobenius (1926: 241-244), and Herskovits and Herskovits (1931: 459-460).

ja-(o)de,   n(i)-igba-ti o   ko ja-(o)de   o   lǫ yǫ   ni idi   rę o
reach-outside; at-time-that she not reach-outside she go appear at waist his she

si di   irere   idi   akikǫ, on na ni o   di   irere
and become tail:feather (of) waist (of) Cock; she also be she become tail:feather

      idi rę titi   di   oni o-l(i)-oni   yi.
(of) waist his until (it) become today that:which-be-today this.

      Ifa ni a-(yi)o fę   obinrin kan, ki   a   ru-(ę)bǫ   ki ęni-kan
      Ifa say we-will love woman one, should we offer-sacrifice that person-one

ma ba   pa obinrin na ni i-pa   fa-(o)ri   mǫ-(ę)ni   l(i)-ǫwǫ. Gbogbo
not should kill woman the, be to-kill shave-head against-person at-hand. All

enia ni yio ma   du   obinrin yi ki   o to   ja mǫ-
people be will (continuative) compete:for woman this before it equal cut against-

(ę)ni l(i)-ǫwǫ. Bi a ba   fę   obinrin na a-(yi)o fi   ewurę   kan, aṣǫ
person at-hand. If we should love woman the we-will take she:goat one, cloth (of)

ara   obinrin na ati ejielogun   ru-(ę)bǫ   ki obinrin na ma
body (of) woman the, and 44,000   (cowries) offer-sacrifice, that woman the not

ba   ku ki awǫn enia si ma sǫ pe owo   run   le obinrin yi
should die that those people and not speak that cowries perish upon woman this

l(i)-ori, ki a ma ba   ma   pe obinrin na mǫ   Egun
at-head, that we not should (continuative) call woman the together:with Egungun

ni ǫjǫ miran.
at day another.

OGUNDA - (I)WORI - 1

      Ko kǫ-(i)le   ko sun ori-(i)gi;   ko kǫ-(i)ṣu ko ję erupę
      "Not build-house not sleep head-(of)-tree; not hoe-yam not eat dirt   (of)

ilę;   agba kan kǫ-(I)fa ko ri obi ti o gbo   ję a   da-(I)fa fun
ground; elder one learn-Ifa not see kola that it grow:old eat" who cast-Ifa for

Ajaolele ti o nlǫ si ode   Oro. Nwǫn ni ki   Ajaolele ru-
Ajaolele that he going to outside (of) Oro. They say should Ajaolele offer-

(ę)bǫ ki o to lǫ si ode   Oro. Nwǫn ni ki   o fi ewurę
sacrifice before he equal go to outside (of) Oro. They say should he take she:goat

ru-(ę)bǫ   akikǫ męta, ayebǫ adię,   abę kan. Ajaolele ru-(ę)bǫ.
offer-sacrifice, cock three, hen   chicken, razor one. Ajaolele offer-sacrifice.

      N(i)-igba-ti o de   ode   Oro, Eṣu yǫ   abę ti o fi
      At-time-that he arrive outside (of) Oro, Eshu pull:out razor that he take (it)

ru-(ę)bǫ   le   l(i)-ǫwǫ. Ija wa da   on pęlu   Qran
offer-sacrifice give (him) at-hand. Fight come cause him together:with Affair,

come out. Instead she turned into the longest feather in his tail, and there she remains until this very day.

Ifa says that we will marry a wife, but that we should sacrifice lest some-one kill her and brag about it to our face. Everyone will be competing for this woman before we win out.[8] If we marry her, we should sacrifice one she-goat, a cloth from her body, and eleven shillings, that she may not die and that people will not say that our money[9] was lost on her, and lest someday we should have to call her to come with the Egungun.[10]

---

8. "It cut against person at hand" is said of a rope that breaks when people are pulling it in opposite directions, as in a tug of war. The figure of speech here compares the attempts to win the woman with a tug of war.

9. The money given as bridewealth.

10. Meaning that she will die. Cf. n. 3, verse 52-4.

---

131 - 1

"One who does not build a house does not have to sleep in the tree top; one who does not hoe yams does not have to eat dirt; an elder who learns[1] Ifa does not have to eat stale kola nuts" was the one who cast Ifa for Ajaolele when he was going to the town of Oro.[2] They said Ajaolele should make a sacrifice before he went to Oro. They said he should sacrifice a she-goat, three cocks, a hen, and one razor. Ajaolele made the sacrifice.

When he reached the town of Oro, Eshu pulled out the razor which Ajaolele had sacrificed and put it in Ajaolele's hand.[3] A fight started between Ajaolele and Affair,

---

1. Note the pun on the words: build (kợ), hoe (kợ), and learn (kợ).

2. There are several towns named Oro, including one near Ido and Ijero in Ekiti.

3. The razor offered as part of the sacrifice is instrumental in getting him into the trouble which brings him wives.

ǫmǫ-(o)binrin   O-l(i)-oro   ti   o   jǫ   pe   Ajaolele   ima
child-woman   (of) One:who-has-Oro that she consent that Ajaolele (continuative)

ba   ra ǫkǫ.   Ǝṣu wa   ti   Qran lu   ǫbǫ
join (her) buy cornstarch:porridge. Eshu come push Affair against knife (of)

ǫwǫ   Ajaolele, o gun Qran.   Nwǫn ni Ajaolele da-(ǫ)ran.   Ǝṣu ni
hand (of) Ajaolele, it stab Affair. They say Ajaolele cause-affair. Eshu say (he)

ko da-(ǫ)ran   o ni ṣe   ni ki   nwǫn fa Qran le Ajaolele l(i)-ǫwǫ
not cause-affair; he say make be should they pull Affair give Ajaolele at-hand

ki   o lǫ ma   tǫ-(o)ju   rǫ.   Nwǫn si fa Qran le   l(i)-
should he go (continuative) care:for-eye hers. They and pull Affair give (him) at-

ǫwǫ pe ki   o lǫ ma   tǫ-(o)ju   rǫ. Bǫ-ni Qran ti   wǫ-
hand that should he go (continuative) care:for-eye hers. So-be Affair have enter-

(i)le-(ǫ)kǫ   ko l(i)-oyun   bǫ-ni ko si bi-(ǫ)mǫ.   N(i)-igba-ti
house-(of)-husband not have-pregnancy; so-be not and bear-child. At-time-that

Qran de   ile   Ajaolele, bi Ajaolele ti   ntǫ-(o)ju   rǫ, bǫ-na
Affair arrive house (of) Ajaolele, as Ajaolele have caring:for-eye hers, so-also

ni o si nba   sun pǫlu.   N(i)-igba-ti o ma
be he and joining (her) sleep together:with (her). At-time-that it (continuative)

to   oṣu mǫta   oyun   han   ni ara   Qran.
reach month three pregnancy appear at body (of) Affair.

      N(i)-igba-ti O-l(i)-Oro   gbǫ   o ni on fi   Qran fun Ajaolele
      At-time-that One:who-has-Oro hear (this) he say he take Affair give Ajaolele

ki   o   ma   ṣe   aya rǫ. Bǫ-na ni igba-(e)keji   O-
should she (continuative) make wife his. So-also be calabash-second (of) One:who-

l(i)-Oro na si fun ni ǫmǫ pǫlu   ati igba-(ǫ)kǫta   O-
has-Oro the and give at child together:with (him) and calabash-third (of) One:who-

l(i)-Oro na si ṣe bǫ gǫgǫ. N(i)-igba-ti o pada de   ilu rǫ, ti   o
has-Oro the and do so just.   At-time-that he return arrive town his, that he

di   ǫ-l(i)-ǫni   o bǫrǫ si jo,   o bǫrǫ si iyǫ.   O wa
become one:who-has-person he begin to dance, he begin to rejoice. He come

di   enia   nla o wa   bǫrǫ si kǫ-(o)rin pe:
become person big he come begin to sing-song that:

                    Ifa mo da r(e)-Oro ṣǫ   Ajaolele,
                    "Ifa I   cast go-Oro happen, Ajaolele,

                    Ifa mo da r(e)-Oro ṣǫ
                    "Ifa I   cast go-Oro happen."

      Ifa ni inu yio dun   ni ohun ti a da   on si yi, o ni a-(yi)o
      Ifa say belly will be:sweet at ohun that we cast him to this; he say we-will

ni iyi a-(yi)o si di   ǫ-l(i)-ǫni   ati pe nwǫn yio fi
have glory; we-will and become one:who-has-person and that they will take

obinrin kan ta-(ǫ)ni   l(i)-ǫrǫ.
woman one sell-person at-gift.

_____

the daughter of the chief of Oro, who had agreed to let Ajaolele buy cornstarch porridge from her. Eshu pushed Affair against the knife in the hand of Ajaolele, and it stabbed Affair. They said Ajaolele had started the trouble.[4] Eshu said that he had not started it; he said that they must put Affair in the charge of Ajaolele, so that he should take care of her until her wound healed. And they put Affair in the charge of Ajaolele so that he could take care of her. It so happened that Affair was already married and living with her husband, but she had not become pregnant and had not born a child. When Affair came to Ajaolele's house, while he was taking care of her, he was also sleeping with her. When the third month arrived, her pregnancy became noticeable.

When the chief of Oro heard this, he said he would give Affair to Ajaolele and that she should be his wife. Likewise the chief second[5] to the chief of Oro gave him one of his daughters, and the chief third to the chief of Oro did the same. When he returned to his own town, Ajaolele had become a person with followers, and he began to dance, he began to rejoice. He had become an important person, and he began to sing:

> "The Ifa that I cast to go to Oro has come to pass, Ajaolele;
> "The Ifa that I cast to go to Oro has come to pass."

Ifa says that we will be happy about the thing for which this figure was cast. He says we will gain glory; and we will become someone with a following, and that we will be given a wife without having to give bridewealth.

---

4. There is a pun here on the trouble or affair of the fight and the name of the daughter of the king.

5. An individual's followers are spoken of as his second, third, and fourth "calabashes" after the order in which, according to their rank, they drink when a calabash of palm wine is passed.

OGUNDA MEJI - 1

O ni   o wọ   wọrọ, mo ni   o tutu dun-dun   o ni   bi kin-ni?
He say, it drag gently; I   say, it cool cold-cold; he say, like what-be (it)?

Mo ni   bi owo   tun-tun ti   a   ma   ni ni,   mo ni kin-
I   say, like cowries new-new that we (continuative) have be (it); I   say, what-

ni ẹbọ?   Ẹiyẹ-(i)le   meji ati egbejila.
be sacrifice? Bird-(of)-house two and 2400   (cowries).

O ni   o wọ   wọrọ, mo ni   o tutu dun-dun   o ni   bi kin-ni?
He say, it drag gently; I   say, it cool cold-cold; he say, like what-be (it)?

Mo ni   bi aya titun ti   a   ma   ni ni,   mo ni kin-ni
I   say, like wife new that we (continuative) have be (it), I   say, what-be

ẹbọ?   O ni   agbebọ adiẹ   meji ati egbejila.
sacrifice? He say, hen   chicken two and 2400   (cowries).

O ni   o wọ   wọrọ, mo ni   o tutu dun-dun, o ni   bi kin-ni?
He say, it drag gently; I   say, it cool cold-cold; he say, like what-be (it)?

Mo ni   bi ọmọ titun ti   a   ma   bi ni,   o ni   akikọ mẹta
I   say, like child new that we (continuative) bear be (it); he say, cock three

ati ẹgbẹtalelọgbọn.   O ni   a-bi-(ọ)mọ-le-(ọ)mọ   ni ti   ṣẹṣẹki,
and 6600   (cowries). He say, to-bear-child-upon-child be that (of) shẹshẹki,

o ni   ọmọ ni din   l(i)-ẹhin obinrin rẹ.
he say, child not lessen at-back woman his.

O ni   o wọ   wọrọ, mo ni   o tutu dun-dun, o ni   bi kin-ni?
He say, it drag gently; I   say, it cool cold-cold; he say, like what-be (it)?

Mo ni   bi ile   tun-tun ti   a   ma   kọ,   o ni   a-da-mọ
I   say, like house new-new that we (continuative) build, he say, to-create-against

a-da-mọ   ni peregun da-(a)ṣọ,   o ni   peregun ki lo aṣọ   esi.
to-create-against be peregun create-cloth, he say, peregun not use cloth (of) last:

O ni   ewurẹ   kan ati ejielogun   l(i)-ẹbọ;   nwọn ni   gbogbo
year. He say, she:goat one and 44,000   (cowries) be-sacrifice; they say, all

aiye yi ni   yio ba   joko   n(i)-ibẹ.
earth this be (it) will join (him) sit:down at-there.

O ni   o wọ   wọrọ, mo ni   o tutu dun-dun, o ni   bi kin-ni?
He say, it drag gently; I   say, it cool cold-cold; he say, like what-be (it)?

Mo ni   bi oye titun ti   a   ma   jẹ ni,   o ni   ki   a   yan
I   say, like title new that we (continuative) eat be (it); he say, should we choose

on l(i)-ẹbọ   ki on ki   on le   jẹ ti   on pẹ: agutan kan,
him at-sacrifice that he should he be:able eat that (of) his be:long: ewe   one,

iti   aṣọ fun-fun,   igba   ẹfun kan, ati ọkanla.
bunch (of) cloth be:white-be:white calabash (of) chalk one, and 22,000 (cowries).

137 - 1

He says, "It is pulling gently." I say, "It is very cool." He says, "Like what?"
I say, "Like new money that we are going to have." I say, "What is the sacrifice?"
Two pigeons and seven pence two oninis.

He says, "It is pulling gently." I say, "It is very cool." He says, "Like what?"
I say, "Like a new wife that we are going to have." I say, "What is the sacrifice?"
He says, "Two hens and seven pence two oninis."

He says, "It is pulling gently." I say, "It is very cool." He says, "Like what?"
I say, "Like a new child that we are going to bear." He says, "Three cocks and one
shilling seven pence eight oninis." He says, "To bear child after child is what the
shẹshẹki plant does."[1] He says children will not decrease in number behind his
wife.

He says, "It is pulling gently." I say, "It is very cool." He says, "Like what?"
I say, "Like a new house that we are going to build." He says, "To grow against
himself, to grow against himself is how Peregun tree grows his cloth";[2] he says,
"Peregun tree never uses last year's clothes." He says, "One she-goat and eleven
shillings is the sacrifice." They say, "The whole world will be sitting down there
with him."

He says, "It is pulling gently." I say, "It is very cool." He says, "Like what?"
I say, "Like a new title that we are going to take." He says we should name the
sacrifice that will enable him to take the title and remain long in office. One ewe,
a bunch of white cloths, a calabash of chalk, and five shillings six pence.

---

1. This refers to the abundance of seeds or fruit of this unidentified plant.
Cf. verse 249-3.

2. This refers to the fact that the peregun tree (Dracaena spp.), which is
used to mark boundaries, gets a new layer of bark each year.

Ori   mi di   ori   ęfun   Ado;
"Head my become head (of) chalk (of) Benin;

Qtękulu   gbogbo ę   wa   yǫ   fun ori mi poro.
"Everybody all   you come rejoice for head my together."

Ifa ni   a-(yi)o ba   ęsę ja.
Ifa say we-will join row reach.

OGUNDA MEJI - 2

Pętę-pętę ni a-irǫ-(ǫ)kǫ   gbǫnrangandan-gbǫnrangandan ni a-irǫ
"Flat-flat be we-strike-hoe, 'gbǫnrangandan-gbǫnrangandan' be we-strike

ada,   l(i)-eji-da l(i)-eji-da ni a-irǫ   agogo   idę,   bi a ki   pa
cutlass, at-two-turn at-two-turn be we-strike gong (of) brass; if we should kill

pǫ   o di   ǫkan-şǫşo giro-giro   a   da fun Qrunmila ti   o wa
together it become one-only   alone-alone" who cast for Qrunmila that he exist

ni ir(ǫ)-ogun   ǫta,   nwǫn ni yio şę-(o)gun   wǫn, nwǫn ni ki   o
at gather-war (of) enemy, they say will make-war (of) them, they say should he

ru   akikǫ męta, ęgbętalelǫgbǫn,   ati asunrun   etu kan.
offer cock three, 6600   (cowries), and bag   (of) etu one.

Ati o-n(i)-iru   ati o-n(i)-iyǫ,   ęnu wǫn sunin-sunin
And one:who-has-locust:bean and one:who-has-salt, mouth their 'sunin-sunin'

ęnu wǫn, nwǫn ni   yio şę wǫn. Ifa ni on yio ba-(ę)ni   şę-(o)gun
mouth their; they say (he) will make them. Ifa say he will join-person make-war

ar(a)-aiye   ni ohun ti   a   da Ifa si yi, o ni a fę   şe ohun kan,
(of) people-(of)-earth at thing that we cast Ifa to this, he say we want do thing one;

o ni on ko ni   ję-ki   a ri ibi   ǫta   n(i)-inu rę,
he say he not be (he) consent-that we see evil (of) enemy at-belly its.

QSA - (O)GUNDA - 1

A-ja-tu-(e)ruku   ęfǫn   a   da fun ǫ-l(i)-ǫdę,   nwǫn ni
"To-fight-loosen-dust (of) buffalo" who cast for one:who-be-hunter; they say

ki   o ru-(ę)bǫ   nitori-pe   yio ri aya kan fę ni ǫdun yi.
should he offer-sacrifice because-that (he) will see wife one love at year this.

Q-l(i)-ǫdę   ru-(ę)bǫ   akikǫ meji, ayebǫ adię   meji, ǫtin
One:who-be-hunter offer-sacrifice (of) cock two, hen   chicken two, liquor (of)

şękętę,   ati ęgbaji.
maize:beer, and 4000 (cowries).

"My head becomes as white as chalk from Benin;[3]
"Everybody, come and rejoice with me because of my head."

Ifa says we will reach the end of our row.[4]

---

3. I will become so old my hair will be white as chalk.
4. That is, find a solution to our problem. The prediction is that the client will get money, a wife, a child, a new house, or a title, depending on which he came to inquire about, if he makes the specified sacrifice.

---

137 - 2

"When we forge a hoe, we beat it out flat; when we forge a cutlass, we beat 'gbǫnrandan-gbǫnrandan';[1] when we forge a brass gong, we turn it over and over and over; if we bring them together, they become only one alone" was the one who cast Ifa for Ǫrunmila when he was going to attack his enemies. They said he would defeat them. They said he should sacrifice three cocks, one shilling seven pence and eight oninis, and one bag made of etu cloth.[2]

Both those who use locust beans and those who use salt, their mouths will be closed 'sunin-sunin,'[3] they say he will defeat them. Ifa says he will help someone defeat the people of the world in this thing for which this figure was cast. He says we want to do something; he says he will not allow us to find the evil of enemies in it.

---

1. The sound made when beating iron on an anvil.
2. Etu is a popular pattern of cotton cloth woven in blue and white on the men's loom.
3. The sound of a person closing his mouth, meaning that no one will be able to say anything against him. It was explained that since everyone uses locust beans or salt in seasoning food, Ǫrunmila will defeat everyone.

---

153 - 1

"To fight and stir up dust like Buffalo" was the one who cast Ifa for Hunter. They said he should make a sacrifice so that he would find a wife to marry during that year. Hunter sacrificed two cocks, two hens, maize beer, and one shilling.

A-(yi)o   wa   egun-iṣu   a-(yi)o   fi   gun   iyan   bọ
We-will   seek   egun-yam   we-will   take (it)   pound   pounded:yam   sacrifice:to

ori.   Ǫ-l(i)-ǫdẹ   ru-(ẹ)bọ.
head.   One:who-be-hunter   offer-sacrifice.

Ni   ǫjǫ   kan   ǫ-l(i)-ǫdẹ   yi   lọ   s(i)-oko,   n(i)-igba-ti   o   gun   egun
At   day   one   one:who-be-hunter   this   go   to-farm,   at-time-that   he   mount   lookout,

o   ri   gidigidi   kan   ṣugbọn   n(i)-igba-ti   o   fẹ   na   ibọn   si,   gidigidi   yi
he   see   Gidigidi   one   but   at-time-that   he   want   stretch   gun   to (it),   Gidigidi   this

ara   pada   o   si   di   wundia   pupa   wẹ;   n(i)-igba-ti   o   bọ   awọ   s(i)-
body   change   it   and   become   maiden   red   fine;   at-time-that   she   take:off   hide   to-

ilẹ   tan,   ǫ-l(i)-ǫdẹ   si   nwo   bi   gidigidi   na   ti   nfi
ground   finish,   one-who-be-hunter   and   looking:at (her)   as   Gidigidi   the   have   taking

awọ   rẹ   pa-mọ   o   si   mọ   ibi-ti   o   fi   pa-mọ   si   ni   ẹhin
hide   hers   kill-against   he   and   know   place-that   she   take (it)   kill-against   to   at   back

igi   kan;   ṣugbọn   o   papa   ko   mọ   pe   ǫ-l(i)-ǫdẹ   yi   nwo
(of) tree   one;   but   she   herself   not   know   that   one:who-be-hunter   this   looking:at

on.
her.

N(i)-igba-ti   gidigidi   na   lọ   tan,   ǫ-l(i)-ǫdẹ   yi   sǫ   ka-
At-time-that   Gidigidi   the   go   finish,   one:who-be-hunter   this   strike   against-

(i)lẹ   l(i)-ori   egun   rẹ   o   si   gbe   awọ   ti   o   bọ   si-(i)lẹ   o
ground   at-head   (of) lookout   his   he   and   take   hide   that   she   take:off   to-ground   he

gbe   s(i)-inu   apo   rẹ   o   si   ntẹle   titi   o   fi   ri   pe   ǫja   ni
carry (it)   to-belly   bag   his   he   and   following (her)   until   he   take   see   that   market   be

o   nlọ;   n(i)-igba-ti   nwọn   de   inu   ǫja,   ǫ-l(i)-ǫdẹ   yi
she   going;   at-time-that   they   arrive   belly   (of) market,   one:who-be-hunter   this

sun-mọ,   o   ki,   o   si   sǫ   fun   pe   on   ni   on   wa
move-against (her),   he   greet (her),   he   and   speak   for (her)   that   she   be   he   seek

wa   si   ǫja;   gidigidi   yi   ti   o   di   obinrin   si   da-(o)hun   o   bi
come   to   market;   Gidigidi   this   that   she   become   woman   and   break-voice   she   ask

lere   pe   Ṣe   ko   si   (ohu)n-kan?   Ǫ-l(i)-ǫdẹ   yi   da-(o)hun   o
(him) (1)   that   "Make   not   be   thing-one?"   One:who-be-hunter   this   break-voice   he

ni   o   nfẹ   lati   fẹ   ni;   gidigidi   da-(o)hun   o   ni   on   ko
say   he   wanting   in:order:to   love (her)   be (it);   Gidigidi   break-voice   she   say   she   not

nfẹ   enia,   n(i)-igba-ti   o   di   igba-(ẹ)kẹta   ti   ǫdẹ   yi   ma
loving   person;   at-time-that   it   become   time-third   that   hunter   this   (continuative)

tǫ   wa   ni   o   wa   bi   ǫdẹ   na   lere   pe   o   ri   (ohu)n-kan   l(i)-
approach (her)   seek   be   she   come   ask   hunter   the   (1)   that   he   see   thing-one   at-

ẹhin   on   dan?
back   hers   (interrogative)?

---

1. Bi . . . lere means "to ask."

We will find some yam cuttings;[1] we will pound yam loaf with them and sacrifice them to our head. Hunter made the sacrifice.

One day this hunter went to the farm. When he climbed to his lookout platform,[2] he saw a Gidigidi,[3] but when he tried to aim his gun at it, this Gidigidi turned into a beautiful reddish maiden. When she had finished taking off her hide, the hunter watched as the Gidigidi hid her hide, and he knew the place where she hid it behind a tree. But she herself did not know that this hunter was watching her.

When the Gidigidi had left, this hunter came down from his lookout and put the hide that she had taken off into his bag; and he followed her until he saw that she was going to market. When they reached the market, this hunter approached her; he greeted her, and told her that he had come to market seeking her. This Gidigidi who had turned into a woman replied, "Is something wrong?" The hunter answered that he wanted to marry her. Gidigidi answered that she was not going to marry anyone. The third time that the hunter approached her in this way, she asked if he had seen anything behind her.[4]

-----

1. There are two yam harvests. At the early harvest, the lower part of some yams is cut off and the rest is replanted. When these mature, they are called egun yams and are used primarily as seed-yams (ebu) for planting in the following year. They are never pounded into yam loaf for eating, but they are commonly used in this form in medicines and for other ritual purposes. Here they are used as a sacrifice to the head, which is for the soul which controls the individual's luck.

2. A platform in a tree reached by a ladder where a hunter watches for game. Note the pun here on "mount the lookout" (gun egun) and "pound yam cuttings" (gun egun).

3. A Gidigidi is a wild animal described by the informant as large and powerful, and similar to a buffalo; it runs from the rain, which it dislikes, and is sometimes seen with its head under a shelter but its body out in the rain. Other informants described it as like a wild goat or like a horse, but stronger. It is identified in the CMS Dictionary as "a large and strong animal," and by Abraham as the Yellowbacked Duiker (Cephalophus Sylvicultrix Sylvicultrix Afzelius). Later in the verse the children of the Gidigidi woman are spoken of as "children of Buffalo," and Buffalo is mentioned in the introductory phrase. Cf. n. 7.

4. That is, whether he had found out anything about her past.

Ọ-l(i)-ọdẹ   na da-(o)hun   o ni   o ri (ohu)n-kan l(i)-ẹhin rẹ.
One:who-be-hunter the break-voice he say he see thing-one at-back hers.

Obinrin gidigidi wa   da-(o)hun   o ni   Kin-ni   o ri l(i)-ẹhin mi? N(i)-
Woman Gidigidi come break-voice she say "What-be he see at-back my?" At-

igba-na ni ọ-l(i)-ọdẹ   sọ   fun   pe ki   o   wa ki on sọ
time-the be one:who-be-hunter speak for (her) that should she come that he speak

ohun ti   on ri l(i)-ẹhin rẹ fun;   n(i)-igba-ti awọn mej(i)-(m)eji si
thing that he see at-back hers for (her); at-time-that those two-two   and

de   ẹhin   ọja   ọ-l(i)-ọdẹ   yi ki   ọwọ bọ   apo o si yọ
arrive back (of) market, one:who-be-hunter this push hand enter bag he and pull:

    awọ rẹ ja-(o)de   o si fi   han   n(i)-igba-ti o ri awọ ti
out hide hers reach-outside he and take (it) appear, at-time-that she see hide that

o bọ   s(i)-inu   igbo l(i)-ọwọ   ọ-l(i)-ọdẹ   yi, o ni
she take:off to-belly (of) forest at-hand (of) one:who-be-hunter this, she say

ki ọ-l(i)-ọdẹ   jọwọ,   o ni on yio fẹ;   obinrin yi
should one:who-be-hunter grant:favor, she say she will love (him); woman this

si pada lọ si ọja   o lọ pa-(i)lẹ   rẹ mọ   o si tẹle ọ-
and return go to market, she go kill-ground hers against, she and follow one:who-

l(i)-ọdẹ yi; ṣugbọn n(i)-igba-ti nwọn nlọ ni ọna o sọ   fun ọ-l(i)-
be-hunter this; but   at-time-that they going at road she speak for one:who-be-

ọdẹ yi pe ko gbọdọ sọ   ọrọ na fun ẹni-k(u)-ẹni,   ọ-l(i)-
hunter this that not must speak word the for person-any-person, one:who-be-

ọdẹ na si sọ   fun   pe on ko ni sọ   fun ẹni-k(u)-ẹni; bayi
hunter the and speak for (her) that he not be speak for person-any-person; thus

ni o di   aya rẹ ti nwọn jọ   ngbe   ile.
be she become wife his that they be:together dwelling:at house.

    Obinrin yi bẹrẹ si bi-(ọ)mọ fun ọdẹ yi; ṣugbọn aya   ọ-l(i)-
    Woman this begin to bear-child for hunter this; but   wife (of) one:who-be-

ọdẹ akọkọ fẹ bẹrẹ si yọ ọ-l(i)-ọdẹ   yi l(i)-ẹnu pe nibo ni
hunter first love begin to pull one:who-be-hunter this at-mouth that where be

ọkọ   on ti ri aya-(e)keji fẹ ti ko sọ   fun on, ọ-l(i)-ọdẹ
husband her have see wife-second love that not speak for her, one:who-be-hunter

yi si sọ   fun   pe ọmọ awọn ti ima   wa ba on ra
this and speak for (her) that child (of) those that (continuative) come join him buy

ẹran l(i)-oko ni,   ṣugbọn iru   ida-(o)hun yi ko tẹ   aya rẹ yi
meat at-farm be (she), but   kind (of) break-voice this not reach wife his this

l(i)-ọrun o si tun bẹrẹ si wadi   pe boya ni ilu yi ni   tabi
at-neck she and then begin to investigate that perhaps at town this be (she) or

ni ilu miran. Ọ-l(i)-ọdẹ   yi si sọ   fun   pe ni ilu miran
at town another. One:who-be-hunter this and speak for (her) that at town another

ni,   ṣugbọn sibẹ-sibẹ ko tẹ   obinrin yi l(i)-ọrun o si bẹrẹ si
be (she), but   still-still not reach woman this at-neck she and begin to

The hunter replied that he had seen something behind her. The Gidigidi woman answered, "What did you see behind me?" Then the hunter told her that she should come with him, so that he could tell her what he had seen behind her. When they got outside the market, the hunter put his hand into his bag and brought out her hide and showed it to her. When she saw the hide that she had taken off in the forest in the hand of the hunter, she said the hunter should take pity on her, that she would marry him. The woman went back to the market and gathered up her goods and set out with the hunter. But while they were on the way, she told the hunter that he must not speak a word about this to anyone; and the hunter told her that he would not tell anyone. Thus she became his wife, and they lived together in his house.

This woman began to bear children for the hunter, but the wife whom the hunter had first married began to tease the hunter by asking him where he had met his second wife, that he had not told her about it. The hunter told her that she was the child of the women who came to the farm to buy meat from him, but this kind of answer did not satisfy his first wife, and she began to inquire whether she had perhaps come from this town or from that town. The hunter told her that she was from a different town, but still this did not satisfy the woman, and she began to

ma   wadi   kiri;   n(i)-inu   ṣ(e)-iṣe bayi ni obinrin gidigidi
(continuative) investigate around; at-belly (of) do-deed thus be woman Gidigidi

yi   bi   ọmọ kinni ti   o   si bi   ekeji.
this bear child first that she and bear second.

    Obinrin yi   wa   lọ ba   ẹgbọn   ọ-l(i)-ọdẹ   yi di ọran
    Woman this come go join elder:sibling (of) one:who-be-hunter this tie affair

na pọ,   ẹgbọn   rẹ si mu   lọ si ode,   o   fun   ni ẹmu
the together, elder:sibling his and take (him) go to outside, he give (him) at palm:

    mu   lọpọ-lọpọ, n(i)-igba-ti o yo   tan   ni ẹgbọn   rẹ
wine drink much-much, at-time-that he be:satisfied finish be elder:sibling his

bere l(i)-ọwọ rẹ pe   nibo ni iwọ ti   ri aya rẹ-(e)keji fẹ?   Ọ-
ask at-hand his that "Where be you have see wife his-second love?" One:who-

l(i)-ọdẹ yi da-(o)hun   o ni gidigidi ni   n(i)-ibi-ti   o gbe nṣọ
be-hunter this break-voice he say Gidigidi be (she), at-place-that he take watching

igi l(i)-oko ni on ti   ri ti   o nbọ   awọ ti on si ti   ko   awọ
tree at-farm be he have see that she taking:off hide that he and have gather hide

rẹ   ti   o si ba   de   ọja   ti   on si fi   awọ rẹ han   ati
hers that he and join (her) arrive market that he and take hide hers appear and

pe lati igba-na ni o ti   di   aya on. N(i)-igba-ti   ẹgbọn
that from time-the be she have become wife his. At-time-that elder:sibling (of)

ọ-l(i)-ọdẹ   yi de   ile o   ko   o   ro   fun aya   ọ-l(i)-
one:who-be-hunter this arrive house he relate he report for wife (of) one:who-be

ọdẹ-(e)keji.
hunter-second.

    N(i)-igba-ti o ṣe   ọ-l(i)-ọdẹ   yi mu-(a)ra o lọ si oko,   ṣugbọn
    At-time-that it make one:who-be-hunter this take-body he go to farm, but

n(i)-igba-ti o di   ọjọ-(ẹ)kẹta ti   o ti   lọ ni eyi iyale   mu igi
at-time-that it become day-third   that he have go be this senior:wife take wood

ti   o si gbe lu-(i)lẹ   o   nfẹ   ṣẹ   igi yi. [Ewọ si ni enia
that she and take strike-ground she wanting break wood this. [Tabu and be people

ko gbọdọ gbe igi lu-(i)lẹ   bẹ ni ile   ọ-l(i)-ọdẹ.]   Eyi
not must take wood strike-ground so at house (of) one:who-be-hunter.] This

obinrin gidigidi yi si da-(o)hun   o ni ṣe   ọkọ   awọn ti   kilọ
woman Gidigidi this and break-voice she say make husband (of) them have warn

fun awọn pe ki   awọn ma-ṣe ṣẹ   igi bẹ mọ   n(i)-inu   ile?   N(i)-
for them that should they not-do break wood so again at-belly (of) house? At-

igba-na ni eyi iyale   da-(o)hun   o ni Ba   ara rẹ   lọ wayi, iwọ
time-the be this senior:wife break-voice she say, "With body yours go, wayi, you

iṣe enia ṣe   ẹranko yi ma   jẹ ma   mu awọ rẹ
make person make animal this, (imperative) eat (imperative) drink hide yours

nbẹ   n(i)-inu   aka.
existing at-belly (of) storehouse."

inquire about. While she was doing this, the Gidigidi woman bore her first child, and her second child.

The first wife went to the hunter's elder brother and discussed the matter with him. The elder brother took the hunter out and gave him lots of palm wine to drink. When the hunter had drunk his fill, his brother asked him, "Where did you meet your second wife?" The hunter replied that she was a Gidigidi, that he had seen her taking off her hide where he was watching from a tree in the farm, and that he had taken her hide and gone to the market with her, that he had shown her the hide, and that from that time on she had been his wife. When the hunter's elder brother came home, he reported this to the hunter's first wife.[5]

After a while, the hunter got ready and went to the farm; but on the second day after he had left, his senior wife took wood and struck it against the ground in order to break it. (It is a tabu that wood must not be struck against the ground in this way in the house of a hunter.) This Gidigidi woman asked whether their husband had not warned them that they must not break wood in this way in his house? Then the senior wife replied with contempt "Take yourself and go away, Wayi![6] You are both a human being and an animal. Eat and drink; your hide is inside the storehouse."

------

5. The Yoruba text says he told the hunter's second wife, but from the context this is clearly an error.

6. An exclamation expressing great contempt.

N(i)-igba-ti obinrin gidigidi yi   gbọ bayi o   ni   Ha! o   si   dakẹ,
At-time-that woman Gidigidi this hear thus she say, "Ha!" she and be:silent,

o   si   mu-(a)ra, o   si   lọ si ori   aka,   n(i)-igba-ti o   de
she and take-body, she and go to head (of) storehouse; at-time-that she arrive

ibẹ, o   ba awọ rẹ n(i)-ibi-ti ọ-l(i)-ọdẹ   gbe fi   pa-
there, she meet hide hers at-place-that one:who-be-hunter take take (it) kill-

mọ si, o   si   gbe awọ rẹ, n(i)-igba-ti o   wo o, o   ti   gbẹ,
against to, she and take hide hers; at-time-that she look:at it, it have dry:out,

o   si   lọ pọn omi, o   ri   i s(i)-inu rẹ, n(i)-igba-ti o   de,   o
she and go draw water, she immerse it to-belly its; at-time-that it be:ready, she

gbe   wọ,   o   si   ni   iwo l(i)-ori, n(i)-igba-na ni o   sa-re ti
take (it) enter (it), she and have horn at-head; at-time-the be she run-go against

iyale   rẹ, o   si   kan a   pa,   n(i)-igba-ti o   kan iyale   rẹ
senior:wife her, she and butt her kill (her), at-time-that she butt senior:wife hers

pa   tan, o   yọ   ọkan s(i)-ilẹ n(i)-inu   awọn iwo rẹ mej(i)-
kill (her) finish, she pull:out one   to-ground at-belly (of) those horn hers two-

(m)eji o   si   mu-(a)ra o   d(a)-ori kọ   oko, n(i)-igba-ti ọ-
two   she and take-body she turn-head turn:toward farm; at-time-that one:who-

l(i)-ọdẹ yi ri ti o   nbọ, o   mọ ti igi ti   bẹ ni ile; n(i)-igba-
be-hunter this see that she coming, he know that wood have cut at house; at-time-

ti o   fẹ kan ọkọ   rẹ, ọkọ   rẹ ni ki   o   ma kan on, o   ni:
that she want butt husband hers, husband hers say should she not butt him, he say:

    Iyan   egun ati ọtin   apẹ
    "Pounded:yam (of) egun and liquor (of) pot,

    Ẹ   p(a)-oko   bo   mi
    "You clean-farm cover me,

    Ẹ   b(a)-ọwọ le   mi.
    "You put-honor upon me."

N(i)-igba-na ni o   wa   bere l(i)-ọwọ   ọ-l(i)-ọdẹ   yi pe bawo
At-time-the be she come ask at-hand (of) one:who-be-hunter this that how

ni iyale   on ti ṣe   mọ   on, n(i)-igba-na ni ọ-l(i)-ọdẹ   yi
be senior:wife his have make know her, at-time-the be one:who-be-hunter this

wa   ko   bi ẹgbọn   on ti ṣe   mu on lọ si ode   ti o   si
come relate as elder:sibling his have make take him go to outside that he and

fun on ni ẹmu   mu yo   ti on ko si mọ igba-ti   on sọ
give him at palm:wine drink be:satisfied that he not and know time-that he speak

fun.   N(i)-igba-na ni o   ni   o dara,   o   ni on ko ni pa,
for (him). At-time-the be she say "it be:good," she say she not be kill (him),

ṣugbọn ki   o   ma   lọ si ile, ati pe n(i)-igba-ku-(i)gba ti
but   should he (continuative) go to house, and that at-time-any-time that

awọn ọmọ on ba   nfẹ   ṣe   ọdun, ki   o   ma   ba   awọn
those child hers should wanting make year, should he (continuative) join those

When the Gidigidi woman heard this, she said, "Ha!" and she kept quiet. She got ready and went to the storehouse. When she got there, she found her hide where the hunter had hidden it, and she brought it out. When she looked at it, it had dried out. She drew some water and put the hide into it. When it was ready, she got into it, and she had horns on her head. Then she ran at the senior wife, butted her, and killed her. When she had butted and killed the senior wife, she pulled off one of her two horns, and then started toward the farm. When the hunter saw her coming, he knew that wood had been broken in his house. When she wanted to butt her husband, her husband said that she must not butt him. He said:

> "Loaf of yam cuttings and pot of maize beer,[7]
> "You cut weeds and cover me,
> "You heap honor upon me."

Then she asked the hunter, how it was that his senior wife had known about her. The hunter told her how his elder brother had taken him out and had given him so much palm wine to drink that he no longer knew what he was saying. Then she said, "It is all right." She said that she would not kill him, but that he should go home and that whenever her children should want to perform their annual festival, he should

---

7. Both the maize beer and the loaf of yam cuttings mentioned here, in an incantation recited by the hunter to prevent the Gidigidi from killing him, were included in the sacrifice he had offered.

ọmọ on   bọ   iwo ti   on yọ   s(i)-ilẹ   ni ile   fun iranti
child hers sacrifice:to horn that she pull:out to-ground at house for remembrance

on   n(i)-igba-ti awọn ba   fẹ   bọ   ori wọn.   Lati igba-na ni
hers at-time-that they should want sacrifice:to head theirs. From time-the be

awọn ọmọ rẹ ti   ma   nbọ   iwo ti nwọn ba   nṣe
those child hers have (continuative) sacrificing:to horn that they should making

ọdun wọn; awọn ti ima   bọ   iwo bayi ni a   ma
year their; those that (continuative) sacrifice:to horn thus be we (continuative)

npe   ti a si nki   ni ọmọ   Ẹfọn   titi di   oni yi.
calling that we and greeting at "child (of) Buffalo" until become today this.

        Ifa ni o ri ire   obinrin kan fun e-l(i)-eyi,   ṣugbọn ki
        Ifa say he see goodness (of) woman one for one:who-be-this, but   should

a ru-(ẹ)bọ   ki obinrin na ma ba   ku n(i)-igba-ti ọmọ rẹ ba
we offer-sacrifice that woman the not should die at-time-that child her should

di   meji; ki o ma ba   ku tan ki iyale   rẹ na ma ba
become two; that she not should die finish that senior:wife her also not should

ku pẹlu;   ki ọkọ   na ma ba   gbe ai-san   ti
die together:with (her); that husband also not should carry not-be:better from

oko wa s(i)-ile ki o ma ba   ku tan ki a ma wi-pe   aya rẹ
farm come to-house that he not should die finish that we not speak-that wife his

ọrun ni o mu   lọ. Ki   a ṣọ-(a)ra   ki a ma f(i)-inu   han
sky be she take (him) go. Should we watch-body that we not take-belly appear

obinrin ni ohun kan ti a nfẹ   ṣe, ki aṣiri   ẹni ti itori   bẹ
woman at thing one that we wanting do, that secret (of) person from because so

tu.
loosen.

QSA MEJI - 1

      Koko de   oju   orokun o pin, ọna de   ori   apata po-ruru
      "Knot arrive face (of) knee he end; road arrive head (of) rock turn-confused"

a da fun Yẹwẹrẹ ni-(ọ)jọ ti o ma   na Ijẹgbẹ ati Ejegbo, nwọn
who cast for Worthless at-day that he (continuative) whip Ijẹgbẹ and Ejegbo, they

ni ki   o ma na nwọn o ni on yio na wọn o si na wọn, n(i)-igba-
say should he not whip them, he say he will whip them he and whip them; at-time-

ti o pada de   ile o ba gbogbo awọn ara   ile rẹ ni ibu-
that he return arrive house he meet all   those people (of) house his at lying-

(i)lẹ   ai-san   o si tọ   awọn babalawo lọ, nwọn ni tani
ground (of) not-be:better he and approach those diviner   go, they say who

Yẹwẹrẹ ba   ja? Nwọn ni afi   bi o ba   ru-(ẹ)bọ   ni o
Worthless join (them) fight? They say unless if he should offer-sacrifice be he

sacrifice with them to the horn that she had pulled off and left at home as a remembrance of her when they might want to sacrifice to their heads. From that
time on, her children have continued to sacrifice to the horn when they perform
their annual festival. Those who sacrifice to horns in this way are the ones that
we call and greet as "Children of Buffalo"[8] until this very day.

Ifa says he sees the blessing of a woman for this person, but that we should
sacrifice, lest the woman die when her children reach two in number; lest she
die and lest her senior wife die with her; lest her husband bring illness home
from the farm; and lest he die and it be said that his wife has taken him away to
heaven. We should be careful not to reveal secrets to a woman[9] regarding something we want to do, lest, through this our secrets be made public.

---

8. According to the informants, this is a sib or lineage name (orilę) in Ifę
whose origin is thus explained. However, a variant of this myth recorded at
Mękǫ, in which a Buffalo (ęfǫn) appears in place of the Gidigidi, identifies the
"Child of Buffalo" as Ǫya, the Goddess of the Niger River and the principal wife
of the God of Thunder. This variant explains why the worshipers or "children"
of Ǫya sacrifice to buffalo horns, and why Ǫya has the praise name Iyansan or
Yansan. Probably this verse also refers to the worshipers of Ǫya, and Gidigidi
is a praise name for Buffalo. Cf. n. 1. Cf. also the versions recorded by Idewu
(1956: 22-25); Danford and Fuja (1960: 7-10); the Walkers (1961: 11-16); and
Fuja (1962: 77-82) in which the animal is identified as a hind or a deer.

9. Cf. verse 18-7.

---

154 - 1

"Knot reaches the knee and ends;[1] road reaches the top of a rock and is lost"[2]
was the one who cast Ifa for Worthless when he was whipping Ijęgbę and Ejegbo.[3]
They said he should not whip them, but he said he would whip them, and he did
whip them. When he returned to his home, he found all his family lying ill upon
the ground. He went to the diviners and they asked with whom Worthless was
fighting. They said that unless he made a sacrifice he

---

1. The knee cap is the only "knot" to be found on the human body.
2. A path may be difficult to follow where it crosses a rock.
3. The meaning of these two names is obscure. Informants suggested that
the latter may mean "face of sore" (oju egbo), and the former may refer to a group
which formerly collected tribute from the people of Ifę for the king.

fi   le   şẹ-(o)gun.   O ru   ẹiyẹ-(i)le   meji, obi mẹsan, abo-
take (them) be:able make-war. He offer bird-(of)-house two, kola nine,   female-

(a)diẹ kan, ati akikọ-(a)diẹ kan. Nwọn wa   ki   Ifa fun   pe:
chicken one, and cock-chicken one. They come recite Ifa for (him) that:

A le   iku   lọ l(i)-ode   ilẹ   yi
"We chase death go at-outside (of) ground this,

Yẹwẹrẹ   iwọ l(i)-o na-(I)jẹgbẹ na Ejegbo rẹ pẹlu
"Worthless you be-who whip-Ijẹgbẹ whip Ejegbo his together:with (him).

A le   arun   lọ l(i)-ode   ilẹ   yi   l(i)-oni
"We chase disease go at-outside (of) ground this at-today,

Yẹwẹrẹ   iwọ l(i)-o na-(I)jẹgbẹ n(a)-Ejegbo rẹ mọ
"Worthless you be-who whip-Ijẹgbẹ whip-Ejegbo his together:with (him),

Yẹwẹrẹ.
Worthless."

Ifa ni ki   ẹni-kan   şọ-(a)ra   ki o ma ja   nitori-ti   bi o
Ifa say should person-one watch-body that he not fight because-that if he

ba   ja   arun   ati ai-san   yio ba   awọn ara   ile   rẹ,
should fight disease and not-be:better will meet those people (of) house his,

ki   ẹni-kan   si ru-(ẹ)bọ   pẹlu   ki awọn a-l(i)-
should person-one and offer-sacrifice together:with (it) that those one:who-be-

ai-san   ile   rẹ ba   le   dide ni ibu-(i)lẹ   nitori-ti
not-be:better (of) house his should be:able arise at lying-ground because-that

ẹbura ni nwọn şẹ.
deity be they offend.

_____

IRẸTẸ ỌKANRAN - 1

Ojẹrẹ   awo   ori   igba   a   da   fun ẹrunlọjọ ẹranko ni ọjọ
New:leaf secret (of) head (of) eggplant who cast for 165   animal at day

ti a-b(i)-awun   nlọ ji ilu   ẹkun   gbe.   A   ni ki
that One:who-like-Miser going steal drum (of) Leopard take (it). They say should

ẹrunlọjọ ẹranko ru-(ẹ)bọ   nitori   a-l(i)-a-ko-wa-ba,
165   animal offer-sacrifice because (of) one:who-be-who-gather-come-meet,

ki nwọn ma ba   ri a-l(i)-a-ko-wa-ba   ni ọdun yi,   ẹdan
that they not should see one:who-be-who-gather-come-meet at year this, (of) rod

eku (ọ)k(an)-ọkan ati ọtọtalugba,   gbogbo ẹranko ru-(ẹ)bọ.
(of) rat one-one   and 260   (cowries); all   animal offer-sacrifice.

Ko l(i)-ọjọ ko l(i)-oşu   ọba   ọrun ran-(i)şẹ   si awọn ẹrunlọjọ
Not at-day not at-month, king (of) sky send-message to those 165

would not be able to conquer them. He offered two pigeons, nine kola nuts, one hen, and one cock. They came and recited Ifa for him as follows:

"We chase Death out of town;
"Worthless, you are the one who is whipping Ijẹgbẹ and also his
    Ejegbo.
"We chase Disease out of town today;
"Worthless, you are the one who is whipping Ijẹgbẹ and also his
    Ejegbo, Worthless."

Ifa says someone should be careful not to fight, because if he should get into a fight, disease and illness will afflict his family; and someone should sacrifice so that those who are ill in his house may be able to get up from where they are lying down because they have offended a deity.

---

166 - 1

"Leaf sprouts,"[1] the diviner of the top of Eggplant was the one who cast Ifa for the 165 kinds of animals[2] on the day that Tortoise[3] was going to steal Leopard's drum. They said that the 165 animals should sacrifice one stick of rats[4] each and 0.78 pence because of a troublemaker,[5] so that they might not see a troublemaker during that year. All the animals sacrificed.

Soon afterward the King of the Sky sent word to the 165 kinds of

---

1. The new leaves or leaf-shoots of any plant.

2. Cf. n. 3, verse 18-4.

3. The real word for Tortoise is ajapa, but he is usually referred to by the name "Miser" (awun, ahun) or one of its derivatives: a-b(i)-awun, a-b(i)-ahun. From Tortoise's stinginess, the women who do petty trading for a very small margin of profit are known as a-l(i)-ajapa, "those who are tortoise."

4. Dried rats and fish are sold impaled on small sticks.

5. A person who brings trouble to someone who doesn't deserve it. The reference is to Tortoise, the trickster of Yoruba folk tales, and the animal counterpart of Eshu, the divine trickster and troublemaker.

ẹranko pe   ki   nwọn wa   ba   on ṣe-(i)re   ki   nwọn si gbe   ilu
animal that should they come join him make-play should they and carry drum

wọn dani; gbogbo ẹranko si se   ilu, n(i)-igba-ti nwọn nlọ,   a-b(i)-
their hold; all   animal and cover drum at-time-that they going, One:who-like-

awun ko ri awọ se   ilu, o ba ilu   ẹkun   n(i)-ibi-ti   o gbe
Miser not see hide cover drum, he meet drum (of) Leopard at-place-that he carry

e si ni oju   ọna ti ẹkun   si lọ wẹ; a-b(i)-awun   ji   ilu
it to at eye (of) road, that Leopard and go wash; One:who-like-Miser steal drum

yi o si gbe   lọ si ọdọ   ọba   ọrun; ilu yi dara   pupọ
this he and carry (it) go to presence (of) king (of) sky; drum this be:good much

o si dun   ju   awọn ilu miran lọ; n(i)-igba-ti awun nlu   ilu
it and be:sweet surpass those drum other go; at-time-that Miser beating drum

yi ni ọdọ   ọba   ọrun ẹnu   ya   awọn ẹranko iy(i)-o-ku
this at presence (of) king (of) sky mouth open those animal this-which-remain

pupọ pe nibo ni awun ti ri iru   ilu   bayi? N(i)-igba-ti ẹkun
much that where be Miser have see kind (of) drum thus? At-time-that Leopard

wa   ilu rẹ titi ti ko ri,   o duro de   awọn ẹranko-(i)y(i)-o-
seek drum his until that not see (it), he stand wait:for those animal-this-which-

ku   ni oju   ọna pe nwọn fẹrẹ   de   na, on yio si ri ẹni-ti
remain at face (of) road that they almost arrive the, he will and see person-that

o ji   on ni ilu   gbe.
he steal him at drum carry (it).

    N(i)-igba-ti gbogbo awọn ẹranko da-(o)ri ti   nwọn mbọ,   erin   ni
    At-time-that all   those animal turn-head that they coming, Elephant be

o tete   de,   ẹkun   si bẹrẹ si kọ-(o)rin pe:
he quickly arrive, Leopard and begin to sing-song that:

    Ọba d(a)-ijọ   are Arekenjan
    "King cause-day (of) play, Arekenjan;

    Ọba d(a)-ijọ   are Arekenjan
    "King cause-day (of) play, Arekenjan;

    K(i)-a   ma   lu k(i)-a   ma   fọn Arekenjan
    "Should-we (continuative) beat, should-we (continuative) blow, Arekenjan.

    Mo r(e)-odo la-wẹ   Arekenjan
    "I   go-river go-wash, Arekenjan;

    E! tete ki n-de   Arekenjan
    "E! quickly that I-arrive, Arekenjan;

    E! tete   ki (e)m(i)-bọ Arekenjan
    "E! quickly that I-come,   Arekenjan.

    Nwọn ma   gbe-(i)lu   lọ Arekenjan
    "They (continuative) carry-drum go, Arekenjan;

    Lu ti-rẹ   ki (e)m(i)-gbọ Arekenjan
    "Beat that-(of)-yours that I-hear,   Arekenjan;

animals that they should come for a dance, and that they should bring their
drums with them. All the animals put new heads on their drums; and when they
were going, Tortoise, who did not find leather with which to cover his drum,
found Leopard's drum on the road where he had left it when he went to wash.
Tortoise stole this drum and took it to the home of the King of the Sky. This
drum was very fine and it sounded better than all the other drums. When Tortoise was beating this drum for the King of the Sky, the other animals gaped in
amazement, wondering where Tortoise had found such a drum. When Leopard
had looked for his drum for a long time without finding it, he waited for the other
animals on the road on which they would soon return, to see who it was that had
stolen his drum.

When all the animals started back, Elephant came first, and Leopard began
to sing:

"The king set the day for a dance, Arekenjan;[6]
"The king set the day for a dance, Arekenjan;
"We should beat our drums, we should blow our trumpets, Arekenjan.
"I went to the river to wash, Arekenjan;
"E! Quickly did I return, Arekenjan;
"E! Quickly did I come back, Arekenjan.
"They took my drum away, Arekenjan;
"Beat yours that I may hear it, Arekenjan;

---

6. Arekenjan has no meaning but is added as the refrain.

Lu   ti-rẹ   ki   (e)m(i)-mọ Arekenjan
"Beat that-(of)-yours that I-know,   Arekenjan.

O di   bombokunbo Arekenjan
"It becomes bombokunbo, Arekenjan;

O ma   di   bombokunbo Arekenjan
"It (continuative) becomes bombokunbo, Arekenjan;

Ilu   mi kọ yi ni Arekenjan
"Drum my not this be, Arekenjan;

Kọja k(i)-o   ma   lọ Arekenjan
"Pass should-you (continuative) go, Arekenjan."

Bayi ni erin   kọja ti o si duro ni apa-kan, ti efọn de   ti
Thus be Elephant pass that he and stand at arm-one, that Buffalo arrive that

ẹkun   si tun kọ-(o)rin b(i)-akan-na, ti on na si tun lu ilu   ti-rẹ,
Leopard and then sing-song like-one-the, that he also and then beat drum that-

rẹ,   ti ẹkun   si tun sọ   fun   pe ki   o kọja ki   o
(of)-his, that Leopard and then speak for (him) that should he pass should he

 ma   lọ ti on na si tun duro ni ẹgbẹ kan; bayi ni gbogbo awọn
(continuative) go that he also and then stand at side one; thus be all   those

ẹranko nde   ti nwọn si nlu   ilu   wọn ti nwọn nkọja ti   nwọn si
animal arriving that they and beating drum their that they passing that they and

nduro   ni ẹgbẹ kan titi o fi   kan awun; n(i)-igba-ti awun yọ   ni awun
standing at side one until it take touch Miser; at-time-that Miser appear be Miser

ti mọ pe on ni   ẹkun   nduro de,   bi ẹkun   si ti ri
have know that he be (whom) Leopard standing wait:for; as Leopard and have see

ilu   rẹ ni o si ti mọ pe ti   on ni ilu   ti awun gbe kọ si
drum his be he and have know that that (of) his be drum that Miser take hang to

ọrun rẹ bi ẹkun   si ti mu awun ti o bẹrẹ si lu   ti o si
neck his; as Leopard and have take Miser that he begin to beat (him) that he and

nha   ni ekanna, ni gbogbo awọn ẹranko pẹlu   nfẹ
scratching (him) at claw, be all   those animal together:with (him) wanting

lu   awun, ṣugbọn bi o ti ni ki on jan   mọ-(i)lẹ   ni awun
beat Miser, but   as he have say that he dash (him) against-ground be Miser

yọ ni ọwọ rẹ o si bọ   s(i)-inu   igbo o si sa lọ. Oju   ekanna
slip at hand his he and enter to-belly (of) forest he and run go. Face (of) claw

    ẹkun   igba-na ni o wa l(i)-ara   awun titi di   oni yi.
(of) Leopard (of) time-the be it exist at-body (of) Miser until become today this.

Ifa ni ọmọ-(ọ)kunrin kukuru pupa kan yio ṣe ohun kan, ki   o ma ba
Ifa say child-man   short red one will do thing one, should he not should

ti ibẹ fi ẹsẹ ko   ohun bu(ru)-buru wa ile ki o ma ba
from there take foot gather thing be:bad-be:bad come house that it not should

ti   mbura si ọrọ na. Ki   agbajọ   awọn enia si ru-(ẹ)bọ
become swearing to word the. Should crowd (of) those people and offer-sacrifice

"Beat yours that I may recognize it, Arekenjan.
"It becomes "bombokunbo,"[7] Arekenjan;
"It is becoming "bombokunbo," Arekenjan;
"This is not my drum, Arekenjan;
"Pass by, you may go on, Arekenjan."

Thus Elephant passed by and waited on one side. Buffalo arrived and Leopard sang the same song, and Buffalo also beat his drum. Leopard told him that he should pass by, and he also stood aside. In this way all the animals arrived, beat their drums, passed by, and stood aside until it became the turn of Tortoise. When Tortoise appeared, he knew that he was the one for whom Leopard was waiting; and when Leopard saw his drum, he knew that it was his own drum that Tortoise had hanging from his neck. And as Leopard seized Tortoise and began to beat him and to scratch him with his claws, all the animals wanted to help him beat Tortoise; but when Leopard said that he was going to dash him to the ground, Tortoise slipped from his hand, escaped into the forest, and ran away. The marks made by Leopard's claws at that time are to be seen on Tortoise's body until this very day."[8]

Ifa says that a short, reddish boy will do something; but he should be careful not to bring home something evil that will make it necessary to take an oath about it. And a crowd of people should sacrifice

---

7. The sound of the drum rhythm.

8. This verse thus explains the marks on Tortoise's shell. For a different explanation see verse 168-1.

pẹlu   ki   nwọn tun şọ-(a)ra   ki   nwọn ma ba   ri   a-
together:with (him) should they then watch-body that they not should see one:who-

l(i)-a-ko-wa-ba   ti   yio mu wọn şe   bi   ẹni-pe   nwọn yio
be-who-gather-come-meet that will take them make like person-that they will

mu   aje   si ohun kan ti   ibi yio ti   ibẹ wọ-(i)le.
drink ordeal to thing one that evil will from there enter-house.

IRẸTẸ - (I)ROSUN - 1

Oropa niga, a ja   tu-(e)ruku   ẹfọn,   eruku gba-gba   ori
"Oropa Niga; to fight loosen-dust (of) Buffalo; dust dry-dry (of) head (of)

ọta   a   da fun ẹkun   ti   nlọ mu ilẹ   ile   ti   nwọn ni
quartz" who cast for Leopard that (he) going take ground (of) house that they say

ki   o ru-(ẹ)bọ   ki   o ma ba   ş(e)-owo   fun olobo
should he offer-sacrifice that he not should make-transaction for another:person

[ori-o-l(i)-ori]   j(ẹ)-ere ki a   ma ba   bẹ   ọwẹ
[head-(of)-one:who-has-head] eat-gain, that they not should request cooperative:

         ẹni-ti   yio ju   ti.   Nwọn ni ki   o ru ọkẹ
work (of) person-that will surpass that (of his). They say should he offer bag (of)

ẹsẹ,   ẹiyẹ-(i)le   mẹrin, ki   o gbe lọ si koto   akurọ.
corn:skin, bird-(of)-house four, should he carry go to bank (of) waterside:garden.

ẹkun   ko ru   nitori-ti   o gbẹkẹle egun   apa rẹ.
Leopard not offer because-that he rely:on bone (of) arm his.

Ni ọjọ kan ẹkun,   obukọ, ati ewurẹ nlọ mu ilẹ   ile, n(i)-
At day one Leopard, He:goat, and She:goat going take ground (of) house; at-

igba-ti obukọ de   ibi   ilẹ,   o şan ilẹ   na o si pada   wa
time-that He:goat arrive place (of) ground, he clear ground the he and return come

si ile rẹ; n(i)-igba-ti o di   ọjọ-(e)keji ẹkun   wa   si ibi   ilẹ
to house his; at-time-that it become day-second Leopard come to place (of) ground

na n(i)-igba-ti o de   ibẹ   ti   o ri pe ẹni-kan   ti şan ilẹ   na
the at-time-that he arrive there that he see that person-one have clear ground the

o ni Ta-ni   ba mi şan ilẹ   mi o si tu   yẹpẹ s(i)-ilẹ o si
he say "Who-be (it) for me clear ground my?" he and loosen dirt to-ground he and

pada   lọ si ile   rẹ; n(i)-igba-ti o di   ọjọ-(e)keji obukọ tun pada
return go to house his; at-time-that it become day-second He:goat then return

wa   si ibi   ilẹ yi o si ri pe nwọn ti   tu   yẹpẹ s(i)-ilẹ
come to place (of) ground this he and see that they have loosen dirt to-ground

o si da-(o)hun pe Ta-ni   ba mi tu   yẹpẹ   ile   mi o na
he and break-voice that "Who-be (it) for me loosen dirt (of) house my?" he also

along with this boy, and they should also be careful, lest they meet a trouble-maker who will cause them to take a trial by ordeal concerning something by means of which evil will enter their house.

---

167 - 1

"Oropa Niga;[1] to fight and stir up dust like Buffalo;[2] parched dust on top of rock" was the one who cast Ifa for Leopard when he was going to take land for a new house. They said that he should make a sacrifice so that someone else should not enjoy the fruits of his labor,[3] and so that someone should not call upon the help of another person in order to get the best of him.[4] They said he should offer a bag of corn-skins[5] and four pigeons, and that he should take the sacrifice to a garden by the waterside. Leopard did not sacrifice, because he depended on the strength of his own arms.

One day Leopard, Goat, and She-goat were going to take land on which to build a new house. When Goat arrived at the piece of land, he cleared the ground and he returned home. On the following day Leopard came to the same piece of land. When he arrived, he found that someone had cleared the ground, and he said, "Who has cleared my land for me?" He dug the ground to make mud for the walls, and then went home. The next day Goat came to this piece of land. He saw that someone had broken the ground, and he asked, "Who has dug the ground for my house for me?" He

---

1. This was interpreted as a name that might be analyzed as "Poison kills Niga" (Oro-pa Niga), with Niga as an unidentified name.

2. Cf. verse 153-1.

3. This refers to the fact that in the tale Goat is the one who lives in the house that Leopard has helped to build.

4. This refers to the fact that in the tale Goat calls upon a hunter's aid to drive Leopard away.

5. The skins of the kernels of corn, taken from the mortar after soaked corn has been pounded.

si bẹrẹ si mọ ogiri o si mọ ile   ogiri kan o si pada lọ s(i)-ile
and begin to build wall he and build layer (of) wall one he and return go to-house

rẹ; n(i)-igba-ti o di   ọjọ-(e)keji ẹkun   lọ si ibi   ilẹ   yi n(i)-
his; at-time-that it become day-second Leopard go to place (of) ground this at-

igba-ti   o de   ibẹ o ba ti ẹni-kan   ti mọ ile   ogiri kan
time-that he arrive there he meet that person-one have build layer (of) wall one

o si da-(o)hun   pe Ta-ni   mọ ile   kan n(i)-inu   ile   ogiri
he and break-voice that "Who-be (it) build layer one at-belly (of) layer (of) wall

    ile   mi? O na si mọ ile   ogiri-(e)keji o si pada lọ si
(of) house my?" He also and build layer (of) wall-second he and return go to

ile; n(i)-igba-ti o di   ọjọ-(e)keji ti obukọ de   ibẹ o ri ti
house; at-time-that it become day-second that He:goat arrive there he see that

nwọn ti mọ ile-(e)keji le ile   na l(i)-ori o si bere pe Ta-ni
they have build layer-second upon layer the at-head he and ask that "Who-be (it)

mọ ile-(e)keji   le ile   mi?
build layer-second upon layer my?"

    Bayi ni nwọn sẹ mọ ogiri titi o fi   pa-(o)ri ti o to   ati kọ   ile
    Thus be they do build wall until it take kill-head that it equal to build house

le   ogiri na l(i)-ori. Obukọ si mu-(a)ra o lọ pa ẹkẹ   o gbe ka-
upon wall the at-head. He:goat and take-body he go kill rafter he carry against-

(i)lẹ si ibi   ile   na n(i)-igba-ti o di   ọjọ-(e)keji ẹkun   na
ground to place (of) house the, at-time-that it become day-second Leopard also

lọ pa okun o si gbe   wa si ibi   ile   na n(i)-igba-ti o de
go kill rope he and carry (it) come to place (of) house the, at-time-that he arrive

ibẹ o ba ti ẹni-kan   ti pa ẹkẹ si ibi   ile   na o si da-
there he meet that person-one have kill rafter to place (of) house the he and break-

(o)hun pe Ta-ni   ba mi pa ẹkẹ wa   si ibi   ile   mi? o si
voice that "Who-be (it) for me kill rafter come to place (of) house my?" he and

gbe okun na s(i)-ilẹ   o si lọ si ile   rẹ; n(i)-igba-ti o di   ọjọ-(e)keji
take rope the to-ground he and go to house his; at-time-that it become day-second

obukọ mu-(a)ra o wa   si ibi   ile   na lati   wa   ro   o si
He:goat take-body he come to place (of) house the in:order:to come roof (it) he and

ba   okun ni ibẹ, o si bere pe Ta-ni   ba on wa   gbe   okun si
meet rope at there, he and ask that "Who-be (it) for him come carry rope to

ibi   ile   on o si bẹrẹ si ro ile   o ro ile   yi tan o si
place (of) house his" he and begin to roof house he roof house this finish he and

lọ si ile;   n(i)-igba-ti o di   ọjọ-(e)keji ẹkun   si wa   si ibẹ lati
go to house; at-time-that it become day-second Leopard and come to there in:

        wa   ro ile   ṣugbọn o ba ti ẹlomiran   ti ro ile,
order:to come roof house but   he meet that another:person have roof house,

o si wi-pe   Ta-ni   o wa ba on ro ile   on? o si bẹrẹ
he and speak-that "Who-be (it) who come for him roof house his?" he and begin

began to build the walls; he built one layer and then went home. Next day Leopard
went to this piece of land. When he arrived, he found that someone had built one
layer of the walls, and he asked, "Who has built one of the layers of the walls of
my house for me?" Then he built the second layer of the walls and went home.
The next day, when Goat came, he found that a second layer had been built upon
that which he had made, and he asked, "Who built another layer for me upon the
one that I built?"

In this way they built the walls until they were completed, and ready to be
roofed. Goat got ready, and he went and cut rafters; and he carried them back to
the place where the house was. On the following day Leopard went to cut ropes,
and he brought them to the site of the house. When he arrived, he found that
someone had brought rafters to the site, and he asked, "Who has brought rafters
to the site of my house for me?" He put the ropes down and went home. The next
day Goat got ready and went to the house to erect the rafters. He found the ropes
there, and asked, "Who has brought ropes to the site of my house for me?" He
began to erect the rafters, and when he had finished doing this he went home.
Next day Leopard came there to erect the rafters, but he found that someone
else had done it. He asked, "Who has erected the rafters of my house for me?"
He began to

si rọ   ni ewe o si rọ   tan.   N(i)-igba-ti o di   ọjọ-(e)keji l(i)-
to thatch (it) at leaf he and thatch finish. At-time-that it become day-second at-

ẹhin   eyi ti obukọ fẹ wa   rọ   ile   ni gbodogi o ba   ti ẹni-
back (of) this that He:goat want come thatch house at gbodogi he meet that person-

kan ti   rọ   ni gbodogi o si bere pe Ta-ni   wa   ba on rọ   ile
one have thatch at gbodogi he and ask that "Who-be (it) come for him thatch house

on ni gbodogi? O ni l(i)-ọla   ni on yio ko   wa   si ile   on.
his at gbodogi?" He say at-tomorrow be he will gather come to house his.

     N(i)-igba-ti o di   ọjọ-(e)keji bi o ti   mbọ   ni o pade ẹkun
     At-time-that it become day-second as he have coming be he meet Leopard

ni ọna ti on na nfẹ   ko   s(i)-ile rẹ pẹlu.   Ẹkun
at road that he also wanting gather to-house his together:with (him). Leopard

bere l(i)-ọwọ obukọ pe Kin-ni o nwa   ni ile on? Obukọ na
ask at-hand (of) He:goat that "What-be he seeking at house his?" He:goat also

bere l(i)-ọwọ   ẹkun   pe Kin-ni o nwa   ni ile   on? Nwọn si fẹ
ask at-hand (of) Leopard that "What-be he seeking at house his?" They and want

bẹrẹ si lati   ja şugbọn ewurẹ ni ki   nwọn ma ja şugbọn ki
begin to in:order:to fight but She:goat say should they not fight but   should

nwọn jọ   jumọ   ma   gbe   ile   na.
they be:together together (continuative) dwell:at house the.

     Bayi ni nwọn jọ   bẹrẹ si jọ   gbe   ile titi o fi   di
     Thus be they together begin to together dwell:at house until it take become

ọjọ kan ti obukọ ri ti ẹkun   gbe oku   ẹranko kan wọ-(i)le
day one that He:goat see that Leopard carry corpse (of) animal one enter-house,

şugbọn n(i)-igba-ti o wo   o ri pe oku   baba on ni ẹkun
but   at-time-that he look:at (it) he see that corpse (of) father his be Leopard

pa ti o si gbe wa si ile. N(i)-igba-ti o di   ọjọ-(e)keji o tun
kill that he and carry come to house. At-time-that it become day-second he then

ri pe ẹkun   tun gbe oku   iya   on wa si ile, o wa   mu-
see that Leopard then carry corpse (of) mother his come to house; he come take-

(a)ra o tọ   ọ-l(i)-ọdẹ   lọ o bẹ   pe ki   o ba on
body he approach one:who-be-hunter go he request (him) that should he for him

pa ẹkun   kan pe bi o ba   le   ba on pa ẹkun   kan on yio fun
kill leopard one that if he should be:able for him kill leopard one he will give (him)

ni ohun kan, ọdẹ yi si mu-(a)ra o si ba obukọ pa ẹkun   kan şugbọn
at thing one; hunter this and take-body he and join He:goat kill leopard one but

n(i)-igba-ti ẹkun   pade obukọ l(i)-ọna ti o ru   oku   ẹkun
at-time-that Leopard meet He:goat at-road that he carry corpse (of) leopard,

ẹru ba   ẹkun   o si bere l(i)-ọwọ   obukọ pe bawo ni o ti   şe
fear meet Leopard he and ask at-hand (of) He:goat that how be he have make

le   pa ẹkun? Obukọ sọ   fun ẹkun   pe on ni akaraba a-wo-pa
be:able kill leopard? He:goat speak for Leopard that he have akaraba to-look:at-kill

thatch the roof with leaves, and he finished thatching it. On the day after this, when Goat came to thatch the house with gbodogi leaves,[6] he found that someone had thatched it with gbodogi and he asked, "Who came and thatched my house with gbodogi leaves for me?" He said, "Tomorrow I will move to my new house."

On the following day, as he was coming, Goat met Leopard on the road, also moving to the new house. Leopard asked Goat, "What are you doing at my house?" And Goat asked Leopard, "What are you doing at my house?" They were about to start fighting, but She-goat said that they should not fight, but that they should live in the house together.

So they began to live together in the house, until one day Goat saw that Leopard had brought home the body of a dead animal. But when he looked at it more closely, he saw that it was the body of his own father that Leopard had killed and brought home to eat. The next day he saw Leopard bring home the body of his mother. Goat got ready and went to see a hunter. He asked him to kill a leopard for him, promising that if he did so, he would give him something. The hunter got ready and killed a leopard for Goat, but when Leopard met Goat on the road carrying the body of the dead leopard, Leopard was frightened, and he asked Goat how he had been able to kill a leopard. Goat told Leopard that he had the evil eye[7]

---

6. A broad leaf (Sarcophrynium spp.) which is used in Ifę for thatching.

7. Akaraba is any kind of medicine which, when pointed at the victim, roots him to one spot so that he cannot move. A-wo-pa is a particular type of this category in which the owner has only to look at his victim in order to kill him.

pe   gbogbo ohun ti   on ba   wo   (ohu)n-kan na ni lati   ku. N(i)-
that all   things that he should look:at, thing-one   the be in:order:to die. At-

igba-ti   ẹkun   gbọ eyi o bẹ si igbo o si sa lọ pata-pata
time-that Leopard hear this he leap to forest he and run go completely-completely

ko si tun pada wa   si ile   na mọ.   Bayi ni obukọ di   o-
not and then return come to house the again. Thus be He:goat become one:who-

n(i)-ile   on ati ewurẹ iyawo   rẹ.
has-house his and She:goat junior:wife his.

        Ifa ni ki ọ-l(i)-ọdẹ   kan ki   o ru-(ẹ)bọ   ki o ma
        Ifa say that one:who-be-hunter one should he offer-sacrifice that he not

ba   pa enia ni ọdun yi; ati pe ẹni-kan   nlọ mu ilẹ   ile
should kill person at year this; and that person-one going take ground (of) house

tabi oko ki   o ru-(ẹ)bọ   ki ẹni-kan   ma ba   bẹ   o-
or   farm should he offer-sacrifice that person-one not should request one:who-

l(i)-ogun   ti   ara wọn ki nwọn ma ba   ri   ija   ogun
has-medicine against body their, that they not should see (a) fight (of) medicine

l(i)-ori ile.   Ọmọde   kan wa n(i)-ibẹ ti a nfi   oju   ọmọde
at-head (of) house. Young:child one exist at-there that we taking eye (of) young:

     wo,   ki   a ma-ṣe fi oju   ọmọde   wo   ọmọ na
child look:at (him); should we not-do take eye (of) young:child look:at child the

nitori-ti   o ni baba n(i)-isalẹ; bi a ba   fi   oju   ọmọde
because-that he have father at-bottom; if we should take eye (of) young:child

wo,   baba-(i)salẹ   rẹ yio fi ori mu-(i)lẹ   yio si
look:at (him), father-(of)-bottom his will take head sink:into-ground will and

fẹrẹ   run   gbogbo enia tan   nitori   ọrọ   ilẹ   ile tabi
almost destroy all   people finish because (of) word (of) ground (of) house or

oko, yi.
farm this.

IRẸTẸ - (Ọ)WỌNRIN - 1

A-l(i)-adin   ko si n(i)-ile kannakanna a gb(e)-ebu
"One:who-have-palm:kernel:oil not be at-house crow   it dwell:at-palm:

                   a   da fun A-b(i)-ahun   Ajapa ti o ma
kernel:oil:factory" who cast for One:who-like-Miser Tortoise that he (continua-

     ba wọn na-(ọ)ja-toku,   nwọn ni ki   o ru-(ẹ)bọ   ki
tive) join them spend-goods-(of)-Toku; they say should he offer-sacrifice that

awo   rẹ ma ba   bajẹ le   e l(i)-ori; ẹiyẹ-(i)le   meji, egbejila
secret his not should spoil upon him at-head; bird-(of)-house two,   2400 (cowries)

so that everything that he looked at had to die. When Leopard heard this he
jumped into the forest and ran away forever; he did not return to the house any
more. Thus Goat and his wife, She-goat, came to own their own house.[8]

Ifa says that a hunter should make a sacrifice so that he will not kill a
human being during this year; and that someone who is going to take land for a
new house or a new farm should make a sacrifice lest someone ask a medicine
man to make medicine against him;[9] and so that he will not get into a fight with
medicine over the house. And there is a child whom we are looking upon as only
a child;[10] we should not treat him as a child because he has a father who stands
behind him. If we should treat him as a child, his father behind him will under-
mine us and almost completely destroy all our family because of the land for
this house or this farm.

---

8. This verse explains why leopards live in the forest, and goats live near
houses. Compare the version of this tale recorded by Frobenius (1926: 248-250).
9. This refers to Goat's boasting of having the evil eye after having been
helped by the hunter. The first prediction refers to the killing of the leopard.
10. This refers to Goat, who, although weaker than Leopard, overcame him
through the help of the hunter.

---

168 - 1

"When the palm kernel oil maker is not at home, crows live in his work-
shop"[1] was the one who cast Ifa for Tortoise, the Miser,[2] when he was trading
at Toku.[3] They said he should make a sacrifice so that his secret would not be
revealed. Two pigeons, seven pence two oninis,

---

1. Ebu is the place where palm kernel oil is made; it must be located outside of town, and when no one is there, crows come to eat what is left.
2. See n. 3, verse 166-1.
3. Informants were unable to clarify the meaning of Toku.

ati akikọ ti   o jẹ pe ko ni jẹ-ki   awo   rẹ ya.   A-b(i)-awun
and cock that it eat that not be consent-that secret his split. One:who-like-Miser

ru   ẹiyẹ-(i)le   meji ati egbejila   ṣugbọn ko ru   akikọ-(a)diẹ
offer bird-(of)-house two and 2400   (cowries) but   not offer cock-chicken

pẹlu   ẹbọ   ti o ru.
together:with sacrifice that he offer.

    Ni igba lai-lai   iyan   mu l(i)-aiye o mu l(i)-ọrun, A-b(i)-awun
    At time ever-ever famine take at-earth it take at-sky,   One:who-like-Miser

wa ọna ti on yio fi   ma   jẹ-(oh)un, o wa da   ọgbọn kan
seek road that he will take (it) (continuative) eat-thing, he seek create wisdom one

o mu-(a)ra o lọ si eti   ọja   n(i)-ibi-ti   ọpẹ   kan wa ti o ni
he take-body he go to ear (of) market at-place-that palm:tree one exist that it have

iho, o sa pa-mọ   s(i)-inu rẹ, n(i)-igba-ti o di   ọrun   ọja,
hole, he run kill-against to-belly its, at-time-that it become fifth:day (of) market,

ti awọn enia pe   si ọja,   ni A-b(i)-ahun   bẹrẹ si kọ-(o)rin
that those people assemble to market, be One:who-like-Miser begin to sing-song

pe:
that:

        Ọpẹ   jo   o-n(i)-imọ   Jo   n-jo
        "Palm:tree dance one:who-have-palm:leaf, Dance I-dance;

        Ọpẹ   tarege tage   o Jo   n-jo
        "Palm:tree stagger stagger, oh, Dance I-dance;

        Ọpẹ   tarege tage   Jo   n-jo
        "Palm:tree stagger stagger, Dance I-dance.

        Ọpẹ   taṣaṣa ka-(ọ)ja   Jo   n-jo
        "Palm:tree flit   go:about-market, Dance I-dance;

        Ọpẹ   tọ biri ka-(ọ)ja   Jo   n-jo
        "Palm:tree twist turn go:about-market, Dance I-dance."

    N(i)-igba-ti A-b(i)-awun   ba   kọ orin bayi, ti nwọn ara
    At-time-that One:who-like-Miser should sing song thus, that those people

      ọja   ba   si gbọ, ti nwọn ba   si ri ọpẹ   ti o nrin
(of) market should and hear, that they   should and see palm:tree that it walking

ka   ọja,   gbogbo ọja   a   bẹ, Ahun a si ja-(o)de   kuro
go:around market, all   market they leap, Miser he and reach-outside depart

n(i)-inu   iho   ọpẹ,   o bẹrẹ si ko   ẹru ati ohun jijẹ, bayi ni
at-belly (of) hole (of) palm:tree, he begin to gather load and thing to:eat, thus be

Ahun ma   nṣe ni ọj(ọ)-ọjọ   ọja   ti o si ma
Miser (continuative) doing at day-day (of) market that he and (continuative)

nko   ohun gbogbo bi onjẹ ti ọwọ rẹ ba   te   ni ọja   ni ọr(un)-
gathering thing all   like food that hand his should alight:on at market at fifth:day-

ọrun   ọja.
fifth-day (of) market.

and a cock was the sacrifice so that his secret would not be disclosed. Tortoise offered the two pigeons and the seven pence two oninis, but he did not offer the cock with the rest of the sacrifice.

Long, long ago there was a famine on earth and in heaven. Tortoise sought a way to get something to eat, and he tried to find a clever trick. He got ready and went to the edge of the market where there was a hollow palm tree, and he hid inside it. When market day[4] arrived and people came to market, Tortoise began to sing:

"The palm tree dances, the one that has palm leaves; Dance, I dance;
"The palm tree staggers about,[5] oh; Dance, I dance;
"The palm tree staggers about; Dance, I dance.
"The palm tree flits about the market; Dance, I dance;
"The palm tree twists and turns through the market; Dance, I dance."

When Tortoise began to sing in this way, and the people in the market heard him and saw the palm tree walking about the market, the whole market broke up. Then Tortoise came out from the hollow of the palm tree and began to gather the traders' goods and things to eat. Tortoise was doing this every market day and gathering all the food that came to his hand each market day.

---

4. Market days are usually every fourth day or, according to the Yoruba system of counting, every fifth day.

5. The words "tarege tage" describe the motion of something that is staggering.

N(i)-igba-ti awọn enia ri eyi, nwọn lọ sọ fun ọba, ọba si ran
At-time-that those people see this, they go speak for king, king and send

Ogun lo si ọja lati lọ mu ohun ti o nṣe iru (ohu)n-kan yi
Ogun go to market in:order:to go take thing that it doing kind (of) thing-one this

wa; ṣugbọn n(i)-igba-ti Ogun na gbọ orin yi ti o si ri ti ọpẹ
come; but at-time-that Ogun the hear song this that he and see that palm:tree

nrin o bẹ lu igbo; bayi ni ọba ran gbogbo awọn irun-(i)mọlẹ ti
walking he leap against forest; thus be king send all those 400-Deity that

nwọn de ibẹ ti nwọn ko si le mu ohun ti o ntu wọn l(i)-
they arrive there that they not and be:able take thing that it scattering them at-

ọja yi. L(i)-ẹhin na ni Eṣu da-(o)hun ti o ni on yio mu n(i)-
market this. At-back the be Eshu break-voice that he say he will take (it); at-

igba-ti o nlọ o so igba irẹrẹ mọ-(a)ra, ṣugbọn n(i)-igba-ti o
time-that he going he tie 200 calabash against-body, but at-time-that he

de ọja ti awọn ara ọja pe ti o si gbọ orin yi
arrive market that those people (of) market assemble that he and hear song this

ti o si ri ọpẹ ti o nrin, on na pẹlu bẹ lu-
that he and see palm:tree that it walking, he also together:with (them) leap against-

(i)gbo, awọn irẹrẹ ti o so mọ-(a)ra si bẹ ku meji, awọn meji na
forest, those calabash that he tie against-body and cut remain two, those two the

si bẹrẹ si wi-pe:
and begin to speak-that:

         Pẹkẹlẹpẹ, gbagidari
         "Pẹkẹlẹpẹ, gbagidari,

         Ko jẹ bayi pẹ gbagidari
         "What eat thus be:long? gbagidari."

N(i)-igba-ti ko le mu ohun na ni ọba wa ran Ọṣanyin pe
At-time-that (he) not be:able take thing the be king come send Ọṣanyin that

ki o lọ mu (ohu)n-kan na wa, n(i)-igba-ti Ọṣanyin nlọ o mu ọgbagbara
should he go take thing-one the come, at-time-that Ọṣanyin going he take burning:

kan dani o si joko ti ina a-l(i)-akara, o fi
iron one hold he and sit:down against fire (of) one:who-have-bean:fritter, he take

ọgbagbara na bọ ina, n(i)-igba-ti o pẹ diẹ, ni o bẹrẹ si gbọ orin
burning:iron the enter fire, at-time-that it be:long small, be he begin to hear song

ti o si ri ti ọpẹ na si nrin, n(i)-igba-ti gbogbo ọja tu
that he and see that palm:tree the and walking, at-time-that all market scatter,

Ọṣanyin joko ko kuro ni ọja, ko si sa pẹlu awọn ara
Ọṣanyin sit:down not depart at market, not and run together:with those people (of)

ọja; n(i)-igba-ti Ahun ri pe ọja tu, o sọ-ka-(i)lẹ o
market; at-time-that Miser see that market scatter, he strike-against-ground he

si bẹrẹ si ko ẹru, ṣugbọn n(i)-igba-ti o de ibi a-l(i)-
and begin to gather load, but at-time-that he arrive place (of) one:who-have-

When the people saw what was happening, they told the king, and the king
sent the God of Iron to the market to bring him whatever was doing this kind of
a thing. But when the God of Iron heard the song and saw the palm tree walking,
he ran into the forest. Thus the king sent all the Four Hundred Deities, and they
went there but were not able to capture the thing that was breaking up the market.
Then Eshu said that he would capture it. When he went he tied 200 small medicine
calabashes[6] on his body, but when he reached the market and the market people
assembled, and he heard the song and saw the palm tree walking, he ran into the
forest with the others. The calabashes of medicine that he had tied on his body
fell off, except for two, and these two began to say:

> "Pękęlępę, gbagidari[7]
> "What is this? gbagidari"

When Eshu could not capture the thing, the king sent the God of Medicine to
go and bring it to him. When the God of Medicine went, he took a burning iron[8]
with him, and he sat down next to the fire of those who sold bean fritters, and he
put the burning iron into the fire. After a little while he began to hear the song
and to see the palm tree walking. When the market people scattered, the God of
Medicine remained seated and did not leave the market; he did not run away with
the market people. When Tortoise saw that the market had scattered, he came
out and began to gather up the goods, but when he came to the place where

---

6. Charms and medicine are kept in small calabashes known as iręrę or
ado.

7. These words represent the sound of the other calabashes falling to the
ground.

8. An iron rod which is heated in order to burn holes through wood.

akara,   ọkan rẹ fẹ jẹ akara,   bi o si ti   na   ọwọ ti o
bean:fritter, heart his want eat bean:fritter, as he and have stretch hand that he

mu akara   kan, Qşanyin yọ   ọgbagbara n(i)-inu   ina o si fi
take bean:fritter one, Qşanyin pull:out burning:iron at-belly (of) fire he and take

tẹ   Ahun ni idi, Ahun wa   da-(o)hun o ni ati Ahun ati igbin di
press Miser at waist, Miser come break-voice he say and Miser and snail become

ẹru   Qşanyin. Qşanyin ni Ahun ni-(ọ)kan ni o mu on ko mu igbin pẹlu
slave (of) Qşanyin. Qşanyin say Miser at-one   be he take he not take snail together:

          ati ọjọ na ni a ti   ma   nfi Ahun bọ   Qşanyin
with (him); from day the be we have (continuative) taking Miser sacrifice:to Qşanyin

titi di   oni yi.
until become today this.

     Ifa ni ki   ẹni-kan   ru-(ẹ)bọ   ki ohun ti o nfẹ   şe gẹgẹ-bi
     Ifa say should person-one offer-sacrifice that thing that he wanting do just-as

awo ma ba   bajẹ mọ   l(i)-ori ti o si ko   itiju bo o.
secret not should spoil against (him) at-head that it and gather shame cover him.

Ifa ni ẹni-kan   nfẹ   şe ohun kan, şugbọn itiju ni   yio kan   bi
Ifa say person-one wanting do thing one, but   shame be (it) will touch (him) if

ko ba   ni ẹbọ   dara-dara.
not should have sacrifice be:good-be:good.

IRẸTẸ QSA[1] - 1

     A r(i)-ọtẹ   tan a nsa,   Kolombo   bi olu   odidẹ,
     "We see-conspiracy finish we running," "Without:covering like chief (of) parrot,"

Abọn   şe   rigidi di   ẹyin,   bi abọn   ko
"Unripe:palm:fruit make bulky become (ripe) palm:fruit, if unripe:palm:fruit not

ba ku   a şe bi ẹ-l(i)-ẹyin   bi o d(i)-ọla   a
should die (it) will make like one:who-be-palm-fruit if it become-tomorrow" who

da fun akere-kokẹyọ ti işe ọmọ   Onişinkọ, nwọn ni ire   meji
cast for Frog-kokẹyọ that make child (of) Onishinkọ; they say goodness two

mbọ wa ba   ki o ru-(ẹ)bọ   ki mej(i)-(m)eji le
coming come meet (him), should he offer-sacrifice that two-two   be:able

tẹ   l(i)-ọwọ. Akere kọ   ko ru-(ẹ)bọ,   o ni igba-ti   on ba
reach (him) at-hand. Frog refuse not offer-sacrifice, he say time-that he should

ri ire   na on yio wa   ru-(ẹ)bọ;   ko si pa   Eşu rara. Nwọn
see goodness the he will come offer-sacrifice; not and appease Eshu at:all. They

---

     1. Also known as A r(i)-ọtẹ sa, meaning "We see a conspiracy and run." See
n. 1, verse 170-1.

bean fritters were sold, he wanted to eat bean fritters. And as he reached out
his hand to take a bean fritter, the God of Medicine pulled the burning iron out of
the fire and pressed it against Tortoise's body. Tortoise cried out, promising
that both Tortoise and Snail would become slaves of the God of Medicine. The
God of Medicine said he would take only Tortoise as his slave and that he would
not take Snail. From that day on, we have been using Tortoise to sacrifice to
the God of Medicine until this very day.[9]

Ifa says someone should make a sacrifice lest the thing he wants to do in
secret be revealed and cover him with shame. Ifa says someone wants to do
something, but shame will come to him if he does not make a very fine sacrifice.

---

9. This verse thus explains the markings on Tortoise's shell, and why
Tortoise is the favorite sacrificial animal of Ǫsanyin (or Ǫşanyin). For a different version of the former, see verse 166-1. Cf. the versions of this tale
recorded by Frobenius (1926: 288-289), Jacobs (1933: 41-45), Itayemi and Gurrey (1953: 79-81), and Fuja (1962: 40-43). A quite different tale (Frobenius,
1926: 40-43) ends in much the same way.

---

170 - 1

"When we have seen a conspiracy we run,"[1] "Naked, like the chief of parrots,"
and "Young palm fruit grows large and becomes ripe palm fruit; if young palm
fruit does not die it will be ripe palm fruit tomorrow"[2] were the ones who cast
Ifa for Frog Kokęyǫ,[3] who was the child of Onishinkǫ.[4] They said two blessings
were coming to him, and that he should sacrifice so that both would be able to
reach him. Frog refused to sacrifice; he said that when he saw the blessings,
he would make the sacrifice. He did not appease Eshu at all. They

---

1. This is derived from an alternative name for this figure, A r(i)-ǫtę sa,
meaning "We see a conspiracy and run."

2. The individual fruits of the oil palm are known as ęyin or ęlęyin when
ripe, and as abǫn or abǫn ęyin when they are small.

3. Akere or ake is a type of frog noted for its ability to jump long distances.
Informants were not sure of the meaning of kokęyǫ, but suggested that it might
mean "not refuse Ǫyǫ," ko-k(ǫ)-Ęyǫ.

4. Onishinkǫ was interpreted as the title of a chief at Ǫyǫ, but from the context it would seem to be a personal or praise name of the Alafin or King of Ǫyǫ.
Frog is identified in the second paragraph as the child of the King of Ǫyǫ. See
also verse 170-3.

ni ki   o ru   obukọ kan, aşọ pupa fẹrẹ-fẹrẹ   o-n(i)-ila,   ati
say should he offer he:goat one, cloth red lightly-lightly which-has-lines, and

ẹgbẹtalelọgbọn.
6600   (cowries).

    Akere jẹ ọmọ   ọba ni ode   Ọyọ, o si ni   obinrin kan ti   o
    Frog eat child (of) king at outside (of) Ọyọ, he and have woman one that she

ti   wa   ni ọdọ   rẹ fun ọjọ gigun şugbọn ko l(i)-oyun   bẹ-ni ko
have exist at presence his for day length but   not have-pregnancy so-be not

si bi-(ọ)mọ ri, ni akoko ti   nwọn ni ki   o ru-(ẹ)bọ   yi gan
and bear-child see, at time that they say should he offer-sacrifice this identical

ni aya   akere yi wa l(i)-oyun,   inu   akere si dun   pupọ.
be wife (of) Frog this come have-pregnancy, belly (of) Frog and be:sweet much.

N(i)-igba-ti o di   ọjọ ti obirin yi ma   bi, oko ni akere
At-time-that it become day that woman this (continuative) bear, farm be Frog

wa   ibẹ ni nwọn si gbe wa   sọ   fun   pe aya rẹ bi ọmọ; n(i)-
exist, there be they and take come speak for (him) that wife his bear child; at-

igba-ti   akere gbọ eyi inu rẹ dun   pupọ, o ni ki   on to   lọ si
time-that Frog hear this belly his be:sweet much, he say before he equal go to

ile   on yio lọ da   ẹmu   on na. Bi akere ti   kuro ni aba ni o-
house he will go cast palm:wine his also. As Frog have depart at barn be one:who-

n(i)-işẹ   ti   ile de   pe nwọn npe   akere ni ile   nitori-ti
have-message from house arrive that they calling Frog at house because-that

ọba ku nwọn si fẹ fi   akere j(ẹ)-oye, nitori-ti   akere ko si ni aba
king die they and want take Frog eat-title, because-that Frog not be at barn

nwọn lọ ba   akere ni inu   oko n(i)-ibi-ti   o gbe nda   ẹmu   ni
they go meet Frog at belly (of) farm at-place-that he take casting palm:wine at

ori   ọpẹ,   n(i)-igba-ti nwọn sọ   fun akere inu rẹ dun   to-
head (of) palm:tree, at-time-that they speak for Frog, belly his be:sweet equal-

bẹ gẹ ti o fi   jẹ-pe   o gbagbe pe ori   ọpẹ   ni o wa   o
so just that he take consent-that he forget that head (of) palm:tree be he exist he

si ja lu-(i)lẹ   o si fi   ẹsẹ şẹ; n(i)-igba-ti nwọn ri pe o fi
and break strike-ground he and take foot break; at-time-that they see that he take

ẹsẹ şẹ   nwọn gbe   wa s(i)-ile şugbọn t(i)-apa   t(i)-itan
foot break they carry (him) come to-house but   that-(of)-arm that-(of)-thigh

rẹ ti şẹ, n(i)-igba-ti nwọn wo   ti ko şe   wo, nwọn fi
his have break; at-time-that they heal (him) that not make heal, they take

ẹlomiran   j(ẹ)-oye na, nwọn si fi   akere s(i)-ilẹ. Lati ọjọ na ni nwọn
another:person eat-title the, they and put Frog to-ground. From day the be they

ti   ma   nwi-pe   Ayọ ayọ-ju   akere f(i)-itan şẹ."
have (continuative) speaking-that "Joy joy-surpass Frog take-thigh break."

said he should sacrifice one he-goat, one red cloth with light stripes, and one shilling seven pence eight oninis.

Frog was the child of the King of Ǫyǫ. He had one wife who had lived with him for some time but who was not pregnant and who had not yet borne a child. At the very time that they said he should make this sacrifice, the wife of Frog became pregnant, and Frog was very happy. When the day came that this woman gave birth, Frog was at his farm, and there they came to tell him that his wife had borne a child. When Frog heard this, he was very happy; he said that before he went home he would tap some palm wine. As Frog left the farm storehouse, a messenger came from home to tell him that they were calling Frog at home, because the king had died and they wanted to make Frog king. Because he was not at the store house, they went and found Frog in the middle of the farm, where he was tapping palm wine at the top of a palm tree. When they told Frog, he was so happy that he forgot that he was up in a palm tree and he fell down and broke his legs. When they saw he had broken his legs, they carried him home, but both his arms and legs were broken. When they tried to cure him and failed, they gave the title to another person, and left Frog alone. From that day on, people have been saying, "Too much happiness broke Frog's legs."[5]

---

5. This is a proverb, which is explained by this verse, as proverbs are often explained by folk tales in Africa. The verse also appears to explain the shape of the legs of this kind of frog.

Ifa ni ire   meji mbọ   wa   ba   ẹni-kan   şugbọn ki   o ru-
Ifa say goodness two coming come meet person:one but   should he offer-

(ẹ)bọ   ki   ire   na ma ba   kọja rẹ nitori   ayọ ayọ-ju;   ki
sacrifice that goodness the not should pass his because (of) joy joy-surpass; that

o ma ba   jẹ-pe   inu   ibu-(i)lẹ   ni yio ti   ma
he not should consent-that belly (of) lying:across-ground be will that (continuative)

gbọ nipa   ti   ire   na.
hear concerning that (of) goodness the.

IRẸTẸ QSA - 2

Ori   l(i)-o kun   ni a-np(e)-a-l(i)-abẹ;   odo   l(i)-okun
"Head be-it be:full (of hair) be we-calling-one:who-has-razor; river have-sea

l(i)-a np(e)-o-tu-(ọ)kọ,   bi o-tu-(ọ)kọ   ko ba   tu
be-we calling-one:who-paddles-boat; If one:who-paddles-boat not should paddle

mi ma   tu-(o)do   lororo,   ma   tu   oju   omi
I (continuative) paddle-river straight, (I) (continuative) paddle eye (of) water

şankala a   da   fun akere nwọn ni ki   iya   rẹ ma ku ni ọdun ni
anyhow," who cast for Frog they say should mother his not die at year be (it)

ki   o ma ba   da   gbese ni ọdun yi na,   nwọn ni ki   o ru   ẹiyẹ-
should he not should cause debt at year this also, they say should he offer bird-

(i)le   mẹrin, ẹgbarin,   obi mẹrin, ko ru-(ẹ)bọ.
(of)-house four, 8000 (cowries), kola four,   not offer-sacrifice.

Ko l(i)-ọjọ ko l(i)-oşu iya   akere ku n(i)-igba-ti o di   ọjọ
Not at-day not at-month mother (of) Frog die; at-time-that it become day

ti o nwu   ode   o ba   awọn Ifẹ mẹr(indilogun)-(m)ẹrindilogun ni ẹnu
that he visiting outside he meet those Ifẹ sixteen-sixteen   at mouth

Geru ni ode   Ẹnuwa, o ni "Kin-ni   şe ẹyin Ifẹ?" O ni ni ọjọ ti
(of) Geru at outside (of) Ẹnuwa, he say "What-be do you Ifẹ?" He say at day that

gbogbo nyin ti   nwa   ojo on le   şe ti ojo ki   o rọ t(i)-
all   you have seeking rain he be:able make that rain should it fall that-(of)-

oni   t(i)-ọla;   n(i)-igba-ti akere lọ tan   ọ-l(i)-ọfin   mu
today that-(of)-tomorrow; at-time-that Frog go finish, one:who-has-palace take

ẹru-(o)binrin mẹrin ati ẹru-(ọ)kunrin mẹrin, amu   ilẹkẹ meji, igba ọkẹ,
slave-woman four and slave-man   four, pot (of) bead two, 200 bag (of

      ati aşọ mẹrindilogun, o fi   ran awọn o-n(i)-işẹ
cowries), and cloth sixteen,   he take (them) send those one:who-have-message

rẹ si akere ki   o jọwọ   ki   o ba   awọn fi wa ojo, n(i)-igba-ti
his to Frog should he grant:favor should he join them take seek rain, at-time-that

Ifa says two blessings are coming to someone, but he should sacrifice lest the blessings pass him by because of too much happiness, and so that he will not be lying ill when he hears about the blessings.[6]

---

6. And be unable to take advantage of them.

---

170 - 2

"When the head is full of hair, we call the barber; when the river is in flood,[1] we call the ferryman; if the ferryman does not paddle, I paddle straight across the river, I paddle across the water anyway" was the one who cast Ifa for Frog.[2] They said he should sacrifice four pigeons, two shillings,[3] and four kola nuts so that his mother would not die during that year, and so that he would not go into debt that year also. He did not sacrifice.

Not long afterward Frog's mother died. On the day when he went out to visit his relatives as part of the funeral ceremonies, he met the sixteen chiefs of Ifẹ at Geru gate in front of the palace of the Ọni,[4] and he asked them, "What are you Ifẹ chiefs doing?" He said that when they wanted rain, he would be able to make rain fall either today or tomorrow. When Frog had gone, the king took four female slaves and four male slaves, two pots of beads, two hundred bags of cowries,[5] and sixteen cloths and sent them with his messengers to Frog to ask if he would please make rain for him. When

---

1. Note the pun on "be it be full" l(i)-o kun and "have sea" l(i)-okun, which means to be flooded or full of water.

2. See n. 3, verse 170-1.

3. Since money is counted by 2000 cowries, there are four units of money as there are four pigeons and four kola nuts.

4. The sixteen major chiefs of Ifẹ—eight inner or palace chiefs and eight outer or town chiefs—met every four days to hear cases in front of the king's palace. Ẹnu Geru is the name of the entrance to the palace, and Ẹnuwa is the name of the square in front of the palace.

5. 200 × 20,000 cowries, or £50.

awǫn o-ni(i)-işẹ   de   ile   akere, akere sun,   nwǫn si
those one:who-have-message arrive house (of) Frog, Frog sleep, they and

ko   gbogbo awǫn (ohu)n-kan nwǫn-yi   s(i)-ilẹ   de   pe bi o
gather all   those thing-one those-this to-ground wait:for (him) that if he

ba   ji   ki   nwǫn ba awǫn ko   fun   pe ǫba ni ki   o
should awake should they join them relate for (him) that king say should he

le   fi   ba wǫn wa   ojo t(i)-oni t(i)-ǫla: n(i)-igba-ti
be:able take join them seek rain that-(of)-today that-(of)-tomorrow; at-time-that

akere ji   ti   o ba   awǫn (ohu)n-kan nwǫn-yi   o ni on ko sǫ   bẹ; ẹru
Frog awake that he meet those thing-one   those-this he say he not speak so; fear

ba   o sa tǫ   awǫn babalawo lǫ, nwǫn ni ẹbǫ   ti   awǫn
meet (him) he run approach those diviner   go, they say sacrifice that they

yan   fun   ri   ko pada, nwǫn ni ki   o wa   ru   ẹbǫ,   n(i)-
choose for (him) before not change, they say should he come offer sacrifice, at-

igba-na ni o to   wa   ru   ẹbǫ   ti nwǫn ti sǫ   fun   ri,
time-that be he equal come offer sacrifice that they have speak for (him) before,

awǫn babalawo si ko   meji fun   n(i)-inu   obi mẹrin na, nwǫn ni
those diviner   and gather two for (him) at-belly (of) kola four the, they say

ki   o lǫ fi   bǫ   iya   rẹ; n(i)-igba-ti o de   oriri
should he go take (them) sacrifice:to mother his; at-time-that he arrive grave (of)

iya   rẹ, n(i)-ibi-ti   o gbe mbǫ   ni ojo gbe ku   giri, o
mother his, at-place-that he take sacrificing:to (her) be rain take sound 'giri,' he

ni "Iya   mi gba mi, yǫ   mi n(i)-inu   ǫran yi, iya   ẹni
say "Mother my help me, pull:out me at-belly (of) affair this, mother (of) person

ni ku f(un)-ẹni   sin"   bi o ti   wi   bẹ tan   ti ojo si ku-o
be die for-person bury"; as he have speak so finish that rain and sound-oh

"Aşoro-o   bu   şuru   oju mpǫn   mi kẹrẹ-kẹrẹ" Ojo bu   lu-(i)lẹ.
"Ashoro-oh, pour plentifully eye being:red me red-red."   Rain pour strike-ground.

Nwǫn ni "A   ko mǫ   ohun ti   akere fi   np(e)-ojo"   Aşoro ni orukǫ
They say "We not know thing that Frog take (it) calling-rain" Ashoro be name

ti iya   akere jẹ.
that mother (of) Frog eat.

      Ifa ni ohun kan npǫn   ni oju, iya   ẹni   ǫrun ni   ki
      Ifa say thing one being:red at eye, mother (of) person (of) sky be (she) should

a bǫ   yio si ran-(ẹ)ni   l(i)-ǫwǫ lati ǫrun wa   lati
we sacrifice:to (her), will and send-person at-hand from sky   come in:order:to

ri ohun na, bi iya   na ki   si wa   l(i)-aiye ki   a bǫ   ori
see thing the; if mother the should and exist at-earth should we sacrifice:to head

rẹ ki iya   na ma ba   ku ni ǫdun yi gan.
her that mother the not should die at year this identical.

———————————————

the messengers came to Frog's house, Frog was asleep. They laid out all the things for him and left word that when he awoke, they should tell him for them that the king said he should make it rain either today or tomorrow. When Frog awoke and found all these things, he said that he hadn't said that he could make rain. He was afraid, and he ran to the diviners. They said that the sacrifice which they had named for him before had not changed. They said he should come and make the sacrifice. After he had made the sacrifice that they had told him to make before, the diviners took two of the four kola nuts and gave them to him; they said that he should go and sacrifice them to his mother. When he arrived at the grave of his mother, where he was sacrificing to her, the rain began to beat down "giri."[6] He said, "My mother, help me. Get me out of this trouble. When one's mother dies, one buries her." As he finished saying this, the rain was beating down, oh! He said, "Ashoro, oh, let the rain pour heavily. I am greatly troubled." The rain poured down. They said, "We don't know what Frog uses to call the rain." Ashoro is the name of Frog's mother.

Ifa says something is troubling someone. His mother in heaven is the one to whom he should sacrifice; she will send help to him in this matter. And if his mother should still be on earth, he should sacrifice to her head so that she may not die this very year.

---

6. The sound of rain falling heavily. Cf. n. 2, verse 17 - 2.

IRẸTẸ ỌSA - 3

Obibẹ   rọra   fo ki   o   ma ba   fi   aṣọ kọ-(i)gi   a   da   fun
"House:bat gently fly that you not should take cloth hang-tree" who cast for

akere ti   yio jẹ Oniṣinkọ l(i)-ẹhin   ọla,   nwọn ni ki   o ru-
Frog that will eat Onishinkọ at-back (of) tomorrow, they say should he offer-

(ẹ)bọ   ki ayọ ayọ-ju   ma ba   pa: ẹiyẹ-(i)le   mẹrin,
sacrifice that joy joy-surpass not should kill (him): bird-(of)-house four,

ẹgbarin,   ati aṣọ pupa fẹrẹ-fẹrẹ   o-n(i)-ila.   Akere kọ
8000   (cowries), and cloth red lightly-lightly one:who-has-lines. Frog refuse

kọ ru-(ẹ)bọ.
not offer-sacrifice.

Ko l(i)-ọjọ ko l(i)-oṣu akere ti   iṣe   ọmọ   ọba ni ode   Ọyọ,
Not at-day not at-month Frog that make child (of) king at outside (of) Ọyọ,

baba rẹ ku, nwọn si lọ mu akere lati   wa   jẹ Oniṣinkọ, ṣugbọn
father his die, they and go take Frog in:order:to come eat Onishinkọ, but

akere ko si n(i)-ile n(i)-igba-ti awọn o-n(i)-iṣe   wa   pe,
Frog not be at-house at-time-that those one:who-have-message come call (him),

o wa   ni oko, nwọn si ni ki iyawo   rẹ ki   o lọ sọ   fun
he exist at farm, they and say that junior:wife his should she go speak for (him)

ni oko, n(i)-igba-ti aya rẹ de   oko ti o sọ   fun akere, akere ni
at farm; at-time-that wife his arrive farm that she speak for Frog, Frog say

ki   o ma pada lọ s(i)-ile ki   o lọ ma   ra gbogbo ẹmu
should she not return go to-house should she go (continuative) buy all   palm:

ti o ba   ba ni ẹnu   ibode   ni ki   o   ra   de
wine that she should meet at mouth (of) town:gate be (it) should she buy (it) wait:

ki   o si lọ pe o-n(i)-ilu   on de   on pẹlu.
for (him) should she and go call one:who-have-drum his wait:for him together:with

(her).

N(i)-igba-ti o fi ma   pada de   ile, aya rẹ ti ṣe gẹgẹ-
At-time-that he take (continuative) return arrive house, wife his have do just-

bi o ti wi de,   n(i)-igba-ti o si de ti o ba o-
as he have speak wait:for (him); at-time-that he and arrive that he meet one:who-

n(i)-ilu rẹ o wi   fun   pe "o ya,   mo fẹ ki   o ba mi
have-drum his he speak for (him) that "it be:ready, I want should you join me

fi ẹsẹ kan ya   ọdọ   gbogbo ọba kiri ki   n-to jẹ ọba
take foot one turn:to presence (of) all   king about before I-equal eat king

nitori-ti   bi mo ba   j(ẹ)-oye tan, n-ko ni ri aye   de   ọdọ
because-that if I   should eat-title finish I-not be see chance arrive presence

wọn mọ lai-lai."   Bayi ni o bẹrẹ si so ogun   egbe   mọ   ara
their again ever-ever." Thus be he begin to tie medicine carrier against body

170 - 3

"Fly carefully, house bat, lest you catch your clothes[1] in a tree" was the one who cast Ifa for Frog who was going to be made Onishinkọ[2] after tomorrow. They said he should sacrifice four pigeons, two shillings, and a red cloth with light stripes, lest too much happiness should kill him. Frog refused to make the sacrifice.

Frog was the child of the King of Ọyọ. Not long afterward his father died, and they went to get Frog to make him Onishinkọ. But Frog was not at home when the messengers came to summon him. He was at the farm, and they told his wife to go to the farm to tell him. When his wife reached the farm and told Frog, Frog said that she should not go straight home, but that she should go and buy all the palm wine that she could find at the town gate, and she should call his drummer to wait for him with her at home.

When he came home, his wife had done just as he had told her and was waiting for him. When he arrived and found his drummer, he told him, "Everything is ready I want you to go about with me at once to visit all the kings before I become king, because after I have taken the title, I will never have a chance to visit them again." He began to tie "carrier medicine"[3] on his body,

_____

1. I.e. wings.
2. Cf. nn. 3 and 4, verse 170-1.
3. A type of medicine which will carry the one who wears it immediately to any place.

rẹ ti   o   si   nso   ọkan mọ   o-n(i)-ilu   rẹ ni ọrun pẹlu
his that he and tying one   against one:who-have-drum his at neck together:with

    ti   o   si   sọ   pe   o   ya,   ki   o   fi   ilu   si   pe:
(him) that he and speak that it be:ready, should he take drum beat that:

     L(i)-ọla,   l(i)-ọla,   l(i)-ọla   akere a   j(ẹ)-Oniṣinkọ
     "At-tomorrow, at-tomorrow, at-tomorrow, Frog will eat-Onishinkọ,

     B(i)-o ba   di   l(i)-ọla   akere a   j(ẹ)-Oniṣinkọ.
     "If-it   should become at-tomorrow, Frog will eat-Onishinkọ."

Bi o ba   si   lu   o-n(i)-ilu   rẹ gba,   o di   Ibadan, n(i)-igba-
As he should and beat one:who-have-drum his strike, it become Ibadan, at-time-

ti   o   ba   de   ibẹ   bi nwọn ni ki   o   duro gba   obi a   ni   ki
that he should arrive there as they say should he stand accept kola he say should

nwọn mu   ba   on ni ile   oye, o tun ni ki   o-n(i)-ilu
they take (it) meet him at house (of) title, he then say should one:who-have-drum

on fi   ilu   gba,   o tun lu   gba   o di   ode   Ọyọ, bayi
his take drum strike, he again beat strike (him) it become outside (of) Ọyọ, thus

ni o nṣe titi o fi   de   Ileṣa; ṣugbọn n(i)-igba-ti   o   npada   bọ,
be he doing until he take arrive Ilesha; but   at-time-that he returning come,

arẹ   ti   mu ogun   egbe   ti   o nlo;   n(i)-igba-ti o ku   diẹ
fatigue have take medicine carrier that he using; at-time-that it remain small

ki   o   de   ile,   egbe   gbe   kọ   ori   igi n(i)-ibi-ti   o
before he arrive house, carrier take hang (him) head (of) tree at-place-that it

rẹ egbe   si, o si gb(e)-iyan-(o)ju titi pe ki   on le   wa   s(i)-ilẹ
tire carrier to, he and take-bold-eye   until that should he be:able come to-ground

ṣugbọn ko le   wa   s(i)-ilẹ.   N(i)-igba-ti o pẹ   ni iro-(i)hin
but   not be:able come to-ground. At-time-that it be:long be report-(of)-news

kan ba   awọn ara   ile,   nwọn si wa   wa   s(i)-ibẹ, n(i)-igba-
touch meet those people (of) house, they and come seek (him) to-there, at-time-

ti   nwọn de   ibẹ   ti   nwọn ri,   nwọn ko   ake ti   igi egungun
that they arrive there that they see (him), they gather axe against tree silk:

      ti   o   wa   l(i)-ori rẹ nwọn si   ge   lu-(i)lẹ,   n(i)-igba-ti
cotton:tree that he exist at-head its they and cut (it) strike-ground, at-time-that

igi wo,   o wo   lu   akere mọ-(i)lẹ   o si   ṣẹ   ni ẹsẹ mej(i)-(m)eji
tree break, it break strike Frog against-ground he and break at foot two-two

ati apa mej(i)-(m)eji n(i)-igba-ti nwọn gbe   akere de   ile,   awọn ara-
and arm two-two   at-time-that they carry Frog arrive house, those people-

ile   rẹ bẹrẹ si wo,   nwọn da   ina ti   titi ilẹ
(of)-house his begin to heal (him), they create fire against (him) until ground

mọ, n(i)-igba-ti ilẹ   mọ   awọn ilu   nreti   pe o fẹrẹ   de   ki   nwọn
clear at-time-that earth clear those town expecting that he almost arrive that they

and he tied one about the neck of his drummer also, and he told the drummer that everything was ready and that he should beat on his drum:[4]

"Tomorrow, tomorrow, tomorrow, Frog will be the Onishinkọ,
"When tomorrow comes, Frog will be the Onishinkọ."

As he struck his drummer, they were suddenly transferred to Ibadan. When he arrived there, they told him to wait while they got him some kola nuts,[5] but he said that they should bring them to his house when he had received his title. Again he told his drummer to beat the drum, and again he struck him, and this time they were in Ọyọ. He kept doing this, until finally they reached Ilesha. But when they were returning from Ilesha, the medicine that he was using wore out. When they were just a little way from home, the medicine dropped him in a tree top, where it wore out. He tried and tried, but could not get down. After a while news of this reached his family, and they came there looking for him; when they got there and saw him, they took axes and chopped down the silk cotton tree in the top of which he had landed. When the tree fell, it threw Frog to the ground, so that he broke both legs and both arms. When they had carried Frog home, his family began to cure him; they built a fire and warmed him by it all night long. When day broke, the townspeople were expecting him to arrive soon, so that they could

---

4. That is, on the "talking drums."
5. It is the custom to give kola nuts to visitors, but Frog could not wait to receive them.

ja   ewe   oye le   l(i)-ori na,   ṣugbọn n(i)-igba-ti nwọn reti   rẹ
break leaf (of) title upon (him) at-head the, but   at-time-that they expect his

titi   ti   nwọn ko ri,   nwọn ran-(i)ṣẹ   wa   si ile   rẹ lati
until that they not see (him), they send-message come to house his in:order:to

wa   pe   pe ki   o ma   bọ,   ṣugbọn n(i)-igba-ti o-
come call (him) that should he (continuative) come, but   at-time-that one:who-

n(i)-iṣẹ   ri   ti o si lọ ro-(i)hin   fun awọn ilu,   nwọn mu
have-message see (him) that he and go report-news for those town, they take

ẹlomiran   nwọn fi   j(ẹ)-oye. Bayi ni akere ko j(ẹ)-oye mọ   ti
another:person they take (him) eat-title. Thus be Frog not eat-title again that

ayọ ayọ-ju   si pa,   ati igba-na ni nwọn ti   ma   nwi-
joy joy-surpass and kill (him), from time-the be they have (continuative) speaking-

pe   "Ayọ ayọ-ju   akere f(i)-itan   ṣẹ."
that "Joy joy-surpass Frog take-thigh break."

    Ifa ni   ire   kan mbọ   wa   ba   ẹni-kan   ṣugbọn ki   o ru-
    Ifa say goodness one coming come meet person-one but   should he offer-

(ẹ)bọ   ki   ayọ ayọ-ju   ma ba   gba ipo   na ni ọwọ rẹ.
sacrifice that joy joy-surpass not should take position the at hand his.

IRẸTẸ - (Q)ṢẸ[1] - 1

    Okunkun gbe adiẹ   mi   t(i)-ori-t(i)-ori   a da fun
    "Darkness take chicken swallow that-(of)-head-that-(of)-head" who cast for

ọ-l(i)-ọdẹ,   nwọn ni oko ni o nlọ   yi; nwọn ni yio ri aya kan
one:who-be-hunter, they say farm be he going this; they say will see wife one

fẹ   n(i)-ibẹ; nwọn ni ki   o ru-(ẹ)bọ   ki o ma ba   ti   ara
love at-there; they say should he offer-sacrifice that he not should from body

    obinrin na ri ibi. O ru-(ẹ)bọ   aja mẹta ati ẹgbẹtalelọgbọn;
(of) woman the see evil. He offer-sacrifice (of) dog three and 6600   (cowries).

ki   o fi ẹgbẹta   rẹ yan ẹkọ.
Should he take 600   (cowries) his buy cornstarch:porridge.

    Q-l(i)-ọdẹ   yi ni aja mẹta ti i ma   mu lọ s(i)-oko
    One:who-be-hunter this have dog three that he (continuative) take go to-farm

    ọdẹ   rẹ; orukọ   ekini a ma   jẹ Okemọkerewu, ekeji   a
(of) hunter his; name (of) first it (continuative) eat Okemọkerewu; second it

ma   jẹ Osọpakagbọmọmi, ati ẹkẹta a ma   jẹ Q-gba-
(continuative) eat Osọpakagbọmọmi, and third it (continuative) eat One:who-sweep-

---

    1. This figure is also known as Iru Ẹkun (Leopard's tail) and as Ẹkun f(i)-
iru na-(i)lẹ (Leopard beats the ground with its tail).

break the leaves of his title over his head. But when they waited and he did not
come, they sent to his house to tell him to come. But when the messenger saw
him and reported his condition to the townspeople, they took another person and
crowned him as king. So it was that Frog never attained the title, because of too
much happiness; and from that time on, people have been saying "Too much happiness broke Frog's legs."[6]

Ifa says that a blessing is coming to someone, but he should make a sacrifice lest too much happiness should take the position meant for him from his
hand.

------

6. A proverb. Cf. verse 170-1, and the tale recorded by Fuja (1962: 17-19).

------

175 - 1

"Darkness swallows up chickens completely" was the one who cast Ifa for
hunter. They said that he was going to the farm; they said he would find a wife
there. They said he should sacrifice that the woman should not bring him evil.
He sacrificed three dogs and one shilling seven pence eight oninis. He should
buy cornstarch porridge with one penny eight oninis of the sacrifice.

This hunter had three dogs,[1] which he used to take hunting with him in the
farm. The first was called Okemọkerewu, the second, Osọpakagbọmọmi, and
the third Ọgba-

------

1. The fact that this hunter, after having sacrificed three dogs, is helped
out of his difficulty by three dogs should be compared with other instances in
which a part of the sacrifice is instrumental in achieving the character's
aims.

(i)lẹ-gba-(i)rawe.   N(i)-igba-ti   ọ-l(i)-ọdẹ   yi   ba   de
ground-sweep-dry:leaves. At-time-that one:who-be-hunter this should arrive

oko, obinrin kan wa   ba   da   oniramọ, ti   si   ma
farm, woman one come join (him) create customer, that (she) and (continuative)

ba   ra gbogbo ẹran ti   o   ba   pa; ṣugbọn ko mọ   pe   ọrọ-
join (him) buy all   meat that he should kill; but   not know that evil:spirit-

(i)gi   ni obinrin na.
(of)-tree be woman the.

     N(i)-igba-ti o di   ọjọ kan, obinrin yi   da-(o)hun   pe ki   ọ-
     At-time-that it become day one, woman this break-voice that should one:who-

l(i)-ọdẹ yi wa   lọ mọ ile   on,   nitori-ti   ọ-l(i)-ode   sọ
be-hunter this come go know house hers, because-that one-who-be-hunter speak

pe   o nfẹ   lati   fẹ   ṣe   aya; n(i)-igba-ti ọ-l(i)-ọdẹ
that he wanting in:order:to love (her) make wife; at-time-that one:who-be-hunter

yi mu-(a)ra tan   lati   ma   ba obinrin yi   lọ, o pe aja
this take-body finish in:order:to (continuative) join woman this go, he call dog

rẹ mẹt(a)-(m)ẹta pe ki   nwọn kalọ,   ṣugbọn obinrin ni   da-(o)hun   pe
his three-three that should they go:along, but   woman this break-voice that

"O nlọ   si iile   aya rẹ o si npe   awọn aja rẹ pe ki   nwọn
"He going to house (of) wife his he and calling those dog his that should they

kalọ?"   O ni ki   ọ-l(i)-ọdẹ   ti il(e)-ẹkun mọ   awọn aja
go:along?" She say should one:who-be-hunter push house-door against those dog

rẹ; nitori-pe   obinrin yi mọ pe awọn aja yi gbona pupọ ati-pe   awọn
his; because-that woman this know that those dog this fierce much and-that those

aja yi ko si ẹranko ti   nwọn ko le   fa-ya.
dog this not be animal that they not be:able pull-split.

     L(i)-ẹhin na ni ọkunrin yi   wọ-(i)le   o si gbe ibọn rẹ, ṣugbọn n(i)-
     At-back the be man   this enter-house he and carry gun his, but   at-

igba-ti   obinrin yi tun ri o ni "Ile   aya rẹ na ni o nlọ ti
time-that woman this again see she say "House (of) wife his the be he going that

o lọ gbe ibọn rẹ o fẹ   lọ j(a)-ogun ni ohun ni?"   Ọ-l(i)-ọdẹ
he go carry gun his, he want go fight-war at there be (it)?" One:who-be-hunter

yi si tun gbe ibọn rẹ s(i)-ilẹ   o si na-(ọ)wọ   mu ada   rẹ ti
this and again take gun his to-ground he and stretch-hand take cutlass his that

o ma   nmu lọ si igbo   ọdẹ   n(i)-igba-ti obinrin yi tun ri
he (continuative) taking go to forest (of) hunter; at-time-that woman this then see

eyi o da-(o)hun   o ni "Ile   aya rẹ ni o nlọ ti   o lọ nmu
this she break-voice she say "House (of) wife his be he going that he go taking

ada,   o fẹ   lọ bẹ wọn l(i)-ori l(i)-ọhun ni?"   Ọ-l(i)-ọdẹ   yi
cutlass, he want go cut them at-head at-there be (it)?" One:who-be-hunter this

lẹgbarawe.[2] When this hunter arrived at the farm, a woman trader came to him
to be his customer, and to buy all the meat that he killed. But he did not know
that this woman was an evil tree-spirit.

One day this woman asked the hunter to come with her to see her home, because the hunter had told her that he wanted her to be his wife. When the hunter
was ready to go with this woman, he called to his three dogs to come along; but
this woman said, "Are you going to your wife's house that you call your dogs to
come along?" She said that the hunter should lock the door on his dogs, because
this woman knew that these dogs were very fierce, and that there was no animal
that they could not tear to pieces. Then this man went into the house and took
his gun, but when the woman saw it, she said, "Are you going to your wife's
house that you take your gun along? Do you want to go to make war there?" And
the hunter put back his gun and took down his cutlass that he used to take hunting
in the forest. When this woman saw it, she said to him, "Are you going to your
wife's house that you take your cutlass along? Do you want to go to cut off someone's head there?" So the hunter

---

2. These names could be only partially translated. The first was said to
mean "One who cuts child of kerewu," o-ke-(ọ)mọ-kerewu; kerewu means cotton
seed, but informants did not know its meaning in this context. The second name
could be translated only as "Osọpaka takes child and swallows it," osọpaka-gb(a)-
ọmọ-mi. The third name means "One who sweeps the ground and sweeps dry
leaves."

tun fi ada   s(i)-ilẹ,   o si wọ   ẹwu dara-dara o si tẹle obinrin
then put cutlass to-ground, he and enter gown fine-fine he and follow woman

yi; ṣugbọn bi o ti   fẹ   bọ   s(i)-ode, aya rẹ ti o ti   fẹ   ṣ(i)-
this; but   as he have want come to-outside, wife his that he have love move-

(w)aju ri   pe   o ni "Ṣe ọdẹ ni ọ, bawo ni o ti   ṣe   yẹ
front before call (him) she say "Make hunter be you, how be he have make suit

pe ki   o ma   ba ẹni-ti   o ko mọ ri   lọ si ibi kan
that should he (continuative) meet person-that he not know before go to place one

ki o ma mu ọbẹ dani?" Nitori-na   o ni ki   o pada lọ si ile,
that he not take knife hold?" Because-the she say should he return go to house,

ki   o si mu ọbẹ rẹ dani. Q-l(i)-ọdẹ   yi si mu ọbẹ i-la-
should he and take knife his hold. One:who-be-hunter this and take knife to-open-

(i)gbẹ yi s(i)-inu   ẹwu rẹ, o si fi   ẹwu bo   mọ-(i)lẹ.
forest his to-belly (of) gown his, he and take gown cover (it) against-ground.

Nwọn si jumọ   nlọ.
They and together going.

    Bayi ni awọn mej(i)-(m)eji jumọ   si lọ titi nwọn fi   de   inu
    Thus be those two-two   together and go until they take arrive belly (of)

igbo, n(i)-igba-ti nwọn de   inu   igbo bẹ ni gbogbo awọn igi bẹrẹ
forest, at-time-that they arrive belly (of) forest so be all   those tree begin

si ki   obinrin yi pe "Ẹ-k(u)-abọ"   ti nwọn si nyọ
to greet woman this that"You-be:greeted-(of)-arrival" that they and appearing

si wọn. N(i)-igba-ti ọ-l(i)-ọdẹ   yi ri eyi, ẹru ba   o si
to them. At-time-that one:who-be-hunter this see this, fear meet (him) he and

fẹ   sa pada ṣugbọn nwọn di   l(i)-ọna nwọn ko si fẹ jẹ-ki   o
want run return but   they tie (him) at-road they not and want consent-that he

lọ nwọn si mu-(a)ra lati   pa;   n(i)-igba-ti o ri pe nwọn fẹ
go, they and take-body in:order:to kill (him); at-time-that he see that they want

pa on o sa gun ori   igi o si bẹrẹ si kọ-(o)rin pe:
kill him he run climb head (of) tree he and begin to sing-song that:

        Aja mi da?   Aja   ọdẹ
        "Dog my where:be (they)? Dog (of) hunter,

        Okemọkerewu, Aja   ọdẹ
        "Okemọkerewu, Dog (of) hunter,

        Osọpakagbọmọmi Aja   ọdẹ
        "Osọpakagbọmọmi, Dog (of) hunter,

        Q-gba-(i)lẹ-gba-(i)rawe   Aja   ọdẹ
        "One:who-sweep-ground-sweep-dry:leaves, Dog (of) hunter,

        Aja mi da?   Aja   ọdẹ
        "Dog my where:be (they)? Dog (of) hunter."

put the cutlass down, and he put on a very fine gown to go with this woman. But
when he came out, his senior wife, whom he had married earlier, called to him
and said, "Are you not a hunter? How can you go somewhere to meet people you
have never known before without carrying a knife?" Therefore, she said, he
should go back to the house and get his knife. The hunter took his bush knife and
put it inside his gown so that the gown hid it. And they went off together.

And so they both went along together until they entered the forest. When
they came into the forest, all the trees began to greet this woman, saying, "Welcome," and came up to them. When the hunter saw this, he was afraid, and he
wanted to run back home. But the trees closed the road and would not let him
go; and they got ready to kill him. When he saw that they were going to kill him,
he ran and climbed to the top of a tree and began to sing:

> "Where are my dogs? The hunter's dogs,
> "Okemǫkerewu, The hunter's dogs,
> "Osǫpakagbǫmǫmi, The hunter's dogs,
> "Qgbalęgbarawe, The hunter's dogs,
> "Where are my dogs? The hunter's dogs."[3]

---

3. This song is sung in the typical West African pattern, with the chorus
singing the refrain, "The hunter's dogs."

N(i)-igba-ti   ǫ-l(i)-ǫdę   yi nkǫ-(o)rin   bayi, l(i)-ęsę kan na ni
At-time-that one:who-be-hunter this singing-song thus, at-foot one the be

awǫn aja męt(a)-(m)ęta sa-re ti   ile   de   ti nwǫn si ba   ǫga
those dog three-three   run-go from house arrive that they and meet master

wǫn n(i)-ibi-ti   o gbe wa n(i)-inu   idamu, ti nwǫn si kǫlu
their at-place-that he take exist at-belly (of) confusion, that they and attack

awǫn ǫta   ǫga wǫn ti nwǫn si ba ǫga   won şę-(o)gun awǫn
those enemy (of) master their, that they and join master their make-war those

ǫrǫ-(i)gi   nwǫn-yi.   Q-l(i)-ǫdę   yi si wa   s(i)-ile
evil:spirit-(of)-tree those-this. One:who-be-hunter this and come to-house

pęlu   awǫn aja rę.
together:with those dog his.

     Ifa ni a-(yi)o ri aya kan fę ti yio wa   l(i)-ori   ęmi   ęni,
     Ifa say we-will see wife one love that will exist at-head (of) breath (of) person

şugbǫn ki   a ru-(ę)bǫ   ki a ma ba   ri ibi lati ǫdǫ
but   should we offer-sacrifice that we not should see evil from presence (of)

obinrin na ti yio fęrę   le   gba ęmi   ęni.
woman the that will almost be:able take breath (of) person.

IRĘTĘ - (Q)ŞĘ - 2

     Efufu lęgę-lęgę   awo   aiye Efufu lęgę-lęgę   awo   ǫrun a
     "Wind sway-sway" secret (of) earth, "Wind sway-sway" secret (of) sky   who

da   fun Qrunmila ni-(ǫ)jǫ ti o nlǫ   si apa   okun ilaji   ǫsa.
cast for Qrunmila at-day that he going to arm (of) sea middle (of) lagoon.

     N(i)-igba-ti Qrunmila nlǫ o sǫ   fun awǫn ǫmǫ-awo   rę pe
     At-time-that Qrunmila going he speak for those child-(of)-secret his that

l(i)-ilǫ   ni on nlǫ yi, nwǫn ko gbǫdǫ sę ǫpǫn   Ifa on titi on yio
at-departure he he going this, they not must tap tray (of) Ifa his until he will

fi   de,   o ni ki   nwǫn ma da   ikin si i-da-si   ǫgęrę   on; n(i)-
take arrive, he say should they not cast ikin to to-cast-to divining:cup his; at-

igba-ti   o di   oşu-(ę)kęta ti o lǫ ni awǫn ǫmǫ-awo   rę sę
time-that it become month-third that he go be those child-(of)-secret his tap

ǫpǫn   idę   rę gbęrę; nwǫn dun yęrę ohun   aro,   nwǫn da ikin si
tray (of) brass his softly; they sound yęrę voice (of) sadness, they cast ikin to

i-da-si   ǫgęrę   rę, apę sǫ-(i)lę   ni m(ǫ)-ǫrun   ai-ku
to-cast-to divining:cup his, sign strike-ground at against-altar (of) not-die (of)

ǫ-l(i)-ǫfin;
one:who-has-palace;

When the hunter sang this song, at once his three dogs came running to him from home, and they found their master in the midst of his difficulties. They attacked the enemies of their master and conquered the evil tree-spirits for him. The hunter went back home with his dogs.[4]

Ifa says we will find a wife who will be with our soul,[5] but we should make a sacrifice so that she will not bring us evil which will almost be able to carry our soul away.

---

4. Cf. the versions of this tale recorded by Frobenius (1926: 233-236), Walker and Walker (1961: 17-19), and Fuja (1962: 155-160).

5. The breath (ẹmi) constitutes one of the multiple souls. See Chapter XI.

---

175 - 2

"Gentle breeze"[1] the diviner of earth, "Gentle breeze" the diviner of heaven was the one who cast Ifa for Ọrunmila when he was going to the shore of the ocean, to the middle of the lagoon.[2]

When Ọrunmila was going, he told his apprentices that after he had gone, they must not tap his divining tray until he returned; he said they should not cast the palm nuts in his divining cup.[3] During the third month of his absence his apprentices tapped his brass divining tray softly; they sang his yẹrẹ song sadly; and they cast the palm nuts in his divining cup. A sign appeared at the shrine kept to prevent the king's death.

---

1. A breeze that makes things sway gently. Cf. verse 255-2.
2. Cf. verse 5-4.
3. That is, they should not attempt to divine until he returned.

Q-1(i)-ọfin   ni "Ha" o ni ki   nwọn lọ pe Qrunmila wa,
One:who-has-palace say "Ha" he say should they go call Qrunmila come,

n(i)-igba-ti awọn o-n(i)-iṣẹ   Q-1(i)-ọfin   de-(i)le
at-time-that those one:who-have-message (of) One:who-has-palace arrive-house

       Qrunmila ti   nwọn ko ba,   nwọn pada de   ọdọ   Q-
(of) Qrunmila that they not meet (him), they return arrive presence (of) One:who-

1(i)-ọfin   nwọn ni awọn ko ba,   nwọn ni ki nwọn ọmọ-awo
has-palace they say they not meet (him), they say that those child-(of)-secret

rẹ mẹt(a)-(m)ẹta ni awọn ba;   Q-1(i)-ọfin   ni ki   nwọn lọ pe
his three-three   be they meet; One:who-has-palace say should they go call

awọn ọmọ-awo   rẹ mẹt(a)-(m)ẹta na wa   ki   nwọn wa   yẹ
those child-(of)-secret his three-three   the come should they come examine

on wo;   n(i)-igba-ti nwọn pe wọn de,   nwọn da Ifa, nwọn da   Irẹtẹ-
him look:at; at-time-that they call them arrive, they cast Ifa, they cast Irẹtẹ-

Qṣẹ,nwọn ni ki   Q-1(i)-ọfin   fi ọkẹ   mẹta, aguntan
Qṣẹ,they say should One:who-has-palace take bag (of cowries) three, ewe

mẹta, ati ẹkun   kan ru-(ẹ)bọ   pẹlu   aṣọ kan; Q-1(i)-
three, and leopard one offer-sacrifice together:with cloth one; One:who-has-

ọfin ni "o dara," o ni ṣugbọn nibo ni o ti   ri ẹkun?
palace say "it be:good," he say but   where be he have see leopard?

   Gbogbo Ifẹ mu-(a)ra, nwọn lọ wo   itẹ nwọn si ka   ẹkun   kan
   All   Ifẹ take-body, they go clear bush they and go:around leopard one

mọ   itẹ nwọn wa   da-(o)hun   pe ki   nwọn lọ pe babalawo ti o
against bush they come break-voice that should they go call diviner   that they

yan   ẹkun   ni ẹbọ   wa ki   nwọn wa   ba wọn mu ẹkun n(i)-
choose leopard at sacrifice come should they come join them take leopard at-

inu   itẹ; n(i)-igba-ti nwọn pe awọn ọmọ-awo   mẹt(a)-(m)ẹta
belly (of) bush; at-time-that they call those child-(of)-secret three-three

de   nwọn ko le   mu ẹkun.
arrive they not be:able take leopard.

   Ni ọjọ na gan   ni Qrunmila sun ni ilu ti o wa ti   orun na
   At day the identical be Qrunmila sleep at town that he exist that sleep the

ko dara,   ti o si mu-(a)ra o tọ   awọn babalawo lọ; nwọn sọ
not be:good, that he and take-body he approach those diviner   go; they speak

fun   pe ki   o tete   mu-(a)ra ki   o ma   lọ si ilu rẹ
for (him) that should he quickly take-body should he (continuative) go to town his

kia-kia,   Qrunmila si ka   ọna ko n(i)-igba-ti o de   ile o bere
quick-quick, Qrunmila and shorten road (1) at-time-that he arrive house he ask

awọn ọmọ-awo   rẹ, nwọn ni o di   ij(ọ)-ẹta ti Q-1(i)-ọfin
those child-(of)-secret his, they say it become day-three that One:who-has-palace

----

   1. Ka . . . ko means "to shorten."

The king said, "Ha!" He said that they should go and tell Qrunmila to come. When the king's messengers came to Qrunmila's house and did not find him, they went back to the king; they said that they could not find him, and that they had found only his three apprentices. The king said they should go and tell the three apprentices to come and examine him. When they had been called and had come, they cast Ifa, and they cast the figure Irẹtẹ Qṣẹ. They said that the king should sacrifice fifteen shillings, three ewes, and one leopard, and also one cloth. The king said, "All right, but where can I find the leopard?"

All the people of Ifẹ got ready; they went and cleared the bush and they surrounded a leopard in the bush. They said that they should call the diviners who had named a leopard as part of the sacrifice to come and capture the leopard in the bush. When they called the three apprentices to come, they could not capture the leopard.

On that very day Qrunmila was sleeping in the town where he was, and he had a bad dream. He got ready and consulted the diviners. They told him that he must get ready quickly and return to his town immediately, and Qrunmila used magic to make the journey shorter. When he got home, he asked his apprentices what was wrong. They said that two days ago[4] the king

---

4. Three days before, according to Yoruba reckoning.

ti   pe   wǫn lǫ pe ki   nwǫn wa   ba   on   mu   ẹkun   n(i)-inu   itẹ,
have call them go that should they come join him take leopard at-belly (of) bush,

nwǫn ko si ti   de;   ṣugbǫn bi awǫn ǫmǫ-awo   ti   de   inu
they not and have arrive; but   as those child-(of)-secret have arrive belly (of)

itẹ ni ẹkun   ti   pa ǫkan n(i)-inu wǫn; n(i)-igba-ti Qrunmila gbǫ bayi o
bush be leopard have kill one at-belly their; at-time-that Qrunmila hear thus he

lǫ ra awǫn kan o gbe   ǫmǫ   ewurẹ sǫ   si inu rẹ, n(i)-igba-ti Qrun-
go buy net one he carry child (of) she:goat throw to belly its, at-time-that Qrun-

mila de   ibẹ   o ju   awǫn na pẹlu   ewurẹ yi s(i)-inu   itẹ;
mila arrive there he throw net the together:with she:goat this to-belly (of) bush;

n(i)-igba-ti ewurẹ ba-(i)lẹ   o ke, n(i)-igba-ti ẹkun   gbǫ igbe
at-time-that she:goat strike-ground it cry; at-time-that leopard hear cry (of)

ewurẹ o sa-re si,   bi o ti   ni ki on gbe ni awǫn yi, n(i)-igba-na
she:goat he run-go to (it), as he have be that he take at net   this, at-time-the

ni Qrunmila bẹrẹ si kǫ-(o)rin pe:
be Qrunmila begin to sing-song that:

> Ẹran ti   o roro
> "Meat that it be:fierce,

> Awǫn ma   yi
> "Net   (continuative) turn (it),

> Ẹran o roro.
> "Meat it be:fierce."

N(i)-igba-ti awǫn yi   tan   ni Qrunmila gbe   ru   ti o si
At-time-that net   turn (it) finish be Qrunmila carry carry (it) that he and

mbǫ   n(i)-ile, ṣugbǫn bi o ti   ngbe   bǫ   ni ẹkun   bẹrẹ si ha
coming at-house, but   as he have carrying (it) come be leopard begin to scratch

ni ekanna; ibi-ti   ẹkun   gbe ha   Qrunmila ni ekanna ni oju mẹrin
(him) at claw;   place-that leopard take scratch Qrunmila at claw   be eye four

ti wa   l(i)-ara   ifa (ekurǫ)   titi di   oni yi, n(i)-igba-ti
that they exist at-body (of) Ifa (palm:nut) until become today this, at-time-that

ẹkun   nha   ni ekanna ni Qrunmila bẹrẹ si kǫ-(o)rin pe:
leopard scratching (him) at claw   be Qrunmila begin to sing-song that:

> O roro
> "It be:fierce,

> Agẹmǫ   ko ṣe jẹ
> "Chameleon not make eat,

> O roro.
> "It be:fierce."

N(i)-igba-ti o gbe   de   ile ni nwǫn ba   lǫ ṣ(e)-ẹbǫ   fun
At-time-that he carry (it) arrive house be they join (him) go make-sacrifice for

Q-l(i)-ǫfin.
One:who-has-palace.

had called them to come and capture a leopard in the bush, and they had not gone; but when they did go to the bush, the leopard had killed one of them. When Qrun- mila heard this, he went and bought a net, and in it he put a young she-goat. When Qrunmila got there, he threw the net, with the she-goat inside it, into the bush. When the she-goat hit the ground, it bleated, and when the leopard heard its cry it ran to it. As it was caught in the net, Qrunmila began to sing:

> "Animal that is very fierce,
> "The net is ensnaring it,
> "Animal is very fierce."

When the net had ensnared the leopard, Qrunmila picked it up and started to carry it home; but as he was carrying it, the leopard began to scratch him with its claws. The places where the leopard scratched Qrunmila with its claws are the four eyes that are to be seen on Ifa (on his palm nuts) until this very day.[5] When leopard was scratching him with his claws, Qrunmila began to sing:

> "It is very bitter,[6]
> "Chameleon is not able to eat it,
> "It is very bitter."

When he had carried the leopard home, they went with him to make the sacrifice for the king.

----

5. This verse thus explains how it came about that the palm nuts used by the diviners have four "eyes" at one end. (See Chapter III).

6. Given as to be fierce (roro) in the text, but interpreted as meaning to be bitter (koro).

Ifa ni   ẹni-kan   nlọ   si idalẹ   kan yio si fi ẹni-kan   de-(i)le
Ifa say person-one going to distance one will and put person-one watch-house

rẹ gẹgẹ-bi a-l(i)-akoso   ti yio duro bi oluwarẹ   na
his just-as one:who-have-control that will stand as person:in:question the

pataki,   ki   a ru-(ẹ)bọ   ki Ṣọpọnna ma ba   pa ẹni-
important:person, should we offer-sacrifice that Shọpọnna not should kill person-

ti a fi s(i)-ile na, ki   ẹni-ti   o lọ si ẹhin   odi   na to
that we put to-house the, before person-that he go to back (of) town:wall the equal

de.   Ki   o ma de   ile   jampo ki nwọn ma   ba   sọ
arrive. Should he not arrive house empty that they (continuative) should speak

pe igbẹ   ma   wa fọ-(ọ)na   o.
that forest (continuative) come break-road his.

Ifa kan wa   ki   a fi ori   le   l(i)-ori ki   a pa igbin
Ifa one exist, should we put shea:butter upon (it) at-head should we kill snail

si ki   a to fi ewurẹ bọ   nitori-ti awọn kan gba-
to (it) before we equal take she:goat sacrifice:to (it) because-that those one take-

(o)ri jọ   ti Ifa yi ma ba   yẹ-(o)ri ni ọrọ wọn nitori-ti   o
head be:together that Ifa this not should avoid-head at word their because-that it

fi ori ti   ọran wọn.
put head against affair their.

OTURA - (Q)BARA[1] - 1

Idi   ṣe b(i)-ire-b(i)-ire   o gun   ori   ẹni, awọn ṣe jẹgẹ-jẹgẹ
"Waist do like-play-like-play it climb head (of) mat; net   do softly-softly

m(u)-ẹru le,   Alukerese rakoro-rakoro o d(i)-agba,   n(i)-igba-ti o
take-load strong," "Alukerese crawl-crawl   it become-elder, at-time-that it

d(i)-agba   tan   o nṣe oju mi eyi, oju mi ọhun" a   da fun Aiye ti
become-elder finish he doing eye my this, eye my there" who cast for Earth that

o nf(i)-ẹkun   oju ṣe irahun   ọmọ nwọn ni yio b(i)-ọmọ nwọn
she taking-tears (of) eye make moaning (of) child; they say will bear-child they

ni gbogbo aiye ni   yio ma   pe   sin ọmọ na yio si
say all   earth be (they) will (continuative) assemble serve child the, will and

de ade ṣugbọn ki iṣe rẹ le   ṣe oju rẹ ni ki   o ru-(ẹ)bọ
cover crown but   that work his be:able dɔ eye her be should she offer-sacrifice

fun. Ewurẹ kan ati aṣọ   ara rẹ ni ẹbọ.
for. She:goat one and cloth (of) body her be sacrifice.

---

1. An alternative name is Etura Oniwara.

Ifa says someone is going to a distant place, and he will leave someone in charge of his house like a director who will stand in his place as an important person. We should sacrifice, lest the God of Smallpox kill this person that we leave at home before the one who goes out of town returns, and so that he does not return to an empty house and be told that the forest has destroyed it.

There is an Ifa;[7] we should put shea butter on top of it and kill a snail on it before we sacrifice a she-goat to it, because some people have been counting on this Ifa not to fail them, because it will help them in this affair.[8]

-----

7. A set of palm nuts (ikin).
8. This translation is uncertain.

-----

181 - 1

"Hips act indifferently,[1] but they get to sit on the mat; nets act gently, but they hold their loads firmly," and "The alukerese vine[2] creeps to maturity; when it is old, it turns its face here and there" were the ones who cast Ifa for Earth when she was weeping and moaning for a child. They said she would bear a child and that the whole world would be gathering to serve it. They said the child would wear a crown but that she should sacrifice so that he would be able to do so while she was still alive to see it. One she-goat and the cloth from her body is the sacrifice.

-----

1. To act as if something does not matter, to do something by indirection, or to feign indifference. To tell important news incidentally in the midst of joking and talking about the point; to gain admission into a crowded room or to reach a desired position in a crowd by moving gradually and joking with those whom one passes; or, as in this case, to move gradually and almost unnoticeably onto a mat.
2. See n. 1, verse 33-2.

Ifa ni   obinrin kan ni-(e)yi, ko si ęni-ti   o tun le   gbagbǫ pe
Ifa say woman one be-this, not be person-that he then be:able believe that

o   le   bi-(ǫ)mǫ mǫ;   yio bi   ǫmǫ-(ǫ)kunrin kan şugbǫn ki   o   ru-
she be:able bear-child again; will bear child-man   one but   should she offer-

(ę)bǫ   ki igba   ǫmǫ na le   şe oju rę; ǫmǫ na yio ję ǫba.
sacrifice that time (of) child the be:able do eye her; child the will eat king.

Aiye kǫ   ko ru-(ę)bǫ   titi o fi ku si oko, ibę ni nwǫn
Earth refuse not offer-sacrifice until she take die to farm, there be they

sin Aiye si n(i)-igba-ti ǫmǫ rę si wa   ni ǫmǫde.   N(i)-igba-ti o
bury Earth to, at-time-that child her and exist at young:child. At-time-that it

pę   titi, igbo kun bo   iboji   ibi-ti   nwǫn sin Aiye si, ko si
be:long until, forest fill cover grave (of) place-that they bury Earth to, not and

si ęni-ti   o mǫ ibę mǫ,   şugbǫn n(i)-igba-ti o pę   ǫmǫ yi
be person-that he know there again, but   at-time-that it be:long child this

di   agba, nwǫn si fi   j(ę)-ǫba; n(i)-igba-yi ni agbę   kan lǫ
become elder, they and take (him) eat-king; at-time-this be farmer one go

da   oko si ibi-ti   nwǫn sin Aiye si, bi o si ti   nfi   kǫ ęran,
create farm to place-that they bury Earth to, as he and have taking hoe heap,

ǫkǫ şa   Aiye l(i)-ori, o si k(e)-igbe pe "Ha   o fi ǫkǫ şa   mi l(i)-
hoe chop Earth at-head, she and cry-cry that "Ha! you take hoe chop me at-

ori?"
head?"

N(i)-igba-ti agbę   yi gbǫ bayi, o fi ǫkǫ s(i)-ilę,   o si sa-re
At-time-that farmer this hear thus, he put hoe to-ground, he and run-go

wa   sǫ   fun ǫba n(i)-ile ti o ri ori gbigbę ti o ns(ǫ)-ǫrǫ   n(i)-
come speak for king at-house that he see head dry   that it speaking-word at-

ibi-ti   o gbe nkǫ ęran. Ǫba ni şe   ki o ran-(i)şę   wa   kalǫ
place-that he take hoeing heap. King say make that he send-message come go:

s(i)-ibę? O ni ki   o ran-(i)şę   tęle   on ati bi awǫn ba
along to-there? He say should he send-message follow him and if they should

de   ibę ti   ko ba   s(ǫ)-ǫrǫ ki ǫba ki   o bę on ni ori;
arrive there that (it) not should speak-word that king should he cut him at head;

ǫba si ran awǫn-(I)mǫlę tęle   lǫ si ibę   şugbǫn n(i)-igba-ti nwǫn
king and send those-Ogboni follow (him) go to there, but   at-time-that they

de   ibę, ori gbigbę ko s(ǫ)-ǫrǫ mǫ, nwǫn si mu agbę   nwǫn si
arrive there, head dry   not speak-word again, they and take farmer they and

bę   l(i)-ori gęgę-bi ileri   rę; şugbǫn bi awǫn-(I)mǫlę ti   bę agbę
cut (him) at-head just-as promise his; but   as those-Ogboni have cut farmer

l(i)-ori tan   ti nwǫn yi ęhin pada ni ori-gbę da-(o)hun   o ni "Ha
at-head finish that they turn back return be head-dry break-voice it say "Ha!

ę   pa enia?"
you kill person?"

Ifa says this is a woman. There is no one who can believe that she is still able to bear children. She will bear a son, but she should make a sacrifice so that his time will come while she is still alive. The child will become king.

Earth refused to sacrifice, and finally she died in the farm, where she was buried when her son was still a young boy. After a while the forest grew up and covered the grave where Earth was buried, and there was no one who knew where it was any more. But after a while her child grew up, and they made him king. At this time a farmer went to make a farm at the place where they had buried Earth, and as he was hoeing yam heaps, his hoe chopped Earth's head, and she cried out, "Ha! Did you chop my head with your hoe?"

When the farmer heard this, he put down his hoe and he ran home to tell the king that he had seen a skull that talked where he was hoeing yam heaps. The king asked whether he should send someone to accompany him there. He said the king should send someone to follow him, and that if they got there and the skull did not talk, the king should cut off his head. The king sent the Ogboni[3] to accompany him to the place, but when they got there, the skull would not talk any more. So they seized the farmer and cut off his head, according to his agreement. But when the Ogboni had cut off the farmer's head and turned to go back, the skull spoke, saying "Ha! Did you kill someone?"

---

3. A group of officials, whose primary functions are to serve as one of the higher courts of justice, and to perform rituals in honor of the earth.

N(i)-igba-ti awǫn-(I)mǫlę si de   ile   nwǫn ro-(i)hin   ohun ti
At-time-that those-Ogboni and arrive house they report-news (of) thing that

awǫn ri fun ǫba nwǫn si sǫ   fun   bi ohun ti   awǫn wi   yi ko
they see for king they and speak for (him) if thing that they speak this not

ba   ri bę ki ǫba ki   o pa awǫn; o si tun ran awǫn Ogungbę le
should see so that king should he kill them; he and then send those Ogungbę upon

nwǫn l(i)-ęhin şugbǫn n(i)-igba-ti nwǫn de   ibę   ori gbigbę tun pa-(ę)nu
them at-back but   at-time-that they arrive there head dry   then kill-mouth

mǫ   ko s(ǫ)-ǫrǫ   mǫ,   awǫn Ogungbę si pa awǫn-(I)mǫlę si ǫhun
against not speak-word again, those Ogungbę and kill those-Ogboni to there

şugbǫn bi wǫn ti   pa wǫn tan ti nwǫn si yi ęhin pada ni ori-gbigbę
but   as they have kill them finish that they and turn back return be head-dry

tun da-(o)hun   ti o si wi-pe   "Ha   ę   pa enia?"
then break-voice that he and speak-that "Ha! you kill person?"

    N(i)-igba-ti awǫn Ogungbę de   ile   nwǫn ko   ohun ti   nwǫn ri   nwǫn
    At-time-that those Ogungbę arrive house they relate thing that they see they

si sǫ   fun ǫba, ǫba si pe awǫn Otu pe ki   nwǫn wa   ba awǫn
and speak for king, king and call those Otu that should they come join those

Ęmęsę lǫ si ibi-ti   ori-gbigbę gbe ns(ǫ)-ǫrǫ.   Şugbǫn ki   awǫn Otu
Ęmęsę go to place-that head-dry   take speaking-word. But   before those Otu

to   lǫ nwǫn mu eji kan ęta   nwǫn tǫ   awǫn babalawo lǫ
equal go they take two touch three (cowries) they approach those diviner   go

awǫn babalawo si sǫ   fun wǫn pe ki   nwǫn ru-(ę)bǫ   agutan
those diviner   and speak for them that should they offer-sacrifice (of) ewe

kan, aşǫ funfun, awin,   ęmu,   ati akara.
one, cloth white, tamarind, palm:wine, and bean:fritter.

    N(i)-igba-ti awǫn Otu de   ibę,   nwǫn bę agutan si,   nwǫn da ęmu
    At-time-that those Otu arrive there, they cut ewe   to (it), they cast palm:

    lu   nwǫn si run   akara   si,   n(i)-igba-ti ori gbigbę
wine against (it), they and crumble bean:fritter to (it); at-time-that head dry

ję tan   o ni o Aiye ni, o ni ki   nwǫn gbe on, nwǫn si gbe
eat finish, it say it Earth be, it say should they carry it, they and carry (it)

s(i)-inu   aşǫ funfun; nwǫn si gbe   wa s(i)-ile nwǫn wa   mǫ
to-belly (of) cloth white; they and carry (it) come to-house, they come know

pe iya   ǫ-l(i)-ǫfin   ni.
that mother (of) one:who-has-palace be (it).

    Ifa ni a-ku-(i)-sin   oku   kan wa, Ifa ni ki   a y(a)-
    Ifa say one:who-die-(not)-bury corpse one exist, Ifa say should we be:quick-

ara lǫ sin oku   na dara-dara ki oku   na ba   ma şe   a-ku-
body go bury corpse the fine-fine   that corpse the should not make one:who-die-

fa enia pupǫ.
pull people many.

When the Ogboni came home, they reported to the king what they had seen, and they told him that if what they had said was not true, the king should kill them. Then the king sent the Ogungbẹ[4] after the Ogboni; but when they got there, the skull again kept silent and would not speak. The Ogungbẹ killed the Ogboni on the spot; but when they had killed them and they turned to come back, the skull again spoke, saying, "Ha! Did you kill someone?"

When the Ogungbẹ came home, they reported what they had seen, telling it to the king. The king called the Otu priests[5] to go with the Ẹmẹsẹ[6] to the place where the skull was talking. But before the Otu priests left, they took five cowries and consulted the diviners; and the diviners told them to sacrifice one ewe, a white cloth, Black Tamarind,[7] palm wine, and bean fritters.

When the Otu arrived there, they cut off the head of the ewe and poured its blood on the skull; they poured palm wine on it; and they crumbled the bean fritters on it. When the skull had finished eating, it said that it was Earth, and it said they should carry it home. They put it in the white cloth and carried it home. Thus they learned that it was the mother of the king.

Ifa says that there is a dead person who has not been buried. Ifa says we should hurry and bury the dead person in fine style, so that it will not draw many people to their death after it.

---

4. A group of officials, whose primary function is to serve as bodyguards of the king and arrest and detain criminals. Cf. n. 4, verse 249-6. Their name means "War society" [Ogun-(ẹ)gbẹ].

5. A group of priests in Ifẹ whose duty it is to dispose of sacrifices for the king. Cf. verse 181-4 for a similar tale in which the meaning of their title is explained.

6. A group of palace officials whose primary functions are to act as messengers of the king and his representatives at the various religious festivals performed by the people of Ifẹ. They are the equivalent of the Ilari of the Ọyọ kingdom. The Ẹmẹsẹ, the Ogungbẹ, and the Ogboni are three sets of officials who assist the king and the chiefs of Ifẹ in governing the capital and the kingdom.

7. A sour fruit, the Black or Velvet Tamarind (Dialium guineense).

OTURA - (Q)BARA - 2

Etura bayi, Qbara bayi a   da   fun omu-(i)ye   meji; nwǫn ni
"Etura thus, Qbara thus" who cast for child-(of)-mother two; they say

ki   awǫn mej(i)-(m)eji ru-(ę)bǫ   ki   ǫran wǫn le   ni   ori; apa-
should those two-two   offer-sacrifice that affair their be:able have head; arm-

kan ru-(ę)bǫ,   apa-kan ko ru.   Awǫn ti   o   ru-(ę)bǫ   n(i)-igba-
one offer-sacrifice, arm-one not offer. Those that they offer-sacrifice at-time-

na ni awǫn ǫmǫ   iya   meji ti   a   ma   nsǫ   pe   Ę   ko
the be those child (of) mother two that we (continuative) speaking that "You not

ri bi (ohu)n-kan wǫn ti   gun?   Awǫn ti   ko ru-(ę)bǫ   n(i)-igba-
see if thing-one their have be:orderly?" Those that not offer-sacrifice at-time-

na ni awǫn ti   a   ma   nsǫ   pe   Nwǫn ba.   Etura ba
the be those that we (continuative) speaking that "They be:worthless. Etura be:

        Qbara ba.   Ęiyę-(i)le   męrin ati ęgbarin   ni
worthless, Qbara be:worthless." Bird-(of)-house four and 8000 (cowries) be

ębǫ.
sacrifice.

Ifa ni ki   awǫn ǫmǫ   iya   meji ru-(ę)bǫ   ki   ǫran wǫn
Ifa say should those child (of) mother two offer-sacrifice that affair their

le   pa-pǫ;   ki   awǫn ar(a)-aiye   ma ba   ma   sǫ
be:able kill-together; that those people-(of)-earth not should (continuative) speak

pe   Nwǫn ba.
that "They be:worthless."

OTURA - (Q)BARA - 3

A ki ini   ititǫ n(i)-inu ki a gb(e)-awǫn ika   si iku   a   da
"We not have truth at-belly that we take-unpaid wickedness to belly" who cast

fun Qsanyin; nwǫn ni ki   o ru-(ę)bǫ   ki ohun kan ki o ma ba
for Qsanyin; they say should he offer-sacrifice that thing one that it not should

pa ohun mǫ   l(i)-ęnu.   Akikǫ-(a)dię męta ati ęgbętalelǫgbǫn   ni
kill voice against (him) at-mouth. Cock-chicken three and 6600   (cowries) be

ębǫ.
sacrifice.

N(i)-igba-ti Qsanyin ma   ru-(ę)bǫ   o ru akikǫ-(a)dię kan;
At-time-that Qsanyin (continuative) offer-sacrifice he offer cock-chicken one;

lati igba-na ni ohun   Qsanyin ko ti   de   oke mǫ ti o si ma
from time-the be voice (of) Qsanyin not have arrive hill again that he and (continu-

nfǫ-(o)hun   fintin-fintin. Ifa ni ki   e-l(i)-eyi   ki   o
ative) speaking-voice tiny-tiny.   Ifa say should one:who-be-this should he

181 - 2

"Etura like this, Qbara like this"[1] was the one who cast Ifa for two children of the same mother. They said that both should make a sacrifice, so that their affairs might be successfully concluded. One side sacrificed; the other side did not. Those that sacrificed at that time are the two children of the same mother,[2] of whom we say, "Don't you see how their things are in order?" Those that did not sacrifice at that time are the ones of whom we say, "They are worthless. Etura is worthless; Qbara is worthless."[3] Four pigeons and two shillings is the sacrifice.

Ifa says that two children of the same mother should make a sacrifice so that they will be able to join forces, and so that people will not be saying, "They are worthless."

_____

1. The diviner's name is derived from the name of the figure. Etura is an alternate form of Otura.

2. Although in the first instance it is implied that there are only two individuals concerned, here it becomes clear that there are at least four.

3. The meaning of this was not clear to informants. The word "ba" was said to be a verb meaning the opposite of "gun" (to be orderly), and hence "worthless." I have followed the informants' interpretation, but I have a suspicion that the name of the diviner should have been given as "Etura ba-yi, Qbara ba-yi" (Etura worthless-this, Qbara worthless-this).

_____

181 - 3

"One does not have the truth in his belly and put wickedness in his stomach for nothing"[1] was the one who cast Ifa for the God of Medicine. They said he should make a sacrifice, lest something should stop the voice in his throat. Three cocks and one shilling seven pence eight oninis is the sacrifice.

When the God of Medicine made the sacrifice, he offered only one cock. From that time on, his voice does not carry far, and he talks with a very tiny voice.[2] Ifa says that this person should

_____

1. A person's character is thought to reside in his stomach, in much the same way that his luck resides in his head. Here it is seen that truth and wickedness are there also. (Cf. Chapter XI.)

2. This verse thus explains why the God of Medicine talks in falsetto, which is one of his widely known characteristics, associated with ventriloquism.

ru-(ẹ)bọ   ki   ohun kan ki   o ma ba   gba   ni ohun ki   a   ma
offer-sacrifice that thing one should it not should take (him) at voice that they not

ba   ma   sọ   pe   "Bawo ni o şe   nfọ-(o)hun   fintin bi ohun
should (continuative) speak that "How be he make speaking-voice tiny   like voice

     Qsanyin bayi?"
(of) Qsanyin thus?"

OTURA - (Q)BARA - 4

Opipi   ye   mọniwọn ki o ba   ri iyẹ   bo
"Featherless (chicken) lay:egg few   that it should see feathers cover

        a   da   fun Aiye. Nwọn ni ki   Aiye ru-(ẹ)bọ   nitori-ti
(them)" who cast for Earth. They say should Earth offer-sacrifice because-that

yio de   ipo   kan şugbọn ki o le   şe oju   iya   rẹ Alaba;
will arrive position one but   that he be:able do eye (of) mother his Alaba;

şugbọn Aiye kọ   ko ru-(ẹ)bọ;   ko pẹ   Alaba, yeye   Aiye, ku
but   Earth refuse not offer-sacrifice; not be:long Alaba, mother (of) Earth, die;

n(i)-igba-ti Aiye d(i)-agba,   nwọn fi   j(ẹ)-ọba.
at-time-that Earth become-elder, they take (him) eat-king.

     Ki   Alaba iya   Aiye to   ku o ni iwọfa kan oju rẹ ni Alaba
     Before Alaba mother (of) Earth equal die she have pawn one, eye his be Alaba

şe   ku o si mọ ibi-ti   nwọn sin   si ni idi   iroko; n(i)-igba-
make die he and know place-that they bury (her) to at base (of) iroko; at-time-

ti iwọfa yi san-(o)wo   tan, bi o ba   ti de   idi   iroko yi
that pawn this repay-cowries finish, as he should have arrive base (of) iroko this

o   ma   fi Alaba şe-(i)re pe   Ori gbigbẹ o nwo   iroko
he (continuative) take Alaba make-play that "Head dry   you looking:at iroko (of)

oko   Alaba ni Alaba? Oj(umọ)-ojumọ ni iwọfa yi   ma   nwi
farm (of) Alaba at Alaba?" Dawn-dawn   be pawn this (continuative) speaking

bayi şugbọn n(i)-igba-ti o di   ọjọ kan bi o ti   wi   bayi tan,   ori
thus but   at-time-that it become day one as he have speak thus finish, head

gbigbẹ da-(o)hun   o ni Iwọfa   Alaba bi o ba   ma   lọ si oko,
dry   break-voice it say "Pawn (of) Alaba if you should (continuative) go to farm,

işẹ ni ki o   ma   şe ẹnu jẹ,   n(i)-igba-ti iwọfa gbọ eyi
make be should you (continuative) make mouth quiet"; at-time-that pawn hear this

o mu-(a)ra o wa s(i)-ile o ni on ri ohun ti oju on ko ri ri
he take-body he come to-house he say he see thing that eye his not see before

ati-pe   ohun ti on ri ju   on lọ o mu-(a)ra o tọ   ọba lọ, o
and-that thing that he see surpass him go; he take-body he approach king go, he

sacrifice, so that something will not take away his voice and so that people will not say, "Why is he talking this way with a tiny voice like that of the God of Medicine?"

---

181 - 4

"A chicken with few feathers lays few eggs, so that its feathers can cover them" was the one who cast Ifa for Earth.[1] They said that Earth would attain an important position but that he should make a sacrifice so that he would be able to do so while his mother was alive to see it; but Earth refused to sacrifice. Not long afterward Alaba, Earth's mother, died; and when Earth grew up, they made him king.

Before she died, Alaba, the mother of Earth, had a pawn.[2] It was in his presence that Alaba died, and he knew the place where they buried her, at the base of an iroko tree.[3] When this pawn had repaid his debt, he used to make fun of Alaba as he passed the iroko tree where she was buried, saying, "Skull, are you looking at the iroko tree in Alaba's farm at Alaba?"[4] Each morning the pawn said this; but one day when he had finished saying it, the skull answered, saying "Pawn of Alaba, when you go to farm, you should keep your mouth shut." When the pawn heard this, he got ready and came home. He said that he had seen something that his eyes had never seen before, and that the thing he had seen passed his understanding. He got ready and went to the king. He

---

1. Cf. the tale of the talking skull in verse 181-1, where Earth appears as the mother of the man who became king. A similar verse with Earth's skull was recorded from an Ifẹ diviner in 1965, and Epega (n.d.: VIII, 14-16) gives a similar tale in a somewhat different verse for the same figure, Otura Qbara. Cf. also the tale of the talking sheep in verse 249-5.

2. An indentured laborer, who works for the creditor in lieu of interest until his loan has been repaid.

3. See n. 4, verse 1-1.

4. An unidentified place-name, distinguished by tone from the name of Earth's mother.

ni   o   ri   ibi-ti   ori   gbigbẹ gbe s(ọ)-ọrọ,   o   ni   bi o   ba   de
say he see place-that head dry   take speak-word, he say if he should arrive

ibẹ   t(i)-o   ko   ba   s(ọ)-ọrọ   ki   ọba   ki   o   bẹ   on   l(i)-ori.
there that-it not should speak-word should king should he cut him at-head.

    Ọba   yan   awọn Ogungbẹ ati awọn Ẹmẹsẹ le   l(i)-ẹhin; n(i)-igba-
    King choose those Ogungbẹ and those Ẹmẹsẹ upon (him) at-back; at-time-

ti   nwọn de   ibẹ   nwọn ni   ki   o   pe   bi o   ti   ma
that they arrive there, they say should he call (it) as he have (continuative)

npe,   o   ni   Ori   gbigbẹ o   nwo   iroko   oko   Alaba ni Alaba,
calling (it), he say "Head dry   you looking:at iroko (of) farm (of) Alaba at Alaba,

o?   Ori   gbigbẹ ko da-(o)hun,   nwọn si   mu,   nwọn pa,   bi nwọn
oh?" Head dry   not break-voice, they and take (him), they kill (him); as they

ti   pa   tan   ni ori-gbigbẹ da-(o)hun o ni   kin-ni   ṣe   ti   ẹ
have kill (him) finish be head-dry   break-voice it say "What-be make that you

fi   pa?   Nwọn ni   Iwọ ta-ni?   O ni   on ori-gbigbẹ ni; nwọn ni
take kill (him)?" They say "You who-be?" It say it head-dry be; they say

Kin-ni   ṣe   ti   o   ko   ti   da-(o)hun   ri?   Ori-gbigbẹ ni   agbere
"What-be make that you not have break-voice before?" Head-dry   say excess (of)

ẹnu   rẹ ni   o   pa.
mouth his be it kill (him).

    N(i)-igba-ti nwọn de   ile   nwọn ro-(i)hin   fun ọba, ọba da-(o)hun
    At-time-that they arrive house they report-news for king, king break-voice

pe   Ta-ni   yio ba on   tu   ori yi?   O   ni   ki   nwọn lọ pe   awọn
that "Who-be will for him appease head this?" He say should they go call those

Otu wa.   Awọn Otu si   tọ   awọn babalawo lọ nwọn si   sọ   ohun ti
Otu come. Those Otu and approach those diviner   go they and speak thing that

nwọn yio ṣe fun wọn; nwọn si   mu   iti   aṣọ   funfun ati agutan; n(i)-igba-
they will do for them; they and take bunch (of) cloth white and ewe;   at-time-

ti   nwọn si   de   ọhun ti   nwọn si   tu   ori-gbigbẹ tan,   nwọn nkọ-
that they and arrive there that they and appease head-dry   finish, they singing-

(o)rin pe:
song that:

      Yeye   Aiye   o   ma   ka   re-(i)le   o
      "Mother (of) Earth you (continuative) should go-house, oh;

      K(i)-o   wa   lọ   ṣe   iwa
      "Should-you seek go make destiny;

      Ẹ   ṣe   hun
      "You make 'hun,'

      Yeye   Aiye   nre-(i)le   o
      "Mother (of) Earth going-home, oh."

said he had seen a place where a skull was talking; he said if he should go there and the skull did not talk, the king should cut off his head.

The king chose the Ogungbẹ and the Ẹmẹsẹ[5] to follow him, and when they got there they told him to call to the skull as he had called it before. He said, "Skull, are you looking at the iroko tree in Alaba's farm at Alaba, oh?" The skull did not answer, and they seized him and killed him. When they had killed him, the skull said, "Why did you kill him?" They asked, "Who are you?" It said it was a skull. They asked, "Why did you not answer before?" The skull replied, "His big mouth killed him."

When they returned home, they reported to the king. The king said, "Who will go and appease this head for me?" He said that they should call the Otu priests. The Otu priests consulted the divners, who told them what they should do. They took a bunch of white cloth and one ewe. When they got there and had appeased the skull, they sang:

> "Mother of Earth, you should go home, oh;
> "Go seek your destiny;
> "You should hum;
> "Mother of Earth is going home, oh."

---

5. See nn. 4-6, verse 181-1, for identification of Ogungbẹ, Ẹmẹsẹ, and Otu.

Eyi ni awǫn Otu ma   nşe   ni ǫjǫ Ferekete titi di   oni yi.
This be those Otu (continuative) doing at day Ferekete until become today this.

     Ifa ni a-ku-(i)-sin   kan wa n(i)-ibę ki   a mu-(a)ra ki
     Ifa say one:who-die-(not)-bury one exist at-there should we take-body should

a tete   sin oku   rę ki o ma ba   ma   şe a-ku-
we quickly bury corpse his that it not should (continuative) make one:who-die-

fa.
pull.

OTURA IROSUN - 1

     Etura ro-ro,   Irosun ro-ro   a   da   fun ęrunlǫjǫ igi
     "Etura bright-bright, Irosun bright-bright" who cast for 165   tree (of)

oko nwǫn ni ki   nwǫn wa   ru-(ę)bǫ   akikǫ męfa-męfa, abęrę
farm; they say should they come offer-sacrifice (of) cock six-six,   needle

męfa-męfa, ati ęgbafa.   Egungun, iroko, apa ati gbogbo awǫn igi
six-six,   and 12,000 (cowries). Egungun, Iroko, Apa, and all   those tree

nla-nla ni oko ni o   ru-(ę)bǫ;   şugbǫn awon igi bi ayinyin, adindin,
big-big at farm be who offer-sacrifice; but   those tree like Ayinyin, Adindin,

ati gbogbo awǫn igi ti ko nla ni oko ko ru-(ę)bǫ   ati gbogbo awǫn
and all   those tree that not big at farm not offer-sacrifice and all   those

igi tęrę-tęrę   inu   oko ati igbo gbogbo ni ko ru   ębǫ
tree slender-slender (of) belly (of) farm and forest all   be not offer sacrifice

yi.
this.

     Ifa ni ki   e-l(i)-eyi   ki   o ru-(ę)bǫ   ki o le
     Ifa say should one:who-be-this should he offer-sacrifice that he be:able

d(i)-agba   ki arun   inu ma pa   si ke(re)-kere.
become-elder that disease (of) belly not kill (him) to small-small.

     Ayani   ni-(e)yi ti   iroko, egungun, apa, ati awǫn igi nla   igbo
     Explanation be-this that Iroko, Egungun, Apa, and those tree big (of) forest

fi nd(i)-agba   şugbǫn ti awǫn kekeke bi ayinyin, adindin ati awǫn
take becoming-elder but   that those small like Ayinyin, Adindin, and those

kekeke ko fi nd(i)-agba   ki nwǫn to   ku, bi nwǫn ba   d(i)-
small   not take becoming-elder before they equal die, if they should become-

agba to   iwǫn   ǫdun męta, (ohu)n-kan-kan a   wǫ inu wǫn a   si
elder equal period (of) year three, thing-one-one will enter belly their will and

da   iho s(i)-inu wǫn a si ma   gun wǫn n(i)-inu, nwǫn a
create hole to-belly their will and (continuative) climb them at-belly, they will

si ku.
and die.

This is what the Otu priests do every Ferekete day until this very day.[6]

Ifa says that there is a dead person who has not been given a burial; we should bury his body quickly so that it will not draw others to their death after it.

---

6. This verse thus explains the song sung by the Otu priests on Ferekete day during the Edi festival, and the meaning of the name Otu, "those who appease" (tu).

---

183 - 1

"Bright red Etura, bright red Irosun"[1] was the one who cast Ifa for the 165 kinds of trees[2] in the farm. They said that they should sacrifice six cocks each, six needles each, and three shillings.[3] The Egungun, Iroko, and Apa[4] and all the very large trees of the forest sacrificed, but the trees like Ayinyin, Adindin,[5] and all the trees that are not large did not, and all the very slender trees in the farm and in the forest likewise did not make this sacrifice.

Ifa says that this person should sacrifice so that he will be able to live to old age, and so that a disease of the stomach will not kill him while he is still very small.

This explains why the Iroko, Egungun, Apa, and the big trees of the forest grow old, but the small trees like Ayinyin, Adindin, and the other small trees die before they grow very old. If they live as long as two years, something bores inside them and makes a hole inside them, and they die.[6]

---

1. Roro is a word that intensifies such verbs as "to be red" (pon, pa) and "to shine, or to be bright" (dan). It is used here to modify the names of the figures Otura and Irosun, both of which are conceived to be red, the latter because of its association with camwood (irosun), from which divining powder is made.

2. Cf. n. 3, verse 18-4.

3. Since cowries are counted by units of 2000, there are six units of money as there are six cocks and six needles.

4. Egungun is the Silk Cotton Tree, also known as Araba (Ceiba pentandra); Iroko, the "African Teak or African Oak" (Chlorophora excelsa); and Apa the Mahogany Bean or Rhodesian Mahogany (Afzelia spp.)

5. Ayinyin and Adindin are unidentified small trees.

6. The explanatory element is made more explicit here than in most verses.

Ifa ni ki   a   ru-(ẹ)bọ   nitori   arun   inu kan, ki o
Ifa say should we offer-sacrifice because (of) disease (of) belly one, that it

ba   le   jẹ-ki   e-l(i)-eyi   d(i)-agba.
should be:able consent-that one:who-be-this become-elder.

OTURA IROSUN - 2

Otura ro-ro,   Irosun ro-ro   a   da   fun aro a   lu-(i)-kin
"Otura bright-bright, Irosun bright-bright" who cast for Dye who beat-ikin

fun olokiti   nwọn ni ki   olokiti   ru-(ẹ)bọ   ki   aro ki   o   ru-
for Mordant they say should Mordant offer-sacrifice that Dye should he offer-

(ẹ)bọ.   Nwọn ni   oyun   kan ni   olokiti   yio ni   yi,   ṣugbọn ki
sacrifice. They say pregnancy one be (it) Mordant will have this, but   should

o   ru-(ẹ)bọ   ki   oyun   na ma ba   le   jo;   olokiti   ko ru-
she offer-sacrifice that pregnancy the not should be:able leak; Mordant not offer-

(ẹ)bọ   n(i)-igba-ti o ṣe   oyun   ohun kan si   dalu   ni idi,
sacrifice, at-time-that it make pregnancy, thing one and puncture (her) at waist,

o   bẹrẹ si iṣe   o si   nro   titi o   fi   ro   tan,   o   nwi   pe
she begin to dribble she and dripping until she take drip finish; she speaking that

on iba   mọ, ki   o   ṣe   ẹbọ   Etura ro, Irosun ro   bayi ni
she should know, should she make sacrifice (of) "Etura drip, Irosun drip"; thus be

o   nwi   titi di   oni yi.
she speaking until become today this.

Bẹ-na   ni aro ko ru-(ẹ)bọ,   nwọn ni iṣe   ti   yio ṣe yi   ti
So-also be Dye not offer-sacrifice, they say work that (he) will do this, that

ẹlomiran   ma ba   ma   fi   ṣe   ẹyẹ,   nwọn ni ki   o
another:person not should (continuative) take (it) make benefit, they say that he

ma ba   si ri arun   ti   yio de   mọ   oju-kan ki   a   si   ṣẹ
not should and see disease that will bind (him) against eye-one that they and break

ọpa le   l(i)-ọwọ. Lati   igba-na nitori-ti   aro ko ru-(ẹ)bọ
staff give (him) at-hand. From time-the because-that Dye not offer-sacrifice

ti   o ba   rẹ aṣọ tan   ẹlomiran   ni ilo   ti   si mu
that he should dye cloth finish, another:person be use (them) that (he) and take

lọ s(i)-ode   awọn enia   a   si   ma   wi-pe   O-ko   ri
(them) go to-outside, those people will and (continuative) speak-that "You-not see

iṣe   aro? Aro ni ọkọ   Aṣọ.   Nwọn a   si   fi   ọpa ro   aro,
work (of) Dye? Dye be husband (of) Cloth." They will and take staff stir Dye,

nwọn a   si fi   ọpa rẹ ti   l(i)-ọrun.
they will and put staff his lean at-neck.

Ifa says we should make a sacrifice because of a stomach disease, so that this person will be able to live to an old age.

---

183 - 2

"Bright red Otura, bright red Irosun"[1] was the one who cast Ifa for Dye and who beat palm nuts for Mordant.[2] They said that Mordant should make a sacrifice, and that Dye should make a sacrifice. They said that Mordant would become pregnant, but that she should sacrifice so that the pregnancy should not leak out. Mordant did not sacrifice. When she became pregnant, something pierced her groin and she began to drip, and she dripped until her pregnancy was all gone.[3] She said that had she known, she would have made the sacrifice of "Etura drips, Irosun drips."[4] And this is what she keeps saying until this very day.

Dye likewise did not sacrifice. They said that he should have sacrificed, so that the fruit of his labor should not be enjoyed by someone else. They said that he should sacrifice, so that he would not see a disease which would confine him to one spot, and so that a staff would not be cut and put into his hand for him to use as a cane. From that time on, because Dye did not sacrifice, when a cloth has been dyed, someone else wears it, and people say, "Don't you see the work of Dye? Dye is the husband of Cloth." And they take a staff to stir Dye, and then lean the staff against Dye's neck.[5]

---

1. Cf. n. 1, verse 183-1.

2. Caustic and fresh wood ashes are placed in a large jar in the bottom of which is a hole covered with a piece of matting. Water is poured over the mixture and allowed to drip slowly out of the bottom to make the mordant (olokiti) for indigo dye (aro). The used caustic and ashes are dried in small cakes and then fired in an oven to produce fresh caustic.

3. Miscarriage of a child is compared here with breaking a hole in the mat so that the water runs through the caustic and ashes too quickly, and the mordant is spoiled.

4. Note the pun here on "drip" (ro) and "bright" (ro-ro).

5. This verse has multiple aeteological elements explaining (1) why mordant drips from the jar; (2) the sound of its dripping; (3) why dye never wears the cloths it colors; (4) why dye is stirred with a stick, which is leaned against the pots when not in use; and (5) why dye pots are kept in one place.

Ifa ni ki   obinrin kan ki   o   ru-(ę)bǫ   ki   oyun   kan ti
Ifa say should woman one should she offer-sacrifice that pregnancy one that

o   ni   bayi ma ba   baję ki o si jo da-nu;   ki   ęni-kan
she have thus not should spoil, that it and leak throw-be:lost; should person-one

si tun ru-(ę)bǫ   ki o ma ba   ri ǫrạn   oju-kan ti a-(yi)o
and then offer-sacrifice that he not should see affair (of) eye-one that we-will

fi   şę   ǫpa le   oluwarę   l(i)-ǫwǫ ki ęlomiran   si gba
make break staff give person:in:question at-hand that another:person and take

işę rę şe; ki ęlomiran   ma j(ę)-ihin   işę rę.
work his make; that another:person not eat-news (of) work his.

OTURA IROSUN - 3

Wuyę-wuyę   a   da fun wǫn ni tibǫ,   nwǫn ni ki   nwǫn ru-
"Quietly-quietly" who cast for them at impasse, they say should they offer-

(ę)bǫ   ki ohun gbogbo ti nwǫn ma   ma   şe ki o   ma
sacrifice that thing all   that they (continuative) (continuative) do that they not

ba   ma   şe tibǫ.   Nwǫn ko ru-(ę)bǫ   ni tibǫ,   nwǫn
should (continuative) make impasse. They not offer-sacrifice at impasse, they

şe ǫran   owo   o di   tibǫ   nwǫn şe ǫran   ǫmǫ o di
do affair (of) cowries it become impasse, they do affair (of) child it become

tibǫ   nwǫn si şe ǫran   aya o di   tibǫ   pęlu;
impasse; they and do affair (of) wife it become impasse together:with (the others);

gbogbo ohun ti   nwǫn nşe ni o   nbǫ   si tibǫ.
all   thing that they doing be they coming to impasse.

Ifa ni ki   e-l(i)-eyi   ru-(ę)bǫ   ki o ma ba   ma
Ifa say should one:who-be-this offer-sacrifice that he not should (continuative)

ri ǫran   tibǫ   ti yio fi ma   mu a-mu-bǫ   ti ǫwǫ
see affair (of) impasse that will take (continuative) take to-take-slip from hand

rę ko si ni tę   ohun-k(u)-ohun.
his not and be press thing-any-thing.

OTURA IROSUN - 4

Abata ko gb(a)-ǫkǫ   a   da fun Yewa ti o nlǫ si igbo   iko,
"Mud   not accept-boat" who cast for Yewa that she going to forest (of) raphia;

nwǫn ni ki   o ru-(ę)bǫ   ki o ma ba   nu   si ǫhun ati-pe
they say should she offer-sacrifice that she not should be:lost to there and-that

Ifa says some woman should make a sacrifice so that the pregnancy which she has will not spoil and leak away; and also that someone should make a sacrifice so that he will not find himself confined to one spot, and have a staff cut for him and placed in his hand; and so that someone else will not enjoy the fruits of his labor, and someone else will not get the credit for what he has accomplished.

---

183 - 3

"Very quietly" was the one who cast Ifa for those at an impasse. They said they should make a sacrifice so that everything that they were doing would not come to an impasse. Those at an impasse did not sacrifice. They tried to get money, it came to an impasse; they tried to get children, it came to an impasse; they tried to get wives, it came to an impasse; everything that they were doing came to an impasse.

Ifa says that this person should make a sacrifice so that he will not see his efforts come to an impasse, and so that things will not slip from his grasp and he will not be able to hold on to anything.

---

183 - 4

"Mud does not float a boat" was the one who cast Ifa for Yewa[1] when she was going to the forest of raphia. They said she should make a sacrifice so that she would not get lost there and so that

---

1. Yewa was interpreted by Ifę informants as a contraction of yeye-wa, "our mother," which is consistent with the funeral song below. However, Yewa is also the goddess of the Yewa River near the Dahomean border, and she is associated with raphia (Raphia spp.), mentioned below.

ki   o   ba   le   pada   wa   s(i)-ile.   Yewa gbǫ   ębǫ   ko ru
that she should be:able return come to-house.   Yewa hear sacrifice not offer (it)

titi   o   fi   lǫ si igbo   iko;   n(i)-igba-ti   o   de   ǫhun,   o   ra
until she take go to forest (of) raphia; at-time-that she arrive there, she disappear

si ibę   ko si   tun pada   de   wa   s(i)-ile mǫ.   Awǫn ęgbę   rę
to there, not and then return arrive come to-house again. Those companion hers

ati awǫn iyawo   ęhin rę   ati awǫn ǫmǫ rę   wa   bǫ   s(i)-ode   nwǫn
and those junior:wife back hers and those child hers come come to-outside they

bęrę si kǫ-(o)rin wi-pe:
begin to sing-song speak-that:

> Yewa l(i)-a   nwa   awa o   ri
> "Yewa be-we seeking we not see;

> Yewa l(i)-a   nwa   o   ye e e e e
> "Yewa be-we seeking, oh, ye e e e e;

> Bę l(i)-a   o   sun,   bę l(i)-a   o   wo
> "So be-we not sleep, so be-we not fall-down;

> Yewa l(i)-a   nwa   o   ye e e e e.
> "Yewa be-we seeking, oh, ye e e e e."

Orin yi   ni awǫn ti   o   ba   nwa   oku   ma   nkǫ   titi
Song this be those that they should seeking corpse (continuative) singing until

di   oni yi   n(i)-igba-ti   oku   ba   ku ni ilę   Yoruba.
become today this at-time-that corpse should die at ground (of) Yoruba.

Ifa ni   ęni-kan   nlǫ   si ibi-kan,   ki   o   ru-(ę)bǫ   ki   o
Ifa say person-one going to place-one, should he offer-sacrifice before he

to   lǫ ki   o   ba   le   pada   de   ile   rę n(i)-ibi-ti   o   ti
equal go that he should be:able return arrive house his at-place-that he have

kuro;   bi ko ba   ru-(ę)bǫ   şe   ni nwǫn yio fi   şe   a-wa-
depart; if not should offer-sacrifice make be they will take make to-seek-(not)-

ri titi lai-lai.   Ęiyę-(i)le   męrin ati ęgbajǫ   ai-din   ni
see until ever-ever. Bird-(of)-house four and 16,000 (cowries) not-lessen be

ębǫ.
sacrifice.

OTURUPǪN - (O)TURA[1] - 1

Aja ni   la-(o)mi   l(i)-ęba, eşinşin o   patę   ilękę, Bi iregun   ba
"Dog be (he) lick-water at-side, fly   not display bead," "If reproach should

kǫ   waju   ęhin l(i)-a-pǫn   si a   d(a)-Ifa f(un)-Osu ti
refuse go:front back be-we-carry:on:back (it) to" who cast-Ifa for-Osu   that

---

1. Also known as Oturupǫn-(o)tura o-tu ewurę (Orurupǫn Otura which
propitiates with a she:goat).

she would be able to return home. Yewa heard, but she did not make the sacrifice, waiting until she had gone to the raphia forest. When she got there, she vanished, and she did not come back home again. Her friends and her junior co-wives and her children came out and began to sing:

> "We are looking for Yewa, we cannot find her;
> "We are looking for Yewa, oh, ye e e e e;
> "So we do not sleep, so we do not rest;
> "We are looking for Yewa, oh, ye e e e e."

This is the song that those who are "looking for the dead" sing until this very day when someone has died in Yoruba land.[2]

Ifa says that someone is going somewhere; he should make a sacrifice before he goes so that he may be able to return home to the place from which he starts; if he does not make the sacrifice, they will be looking for him in vain for ever. Four pigeons and four shillings, no less, is the sacrifice.[3]

---

2. This verse thus explains one of the songs sung during the part of the funeral ceremonies known as "looking for the dead person" (iwa oku).

3. For the manner in which this sacrifice is performed, see the end of Chapter VI.

---

204 - 1

"Dog laps up water on the side of his mouth; fly does not display beads for sale" and "If reproach refuses to go forward, then we carry it backward" were the ones who cast Ifa for Osu, who

şe   ǫmǫ   ǫba l(i)-Ęyǫ, Ajǫri, t(i)-o   ni on   rǫ-(ǫ)mǫ-bi   t(i)-
make child (of) king at-Qyǫ, Ajǫri, that-she be she (not) pain-child-bear that-

o   nsǫ-(ę)kun   a-l(i)-ai-bi-(ǫ)mǫ.
she shedding-tears (of) one:who-be-not-bear-child.

        Aja ni   la-(o)mi   l(i)-ęba, ęşinşin ko patę   ilękę, Bi iregun   ba
        "Dog be (he) lick-water at-side, fly   not display bead," "If reproach should

kǫ   waju   ęhin l(i)-a-pǫn   si a   d(a)-Ifa f(un)-Arera ti
refuse go:front back be-we-carry:on:back (it) to" who cast-Ifa for-Arera   that

şe   ǫmǫ   ǫba ni Ifę ti   nsǫ-(ę)kun   a-l(i)-ai-bi-(ǫ)mǫ.
make child (of) king at Ifę that shedding-tears (of) one:who-be-not-bear-child.

        Ębǫ   ti   Arera ni agbo kan. Ębǫ   ti   Osu ni agutan kan.
        Sacrifice that (of) Arera be ram one. Sacrifice that (of) Osu be ewe   one.

Eyi-ti   wǫn yio ma   sin ni   fun Arera, agbo ke(re)-kere; eyi-
This-that they will (continuative) raise be (it) for Arera, ram small-small; this-

ti   wǫn yio ma   sin ni   fun Osu, agutan ke(re)-kere.
that they will (continuative) raise be (it) for Osu, ewe   small-small.

        Awǫn mej(i)-(m)eji ni nwa   ǫmǫ nwǫn si pade Arera do   Osu
        Those two-two   be seeking child they and meet; Arera copulate:with Osu

l(i)-oyun.   Arera sǫ   fun Osu pe Ojodu l(i)-ǫmǫ on yio ma
have-pregnancy. Arera speak for Osu that Ojodu be-child his will (continuative)

ję. Ko pę   l(i)-ęhin   eyi ǫtę   tę   Ojudu ni awǫn ara
eat. Not be:long at-back (of) this conspiracy conspire Ojudu be those people (of)

Ile-Ifę ba   fę   ra a   (fun Qni) pe ki   on fi   şe   ębǫ.
Ile-Ifę meet (him) want buy him (for Qni) that should he take (Ojudo) make sacrifice.

N(i)-igba-ti wǫn so Ojudo mǫ-(i)lę   o bęrę si sǫ-(ę)kun pe ni ilu   on
At-time-that they tie Ojudo against-ground, he begin to shed-tears that at town his

ni wǫn mu on wa   ni Qni ba   fun   ni obi męjǫ ni męrin d(i)-
be they take him come, be Qni should give (him) at kola eight, be four   become-

oju-de   męrin şi-(o)ju si oke, ni wǫn ba   nkǫ-(o)rin bayi:
eye-cover four open-eye to hill, be they should singing-song thus:

              Ojudo de,   ǫmǫ   Arera
              "Ojudo arrive, child (of) Arera;

              Ojudo de,   ǫmǫ   Arera
              "Ojudo arrive, child (of) Arera;

              Ę ba mi dupe   l(i)-ǫwǫ obi ti o yan.
              "You join me give:thanks at-hand kola that it be:good.

              Ojudo de,   ǫmǫ   Arera
              "Ojudo arrive, child (of) Arera;

              Ęran ni   k(i)-o   gba
              "Meat be (it) should-you take;

              Ma ma   gba ori   ǫmǫ.
              "Not (continuative) take head (of) child.

was the child of the King of Qyọ, Ajọri,[1] who had not experienced the pains of childbirth, and who was weeping because she had not borne a child.

"Dog laps up water on the side of his mouth; fly does not display beads for sale," and "If reproach refuses to go forward, then we carry it backward" were the ones who cast Ifa for Arera, who was the child of the King of Ifẹ and who was weeping because he had not begotten a child.

The sacrifice of Arera was one ram. The sacrifice of Osu was one ewe. Arera should raise his little ram.[2] Osu should raise her little ewe.

Both were trying to get children; they met and Arera had intercourse with Osu, and Osu became pregnant. Arera told Osu that his child should be called Ojodu. Not long after this, there was a conspiracy against Ojodu. The people of Ifẹ wanted to buy him so that the Qni could sacrifice him. When they tied Ojodu down, he began to weep that he had been taken to his own town as a captive. He said that the Qni should give him eight kola to cast, and if they should come out four face down and four face up, they should begin to sing:

> "Ojudo comes, the child of Arera;
> "Ojudo comes, the child of Arera;
> "You should give thanks with me that the kola turned out good.[3]
> "Ojudo comes, the child of Arera;
> "You should take an animal as the sacrifice;
> "You should not take the head of a kinsman.

———————

1. This verse was recorded in Igana. Ajọri was said to be another name for Osu, the daughter of the king of Qyọ.

2. That is, he should take a young ram and raise it until it was full grown, when he should sacrifice it.

3. That is, the divination turned out propitiously, with four kola face up and four face down.

Ęran ni   k(i)-o   gba,
"Meat be (it) should-you take;

Ma   ma   gba ori   ǫmǫ
"Not (continuative) take head (of) child;

Ojudo de   ǫmǫ   Arera.
"Ojudo arrive, child (of) Arera."

Lati-(i)gba na ni a ba   ti   nfi   ewurę bǫ   Ifa.
From-time the be we should have taking she:goat sacrifice:to Ifa.

IKA MEJI - 1

Opopo męta   ile   Ila, ǫna   Ojomo odo; męta de-(i)le,
"Street three (of) house (of) Ila, road (of) Ojomo odo; three arrive-house,

męta ko de-(i)le,   Qpę   ke(re)-kere   ile   Irojo a b(i)-
three not arrive-house" "Palm:tree small-small (of) house (of) Irojo it bear-

ęmu   rojo-rojo a   da   fun nwǫn ni Ilabęsan ni ǫjǫ ti   ǫba wǫn wǫ-
palm:wine good-good" who cast for those at Ilabęsan at day that king their enter-

(i)le-eji   nwǫn ni ki   nwǫn lǫ mu erin   wa   ki   wa   fi
house-(of)-rain that   say should they   go take elephant come should come take (it)

ş(e)-ębǫ;   gbogbo awǫn ǫ-l(i)-ǫdę   şe ti,   awun ni on yio şe, o
make-sacrifice; all   those one:who-be-hunter do not, Miser say he will do, he

mu gbogbo ohun ti ęnu ję, o lǫ gbe   ba erin,   n(i)-igba-ti
take all   thing that mouth eat, he go carry (them) meet Elephant, at-time-that

erin   tǫ   wo   o ni Ohun ti iwǫ erin   yio ma
Elephant taste (them) look:at he say "Thing that you, Elephant, will (continuative)

ję ni-(e)yi bi o   ba   de   ile   ti   nwǫn ba   fi   ǫ   j(ę)-ǫba nitori-
eat be-this, if you should arrive house that they   should take you eat-king because-

ti   ǫba   ilu   Ilabęsan ku, iwǫ ni nwǫn si   nfę   fi   j(ę)-ǫba.
that king (of) town (of) Ilabęsan die, you be they and wanting take (you) eat-king."

N(i)-igba-ti erin   gbǫ bayi inu rę dun   o si tęle a-b(i)-
At-time-that Elephant hear thus, belly his be:sweet, he and follow One:who-like-

awun, a-b(i)-awun   si kǫ-(o)rin wi-pe:
Miser, One:who-like-Miser, and sing-song say-that:

A-(yi)o m(u)-erin   j(ę)-ǫba Şękurębęlę
"We-will take-Elephant eat-king, Shękurębęlę;

A-(yi)o m(u)-erin   j(ę)-ǫba Şękurębęlę.
"We-will take-Elephant eat-king, Shękurębęlę.

Bayi ni a-b(i)-awun   bęrę si kǫ-(o)rin titi awǫn mej(i)-(m)eji
Thus be One:who-like-Miser begin to sing-song until those two-two

"You should take an animal as the sacrifice;
"You should not take the head of a kinsman;
"Ojudo comes, the child of Arera."

From that time on, we have sacrificed she-goats to Ifa.[4]

---

4. This verse explains why human sacrifices are no longer made to Ifa, and why she-goats are sacrificed instead.

---

222 - 1

"Three streets of the house in Ila, roads of Ojomo odo;[1] three reach home, three don't reach home" and "Very small palm tree of the house of Irojo yields very good palm wine" were the ones who cast Ifa for the people of Ilabẹsan on the day their king died.[2] They said they should bring an elephant with which to make a sacrifice. All the hunters of the town tried to catch an elephant, but failed; Tortoise said that he would do it. He took all the things that the mouth eats and carried them out to Elephant. When Elephant had tasted them, Tortoise said, "These are the things that you, Elephant, will be eating if you come home so that they can make you king, because the king of the town of Ilabẹsan has died, and you are the one they want to make king." When Elephant heard this, he was happy, and he followed Tortoise, and Tortoise sang:

"We will take Elephant and make him king, Shẹkurẹbẹlẹ;[3]
"We will take Elephant and make him king, Shẹkurẹbẹlẹ."

Thus Tortoise sang until these two

---

1. Ojomo odo is an unidentified town; Ila is a town about forty-five miles northeast of Ifẹ.
2. The euphemism used here is "entered the house of rain." Ilabẹsan is an unidentified town.
3. Shẹkurẹbẹlẹ has no meaning but is added as the refrain "to make the song sound sweet."

fi   de   ile;   n(i)-igba-ti nwǫn wǫ   inu   ilu   ti   awǫn ara
take arrive house; at-time-that they enter belly (of) town that those people (of)

ilu ri erin   nwǫn pariwo ye, ęru si   ba   erin   şugbǫn a-b(i)-
town see Elephant they shout "Ye," fear and meet Elephant but   One:who-like-

awun da   l(i)-ǫkan-le   pe   o   ko ri awǫn ara   ilu bi
Miser cause (him) at-heart-strong that "You not see those people (of) town how

inu wǫn ti   dun   lati ri ǫ?   Şugbǫn ki   erin   ati a-
belly their have be:sweet to see you?" But   before Elephant and One:who-

b(i)-awun to   wǫ ilu ni awǫn ara   ilu ti   gbę ǫfin s(i)-ilę
like-Miser equal enter town be those people (of) town have dig pitfall to-ground

de   wǫn gęgę-bi a-b(i)-awun   ti   kǫ wǫn ki   o   to   lǫ si
wait:for them just-as One:who-like-Miser have teach them before he equal go to

inu   igbo pe on yio lǫ mu erin   wa.   N(i)-igba-ti erin   wǫ
belly (of) forest that he will go take Elephant come. At-time-that Elephant enter

ilu, awǫn ara   ilu ti   tę   ęni le   ori   ǫfin na nwǫn si
town, those people (of) town have spread mat upon head (of) pitfall the, they and

ni ki   erin   wa   joko   le   l(i)-ori nitori-ti   ori   itę
say should Elephant come sit:down upon (it) at-head because-that head (of) spread

ni o ni lati joko   si.   Bi erin   ti   fę lati joko   le   ori
be he be to sit:down to (it). As Elephant have want to sit:down upon head (of)

ęni yi, ni ęni jin   s(i)-inu   ǫfin ti   erin   na si şubu s(i)-inu
mat this, be mat fall:down to-belly (of) pitfall that Elephant also and fall to-belly

ǫfin pęlu;   n(i)-igba-ti awǫn ara   ilu ri ti   erin
(of) pitfall together:with (it); at-time-that those people (of) town see that Elephant

şubu s(i)-inu   ǫfin nwǫn ko igi ti   nwǫn si pa.   Bayi
fall to-belly (of) pitfall they gather tree against (him) they and kill (him). Thus

ni awǫn ara   ilu   Ilabęsan fi erin   ru-(ę)bǫ   si ilu wǫn
be those people (of) town (of) Ilabęsan take Elephant offer-sacrifice to town their

nipa   iran-l(i)-ǫwǫ   a-b(i)-awun   ti   ilu wǫn si bęrę si
concerning sending-at-hand (of) One:who-like-Miser that town there and begin to

to-ro.
be:in:order-stand.

     Ifa ni ęni-kan   wa   ti   ori rę ngbe   lǫ de   ipo   kan,
     Ifa say person-one exist that head his carrying (him) go arrive position one,

şugbǫn ęni-ti   yio ran-l(i)-ǫwǫ ojiji   ni   yio wa, yio si ję
but   person-that will send-at-hand suddenly be (he) will come, will and eat

ęni-ti   a ko gb(e)-oju le   on ni yio ję olu-ran-l(i)-ǫwǫ   na.
person-that we not take-face upon him be will eat one:who-send-at-hand the.

reached home. When they entered into town, the townspeople saw Elephant and began to cheer, "Ye!" Elephant was frightened, but Tortoise encouraged him, saying, "Don't you see how happy the townspeople are to see you?" But before Elephant and Tortoise entered the town, the townspeople had dug a pitfall for them, just as Tortoise had instructed before he went into the forest to get Elephant. When Elephant entered the town, the townspeople had spread a mat on top of the pitfall. And they said that Elephant should come and sit upon it, because the mat was to be the throne on which he was to sit. When Elephant tried to sit down on the mat, the mat fell into the pitfall, and Elephant fell into the pitfall with it. When the townspeople saw that Elephant had fallen into the pitfall, they took sticks and killed him. Thus the people of the town of Ilabęsan were able to sacrifice an elephant for the good of their town, with the help of Tortoise, and their town began to run smoothly again.[4]

Ifa says there is someone whose head[5] will place him in an important position, but the person who will help him will come to his aid suddenly, and someone he does not expect will be his helper.

-----

4. Cf. the versions of this folk tale recorded by Frobenius (1926: 289-292); Ogumefu (1929: 65-68; n.d. 7-9); Jacobs (1933: 9-11); and Walker and Walker (1961: 61-63).
5. That is, his luck or destiny; an important position or office is in store for this person.

IKA MEJI - 2

Jikelewi   awo   ologbo a   da   fun ologbo ni ọjọ ti   o   nfi   oj(umọ)-
"Pouncing," secret (of) Cat   who cast for Cat   at day that he taking dawn-

ojumọ ṣe   owo   a-mu-bọ,   nwọn ni ki   o   ru   abẹrẹ mẹfa,
dawn   make transaction (of) to-take-slip, they say should he offer needle six,

ẹiyẹ-(i)le   mẹfa ati ẹgbafa.   O ru-(ẹ)bọ.   Lati igba-na ni
bird-(of)-house six, and 12,000 (cowries). He offer-sacrifice. From time-the be

ologbo ko ti   mu a-mu-bọ   mọ.
Cat   not have take to-take-slip again.

Ifa ni ẹni-kan   wa   ti o ti   nmu ohun gbogbo ni a-mu-bọ,
Ifa say person-one exist that he have taking thing all   at to-take-slip,

ki   o ru-(ẹ)bọ   ki o ma ba   ma   mu a-mu-bọ   mọ.
should he offer-sacrifice that he not should (continuative) take to-take-slip again.

IKA MEJI - 3

I-ba-re-re   awo   ina a   da   fun ina; nwọn ni ibi-
"To-pay:homage-far-far" secret (of) Fire who cast for Fire; they say place-

k(u)-ibi ti ina ba   fi   ori le,   ni yio jẹ ọna fun,   nwọn ni
any-place that Fire should take head appear, be will eat road for (him), they say

ori rẹ yio la   ọna fun.   Nwọn ni ki   o   ru   akiko adiẹ   mẹta,
head his will open road for (him). They say should he offer cock chicken three,

ẹgbẹtalelọgbọn   ati epo   pupọ. Ina ru-(ẹ)bọ.
6600   (cowries) and palm:oil much. Fire offer-sacrifice.

Ifa ni ẹni-kan   nfẹ   ṣe ohun kan, ki   oluwarẹ   ru-
Ifa say person-one wanting do thing one, should person:in:question offer-

(ẹ)bọ   ki   ọna ba   le   la fun   nitori-ti   bi oluwarẹ
sacrifice that road should be:able open for (him) because-that if person:in:

        ba   ru-(ẹ)bọ   ohun-k(u)-ohun ti o nfẹ,   iba-ṣe
question should offer-sacrifice thing-any-thing that he wanting, should-make

iṣẹ ni   tabi bi o ba   fẹ   ṣe ohun pataki   kan ohun na yio ṣe iṣẹ.
work be (it) or   if he should want do thing important one, thing the will do to:be:
done.

---

222 - 2

"Pouncing," the diviner of Cat, was the one who cast Ifa for Cat when he was trading every day, but having his profits slip from his grasp. They said he should sacrifice six needles, six pigeons, and three shillings.[1] He made the sacrifice. From that time on, Cat has never again had things slip from his grasp.[2]

Ifa says there is someone who is having everything slip from his grasp; he should sacrifice so that things will never slip from his grasp again.

---

1. Since cowries are counted by units of 2000, there are six units of cowries here, as there are six needles and six pigeons.

2. It is understood that the needles became Cat's claws, with which he keeps things from escaping from his grasp. This verse thus explains how cats came to have claws, and why they can hold things tightly.

---

222 - 3

"To pay homage from afar"[1] the diviner of Fire, was the one who cast Ifa for Fire. They said wherever Fire should turn, there would be a way for him; they said his head would open the way for him.[2] They said he should sacrifice three cocks, one shilling seven pence eight oninis, and plenty of palm oil.[3] Fire made the sacrifice.

Ifa says someone wants to do something; he should make a sacrifice, so that the way will be clear for him, because if he should sacrifice, he will be able to do whatever he wants — whether it is work or an important thing that he wants to do.

---

1. The imagery here compares the way one rubs his hands to warm them before the fire with the way in which one "rubs his hands" in paying homage to a ruler. Cf. n. 5, verse 111-1 and n. 2, verse 2-2.

2. The meaning is that Fire will burn its own path wherever it goes.

3. Cf. verse 245-1, where it is specifically stated that the palm oil is poured on Fire to keep him alive.

ỌṢẸ OGBE[1] - 1

Alamurin-rindin-rindin a   da   fun a-l(i)-agẹmọ   ye t(i)-
"Lizard-silly-silly"   who cast for One:who-be-chameleon that that-(of)-

igbi gbẹ,   ọran   a-l(i)-agẹmọ,   ọran   a-l(i)-agẹmọ
time olden; affair (of) One:who-be-chameleon, affair (of) One:who-be-chameleon

bi eyi-ti   a ṣ(e)-epe   sọ. Gbajumọ enia kan wa ti gbogbo aiye
like this-that we make-curse talk. Gentleman person one exist that all   earth

nro   ibi si,   o ru-(ẹ)bọ   ko fin,   o ṣ(e)-ogun,   ko
thinking evil to (him), he offer-sacrifice, not come:to:pass, he make-medicine, not

jẹ fun u. Ki   o ru ẹiyẹ-(i)le   meji ati ẹgba   marun ki
eat for him. Should he offer bird-(of)-house two and 2000 (cowries) five   that

ori rẹ ma ba   buru pata-pata   nitori ti ori bu(ru)-buru
head his not should be:bad completely-completely, because that head be:bad-be:bad

ni   o gbe ti   ọrun wa.
be (it) he carry from sky come.

Ewe   Ifa rẹ: A (yi)o wa a-tẹ-yun   a-tẹ-wa   gbẹgidina ati
Leaf (of) Ifa its: We will seek to-press-go to-press-come gbẹgidina and

ọṣẹ; a-(yi)o gun ẹiyẹ-(i)le   kan mọ;   a-(yi)o si wa   igba
soap; we-will pound bird-(of)-house one against (it); we-will and seek calabash

a-de-mu   kan, a-(yi)o wẹ ori   ẹni   na s(i)-inu rẹ a-(yi)o lọ
to-cover-drink one; we-will wash head (of) person the to-belly its; we-will go

da   si odo ti o ba   nṣan.
pour (it) to river that it should flowing.

Ifa ni ẹni-kan   wa ti o dabi   ẹni-pe   o ngbe ṣ(e)-epe,
Ifa say person-one exist that he resemble person-that they taking make-curse,

ki   ẹni   na lọ wẹ   ori rẹ si odo.
should person the go wash head his to river.

ỌṢẸ OGBE - 2

Koriko nde,   ẹruwa dide   dide   ki o   ma   jo   niṣo
"Grass standing, grass standing, standing that you (continuative) dance proceed

ni-(i)le, ọba nla alẹ   ana   p(a)-ẹran jẹ a   da fun ọ-
at-house, king big (of) evening (of) yesterday kill-meat eat" who cast for one:who-

l(i)-ọfin   a   lu-(i)kin fun Ameri, aya rẹ.
has-palace who beat-ikin for Ameri, wife his.

---

1. Also known as Ọṣẹ-l(u)-Ogbe, meaning Ọṣẹ-against-Ogbe.

225 - 1

"Foolish lizard" was the one who cast Ifa for Chameleon long, long ago. "Chameleon's trouble, Chameleon's trouble"—like this a curse is pronounced. There is a gentleman of whom all the world is thinking evil; he makes a sacrifice, but it has no effect; he makes medicine, but it does not work for him. He should sacrifice two pigeons and two shillings six pence, that his luck may not be completely bad, because he has come from heaven with a bad head.[1]

Ifa's leaves: We will hunt for some gbẹgidina[2] that have been trampled by much coming and going, and some soap; we will pound one pigeon with these; we will take a covered calabash; we will wash the person's head in this mixture in the calabash; we will pour the rest into a river that is flowing.

Ifa says there is someone who is behaving as if he had been cursed; the person should go and wash his head at the river.

---

1. In this case a person who has been given bad luck as part of his destiny is told to sacrifice so that his luck will not be as bad as it might be if he does not sacrifice. (Cf. Chapter XI.)

2. An unidentified kind of grass.

---

225 - 2

"Grass standing, ẹruwa grass[1] standing, stand up and dance home ahead of them; last night the great king killed meat to eat" was the one who cast Ifa for the king and who beat palm nuts for Ameri, his wife.

---

1. Probably <u>Andropogon Gayanus</u> (eruwa funfun) or <u>A</u>. <u>tectorum</u> (eruwa dudu). "Koriko" is a general term for grass.

Ẹni-kan   wa   ti   o   nfi   ohun-gbogbo ṣ(e)-ikẹ   ṣ(e)-igẹ
Person-one exist that he taking thing-all   make-indulgence make-petting

o-l(i)-obinrin   kan, ṣugbọn ajẹ   ni o-l(i)-obinrin   na, ko njẹ
(of) one:who-be-woman one, but   witch be one:who-be-woman the, not consent-

ki (ohu)n-kan   ẹni   ma   gun;   a ru-(ẹ)bọ   ko
ing that thing-one (of) person (continuative) be:orderly; he offer-sacrifice not

fin,   o ṣ(e)-ogun   ko jẹ, ki   a ru-(ẹ)bọ   nitori
come:to:pass, he make-medicine not eat; should he offer-sacrifice because (of)

rẹ ọrọmọ-adiẹ   mẹfa, ọpa   ate   mẹfa, iṣu ẹbẹ; nwọn ni ki
her young-(of)-chicken six,   staff (of) birdlime six,   yam ẹbẹ; they say should

o   ma   gbe   lọ s(i)-inu   oko rẹ, o gbe   ẹbẹ na lọ s(i)-
he (continuative) carry (them) go to-belly (of) farm his, he carry ẹbẹ the go to-

inu   oko rẹ, o si so ọrọmọ-adiẹ   na mọ   atẹtẹ   o
belly (of) farm his, he and tie young-(of)-chicken the against basketry:tray, he

si so awọn ate   na mọ   eti   atẹtẹ   na. Iyale
and tie those birdlime the against ear (of) basketry:tray the. Senior:wife (of)

aya   ọkunrin yi si wa   di   ẹiyẹ, o si fo lọ si oko; n(i)-igba-ti
wife (of) man   this and come become bird, she and fly go to farm; at-time-that

o de   oko, o gbọ igbe   awọn ọrọmọ-adiẹ,   o si fo s(i)-ilẹ,
she arrive farm, she hear cry (of) those young-(of)-chicken, she and fly to-ground,

o ri ẹbẹ, bi o ti   bẹrẹ si jẹ,   bẹ-ni ate   si mu,   o si ku.
she see ẹbẹ, as she have begin to eat, so-be birdlime and take (her), she and die.

Ifa ni ẹ-l(i)-ẹiyẹ   obinrin kan wa   ti   o si duro ti-(ẹ)ni,
Ifa say one:who-be-bird woman one exist that she and stand against-person;

Ifa ni ẹbọ   ti o ma le   pa-(ẹ)ni   ni ki   a ru,   Ifa ni a
Ifa say sacrifice that she not be:able kill-person be should we offer; Ifa say we

ngb(e)-im(ọ)-ọran   kan, ṣugbọn ọta   ẹni   ni a ngb(e)-
taking-knowledge-(of)-affair one, but   enemy (of) (of) person be we taking-

im(ọ)-ọran   na le   l(i)-ọwọ; nitori-na   ki   a ṣọ-(a)ra
knowledge-(of)-affair the upon (him) at-hand; because-the should we watch-body

ki a ma ba   s(ọ)-ọrọ   ni oju   ẹni-ti   yio ṣe   ofofo
that we not should speak-word at face (of) person-that will make tale:bearer (of)

ẹni.
person.

QṢẸ OGBE - 3

Ọṣẹ tu-(e)rutu   a   da   fun A-l(i)-ara   n(i)-igba-ti o nsun-
"Ọṣẹ loosen-dust" who cast for One:who-has-Ara at-time-that he shedding-

(ẹ)kun   a-l(i)-ai-l(i)-owo   l(i)-ọwọ, nwọn ni ki   o ru-
tears (of) one:who-be-not-have-cowries at-hand, they say should he offer-

There is someone who is favoring and indulging a woman with everything; but the woman is a witch. She will not allow his affairs to straighten out. He makes a sacrifice, but it has no effect; he makes medicine, but it does not work. He should sacrifice six baby chickens, six sticks of birdlime,[2] and seasoned mashed yams because of this woman. They said he should carry them into his farm. He carried the seasoned mashed yams into his farm, and he tied the chicks to a basketry tray; he tied the sticks of birdlime to the edge of the tray. The senior wife of this man turned into a bird and she flew to the farm. When she reached the farm, she heard the cries of the baby chickens and flew down to the ground; she saw the seasoned mashed yams and, as she began to eat them, she stuck to the birdlime and she died.[3]

Ifa says there is a bird-woman[4] who is standing beside this person. Ifa says that he should make a sacrifice, so that she will not be able to kill him. Ifa says that we are seeking advice about a matter, but that the person from whom we are seeking advice is an enemy; therefore we should be careful not to speak of it in front of this person, who will prove to be a tale-bearer.

---

2. A sticky substance made from the sap of a tree and used with a decoy to catch parrots in the cornfield. Cf. verse 245-2.

3. Note that all of the items sacrificed are instrumental in catching the witch.

4. A witch. Witches are believed to have birds and other animal familiars and, as stated in this verse, to be able to turn themselves into birds.

---

225 - 3

"Qṣẹ[1] stirs up dust" was the one who cast Ifa for the King of Ara when he was weeping because he had no money. They said he should sacri-

---

1. Qṣẹ is from the name of the figure.

(ẹ)bọ,   o   ru   ẹiyẹ-(i)le   mẹrin ati ekuru funfun. Nwọn ni   ibi
sacrifice; he offer bird-(of)-house four   and ekuru white.   They say if   (not)

ti-rẹ   ni   a-(yi)o f(i)-owo   nini   ti   si.
that-(of)-his be (it) we-will take-cowries having lean to.

      O   l(i)-owo   tan   o   ku   ki   o   ni   aya, o   tun   ru   ayebọ
      He have-cowries finish it remain that he have wife, he then offer hen

adiẹ   meji,   ẹgbẹrindinlogun   ati ẹgbẹrindilọgbọn,   ati keregbe kan, o
chicken two, 3200   (cowries) and 5200   (cowries), and calabash one, he

ni   aya.
have wife.

      Nwọn ni ki   o   ru-(ẹ)bọ   ọmọ bibi   ago   akikọ
      They say should he offer-sacrifice (of) child to:be:born (of) coop (of) cock

adiẹ   kan, ẹtala,   o si bi-(ọ)mọ.
chicken one, 26,000 (cowries), he and bear-child.

      O   ni   ki   on jẹ oye, o   tun ru   ẹbọ   agbo kan, igan
      They say should he eat title, he then offer sacrifice (of) ram one, piece (of)

aṣọ   funfun kan, igba   ẹfun kan.
cloth white   one, calabash (of) chalk one.

      O   ni   ki   o   pẹ   l(i)-ori   oye, o   ru   ẹiyẹ-(i)le   funfun
      They say should he be:long at-head (of) title, he offer bird-(of)-house white

mẹrin, aṣọ   funfun, ẹgbarin,   o d(i)-agba   a   si   nsa   l(i)-
four,   cloth white, 8000   (cowries); he become-elder we and drying (him) at-

orun.
sun.

      Ifa ni ọmọ ke(re)-kere kan wa   yio ba   ẹṣẹ ja-(o)ri.
      Ifa say child small-small one exist, will with row reach-head.

                (E)m(i)-a y(an)-owo,   y(an)-ọmọ
                "I-will   choose-cowries, choose-child,

                E   si ye   mo le   yinnu
                "Not be that I   be:able leave;

                (E)m(i)-a y(an)-owo,   y(an)-ọmọ
                "I-will   choose-cowries, choose-child,

                E   si ye   mo le   yinnu
                "Not be that I   be:able leave."

Ifa ni ọba   ọrun da   ọja   kan fun a-l(i)-agba   kan, ki   iwa
Ifa say King (of) Sky   create market one for one:who-be-elder one, that destiny

rẹ   ma bajẹ ni oju rẹ l(i)-aiye ni ki   o   ru-(ẹ)bọ   fun.
his not spoil at eye his at-earth be should he offer-sacrifice for (it).

---

fice; he sacrificed four pigeons and white steamed beans. They said no one would have as much money as he.

He got money, but he still needed wives. He sacrificed two hens, nine pence six oninis, and one shilling three pence six oninis, and one calabash. He got wives.

They said he should sacrifice a coop full of cocks and six shillings six pence, so that he might have children, and he got children.

They said he would take a title; then he sacrificed one ram, one length of white cloth, and one calabash of chalk.

They said he would remain in office for a long time; he sacrificed four white pigeons, a white cloth,[2] and two shillings. He grew so old that they had to warm him in the sun.[3]

Ifa says there is a very small child who will complete his task.

> "I will choose money, I will choose children;
> "I will not be able to depart.[4]
> "I will choose money, I will choose children;
> "I will not be able to depart."

Ifa says that the King of the Sky will "create a market"[5] for an old person; so that his destiny[6] may not spoil while he is still alive on earth, he should make a sacrifice.

---

2. Note the recurrence of the color white: white steamed beans, a piece of white cloth, a calabash of chalk, four white pigeons, and a white cloth. The figure ọṣẹ is associated with the color white, because of the similarity of its name to the Yoruba for soap (ọṣẹ) which, though black, yields white suds.

3. Literally, to dry him out in the sun.

4. Probably, to leave this earth; to die.

5. This is a figure of speech for giving him a large family and many followers, as numerous as the crowds in the market.

6. The implication is that this destiny includes money, children, a title, and long life.

ỌṢẸ OGBE - 4

Kere-tọ-gburu-wọ-amu   a   da   fun Q-l(i)-ọfin-l(i)-
"Dipper-jump-continuously-enter-jar" who cast for One:who-has-palace-has-

aga-oyinbo   ti a   ni ki   o wa   ru-(ẹ)bo   nitori
chair-(of)-whiteman that they say should he come offer-sacrifice because (of)

a-b(i)-oyun   ile rẹ. Ifa ni a-b(i)-oyun   kan ni-
one:who-bear-pregnancy (of) house his. Ifa say one:who-bear-pregnancy one be-

(e)yi ki   o   ma ṣe   eṣe   lai. Nwọn ni ki   o   ru   igiripa
this should she not make calamity, alas! They say should he offer full:grown

obukọ kan, amu   omi kan, egbejila   ati aṣọ   idi   obinrin
he:goat one, jar (of) water one, 2400   (cowries) and cloth (of) waist (of) woman

na, Q-l(i)-ọfin   ko ru-(ẹ)bọ.
the; One:who-has-palace not offer-sacrifice.

    N(i)-igba-ti a-b(i)-oyun   yi ma   bi, o bi
    At-time-that one:who-bear-pregnancy this (continuative) bear, she bear

ọmọ-(ọ)kunrin kan, nwọn si sọ   orukọ rẹ ni Ade-rin-mọ-(ọ)la.   N(i)-
child-man   one, they and speak name his be Crown-walk-against-honor. At-

igba-ti   ọmọ yi to   s(ọ)-ọrọ,   ko s(ọ)-ọrọ; n(i)-igba-ti o di
time-that child this equal speak-word, not speak-word; at-time-that he become

agba tan   o ya(n)-(o)di;   nwọn ṣe titi ko le   s(ọ)-ọrọ;   nwọn mu
elder finish he become-dumb; they do until not be:able speak-word; they take

   fun a   pa ẹfọn pe ki   nwọn mu   lọ si oko   ẹfọn
(him) for those:who kill buffalo that should they take (him) go to farm (of) buffalo

pe boya   yio le   s(ọ)-ọrọ; ẹfọn fọn mọ   titi ko
that perhaps (he) will be:able speak-word; buffalo blow against (him) until not

s(ọ)-ọrọ,   nwọn mu   fun awọn a p(a)-erin   pe boya   bi erin
speak-word. They take (him) for those who kill-elephant that perhaps if elephant

ba ke mọ   boya o le   s(ọ)-ọrọ ṣugbọn ko le   s(ọ)-
should cry against (him) perhaps he be:able speak-word but   not be:able speak-

ọrọ; n(i)-igba-ti gbogbo wọn ṣe ti ni ahun da-(o)hun ti o ni on yio
word; at-time-that all   them do not, be Miser break-voice that he say he will

ṣe   ọmọ na yio si s(ọ)-ọrọ,   Q-l(i)-ọfin   ni bi ahun ba
do (it) child the will and speak-word. One:who-has-palace say if Miser should

le   ṣe ti   o si s(ọ)-ọrọ   on yio da ile   on si meji-meji on
be:able do (it) that he and speak-word, he will break house his to two-two   he

yio si fi   jin.
will and take (it) give (him).

    N(i)-igba-ti o mu ọmọ yi de   ile o ni ki   nwọn ba on wa
    At-time-that he take child this arrive home he say should they join him seek

ẹru   ọpa   atori meji ati (l)ọpọ-lọpọ oyin   igan, nwọn si ko
load (of) staff (of) atori two and much-much honey (of) bee; they and gather

225 - 4

"The dipper jumps in and out of the water jar"[1] was the one who cast Ifa for the King who has a Whiteman's chair.[2] They said he should make a sacrifice on behalf of a pregnant woman in his house. Ifa says this concerns a pregnant woman; do not let her meet with calamity,[3] alas! They said he should sacrifice one full grown he-goat, one jar of water,[4] seven pence two oninis, and the cloth from the woman's waist. The king did not sacrifice.

When this pregnant woman gave birth, she gave birth to a boy; they said his name was "Crown walks with honor." When he was old enough to talk, he did not talk; and when he grew up, he was a dumb mute. They tried and tried but could not get him to speak. They took him to the buffalo hunters to have them take him to the place where the buffalo live, hoping that perhaps he would be able to talk; the buffalo bellowed at him, but he did not speak. They took him to the elephant hunters, hoping that perhaps if the elephants should trumpet at him, he would be able to talk; but he could not talk. When all of them had tried and failed, Tortoise said that he would do it, and that the child would talk. The king promised that if Tortoise was able to do it, and the child did speak, he would divide his house in two, and give half to Tortoise.

When Tortoise brought this child home, he said that they should find him two loads of switches[5] and lots of honey.[6] They gathered

----

1. The amu is a large, narrow-necked pot in which water is stored; the kere is a dipper, which was formerly made of a snail shell.
2. Chairs of European manufacture were used as thrones by some Yoruba kings.
3. The phrase "şe eşe" is used to refer to the death of pregnant women, an especially evil event requiring removal of the foetus before burial, or for those killed accidentally by hunters and, today, for those killed in automobile accidents. Here it refers to the birth of a dumb mute.
4. Note the reference to the name of the diviner.
5. Switches made from the atori bush. See n. 4, verse 33-1.
6. Igan was explained as meaning the honey bee, also known as oyin. Cf. n. 3, verse 18-8.

gbogbo rẹ wa   fun.   N(i)-igba-ti ahun ri oyin yi   gba   o
all   his come for (him). At-time-that Miser see honey this (he) accept (it) he

gbe   lọ si oju   ọna gbogbo ẹni-ti   o ba   nkọja lọ ntọ
carry (it) go to eye (of) road all   person-that he should passing go tasting (it)

la   ṣugbọn n(i)-igba-ti Ade-rin-mọ-(ọ)la   de   ibẹ ti o fi ọwọ
lick but   at-time-that Crown-walk-against-honor arrive there that he put hand

bọ   oyin yi ti o si tọ-la,   ahun ti o ti sa pa-mọ
enter honey this that he and taste-(it)-lick, Miser that he have run kill-against

s(i)-inu   igbo yọ   si   o si da   ni ọwọ ni, o si sọ   fun
to-belly (of) forest appear to (him) he and hold (him) at hand (1), he and speak for

        pe o ji   on ni oyin. Bayi ni ahun mu   ni ole ti o si
(him) that he steal him at honey. Thus be Miser take (him) at thief that he and

ko   ọpa bo   ti o si bẹrẹ si lati na,   n(i)-igba-ti o pẹ
gather staff cover (him) that he and begin to to whip (him), at-time-that it be:

     ti o ti nna,   o na   ni ọrun, n(i)-igba-ti o na
long that he have whipping (him), he whip (him) at neck, at-time-that he whip (him)

ni ọrun, o dun ọmọ yi pupọ o si ke gbo,   o ni:
at neck, it pain child this much he and cry loudly, he say:

        Ade-rin-mọ-(ọ)la   ọmọ   Ọṣin
        "Crown-walk-against-honor, child (of) Ọshin,

             Ọmọ   Ọṣin
             Child (of) Ọshin;

        Mo b(a)-erin   de-(i)gbo   erin
        "I   join-elephant arrive-forest (of) elephant,

             Ọmọ   Ọṣin
             Child (of) Ọshin;

        Mo b(a)-efọn   r(e)-oko   i-p(a)-ẹfọn
        "I   join-buffalo go-farm (of) to-kill-buffalo,

             Ọmọ   Ọṣin
             Child (of) Ọshin;

        Mo b(a)-ogodo   r(e)-oko   iyo
        "I   join-young:animal go-farm (of) Iyo,

             Ọmọ   Ọṣin
             Child (of) Ọshin.

        Ogodo   ni mo j(i)-oyin   jẹ
        "Young:animal be I   steal-honey eat,

             Ọmọ   Ọṣin
             Child (of) Ọshin;

_____

1. Da . . . ni means "to hold."

the things and brought them to him. Tortoise took the honey, and carried it to a
path. Everyone passing by tasted it, but when "Crown walks with honor" came
there and put his finger into the honey and licked it, Tortoise, who had hidden in
the forest, came out and seized him, and accused him of stealing his honey. Thus
did Tortoise catch him as a thief, and he picked up the switches and covered him
with blows, beginning to whip him. When he had been whipping him for a long
time, he whipped him on the neck. When he whipped him on the neck, it hurt this
child very much, and he cried out loudly, saying:

> "Crown walks with honor, child of Qshin,
>> Child of Qshin;
> "I went with elephants to the forest of elephants,
>> Child of Qshin;
> "I went with buffalo to the farm where they hunt buffalo,
>> Child of Qshin;
> "I went with a young animal[7] to the farm of Iyo,[8]
>> Child of Qshin.
> "I stole the young animal's honey to eat,
>> Child of Qshin;

---

7. This refers to Tortoise, as is shown in the following line.
8. This was explained only as the name of the farm.

Ade-rin-mọ-(ọ)la   ọmọ   Ọṣin
"Crown-walk-against-honor, child (of) Ọshin,

    Ọmọ   Ọṣin
    Child (of) Ọshin;

Yesi l(i)-o   l(i)-ogodo?   Yesi l(i)-o   l(i)-oyin?
"Who be-who have-young:animal? Who be-who have-honey?

    Ọmọ   Ọṣin
    Child (of) Ọshin;

Baba   mi l(i)-o   l(i)-ogodo   on l(i)-o   l(i)-oyin,
"Father my be-who have-young:animal, he be-who have-honey,

    Ọmọ   Ọṣin.
    Child (of) Ọshin."

Bayi ni Ade-rin-mọ-(ọ)la   bẹrẹ si kọ-(o)rin ti   o si bẹrẹ si s(ọ)-
Thus be Crown-walk-against-honor begin to sing-song that he and begin to speak-

ọrọ titi o pẹlu   ahun fi   de   ile.   N(i)-igba-ti Ọṣin ri
word until he together:with Miser take arrive house. At-time-that Ọshin see (him)

inu rẹ dun   pupọ o si da   ile   ati ọna rẹ si meji-meji o si
belly his be:sweet much he and break house and road his to two-two   he and

ko   fun ahun.
gather (half) for Miser.

Ifa ni ki   a   ru-(ẹ)bọ   nitori   obinrin a-b(i)-oyun   kan,
Ifa say should we offer-sacrifice because woman one:who-bear-pregnancy one,

ki ọmọ   inu rẹ ma ba   ya(n)-(o)di, ki o   si na   ni owo
that child (of) belly hers not should become-dumb, that she and spend at cowries

pupọ.
much.

QṢẸ - (O)TURA - 1

Kọlọbọ   ti   ẹnu   awo gba ire   a   da   fun gbogbo
"Throat:disease from mouth (of) plate take goodness" who cast for all

aiye n(i)-igba-ti ai-san   nja.   Ẹṣu ni ẹbọ   yio ma
earth at-time-that not-be:better fighting. Eshu say sacrifice will (continuative)

fin   bi awọn enia   aiye ba   fi   ti   on ṣe. Awọn enia
come:to:pass if those people (of) earth should take that (of) his do. Those people

    aiye si wa   fi agbọn   igbin kan, agbo kan, ẹgba   meje
(of) earth and come take basket (of) snail one, ram one, 2000 (cowries) seven

ru-(ẹ)bọ   na; lati igba-na ni aiye ti   bẹrẹ si dara.
offer-sacrifice the; from time-the be world have begin to be:good.

"Crown walks with honor, child of Qshin,
      Child of Qshin;
"Whose is the young animal? Whose is the honey?
      Child of Qshin;
"My father owns the young animal, he owns the honey,
      Child of Qshin."[9]

In this way "Crown walks with honor" began to sing and he began to talk until he and Tortoise came back home. When Qshin, the king, saw that he was talking, he was very happy and divided his house and home[10] in two and gave half to Tortoise.

Ifa says we should sacrifice because of a pregnant woman, lest the child within her be a dumb mute and lest she spend much money because of it.

---

9. This is a song sung in typical leader-chorus pattern, with "Child of Qshin" as the refrain sung by the chorus.

10. The Yoruba idiom is "his house and road," meaning all his possessions. Cf. the versions of this tale recorded by Bouche (1885: 225-226); Ellis (1894: 263-265); Frobenius (1926: 237-238); Jacobs (1933: 28-30); and Itayemi and Gurrey (1953: 51-53).

---

236 - 1

"Sore throat takes the good from the plate"[1] was the one who cast Ifa for all the people on earth when they were afflicted with illness. Eshu says that the sacrifice will be effective if they will do as he says. The people on earth came and sacrificed one basket of snails, one ram, and three shillings six pence. From that time on, the world began to be good.

---

1. Kǫlǫbǫ was described by informants as a throat disease which turns the throat and tongue black and prevents one from eating. Abraham equates it with efu, which he defines as "thrush (a disease causing white patches on the tongue and mouth and preventing one eating pepper)." In either case, it spoils the joy of eating. This verse was recorded from Araba of Modakękę, a suburb of Ifę founded by refugees from the Qyǫ area during the wars of the last century.

ỌṢẸ MEJI - 1

Akọda awo   ẹ-l(i)-ẹrupẹ,   Ọdọrọgi awo   o-d(a)-
"Akọda, secret (of) one:who-has-dirt," "Too:long, secret (of) one:who-cause-

oro a   da f(un)-Ọrunmila n(i)-ọjọ ti ibi gbogbo   inu   aiye fẹ
pain" who cast for-Ọrunmila at-day that evil all   (of) belly (of) earth want

mu   lọ. O ni on na ni   ọga   bi ti   wọn na, ti o si
take (him) go. He say he also have master as that (of) them also, that he and

ma   gba   l(i)-ọwọ wọn ti   ko ni jẹ-ki   nwọn mu on
(continuative) take (him) at-hand their that (he) not be consent-that they take him

lọ.
go.

O tọ   awọn ẹiyẹ fin-fin   inu   ọgan   lọ, ẹiyẹ
He approach those bird be:white-be:white (of) belly (of) termite:hill go, bird

ma-fin-ma-fin   apa osi ẹiyẹ fin-fin   ti o ti   inu
not-be:white-not-be:white (of) arm left, bird be:white-be:white that they from belly

ọgan   fo wa s(i)-aiye. Ẹiyẹ fin-fin   inu   ọgan
(of) termite:hill fly come to-earth. Bird be:white-be:white (of) belly (of) termite:

ni o ni ki   Ọrunmila mu obi ifin wa.   Ẹiyẹ ma-fin-ma-
hill be who say should Ọrunmila take kola white come. Bird not-be:white-not-

fin   apa osi on ni o ni ki   Ọrunmila mu obi ipa wa.   Ẹiyẹ
white (of) arm left his be who say should Ọrunmila take kola red come. Bird

fin-fin   ti o ti inu   ọgan   fo w(a)-aiye ni ki
be:white-be:white that they from belly (of) termite:hill fly come-earth say should

Ọrunmila mu atare   wa,   nwọn fi   g(un)-egiri fun Ọrunmila. Nwọn
Ọrunmila take Guinea:pepper come; they take (it) pound:egiri for Ọrunmila. They

ni   ori ki ifọ   awun, ẹdọ ki idun igbin, etu ki ipa ọta   ni ilẹ
say, "Head not break Miser, liver not pain snail, cold not kill quartz at ground (of)

odo.   Nwọn ni ibi ko ni   le   mu.   Yio da iyẹ-
river." They say evil not be (it) be:able take (him). Will cast wood:dust-(of)-

(i)rosun na si ọbẹ na yio jẹ.
irosun   the to stew the will eat (it).

ỌṢẸ MEJI - 2

A-(yi)o fi   ẹfun ati osun   tẹ   Ọṣẹ Meji s(i)-ara   ogiri.
We-will take chalk and camwood press Ọṣẹ Meji to-body (of) wall.

Ewu   f(i)-ori   arugbo   ṣe-(i)le,   imọ   gbigbẹ ko ni
"Grey:hair take-head (of) old:person make-house, palm:leaf dry   not have

ọran   atiro l(i)-ọrun, a   da   Ifa fun obi ti o nti   ode
affair (of) basket at-neck" who cast Ifa for Kola that they leaving outside (of)

239 - 1

Akǫda,[1] the diviner of "One who owns soil," and "Too long,"[2] the diviner of "Causer of pain," were the ones who cast Ifa for Ǫrunmila on the day that all the evil spirits in the world wanted to carry him away. He said that he, too, had a master[3] as they did, and that his master would deliver him from their hands and not let them carry him away.

He went to the white birds inside the termite hill, to the white-spotted birds on the left side, and to the white birds who flew to earth from inside the termite hill. The white birds inside the termite hill said that Ǫrunmila should bring white kola. The white-spotted birds on the left side said Ǫrunmila should bring red kola. The white birds who flew to earth from inside the termite hill said that Ǫrunmila should bring Guinea pepper.[4] They pounded these things to make egiri medicine[5] for Ǫrunmila. They said, "The head of tortoise does not ache; the liver of snail does not hurt him; the stone at the bottom of the river does not feel cold." They said that the evil spirits would not be able to carry him away. We will pour the divining powder into the stew and eat it.[6]

---

1. The title of one of the diviners of the King of Ifę. (See Chapter X.)
2. Something that is too long.
3. The ancestral guardian soul is sometimes referred to as one's "master" (ǫga).
4. Aframomum melegueta, also known as Maleguetta pepper or "Alligator pepper."
5. Egiri is a kind of medicine to prevent death.
6. After the figure Ǫsę Meji is marked in the divining powder and this verse has been recited, the powder is added to a stew made of a small tortoise and a small snail, which are removed from their shells, and white kola, red kola, Guinea pepper, salt, pepper, and palm oil. This is a charm or medicine to prevent death known as "not-die" (aiku) or "not-see-death" (ariku, a ri iku); egiri, mentioned in the verse was said to be another name for such a charm. Cf. the verse recorded by Lijadu (1923: 26).

---

239 - 2

We will mark Ǫsę Meji on the side of a wall with chalk and camwood.[1]

"Grey hairs make their home on the heads of the aged; dry palm leaves cannot carry burdens[2] on their shoulders" was the one who cast Ifa for Kola, when they were coming from

---

1. The figures Ǫsę meji and Ofun meji can be seen drawn for protection in chalk and camwood on the wall of houses. Cf. verse 256-6.
2. Literally "do not see the affair of an atiro," which is a basketry framework used for carrying bundles.

ọrun bọ   ni ode   aiye,   nwọn ni   ki   nwọn ru-(ẹ)bọ   ki-(a)r(a)-
sky   come at outside (of) earth; they say should they offer-sacrifice that-people-

aiye   ma le   pa wọn,   aburo   wọn ke(re)-kere ni o   ru
(of)-earth not be:able kill them, junior:sibling their small-small be who offer

ẹbọ;   awọn ẹgbọn   ko ru   Aburo   wọn ni awẹ   ke(re)-
sacrifice; those elder:sibling not offer. Junior:sibling their be section small-

kere ti   a   ma   nyọ   si ọtọ.   Lati igba-na ni ar(a)-
small that we (continuative) pulling:out to aside. From time-the be people-(of)-

aiye ti   ma   npa   obi.
earth have (continuative) killing kola.

      A-(yi)o jẹ obi fọn   l(i)-ẹhin   igba-ti   a   ba   ti tẹ   tan,
      We-will eat kola blow (it) at-back (of) time-that we should have press finish,

pe ki   apa   ar(a)-aiye   ma le   ka-(ẹ)ni.   Akikọ mẹta
that should arm (of) people-(of)-earth not be:able go:around-person. Cock three

ati ẹgbẹdogun   ni ẹbọ.
and 3000   (cowries) be sacrifice.

OFUN OGBE[1] - 1

      Ẹ-ra-ni-dẹdẹ   l(i)-o d(a)-Ifa ko-(I)gun ti o nlọ si ilu   Igbo
      "You-fly-at-low" be-who cast-Ifa for-Vulture that he going to town (of) Igbo

      dẹdẹ, nwọn ni arẹ   ko ni mu,   nwọn ni ko ni ri   idagiri
(of) low;   they say fatigue not be take (him), they say not be see catastrophe (of)

ojojo,   nwọn ni ni akoko ti   ebi   ba   ma   pa   ni Olodu-
sickness, they say at time that hunger should (continuative) kill (him) be Olodu-

mare yio ma   gba onjẹ ti   yio jẹ ko.   Igun   ru   i-
mare will (continuative) carry food that (he) will eat meet (him). Vulture offer to-

san-mọ-(i)di   aṣọ   idi rẹ, oru   epo   kan, obukọ kan; Igun
wrap-against-waist cloth (of) waist his, pot (of) palm:oil one, he:goat one; Vulture

ru-(ẹ)bo.   Bi o ba   da   ki ebi   pa Igun,   idagiri   yio
offer-sacrifice. If it should happen that hunger kill Vulture, catastrophe will

da   ni ilu.
occur at town.

      Ifa ni a   nlọ   ṣe ohun kan, o ni   on ko ni jẹ-ki   a   ri ojojo
      Ifa say we going do thing one, he say he not be consent-that we see sickness

ni ibi   (ohu)n-kan na, o ni e-l(i)-ekeji   ẹni   ọrun yio
at place (of) thing-one the, he say one:who-be-second (of) person (of) sky will

ti-(ẹ)ni   l(i)-ẹhin ni idi   (ohu)n-kan na, oju ko ni ti-(ẹ)ni.
push-person at-back at waist (of) thing-one the, eye not be push-person.

---

1. Also known as Ofun-na-(O)gbe, meaning Ofun-reaches-Ogbe.

---

heaven to earth. They said that they should sacrifice so that human beings would not be able to kill them. Their little junior siblings were the ones who made the sacrifice; the elder siblings did not sacrifice. The junior siblings are the small sections of kola nuts[3] that we set aside. From that time on, people have been killing Kola.[4]

We will chew kola and blow it out after we have marked the figure on the wall, so that witches will not be able to take this person.[5] Three cocks and nine pence is the sacrifice.

----

3. The tiny bits or natural segments (awẹ) of the kola nut (Cola acuminata) are not eaten but picked out and set aside. The verse explains why this is so, and why the larger segments are eaten.

4. To split kola is spoken of as to "kill it"; the meaning is that it is eaten.

5. Literally "to encircle," referring to the fact that a kola nut can be enclosed in the hand; but the meaning here is that they will not be able to kill him.

----

241 - 1

"Fly low" was the one who cast Ifa for Vulture when he was going to the town of low Igbo.[1] They said that he would not become tired. They said he would not meet with the misfortune of sickness. They said that when he became hungry, the Sky God would bring food for him to eat. Vulture sacrificed the sash from his waist, a small pot of palm oil, and one he-goat. Vulture made the sacrifice. If it happens that Vulture is hungry, a catastrophe will occur in the town.[2]

Ifa says we are going to do something. He says that he will not allow us to meet with sickness there. He says our spiritual double in heaven[3] will assist us in this thing, and we will not be disgraced.

----

1. According to Ifẹ tradition the Igbo were a group of people located toward the south, who fought with Ifẹ until they were defeated by Mọrẹmi. See n. 5, verse 24-1.

2. Cf. verses 5-2, 248-1. This explains why any disaster in town benefits Vulture, who feeds on the bodies of dead animals and on the sacrifices offered to bring the disaster to an end.

3. The ancestral guardian soul.

OFUN OGBE - 2

Ọjẹrẹ   agbado f(i)-ori   j(ọ)-Egun   ko le   ṣe iṣe
"Sprout (of) corn   with-head resemble-Egungun, not be:able do deed (of)

Egungun a   da   fun Itọ,   a   lu   fun Itọ a   da   fun Atọ   ti   iṣe
Egungun" who cast for Urine, who beat for Spit, who cast for Semen that make

ọmọ ik(an)-ẹhin   wọn; nwọn ni ki   awọn mẹt(a)-(m)ẹta ru-(ẹ)bọ
child standing-back (of) them; they say should those three-three   offer-sacrifice

ki nwọn ba   ma   di   odidi,   adiẹ   mẹwa-mẹwa ati
that they should (continuative) become entire, (of) chicken ten-ten   and

ẹgb(awa)-ẹgbawa.   Nwọn ni ki ọran wọn ba   le   ma
20,000-20,000   (cowries). They say that affair their should be:able (continuative)

ni   ori. Itọ ko ru-(ẹ)bọ   bẹ-ni   Itọ ko pa-(E)ṣu.   Atọ
have head. Urine not offer-sacrifice, so-be (it) spit not appease-Eshu. Semen

ti   iṣe   ọmọ ik(an)-ẹhin   wọn ru adiẹ   mẹwa ati ẹgbawa
that make child standing-back (of) them offer chicken ten   and 20,000 (cowries)

ti-rẹ.
that-(of)-his.

N(i)-igba-ti o ṣe   bi Itọ ba   ba-(i)lẹ   o p(a)-ora,
At-time-that it make (later) as Spit should strike-ground he kill-disappearance,

bi Itọ ba   ba-(i)lẹ   a wọ-(i)lẹ   lọ, Atọ ba-(i)lẹ   o di
as Urine should strike-ground he enter-ground go, Semen strike-ground he become

ọmọ kandi-kandi.
child healthy-healthy.

Ta   l(i)-o bi   nwọn-yi wẹrẹ?
"Who be-who bear those-this tiny?

Atọ   l(i)-o bi   nwọn-yi wẹrẹ, Atọ
"Semen be-who bear those-this tiny, Semen."

Ifa ni awọn mẹta kan wa   ti   iṣe   ọmọ   iya   kan na, ki   nwọn
Ifa say those three one exist that make child (of) mother one the, should they

ru-(ẹ)bọ   ki nwọn ma ba   ra   mọ   aiye l(i)-ara ki o si
offer-sacrifice that they not should disappear against earth at-body that it and

ku   eyi a-bi-k(an)-ẹhin   wọn.
remain this one:who-born-stand-back (of) them.

OFUN OGBE - 3

Ijanwọn   irin, Ijanwọn   irin, ariwọ   irin ko ni   a-fa-ya
"Scraps (of) iron, Scraps (of) iron, hook (of) iron not be (it) to-pull-split"

a   da   fun Oriṣala Ọṣẹrẹgbo nwọn ni ki   o wa   ru-(ẹ)bọ
who cast for Orishala Ọshẹrẹgbo, they say should he come offer-sacrifice (of)

241 - 2

"Corn tassels look like an Egungun[1] but cannot do what Egungun can" was the one who cast Ifa for Urine, beat palm nuts for Spit, and cast Ifa for Semen,[2] who was their younger sibling. They said that these three should sacrifice ten chickens each and five shillings each so that they might become whole persons,[3] and so that their affairs might be able to come to a successful conclusion. Urine did not sacrifice, nor did Spit appease Eshu. Semen, the youngest born of these three, sacrificed his ten chickens and five shillings.

Afterward, whenever Spit touches the ground, he disappears; and when Urine touches the ground, he goes into it; but when Semen touches the ground,[4] he turns into a healthy child.

"Who is it that begets these tiny children?
"Semen is the one who begets these tiny children, Semen."

Ifa says there are three people who are children of the same mother; they should make a sacrifice so that they will not disappear from the face of the earth, leaving only the last born among them.

---

1. That is, the corn stalk has a decoration on top like the headpiece of an Egungun costume. Ǫjẹrẹ, though referring here to the tassel, was said to mean, more generally, new sprouts or leaves of any plant. Cf. verse 166-1.

2. Note the pun on Urine (Itǫ), Spit (Itǫ), and Semen (Atǫ).

3. So that they might become children as Semen does.

4. It is understood that this means when it enters the womb. The verse thus explains why only semen can produce children.

---

241 - 3

"Scrap iron, scrap iron, iron hooks do not break"[1] was the one who cast Ifa for the God of Whiteness. They said that he should come and make a sacrifice

---

1. Like the usual ones, made of wood. Cf. n. 1, verse 4-4.

awǫn ǫmǫ rẹ meji wẹrẹ-wẹrẹ, o ni on ko le   ru-(ẹ)bǫ,   o ni on
those child his two tiny-tiny,   he say he not be:able offer-sacrifice, he say he

ni on da   ẹru ti on si da   ǫmǫ; ko pẹ   o ran awǫn ǫmǫ nwǫn-
be he create slave that he and create child; not be:long he send those child those-

yi ni oko, n(i)-igba-ti nwǫn de   ǫna, odo gbe   ǫkan lǫ n(i)-inu nwǫn,
this at farm, at-time-that they arrive road, river carry one go at-belly their,

n(i)-ibi-ti   nwǫn wa nwǫ ki,   ina bǫ s(i)-ile   ǫkan
at-place-that they come flocking greet (him), fire come to-house (of) one

ti o ku   si jona   s(i)-inu   ile na.
that he remain and burn (him) to-belly (of) house the.

    Ifa ni awǫn ǫmǫ meji kan wa ki   baba wǫn ru akikǫ meji, ẹgbafa,
    Ifa say those child two one exist should father their offer cock two, 12,000

        ati agbǫn   ẹkǫ   kan ki awǫn ǫmǫ na ma ba
(cowries), and basket (of) cornstarch:porridge one that those child the not should

ku; tabi ki   a sǫ-(a)ra nitori   awǫn ǫmǫ meji kan, ki ǫkan ma
die; or should we watch-body because (of) those child two one, that one not

ba   jona ki ekeji ma ku s(i)-odo.
should burn that second not die to-river.

OFUN OGBE - 4

    A-ta-(ẹ)kan-si-ǫja   a   da fun-(i)gba-(o)ri   ti
    "One:who-sell-once-to-market" who cast for-calabash-(of)-shea:butter that

o nlǫ si ǫja   Ejigbomẹkun, nwǫn ni ki   o ru-(ẹ)bǫ   nitori
he going to market (of) Ejigbomẹkun, they say should he offer-sacrifice because

    awǫn ẹgbẹ   rẹ   ǫrun mẹta. Ekini a ma   jẹ I-mu-(i)na-
(of) those companion his (of) sky three. First it (continuative) eat "It-take-fire-

mu-(i)na-yanran-yanran. Ekeji a ma   jẹ Imǫrimǫ-kǫ-yẹri-
take-fire-bright-bright." Second it (continuative) eat "Lightning-flash-sparkle-

yẹri.   Ẹkẹta a ma   jẹ A-gbe-(i)nu-ile-p(a)-
sparkle." Third it (continuative) eat "One:who-dwell:at-belly-(of)-house-kill-

ẹya.   Igba   ori   ko ru-(ẹ)bǫ   ẹiyẹ-(i)le   mẹta
yamstick." Calabash (of) shea:butter not offer-sacrifice (of) bird-(of)-house three,

ẹgbẹrindilogun   A-(yi)o lǫ sǫ   igba-(o)wo   ori rẹ si oju   ǫna.
3200   (cowries). We-will go throw 200-cowries (of) head its to eye (of) road.

    A-l(i)-ai-ru-(ẹ)bǫ   igba   ori   ni o jẹ
    One:who-be-not-offer-sacrifice (of) calabash (of) shea:butter be who consent

ki o jẹ ẹkan ni a fi   fi igba   ori   ta ori   ti
that it eat once be we make take calabash (of) shea:butter sell shea:butter that

for his two very small children. He said he was not able to sacrifice; he said that
he was the one who created both slaves and free born.[2] Not long afterward he sent
his two children to the farm. When they reached the road, the river carried one
of them away; and where people were coming to greet the other, a fire started in
his house and burned him to death in the house.

Ifa says there are two children whose father should sacrifice two cocks, three
shillings, and a basket of cornstarch porridge, so that these children will not die.
Or we should be careful of two children, lest one be burned to death and the other
be drowned in a river.

---

2. See n. 3, verse 5-1, and n. 3, verse 9-1.

---

241 - 4

"Sold once in the market" was the one who cast Ifa for Calabash of Shea
Butter when he was going to the market of Ejigbomękun.[1] They said he should
make a sacrifice because of his three comrades in heaven. The first is called
"It seizes fire[2] very brightly"; the second is called "Lightning flashes and spar-
kles";[3] the third is called "One who lives in the house and cuts yam sticks."[4]
Calabash of Shea Butter did not make the sacrifice of three pigeons and nine
pence six oninis. We will throw the six oninis (200 cowries) into the road.

The failure of Calabash of Shea Butter to sacrifice is the reason why we
use a calabash only once to sell shea butter, and why

---

1. Cf. n. 5, verse 24-1.
2. Imunamuna was freely translated as "very fierce," but in this context it
should be compared with imọnamọna, meaning lightning.
3. Imọrimọ refers to a flash of lightning; kọ means to flash, as lightning;
yęri-yęri means to sparkle, like the sparklers used in fireworks.
4. The sticks to which yam plants are trained.

ẹni-ti   o   ra   igba   ori   si gbe igba   na lọ pẹlu
person-that who buy calabash (of) shea:butter and take calabash the go together:

      ori.
with shea:butter.

      Ifa ni   a   nlọ   ṣe   owo   kan, ki   a   ṣọ-(a)ra   ki ẹni-
      Ifa say we going make transaction one, should we watch-body that person-

(e)keji   ẹni   ọrun ma ba   ma   ba owo   na jẹ
second (of) person (of) sky not should (continuative) spoil transaction the (1)

mọ-(ẹ)ni   l(i)-ọwọ nitori-ti   n(i)-igba-ti awọn ẹgbẹ   igba
against-person at-hand because-that at-time-that those companion (of) calabash

      ori   mẹt(a)-(m)ẹta ba   ti   fi oju kan igba   ori,
(of) shea:butter three-three   should have take eye touch calabash (of) shea:butter,

ori rẹ a   bajẹ.
head his will spoil.

OFUN - (I)WORI[2] - 1

      Ofun pa Iwori wara   Mọ mu mi l(i)-ọwọ, emi ko wọ   kanki,
      "Ofun kill Iwori immediately" "Not take me at-hand, I   not enter shorts;

yin   mi l(i)-ẹsẹ nu, bẹ-ni emi ko bọ   ṣokoto   a   da   fun Ewe-gbe-mi-
leave me at-foot (3), so-be I   not wear trousers" who cast for "Leaf-assist-me-

awala-wulu   ọmọ   A-gb(ọ)-Egun   ko fọ,   Lubayẹmi, ọmọ
mumble-mumble," child (of) "One:who-hear-Egun not speak," Lubayẹmi, child (of)

A   fi igba ata   ṣẹ-(o)gun, A-fin-(o)ju   ẹ-l(i)-ẹwa
"One:who take 200 pepper make-war," "One:who-decorate eye one:who-has-beauty

ru-(i)l(e)-ẹkun   ọrun gbọngan-gbọngan, nwọn ni ti   ar(a)-aiye
open-house-door (of) sky 'gbọngan-gbọngan'"; they say that (of) people-(of)-earth

ti   ara-(ọ)run   on l(i)-o ma   j(ẹ)-ọba fun wọn.
that (of) people-(of)-sky he be-who (continuative) eat-king for them.

      Ifa ni ọkunrin kan ni o   nrin   kiri ile bi   were   bi were
      Ifa say man   one be who walking about house like insane:person like insane:

      yi, Ifa ni on ni   yio ni ile   na-(i)gb(a)-ẹhin, Ifa ni   t(i)-
person this; Ifa say he be (who) will have house the-time-back;   Ifa say that-(of)-

ọkunrin t(i)-obinrin   ile   na ni o   ma   ma   pe
man   that-(of)-woman (of) house the be who about:to (continuative) assemble

---

      1. Ba . . . jẹ means "to spoil."
      2. Also known as Ofun pa Iwori, meaning Ofun kills Iwori. Cf. n. 1, verse
243-1.
      3. Yin . . . nu means "to leave."

the person who buys shea butter takes the calabash along with the shea butter.[5]

Ifa says we are going to do some business; we should be careful lest our spiritual double in heaven spoil the transaction for us because, when Calabash of Shea Butter's three comrades in heaven look upon Calabash of Shea Butter, his head spoils.[6]

---

5. When shea butter melts, it spoils the calabash. Therefore, when shea butter is sold in the market, the buyer takes the calabash home with him and discards it when the shea butter is finished. This passage explains both this and the name of the diviner, "Sold (only) once in the market."

6. As is indicated by their names, the first two of these comrades refer to lightning and heat, which can melt shea butter and spoil the calabash in which it is kept.

---

243 - 1

"Ofun kills Iwori[1] immediately," and "Don't hold my hand, I am not putting on shorts;[2] let go of my feet, I am not wearing trousers" were the ones who cast Ifa for "Leaves help me 'mumble, mumble'"[3] the child of "One who understands the Egun language but does not speak it," Lubayẹmi, the child of "One who conquers with two hundred peppers," "Beautiful neat person opens the door of the sky so that it sounds 'gbọngan-gbọngan'."[4] They said that he would become king of the people of earth and the people of heaven.

Ifa says there is a man who is going about the house like a person who is insane. Ifa says he is the one who will own the house after a while. Ifa says that both the men and women of the house are going to assemble

---

1. This is an alternative name for the figure Ofun Iwori, appearing here in the name of one of the diviners.

2. Kanki are short trousers reaching about to the knee, while ṣokoto reach to the ankle. The whole name is said to mean "Leave me alone, I don't want to fight."

3. Awala-wulu represents the sounds made when someone tries to speak a language that he does not know, such as Egun, the language spoken by the people of Porto Novo, referred to later, or to the scribbling of a child who does not yet know how to write. In this context it refers to the sound of thunder.

4. Gbọngan-gbọngan represents the noise of a door vibrating after it has been slammed shut. Here it refers to the sound of thunder. These four names are associated with Shango, the God of Thunder, identified below.

sin   k(an)-ęhin on ni   yio si j(ę)-ǫba le   wǫn l(i)-ori.   Ewe-
serve (him) stand-back; he be (who) will and eat-king upon them at-head. "Leaf-

gbe-mi   ni orukǫ ti   a   pe   Şǫngo.
assist-me" be name that we call Shango.

   Agbo kan, ętala   igba akǫ okuta ni ębǫ.   Şǫngo si   ru-
   Ram one, 26,000 (cowries), 200 male stone be sacrifice. Shango and offer-

(ę)bǫ   lati igba-na ni ko si ęni-ti   o   le   duro de   l(i)-
sacrifice, from time-the be not be person-that he be:able stand wait:for (him) at-

aiye l(i)-ǫrun.
earth at-sky.

OFUN - (I)WORI - 2

   Ofun do-do-do,   Iwori win   a   da   fun Kannike ti   o
   "Ofun empty-empty-empty, Iwori very:heavy" who cast for Kannike that he

ma   tori   t(i)-(ow)o-kan   kun-(i)gbę lǫ nwǫn ni ki
(continuative) because (of) that-(of)-cowry-one enter-forest go, they say should

o ru   ęiyę-(i)le   męrin ati ęgbarin   ki o ma ba   şe işe   a
he offer bird-(of)-house four and 8000   (cowries) that he not should do work to

şe da-nu.   Kannike ko ru-(ę)bǫ.   Kannike ni orukǫ ada   ję
do throw-be:lost. Kannike not offer-sacrifice. Kannike be name Cutlass eat;

lati igba-na bi ada   ba   kǫ-(i)şu,   şan   agbado tan,   nwǫn
from time-the if Cutlass should hoe-yam, clear (bush) (of) corn   finish, they

y(ǫ)-ǫwǫ   n(i)-inu rę, ęlomiran   a   wa, a   si ko   ere rę ję.
pull:out-hand at-belly his, another:person will come, will and gather gain his eat

(it).

   Ifa ni ǫkunrin kan ni yi, ki   o ma le   ma   şe işe a-
   Ifa say man   one be this, should he not be:able (continuative) do work to-

şe-da-nu,   lai. Gbogbo işe ti o nşe   ko nri   ori rę, ęlomiran
do-throw-be:lost, alas! All   work that he doing not seeing head its, another:

    ni o nko   ere rę ję.
person be he gathering gain its eat (it).

OFUN - (I)WORI - 3

   Ofun awo   Igando, Iwori awo   Igando, Mǫşamǫşa   l(i)-aşǫ
   Ofun, secret (of) Igando, Iwori secret (of) Igando, "Varicolored:cloth be-cloth

aję   a   da   fun a-l(i)-akara   Eriwǫn, nwǫn ni ǫkan-şoşo
(of) witch" who cast for one:who-has-bean-fritter (of) Eriwǫn; they say one-only

to serve him afterward, and he will be king over them. "Leaves help me" is the name we call the God of Thunder.

One ram, six shillings six pence, and 200 male stones[5] is the sacrifice. The God of Thunder made the sacrifice, and from that time on, no one has been able to stand and face him[6] either on earth or in heaven.

---

5. "Male stones" were identified as white pebbles of quartzite (ọta).

6. That is, no one has dared to oppose him; no one can hear his thunder and not run from him. The verse thus explains how Shango came to have so much power and respect.

---

243 - 2

"Empty, empty Ofun; very heavy Iwori"[1] was the one who cast Ifa for Kannike when he was going to run into the forest because of one cowry.[2] They said he should sacrifice four pigeons and two shillings so that he might not lose the benefits of his work. Kannike did not make the sacrifice. Kannike is the name of Cutlass, and from that time on, if Cutlass grows yams or clears the land for corn, he is put aside and someone else comes and takes the fruits of his labor.[3]

Ifa says this is a man. Let him not lose the benefits of his work, alas! Everything that he is doing is not coming to a successful conclusion, and some-one else takes the fruits of his labor.

---

1. The diviner's name is derived from the name of the figure.

2. That is, to escape his creditors. Cf. verse 255-3, where a character in similar circumstances borrowed money to make the sacrifice and became wealthy.

3. This verse explains why a cutlass (machete) does not eat the yams and corn that it helps to grow.

---

243 - 3

Ofun, the diviner of Igando; Iwori[1] the diviner of Igando; and "A cloth of many colors[2] is the cloth of a witch" were the ones who cast Ifa for the seller of bean fritters in the town of Eriwọn. They said that only

---

1. The name of the figure, Ofun Iwori, appears in the names of the divin-ers.

2. This was described as a cloth with small areas of different colors.

Qla   qmq   rę   yi   ni ębq   bq   (ębq   mu),   nwqn ni   ki
"Honor," child hers this, be sacrifice sacrifice:to (sacrifice take); they say should

o   ru   ewurę   kan, ejilelogun   ati aşq rę ki qmq na ma ba
she offer she:goat one, 44,000   (cowries) and cloth her that child the not should

ku.   O   ru-(ę)bq.
die. She offer-sacrifice.

      Ifa ni ki   e-l(i)-eyi   ru-(ę)bq   nitori   qmq kan-na ti
      Ifa say should one:who-be-this offer-sacrifice because (of) child one-the that

o bi,   ki o ma ba   ri iku ojiji,   iku ti o ma   pa qmq
he bear, that he not should see death suddenly, death that it (continuative) kill child

na a   ko ni mq   rara.
the we not be know (it) at:all.

OFUN - (I)WORI - 4

Ofun awo   Igando, Iwori awo   Igando, Oyakatayaka aba
Ofun, secret (of) Igando, Iwori secret (of) Igando, "Huge   storehouse

ni   p(a)-o-l(i)-oko   l(i)-ęrin   a   da   fun Ęfunşeku ti işe
be (it) kill-one:who-have-farm at-laughter" who cast for Ęfunşeku that make

o-l(i)-ori   agan   Ile-Ifę, nwqn ni ire   aiye
one:who-be-head (of) barren:women (of) Ile-Ifę; they say goodness (of) earth

ire   qrun ma   to   l(i)-qwq l(i)-qdun-ni, nwqn ni ki   o
goodness (of) sky (continuative) reach at-hand at-year-this, they say should she

ru-(ę)bq   at(i)-ęnu-ję   ki nwqn ma ba   fun   ni ogun
offer-sacrifice (of) from-mouth-eat that they not should give (her) at medicine

ję. O-l(i)-ori   agan   Ife-Ifę ni a-pe   aba.   N(i)-
eat. One:who-be-head (of) barren:women (of) Ife-Ifę be we-call Storehouse. At-

igba-ti   a   ba   ko   işu, agbado, awuję ati (l)qpq-lqpq (ohu)n-kan s(i)-
time-that we should gather yam, corn,   awuję and much-much thing-one to-

inu   aba,   inu rę a   ma   dun,   şugbqn e-l(i)-
belly (of) Storehouse, belly her will (continuative) be:sweet, but   one:who-be-

eyi a de,   a   mu işu, ti e-l(i)-eyi   ba   de   a   mu igbado
this will arrive, will take yam, that one:who-be-this should arrive will take corn,

bę-bę nwqn da   oju   aba   de-(i)lę   janpo.
so-so they break eye (of) Storehouse arrive-ground empty.

      Ifa ni ęni-kan   wa   ti o fę şe işę kan ti Q-l(i)-qrun   yio
      Ifa say person-one exist that he want do work one that One:who-has-sky will

da ori   qla kq   ki o ru-(ę)bq   ki o ma ba
turn head (of) honor turn:toward (him), should he offer-sacrifice that he not should

"Honor," her child, was acceptable as a sacrifice.[3] They said she should offer one she-goat, eleven shillings, and her cloth so that the child would not die. She made the sacrifice.

Ifa says that this person should make a sacrifice because of his only child, lest it meet with sudden death; the death that will kill the child is one of which we will know nothing whatsoever.[4]

---

3. This statement, contradicted in the following sentence, was explained as meaning that although the child is the only sacrifice the gods will accept, it may be possible to change their minds by making the other sacrifice suggested.

4. That is, we will never learn what has killed the child.

---

243 - 4

Ofun, the diviner of Igando; Iwori, the diviner of Igando;[1] and "A huge storehouse makes the farmer laugh"[2] were the ones who cast Ifa for Ẹfunsheku who was "The head of the barren women of Ifẹ." They said that blessings of heaven and blessings of earth would come to her during that year. They said she could sacrifice against "eat from mouth"[3] so that she might not be given medicine to eat. "The head of the barren women of Ifẹ" is what we call Storehouse. When we gather yams, corn, awujẹ beans,[4] and many other things and store them inside Storehouse, she is happy; but someone comes and takes the yams, someone comes and takes the corn; and so they disgrace Storehouse and let her fall down empty.[5]

Ifa says there is someone who wants to do some work; the Sky God will direct honor toward him. He should sacrifice lest he

---

1. See n. 1, verse 243-3.

2. A large, full storehouse makes a farmer happy.

3. A type of bad medicine which, as explained by informants and by the verse, is given to someone to eat. It would also seem to mean a medicine whose purpose is to be able to take food from someone.

4. Probably butter beans (Phaseolus lunatus), but the name awujẹ is also applied to other kinds of beans. (See Dalziel, 1937: 240, 254, 255.)

5. This verse explains why the possessions of Storehouse are taken away and it is deserted and left to fall apart. The implication is clear that Storehouse did not make the prescribed sacrifice.

ri ęni-ti   yio fun   ni ogun   ję. Gbogbo owo   ile   (ati)
see person-that will give (him) at medicine eat. All   cowries (of) house (and)

ǫna yio si tan   l(i)-ęhin na ki o ma ba   ku. Agutan kan, ǫkanla,
road will and finish at-back the that he not should die. Ewe   one, 22,000

            amu   epo,   ati aʂǫ   ara rę ni ębǫ.
(cowries), jar (of) palm:oil, and cloth (of) body his be sacrifice.

OFUN - (E)DI - 1

O-fun-(i)di   o nso,   o ʂai fun-(i)di   o nso,   o
"You-squeeze-waist you flatulating, you not sqeeze-waist you flatulating; you

ʂe   ǫran o ko bę-bę   Iwo ko bę-bę   ǫran iwǫ nʂe
make affair you not request-request, You not request-request affair you making

o-ni-k(?)-oju   yanran-yanran a d(a)-Ifa ko Ʂakeu ti iʂe   ǫmǫ
one:who-be-(?)-eye 'yanran-yanran'" who cast-Ifa for Shakeu that make child (of)

Ibagboloro ni ǫjǫ ti o nlǫ mu ǫta   oye l(i)-oke, nwǫn ni ki   o
Ibagboloro at day that he going take quartz (of) title at-hill; they say should he

ru-(ę)bǫ   ki-(a)r(a)-aiye   ma ba   da   n(i)-iji, agutan
offer-sacrifice that-people-(of)-earth not should cause (him) at-dread, ewe

kan, ętalelogun,   aʂǫ funfun kan, Ʂakeu ko ru.
one, 46,000   (cowries), cloth white one; Shakeu not offer.

Ʂakeu ję ǫmǫ   ǫba o si la   pupǫ, n(i)-igba-ti ǫba ku,
Shakeu eat child (of) king he and be:wealthy much, at-time-that king die,

Ʂakeu ni ta-ni on tun le   du   oye de ǫdǫ   rę mǫ
Shakeu say who-be he then be:able compete:for title arrive presence his again

n(i)-inu   aiye yi, o si ko   gbogb(o)-ohun ti a fi
at-belly (of) earth this, he and gather all-thing   that we take (them)

idu-(o)ye,   ki a iko   fun awǫn-(i)j(ę)-oye, lǫ si ǫrun, o ta
competition:for-title, that we gather give those-eat-title, go to sky; he suspend

okun o gun   lǫ si ǫrun. N(i)-igba-ti o de   ǫrun Q-l(i)-ǫrun   ni iwǫ
rope he climb go to sky. At-time-that he arrive sky One:who-has-sky say "You

ko ri ęni-ti   iwǫ yio du-(o)ye   l(i)-ǫdǫ ni gbogbo aiye mǫ?
not see person-that you will compete:for-title at-presence at all   earth again?"

O ni ki   o ma ʂe bayi mǫ. N(i)-igba-ti Ʂakeu npada   bǫ   wa si
He say should he not do thus again. At-time-that Shakeu returning come come to

aiye, okun ti o fi   gun oke lǫ si ǫrun, Eʂu ja,   n(i)-igba-ti o
earth, rope that he take (it) climb hill go to sky, Eshu cut (it); at-time-that he

ni ki o tun pada s(i)-oke, Eʂu tun ja eyi-ti   iba fi   gun
say that he then return to-hill, Eshu then cut this-that (he) should take (it) climb

meet someone who will give him bad medicine to eat, and all the money of his house and home[6] be spent to keep him from dying. One ewe, five shillings six pence, a jar of palm oil, and the cloth from his body is the sacrifice.

---

6. See n. 10, verse 225-4.

---

244 - 1

"You contract your anus, and you flatulate; you do not contract your anus, and you flatulate" and "You get into trouble and you don't beg forgiveness; you don't beg forgiveness, and you deny your guilt"[1] were the ones who cast Ifa for Shakeu, who was the child of Ibagboloro, on the day that he was going to the hill to take the stone of a title.[2] They said he should sacrifice one ewe, eleven shillings six pence, and one white cloth, so that people would not frighten him. Shakeu did not make the sacrifice.

Shakeu was the king's son, and he was very rich. When the king died, Shakeu asked, "Who else is there on earth for me to visit in competing for this title?"[3] He gathered together everything with which we compete for a title, and which we take as gifts to the chiefs, and he went to heaven. He hung a rope from the sky and climbed up it. When he reached heaven, the Sky God said, "Isn't there anyone else for you to visit on the whole earth?" He said he must never do this again. When Shakeu was returning to the earth, Eshu cut off the bottom of the rope with which he had climbed up to heaven. When he started to go back up, Eshu cut off the top of the rope with which he was going to climb

---

1. "Yanran-yanran" was said to describe the facial expression of a person making an indignant denial.

2. Going to the top of a hill and taking a stone is a part of the installation ceremony; it should be compared with the Qni's visit to Oke Ora during his installation.

3. Candidates for a titled position visit the other chiefs, bringing them presents and food; the candidates also entertain the other chiefs in their own homes, hoping to make a better impression than their rival candidates. In campaigning to succeed his father, and having visited all the chiefs on earth that he considered worthy of his notice, Shakeu presumed to see the Sky God himself.

oke   ǫrun, Şakeu wa   duro si agbedemeji   ǫrun, orun npa.   N(i)-
hill (of) sky, Shakeu come stand to middle   (of) sky, sun killing (him). At-

igba-ti   ebi   ma   pa   ku ni o fi   igbe bǫ-(ę)nu   pe:
time-that hunger (continuative) kill (him) die, be he take cry enter-mouth that:

        Emi Şakeu de   o   ǫmǫ   Ibagboloro
        "I   Shakeu arrive, oh, child (of) Ibagboloro;

        Ebi   ma   npa   emi ǫmǫ   oye l(i)-oke o.
        "Hunger (continuative) killing me, child (of) title at-hill, oh."

    Ifa ni Q-l(i)-ǫrun   fę gbe atupa   iwa   fun ęni-kan,   ki
    Ifa say One:who-has-sky want take lamp (of) destiny give person-one, should

o şǫ-(a)ra   ki o ma ba   fi   a-şe-ju   baję,   ki o ma ba
he watch-body that he not should take to-do-surpass spoil (it), that he not should

ja okun di-(o)ju.
cut rope close-eye.

OFUN - (E)DI - 2

    A-ta-koro   awo   wǫn l(i)-ode Igbade l(i)-o da   fun
    "One:who-kick-at:once," secret (of) those at-outside Igbade be-who cast for

wǫn l(i)-ode   Igbade ni-(ǫ)jǫ ti   mu-(ę)ni-mu-(ę)ni   ǫrun de,
them at-outside (of) Igbade at-day that take- person-take-person (of) sky arrive,

ti ęmimǫ   ǫrun nhan;   A-ta-koro   ni ire   de
that evil:thing (of) sky appearing; "One:who-kick-at:once" say goodness arrive

fun wǫn ni ǫdun yi ni ode   Igbade, nwǫn ni alafia,   inu wǫn
for them at year this at outside (of) Igbade; they say contentment, belly their

dun,   nwǫn yǫ.
be:sweet, they rejoice.

    Alapa-ko-wo-n(i)-ile-ki-o-lǫ-si-oko-lǫ-pa-(ę)ni,   on na ję
    "Wall-not-break-at-house-that-it-go-to-farm-go-kill-person," he also eat

babalawo ni ode   Igbade, o ni ha, o ni ębǫ   e-l(i)-e-
diviner   at outside (of) Igbade, he say 'Ha!,' he say sacrifice (of) one:who-be-who-

mu   ǫrun ni nwǫn iba   ru. Egbejila,   akikǫ-(a)dię, ati ęran-
take (of) sky be they should offer. 2400   (cowries), cock-chicken, and twisted-

(o)kun ni nwǫn iba   ru.
rope be they should offer.

    O ni e-l(i)-e-mu   ǫrun de   ti yio ma   mu
    He say one:who-be-who-take (of) sky arrive that will (continuative) take

wǫn, nwǫn ki   mǫ-(i)lę,   nwǫn bęrę si lu,   nwǫn ni ęni-
them; they push (him) against-ground, they begin to beat (him), they say person-

up to heaven. Shakeu was left hanging in mid-air, and the sun was beating down on him. When he was dying of hunger, he cried out:

> "I, Shakeu come, oh; child of Ibagboloro;
> "I am dying of hunger; child of a chief above, oh."

Ifa says the Sky God wants to give the lamp of destiny to someone. He should be careful lest he spoil his opportunity by being overambitious, and lest he break the string and clog up the beads.[4]

---

4. A metaphor for spoiling everything. See n. 2, verse 14-2.

---

244 - 2

"Jump at once," diviner of the town of Igbade, was the one who cast Ifa for the people of Igbade on the day that evil spirits who seize people were coming from heaven, when evil beings from heaven were appearing. "Jump at once" said that blessings would come to the people of Igbade during that year.[1] They said, "All is well"; they were happy and they rejoiced.

"The wall which collapses at home does not kill someone in the farm" was also a diviner at Igbade. He said "Ha!" He said that they should offer a sacrifice against evil spirits from heaven that would seize them. Seven pence two oninis, a cock, and twisted ropes is what they should sacrifice.

He said that evil spirits were coming from heaven to seize them and carry them away. The people shoved him to the ground and they began to beat him.[2] they said, "The

---

1. That is, he divined falsely, and failed to warn them of the impending danger.
2. Because they did not want to hear the truth about their danger.

ti   awǫn pe   sǫ   pe   ire   aya,   ire   aje,   şugbǫn iwǫ ni
that they call speak that goodness (of) wife, goodness (of) money, but   you say

e-l(i)-e-mu   ǫrun de.
one:who-be-who-take (of) sky   arrive.

    Nwǫn si   de   e,   n(i)-ibi-ti   nwǫn de e   mǫ,   ni Eşu da   eruku
    They and bind him,   at-place-that they bind him against, be Eshu cast   dust

s(i)-inu   igbo,   o pa-(a)tę mǫ,   t(i)-igbo   t(i)-iju
to-belly (of) forest, he clap-palm against (it), that-(of)-forest that-(of)-dense:

    di   ogun,   ogun   ba   ko   gbogbo   wǫn.   Nwǫn wa   sǫ
forest become warrior, warrior meet gather all   (of) them. They come speak

pe babalawo yi   wi   bę, n(i)-igba-na ni Eşu da-(o)hun   pe babalawo na
that diviner   this speak so, at-time-the be Eshu break-voice that diviner   the

da?   Nwǫn ni o ni awǫn de   mǫ-(i)lę   yi.
where:be (he)?   They say he be they bind against-ground this.

    Awǫn ogun   kan sa-re si babalawo na, nwǫn ni   ǫkunrin ni.   Awǫn
    Those warrior one run-go to diviner   the, they say man   be (he). Those

ogun   sǫ   fun babalawo na pe ki   o şe   Ifa fun awǫn ki   awǫn le
warrior speak for diviner   the that should he make Ifa for them that they be:able

ri   ilu   miran ko,   o ni afi   bi nwǫn ba   ma   da   awǫn
see town another gather, he say unless if they   should (continuative) release those

ara   ode   Igbade fun on, nwǫn wa   da   awǫn ara   ode
people (of) outside (of) Igbade for him, they come release those people (of) outside

    Igbade fun,   o wa   sǫ   fun awǫn ara   ode   Igbade pe
(of) Igbade for (him), he come speak for those people (of) outside (of) Igbade that

ki   wǫn lǫ mu egb(ejila)-egbejila   ati ęran-(o)kun-(ǫ)k(an)-ǫkan ati
should they go take 2400-2400   (cowries) and twisted-rope-one-one   and

akikǫ fun on.
cock for him.

    Ifa ni   awǫn agbo kan wa,   ki   nwǫn lǫ bǫ   Ifa kan bayi nitori
    Ifa say those flock one exist, should they go sacrifice:to Ifa one thus because

ki e-l(i)-e-mu   ǫrun ma ba   mu wǫn lǫ ni ǫdun yi, ki
that one:who-be-who-take (of) sky not should take them go at year this, should

wǫn fi   ęran-(o)kun-(ǫ)k(an)-ǫkan, egb(ejila)-egbejila,   ati akikǫ-(ǫ)k(an)-
they take twisted-rope-one-one   2400-2400   (cowries), and cock-one-

ǫkan ru-(ę)bǫ.
one   offer-sacrifice.

---

other diviner we called promised us blessings of wives and blessings of money, but now you tell us that something from heaven is coming to seize us."

They tied him up, and at the place where they left him tied up, Eshu threw dust into the forest and clapped his hands at it.[3] The forest turned into warriors, and the warriors captured all the people. The people said that a diviner had warned them of just this thing.[4] Then Eshu spoke, asking, "Where is this diviner?" They said that they had tied him up and left him.

The warriors ran to the diviner; they said, "He's a real man!" The warriors told the diviner to make Ifa for them, so that they would be able to capture another town. He said that they could not do so unless they released the people of Igbade for him. They released the people of Igbade for him, and he told the people of Igbade that they should each go and get seven pence two oninis, a twisted rope, and a cock for him.

Ifa says that there is a group of people who should sacrifice to an Ifa because evil spirits from heaven are coming to seize them during this year; they should each sacrifice a twisted rope, seven pence two oninis, and one cock.

––––––––––

3. A method used by Eshu to accomplish magical transformations. Cf. verse 1-10.

4. By creating the warriors, Eshu not only rescues the diviner but makes his prediction come true.

OFUN - (Q)BARA - 1

O-fun   bala-bala   a   da   fun ina ni-(ǫ)jǫ ti   o nlǫ   ję oye
"It-be:white spotted:spotted" who cast for Fire at-day that he going eat title

ǫmǫ ni rǫ-rǫ ni-(ǫ)jǫ ti   aiye   ina ko dara.   Nwǫn ni ki   o
(of) child at up-up at-day that earth (of) Fire not be:good. They say should he

ru   akikǫ męta, oru   epo,   ati ęgbędǫgbǫn   ki aiye rę ba
offer cock three, pot (of) palm:oil, and 5000   (cowries) that earth his should

le   dara;   ina ru-(ę)bǫ.   N(i)-igba-ti o ba   ku   dię ki
be:able be:good; Fire offer-sacrifice. At-time-that it should remain small that

ina ku, bi a ba   bu epo   si,   a bęrę si jo   rǫ-rǫ.
Fire die, if we should dip palm:oil to (it), it begin to dance up-up.

Ifa ni ǫkunrin kan wa   ti Q-l(i)-ǫrun   gbe iwa   fun,   bę-ni
Ifa say man   one exist that One:who-has-sky take destiny give (him), so-be

o fęrę di   arugbo   tan,   ina   oluwarę   na yio ma
he almost become old:person finish, fire (of) person:in:question the will (continua-

jo   rǫ-rǫ. Şugbǫn ki   o ru-(ę)bǫ.
tive) dance up-up. But   should he offer-sacrifice.

OFUN - (Q)BARA - 2

Igbo   didi ni a gbe j(a)-agba   ibanbalę ni nwǫn gbe fa-(o)kun a   da
"Forest tied be we take break-agba; low:down be they take pull-rope" who cast

fun eşinşin ni ǫjǫ ti   o   ma   gbe ate   n(i)-iyawo,   bę-ni
for Fly   at day that he (continuative) take Birdlime at-junior:wife so-be (she)

ko ni kǫ,   ko si ni fun   ni alafia.   Eşinşin ni   ko buru
not be divorce (him), not and be give (him) at contentment. Fly   say "not be:

on yio fę   bę, ni ǫjǫ ti   o fę ate,   n(i)-igba-ti o ni ki o
bad" he will love (her) so, at day that he love Birdlime, at-time-that it be that he

fi   ǫwǫ kan,   ate   mu,   bi o ba   ni ki on fi   ęsę kan,
take hand touch (her), Birdlime take (him), if it should be that he take foot touch

ate   a   mu.   Eşinşin wa   fi   ori yi ate   kitikiti,
(her) Birdlime will take (him). Fly   come take head turn Birdlime completely,

n(i)-igba-na ni eşinşin bęrę si wi-pe:
at-time-the be Fly   begin to speak-that:

Emi ni mo fę   ǫ-ǫ-ǫ.
"I   be I   love you-u-u."

Bayi ni eşinşin wi   titi o fi   ku si oju   ate.
Thus be Fly   speak until he take die to eye (of) Birdlime.

245 - 1

"It is white, flickering"[1] was the one who cast Ifa for Fire on the day when he was going to take the title of "Child up high,"[2] on the day that things were not going well for Fire. They said he should sacrifice three cocks, a pot of palm oil, and one shilling three pence, so that things might go well for him. Fire sacrificed. When Fire is about to die, if we pour palm oil on him he begins to dance up high.[3]

Ifa says there is a man to whom the Sky God will give his destiny; even though he is almost an old man, the "fire" of his destiny will continue to dance up high. But he should offer a sacrifice.

---

1. Bala-bala means "spotted with mud," when applied to a cloth, and "flickering," when applied to a fire. In this context both meanings are implied, since it modifies directly the verb "to be white," and since it is a part of the name of Fire's diviner.

2. "Child up high" or "Child at up-up" is a praise-name of Fire; as seen below, it means that the fire will burn high.

3. Meaning that the flames will burn high. Note that the palm oil included in the sacrifice is instrumental in making the prediction come to pass. Cf. verse 222-3.

---

245 - 2

"It is in the dense forest that we pluck twine; it is down that we pull rope"[1] was the one who cast Ifa for Fly on the day that he was going to take Birdlime[2] as his wife. They warned him that she would neither divorce him nor give him peace. Fly said "All right," he would marry her anyway. On the day that he married Birdlime, when he touched her with his hand, Birdlime seized him; and when he touched her with his foot, Birdlime seized him. Fly rolled his head[3] against her and was stuck completely. Then Fly began to say.

"I-I-I lov-v-ve you-u-u."[4]

Fly kept saying this until he died in the Birdlime.

---

1. Both agba and okun were given as words for rope and twine. The reference here is to the gathering of vines or lianas for use as rope, as these are pulled down from the large trees of the forest.

2. Cf. n. 2, verse 225-2. A sticky substance like that on flypaper.

3. As a fly twists or turns its head on its neck. Cf. the Tar Baby story.

4. This is said to be what fly says when it buzzes. When this line is repeated, all the final vowels are nasalized as follows: "emin nin mon fẹn ọ-ọ-ọn," to imitate the buzzing sound. The verse explains why flies buzz as they do, and why they stick in birdlime.

Ifa ni a-(yi)o fẹ   obinrin dara-dara kan, n(i)-igba-ti obinrin yi   ko ni
Ifa say we-will love woman fine-fine   one, at-time-that woman this not be

kọ-(ẹ)ni   tan,   ọkunrin na ko si ni ni   alafia   l(i)-ara   obinrin
divorce-person finish, man   the not and be have contentment at-body (of) woman

yi titi ọkunrin na yio fi   ku. Akikọ mẹta ati ẹgbẹdọgbọn   ni ẹbọ   ti
this until man   the will take die. Cock three and 5000 (cowries) be sacrifice that

a   yan   fun eşinşin şugbọn ko ru   ẹbọ   na, bi o ba   şe   pe o
they choose for Fly   but   not offer sacrifice the, if it should make that he

ru   ẹbọ   na, eşinşin ki ba   ti   ma   ku si ori   ate.
offer sacrifice the, Fly   not should have (continuative) die to head (of) Birdlime.

OFUN -(Q)BARA - 3

Lile   oşu   ọmọ ni dederede, ai-le   oşu   ọmọ
"Appearance (of) month (of) child at plainly;   not-appear (of) month (of) child

ni dedere a   da   fun Qrunmila ti   o nni-(ọ)kan mu igba   obi ti o
at plainly" who cast for Qrunmila that he being-one take calabash (of) kola that he

nni-(ọ)kan mu-(i)gba   ata;   nwọn ni ki   Qrunmila ru-(ẹ)bọ
being-one take-calabash (of) pepper; they say should Qrunmila offer-sacrifice

pe ni oşu ti o ma   le   yi ni Q-l(i)-ọrun   gbe igba
that at month that it (continuative) appear this be One:who-has-sky take calabash

    iwa   le   l(i)-ọwọ, ẹiyẹ-(i)le   mẹrin ati ẹgbarun,
(of) destiny upon (him) at-hand, bird-(of)-house four   and 10,000 (cowries),

igbin meji, ati ekuru   fun-fun.   O ru-(ẹ)bọ.   N(i)-igba-
snail two, and steamed:beans be:white-be:white. He offer-sacrifice. At-time-

ti   Qrunmila ru-(ẹ)bọ   yi tan ni owo   ba   de   si,   n(i)-
that Qrunmila offer-sacrifice this finish, be cowries should arrive to (him); at-

igba-ti o wa   di   o-l(i)-owo   tan ti o ni ẹru   ti
time-that he come become one:who-have-cowries finish that he have slaves that

o ni   iwọfa, ni o bẹrẹ si wi-pe:
he have pawns, be he begin to speak-that:

Iya   o ba   ti   ya   mi l(i)-oşu yi, o,
"Pawning he should have pawned me at-month this, oh,

Agba-(a)gba a ki f(i)-ara   ş(e)-ọfa   k(i)-a r(ṭ)-oju sin-(i)kin   ẹni.
"Elder-elder we not take-body make-pawn that-we see-eye serve-ikin (of) person."

Ifa ni ẹni-kan   nfẹ   di   o-l(i)-owo,   ti yio fi   a-
Ifa say person-one wanting become one:who-have-cowries, that will take one:

l(i)-ai-j(ẹ)-oye,   yio si ju   o-l(i)-oye   lọ, gbogbo ohun ti o
who-be-not-eat-title, will and surpass one:who-has-title go, all   thing that he

Ifa says someone will marry a very beautiful woman; but when this woman refuses to divorce him, the man will not have peace with this woman until he dies. Three cocks and one shilling three pence is the sacrifice that they chose for Fly, but he did not make it. If Fly had made this sacrifice, he would not always get stuck in birdlime.

---

245 - 3

"The new moon appears clearly; the new moon does not appear clearly"[1] was the one who cast Ifa for Qrunmila when he had to carry his calabash of kola nuts by himself and to carry his calabash of pepper by himself.[2] They said Qrunmila should sacrifice four pigeons, two shillings six pence, two snails, and white steamed beans so that the Sky God might put the calabash of destiny into his hands during the present month. He made the sacrifice. When Qrunmila had completed the sacrifice, money came to him; when he became rich and had slaves and "pawns,"[3] he began to say:

"They were going to pawn me this month, oh;
"Elders, we do not pawn ourselves and have time to serve our palm nuts."[4]

Ifa says someone wants to be a man with money; he will not have a title, but he will be more important than a chief. He will have everything

---

1. Cf. Clarke, 1939: 247.
2. Because he was poor and had no relatives or followers to help him.
3. See n. 2, verse 181-4.
4. This again is obscure. One informant interpreted it as meaning that before Qrunmila sacrificed, his status was no better than that of a "pawn" or indentured servant. It also seems to imply that Qrunmila had been so poor that he was about to be pawned. In either case it is clear that he is concerned about sacrificing to his divining nuts, which would have been difficult if he were a pawn.

nfẹ   ni ode   aiye ni   yio ri,   şugbọn l(i)-oni yi oluwarẹ
wanting at outside (of) earth be (he) will see, but   at-today this person:in:

          ni-(ọ)kan mu-(i)gba   o nni-(ọ)kan mu awo.
question be-one   take-calabash he being-one take plate.

OFUN - (Q)BARA - 4

   Akikara-(i)gba   fọ   o di   o-n(i)-ipa   mu-(i)pa,
   "Broken:piece-(of)-calabash break, it become one:who-have-path take-path,

o-n(i)-iya   mu-(i)ya   a   da fun Oluw(a)-ẹri   ni-(ọ)jọ ti o
one:who-has-turning take-turning" who cast for Lord-(of)-river at-day that he

 ma   gba obinrin   Keso, nwọn ni ki   Oluw(a)-ẹri   ru-
(continuative) take woman (of) Keso, they say should Lord-(of)-river offer-

(ẹ)bọ   ki o ma jẹ-pe   nitori-ti   obinrin yi ni t(i)-ile
sacrifice that he not consent-that because-that (of) woman this be that-(of)-house

t(i)-ọna   rẹ ma   pa-run   si.   Oluw(a)-ẹri   ni on yio
that-(of)-road his (continuative) kill-perish to (her). Lord-(of)-river say he will

gba.   Nwọn ni ki   o ru   ewurẹ,   amu   ori,   igba igbin,
take (her). They say should he offer she:goat, jar (of) shea:butter, 200 snail,

ejielogun.
44,000 (cowries).

   Oluw(a)-ẹri   ko ru-(ẹ)bọ   o si gba obinrin   Keso, n(i)-igba-
    Lord-(of)-river not offer-sacrifice, he and take woman (of) Keso, at-time-

ti o di   oşu-(ẹ)kẹta ti Oluw(a)-ẹri   ti   gba aya   Keso ni Igun
that it become month-third that Lord-(of)-river have take wife (of) Keso be Igun

wa   ki   Keso, Keso si se   işu, n(i)-igba-ti işu jinna,   ni Keso ni
come greet Keso, Keso and cook yam, at-time-that yam be:done, be Keso say

ki   Igun wa   ma   wo işu si odo   fun on, Igun ni bawo ni o
should Igun come (continuative) peel yam to mortar for him, Igun say how be he

ti   ri? O ni   aya rẹ nkọ?   Keso ni Oluw(a)-ẹri   ti   gba
have see? He say, "Wife his what:about?" Keso say Lord-(of)-river have take

   ni ọwọ on, o ni   ki-ni-şe   ti   ko ti   wi   fun on
(her) at hand his, he say "What-be-(it)-make that (he) not have speak for him

lati igba-ti   on ti   de?
from time-that he have arrive?"

   N(i)-igba-ti Igun gbọ bayi, ko le   duro mọ, o lọ pe Aidan ati
   At-time-that Igun hear thus, not be:able stand again, he go call Aidan and

Ata-wẹrẹ,   n(i)-igba-na ni awọn mẹr(in)-(m)ẹrin dide: Igun, Keso, Ata-
Pepper-wẹrẹ, at-time-the be those four-four   arrived: Igun, Keso, Pepper-

wẹrẹ ati Aidan nwọn lọ kọlu ile   Oluw(a)-ẹri   n(i)-igba-ti nwọn
wẹrẹ and Aidan, they go attack house (of) Lord-(of)-river; at-time-that they

he wants on earth, but at present he has to carry his calabash by himself and carry his plate by himself.

---

245 - 4

"The broken piece of calabash breaks again; it is time for each to take his own path, for each to take his way" was the one who cast Ifa for Lord of the River[1] on the day he was about to seduce the wife of the Keso. They said that the Lord of the River should make a sacrifice lest his house and home[2] be destroyed because of her. The Lord of the River said he would seduce her. They said he should sacrifice a she-goat, a jar of shea butter, 200 snails, and eleven shillings.

The Lord of the River did not sacrifice, and he took Keso's wife. After two months had passed since the Lord of the River had taken Keso's wife, Igun came to greet Keso. Keso cooked yams, and when they were done, Keso told Igun to peel them into the mortar for him. Igun asked, "What is the meaning of this?" He said, "Where is your wife?" Keso said that the Lord of the River had taken her from him. Igun said, "Why didn't you tell me this when I first arrived?"

When Igun heard this, he could wait no longer; he went and called the Aidan and Ata-werę. When these four came together—Igun, Keso, Ata-werę and Aidan— they went to attack the house of the Lord of the River. They

---

1. The "Lord of the River" is the "father of the fishes," but he is not a deity.
2. All his possessions. See n. 10, verse 225-4.

kǫlu,   ẹja nla, isin,   ẹja wẹrẹ, ǫmǫ   Oluw(a)-ẹri   ni nwǫn ṣe,   n(i)-
attack, fish big, minnow, fish tiny, child (of) Lord-(of)-river be they make; at-

igba-ti   nwǫn kǫlu wǫn, nwǫn run   wǫn ṣẹmu-ṣẹmu,   gbogbo
time-that they attack them, they destroy them completely-completely, all

awǫn ǫmǫ   Oluw(a)-ẹri   ku tan.   N(i)-igba-ti nwǫn mbǫ   ni nwǫn
those child (of) Lord-(of)-river die finish. At-time-that they coming be they

bẹrẹ si kǫ-(o)rin wi-pe:
begin to sing-song speak-that:

> Keso o   ma-ṣ(e)-ai   ja
> "Keso, oh, (imperative)-do-not fight;

> Aidan ma-ṣ(e)-ai   ja.
> "Aidan, (imperative)-do-not fight."

    Ifa ni ẹni-kan   fẹ gba obinrin kan, ki   o ṣǫ-(a)ra   ki o ma
    Ifa say person-one want take woman one, should he watch-body that he not

jẹ-pe   t(i)-ile   ti-(ǫ)na   ǫkunrin na ni   yio run
consent-that that-(of)-house that-(of)-road (of) man   the be (it) will perish

nitori   obinrin ti   a fẹ gba yi, ki   o ru-(ẹ)bǫ   dara-dara.
because (of) woman that he want take this, should he offer-sacrifice be:good-be:good.

Nwǫn ti   ro   ǫkǫ   pin pe   ko le   ṣe ohun-k(u)-ohun, ṣugbǫn
They have think husband end that (he) not be:able do thing-any-thing, but

enia   ẹhin   ǫkǫ   ni   yio gbe-ja   ǫkǫ   obinrin na ti
people (of) back (of) husband be (he) will assist-fight husband (of) woman the that

    ile   wǫn yio fi   run   tan pata-pata   t(i)-ǫmǫ   t(i)-
(of) house their will take perish finish completely-completely that-(of)-child that-

aya.   Lati igba-na li o ti   jẹ-pe   awǫn ǫmǫ   ar(a)-aiye
(of)-wife. From time-the be it have consent-that those child (of) people-(of)-earth

ti   ma   gun   odo, ti nwǫn ma   nfi Igun, Aidan, Keso
have (continuative) poison river, that they (continuative) taking Igun, Aidan, Keso

ati Ata-wẹrẹ   gun   odo ti nwǫn si ma   npa ẹja   inu
and Pepper-wẹrẹ poison river that they and (continuative) killing fish (of) belly (of)

odo.
river.

---

attacked the big fish, the minnows, and the small fish, who were the Lord of the
River's children. They attacked them and completely destroyed them, and all the
children of Lord of the River were killed. When they were returning, they began
to sing:

"Keso, oh, you must not fight;
"Aidan, you must not fight."

Ifa says someone wants to seduce a woman; he should be careful lest his
house and home be destroyed because of this woman that he wants to seduce; he
should make a very fine sacrifice. People have thought that the husband is
finished, and that he can't do anything; but people in back of the husband will assist him in fighting the seducer of his wife, and will completely destroy the seducer's home, including his wives and his children. From that time on, human
beings have been using fish poison in the river, and using Igun, Aidan, Keso, and
Ata-wẹrẹ as poison to kill the fish in the river.[3]

3. This verse explains the origin of fish poison, and why the plants are used
for this purpose. Dalziel records the use of all for fish poison except keso, an
unidentified fruit that is also a quick-acting purgative. Igun is the Fish Poison
Bean (Tephrosia Vogelii or T. densiflora) or another plant (Mundulea sericea)
known by the same name; leaves of both are used as fish poison. Ata-wẹrẹ or
"Wẹrẹ peppers" possibly refers to the pods of the Fish Poison Bean, for which
Dalziel gives "wẹrẹ" as an alternative name. Aidan or aridan is a fruit (Tetra-
pleura tetraptera).

OFUN - (Q)KANRAN¹ - 1

O-finran   Ẹkun   ni   t(ẹ)-ọna   ni ọsan   ganranin-ganranin
"One:who-provokes, Leopard, be (he) press-road at midday upright-upright"

a   da   fun Qrunmila ni-(ọ)jọ ti   nwọn nran-(i)şẹ   iku   pe
who cast for Qrunmila at-day that they sending-message (of) death call (him)

l(i)-ọrun Eşinrinmọgbọ.
at-sky   Eshinrinmọgbọ.

        Mi ko ni   rin-(ọ)na k(o)-Q-1(i)-ọrun
        "I   not be (who) walk-road meet-One:who-has-sky;

        Agogo   idẹ   n(i)-igba-ti o ba   nro   goro-goro-goro
        "Gong (of) brass at-time-that it should sounding 'goro-goro-goro,'

        Ki f(i)-oju kan Orişa
        "Not take-eye touch Orisha;

        Mi ko ni   jẹ ipe   Q-1(i)-ọrun
        "I   not be (who) eat call (of) One:who-has-sky;

        Aja ti   ko ba   ni   ọmọ n(i)-inu
        "Bell that not should have child at-belly,

        Ki jẹ ipe   Orişa.
        "Not eat call (of) Orisha."

Ifa ni   ẹni-kan   ni gbogbo ar(a)-aiye   k(o)-ẹbọ   k(o)-edi
Ifa say person-one be all   people-(of)-earth gather-sacrifice gather-to:tie

ti   yi, o ni yẹ-yẹ   ni nwọn nşe,   ọwọ wọn ko ni le   tẹ,
against this; he say empty-empty be they making, hand their not be be:able press

        ọrun ni Q-1(i)-ọrun   ti   ran   wa,   oju rẹ ni gbogbo awọn
(him), sky be One:who-has-sky have send (him) come, eye his be all   those

ti nko   ẹbọ   ko   edi   ti   yio şe ku tan.
that gathering sacrifice gather to:tie against (him) will make die finish.

OFUN - (Q)KANRAN - 2

O-fun   tin   a   da   fun Ade-g(un)-ori-oye   ọmọ
"It-be:white very:white" who cast for Crown-mount-head-(of)- title, child (of)

Qrangunaga nwọn ni ko ni parun ni ode   aiye rẹ, (A)de-g(un)-ori-
Qrangunaga; they say not be perish at outside (of) earth his, Crown-mount-head-

oye   ni orukọ ti a pe ipe,   nwọn ni ki   o ru   obukọ kan,
(of)-title be name that we call trumpet; they say should he offer he:goat one,

---

1. Also known as Ofinran Ẹkun, meaning "One who provokes Leopard." Cf.
n. 1, verse 246-1.

246 - 1

"The leopard looking for a fight[1] goes walking at high noon"[2] was the one who cast Ifa for Qrunmila on the day they were sending Death to call him to heaven, Eshinrinmọgbọ.[3]

> "I do not meet the Sky God when I go walking;
> "When a brass gong is sounding 'goro-goro-goro,'[4]
> "It does not look at the God of Whiteness;[5]
> "I do not answer the call of the Sky God;[6]
> "A bell that has no clapper
> "Does not answer the call of the God of Whiteness."[7]

Ifa says there is someone against whom everyone is making sacrifices and making charms.[8] He says they are doing it in vain; they will not be able to hold him down. From heaven the Sky God has sent him, and he will live to see all those who are making sacrifices and charms against him die.

---

1. Ofinran Ẹkun is an alternative name for the figure Ofun Qkanran, meaning "one who provokes leopard." In this context, however, it is the leopard that is looking for a fight, by appearing in the daytime, when he is most apt to meet people on the road.
2. Qsan (mid-day) covers a period from about 10:00 A.M. to 4:00 P.M. Ganranin-ganranin or gan-gan refers to the position of the sun overhead, or perhaps to the intensity of its heat. Together the two terms cover the period from about noon to 2:00 P.M.
3. Identified only as a title or praise-name (oriki) of heaven.
4. The sound made by the gong, which is a large, clapperless bell beaten with a stick.
5. As informants explained, "because it has no eye." The implication, however, is probably that another type of bell (aja), mentioned below, is used in the worship of Orishala.
6. I am not going to die yet; my time to die has not yet come.
7. A bell (aja) that has lost its clapper is not useful to Orishala.
8. A type of charm (edi) to tie a person to a spot, or to make him do evil against his will.

---

246 - 2

"It is very white"[1] was the one who cast Ifa for "Crown mounts title," the child of Qrangunaga.[2] They said he would not perish within his world. "Crown mounts title" is the name that we call trumpet.[3] They said he should sacrifice one he-goat,

---

1. This is derived from Ofun in the name of the figure.
2. The title of the king of Ila, forty-five miles northeast of Ifẹ.
3. These are small ivory trumpets on which are blown the titles of a chief in saluting him.

ẹgbẹtalelọgbọn   aṣọ   i-san-mọ-(i)di   rẹ, o ru-(ẹ)bọ.
6600   (cowries), cloth to-wrap-against-waist his, he offer-sacrifice.

    Ifa ni   ọkunrin a-l(i)-agba   kan ni-yi   ti   o   ma   ri
    Ifa say man   one:who-be-elder one be-this, that he (continuative) see

obinrin arugbo   kan fẹ   ti   gbogbo enia   ro   pe   ko le   bi-(ọ)mọ
woman old:person one love that all   people think that not be:able bear-child

mọ, ni oju   obinrin yi ni ọmọ ti   o   ma   bi yio ṣe   j(ẹ)-
again, at eye (of) woman this be child that she (continuative) bear will make eat-

oye ti   nwọn yio si   ma   fun ipe   fun   ti   nwọn yio si
title that they will and (continuative) blow trumpet for (him) that they will and

fi   oro de   e   l(i)-ori, bẹ-ni   gbogbo enia   ni nwọn nfi   ọkunrin
take miter cover him at-head, so-be (it) all   people be they taking man

yi ṣe-(i)re   bayi, nitori-ti   ko ni   igba   tabi awo.
this make-play thus, because-that not have calabash or plate.

OFUN - (Q)KANRAN - 3

    Pẹrẹṣipẹ,   pẹrẹṣipẹ,   Ifa l(i)-o-ṣe   ohun ti   a ba   gbọ, igede
    "To:open:flat, to:open:flat, Ifa be-who-make thing that we should hear, curse

ni-(ọ)kan ni   ko ju   mọ, Igede l(i)-ohun   Ifẹ a   da   fun Wa-
be-one   be (we) not surpass know, Curse be-voice (of) Ifẹ" who cast for Come-

(i)le-(e)lu   A-ji-ṣ(e)-ọmọ,   ọmọ   A-l(i)-abẹbẹ
house-(of)-stranger One:who-awake-make-child, child (of) One:who-has-fan

oyoro.   Nwọn ni ki   Wa-(i)le-(e)lu   ru   ẹiyẹ-(i)le
glittering. They say should Come-house-(of)-stranger offer bird-(of)-house

mẹrin, ẹgbarun.   Nwọn ni nitori-ti   ẹjọ kan li o ma
four, 10,000 (cowries). They say because-that case one be it (continuative)

digbolu   yi, n(i)-inu   ẹjọ na ni o gbe ma   la.
come:against (him) this, at-belly (of) case the be he take (continuative) be:wealthy.

    N(i)-igba-ti o ru   ẹbọ   tan,   ni nwọn pe   l(i)-ẹjọ, o-l(i)-
    At-time-that he offer sacrifice finish, be they call (him) at-case, one:who-has-

ọfin   ni ki   nwọn lọ mu   wa,   bi nwọn ti   mu   de   ti
palace say should they go take (him) come; as they have take (him) arrive that

nwọn kun-(i)lẹ   ti   o nro-(ẹ)jọ,   ni o jin   si ilẹ   akun,
they kneel-ground that he reporting-case, be he fall:down to earth (of) bead,

ọ-l(i)-ọfin   ni ki   o   ma   gbọn   akun na, nitori-pe
one:who-has-palace say should he (continuative) scoop:out bead the, because-that

ki ṣe   on ni-(ọ)kan ni on ọ-l(i)-ọfin   kọkọ pe pe ki   o wa
not make he be-one   be he one:who-has-palace first call that should he come

one shilling seven pence eight oninis, and the sash from his waist. He made the sacrifice.

Ifa says this is an old man who is going to marry an old woman who everyone thinks can no longer bear children. This woman will live to see the child that she is about to bear become a chief; they will blow trumpets for him and put a miter[4] on his head. Everyone is making fun of this man because he does not have even a calabash or a plate.

---

4. A type of hat, made of finely plaited straw and decorated with leather appliquéd to velvet, which is worn by the principal diviners and town chiefs (Ifẹ). (See Chapter X.)

---

246 - 3

"Open for all to see, open for all to see; Ifa is the one who does things we can hear about; only curses we should not know about; curses are the voice of Ifẹ"[1] was the one who cast Ifa for "Come to the foreigner's house, who wakes and makes a child," the child of "One who has a glittering fan." They said that "Come to the foreigner's house" should sacrifice four pigeons and two shillings six pence. They said he should sacrifice because of a case that would be brought against him in court, through which he would become rich.

When he had completed the sacrifice, they called him to court. The king said that they should go to bring him, and when he was brought and knelt down to state his case, he broke through the ground into a pit of beads.[2] The king said he should take the beads, because he was not the first nor the only one whom the king had called to come

---

1. This means that the Ifa diviners do not work with bad medicine or do other evil things which have to be concealed, while those who use curses keep their work a secret. Ifẹ is reputed as a place where curses are strong and commonly used, as the Ijẹbu people are known for using bad medicine (ogun). Spells or incantations (ọfọ) whose purpose is to kill someone are known as igede, ogede, or ẹgede.

2. See n. 5, verse 3-1.

ro-(ẹ)jọ.   Bayi-ni Wa-(i)le-(e)lu   bẹrẹ si gbọn   akun na ti
report-case. Thus-be Come-house-(of)-stranger begin to scoop:out bead the that

o si ti   ibẹ di   ọ-l(i)-ọla.   Wa-(i)le-(e)lu
he and from there become one:who-have-wealth. Come-house-(of)-stranger

wa   bẹrẹ si wi-pe: N-ko mọ pe a-pe-jin   ni erin   pe on.
come begin to speak-that: "I-not know that to-call-give be Elephant call him."

    Ifa ni ẹni-kan   wa   ti   ọran kan ha   mọ,   tabi ti o
    Ifa say person-one exist that affair one press against (him), or that he

 ma   ro-(ẹ)jọ   kan yi, Ifa ni n(i)-inu   ẹjọ na ni oluwarẹ
(continuative) report-case one this; Ifa say at-belly (of) case the be person:in:

       yio ti   di   ọ-l(i)-ọla.
question will have become one:who-have-wealth.

OFUN - (Q)KANRAN - 4

    Ejo   tere nnako tere nna a   da fun ẹrunlọjọ eku ni-(ọ)jọ ti   Ọfọn
    "Snake tere nnako tere nna" who cast for 165   rat at-day that Mouse

nlọ ji   ogiri   Orişa jẹ, nwọn ni ki   nwọn ru   akikọ
going steal boiled:locust:bean (of) Orisha eat, they say should they offer cock

(ọ)k(an)-ọkan ati ẹgb(ẹsan)-ẹgbẹsan.   Gbogbo awọn eku ru-(ẹ)bọ
one-one   and 1800-1800   (cowries). All   those rat offer-sacrifice

şugbọn Ọfọn ni-(ọ)kan ni   ko ru-(ẹ)bọ.
but   Mouse be-one   be (he) not offer-sacrifice.

    N(i)-igba-ti o di   ọjọ kan ogiri   Orişa nu,   Orişa
    At-time-that it become day one boiled:locust:bean (of) Orisha be:lost, Orisha

wa   sọ-pe   awọn eku ni o   ji   on ni ogiri   jẹ, o kẹ irin
come speak-that those rat be who steal him at boiled:locust:bean eat, he set trap

s(i)-ilẹ   o ni ki   gbogbo eku wa   kọja ni oju   irin na, o ni ẹni-
to-ground he say should all   rat come pass at eye (of) trap the, he say person-

ti o ba ji   on ni ogiri   jẹ, irin yio mu.   Ẹmọ ni
that he should steal him at boiled:locust:bean eat, trap will take (him). Ẹmọ be

o   kọkọ kọja o si nk(ọ)-orin   pe:
who first pass he and singing-song that:

              Ejo   tere nnako tere nna
              "Snake tere nnako, tere nna;

              Ẹmọ l(i)-ori   eku Tere nna
              "Ẹmọ be-head (of) rat Tere nna;

              Akọsin l(i)-ako   wọn jẹ Tere nna
              "Akọsin be-leader their eat, Tere nna.

and state his case.[3] So "Come to the foreigner's house" began to scoop up the beads, and in this way he became a wealthy man. "Come to the foreigner's house" began to say: "I didn't know that the Elephant called me to give me a present."[4]

Ifa says there is someone whose affairs are troubling him, or that someone has been called to state his case in court. Ifa says that through this case, he will become wealthy.

---

3. Because they had not been found by the many others who had knelt in the same spot, the beads must have been meant for him. Usually the king claims half of any beads found in this way.

4. He expected, rather, to be punished. Elephant is a praise-name of the king.

---

246 - 4

"Snake tere nnako, tere nna"[1] was the one who cast Ifa for the 165 kinds[2] of rats on the day that Mouse was going to steal and eat the boiled locust beans[3] of the God of Whiteness. They said they should sacrifice one cock each and five pence four oninis apiece. All the rats made the sacrifice except Mouse who alone did not sacrifice.

One day the boiled locust beans of the God of Whiteness were missing. The God of Whiteness said that rats were the ones who had stolen and eaten his boiled locust beans; and he set a trap and told all the rats to come and pass over it. He said that the ones who had stolen his boiled locust beans would be caught in the trap. The Ẹmọ rat[4] was the first to pass over, and as he went he sang:

> "Snake, tere nnako, Tere nna;
> "Ẹmọ is head of the rats, Tere nna;
> "Akọsin[5] is their leader, Tere nna.

---

1. These words have no meaning, but are added to the song which goes with this verse "to make it sweet." "Tere nna" is the refrain in which the chorus joins.

2. See n. 3, verse 18-4.

3. Ogiri are boiled and fermented oil seeds used in preparing stew sauce. Egunsi or melon seeds (Citrullus vulgaris) are commonly used but iru or African locust beans (Parkia filicoidea) are regarded as "sweeter" and are specified in the song below. Both egunsi stew and fried locust beans are favorite foods of the God of Whiteness, identified here only as Orisha. Cf. n. 3, verse 5-1.

4. A small brown rat; Tullberg's rat (Praomys Tullbergi).

5. An unidentified kind of rat who "goes in front when rats are looking for food.

Bi mo ba   ji-(i)ru   ana   ję Tere nna
"If I   should steal-locust:bean (of) yesterday eat, Tere nna;

Ki-(i)rin   kan   mi l(i)-a-kan-pa   Tere nna
"Should-trap knock me at-to-knock-kill, Tere nna.

Bi mi ko ba   ji-(i)ru   ana   ję Tere nna
"If I   not should steal-locust:bean (of) yesterday eat, Tere nna;

Ki-(i)rin   kan   mi l(i)-a-kan-yǫ   Tere nna
"Should-trap knock me at-to-knock-slip, Tere nna;

Ejo   tere nnako Tere nna.
"Snake tere nnako, Tere nna."

Bayi ni Ęmǫ kǫja ti   irin ko si mu,   gbogbo eku si nkǫ-(o)rin   bayi,
Thus be Ęmǫ pass that trap not and take (him), all   rat and singing-song thus,

nwǫn si nkǫja   ni oju   irin titi ti   o fi   kan   Qfǫn,   şugbǫn n(i)-igba-
they and passing at eye (of) trap until that it take touch Mouse, but   at-time-

ti   o ni ki   on kǫja irin si mu   n(i)-igba-ti nwǫn tu   Qfǫn
that he say should he pass, trap and take (him), at-time-that they loosen Mouse

tan, o ja   lu   igbo, lati igba-na ni Qfǫn ko ti   nba   eku
finish, he jump strike forest; from time-the be Mouse not have meeting rat

pe   mǫ.
assemble again.

Ifa ni ki   awǫn kan ru-(ę)bǫ   nitori-ti   bi ǫran   kan bi ęni
Ifa say should those one offer-sacrifice because-that as matter one if person

mu aje   ole, ki   ęni-kan   ma fi ęsę ko   (ohu)n-kan ba
drink ordeal (of) thief, should person-one not take foot gather thing-one   meet

wǫn. Ifa ni ole kan yio ja,   şugbǫn ki   e-l(i)-eyi   ru-
them. Ifa say thief one will reach (us), but   should one:who-be-this offer-

(ę)bǫ ki a ma ba   mu   ni ole. Ęni-kan   wa   ni ipo
sacrifice that we not should take (him) at thief. Person-one exist at position (of)

oye kan l(i)-oni, o nji   iru, ni oşu   męta l(i)-oni ni Olodumare yio fi
title one at-today, he waving tail, at month three at-today be Olodumare will put

ęlomiran   si ori   ipo   na.
another:person to head (of) position the.

OFUN - (I)ROSUN - 1

Oşuşu   ǫwǫ   a b(i)-ęnu   l(i)-apa kan a   da   fun Ofun
"Bunch (of) midrib:of:palm:leaf it bear-mouth at-arm one" who cast for Ofun

ti   o ma   mu ǫbuntun   adugbo wa s(i)-ile nwǫn ni ki
that he (continuative) take bride   (of) quarter come to-house; they say should

"If I stole the locust beans yesterday to eat, Tere nna;
"May the trap catch me, Tere nna.
"If I did not steal the locust beans yesterday to eat, Tere nna;
"May the trap let me escape, Tere nna;
"Snake tere nnako, Tere nna."

In this way the Ẹmọ rat passed over and the trap did not catch him; and all the rats sang this song and passed over the trap until it was the turn of Mouse. But when the God of Whiteness said that Mouse should pass over, the trap caught him. When they released Mouse, he ran away. From that time on, Mouse has not associated with the rats any more.[6]

Ifa says a group of people should make a sacrifice so that if someone takes an ordeal to prove he is not a thief, he may not bring evil home to them. Ifa says that we will encounter a thief, but this person should make a sacrifice lest he himself be taken as the thief. There is someone who has a title today; he is waving a horse-tail switch;[7] two months from today the Sky God will put another person in his place.

---

6. The verse thus explains why Mouse lives in the house and not with the other rats.

7. Chiefs use whisks similar to those of the babalawo, but made of horse tails rather than cow tails. This prediction involves a pun on "steal locust beans" (ji iru) and "wave tail" (ji iru); the latter would more commonly be given as ju irukẹrẹ. Cf. n. 5, verse 54-4.

---

247 - 1

"Broom's mouth is on one side"[1] was the one who cast Ifa for Ofun when he was going to bring home a bride from his quarter. They said

---

1. Yoruba brooms or besoms are made of the midribs (ọwọ) of palm leaves, tied together with a string around the middle. The butt or base of the broom is usually not perpendicular to its axis, but slanted at an angle, to which this name refers.

o ru   ayebǫ meji, ęgbędǫgbǫn,   Ofun ru-(ę)bǫ,   bayi ni o do
he offer hen   two,   5000   (cowries); Ofun offer-sacrifice, thus be he copulate:

   Irosun   l(i)-oyun.
with Irosun (she) have-pregnancy.

   Ifa ni ęni-kan   ma   fę   obinrin kan, işe   ni o   ma
   Ifa say person-one (continuative) love woman one, make (it) be he (continuative)

ji   obinrin na do   ti   obinrin na yio si l(i)-oyun,   n(i)-
steal woman the copulate:with (her), that woman the will and have-pregnancy; at-

igba-na ni   yio si di   aya rę.
time-the be (she) will and become wife his.

OFUN - (I)ROSUN - 2

   Şofe l(i)-awo   Ewi, A-rin-(ǫ)na-ko   awo   Qfa. Şofe nş(e)-
   Shofe be-secret (of) Ewi, To-walk-road-meet secret (of) Qfa. Shofe making-

awo   fun Ewi, o si ndo   aya rę, gbogbo ohun ti   o nşe   fun
secret for Ewi, he and copulating:with wife his, all   thing that he doing for

Ewi ko gba bę-ni ko ję mǫ.   N(i)-igba-na ni Ewi ni ki   a   lǫ pe A-
Ewi not take so-be not eat again. At-time-the be Ewi say should they go call To-

rin-(ǫ)na-ko   awo   Qfa wa   pe ki   o wa   şe (ohu)n-kan fun on,
walk-road-meet, secret (of) Qfa, come that should he come do thing-one for him,

boya   ohun ti   o wa   şe fun on yio gba.
perhaps thing that he come do for him will take.

   N(i)-igba-ti Şofe gbǫ pe Ewi lǫ ran-(i)şę   pe babalawo miran, o
   At-time-that Shofe hear that Ewi go send-message call diviner   another, he

si mǫ pe bi o ba   de   yio bo-(o)ri rę Şofe ji   wa si
and know that if he should arrive will cover-head his, Shofe awake come to

odo   Ewi, o sǫ   fun   pe babalawo kan nbǫ   ni ǫdǫ   rę
presence (of) Ewi, he speak for (him) that diviner   one coming at presence his

l(i)-oni, babalawo na ni ębǫ,   nitori-na   Ewi ran-(i)şę   lǫ s(i)-oju
at-today, diviner   the be sacrifice, because-the Ewi send-message go to-eye

   ǫna, bi A-rin-(ǫ)na-ko   ti nbǫ   o bǫ si ǫwǫ   awǫn o-
(of) road, as To-walk-road-meet have coming he come to hand (of) those one:who-

n(i)-işę   Ewi, nwǫn si mu   N(i)-igba-na ni A-rin-(ǫ)na-ko
have-message (of) Ewi, they and take (him). At-time-the be To-walk-road-meet

da-(o)hun, o ni, ile   on ni on wa   ti Ewi wa   ran-(i)şę   pe on,
break-voice, he say house his be he exist that Ewi come send-message call him,

abi enia   a   ma   pe   ni   pa?
or people they (continuative) call (one) be (they) kill (him)?

he should sacrifice two hens and one shilling three pence. Ofun made the sacrifice, and in this way he had intercourse with Irosun[2] and she became pregnant.

Ifa says someone loves a woman. He should "steal" the woman[3] and have intercourse with her, so that she will become pregnant. Then she will become his wife.

---

2. The name of the figure is explained here in terms of the sexual union of Ofun and Irosun.

3. Have an illicit affair with her.

---

247 - 2

Shofe, the diviner of the Ewi; "Meet walking along the road," the diviner of Qfa.[1] Shofe was divining for the Ewi, and he was having intercourse with his wife; everything that he did for the Ewi did not take effect and did not work any more.[2] Then Ewi said they should go and call "Meet walking along the road," the diviner of Qfa, to come and do something for him, hoping that perhaps what he did would take effect.

When Shofe heard that the Ewi had sent to call another diviner, he knew that if he arrived, the other diviner would outdo him. Shofe awoke and went to see the Ewi; he told him that a diviner was coming to see him that day, and that the diviner was required as a sacrifice.[3] Thereupon the Ewi sent his messengers to the road, and as "Meet walking along the road" was coming, he fell into the hands of Ewi's messengers. They seized him. Then "Meet walking along the road" spoke, saying, "The Ewi sent to my own house to call me. Do people invite someone to come, and then kill him?"

---

1. Ewi is the title of the King of Ado Ekiti, a town about fifty miles east of Ifę, while Qfa is a town about the same distance to the north. This verse begins simply by naming the two central characters in the tale, both of whom are diviners, without the usual statement of problem and divination to serve as a precedent.

2. As stated more explicitly later in the verse, it is a tabu for a diviner or for a medicine man or doctor to commit adultery with the wife of a client, the consequence being that their predictions will not come true and their charms and medicines will not work.

3. He falsified Ifa's message to protect himself.

N(i)-igba-na ni A-rin-(ọ)na-ko   wa   sọ   fun Ewi pe babalawo ti
At-time-the be To-walk-road-meet come speak for Ewi that diviner   that

o nd(a)-Ifa   fun   ni ko jẹ   ki aiye   Ewi gun,   nitori-
he casting-Ifa for (him) be not consent that earth (of) Ewi be:orderly, because-

ti o ndo   ni obinrin, n(i)-igba-na ni Ṣofe, ti iṣe babalawo
that he copulating:with (him) at woman, at-time-the be Shofe, that make diviner

     Ewi, da-(o)hun   pe nibo ni on ti   gbe ndo   aya   Ewi ti
(of) Ewi, break-voice that where be he have take copulating:with wife (of) Ewi that

A-rin-(ọ)na-ko   ri on? A-rin-(ọ)na-ko   da-(o)hun, o ni ki
To-walk-road-meet see him? To-walk-road-meet break-voice, he say should

gbogbo awọn aya   Ewi lọ ma   ko   ọkẹ   aṣọ   wọn wa,   n(i)-
all   those wife (of) Ewi go (continuative) gather bag (of) cloth their come; at-

igba-ti   nwọn ko   wọn de,   ni gbogbo wọn ntu   ọkẹ wọn, nwọn
time-that they gather them arrive, be all   them loosening bag their, they

nko   aṣọ   inu wọn s(i)-ilẹ, n(i)-ibi-ti   nwọn gbe nko   aṣọ
gathering cloth (of) belly their to-ground; at-place-that they take gathering cloth

s(i)-ilẹ   ni nwọn ri i-san-mọ-(i)di   aṣọ   Ewi kan n(i)-inu   ọkẹ
to-ground be they see to-wrap-against-waist cloth (of) Ewi one at-belly (of) bag

     obinrin   Ewi kan,
(of) woman (of) Ewi one;

     N(i)-igba-na ni Ewi da-(o)hun   pe n(i)-igba-ti o sọ   pe iwọ ko fẹ
At-time-the be Ewi break-voice that"At-time-that you speak that you not love

mi l(i)-aya, bawo ni aṣọ yi ṣe   de   inu   ọkẹ   aya on yi, nitori-
me at-wife, how be cloth this make arrive belly (of) bag (of) wife his this, because-

ti on ti   fi aṣọ yi ru-(ẹ)bọ   l(i)-ọwọ iwọ, Ṣofe, o si ti
that he have take cloth this offer-sacrifice at-hand (of) you, Shofe, you and have

jẹ   l(i)-eru   lọ, bayi ni nwọn ki Ṣofe mọ-(i)lẹ   ti nwọn de e,
eat (it) at-payment go"; thus be they push Shofe against-ground that they bind him,

Ewi si ni ki   nwọn lọ ma   gbẹ ilẹ   n(i)-inu   gbagede on
Ewi and say should they go (continuative) dig ground at-belly (of) backyard his

ki on ba fi   nu-(i)lẹ,   ki   on fi   ṣe   ebọ
that they should take (him) put:in-ground, should they take (him) make sacrifice

ti   nwọn wi.
that they speak.

     Ṣofe bẹ   A-rin-(ọ)na-ko   pe ki   o gba on, A-rin-(ọ)na-ko
Shofe request To-walk-road-meet that should he help him, To-walk-road-meet

wa   sọ   fun   pe, ṣe o mọ n(i)-igba-ti o fi yan   on ni
come speak for (him) that, "Make you know at-time-that you take choose him at

ẹbọ?   O ni on ko mọ, n(i)-igba-ti o bẹ   titi A-rin-(ọ)na-ko
sacrifice?" He say he not know, at-time-that he request until, To-walk-road-meet

Then "Meet walking along the road" told the Ewi that the diviner who was casting Ifa for him was preventing his affairs from being in order because he was having intercourse with one of his wives. Then Shofe, who was the Ewi's diviner, replied, "Where have I been having intercourse with the Ewi's wife, that you saw me?" "Meet walking along the road" answered, saying that all the wives of the Ewi should bring out their bags of clothes. When they had brought them, they began to undo them and to empty the clothes inside them onto the ground. As they were doing this, they saw a sash of the Ewi in the bag of one of the Ewi's wives.

Then the Ewi spoke: "You said that you were not making love to my wife. How, then, did this cloth get inside my wife's bag? Because I used it to make a sacrifice which you prescribed, Shofe, and you took it away as payment." So they forced Shofe to the ground and tied him up. The Ewi said they should go and dig a hole in the back yard, and bury him in it, and that Shofe should be used to make the sacrifice which he himself had prescribed.

Shofe begged "Meet walking along the road" to help him. "Meet walking along the road" replied, "Don't you remember when you said I should be sacrificed?" Shofe said he didn't remember. When he had pleaded and pleaded, "Meet walking along the road"

gbe Şofe g(un)-odi   Şofe si sa-lǫ. A-rin-(ǫ)na-ko   wa   pa
carry Shofe climb-townwall, Shofe and run-go. To-walk-road-meet come kill

ewurę nu-(i)lę   o si sǫ   fun Ewi pe on ti   pa.
she:goat put:in-ground he and speak for Ewi that he have kill (him).

   N(i)-igba-ti o pę   nwǫn wa   ngburo   Şofe ka-kiri,
   At-time-that it be:long they come hearing:news (of) Shofe go:around-about,

Ewi si bi A-rin-(ǫ)na-ko   lere pe   şe o ni o ti pa Şofe ru-
Ewi and ask To-walk-road-meet (1)   that "Make you say you have kill Shofe offer-

(ę)bǫ?   O ni bę ni,   boya   ogun   li o fi   da
sacrifice? He say so be (it), perhaps medicine be he take (it) transform (himself)

lǫ, Şofe wa   bęrę si wi-pe:
go, Shofe come begin to speak-that:

      A-rin-(ǫ)na-ko   o ma   şe-(oh)un, o şe enia
      "To-walk-road-meet you indeed make-thing, you make person;

      O ko ję-ki   a mu Şofe   Ewi ş(e)-ębǫ.
      "You not consent-that they take Shofe (of) Ewi make-sacrifice."

Ifa ni ęni-kan   wa ai-san   nşe,   ki   o kiyesi ara, ęni-
Ifa say person-one exist not-be:better making, should he heed body, person-

ti nşe   Ifa tabi ogun   fun-(ę)ni ko ję-ki   o san,   o nfę
that making Ifa or   medicine for-person not consent-that he be:better, he loving

   ni obinrin, obinrin   a-l(i)-ai-san   na si nd(o)-
(him) at woman, woman (of) one:who-be-not-be:better the and copulating:with-

ǫkǫ   mǫ   l(i)-ara, nitori-na gbogbo ogun   tabi Ifa ti o
husband against (him) at-body, because-the all   medicine or   Ifa that he

nşe   ko le   ję. Ewurę kan, ejielogun   aşǫ   ara rę ni
making not be:able eat. She:goat one, 44,000 (cowries), cloth (of) body his be

ębǫ.
sacrifice.

   Ifa ni a-(yi)o pe ęni-kan   lǫ si ęhin   odi   kan lǫ şe
   Ifa say they-will call person-one go to back (of) townwall one go make

ogun   tabi Ifa kan, ki   o şǫ-(a)ra ki o ma ba   ko   ekona
medicine or   Ifa one, should he watch-body that he not should meet evil:spirit

n(i)-ibi-ti o nlǫ, nitori-ti   oluwarę   yio ba   enini
at-place-that he going, because-that person:in:question will meet enemy (of)

ęni-ti   o ti nşe   Ifa tabi ogun   fun a-l(i)-ai-san   na
person-that he have making Ifa or   medicine for one:who-be-not-be:better the

pade, nitori-na ki   o ru aguntan kan ati aşǫ kan pęlu   ętala.
meet, because-the should he offer ewe   one and cloth one together:with 26,000

(cowries).

---

1. Bi . . . lere means "to ask."

---

took Shofe to the town wall, and let Shofe climb the town wall and run away. "Meet walking along the road" came back and killed a she-goat and buried it in the hole; and he told the Ewi that he had killed Shofe.

After a while they heard news that Shofe was still alive, and the Ewi asked "Meet walking along the road": "Didn't you say you had killed Shofe as a sacrifice? He said, "Yes, but perhaps he had medicine to bring himself back to life." Shofe then began to say:

"'Meet walking along the road,' you were kind indeed; you are truly human;
"You did not let them take Ewi's Shofe to make the sacrifice."

Ifa says there is someone who is not well; he should be careful. The person who is making Ifa or making medicine for him does not let him get well, because he is making love to his wife; and the wife of the sick person is committing adultery against him. Therefore all the medicine and the Ifa that he is making are not able to work. One she-goat, eleven shillings, and the cloth from his body is the sacrifice.

Ifa says someone will be called out of town to make medicine or Ifa. He should be careful lest he meet an evil spirit where he is going, because he will meet with the enemy of the sick person for whom he is making Ifa or medicine. Therefore he should sacrifice one ewe and one cloth, plus six shillings six pence.

OFUN - (I)ROSUN - 3

A-kǫ-(e)be-le-(e)be   awo   inu   oko   a   da   fun
"To-pile-yam:heap-upon-yam:heap," secret (of) belly (of) farm who cast for

Etitan   ni-(ǫ)jǫ ti   Etitan   wa   ni on ni-(ǫ)kan ti   ko n(i)-
Refuse:Heap at-day   that Refuse:Heap exist at he be-one   that (he) not have-

igba   ti   ko l(i)-awo   nwǫn ni aya kan ni o   ma   ri fę
calabash that (he) not have-plate, they say wife one be he (continuative) see love

yi, n(i)-igba-ti o ba   fę   aya na tan   ni t(i)-ęru   t(i)-ǫmǫ
this; at-time-that he should love wife the finish be that-(of)-slave that-(of)-child

yio ma   pe   sin,   nwǫn ni ki   o ru   eku, ęja, ori,
will (continuative) assemble serve (him); they say should he offer rat, fish, shea:

       obukǫ kan, ęgbęrindinlogun,   Etitan   ru-(ę)bǫ.
butter, he:goat one, 3200   (cowries); Refuse:Heap offer-sacrifice.

N(i)-igba-ti Etitan   ru-(ę)bǫ   tan o ri obinrin kan ti   orukǫ
At-time-that Refuse:Heap offer-sacrifice finish he see woman one that name

rę nję   Gborongaga fę, n(i)-igba-na ni o di   pe gbogbo enia   ngba
her eating Gborongaga love, at-time-the be it become that all   people sweeping

ile   gba ode wa   da   s(i)-inu Etitan   ti ifa
house sweep outside come cast (it) to-belly (of) Refuse:Heap that windfall (of)

ile   ati ti   ode di   ti   Atitan.   Olu   a-wu-
house and that (of) outside become that (of) Refuse:heap. Mushroom to-sprout-

ka-(a)lę   ori   Atitan   ni   ję Gborongaga.
around-evening (of) head (of) Refuse:heap be (who) eat Gborongaga.

Ifa ni ęni-kan   wa ti ko ni   (ohu)n-kan-kan nisisiyi, yio ri
Ifa say person-one exist that not have thing-one-one right:now, will see

obinrin kan fę   n(i)-igba-ti o ba   fę   tan ni ifa   yio ma
woman one love; at-time-that he should love (her) finish be windfall will (continu-

       ti   gbogbo ilu wa   ba.
ative) from all   town come meet (him)

Yesi gbe Gborongaga ni iyawo?
"Who take Gborongaga at junior:wife?

Atitan   ga-ga-ga   l(i)-o gbe Gborongaga ni iyawo.
"Refuse:Heap be:high-be:high-be:high be-who take Gborongaga at junior:wife."

OFUN - (I)ROSUN - 4

Ęrun   ipǫn-(ǫ)na   o f(i)-oju j(ǫ)-ikin   ko ri ęję ję
"Palm:nut (of) mouth-(of)-road it take-eye resemble-ikin, not see blood eat

bi ikin a   da   fun Ofun O-l(i)-osun   a f(i)-ęfun s(i)-oju sǫ-(ę)kun
like ikin" who cast for Ofun Who-has-camwood who take-chalk to-eye   shed-tears

247 - 3

"Pile yam heap upon yam heap," the diviner inside the farm, was the one who cast Ifa for Refuse Heap in the days when Refuse Heap lived all alone, and had neither a calabash nor a plate.[1] They said he would find a woman to marry, and that when he had married her, both slaves and children would assemble to serve him.[2] They said he should sacrifice a rat, a fish, shea butter, one he-goat, and nine pence six oninis. Refuse Heap made the sacrifice.

When Refuse Heap had completed the sacrifice, he met a woman whose name was Gborongaga and married her. Then it happened that everyone sweeping their houses and sweeping the streets came and threw their sweepings on Refuse Heap, and that the windfalls[3] from the house and the street belonged to Refuse Heap. The mushroom that springs up overnight on Refuse Heap is what is called Gborongaga.

Ifa says there is someone who does not own anything at present; he will find a woman to marry; when he has married her, he will receive windfalls from everyone in town.

"Who married Gborongaga?
"Refuse Heap, very tall, was the one who married Gborongaga."

---

1. That is, he had no property and no family, friends, or followers.
2. They will work for him, as a subject serves a king, or a child his father.
3. Property that comes into one's possession unexpectedly, without payment, and even without his knowing how or from where it came.

---

247 - 4

"Palm nuts embedded in the path are like the palm nuts of Ifa, but they do not drink blood like Ifa's palm nuts"[1] was the one who cast Ifa for Ofun with Camwood[2] who had put chalk on her face while weeping

---

1. See n. 3, verse 6-3. Palm nuts are known both as ẹrun and as ekurọ.
2. The character's name, Ofun Olosun, is a pun on the name of the figure, Ofun Irosun, as are the white chalk (ẹfun) and the red "camwood" or barwood (osun) with which the client is instructed to mark her face. Cf. n. 5, verse 111-2.

ǫmǫ,   nwǫn ni ki   o   ru-(ę)bǫ   pe   ire   ǫmǫ de   si
(of) child; they   say should she offer-sacrifice that goodness (of) child arrive to

    ni ǫdun-ni.   O   ru-(ę)bǫ.
(her) at year-this.   She offer-sacrifice.

     Ifa ni   obinrin kan wa   ti   nwa   ǫmǫ ori   rę gba ayebǫ adię   kan.
     Ifa say woman one exist that seeking child, head her take hen   chicken one.

Ki   o   fi   ęfun   sa   oju ǫtun, ki   o   fi   osun   sa   oju osi n(i)-
Should she take chalk mark eye right, should she take camwood mark eye left at-

igba-ti   o   ba   fę   bǫ   ori na. Ifa ni ire   ǫmǫ de
time-that she should want sacrifice:to head the. Ifa say goodness (of) child arrive

si   ni ǫdun-ni.
to (her) at year-this.

OFUN - (I)ROSUN - 5

     "Ofun Ojuro, yękę ǫtita" a   da   fun Ojuro iya   Efurę ti   a   nlǫ
     "Ofun Ojuro, tipped stool" who cast for Ojuro mother (of) Efurę that she going

b(a)-O-l(i)-okun   p(a)-ęsan   ǫdun, nwǫn ni ki   o   ru-(ę)bǫ
join-One:who-has-sea kill-festival (of) year; they say should she offer-sacrifice

ki   ǫna i-şi-(ǫ)na   ko ba   ba,   ko ru-(ę)bǫ   ęiyę-
that road to-miss-road not should join (her), (she) not offer-sacrifice (of) bird-

(i)le   meji, ati ęgbędǫgbǫn.
(of)-house two, and 5000   (cowries).

     Ko ru-(ę)bǫ,   o   ni ki şe   oni   ni on ti   ma   nlǫ
     Not offer-sacrifice, she say not make today be she have (continuative) going

ba O-l(i)-okun   ş(e)-ǫdun o   ni nwǫn sęsę wa   ni ki   o   ru-
with One:who-has-sea make-year; she say they just come say should she offer-

(ę)bǫ   ni ǫdun-ni. N(i)-igba-ti o   nlǫ Eşu na   ǫpa si igbo, o
sacrifice at year-this. At-time-that she going Eshu stretch staff to forest, she

o   şi-(ǫ)na   si igbo.
and miss-road to forest.

     Şugbǫn n(i)-igba-ti o   lǫ tan,   awǫn ara   ile   rę wa   ru-
     But   at-time-that she go finish, those people (of) house hers come offer-

(ę)bǫ,   n(i)-igba-ti Ojuro şi-(ǫ)na   şi-(ǫ)na   s(i)-inu   igbo, ibi-
sacrifice, at-time-that Ojuro miss-road miss-road to-belly (of) forest, place-

ti   o gbe nrin   kiri n(i)-inu   igbo o   wa   ba   eko
that she take walking around at-belly (of) forest she come meet tail:feather (of)

odidę ni ilę,   o ga   gegerege, o wa tę   aşǫ rę s(i)-ilę   o
parrot at ground, it be:high very:high, she come spread cloth hers to-ground she

because she had no child. They said she should sacrifice so that the blessing of a child might come to her during that year. She sacrificed.

Ifa says there is a woman who is seeking a child; her head needs a hen as sacrifice.[3] She should mark her right eye with chalk and her left eye with cam-wood when she sacrifices to her head. Ifa says the blessing of a child will come to her during this year.

----

3. This sacrifice to the ancestral guardian soul is in addition to those made annually. See Chapter XI.

----

247 - 5

"Ofun of Ojuro, tipped stool"[1] was the one who cast Ifa for Ojuro, the mother of Efurę[2] on the day that she was going with the Sea Goddess to perform her annual festival. They said she should make a sacrifice, lest she miss her way; she did not make the sacrifice of two pigeons and one shilling three pence.

She did not sacrifice. She said that today was not the first time that she had gone with the Sea Goddess to perform her festival.[3] She said the diviners were only saying that she should sacrifice this year.[4] When she was going, Eshu pointed his staff toward the forest, and she lost her way in the forest.

But when she had gone, her relatives came to make the sacrifice. When Ojuro lost her way inside the forest, she came across parrot's red tail-feathers lying on the ground where she was wandering about, and there was a high pile of them. She spread her cloth on the ground

----

1. A stool (ǫtita, apoti) made from a section of the trunk of a tree or in the shape of a box, tipped on its side. The meaning of the full name is obscure, but Ofun refers to the name of the figure.

2. An unidentified vine used as a rope. Ojuro was said to mean face or eye spoils (oju-ro), and is identified below.

3. And she had never got lost before or had to make a sacrifice.

4. That is, she suspected the diviners of making up this prediction when there was no real basis for it, because they wanted the money.

bẹrẹ si ki-bọ,   ko mọ pe ibẹ ni ọba   odidẹ gbe sun, n(i)-igba-
begin to push-enter, not know that there be king (of) parrots take sleep, at-time-

ti awọn ara   ile rẹ wa ti nwọn ko ri   nwọn bẹrẹ si kọ-
that those people (of) house hers come that they not see (her) they begin to sing-

(o)rin pe:
song   that:

A ma ri Ojuro
"We not see Ojuro,

Ojuro, Ojuro
"Ojuro, Ojuro."

N(i)-igba-ti Ojuro ki   eko   bọ aṣọ o wa ri oju   ọna
At-time-that Ojuro push tail:feather enter cloth she come see eye (of) road

n(i)-igba-ti o ja-(o)de   si oju   ọna o fi aṣọ rẹ b(o)-ori
at-time that she reach-outside to eye (of) road she take cloth hers cover-head,

awọn enia rẹ wa ri   nwọn bẹrẹ si kọ-(o)rin pe:
those people hers come see (her), they begin to sing-song that:

A ma   ri Ojuro o
"We indeed see Ojuro, Oh,

Ojuro, Ojuro
"Ojuro, Ojuro."

Nwọn bẹrẹ si pa   abẹbẹ nwọn si njo,   n(i)-igba-na ni O-1(i)-okun   fa
They begin to clap fan   they and dancing, at-time-the be One:who-has-sea pull

ọmọ rẹ obinrin kan o   fi   fun Ojuro. Ojuro ni Oluyare jẹ.
child her woman one she take (it) give Ojuro. Ojuro be Oluyare eat.

Ifa ni ẹni-kan   nṣe ohun kan bi ẹni   ṣi-(ọ)na,   ki   o lọ
Ifa say person-one doing thing one like person miss-road, should he go

bọ   si ẹbura kan bi e-1(i)-eko-(o)didẹ   bayi, on ni o
sacrifice to deity one like one:who-have-tail:feather-(of)-parrot thus; he be who

ma   mu ori   ẹni   ja-(ọ)na, ki   oluwarẹ   wa
(continuative) take head (of) person reach-road; should person:in:question come

ile   rẹ wo.   Gbogbo ohun ti e-1(i)-eyi   iba   ni   ni ẹbura
house his look:at (it). All   thing that one:who-be-this should have be deity

na ngba 1(i)-ọwọ rẹ ti   ko jẹ-ki   o ni.
the taking at-hand his that not consent-that he have (them).

and began to fill it with the feathers. She did not know that this was where the
king of the parrots was wont to sleep. When her relatives came and did not find
her, they began to sing:

> "We cannot find Ojuro;
> "Ojuro, Ojuro."

When Ojuro had put the feathers into her cloth, she found the way to the
road, and when she reached the road, she covered her head with the cloth. Her
people found her and began to sing:

> "We did find Ojuro, oh;
> "Ojuro, Ojuro."

They began to beat their fans,[5] and they were dancing. Then the Sea Goddess
took one of her daughters and gave it to Ojuro. Ojuro is what the Oluyare[6] are
called.

Ifa says someone is doing something like·one who has lost his way; he
should go and sacrifice to a deity that has parrots' red tail-feathers;[7] for it is
the one who will lead him to the right road. This person should examine his
house carefully. All the things that this person has, this deity is taking away
from him and it will not let him have them.

---

5. Fans are clapped or beaten against the palm of the hand to keep time
with singing.

6. This verse explains the origin of the Oluyare costumes. The Oluyare
are masked dancers who appear during the Edi festival in honor of Qsangangan
Qbamakin; they represent the Igbo people who attacked Ifẹ until they were defeated by Mọremi. See n. 5, verse 24-1. Here it is implied that Ojuro is masculine, like the Oluyare and Qsangangan Qbamakin, and has taken the Sea Goddess'
daughter as his wife; but initially Ojuro is identified as the mother of Efurẹ.

7. The red tail-feathers of the African Grey Parrot are used on the costumes of the Oluyare, and they are associated with the worship of Ifa, Qshun,
and other deities.

OFUN - (Q)WǪNRIN[1] - 1

Ofun-(Q)wǫnrin-(Q)wǫnrin, awo   Igun   l(i)-o   d(a)-Ifa fun Igun a
"Ofun-Qwǫnrin-Qwǫnrin,"   secret (of) Vulture be-who cast-Ifa for Igun who

bu   fun Qşin ni-(ǫ)jǫ ti   mu-(ę)ni-mu-(ę)ni   ǫrun de,   ni-
shared (it) for Eagle at-day that take-person-take-person (of) sky arrive, at-

(ǫ)jǫ ti   ęmimǫ   ǫrun nhan,   nwǫn ni ki   nwǫn ru-(ę)bǫ
day that evil:thing (of) sky appearing they say should they offer-sacrifice

nitori   iku   a-şi-ku   Qşin kǫ   ko ru-(ę)bǫ   Igun
because (of) death (of) to-miss-die, Eagle refuse not offer-sacrifice, Vulture

ru-(ę)bǫ   obukǫ (ǫ)k(an)-ǫkan, ęgbę(dǫgbǫn)-(ę)gbędǫgbǫn,   oru
offer-sacrifice (of) he:goat one-one,   5000-5000   (cowries), pot

   epo   (ǫ)k(an)-ǫkan, i-san-mǫ-(i)di   aşǫ wǫn, Qşin ni ohun ti
(of) palm:oil one-one,   to-wrap-against-waist cloth their; Eagle say thing that

Q-1(i)-ǫrun   ba   ti   şe,   ki işe ku;   Igun   ni ori   rę
One:who-has-sky should have made, (he) not make remain; Vulture say head his

ko dara,   o ni on yio ru   ębǫ,   o ru   ębǫ.
not be:good, he say he will offer sacrifice, he offer sacrifice.

N(i)-igba-ti Igun   ru-(ę)bǫ   tan awǫn babalawo ni ki   o lǫ
At-time-that Vulture offer-sacrifice finish those diviners say should he go

ma   rin ki   o lǫ ma   yan,   nwǫn ni ko ni ku iku
(continuative) walk should he go (continuative) be:bold; they say not be die death

     a-şi-ku   nwǫn ni ebi   ko ni   pa,   nwǫn ni akoko ti   ebi
(of) to-miss-die, they say hunger not be (it) kill (him), they say time that hunger

ni   npa   ni ęni-(e)keji   rę   ǫrun yio ranti   rę, nwǫn ni
should killing (him) be person-second his (of) sky will remember his, they say

a ko ri ati ku   Igun lai-lai.   Lati igba-na bi Igun   ba   ba
we not see to die (of) Vulture ever-ever. From time-the if Vulture should alight

ti   enia   ko ba   f(i)-ǫwǫ kan,   bi Qşin ba   ni ki   on ba,
that people not should take-hand touch (him); if Eagle should say that he alight,

ǫmǫ   ar(a)-aiye   a ki   mǫ-(i)lę   nwǫn a   pa,
child (of) people-(of)-earth will push (him) against-ground they will kill (him),

nwǫn a si se   ję.   Ęiyę ti o ba   fi   ara we   Igun,
they will and cook (him) eat (him). Bird that he should take body imitate Vulture,

ęhin   aro ni   sun.
back (of) hearth be (he) sleep.

Ifa ni awǫn meji kan wa, ki   nwǫn ru-(ę)bǫ   nitori   iku
Ifa say those two one exist, should they offer-sacrifice because (of) death

a-şi-ku.
to-miss-die.

---

1. Ofun Elerin is an alternative name for this figure.

248 - 1

"Ofun Qwǫnrin-Qwǫnrin,"[1] the diviner of Vulture, was the one who cast Ifa for Vulture and shared it with Fish Eagle[2] on the day that evil spirits who seize people were coming from heaven, when evil beings from heaven were appearing. They said they should sacrifice to avert accidental death. The Fish Eagles refused to sacrifice, but the Vultures sacrificed one he-goat each, one shilling three pence each, one pot of palm oil each, and the sashes from their waists. Fish Eagle said that whatever the Sky God has made, he has not left unfinished. Vulture said that his luck was not good; he said that he would make the sacrifice; and he made it.

When Vulture had completed the sacrifice, the diviners told him to walk about bravely.[3] They said that he would not meet an accidental death. They said he would not be hungry; they said that whenever he was hungry, his spiritual double in heaven would remember him.[4] They said we never see how Vulture dies.[5] From that time on, when Vulture alights, one must not lay a hand upon him; but when a Fish Eagle alights, human beings catch him and kill him, and they cook him to eat. A bird who tries to imitate Vulture, will "sleep behind the hearth."[6]

Ifa says that there are two people; they should make a sacrifice to avert accidental death.

---

1. Derived directly from the name of the figure, Ofun-(Q)wǫnrin; there is no meaning to the reduplication.
2. The Vulturine Fish-Eagle (Gypohierax angolensis).
3. He should walk boldly among human beings without fear of being killed. As this verse explains below, Vulture must not be killed. Igun is the Common or Hooded Vulture (Necrosyrtes monachus monachus) of whom Fairbairn (1933: 12) says, "Since it is unharmed by man, it is bold and can be seen thronging markets, refuse heaps and the neighbourhood of butchers' slabs, doing its useful work as a scavanger."
4. This refers, as in verses 5-2 and 241-1, to the fact that Vulture has much to eat when a town suffers from an epidemic or other catastrophe.
5. Informants say that the bodies of dead vultures are never seen. Cf. verse 5-2.
6. Meaning that it will be cooked and eaten if it tries to be as bold as Vulture. This verse explains why Fish Eagle is killed and why Vulture is not; why Vulture never goes hungry; why he walks boldly among human beings; and why dead Vultures are never seen.

OFUN - (Q)WǪNRIN - 2

"Koto şale,   gegele şale   a   da   fun wǫn ni ilu   Gęsi
"Hole be:suddenly, hillock be:suddenly" who cast for them at town (of) Gęsi

kiki   irukęrę, nwǫn ni ki   nwǫn ru-(ę)bǫ   nitori   ire
altogether tail;   they say should they offer-sacrifice because goodness (of)

ǫmǫ de   si wǫn ni ǫdun-ni.   Ara   ilu   Gęsi kiki
child arrive to them at year-this. People (of) town (of) Gesi altogether

irukęrę ni orukǫ ti   a   pe   agbado.
tail   be name that we call corn.

    Ifa ni   awǫn enia   kan wa   ni agbo, ki   nwǫn ru-(ę)bǫ,   ire
    Ifa say those people one exist at flock, should they offer-sacrifice; goodness

        ǫmǫ de   si wǫn ni ǫdun-ni, ki   nwǫn ru   ęgb(ęfa)-ęgbęfa,
(of) child arrive to them at year-this; should they offer 12,000-12,000 (cowries),

ęiyę-(i)le   (ǫ)k(an)-ǫkan, nwǫn ru-(ę)bǫ.   Lati igba-na ni ǫmǫ
bird-(of)-house one-one,   they offer-sacrifice. From time-the be child (of)

agbado ti   ma   npǫ.
corn   have (continuative) being:many.

OFUN - (Q)WǪNRIN - 3

    Ferefere ta-(i)di   bǫnun bǫnun a   da   fun Q-l(i)-ǫrun   okolo ti   o
    "Ferefere kick-waist stiff   stiff" who cast for One:who-has-sky Okolo that he

nlǫ   fę   Şebeje, obinrin   Oju. Nwǫn ni ki   o ru-(ę)bǫ   nitori
going love Shebeje, woman (of) Eye. They say should he offer-sacrifice because

    obinrin kan.
(of) woman one.

    Ifa ni   ire   aya kan de,   ęni-kan   yio ri aya kan bi   wundia
    Ifa say goodness (of) wife one arrive, person-one will see wife one like maiden

bayi he,   ti   oju ti   foru,   Ifa ni ki   a   şe   sara nitori
thus gather, that eye have overlook; Ifa say should we make feast because (of)

obinrin na,   ayebǫ meji, ęgbęrindilogun.
woman the: hen   two, 3200   (cowries).

248 - 2

"Unexpected holes, unexpected bumps"[1] was the one who cast Ifa for the people of the town of "Gẹsi entirely of cow-tail switches."[2] They said they should make a sacrifice so that the blessing of children might come to them during that year. The people of the town of "Gẹsi entirely of cow-tail switches" is what we call corn.

Ifa says that there is a group of people who should make a sacrifice. The blessing of children is coming to them during this year. They should sacrifice three shillings each, and one pigeon each. They[3] made the sacrifice, and from that time on, the children[4] of corn have always been numerous.

---

1. As on a rough or uneven road, over which one stumbles in the dark.
2. Gẹsi usually refers to the English, but its meaning in this context was not understood by informants. The cow tail switches, such as are carried by diviners, refer here to corn tassels, and the "town" is a corn field.
3. That is, the maize plants.
4. The verse thus explains why corn or maize bears many kernels.

---

248 - 3

"Ferefere[1] sticks out his buttocks[2] stiffly"[3] was the one who cast Ifa for the Sky God Okolo[4] when he was going to marry Shebeje, the wife of Eye. They said he should make a sacrifice because of a woman.

Ifa says the blessing of a wife is coming. Someone will find a virgin to take as a wife who has been overlooked by the eyes[5] of others. Ifa says that we should make a feast[6] because of the woman: two hens and nine pence six oninis.

---

1. This could not be translated or interpreted by informants.
2. As in the Yoruba manner of dancing.
3. Like a sail that stiffens in the breeze.
4. This could not be translated or interpreted by informants.
5. Note the reference here to Eye, the husband of Shebeje.
6. Sara is a Hausa word, indicating a feast that is given instead of making a sacrifice. In this case the hens are to be used in preparing it.

OFUN - (Q)WǪNRIN - 4

Ohanhan   nsun-(ẹ)kun   ifun,   nwǫn ni aiyan   ni o nṣe,
"Ohanhan (bird) shedding-tears (of) intestines, they say anxiety be he making,"

Ogbigbo ru   ẹru   Oriṣa, bẹ-ni   ko sǫ,   Odidẹrẹ ba-
"Ogbigbo carry load (of) Orisha, so-be (he) not put:down (it)," "Parrot alight-

(i)lẹ   tẹjẹ-tẹjẹ-tẹjẹ   a   da fun Qrunmila ni-(ǫ)jǫ ti   o   pẹlu
ground wobble-wobble-wobble" who cast for Qrunmila at-day   that he together:

    Qna-(I)ledi   nṣ(e)-ǫta,   nwǫn ni ki   o ru-(ẹ)bǫ   ki   o
with Road-(of)-Iledi making-enemy, they say should he offer-sacrifice that he

ba   le   ṣẹ-(o)gun rẹ. Eku, ẹja, igbin, ayebǫ adiẹ,   ẹgbata   ni
should be:able make-war his. Rat, fish, snail, hen   chicken, 6000 (cowries) be

ẹbǫ.
sacrifice.

    Ifa ni ẹni-kan   wa   ti o nṣe a-bi-(i)nu-ku   ẹni   n(i)-inu
    Ifa say person-one exist that he doing to-vex-belly-die person at-belly (of)

ile   ẹni,   Ifa ni ko jẹ   ki ǫwǫ   ẹni   lǫ si iwaju, ko si
house (of) person, Ifa say not consent that hand (of) person go to front, not and

jẹ-ki   ǫwǫ   ẹni   lǫ s(i)-ẹhin. Ifa ni ki   a ru-(ẹ)bǫ   ki
consent-that hand (of) person go to-back.   Ifa say should we offer-sacrifice that

Q-l(i)-ǫrun   ba   le   ba-(ẹ)ni   ṣẹ-(o)gun rẹ.
One:who-has-sky should be:able join-person make-war his.

    Epe   kan wa l(i)-ǫwǫ   Qna-Iledi,   o ni on fi   nba   Qrunmila
    Curse one exist at-hand (of) Road-(of)-Iledi, he be who take joining Qrunmila

ja,   ni-(ǫ)jǫ kan bi Qna-(I)ledi   ti   fi   epe ba-(ẹ)nu   ti o fẹ
fight, at-day one as Road-(of)-Iledi have take curse touch-mouth that he want

ṣẹ   le   Qrunmila l(i)-ori, ni Qrunmila ko   eku, ẹja, igbin s(i)-ilẹ   ti
curse upon Qrunmila at-head, be Qrunmila gather rat, fish, snail to-ground that

o fẹ   fi   bǫ   oke ipǫnri   rẹ, Qrunmila si pe
he want take (them) sacrifice:to hill (of) guardian:soul his, Qrunmila and call

Qna-(I)ledi   pe ki   o sure fun on, ṣugbǫn nitori-ti   Qna-(I)ledi
Road-(of)-Iledi that should he bless for him, but   because-that Road-(of)-Iledi

ko le   duro li oju rẹ ki o ma   ṣ(e)-epe   le   l(i)-ori,
not be:able stand at eye his that he (continuative) make-curse upon (him) at-head,

Qna-(I)ledi   bẹrẹ si sure fun Qrunmila, o ni   yio ṣẹ-(o)gun   ǫta
Road-(of)-Iledi begin to bless for Qrunmila, he say (he) will make-war (of) enemy

rẹ, n(i)-igba-ti o di   ǫjǫ-(ẹ)kẹta ni Qna-(I)ledi   ku.
his, at-time-that it become day-third   be Road-(of)-Iledi die.

    Ifa ni ǫta   wa kan yio ku bi o ba   le   tun ma   fi
    Ifa say enemy our one will die if he should be:able then (continuative) take

ohun bu(ru)-buru   ma   pe-(o)ri   ẹni   Qrunmila wa
thing be:bad-be:bad (continuative) call-head (of) person. Qrunmila come

248 - 4

"The Ohanhan bird weeping because of his intestines; they say he is worrying unnecessarily," "The Ogbigbo bird[1] carries a deity's load, and does not put it down," and "The Parrot alights on the ground wobbly, wobbly, wobbly"[2] were the ones who cast Ifa for Qrunmila on the day that he and Qna-Iledi[3] were enemies. They said Qrunmila should make a sacrifice so that he would be able to defeat him. A rat, a fish, a snail, a hen, and one shilling six pence was the sacrifice.

Ifa says there is a person who is angry enough to kill someone in his own house; he does not let him go forward, and he does not let him go backward. Ifa says we should make a sacrifice so that the Sky God will help us defeat him.

Qna-Iledi knew a curse,[4] and he was the one who was fighting with Qrunmila. One day as Qna-Iledi touched it to his mouth to pronounce the curse upon Qrunmila's head, Qrunmila gathered a rat, a fish, and a snail together in order to sacrifice to his ancestral guardian soul, and he called Qna-Iledi to come and bless him. But because Qna-Iledi could not stand before him and curse him to his face, Qna-Iledi began to bless Qrunmila, saying that he would defeat his enemies. Two days later Qna-Iledi died.[5]

Ifa says our enemy will die if he should invoke evil on our head.[6] Qrunmila comes

---

1. Ohanhan and Ogbigbo are two unidentified birds with large hooked bills, the latter being larger.

2. Tẹjẹ-tẹjẹ-tẹjẹ describes the wobbling motion of a parrot walking.

3. This name was interpreted by informants as meaning the Road to the town of Iledi.

4. Epe is usually translated as a curse (like igede; cf. verse 246-3), but as explained here, it involves a charm or medicine that is touched to the lips while the curse is uttered.

5. Qna-Iledi, having made medicine to make his statements come true, causes his own death when he says that Qrunmila's enemies will die.

6. According to informants, this need not involve the use of any medicine. It may consist simply of saying that someone has a bad head (olori buruku, olori buburu), which is regarded as an insult approaching a curse.

da-(o)hun   o ni ki   a ko   obi fun a-ş(e)-ika   ki   o
break-voice he say should we gather kola for one:who-do-wickedness that he

fi   ęnu   ara rę wure.
take mouth (of) body his bless.

OFUN - (O)GUNDA[1] - 1

Qdę   dudu ni   ta-(ǫ)fa   oro,   ile   Imǫlę ni a k(ǫ)-
"Hunter black be (who) shoot-arrow (of) poison"; "House (of) Ogboni be we hang-

apo wǫjǫ-wǫjǫ wǫ,   bi ǫmǫde   ba   gb(o)-oju ki   Ifa bi ko gb(o)-
bag bulge-bulge enter"; "If young:child should harden-eye greet Ifa, if not harden-

oju ki   Ifa, ki   a fi   Ofun Eko lǫ wo   a da fun irun-(i)mǫlę
eye greet Ifa, should we take Ofun Eko go look:at (it)" who cast for 400-Deity   (of)

oju-k(an)-ǫtun a   bu   fun igba-(i)mǫlę oju-k(an)-osi, nwǫn ni ki   nwǫn
eye-touch-right who share for 200-Deity   eye-touch-left, they say should they

ki   o   ru-(ę)bǫ   ki ǫrǫ wǫn le   ni ǫjǫ-wa, nwǫn ru   eku,
should they offer-sacrifice that word their be:able have day-come, they offer rat,

ęja, igbin, obi, ati ęgbędǫgbǫn.
fish, snail, kola, and 5,000   (cowries).

Awǫn orişa ti o ru-(ę)bǫ   n(i)-igba-na ni awǫn orişa ti   a
Those orisha that they offer-sacrifice at-time-the be those orisha that we

nlu   igbin fun   titi di   isisiyi; awǫn ti   ko ru-(ę)bǫ   n(i)-
beating igbin for (them) until become right:now; those that not offer-sacrifice at-

igba-na ni awǫn ti   a npe   ni Orişa   Agbala titi di   oni yi.
time-the be those that we calling at Orisha (of) Backyard until become today this.

Ifa ni   awǫn kan nlǫ   şe ohun kan bi işę   aje   bayi, ki   a
Ifa say those one going do thing one like work (of) money thus, should we

ru-(ę)bǫ   ki ǫran   ęni   le   ni ęhin ni ohun na, ki ǫmǫ
offer-sacrifice that affair (of) person be:able have back at thing the, that child (of)

ęhin ma ba   gbǫn-(ę)ni   lǫ. Ifa ni ki   a ba   le   di
back not should surpass-person go. Ifa say should we should be:able become

ęni   a-pe-sin,   bi ęni-kan   ko ba   si ru-(ę)bǫ   yi,
person to-assemble-serve, if person-one not should and offer-sacrifice this,

yio di   ęni   kǫrǫ ni oju   awǫn ęgbę   rę.
will become person (of) corner at eye (of) those companion his.

---

1. Alternate names for this figure are Ofun Eko (see n. 2, verse 249-1),
Ofuntǫla "Loss then wealth" (see n. 3, verse 249-2), and Ofuntǫpola "Ofun tastes
palm oil" (see n. 1, verse 249-3).

to tell us to take kola and give it to the one who is doing evil to us, so he will
bless us with his own mouth.

---

249 - 1

"Black hunter shoots poisoned arrows," "Entering the Ogboni house we hang
up bulging bags"[1] and "To find out if a child is brave enough to recite Ifa, or if he
is not brave enough to recite Ifa, we use Ofun Eko to test him"[2] was the one who
cast Ifa for the Four Hundred Deities on the right and the Two Hundred Deities
on the left.[3] They said they should make a sacrifice so that their words might
come true. They sacrificed a rat, a fish, a snail, kola, and one shilling three
pence.

The orisha who sacrificed at that time are those for whom we have been
beating igbin drums until this very day; those who did not make the sacrifice
then are those whom we have been calling Deities of the Backyard[4] until this
very day.

Ifa says a group of people are going to do something like working for money;
we should make a sacrifice so that it may reach a successful conclusion, and so
that someone's inferiors may not surpass him. Ifa says we will be able to become a person whom others gather to serve; but if someone does not make this
sacrifice, his companions will regard him as of no importance.

---

1. This refers to the large amounts of food eaten at the Ogboni house. (See
n. 3, verse 181-1.)

2. Ofun Eko is one of the alternative names for Ofun Ogunda. Its verses are
regarded as very dangerous, and even experienced diviners must make an atonement (etutu) before reciting them. They must not be recited "for nothing" or "empty
mouthed." (See Chapter IX and verse 249-3.)

3. Usually these phrases refer to any of the deities, but here they appear to
refer to the "white deities" (cf. n. 3, verse 5-1) because of the reference to Orisha
Agbala and to igbin drums. Igbin is a type of drum which is used in the worship of
the "white deities," but the verse implies that it is not used for Orisha Agbala.

4. Orisha Agbala, the Deity of the Backyard, is one of the lesser "white deities."
He is considered to be a younger brother of Orisha Oko, the Deity of the Farm, and
he is also known as Alataporipo, a praise-name whose meaning could not be interpreted. A simple shrine to him is said to be found in the backyard of every compound in Ifẹ, marked by a peregun tree (Dracaena spp.), near which sacred materials
are buried in the ground. He can be worshipped by anyone, and he often receives
adimu at the instruction of the babalawo (see Chapter V). But there seem to be no
myths about him, and he has no central shrine, no priests or priestesses, no cult
group, and no annual festivals. According to some informants there are several
minor deities known by this term, and the verse, which explains why they are less
important than the other "white deities," supports this view. Cf. verse 103-2.

OFUN - (O)GUNDA - 2

Abata a-b(i)-aiya   gbędę-gbędę   a   da   fun Qrunmila ti   o   ti
"Mud   which-bear-chest mushy-mushy" who cast for Qrunmila that he have

nşe   ofun ęgbę-l(e)-ęgbę lai-lai,   nwǫn ni ki   o ru-(ę)bǫ   pe ni
making loss side-upon-side ever-ever; they say should he offer-sacrifice that at

ǫdun-ni   ni Q-1(i)-ǫrun   san   gbogbo (ohu)n-kan rę ti   o   ti   nşe
year-this be One:who-has-sky repay all   thing-one   his that they have making

ofun fun.   O ru   eku, ęja, igbin, ayebǫ adię,   ati egbejila.
loss for (him). He offer rat, fish, snail, hen   chicken, and 2400   (cowries).

N(i)-igba-ti Qrunmila ru-(ę)bǫ   yi tan, o ko   ori   eku,
At-time-that Qrunmila offer-sacrifice this finish, he gather head (of) rat,

ori   ęja, ori   adię   ati aşę   igbin na s(i)-inu   ohun kan
head (of) fish, head (of) chicken and antenna (of) snail the to-belly (of) thing one

o gbe   s(i)-ilę   n(i)-igba-ti ilę   fi   ma   mǫ, awǫn erun
he take (it) to-ground; at-time-that ground take (continuative) clear, those ant

(ijalǫ)   ti şu   mǫ,   bi o ti   ni ki o gba   wǫn kuro   ni
(driver:ant) have gather against (it) as he have say that he sweep them depart be

o jin   s(i)-ilę   O-1(i)-okun,   bayi ni Qrunmila bęrę si gbǫn
he fall:down to-ground (of) One:who-has-sea; thus be Qrunmila begin to scoop:up

akun. N(i)-igba-ti awǫn ti o ba   ję-(oh)un ni ana   wa ki
bead. At-time-that those that they join (him) eat-thing at yesterday come greet

pe   o   ku   ina-(o)wo   ati pe Q-1(i)-ǫrun
(him) that "You be:greeted (of) spending-(of)-cowries" and that "One:who-has-sky

yio sǫ   ofun rę di   ǫrǫ   Qrunmila da-(o)hun o ni ofun ti o
will change loss his become riches"; Qrunmila break-voice he say loss that he

şe   l(i)-ana   ko t(o)-ǫla,   lati igba-na ni a ti   npe   odu
make at-yesterday not equal-wealth, from time-the be we have calling figure

yi Ofun-t(i)-ǫla.
this Loss-that-(of)-wealth.

Ifa ni ęni-kan   ti   nşe   ofun ri,   şugbǫn ni ǫdun yi ni Q-
Ifa say person-one have making loss before, but   at year this be One:who-

l(i)-ǫrun yio sǫ ofun na di,   ti gbogbo chun ti o ti sǫ-nu   ni
has-sky will fill loss the close, that all   thing that he have throw-be:lost at

ǫwǫ rę yio bǫ   si-(a)po pata-pata.
hand his will come to-pouch completely-completely.

----

249 - 2

"Mud has a mushy[1] chest" was the one who cast Ifa for Qrunmila when he had been suffering losses on all sides from the beginning of time. They said that he should sacrifice so that during that year the Sky God might repay him for all his losses. He sacrificed a rat, a fish, a snail, a hen, and seven pence two oninis.

When Qrunmila had completed this sacrifice, he put the head of the rat, the head of the fish, the head of the hen, and the feelers of the snail in something and left it on the ground. When dawn was breaking, ants (driver ants) gathered and covered the sacrifice; and when Qrunmila began to sweep them away, he broke through the ground into a pit of the Sea Goddess.[2] So Qrunmila began to scoop up beads from the pit. When those who had eaten with him the day before came to greet him, saying, "Greetings on spending money" and "The Sky God will change your losses into riches," Qrunmila answered that the losses he had suffered in the past did not equal the wealth he had gained. From that time on, we have called this figure of Ifa "Loss then Wealth."[3]

Ifa says that someone has been suffering losses in the past, but this year the Sky God will fill up his losses,[4] and everything that has been lost from his hand will come into his pouch.

---

1. Soft and wet.

2. The Sea Goddess, renowned for her wealth, is here associated with the pits of sẹgi beads through which one may attain wealth (cf. n. 2, verse 1-1; n. 5, verse 3-1). Archaeological excavations have shown that the sacred grove of the Sea Goddess at Ifẹ was a site where glass making, in a variety of colors, flourished in ancient times (Frobenius, 1912: I, f. 337; Frobenius, 1913: I, 92-94; Fagg and Willett, 1960: 29). "Here evidently had been the centre of the great glass making industry which had spread segi beads across West Africa" (Willett, 1960: 237).

3. The verse thus explains one of the alternative names of the figure Ofun Ogunda, Ofun-t(i)-ọla.

4. Note the pun here on "fill up" (sọ . . . di) and "change into" (sọ . . . di) above, and "lost" (sọ-nu) below.

OFUN - (O)GUNDA - 3

Ofun-tǫ-(e)po-la,   awo   A-l(i)-ara   d(a)-Ifa fun A-
"Ofun-touch-palm:oil-lick," secret (of) One:who-has-Ara, cast-Ifa for One:who-

l(i)-ara   nwǫn ni   ire   aje   de   si   ni ǫdun yi,   nwǫn ni
has-Ara; they say goodness (of) money arrive to (him) at year this; they say

ki   o ru-(ę)bǫ,   A-l(i)-ara   gbǫ o si ru   ęiyę-(i)le
should be offer-sacrifice; One:who-has-Ara hear he and offer bird-(of)-house

meji egbejila.   Nwǫn ni gbogbo ara   ṣę-fun-ṣę-fun
two, 2400   (cowries). They say all   body (of) make-be:white-make-be:white

fi   ṣe   aje.
take (it) make money.

A-da-iṣ(e)-ai-tǫ-(e)po-la,   awo   Ajero, da   fun Ajero, nwǫn
"To-cast-do-not-touch-palm:oil-lick," secret (of) Ajero, cast for Ajero; they

ni ire   aya de   si   ni ǫdun-ni, nwǫn ni ki   o ru.
say goodness (of) wife arrive to (him) at year-this; they say should he offer.

Ajero ru-(ę)bǫ   ayebǫ adię   meji, ęgbęrindinlogun.   Nwǫn ni
Ajero offer-sacrifice (of) hen   chicken two, 3200   (cowries). They say

ewe ba-mi-m(u)-ǫbuntun ko mu   ti, n(i)-igba-ti Ajero ru-(ę)bǫ
leaf join-me-take-bride not take (her) not; at-time-that Ajero offer-sacrifice

tan   o bęrę si ni   obinrin.
finish he begin to have woman.

Ki   a da Ifa ki   a to   f(i)-ęnu   bǫ-(e)po   a da fun
"Should we cast Ifa before we equal take-mouth dip-palm:oil" who cast for

Olǫṣǫṣa,   ǫmǫ   Ajirawǫkin-beje-beje, nwǫn ni ire   ǫmǫ de
Oloshosha, child (of) Ajirawǫkin-beje-beje; they say goodness (of) child arrive

si   ni ǫdun-ni, nwǫn ni ki   o ru ago   akikǫ adię,   ati ęgbafa.
to (him) at year-this, they say should he offer coop (of) cock chicken, and 12,000

Nwǫn ni a-bi-(ǫ)mǫ-le-(ǫ)mǫ   ni ti   ṣęṣęki, nwǫn ni bi
(cowries). They say to-bear-child-upon-child be that (of) shęshęki, they say as

awǫn obinrin yio ti   ma   bi ǫmǫ rere, bę na ni nwǫn (yi)o
those woman will have (continuative) bear child good, so also be they will

ma   ri ǫmǫ rere gbe pǫn.
(continuative) see child good carry carry:on:back.

Ifa ni on ri ire   aje   ire   aya ati ire   ǫmǫ.
Ifa say he see goodnes (of) money, goodness (of) wife, and goodness (of) child.

---

249 - 3

"Ofun tastes palm oil,"[1] the diviner of the King of Ara, was the one who cast Ifa for the King of Ara. They said that the blessing of money would come to him during that year. They said he should make a sacrifice. The King of Ara heard, and he sacrificed two pigeons and seven pence two oninis. They said the whole body of the "Be white, be white" leaf was like money.[2]

"To cast but not taste palm oil," the diviner of Ajero, was the one who cast Ifa for Ajero, the King of Ijero. They said that the blessing of wives would come to him during that year. They said he should sacrifice. Ajero sacrificed two hens and nine pence six oninis. They said the leaf "With me take a wife"[3] would not fail to take her. When Ajero had completed his sacrifice, he began to have wives.

"If we cast this Ifa, we should not recite it before we put palm oil in our mouth" was the one who cast Ifa for Oloshosha, child of Ajirawǫkin-beje-beje.[4] They said that the blessing of children would come to him during that year. They said he should sacrifice a coop full of cocks and three shillings. They said that bearing child after child is what the shǫshǫki plant does.[5] They said: as his wives will bear good children, so they will also have good children to carry on their backs.

Ifa says that he sees the blessing of money, the blessing of wives, and the blessing of children.

---

1. This is another alternative name for the figure Ofun Ogunda, referring to the fact that before reciting this verse the diviner puts his finger in palm oil and licks it as an atonement (cf. n. 2, verse 249-1). The names of the other two diviners also refer to tasting or not tasting palm oil when divining. Palm oil is tasted before reciting the first and third part, but not the second.

2. An alternative name for ǫfunlǫ (Evolvus alsinoides), whose white leaves resemble cowries. See n. 3, verse 111-2.

3. An unidentified plant with which informants were not familiar but which they believed to be a sticky plant used, as the name suggests, in making love charms.

4. This character could not be identified, nor his name translated. The two previous characters are Ekiti kings, whose towns lie about forty and forty-five miles northeast of Ifǫ.

5. An unidentified plant said to bear many fruit. Cf. n. 1, verse 137-1. Note the imitative magic in using a white leaf for money, a sticky leaf for wives, and a fruitful plant for children.

OFUN - (O)GUNDA - 4

A   da   f(i)-ęnu   bǫ-(e)po   Irosun   a   da   fun Qrunmila ti   o
"To cast take-mouth dip-palm:oil (of) Irosun" who cast for Qrunmila that he

ma   mu   ilę   ni Mǫpę ni ile   baba   rę. Ję-n-joko
(continuative) take ground at Mǫpę at house (of) father his. Consent-I-sit:down

o   ba   ję-n-joko   mi.   Ęni   ęni   ki iyan-(ę)ni   han
you should consent-I-sit:down my. Person (of) person not betray-person appear

ęni   ęni.
person (of) person.

Ifa ni   on ko ni ję-ki   a   ri   ohun ti   yio gbo-(ę)ni   ni ijoko
Ifa say he not be consent-that we see thing that will disturb-person at sitting:

ile   ęni.   Enia   ęni   kan wa   ti   o   nfi   ori
down (of) house (of) person. Person (of) person one exist that he taking head

mu-(i)lę   şe-(ę)ni   ni ibu-(i)joko   ęni   na. Obukǫ kan
sink:into-ground make-person at place-(of)-sitting (of) person the. He:goat one

ati   ęgbętalelǫgbǫn   ni ębǫ.
and 6600   (cowries) be sacrifice.

A-(yi)o   ja   ewe Ję-n-joko,   a-(yi)o gbę ilę   a-(yi)o ri
We-will break leaf Consent-I-sit:down, we-will dig ground; we-will put:in

ori   obukǫ na mǫ   ibę, a-(yi)o ko   ewe Ję-n-joko   bo
head (of) he:goat the against there; we-will gather leaf Consent-I-sit:down cover

mǫ-(i)lę   ki   a   to   ko   ilę   bo.
(it) against-ground before we equal gather earth cover (it).

OFUN - (O)GUNDA - 5

"Ofun-t(i)-ǫla"   a   da   fun Logun-(I)rangan ti   o   ni   aguntan
"Loss-that-(of)-wealth" who cast for Logun-Irangan   that he have ewe

ti   o   ns(ǫ)-ǫrǫ   bi enia, nwǫn ni ki   o   ru-(ę)bǫ   ki oto
that he speaking-word like person; they say should he offer-sacrifice that boast

ma   ba   tę   Logun-Irangan ru-(ę)bǫ.   Ifa ni ki   ęni-
not should disgrace (him); Logun-Irangan offer-sacrifice. Ifa say should person-

kan ru-(ę)bǫ   ki oto ma ba   tę   n(i)-iwaju   enia   ni
one offer-sacrifice that boast not should disgrace (him) at-front   (of) people at

agbajǫ   ilu.   Logun-Irangan ni orukǫ ti   a   pe   Lǫwa Ijaruwa.
crowd (of) town. Logun-Irangan be name that we call Lǫwa Ijaruwa.

L(i)-ęhin na ni nwǫn lǫ sǫ   fun Qni pe   Logun-Irangan ni   aguntan kan
At-back the be they go speak for Qni that Logun-Irangan have ewe   one

ti   ns(ǫ)-ǫrǫ   bi enia, Qni si ran-(i)şę   pe e, o si bi-lere
that speaking-word like person; Qni and send-message call him, he and ask

249 - 4

"To cast and taste the palm oil[1] of Irosun" was the one who cast Ifa for Qrun-mila when he was going to move to Mǫpę[2] near the house of his father. "Let me sit down," you should let me sit down as I am.[3] One's relatives should not betray one.[4]

Ifa says he will not let us meet something that will not give someone a chance to sit down in peace at home. There is someone among his relatives who is undermining his seat. One he-goat and one shilling seven pence eight oninis is the sacrifice.

We will pluck "Let me sit down" leaves.[5] We will dig a hole in the ground; we will put the goat's head into the hole. We will cover it with the "Let me sit down" leaves before we cover it again with dirt.

---

1. Cf. n. 1, verse 249-3. Before reciting this verse, the diviner must put palm oil into his mouth as atonement.

2. An unidentified place name.

3. This is a pun, referring both to the name of the leaf "Let me sit down" (Cissampelos owariensis and C. mucronata) and to the fact that someone's enemy will not let him sit down and rest.

4. This is an oversimplified translation of a complex play on the word "ęni."

5. The use of "Let me sit down" leaves to enable a person to get a chance to sit down and rest is another example of word magic.

---

249 - 5

"Loss then wealth"[1] was the one who cast Ifa for Logun-Irangan[2] who had a ewe who talked like a human being. They said he should sacrifice, lest empty boasting cause him disgrace; Logun-Irangan made the sacrifice. Ifa says that someone should make a sacrifice lest empty boasting bring him to disgrace before the whole town. Logun-Irangan is the name that we call Lǫwa Ijaruwa.

Afterward they told the Qni that Logun-Irangan had a ewe that talked like a human being, and the Qni sent word for him to come. He asked

---

1. An alternative name for the figure Ofun Ogunda. See n. 3, verse 249-2.

2. As explained later, Logun-Irangan is an alternative name for Lǫwa Ijaruwa, more commonly called Lǫwa, who is the head of the inner or palace chiefs of Ifę.

pe,   l(i)-otǫ ni o   ni   aguntan kan ti   ns(ǫ)-ǫrǫ   bi   enia   bi? O
that "At-truth be you have ewe   one that speaking-word like person if?" He

si   da-(o)hun   pe   nitotǫ ni,   Qni si   sǫ   fun   pe bi o ba
and break-voice that truly be (it), Qni and speak for (him) that if it should

di   ǫjǫ marun Qja-Ifę   ki   o   mu aguntan na wa,   o ni bi
become day five Market-(of)-Ifę should he take ewe   the come, he say if

aguntan na ba   s(ǫ)-ǫrǫ,   o ni on yio da   ohun   ini
ewe   the should speak-word, he say he will break thing (of) possession (of)

ile   on si meji, on yio si ko   fun Lǫwa o ni şugbǫn bi aguntan
house his to two, he will and gather (them) give Lǫwa, he say but   if ewe

na ko ba   s(ǫ)-ǫrǫ,   o ni on yio so Lǫwa rǫ   on (yi)o si da
the not should speak-word, he say he will tie Lǫwa hang (him) he will and create

ina sun Lǫwa, Lǫwa si şe   ileri   pe aguntan na yio s(ǫ)-ǫrǫ   ni ǫjǫ
fire roast Lǫwa, Lǫwa and make promise that ewe   the will speak-word at day

na. N(i)-igba-ti o di   ǫrun   ǫja,   Lǫwa mu aguntan na wa,
the. At-time-that it become fifth:day (of) market, Lǫwa take ewe   the come,

Lǫwa ba   aguntan na s(ǫ)-ǫrǫ   titi,   şugbǫn aguntan na ko da   l(i)-
Lǫwa join ewe   the speak-word until, but   ewe   the not break (him) at-

ohun rara, n(i)-igba-ti Lǫwa ba   s(ǫ)-ǫrǫ   titi ti   ko da-(o)hun,
voice at:all; at-time-that Lǫwa join (it) speak-word until that (it) not break-voice,

n(i)-igba-na ni nwǫn gbe Lǫwa lu-(i)lę,   nwǫn si de e, nwǫn si bęrę
at-time-the be they take Lǫwa strike-ground, they and bind him they and begin

si fi   ęhin rę ra ina, n(i)-igba-ti o di   igba-męta ti   nwǫn ma
to take back his rub fire, at-time-that it become time-three that they (continua-

   fi   ęhin rę ra ina, n(i)-igba-na ni aguntan rę yi da-(o)hun   o ni
tive) take back his rub fire, at-time-the be ewe   his this break-voice, he say

A-a, ę   ma   pa (ę)ni?
"A-a!, you (continuative) kill person?"

   N(i)-igba-ti aguntan sǫ   bayi, awǫn enia   si da-(o)hun   pe   aguntan
   At-time-that ewe   speak thus, those people and break-voice that "Ewe

s(ǫ)-ǫrǫ,   aguntan s(ǫ)-ǫrǫ.   Qni si da   ohun   ini   ile
speak-word, ewe   speak-word." Qni and break thing (of) possession (of) house

rę si ǫna meji, o si ko   fun Lǫwa; n(i)-igba-ti Lǫwa nmu aguntan
his to road two, he and gather (one) give Lǫwa; at-time-that Lǫwa taking ewe

rę yi lǫ si ile,   Lǫwa bi i   lere pe ki-ni   şe ti iwǫ aguntan
his this go to house, Lǫwa ask him (1) that "What-be (it) make that you ewe

yi şe   ję-ki   nwǫn fi ęhin on ra ina n(i)-igba-męta? Aguntan rę
this make consent-that they take back his rub fire at-time-three? Ewe   his

---

1. Bi . . . lere means "to ask."

him "Is it true that you have a ewe that talks like a human being?" Lǫwa answered that it was truly so. The Qni told him that in four days, on the day of the
Ifẹ Market,[3] he should bring the ewe to him. He said that if the ewe talked, he
would divide all his possessions in half and give one half to Lǫwa. But he said
that if the ewe did not talk, he would tie Lǫwa and hang him up, and build a fire
to roast him on. Lǫwa promised that the ewe would speak on the appointed day.
When the fourth day arrived, Lǫwa brought the ewe to the king. Lǫwa talked and
talked with the ewe, but the ewe would not answer at all. When Lǫwa had talked
and talked without the ewe answering, they threw Lǫwa to the ground, bound him,
and began to pass him slowly back and forth across the fire. As they were passing him across the fire the third time, his ewe spoke, saying, "Ah! ah! Are you
killing someone?"[4]

When the ewe said this, the people shouted, "The ewe is talking! The ewe is
talking!" And the Qni divided all his possessions into two parts, and he gave
half to Lǫwa. When Lǫwa was taking his ewe home, Lǫwa asked him "Why did
you let them pass me back and forth across the fire three times?" His ewe

---

3. The first day of the four-day week is called ǫjǫ Qjaifẹ or "day of the
Market of Ifẹ," after the principal market.

4. Cf. the tale of the talking skull that refused to talk in verses 181-1 and
181-4.

si da-(o)hun   pe: Ki   o da   ọ   l(i)-ohun l(i)-ẹkan-ṣoṣo ki   o si
and break-voice that, "Should he break you at-voice at-once-only   that he and

ko   gbogbo ẹru   yẹn l(i)-ẹsẹ-k(u)-ẹsẹ lai ri iya?   O ni "Owo
gather all   loads this at-foot-any-foot not see punishment?" He say, "Trans-

       ti a ba   ma   ṣe la,   a ko ni ri apa rẹ l(i)-
action that we should (continuative) make be:wealthy, we not be see scar its at-

ara ni?
body be (it)?

OFUN - (O)GUNDA - 6

Emini, awo   aja-(i)lẹ   a   da   fun ẹrunlọjọ ẹranko ni ọjọ
Emini, secret (of) ceiling-(of)-ground, who cast for 165   animal at day

ti nwọn nlọ   fẹ   Laduntan ọmọ   O-l(i)-okun   Nwọn ni ki   wọn
that they going love Laduntan child (of) One:who-has-sea. They say should they

ru   ewurẹ kan, ati ẹgbawa,   aṣọ dudu kan.
offer she:goat one, and 20,000 (cowries), cloth black one.

     Ifa ni a   nṣe   ọpalaye   ọran   aya kan, o so   ko ju
     Ifa say we making court:case (of) affair (of) wife one, "it bear:fruit not surpass

ka,   o wọ   ko ju   he.   Ifa ni ọrẹ ni   yio
pluck (it), it shed (fruit) not surpass pick:up (it)." Ifa say friend be (who) will

jẹ-ki   ọran   aya na ṣe iṣe,   ẹni-ti   o nfẹ   gba aya yi ko
consent-that affair (of) wife the do work; person-that he wanting take wife this not

ni owo,   bẹ-ni oju   awọn ara   ile   obinrin yi ko to
have cowries, so-be eye (of) those people (of) house (of) woman this not equal

ile   ale   ọmọ wọn.
house (of) concubine (of) child their.

     O-l(i)-okun   ni ẹni-ti   o ba   le   fun aka   on dun
     One:who-has-sea say person-that he should be:able blow granary her sound

ni on yio fi   ọmọ on   fun.   A-b(i)-awun   ni on a   ri ṣe.
be she will take child hers give (him). One:who-like-Miser say he will see do (it).

Ẹbọ: akiko meji, pẹrẹ   epo   kan, egbejila,   ati araba
Sacrifice: cock two, pot (of) palm:oil one, 2400   (cowries), and loaf   (of)

iyan   kan.
pounded:yam one.

     O-l(i)-okun   ni bi o ba   di   ọla,   O-l(i)-okun   ni
     One:who-has-sea say if it should become tomorrow; One:who-has-sea say

ki   nwọn wa   pe aka   on. Ki   ilẹ   to   mọ,   A-b(i)-
should they come call granary her. Before ground equal clear, One:who-like-

replied, "Should I have answered you the very first time, and have you get all this property at once without any suffering?" He said, "If one becomes rich through trade, do we not see its scars on one's body?"

---

249 - 6

Dampness,[1] the diviner of Dungeon,[2] was the one who cast Ifa for the 165 kinds[3] of animals on the day that they were going to love Laduntan, the child of the Sea Goddess. They said they should sacrifice one she-goat, five shillings, and one black cloth.

Ifa says we will be brought to court because of an affair with a woman. "It bears fruit, we cannot pick it; the fruit falls, we cannot gather it."[4] Ifa says there is a friend who will allow the affair with this woman to reach a successful conclusion. The one who wants to marry this woman has no money, and the parents of this woman do not know where their child's lover lives.

The Sea Goddess said that the person who would be able to make her granary speak would be the one to whom she would give her child in marriage. Tortoise said he would try to do it. The sacrifice is two cocks, one pot of palm oil, seven pence two oninis, and one yam loaf.

The Sea Goddess said that they should come the next day to call to her granary to speak. Before day break,

---

1. Informants were unable to give the meaning of emini, but from the name and from the verse itself (see n. 4) it appears to mean dampness or dew, usually given as ǫnini, enini, eni, or iri.

2. A subterranean chamber, such as that used by the Ogungbę (see n. 4, verse 181-1), for detaining convicted criminals until their fines have been paid.

3. See n. 3, verse 18-4.

4. Used here like a proverb implying that it will be difficult for him to marry the woman, this is a Yoruba riddle, whose answer is "Dew." Bascom (1949: 12). Cf. n. 1, above.

awun ti   ko   s(i)-inu   aka,   o si fi   ara pa-mǫ,   bi o ti
Miser have enter to-belly (of) granary, he and take body kill-against; as it have

d(i)-ǫjǫ-(e)keji,   bi O-l(i)-okun   ti sǫ   pe Aka,   o, A-
become-day-second, as One:who-has-sea have speak that "Granary, oh," One:who-

b(i)-awun da-(o)hun   n(i)-inu   aka   pe Aka,   aka   awa l(i)-a
like-Miser break-voice at-belly (of) granary that "Granary, Granary we be-who

f(a)-aka   ǫba,   aka   awa l(i)-a f(a)-aka   ǫba. N(i)-igba-na
pull-granary (of) king; granary we be-who pull-granary (of) king." At-time-the

ni nwǫn wa   fi   obinrin yi fun Ǫrunmila.
be they come take woman this give Ǫrunmila.

    Ifa ni aya kan ni a nfǫ   fǫ yi, ǫrǫ   ǫni   ni   yio ba-
    Ifa say wife one be we wanting love this, friend (of) person be (who) will join-

(ǫ)ni   di awo   idi rǫ ti   yio fi   le   fǫ-(ǫ)ni.
person tie secret (of) base its that (she) will take (him) be:able love-person.

OFUN - (Ǫ)SA - 1

    O-fun-şai   o-mu-gba   ko f(i)-ǫwǫ
    "It-be:white-very:white, one:who-know-sweep not take-midrib:of:palm:leaf

gba ǫrun a   da fun Aganna ti işe osa   A-f(o)-ojo   l(i)-
sweep sky" who cast for Aganna that make assistant (of) One:who-clear-rain at-

Ǫyǫ, nwǫn ni Ǫ-l(i)-ǫrun   yio da ori   ire   kan si   ni ǫdun-
Ǫyǫ; they say One:who-has-sky will turn head (of) goodness one to (him) at year-

ni,   şugbǫn ki   o ru-(ǫ)bǫ   ki ar(a)-aiye   ma ba   da
this, but   should he offer-sacrifice that people-(of)-earth not should cause (him)

l(i)-ǫja,   nitori-ti   ire   na ko ni tan   ni ǫwǫ rǫ ati ǫmǫ
at-frustration, because-that goodness the not be finish at hand his and child (of)

ǫmǫ rǫ lai-lai.   Aganna ni irǫ ni nwǫn npa,   ko ru   ęiyę-(i)le
child his ever-ever. Aganna say lie be they killing, not offer bird-(of)-house

meji, adię   meji, ati ęgbęrinlelogun.
two, chicken two, and 4800   (cowries).

    N(i)-igba lai-lai   ni ode   Ǫyǫ ni ǫd(un)-ǫdun ti ǫba   Ǫyǫ ba
    At-time ever-ever at outside (of) Ǫyǫ at year-year   that King (of) Ǫyǫ should

nşe   ǫdun ti o ba   si di   ǫjǫ ti o ma   şe   ęyę
making year that it should and become day that he (continuative) make decoration

ja-(o)de,   ojo ki iję-ki   o r(i)-aye ja-(o)de   bę-ni
reach-outside, rain not consent-that he see-chance reach-outside, so-be (it)

Aganna işę   ojo fifo   ni   işe, ǫba Ǫyǫ sǫ   fun   pe bi
Aganna work (of) rain clearing be (he) do, King (of) Ǫyǫ speak for (him) that if

Tortoise had entered the granary and hidden himself in it. When the next day came, and as the Sea Goddess called, "Granary, oh!", Tortoise answered from inside the granary "Granary, Granary; we pull the king's granary;[5] Granary, we pull the king's granary." Then they gave this woman to Qrunmila.[6]

Ifa says there is a woman whom we want to marry. Someone's friend will keep the secret for him so that she will be able to marry him.[7]

---

5. The informant translated f'aka as "pull-granary" (fa-aka), but the context suggests that it should be translated as "blow-granary" (fun-aka), meaning to make the granary speak.

6. There is an inconsistency here. Qrunmila is not an animal, but the verse says that it was the 165 animals who were trying to win the hand of Laduntan. As it stands, however, Tortoise was not trying to marry Laduntan himself, but was simply aiding Qrunmila.

7. As Tortoise did for Qrunmila.

---

250 - 1

"It is very white,[1] one who knows how to sweep does not use a broom to sweep the sky," was the one who cast Ifa for Aganna, who was the assistant to the "One who prevents rain" at the town of Qyǫ.[2] They said the Sky God would direct a blessing to him during that year, but that he should make a sacrifice so that the people of the earth would not frustrate him, because this blessing would never end, but would benefit both himself and his children's children forever. Aganna said the diviners were telling lies. He did not make the sacrifice of two pigeons, two chickens, and one shilling two pence four oninis.

From the beginning of time in Qyǫ, each year when the King of Qyǫ was going to make his annual festival, when the day came and he put on his finery to go out, the rain did not let him have a chance to go outside. As Aganna's work was preventing rain, the King of Qyǫ told him that if

---

1. Note that this is derived from the name of the figure, Ofun-(Q)sa. The meaning of the phrase as it is used here is that it is something that is very clean like the ground which has just been swept, or like the sky from which clouds have cleared.

2. As important as the power of a rainmaker (cf. verse 170-2) is the power to prevent rain from interfering with an important ritual occasion. In both verses to which these powers are referred, they are ineffective.

o ba   le   ja-(o)de,   ti ojo ko si rǫ titi   di   akoko
he should be:able reach-outside, that rain not and fall until (it) become time   (of)

ǫja   alę,   on yio fun Aganna ni ǫmǫ-(o)binrin kan, amu   ilękę,
market (of) evening, he will give Aganna at child-woman one, jar   (of) bead,

ogun așǫ,   ęgbęwa ǫkę,   ogun ęwu, ati ga   malu kan.
twenty cloth, 2000   bag (of cowries), twenty gown, and cattle:pen cow one.

   N(i)-igba-ti ǫba tę   itę   lǫ bi ilę   bi ęni, ti o si gunwa
   At-time-that king spread spread go like ground like mat, that he and sit:in:

        tan ni ojo bęrę si rǫ nitori-ti   Aganna ko ru-(ę)bǫ
splendor finish be rain begin to fall because-that Aganna not offer-sacrifice

ki   o to   lǫ, bę-ni   Aganna ti   șe   ileri   ki   o to   lǫ pe
before he equal go, so-be (it) Aganna have make promise before he equal go that

ojo ko ni rǫ, bayi ni Aganna bę   lu-(i)gbo   n(i)-igba-ti ojo bęrę si rǫ,
rain not be fall, thus be Aganna jump strike-forest at-time-that rain begin to fall,

ko si ri aye   ko   gbogbo (ohu)n-kan ti ǫba   Qyǫ ko   fun.
not and see chance gather all   thing-one that King (of) Qyǫ gather give (him).

   Ifa ni ęni-kan   wa ti Q-l(i)-ǫrun   fę ti   l(i)-ęhin
   Ifa say person-one exist that One:who-has-sky want push (him) at-back

de ibi-ti   yio ti   ri ire   kan, șugbǫn ki   o ru-
arrive place-that (he) will from (it) see blessing one, but   should he offer-

(ę)bǫ ki ar(a)-aiye   ma dan,   ki ileri   rę ma ba
sacrifice that people-(of)-earth not thwart (him), that promise his not should

di   ofo.
become emptiness.

OFUN - (Q)SA - 2

   A-ya-nu   awo   ǫjǫ a da fun ǫjǫ; A-ya-nu,   awo
   To-split-be:lost, secret (of) Day, who cast for Day; To-split-be:lost, secret

      oșu   a da fun oșu; Ijihęri awo   ǫlǫ   a da f(un)-
   (of) month, who cast for Month; Ijihęri, secret (of) Grindstone, who cast for-

ǫlǫ;   Eji   rǫ da-(a)kurǫ   si a da fun Yeye
Grindstone; "Rain (not) fall miss-waterside:garden (1)" who cast for Mother

Qni-rǫ-l(i)-o-rǫ-mǫ,   nwǫn ni ti   ojo
Person-be:soft:for-(him)-be-it-be:soft:for-(him)-again; they say that (of) rain

ti   ęrun   ko ni ni   l(i)-ara, nwǫn ni n(i)-igba-ti o ba
that (of) dry:season not be press (him) at-body; they say at-time-that it should

---

1. Da . . . si means "to miss."

he would be able to go out, and if the rain did not fall until the time of the evening market, he would give Aganna one girl, a jar full of beads, twenty cloths, two thousand bags of cowries,[3] twenty gowns, and a pen full of cows.

When the king had spread out his cloths on the ground like a mat, reaching far and wide, and had seated himself on them in full royal splendor,[4] rain began to fall because Aganna had not made the sacrifice before the king went out. But Aganna had made a promise before the king went out that it would not rain. So Aganna fled into the forest when rain began to fall, and he did not have a chance to take with him all those things that the King of Ọyọ had given him.

Ifa says there is someone whom the Sky God wants to help reach a place where he will find a blessing, but he should make a sacrifice so that the people on earth will not thwart him, and that his promises should not become empty.

---

3. £500. Each bag contains 20,000 cowries, worth five shillings.
4. See n. 2, verse 52-1.

---

250 - 2

Loss the diviner of Day, was the one who cast Ifa for Day; Loss the diviner of Month, was the one who cast Ifa for Month; Ijihẹri[1] the diviner of Grindstone, was the one who cast Ifa for Grindstone; "When rain falls, it does not miss the waterside garden" was the one who cast Ifa for Mother "One who has it easy, always has it easy."[2] They said that neither the rains nor the dry season would be hard for him. They said that after it

---

1. This word represents the sound made when grinding on the metate-like grindstone.
2. The idea here is to be compared with "wealth begets wealth." Note the play on the words "fall" (like rain; rọ) and "be soft for" (rọ).

rǫ   l(i)-ǫrun tan   yio tun rǫ   a-l(i)-a-ro-
be:soft:for (him) at-neck   finish (it) will then be:soft:for one:who-be-who-stand-

ti   rę l(i)-ǫrun pęlu.   Qni-rǫ-l(i)-o-rǫ-
support his at-neck together:with (him). Person-be:soft:for-(him)-be-it-be:soft:

mǫ   ni orukǫ a pe Akurǫ.   Igbin męrin, ęiyę-(i)le
for-(him)-again be name we call Waterside:garden. Snail four,   bird-(of)-house

męrin, oru   epo   kan, ati ęgbędǫgbǫn.
four, pot (of) palm:oil one, and 5000   (cowries).

     O ru-(ę)bǫ   lati igba-na ni Akurǫ   ko ti gbę   ti
     He offer-sacrifice; from time-the be Waterside:garden not have dry:out that

     ojo ti   ęrun.   N(i)-igba-ti o rǫ   l(i)-ǫrun tan, ni
(of) rain that (of) dry:season. At-time-that it be:soft:for (him) at-neck finish, be

o njo   ti o nyǫ   ti o si nkǫ-(o)rin   bayi pe:
he dancing that he rejoicing that he and singing-song thus that:

          Airan l(i)-okun   ade   o
          "Airan be-rope (of) crown, oh,

          Airan l(i)-okun   aja
          "Airan be-rope (of) king.

          Qni-rǫ-l(i)-o-rǫ-mǫ   o
          "Person-be:soft:for-(him)-be-it-be:soft:for-(him)-again, oh,

          Airan l(i)-okun   aja.
          "Airan be-rope (of) king."

     Ifa ni ęni-kan   wa ti o ję-pe lati ǫrun ni Q-l(i)-ǫrun   ti
     Ifa say person-one exist that he eat-that from sky be One:who-has-sky have

fi irǫ-(ǫ)run   fun   wa,   n(i)-igba-ti o ba   rǫ
take softness-(of)-neck give (him) come; at-time-that it should be:soft:for (him)

l(i)-ǫrun tan   yio si tun rǫ   a-l(i)-a-ba-rin   rę l(i)-
at-neck   finish will and then be:soft:for one:who-be-who-join-(him)-walk his at-

ǫrun pęlu.   Qla   rę yio si ran gbogbo a-l(i)-a-ba-
neck together:with (him). Honor his will and send all   one:who-be-who-join-

rin   rę.
(him)-walk his.

OFUN - (Q)SA - 3

     Ofun sa   wo   bi   a ję bi ko ni ję   a   da fun
     "Ofun apply:medicine look:at (it) if (it) will eat if not be eat" who cast for

ęrunlǫjǫ ewe, nwǫn ni ki   nwǫn ru akikǫ (ǫ)k(an)-ǫkan, abę   (ǫ)k(an)-ǫkan,
165   leaf; they say should they offer cock one-one,   razor one-one,

ǫgb(ǫkanla)-ǫgbǫkanla   ki oto ma ba   tę   wǫn. Eyi-ti o
2200-2200   (cowries) that boast not should disgrace them. This-that they

was easy for him, it would be easy for his companions also. "One who has it easy, always has it easy" is the name of Waterside Garden. Four snails, four pigeons, one pot of palm oil, and one shilling three pence is the sacrifice.

He made the sacrifice, and from that time on, Waterside Garden has never dried up, either in the rains or in the dry season. When it was easy for him, he was dancing and rejoicing, and he was singing:

> "Airan[3] is the rope of crowns, oh,
> "Airan is the rope of kings.
> "One who has it easy, always has it easy, oh,
> "Airan is the rope of kings."[4]

Ifa says there is someone who was given an easy lot by the Sky God when he came from heaven. When things have become easy for him, they will also be easy for his associates. And his honor will help all who associate with him.

---

3. An unidentified grass which is eaten by horses.
4. The meaning of this song was not at all clear to informants.

---

250 - 3

"Ofun applies medicine[1] and looks to see if it works or not" was the one who cast Ifa for the 165 kinds[2] of leaves. They said they should offer one cock each, one razor each, and six pence six oninis each, so that empty boasting would not disgrace them. Those

---

1. Note the pun here on the name of the figure, Ofun-(Q)sa; and the fact that the name of the diviner is in this case closely associated with the meaning of the rest of the verse.
2. See n. 3, verse 18-7.

ru n(i)-inu   awǫn ewe ni eyi-ti   a fi   şe ogun   ti o
offer at-belly (of) those leaf be this-that we take (them) make medicine that it

ję, ti a nwi-pe   ewe yi ma   ję o.
eat, that we speaking-that "Leaf this indeed eat, oh."

   Ifa ni ohun ti a da Ifa si   yi, ki (ohu)n-kan na le   dara
   Ifa say thing that we cast Ifa to (it) this, that thing-one the be:able be:good

ni a da ębǫ   si.   Ifa ni on ko ni ję-ki   oju ki   o ti-
be we cast sacrifice to (it). Ifa say he not be consent-that eye should it push-

(ę)ni nipa   ǫrǫ na. O ni ki   a ru-(ę)bǫ   ki (ohu)n-kan
person concerning word the. He say should we offer-sacrifice that thing-one

na le   dara ja-(i)lę.
the be:able be:good reach-ground.

OFUN - (Q)ŞĘ - 1

   "O-fun-şę   ęla   yun   a   da fun Olobutu ti işe
   "It-be:white-abruptly, whiteness continuously" who cast for Olobutu that make

ǫba   ęiyę l(i)-oko nwǫn ni ni ǫdun yi ni ori rę yio ti   de
king (of) bird at-farm; they say at year this be head his will push (him) arrive

ibi-ti   yio gbe şe iwa   şugbǫn ębǫ   ki o ma ri e-
place-that (he) will take make destiny but   sacrifice that he not see one:who-

l(i)-enini ti yio ti   kuro ni ipo   na ni ki   o şe;   ęwu
has-enmity that will push (him) depart at position the be should he make; gown

pupa   ǫrun rę ti o fi   şe   ęyę,   aguntan kan, ęgbafa,
red   (of) neck his that he take (it) making decoration, ewe   one, 12,000 (cowries),

ati amu   epo   kan ni ębǫ.
and jar   (of) palm:oil one be sacrifice.

   Olobutu ko ru   ębǫ,   n(i)-igba-ti nwǫn fi   j(ę)-ǫba ti ko şe
   Olobutu not offer sacrifice; at-time-that they take (him) eat-king that not do

rere ni gbogbo ęiyę ba yǫ   ni oye. Ęwu   igba-na ni o wa   ni
good be all   bird did pull:out (him) at title. Gown (of) time-the be it exist at

ǫrun   g(un)-osun-(g)un)-osun   titi   di   oni yi, nwǫn si
neck (of) pound-camwood-pound-camwood until (it) become today this, they and

fi ǫkin si ipo   rę.
put ǫkin to position his.

   Ifa ni Q-l(i)-ǫrun   ma   gbe ęni-kan   de ipo   kan,
   Ifa say One:who-has-sky (continuative) take person-one reach position one,

şugbǫn ki   o ru-(ę)bǫ   ki o ma ba   ri e-l(i)-enini
but   should he offer-sacrifice that he not should see one:who-has-enmity

among the leaves who sacrificed are the ones from whom we can make medicine
that works, and of whom we say, "This leaf really works, oh."[3]

Ifa says that there is something for which we have cast Ifa, and that it will
turn out well if we sacrifice because of it. Ifa says he will not allow us to be
disgraced in this matter. He says we should make a sacrifice so that the thing
can turn out well from top to bottom.

---

3. This verse thus explains why some leaves are useful in making medicine
while others are not.

---

255 - 1

"It is suddenly white,[1] was the one who cast Ifa for Olobutu, the king of the
birds in the farm. They said that during that year his head would bring him to
a place where he would achieve his destiny, but that lest he meet an enemy
who would push him out of the position, a sacrifice should be made. The red
gown from his back with which he decorated himself, one ewe, three shillings,
and one jar of palm oil was the sacrifice.

Olobutu did not make the sacrifice. When they made him king and he did
not do good, all the birds took the title away from him. The gown which he did
not sacrifice can still be seen on the neck of "Pound camwood pound camwood"[2]
until this very day. And they put the okin bird in his position.

Ifa says that the Sky God is going to place someone in an important position, but that he should make a sacrifice, lest he meet an enemy

---

1. Note the pun here on the name of the figure Ofun-(Q)sę. White is associated with both Ofun and Qsę, and the okin is a white bird.

2. This is another name for olobutu, an unidentified bird, referring to the
band of red feathers (its red "gown") on its neck. This verse thus explains how
it came to have this marking and how the okin came to be regarded as "king of
the birds." The okin, identified by Abraham as an egret, is described as a
white bird whose highly prized feathers are fastened to king's crowns.

ti   yio yǫ   ni ipo   rę na. Ifa ni ęni-kan   wa   l(i)-ori
that will pull:out (him) at position his the, Ifa say person-one exist at-head (of)

ipo   kan n(i)-isisiyi, şugbǫn bi ęni   ikǫkǫ ba   ni   ębǫ   yio
position one at-right:now, but   if person (of) corner should have sacrifice will

gba ipo   na l(i)-ǫwǫ rę ni oju   ara   rę.
take position the at-hand his at eye (of) people his.

OFUN - (Q)ŞĘ - 2

   Afęręfę-lęgę-lęgę ti   ori   oko wa-(i)lę,   ojo   Apa ni
   "Breeze-sway-sway from head (of) farm come-ground; rain (of) Apa be (it)

irǫ ni ibubu   a   da fun Şereke ǫmǫ   a-ş(e)-oro   p(a)-
fall at sideways" who cast for Shereke, child (of) one:who-make-ritual kill-

ęgbęrin awun ję. Ojo dudu ni   ti-(i)rǫ l(i)-Apa ni   ko ję-ki
800   Miser eat. Rain black be (it) have-fall at-Apa be (it) not consent-that

nwǫn ri ǫmǫ tun-tun gbe ş(e)-ere, n(i)-igba-ti ojo funfun ba   nrǫ
they see child new-new take make-play, at-time-that rain white should falling

l(i)-Apa nwǫn a   ri ǫwǫ tun-tun gbe ş(e)-ere.
at-Apa   they will see child new-new take make-play.

   Ifa ni ęni-kan   wa ti o ni   aya pupǫ şugbǫn ti   awǫn aya rę
   Ifa say person-one exist that he have wife many, but   that those wife his

wǫn-yi   ko bi ǫmǫ, Ifa ni on yio şi   ǫna   ǫmǫ fun   ni ǫdun
those-this not bear child; Ifa say he will open road (of) child for (him) at year

yi, ki oluwarę   na şe   alafia   ǫmǫ. Ębǫ
this, that person:in:question the make contentment (of) child. Sacrifice (be)

ewurę   kan, ejielogun,   yio mu ewurę yi lǫ si odo kan ti
she:goat one, 44,000   (cowries); (we) will take she:goat this go to river one that

ko nşan   ti ko jina si,   ki   gbogbo enia si tęle   lǫ si
not flowing that not be:far to (him); should all   people and follow (him) go to

ibę ki   o fi   bǫ,   ki   babalawo ję owo   na ni eru.
there should they take (it) sacrifice; should diviner eat cowries the at payment.

OFUN - (Q)ŞĘ - 3

"Otere   omi   Qşę, abuku   odo ni   d(i)-abata,   ikasin
"Trickle (of) water (of) Qshę, disgrace (of) river be (it) become-mud"; Left:

   omi gbe-(i)le   Q-l(i)-ǫrǫ   kan a   da fun Abǫnun
over water dwell:at-house (of) One:who-has-riches sour" who cast for Abǫnun

who will take him from the position. Ifa says there is someone in an important position at the present time, but if someone who now stays in the corner should make a sacrifice, he will take the post from him while his relatives are alive to see it.

---

255 - 2

"Gentle breeze[1] comes to earth from the top of the farm; rain at Apa[2] falls on a slant" was the one who cast Ifa for Shereke, the child of the "Priest who kills 800 tortoises to eat." The black rain that falls at Apa does not let the people of Apa have new-born children to celebrate; when white rain[3] falls at Apa, they will have new-born children to celebrate.

Ifa says there is someone who has many wives, but that his wives have not born children. Ifa says he will open the road of children for him during this year, so that this person can find the contentment of children. The sacrifice is one she-goat and eleven shillings. We will take this she-goat to a nearby body of still water; all his people should follow him and they should sacrifice the she-goat there. The diviner should keep the money as his payment.

---

1. Cf. n. 1, verse 175-2.
2. "Apa," whose meaning was given as wastrel or prodigal, was interpreted here as the name of an unidentified town.
3. Informants did not know the significance of black and white rain, and the whole introduction is obscure.

---

255 - 3

"Trickle of water at Qshẹ,[1] river's disgrace is to become mud" and "Yesterday's water in the house of a rich man is stale"[2] were the ones who cast Ifa for Abọnun,

---

1. "Qshẹ," one of the elements in the name of this figure, was interpreted here as the name of an unidentified town. "Otere" was said to mean something that flows in a small stream, like a spring.
2. A rich man can afford to complain if his water is not fresh every day, and to regard water left over from the day before as "sour" or stale.

ti   işe   ọmọ   Olodumare ni ọjọ ti   ọmọ   inu   aiye   nro
that make child (of) Olodumare at day that child (of) belly (of) earth thinking (he)

pin.
end.

    Ifa ni   ẹni-kan   wa   ti   o   di   arugbo   ti   gbogbo awọn ara
    Ifa say person-one exist that he become old:person that all   those people

ile   rẹ ko ka   si,   ti   nwọn nfi   şe   ẹ-l(i)-
(of) house his not count to (him), that they taking (him) make one:who-have-

ẹya,   ni ọdun yi ni Q-l(i)-ọrun   yio şi   ọna   owo   fun
ridicule, at year this be One:who-has-sky will open road (of) cowries for (him)

ti   gbogbo enia yio si   ma   fi   ori ba-(i)lẹ   fun
that all   people will and (continuative) take head touch-ground for (him)

pẹlu   awọn ij(ẹ)-oye. Ifa kan ti   ko   gbogbo iwa   ẹni   pa-
together:with those eat-title. Ifa one have gather all   destiny (of) person kill-

mọ,   ki   a   tọ-(o)ju   Ifa na ki o ba   le   şi   ọna fun-
against, should we care:for-face (of) Ifa the that it should be:able open road for-

(ẹ)ni.   A-(yi)o fi   ewurẹ   kan bọ   Ifa.
person.   We-will take she:goat one sacrifice:to Ifa.

    Abọnun jẹ talaka   o si   jẹ arugbo,   ẹ-l(i)-ẹya   ni awọn
    Abọnun eat poor:man he and eat old:person, one:who-have-ridicule be those

ara   ile   rẹ ma   fi   şe   nşe,   n(i)-igba-ti Abọnun
people (of) house his (continuative) take (him) make making; at-time-that Abọnun

tọ   babalawo lọ pe ki   nwọn yẹ   on wo,   nwọn ni   Ifa
approach diviners go that should they examine him look:at (him), they say Ifa

gba ewurẹ   ni ọwọ rẹ, o wa   lọ si ọja,   o ra ewurẹ   kan ni awin,
take she:goat at hand his; he come go to market, he buy she:goat one at unpaid,

o   ni b(i)-o ba   di   ọtunla   ki   e-l(i)-ewurẹ
he say if-it   should become day:after:tomorrow should one:who-has-she:goat

wa   gb(e)-owo,   n(i)-igba-ti o de   ile,   o pa ewurẹ, n(i)-igba-ti
come take-cowries; at-time-that he arrive house, he kill she:goat, at-time-that

o di   ọjọ-(e)keji, o ha   ewurẹ yi ka   gbogbo ile,   n(i)-igba-ti
it become day-second, he share she:goat this around all   house; at-time-that

o di   ọjọ-(ẹ)kẹta o sa pa-mọ   s(i)-inu   igbo nitori-ti   o ri
it become day-third he run kill-against to-belly (of) forest because-that he see

pe on ko ni   ri owo   ewurẹ yi san   fun e-l(i)-ewurẹ.
that he not have see cowries (of) she:goat this repay for one:who-has-she:goat.

    N(i)-ibi-ti   o gbe nrin   lọ, n(i)-inu igbo ni o jin   s(i)-ilẹ
    At-place-that he take walking to, at-belly forest be he fall:down to-ground

akun, n(i)-igba-ti e-l(i)-ewurẹ   de   ile   Abọnun ti
(of) bead; at-time-that one:who-has-she:goat arrive house (of) Abọnun that (she)

ko ba,   awọn ara   ile   Abọnun da-(o)hun, nwọn sọ   fun
not meet (him), those people (of) house (of) Abọnun break-voice, they speak for

who was the child of the Sky God, on the day that people on earth thought he was all through.[3]

Ifa says there is someone who has grown old; none of his relatives take any account of him, and they are making fun of him. During this year the Sky God will open the road of money for him, and everyone will prostrate themselves before him, including the chiefs. An Ifa has taken all his destiny and hidden it; we should take care of the Ifa so that it will be able to open the road for him. We will sacrifice one she-goat to Ifa.

Abọnun was a poor man and he was very old. His relatives were making fun of him. When Abọnun consulted the diviners, so that they might examine his case, they told him that Ifa wanted a she-goat from him. He went to the market, and bought a she-goat on credit. He told the goat-seller that she should come to collect the money on the day after tomorrow. When he reached home, he killed the goat. The next day he shared the goat among all the people of his house. And on the following day he ran into the forest to hide, because he saw that he had not found the money to pay the goat-seller for the goat.

In the forest he was walking about, he broke through the ground into a pit of beads. When the goat-seller came to Abọnun's house and did not find him, the people of Abọnun's house said to

---

3. Literally, "ended" or "finished," meaning that he did not count for anything any more.

546 Ofun - (Q)şę - 3

e-l(i)-ewurę pe Ki-ni iwǫ na ta ewurę fun si?
one:who-has-she:goat that "What-be you the sell she:goat for (him) to (him)?

Nibo ni yio ti ri owo san fun ǫ?
Where be (he) will have see cowries repay for you?"

    N(i)-igba-na ni e-l(i)-ewurę dogo de Abǫnun si ile, n(i)-igba-
    At-time-the be one:who-has-she:goat stay wait:for Abǫnun to house; at-time-

ti Abǫnun de ile ti o ba e-l(i)-ewurę o gbe gbirin
that Abǫnun arrive house that he meet one:who-has-she:goat, he take package (of)

akun fun E-l(i)-ewurę ba lǫ pęlu ija-(ai)ya, n(i)-
bead give (her). One:who-has-she:goat join (it) go together:with break-chest; at-

igba-ti o fi ma di ǫdun-(e)keji Abǫnun ti di ǫ-
time-that it take (continuative) become year-second Abǫnun have become one:who-

l(i)-ǫrǫ n(i)-igba-ti o ma bǫ Ifa rę, malu ni o pa o
have-riches; at-time-that he (continuative) sacrifice:to Ifa his, cow be he kill he

si pa-(a)şę pe ki nwǫn fi se ǫbę, n(i)-igba-ti ǫbę jina
and kill-command that should they take (it) cook stew; at-time-that stew cooked

ni Abǫnun joko ti i ti o si bęrę si kǫ-(o)rin wi-pe:
be Abǫnun sit:down against it that he and begin to sing-song speak-that:

    Ę m(u)-awo wa, ę la gba o
    "You take-plate come, you come accept, oh;

    A-ro-(ę)ni-pin m(u)-awo wa
    "One:who-think-person-end take-plate come;

    Ę la gba o A-ro-(ę)ni-pin
    "You come take, oh, One:who-think-person-end."

    Ifa ni ęni-kan wa ti awǫn enia nsǫ pe ko nilari,
    Ifa say person-one exist that those people speaking that not become:lucky,

şugbǫn Ǫ-l(i)-ǫrun ma şi-(ǫ)na owo ati alafia
but One:who-has-sky (continuative) open-road (of) cowries and contentment

fun, gbogbo enia ni yio ma pada lati wa tun bu
for (him), all people be (they) will (continuative) return to come then share

ǫla fun ti nwǫn yio si ma tę-(o)ri-ba fun bi ko
honor for (him) that they will and (continuative) press-head-touch for (him) if not

j(ę)-oye yio ni ǫla ju ęni-ti o ję oye lǫ.
eat-title will have honor surpass person-that he eat title go.

---

her, "Why did you sell <u>him</u> a goat? Where will <u>he</u> find the money to pay you?"

Then the goat-seller sat down to wait for[4] Abǫnun at his house. When Abǫnun came home and found the goat-seller, he gave her a package of beads wrapped in leaves. The goat-seller took it away with fear in her heart.[5] By the next year Abǫnun had become a rich man, and when he sacrificed to his Ifa, he killed a cow.[6] He ordered that it be made into a stew. When the stew was cooked, Abǫnun sat down beside it and began to sing:

> "Bring your plates, come and eat, oh;
> "You who thought that I was all through, bring your plates;
> "Come and eat, oh, you who thought I was all through."

Ifa says there is someone who people say will never have any luck, but the Sky God is about to open the road of money and contentment for him. Everyone will come back to him in order to pay him honor, and they will bow down for him. Even if he is not made a chief, he will have more honor than those who are chiefs.

---

4. "Dogode" is used to describe the activities of a creditor in dunning a debtor. It is the equivalent of "camping on the doorstep," and may mean to sit (joko), stand (duro), or lie down [dubu-(i)lę].

5. That is, she was afraid that she was being paid with stolen goods, and might be involved in a legal case. The Yoruba idiom "break-chest" refers to the beating of her heart; the chest is the seat of courage in much the same way that the head is the seat of luck and the stomach the seat of one's disposition.

6. Only kings and very wealthy people could afford to use a cow as sacrifice.

OFUN - (Q)ŞĘ - 4

O-fun-şunin   awo   aşǫ   l(i)-o   da   fun aşǫ   ni ǫjǫ ti   o
"To-squeeze-'shunin,'" secret (of) Cloth be-who cast for Cloth at day that she

nsǫ-(ę)kun   a-l(i)-ai-ri-ǫmǫ-bi,   nwǫn ni   yio l(i)-
shedding-tears (of) one:who-be-not-see-child-bear; they say (she) will have-

oyun   kan, şugbǫn ębǫ   ar(a)-aiye   ni ki   o   ru   aşǫ
pregnancy one, but   sacrifice (of) people-(of)-earth be should she offer cloth

i-ro   kan, ewurę   kan, ati ęgbędǫgbǫn.
to-wrap one, she:goat one, and 5000   (cowries).

Aşǫ   gbǫ   ko ru-(ę)bǫ,   n(i)-igba-ti aşǫ   ba   l(i)-oyun
Cloth hear not offer-sacrifice, at-time-that Cloth should have-pregnancy,

oyun   na a   si ra   mǫ   l(i)-ara, n(i)-igba-na ni aşǫ
pregnancy the will and disappear against (her) at-body; at-time-the be Cloth

bęrę si wi-pe   on iba   mǫ ki   o   şe   ębǫ   O-fun-
begin to speak-that "She should know should she make sacrifice (of) To-squeeze-

şunin n(i)-ijǫsi   o si bęrę si k(i)-a-ba-mǫ   pe ki-ni   on
'shunin' at-other:day," she and begin to that-we-should-know that "What-be she

şe yi?
do this?"

Ifa ni obinrin kan ni-(e)yi ti   yio l(i)-oyun,   şugbǫn ki   o   ru-
Ifa say woman one be-this that will have-pregnancy, but   should she offer-

(ę)bǫ   ar(a)-aiye   ki oyun   na ma ba   ra   mǫ
sacrifice (of) people-(of)-earth that pregnancy the not should disappear against

l(i)-ara. Obinrin kan si tun ni-(e)yi ki   o   ru-(ę)bǫ   ki
(her) at-body. Woman one and then be-this should she offer-sacrifice that

oyun   ti o   ni yi ma jo mǫ   l(i)-ara.
pregnancy that she have this not leak against (her) at-body.

OFUN MEJI - 1

A sa-re a ka-(ǫ)san a fi-(i)rin   gbęrę-gbęrę ka-(ǫ)san, a ki
"We run-go we pluck-ǫsan, we take-walking slowly-slowly pluck-ǫsan, we not

ni ęni   ni (i)m(u)-ǫsan   k(i)-a m(u)-ai-pǫn   a   da fun oju ti
have person at place-(of)-ǫsan that-we drink-not-be:ripe" who cast for Eye that

o nlǫ   j(ę)-ǫ-l(i)-ǫja   l(i)-arin   ara; nwǫn ni ki   oju
he going eat-one:who-has-market at-middle (of) people; they say should Eye

ki   o ru-(ę)bǫ   ęiyę-(i)le   meji, ęyin-(a)dię   meji,
should he offer-sacrifice (of) bird-(of)-house two, egg-(of)-chicken two,

ęgbęrindinlogun   ati ǫbǫtǫ   ori   a-(yi)o lǫ   ori   mǫ
3200   (cowries), and lump (of) shea:butter, we-will grind shea:butter against

255 - 4

"To wring out 'shunin,'"[1] the diviner of Cloth, was the one who cast Ifa for Cloth when she was weeping because she was childless. They said she would become pregnant, but that as a sacrifice against witches[2] she should offer one cloth wrapper,[3] one she-goat, and one shilling three pence.

Cloth heard but did not make the sacrifice. When Cloth became pregnant, the pregnancy disappeared from her body. Then Cloth began to say, "Had I but known, I would have made the sacrifice of To wring out 'shunin' the other day," and she began to regret, saying, "Why did I do this?"

Ifa says this is a woman who will become pregnant; but she should make a sacrifice against witches, so that the pregnancy will not disappear from her body. And then again there is a woman who is already pregnant who should make a sacrifice so that her pregnancy will not leak away.[4]

---

1. "Shunin" is the sound made when a cloth is squeezed or wrung dry. The name of the diviner is a play upon the name of the figure [Ofun-(ọ)ṣẹ]. The imagery involved in the diviner's name is carried consistently through the verse. The water dripping from the cloth refers to the tears of Cloth, weeping for children. The air bubbles that appear when a cloth is wrung out are referred to as Cloth becoming pregnant, a condition which never lasts because Cloth failed to sacrifice; and the verse explains why this happens. And there is a danger that the client's pregnancy may also leak away.

2. Ar(a)-aiye is a euphemism for witches.

3. A large, rectangular piece of cloth that is wrapped around the waist as a skirt.

4. Cf. verse 183-2, where the pregnancy of the mordant used in dyeing also leaks away.

---

256 - 1

"We run to pick star apples,[1] we walk leisurely to pick star apples; but since we don't have anyone at the place where star apples grow, we always have to eat them unripened"[2] was the one who cast Ifa for Eye when he was going to be made king. They said Eye should sacrifice two pigeons, two chicken eggs, nine pence six oninis, and a lump of shea butter. We will grind the shea butter with

---

1. See n. 3, verse 54-5.

2. Because we have no one to watch them, the star apples are stolen as they ripen, leaving us only unripened ones.

ewe jẹ-n-joko   a-(yi)o pa ọkan si   n(i)-inu   awọn ẹiyẹ-
leaf consent-I-sit:down, we-will kill one   to (it) at-belly (of) those bird-(of)-

(i)le meji na a-(yi)o fọ   ẹyin-(a)diẹ   kan si   a-(yi)o ma
house two the, we-will break egg-(of)-chicken one to (it), we-will (continuative)

fi   pa ara. Oju ru-(ẹ)bọ.
take (it) rub body. Eye offer-sacrifice.

   Ifa ni ẹni-kan   wa ti Q-l(i)-ọrun   yio da   ọja   iwa
   Ifa say person-one exist that One:who-has-sky will create market (of) destiny

nla kan fun   ti yio kan gbogbo awọn ara   ile rẹ gẹgẹ-bi oju
big one for (him) that will touch all   those people (of) house his just-as Eye

ti ri fun gbogbo ara;   ọmọde   kan si wa ti Q-l(i)-ọrun   yio
have see for all   people; young:child one and exist that One:who-has-sky will

mu de   ipo   nla kan, ṣugbọn ki   o ru-(ẹ)bọ   dara-dara
take arrive position big one, but   should he offer-sacrifice be:good-be:good

nitori   e-l(i)-enini.
because (of) one:who-has-enmity.

OFUN MEJI - 2

   "B(i)-a   ṣe iwọ bi   yio ṣe emi ki jẹ-ki   a ṣu   si
   "If-(it)-will make you if (it) will make me, not consent-that we defecate to

oko   a-l(i)-ai-r(i)-oju,   bi a ba   ṣu   si oko   a-l(i)-
farm (of) one:who-be-not-see-eye; if we should defecate to farm (of) one:who-be-

ai-r(i)-oju, ebi-ala   rẹ ni a ko gbọdọ rin, bi a ba   rin ebi-
not-see-eye edge-(of)-boundary his be we not must walk; if we should walk edge-

ala   rẹ iṣu rẹ ni a ko gbọdọ jẹ, a da fun Oniwọnranole ti
(of)-boundary his, yam his be we not must eat" who cast for Oniwọnranole that

ar(a)-aiye   nfi   ṣe ẹ-l(i)-ẹya   ẹgbagun,
people-(of)-earth taking (him) make one:who-have-ridicule (of) 40,000 (times),

ti nwọn nfi   ṣe ẹ-l(i)-ẹya   ẹgbagbọn   nwọn
that they taking (him) make one:who-have-ridicule (of) 60,000   (times); they

ni gbogbo aiye ni   yio pe   sin   n(i)-igb(a)-ẹhin oju-
say all   earth be (it) will assemble serve (him) at-time-back   face-(of)-

alẹ   rẹ. Oniwọnranole ni orukọ ti a pe Ifa. Ewurẹ kan, eku, ẹja,
evening his. Oniwọnranole be name that we call Ifa. She:goat one, rat, fish,

ayebọ adiẹ   ati obi ni ẹbọ.
hen   chicken, and kola be sacrifice.

   Ifa ni ẹni-kan   ni gbogbo awọn ara   ile rẹ nbu   ti nwọn
   Ifa say person-one be all   those people (of) house his insulting that they

the leaf "let me sit down";[3] we will kill one of the two pigeons and add its blood; we will break one egg onto the mixture; and with it we will rub our body. Eye made the sacrifice.

Ifa says that there is someone for whom the Sky God will create a large market of destiny, which will affect all his family, just as Eye sees for everyone.[4] And there is a young child whom the Sky God will place in a very important position; but he should make a very good sacrifice to avoid an enemy.

---

3. See n. 3, verse 249-4.

4. This verse thus explains that, because he made the sacrifice, no one can see without eyes.

---

256 - 2

"Whether it is you or whether it is I, we are not permitted to defecate on the farm of one who is too busy to look after it;[1] if we do defecate on the farm of one who is too busy to look after it, we must not walk along the boundary of his farm; if we do walk along the boundary of his farm, we must not eat his yams"[2] was the one who cast Ifa for Oniwǫnranole when people were ridiculing him 40,000 times, when they were ridiculing him 60,000 times. They said all the world would gather to serve him in his old age. Oniwǫnranole is the name that we call Ifa.[3] One she-goat, a rat, a fish, a hen, and kola is the sacrifice.

Ifa says there is someone whom all the people of his house are insulting

---

1. Alairoju was interpreted as meaning one who is so busy that he doesn't have time to look after his farm; but the reference may be to a blind man.

2. Prohibitions of this type are known as ǫhun. Informants compared them to tabus (ewǫ), but were unable to differentiate between them. If either is broken, one suffers the consequences (ję ewǫ, ję ǫhun). Abraham gives "I suffered the penalty" for ǫhun hun mi.

3. It is understood that Ifa became so important because he made the sacrifice.

si npe   ni ǫlę   yi, oluwarę   na ni   yio ni
and calling (him) at lazy:person this, person:in question the be (who) will have

gbogbo ile   na ni igb(a)-ęhin   ǫla;   a si nfę   şe ohun kan, ohun
all   house the at time-back (of) tomorrow; we and wanting do thing one, thing

na yio ni   ere n(i)-ik(an)-ęhin.   Gbogbo ile   ni   yio ma
the will have gain at-standing-back. All   house be (it) will (continuative)

pe   sin   ęni-kan   ni ęhin-ǫla.
assemble serve person-one at back-(of)-tomorrow.

OFUN MEJI - 3

"Afinkin ni   p(a)-ęru, ilę   dida   ni   p(a)-ǫrę, epe ni   p(a)-
"Afinkin be (it) kill-slave, ground broken be (it) kill-friend, curse be (it) kill-

ole, a-jǫ-bi   ni   pa   iye-kan,   b(i)-
thief, those:who-be:together-bear be (they) kill (those) (of) mother-one," "If-

ǫja   ba   tu   pę   a k(u)-ero   kata-kata,   a ku-
market should loosen suddenly, it remain-stranger scattered-scattered, it remain-

(a)-na-(ǫ)ja,   a ku-(a)-p(a)-atę   a   da   fun Irun-(I)mǫlę
those:who-spend-goods, it remain-those:who-kill-tray" who cast for 400-Deity

ti Olodumare nran-(i)şę   iku pe wǫn igb(a)-(og)oji ti o nran-
that Olodumare sending-message (of) death call them time-forty   that he sending-

(i)şę   iku pe wǫn igb(a)-(ǫg)ǫta.
message (of) death call them time-sixty.

N(i)-igba-ti Olodumare nran-(i)şę   iku pe gbogbo Irun-(I)mǫlę,
At-time-that Olodumare sending-message (of) death call all   400-Deity,

Qrunmila pe   gbogbo wǫn, o se   ikoko   igbin kan, ikoko   ęja kan, ikoko
Qrunmila call all   them, he cook pot   (of) snail one, pot   (of) fish one, pot

eku kan, o yan   agbǫn   ori   kan o si pǫn amu
(of) rat one, he choose basket (of) cornstarch:porridge one he and draw jar (of)

omi kan ti   wǫn; n(i)-igba-ti wǫn ję ti wǫn mu   tan,   Qrunmila
water one against them; at-time-that they eat that they drink finish, Qrunmila

sǫ   fun wǫn pe l(i)-ilǫ   ti nwǫn nlǫ   si ǫrun yi, ki   awǫn ma şe
speak for them that at-departure that they going to sky this, should they not do

şe   ara awǫn ni ęyǫbęyǫ, ki   a   şe   ara wǫn ni şirimu, ki
make body their at one:by:one, should they make body their at united, should

awǫn si jǫ   ma   rin lǫ, ki   awǫn ma-şe rin l(i)-ǫk(an)-
they and be:together (continuative) walk go, should they not-do walk at-one-

ǫkan, o ni nitori-ti   bi awǫn ba   fi   ara awǫn şe   ǫkan, Olodumare
one, he say because-that if they should take body their make one, Olodumare

and are calling lazy; this person will own the entire house in the near future.
And we want to do something; this thing will yield a profit eventually. The whole
house will gather to serve someone in the near future.

---

256 - 3

"Afinkin[1] is what kills slaves; broken oaths[2] are what kill friends; curses[3]
are what kill thieves; and ancestors are what kill relatives"[4] and "If the market
breaks up suddenly, foreigners are left scattered here and there, traders remain, and those who have spread their wares for sale remain"[5] were the ones
who cast Ifa for the Four Hundred Deities when the Sky God was sending Death
to call them forty times, when he was sending Death to call them sixty times.
    When the Sky God sent Death to call all the Four Hundred Deities, Qrun-
mila called them together. He cooked one pot of snails, one pot of fish, one pot
of rats, and he bought one basket of cornstarch porridge and drew one jar full of
water for them. When they had finished eating and drinking, Qrunmila told them
that when they went to heaven this time, they should not go singly; they should go
together and stand united; they should not walk alone. He said, because if they
stayed together, the Sky God

---

1. This could not be explained by informants; but from the context it would
seem to be something comparable to an oath or a curse. Idowu (1962: 52) gives
it as Afinti, which he translates as tale-bearing, in a very similar introduction
to a verse which he ascribes to Ogbe Meji.
    2. To take an oath is called to "drink ground" (mulę, mu ilę), and to break
an oath to "break ground" (da ilę).
    3. See n. 4, verse 248-4.
    4. According to informants "those born together" (ajǫbi) refers to the an-
cestors, and "those of one mother" (iyekan) is used loosely here to mean those
related by either the father or the mother. A person who is accused of making
bad medicine against such a relative or of having sexual relations with a relative's
wife is made to take an oath of his innocence. He must eat kola in the main chamber of the compound and repeat "May the ancestors kill me" (if I am guilty) [Ki
ajǫbi pa mi]. This type of an oath, taken only when there is a dispute within the
family, is considered extremely dangerous, even more so than the public oaths by
the Ogunladin in the Qni's palace. Idowu (1962: 52) gives Alajǫbi, translated as
consanguinity.
    5. When something happens in the market, the customers leave, but those
who sell in the market stay to protect their wares, and people who have come from
other towns remain because they have nowhere else to go.

ko ni le   da   ǫkan duro tabi ki o mu ǫkan s(i)-ilę   n(i)-inu awǫn.
not be be:able cause one stand or that he take one to-ground at-belly their.

    N(i)-igba-ti nwǫn de   ǫdǫ   Olodumare, gbogbo awǫn Irun-(I)mǫlę
    At-time-that they arrive presence (of) Olodumare, all   those 400-Deity

sǫ   fun Olodumare pe ǫkunrin dudu ti o gbe   ide k(a)-ǫrun   yi ni o
speak for Olodumare that man   black that he carry ide around-neck this be he

nru   aiye nitori-na   ki   Olodumare ki   o mu   s(i)-ilę   ni
disturbing earth because-the should Olodumare should he take (him) to-ground at

ǫrun ki   o ma-şe ję-ki   o tun pada   lǫ si aiye mǫ.
sky   should he not-do consent-that he then return go to earth again.

    N(i)-igba-ti Olodumare gbǫ bayi o pe Eşu o bere   l(i)-ǫwǫ rę
    At-time-that Olodumare hear thus he call Eshu, he ask (him) at-hand his

pe iwǫ ni   mo fi şǫ wǫn, bawo ni o ti ri ęni-ti   nwǫn
that you be (who) I   take watch them, how be you have see person-that they

wi   yi si? Eşu da-(o)hun   o ni irǫ ni nwǫn npa   mǫ   Qrunmila, o
speak this to? Eshu break-voice he say lie be they killing against Qrunmila, he

ni bi ęni-kan   ba   nşe   ai-san   n(i)-inu nwǫn ęni-ti nwǫn
say if person-one should doing not-be:better at-belly their, person-that they

wi   yi ni   ima   tǫ-(o)ju   rę, bi o ba   si gba eku
speak this be (who) (continuative) care:for-eye his, if he should and accept rat

tabi ęja on na ni   ma   ję,   Eşu si tun sǫ   pe n(i)-
or   fish, his the be (he) (continuative) eat (them), Eshu and then speak that at-

igba-ti awǫn nbǫ   ni ǫdǫ   Olodumare yi, o se ikoko   eku,
time-that they coming at presence (of) Olodumare this, he cook pot   (of) rat,

ikoko   ęja, ikoko   igbin, amu   omi o si yan   agbǫn   ori
pot   (of) fish, pot   (of) snail, jar (of) water, he and choose basket (of) corn-

         kan si,   awǫn ję awǫn si mu ki   awǫn to   bǫ   ni
starch:porridge one to (it), they eat they and drink before they equal come at

ǫdǫ   iwǫ, Olodumare.
presence (of) you, Olodumare.

    N(i)-igba-ti ǫba   ǫrun gbǫ bayi, o ko   gbogbo awǫn Irun-(I)mǫlę
    At-time-that King (of) sky hear thus, he gather all   those 400-Deity

o de wǫn mǫ-(i)lę   si ǫrun, o ni ki   Qrunmila ati Eşu ma
he bind them against-ground to sky, he say should Qrunmila and Eshu (continua-

      lǫ si aiye. N(i)-igba-ti awǫn mej(i)-(m)eji de   inu   aiye, inu
tive) go to earth. At-time-that those two-two   arrive belly (of) earth, belly

    Qrunmila dun,   o si bęrę si yin   awǫn babalawo rę o si nkǫ-
(of) Qrunmila be:sweet, he and begin to praise those diviners his he and singing-

(o)rin pe:
song that:

would not be able to stop any one of them or be able to detain any one of them.

When they came to the Sky God, all the Four Hundred Deities told him that a black man who was wearing ide beads[6] around his neck was the one who was upsetting the world, and that therefore the Sky God should keep him in heaven and not let him return to earth any more.

When the Sky God heard this, he called Eshu; he asked him "You are the one I have set to watch them. What do you know about this person of whom they speak?" Eshu answered, saying they were telling lies against Qrunmila. He said that whenever any one was ill, the one they said these things about was the one who cured them, and if he received rats or fish as a sacrifice, he only ate those that were meant for him. And then Eshu said that when they were coming to the Sky God this time, "Qrunmila cooked a pot of rats, a pot of fish, and a pot of snails, and he drew a jar of water and bought a basket of cornstarch porridge for them; and they ate and drank before they came before you, oh Olodumare."

When the King of the Sky heard this, he took all the Four Hundred Deities and tied them down in the sky; and he said that Qrunmila and Eshu should go back to earth. When these two arrived on earth, Qrunmila was happy and he began to praise his diviners and to sing:

----

6. Ide are the kind of beads worn by babalawo (see Chapter IX), identifying the "black man" as Qrunmila.

A   gb(e)-ori-(i)lę   a j(ę)-eku o
"We dwell-at-head-(of)-ground we eat-rat, oh;

A   gb(e)-ori-(i)lę   a ję-(ę)ja
"We dwell:at-head-(of)-ground we eat-fish;

A   mu-(i)gba   odu a ję-(i)gbin
"We drink-calabash (of) odu we eat-snail.

A-şę   d(i)-ǫwǫ   ilę   a jǫ   mu
"That:which-happen become-hand (of) ground we be:together drink;

Ę   gb(e)-ori-(i)lę   ę da   mi
"You dwell:at-head-(of)-ground you break (ground) my;

A-şę   d(i)-ǫwǫ   ilę   a jǫ   mu
"That:which-happen become-hand (of) ground we be:together drink."

Ifa ni ki   a   ma da   ilę   ǫrę ki a   ma ba   ku iku
Ifa say should we not break ground (of) friend that we not should die death (of)

ai-ro-tęlę,   a ba ęni-kan   p(a)-ero   ǫrǫ kan, oluwarę
not-think-beforehand; we join person-one kill-thought (of) word one, person:in:

        nfę   da-(i)lę   si-(ę)ni, ara   ǫrun ni   yio şe i-
question wanting break-ground to-person, people (of) sky be (who) will make to-

da-(ę)jǫ   ǫrǫ rę; ęni-kan   si tun wa   ti o nşe ai-san
cause-case (of) word his; person-one and then exist that he doing not-be:better,

    ko ni ku, ęni-ti   a ko gb(e)-oju le ni   yio ku. Gbogbo ohun
(he) not be die, person-that we not take-eye upon be (he) will die. All   thing

ti Qrunmila fi   ru-(ę)bǫ   n(i)-igba-na ni gbogbo enia   fi
that Qrunmila take (them) offer-sacrifice at-time-the be all   people take (them)

nbǫ   nisisiyi.
sacrificing right:now.

(Ękǫ   inu   Ifa yi: Iwǫ ko gbǫdǫ j(ę)-ęri   eke   si
(Lesson (of) belly (of) Ifa this: You not must eat-witness (of) falsehood to

ǫmǫnikeji rę.)
companion yours.)

OFUN MEJI - 4

Iku   nda-(i)na   epin, arun   nda-(i)na   ita; aję on Eşu
"Death creating-fire (of) epin; disease creating-fire (of) ita; witch and Eshu

nda-(i)na   munrun-munrun a   da fun Qrunmila n(i)-igba-ti ara
creating-fire (of) munrun-munrun" who cast for Qrunmila at-time-that body (of)

ǫmǫ rę ko da;   nwǫn ni ki   o ru-(ę)bǫ   ęiyę-(i)le   kan,
child his not be:good; they say should he offer-sacrifice (of) bird-(of)-house one,

"We live on earth, we eat rats, oh;
"We live on earth, we eat fish;
"We drink calabashes of odu,[7] we eat snails.
"Whatever happens concerns the oath that we took together;
"You lived on earth, you broke your oath to me;
"Whatever happens concerns the oath that we took together."

Ifa says that we should not break an oath with a friend, lest we meet death unexpectedly. We have discussed something with someone who wants to break his oath to us, but the people in heaven will judge and punish him. And then there is someone who is ill, he will not die; but someone else whom we have not even noticed is the one who will die. All the things that Qrunmila sacrificed at that time are what everyone uses in sacrificing at the present time.[8]

(The lesson[9] of this Ifa verse is that "You must not bear false witness against your companions.")

7. Informants could not explain the meaning of odu in this context.

8. The verse explains why snails, fish, rats, cornstarch porridge, and water are used in sacrifices to Qlqrun, and why Ifa and Eshu are so important on earth.

9. This moral, which is not recited by the diviners as part of the Ifa verse, was added by the interpreter.

256 - 4

"Death kindles a fire of epin wood; disease kindles a fire of ita wood; Witches and Eshu kindle a fire of munrun-munrun wood"[1] was the one who cast Ifa for Qrunmila when his child's health was not good. They said he should sacrifice one pigeon,

1. Munrun-munrun is an unidentified tree. Firewood from the ita tree (Celtis Soyauxii, C. Zenkeri, C. Adolfi-Frederici) is important among the gifts to the wife's relatives at marriage. Epin is the Sandpaper tree (Ficus asperifolia).

akiko adię   kan, obi męfa, ęgba   męfa, ki omo rę ma ba   ku.
cock chicken one, kola six,   2000 (cowries) six,   that child his not should die.

O ru   omo rę na si ye.   Ifa ni ki   a ru-(ę)bo   ki ai-san
He offer, child his the and live. Ifa say should we offer-sacrifice that not-be:

        ma le   şe-(ę)ni.
better not be:able make-person.

OFUN MEJI - 5

Aşinşinrin ni   ş(e)-awo   ilu   o-d(a)-oro   ikandu
Ashinshinrin be (who) make-secret (of) town (of) one:who-cause-spite, Ikandu

ni   ş(e)-awo   ilu   o-ş(e)-ika   ęta fi   iru
be (who) make-secret (of) town (of) that:which-make-wickedness, "Ęta take tail

gba-(i)lę   gęręgę, o nre   mogan a   da fun Oşu-fun-mi-l(i)-ayo, a
sweep-ground 'gęręgę' he going Mogan" who cast for "Oshu-give-me-at-joy, who

bi ija wara   n(i)-igba-ti o nlo si Agege, nwon ni ki   o ru
as fight immediately" at-time-that he going to Agege; they say should he offer

eku meje, ęja meje, ęgbaje owo   ęyo, o ru   ębo.
rat seven, fish seven, 14,000 cowries ęyo, he offer sacrifice.

Ifa ni ki   a ru-(ę)bo   irin   ajo   ti a np(a)-
Ifa say should we offer-sacrifice (of) walking (of) journey that we killing-

ete   lati lo, ki a ba   le   pada wa si ile   ni alafia.
intention to   go, that we should be:able return come to house at contentment.

OFUN MEJI - 6

A-(yi)o fi   ęfun ati osun   tę   Ofun Meji s(i)-ara   ogiri.
We-will take chalk and camwood press Ofun Meji to-body (of) wall.

Ayę, Odogbonikanran, A-dęgbęlu,   A-lu-wi   Apakenija
"Ole, Odogbonikanran, One:who-collapses, One:who-beat-speak, Apakenija

A-ja-koro-(w)a-(i)le,   A-tu-gbe   ni tuku tu   ębo,
One:who-reach-at:once-come-house,To-loosen-be:lost be boar loosen sacrifice,

ibi-ti   ewu ba   so-(i)lę   si ni   ku si.
Place-that rodent should strike-ground to be (it) die to."

A-(yi)o ję obi a-(yi)o tu   fon a-(yi)o wi-pe   ibi-k(u)-ibi   ti
We-will eat kola; we-will spit (it) blow; we-will speak-that evil-any-evil that

o ba   fi ori şę   mi ibę ni ki   o ku si ki   o ma le   ran
it should take head make me, there be should it die to, should it not be:able affect

mi.
me.

---

one cock, six kola nuts, and three shillings, so that his child might not die. He made the sacrifice and his child lived. Ifa says we should make a sacrifice so that someone will not become ill.

---

256 - 5

Ashinshinrin, who was the diviner of the town of Revenger; Ikandu, who was the diviner of the town of Evil Doer; and "Ęta[1] sweeps the ground with its tail 'gęręgę,'[2] he is going to Mǫgan"[3] were the ones who cast Ifa for "'Ǫshu gives me happiness' who is like a sudden fight" when he was going to Agege.[4] They said he should sacrifice seven rats, seven fish, and three shillings six pence. He made the sacrifice.

Ifa says we should make a sacrifice because of a journey on foot that we intend to make, so that we may be able to return home in contentment.

---

1. Ęta is identified by Abraham as the civet-cat from which musk (işeta, eşeta) is obtained. Ashinshinrin is a bad-smelling rat; and ikandu is a large, bad-smelling ant. The two towns mentioned could not be identified by informants.
2. This word describes the motion of the tail in sweeping the earth.
3. Interpreted as the name of an unidentified town.
4. A town about fifteen miles inland from Lagos on the road to Abęokuta and Ibadan.

---

256 - 6

We will mark Ofun Meji on the wall in chalk and camwood.[1]
"Ole! Odogbonikanran! The one who slumps![2] The one who beats and speaks![3] Apakenija! The one who comes home as soon as he gets there! The wild boar[4] scatters sacrifices so that they stay scattered! Where the ewu[5] touches the ground is where it dies!"

We will chew kola and blow it from our mouth; we will say, "Whatever evil may befall me should perish; it should not be able to affect me."

---

1. This is not a usual verse recited as a part of divination, but one of the medicines learned by the diviners; see n. 1, verse 239-2. In large part it consists of verbal incantations whose meaning is obscure even when they can be translated, which give efficacy to the marks made on the wall.
2. As when one pretends to collapse or fall against a wall when he is given a playful shove.
3. This probably refers to Ǫrunmila beating palm nuts.
4. Identified in Abraham as the Red River-hog (ęlędę odo).
5. Described by informants as a nocturnal rodent-like animal, which may be arboreal; Abraham gives ewu as a synonym for okete, the Giant Rat or Pouched Rat (Cricetomys gambianus).

PARODIES - 1

Qna tọ   tara   ma ya   a   da   fun Reluwe ni-(ọ)jọ ti   o
"Road be:straight straight not turn" who cast for Railway at-day that he

nṣ(e)-awo   r(e)-odo ti o nlọ b(a)-Oyinbo ṣ(e)-owo.   Nwọn
making-secret go-river that he going join-Whiteman make-transaction. They

ni gbogbo ẹru   Oyinbo,   Reluwe ni   yio ni,   nwọn ni ki
say all   load (of) Whiteman, Railway be (he) will have (them); they say should

o ru-(ẹ)bọ,   nwọn ni ati oyinbo   ati a-kọ-(i)we,   Reluwe ni
be offer-sacrifice, they say and Whiteman and One:who-write-book, Railway be

      yio ni   ẹru wọn.
(who) will have load their.

Reluwe kọ   ko ru-(ẹ)bọ.   Lati igba-na bi gbogbo enia   ba
Railway refuse not offer-sacrifice. From time-the if all   people should

ko   ẹru s(i)-inu   Reluwe, n(i)-igba-ti nwọn ba   sọ   nwọn a   si
gather load to-belly (of) Railway, at-time-that they should alight, they will and

ko   ẹru wọn kuro n(i)-inu rẹ.
gather load their depart at-belly his.

Ifa ni ẹni-kan   nlọ si ẹhin   odi   kan, nwọn ni ki   o ru-
Ifa say person-one going to back (of) townwall one, they say should he offer-

(ẹ)bọ   ki ole ma ba   gba ẹru rẹ ni ọwọ rẹ.
sacrifice that thief not should take load his at hand his.

PARODIES - 2

Qna tọ   tara   ma ya   l(i)-o da-(I)fa fun Reluwe ni ọjọ ti
"Road be:straight straight not turn" be-who cast-Ifa for Railway at day that

o nsọ-(ẹ)kun   a-l(i)-ai-l(i)-ẹni   nwọn ni ki   o ru-
he shedding-tears one:who-be-not-have-person, they say should he offer-

(ẹ)bọ   yio ni   ẹni   akikọ mẹta, ẹgbafa   ati aṣọ   ara rẹ.
sacrifice will have person, cock three, 12,000 (cowries) and cloth (of) body his.

Reluwe ru   ẹgbafa   ati aṣọ   ara rẹ, ṣugbọn ko ru
Railroad offer 12,000 (cowries) and cloth (of) body his, but   not offer

akikọ mẹta ti o jẹ-pe   ki   awọn enia na ba   ba   k(a)-
cock three that it consent-that should those people the should join (him) around-

alẹ.   Reluwe bẹrẹ si di   ẹ-l(i)-ẹni;   bi gbogbo enia   ba
evening. Railway begin to become one:who-have-person; if all   people should

wọ   inu   Reluwe, bi o ba   di   alẹ   nwọn a   kuro n(i)-inu
enter belly (of) Railway, if it should become evening they will depart at-belly

rẹ, onikaluku   a   si lọ si ile   rẹ. Lati igba-na ni gbogbo ero
his; everyone:else will and go to house his. From time-the be all   traveller

257 - 1

"The road is very straight, it does not turn"[1] was the one who cast Ifa for
Railway on the day that he was divining and going down to trade with Whiteman.
They said that all the loads of Whiteman would belong to Railway. They said he
should make a sacrifice. They said that Railway would own the loads of both
Whiteman and Clerk.[2]

Railway refused, he did not make the sacrifice. From that time on, if everyone puts his load inside Railway, when he gets off the train he takes his load off
and carries it away from Railway.[3]

Ifa says that someone is going out of town. They say he should make a sacrifice lest a thief should steal his loads from him.

---

1. This introductory phrase is taken directly from verse 20-2. Here it is
more meaningfully applied to Railway, whose tracks are straighter than the traditional paths and streets. Cf. also verses 17-3 and 257-2.

2. The clerks or "ones who write books" were mainly employed by European
trading firms and in government service. Like the Europeans they traveled by
railway rather than by foot, with their "loads" or baggage with them.

3. Although this parody specifies no sacrifice, it has the typical explanatory
element, to show why baggage is taken away from the railway train on which it is
carried. Cf. verse 243-4.

---

257 - 2

"The road is very straight, it does not turn"[1] was the one who cast Ifa for
Railway on the day he was weeping because he did not have followers. They said
he would have followers if he sacrificed three cocks, three shillings, and the cloth
from his body.

Railway offered three shillings and the cloth from his body, but did not offer
the three cocks to let people stay with him overnight. Railway began to become a
person with followers, but after everyone went into Railway, when it became evening his followers went away again, everyone going to his own home. From that
time on, all travelers

---

1. Cf. n. 1, verse 257-1.

ti   ma   nwǫ   inu   Reluwe   ti   nwǫn si   ma   nkuro
that (continuative) entering belly (of) Railway that they and (continuative) departing

n(i)-inu rę ni al(ę)-alę.
at-belly his at evening-evening.

    Ifa ni a-(yi)o di   ę-l(i)-ęni   şugbǫn ki   a   ru-(ę)bǫ
    Ifa say we-will become one:who-have-person, but   should we offer-sacrifice

ki   ęni   ti a ni   ma ba   fi-(ę)ni   s(i)-ilę.
that person that we have not should put-person to-ground.

PARODIES - 3

    Okunkun ję-ki   agba ri-(ǫ)na   a   da-(I)fa fun Oyinbo   ti   a
    "Darkness consent-that elder see-road" who cast-Ifa for Whiteman that they

ma   gba atupa   ǫwǫ rę nwǫn ni atupa   ǫwǫ rę ni ębǫ.
(continuative) take lamp (of) hand his; they say lamp (of) hand his be sacrifice.

Oyinbo   fi   atupa   ǫwǫ rę ru-(ę)bǫ.
Whiteman take lamp (of) hand his offer-sacrifice.

    Ifa ni ki   ęni-kan   fi   atupa   ǫwǫ rę ru-(ę)bǫ.   N(i)-igba-
    Ifa say should person-one take lamp (of) hand his offer-sacrifice. At-time-

ti   agba ko ri-(ǫ)na, o   da Ifa fun Oyinbo   o si fę   gba atupa   ǫwǫ
that elder not see-road, he cast Ifa for Whiteman he and want take lamp (of) hand

rę.
his.

PARODIES - 4

    Bi o   ba   rin pę   titi, ebi   a   pa ǫ   pę   titi   a
    "If you should laugh be:long until, hunger will kill you be:long until" (be) who

da   fun Ǫ-l(i)-ǫgędę-agbagba ti o ş(e)-ǫmǫ   kǫrǫgun-kǫrǫgun. Nwǫn ni
cast for One:who-has-plantain that he make-child thick-thick.   They say

ǫgędę ti o wa   ni agbala ti o yǫ   ǫmǫ on ni ębǫ.
plantain that he exist at backyard that it sprout child hers be sacrifice.

    Babalawo ti ebi   npa   ni o ki   Ifa yi fun ǫkunrin kan ti
    Diviner   that hunger killing (him) be who greet Ifa this for man   one that

o ni   ǫgędę ti o yǫ   ǫmǫ ni agbala   rę.
he have plantain that it sprout child at backyard his.

who enter Railway have been leaving again each evening.[2]

Ifa says we will become a person who has followers, but we should make a sacrifice so that the followers that we have should not leave us.

---

2. The explanatory element here tells why the passengers leave the train each night. This parody includes a characteristic implication, that when a sacrifice is only partially made, the desired effect is not permanently attained.

---

257 - 3

"Darkness lets the elder see the road" was the one who cast Ifa for Whiteman when they were going to take the lamp from his hand.[1] They said that the lamp in his hand was the sacrifice. Whiteman sacrificed the lamp in his hand.

Ifa says someone should make a sacrifice of the lamp in his hand. When the elder could not see the road, he cast Ifa for Whiteman, and he wanted to take the lamp in his hand.

---

1. The implication, stated more specifically later, is that the diviner wanted the lamp (or flashlight) which he knew the Whiteman had, and therefore falsely, and unethically, said that it was required as a sacrifice.

---

257 - 4

If you laugh long, you will hunger long" was the one who cast Ifa for one who had a plantain with very thick children.[1] They said that the plantain that was in his backyard which had children was the sacrifice.[2]

The diviner who was suffering from hunger was the one who recited this verse for a man who had a plantain with children in his backyard.[3]

---

1. I.e. the fruit.
2. Cf. verse 2-2.
3. Cf. n. 1, verse 257-3.

REFERENCES CITED

ABIMBQLA, 'WANDE
n. d.   "16 Principal Odu of Ifa." (Typewritten manuscript).

ABRAHAM, R. C.
1940   The Tiv People. 2d ed. London: Crown Agents for the Colonies.
        Pp. x plus 177.
1958   Dictionary of Modern Yoruba. London: University of London Press.
        Pp. xli plus 776.

AINSLIE, J. R., et al.
1936   Vocabulary of Nigerian Names of Trees, Shrubs and Herbs. Lagos:
        Government Printer. Pp. 64.

ALAPINI, JULIEN
1950   Les Noix Sacrées. Etude complète de Fa-Ahidégoun. Génie de la
        Sagesse et la Divination au Dahomey. Monte-Carlo: Regain. Pp. 126.

ANONYMOUS
1930   African Folk Tales. Book 2. Lagos: Church Missionary Society's
        Bookshop. Pp. 72.

ATAIYERO, SAMUEL O. S.
1934   Iwe Qfọ Ayajọ Odu Iwosan Jẹminiho. Lagos: The Union Press. Pp. 18.

AUGUSTINY, JULIUS
1925   "Kambamärchen," Zeitschrift für Eingeborenen-Sprachen, XV, 81-116,
        213-223.

BADIBANGA
1931   L'Éléphant qui marche sur des oeufs. Bruxelles: L'Eglantine. Pp. 90.

BARKER, W. H., AND CECILIA SINCLAIR
1917   West African Folk-Tales. London: George G. Harrap & Co. Pp. 184.

BASCOM, WILLIAM
1941   "The Sanctions of Ifa Divination," Journal of the Royal Anthropological
        Institute, LXXI (1/2), 43-54.
1942   "Ifa Divination: Comments on the Paper by J. D. Clarke," Man, XLII
        (21), 41-43.
1943   "The Relationship of Yoruba Folklore to Divining," Journal of American
        Folklore, LVI (220), 127-131.
1944   The Sociological Role of the Yoruba Cult-Group. Memoirs of the Ameri-
        can Anthropological Association, LXIII. Pp. 75.
1949   "Literary Style in Yoruba Riddles," Journal of American Folklore, LXII
        (243), 1-16.
1951a   "Yoruba Cooking," Africa, XXI (2), 125-137
1951b   "Social Status, Wealth and Individual Differences among the Yoruba,"
        American Anthropologist, LIII (4), 490-505.
1952   "Two Forms of Afro-Cuban Divination," in Acculturation in the Americas,
        Sol Tax (ed.). Proceedings and Selected Papers of the XXIXth Interna-
        tional Congress of Americanists, I, 63-69. Chicago: University of Chi-
        cago Press.

1954   "Four Functions of Folklore," Journal of American Folklore, LXVII
        (266), 333-349.
1960   "Yoruba Concepts of the Soul," in Men and Cultures, A. F. C. Wallace
        (ed.). Selected Papers of the Fifth International Congress of Anthro-
        pological and Ethnological Sciences, pp. 401-410. Philadelphia: Uni-
        versity of Pennsylvania Press.
1961   "Odu Ifa: The Order of the Figures of Ifa," Bulletin de l'Institut
        Français d'Afrique Noire, XXIII (3/4), 676-682.
1965   "The Forms of Folklore: Prose Narratives," Journal of American Folk-
        lore, LXXVIII (303), 3-20.
1966   "Odu Ifa: The Names of the Signs," Africa, XXXVI (4), 408-421.

BASCOM, WILLIAM, AND PAUL GEBAUER
1953   Handbook of West African Art, Popular Science Handbook Series, No. 5,
        Robert E. Ritzenthaler (ed.). Milwaukee: Milwaukee Public Museum.
        Pp. 83.

BASDEN, G. T.
1921   Among the Ibos of Nigeria. Philadelphia: J. B. Lippincott. Pp. 315.

BASTIDE, ROGER
1958   Le Condomblé de Bahia (Rite Nagô). Le Monde d'Outre-Mer Passé et
        Présent, Première Serie: Études V. Paris: Mouton & Co. Pp. 260.

BAUDIN, NOËL
1884   "Le Fétichisme, ou la Religion des Nègres de la Guinée," Les Missions
        Catholiques, XVI, 190-260 passim.
1885   Fetichism and Fetich Worshippers. New York: Benziger Brothers.
        Pp. 127. (Originally published in 1884 as two articles in Les Missions
        Catholiques, XVI, 190-260, 321-358 passim.)

BERTHO, JACQUES
1936   "La Science du Destin au Dahomey," Africa, IX (3), 359-378.

BEYIOKU, FAGBENRO
1940   Ifa. Lagos: The Hope Rising Press. Pp. 36.
1943   Iwe Kini Agbọniregun. Lagos: Alafia Press. Pp. 13.

BLOXAM, G. W.
1887   "Exhibition of West African Symbolic Messages," Journal of the Anthro-
        pological Institute, XVI, 295-299.

BOSMAN, WILLIAM
1705   A New and Accurate Description of the Coast of Guinea, Divided into
        the Gold, the Slave, and the Ivory Coasts. London: James Knapton and
        Dan. Midwinter. Pp. 493 plus index. (First published in Utrecht in
        1704 as Nauwkeurige Beschrijvinge van de Guinese.)

BOUCHE, PIERRE
1884-1885 "Contes Nagos," Melusine, II, 49-60, 121-129, 313-320.
1885   Sept Ans en Afrique Occidentale. La Côte des Esclaves et Le Dahomey.
        Paris: E. Plon, Nourrit et Cie. Pp. viii plus 403.

BOUVEIGNES, O. DE (Nom-de-plume of Léon Guébels)
1938   Entendu dans la Brousse. Contes Congolais. Les Joyaux de l'Orient, X.
        Paris: Librairie Orientaliste Paul Geuthner. Pp. 209.

BOWEN, T. J.
    1857   Central Africa. Adventures and Missionary Labors in Several Coun-
            tries in the Interior of Africa, from 1849-1856. Charleston: Southern
            Baptist Publication Society. Pp. 359.
    1858   Grammar and Dictionary of the Yoruba Language. Smithsonian Con-
            tributions to Knowledge, X (4). Pp. xxi plus 136.

BRADBURY, R. E.
    1957   The Benin Kingdom and the Edo-Speaking Peoples of South-Western
            Nigeria. Ethnographic Survey of Africa, Western Africa, XIII, Daryll
            Forde (ed.). London: International African Institute. Pp. 1-171.

BURTON, RICHARD F.
    1863   Abeokuta and the Cameroons Mountains, I-II. London: Tinsley Broth-
            ers. Pp. xvi plus 333; v plus 306.
    1893   A Mission to Gelele, King of Dahomey, I-II. London: Tylston and Ed-
            wards. Pp. xxi plus 256; viii plus 305. (Memorial edition; first pub-
            lished in 1864.)

BURTON, W. F. P.
    1961   The Magic Drum. Tales from Central Africa. London: Methuen & Co.
            Pp. 196.

CAMPBELL, ROBERT
    1861   A Pilgrimage to My Motherland. An Account of a Journey among the
            Egbas and Yorubas of Central Africa, in 1859-60. New York: Thomas
            Hamilton. Pp. 145.

CAMPHOR, A. P.
    1909   Missionary Story Sketches and Folk Lore from Africa. Cincinnati:
            Jennings and Graham. Pp. 346.

CARDINALL, A. W.
    1931   Tales Told in Togoland. London: Oxford University Press. Pp. 290.

CHAUSSE, HENRY AND HOLLEY
    1885   "Voyage dans le Yoruba," Les Missions Catholiques, XVII, 16-103
            passim.

CLARKE, J. D.
    1939   "Ifa Divination," Journal of the Royal Anthropological Institute, LXIX
            (2), 235-256.

CLARKE, KENNETH W.
    n.d.   "A Motif-Index of the Folktales of Culture-Area V, West Africa," Ph.D.
            dissertation (1958), Indiana University. Pp. 589. (Ann Arbor: Uni-
            versity Microfilms, 1963.)

CMS
    1937   Dictionary of the Yoruba Language. Lagos: Church Missionary Socie-
            ty Bookshop. Pp. 218 plus 243. (First published in 1913; reprinted as
            A Dictionary of the Yoruba Language, London: Oxford University Press,
            1950 and 1957.)

COLE, J. A. ABAYOMI
    1898   Astrological Geomancy in Africa, (Not available; quoted in Dennett,
            1906: 269-271.)

COURLANDER, HAROLD
    1963   The King's Drum. London: Rupert Hart-Davis. Pp. 125.

COURLANDER, HAROLD, AND ALBERT KOFI PREMPEH
    1957   The Hat-Shaking Dance. New York: Harcourt, Brace & Co. Pp. 115.

CROWTHER, SAMUEL
    1852   A Vocabulary of the Yoruba Language. London: Seeleys. Pp. v plus
            38 plus 287.

DALZIEL, J. M.
    1937   The Useful Plants of West Tropical Africa. London: The Crown Agents
            for the Colonies. Pp. xii plus 612.

DAMMANN, ERNST
    1935-1936. "Digo-Märchen," Zeitschrift für Eingeborenen-Sprachen, XXVI (2/3),
            81-86, 202-231.

DANFORD, J. A. AND S. A.
    1960   Folklore and Fables. Lagos: Ministry of Information. Pp. 31. (First
            published in 1953.)

DAPPER, O.
    1668   Naukeurige Beschrijvinge der Afrikaensche Gewesten. Amsterdam:
            Jacob van Meurs. Pp. 728.

DAYRELL, E.
    1913   Ikom Folk Stories from Southern Nigeria. Royal Anthropological Insti-
            tute, Occasional Papers, III. Pp. viii plus 100.

DELANO, ISAAC O.
    1937   The Soul of Nigeria. London: T. Werner Laurie Ltd. Pp. 252.

DENNETT, R. E.
    1906   At the Back of the Black Man's Mind. London: Macmillan & Co. Pp.
            xv plus 288.
    1910   Nigerian Studies, or the Religious and Political System of the Yoruba.
            London: Macmillan & Co. Pp. xiii plus 235.

DOKE, CLEMENT M.
    1927   Lamba Folk-Lore. Memoir of the American Folk-Lore Society, XX.
            Pp. xvii plus 570.

DOWNES, R. M.
    1933   The Tiv Tribe. Kaduna: The Government Printer. Pp. 101.

ELLIS, A. B.
    1887   The Tshi-Speaking Peoples of the Gold Coast of West Africa. London:
            Chapman and Hall. Pp. vii plus 343.
    1890   The Ewe-Speaking Peoples of the Slave Coast of West Africa. London:
            Chapman and Hall. Pp. 331
    1894   The Yoruba-Speaking Peoples of the Slave Coast of West Africa.
            London: Chapman and Hall. Pp. vii plus 402.

EPEGA, D. QNADELE
    1931   The Mystery of the Yoruba Gods. Lagos: The Hope Rising Press.
            Pp. 39.
    1937   Iwe Ifa ati Itumọ Ala. Lagos: The Hope Rising Press. Pp. 15.

n.d.   "Ifa - Amọna Awọn Baba Wa," I-XVI. Ode Rẹmọ: Imọlẹ Oluwa Institute. (1948-1957, typewritten.)

FAGG, WILLIAM, AND FRANK WILLETT
    1960   "Ancient Ife. An Ethnographical Summary," Odu, No. 8, 21-35.

FAIRBAIRN, W. A.
    1933   Some Common Birds of West Africa. Lagos: Church Missionary Society Bookshop. Pp. xii plus 106.

FARROW, STEPHEN S.
    1926   Faith, Fancies and Fetich, or Yoruba Paganism. London: Society for Promoting Christian Knowledge. Pp. xi plus 180.

FIELD, M. J.
    1937   Religion and Medicine of the Gã People. London: Oxford University Press. Pp. viii plus 214.

FINNEGAN, RUTH
    1967   Limba Stories and Story-Telling. Oxford Library of African Literature. Oxford: Clarendon Press. Pp. xii plus 352.

FISCHER, OSKAR
    1929   Divinations-Formen der Primitiven Afrikas. München: Parcus Buchdruckerei. Pp. 117.

FORDE, DARYLL, AND RICHENDA SCOTT
    1946   The Native Economies of Nigeria. M. Perham (ed.). London: Faber and Faber. Pp. xxiv plus 312.

FROBENIUS, LEO
    1912-1913. Und Afrika Sprach, I-III. Berlin-Charlottenburg: Vita, Deutsches Verlagshaus. Pp. xxv plus 402; ix plus 391; xxiv plus 508.
    1913   The Voice of Africa, I-II. London: Hutchinson & Co. Pp. xxiii plus 349; viii plus 353-682.
    1924a   Dämonen des Sudan. Atlantis VII. Pp. 373.
    1924b   Volkserzählungen und Volksdichtungen aus dem Zentral-Sudan. Atlantis IX. Pp. 427.
    1924c   Volksdichtungen aus Oberguinea. Atlantis XI. Pp. 356.
    1926   Die Atlantische Götterlehre. Atlantis X. Pp. xix plus 318.

FROBENIUS, LEO, AND DOUGLAS C. FOX
    1937   African Genesis. New York: Stackpole Sons. Pp. 236.

FUJA, ABAYOMI
    1962   Fourteen Hundred Cowries. London: Oxford University Press. Pp. vii plus 164.

GARNIER, CHRISTINE, AND JEAN FRALON
    1951   Le Fétichisme en Afrique Noire (Togo-Cameroun). Paris: Payot. Pp. 213.

GORER, GEOFFREY
    1935   Africa Dances. New York: Alfred A. Knopf. Pp. xv plus 337 plus viii.

GRANDIN, LEONCE
    1895   A l'Assaut du Pays du Noirs: Le Dahomey, I-II. Paris: René Haton. Pp. xxv plus 285; 307.

570   References Cited

HAMILTON, JAMES
    1856   Wanderings in North Africa. London: John Murray. Pp. xxiv plus 320.

HARRIS, JOEL CHANDLER
    1892   Uncle Remus and His Friends. New York: Houghton, Mifflin and Co.
            Pp. xvii plus 357.

HERSKOVITS, MELVILLE J.
    1938   Dahomey. An Ancient West African Kingdom, I-II. New York: J. J.
            Augustin. Pp. xxi plus 402; xiv plus 407.

HERSKOVITS, MELVILLE J. AND FRANCES S.
    1931   "Tales in Pidgin English from Nigeria," Journal of American Folklore,
            XLIV (174), 448-466.
    1958   Dahomean Narrative. African Studies, I. Evanston: Northwestern Uni-
            versity Press. Pp. xvi plus 490.

HOFFMAN, C.
    1915-1916 "Märchen und Erzählungen der Eingeborenen in Nord-Transvaal,"
            Zeitschrift für Kolonialsprachen, VI, 28-54, 124-153, 206-243, 285-331.

IDEWU, OLAWALE
    1956   "The Hunter and the Hind (Folklore)," The Blackburn Scroll, II, 22-25.

IDOWU, E. BOLAJI
    1962   Olódùmarè. God in Yoruba Belief. London: Longmans. Pp. viii plus
            222.

IRVING, DR.
    1853   "The Yoruba Mission," Church Missionary Intelligencer, IV, 123-137,
            185-190, 227-237.

ITAYEMI, PHEBEAN, AND P. GURREY
    1953   Folk Tales and Fables. Penguin West African Series, WA3. London:
            Penguin Books. Pp. 123.

JABLOW, ALTA
    1961   Yes and No. The Intimate Folklore of Africa. New York: Horizon Press.
            Pp. 223.

JACOBS, D. ABIOLA
    1933   Itan Abahun Ijapa. Ibadan: Lisabi Press. Pp. 60.

JAULIN, ROBERT
    1957   "Essai d'analyse formelle d'un procédé géomantique," Bulletin de l'In-
            stitut Français d'Afrique Noire, Série B: Sciences Humaines, XIX, 43-
            71.
    1966   La Géomancie. Analyse formelle. Cahiers de l'Homme, Ethnologie—
            Géographie—Linguistique, N.S., IV. Paris: Mouton & Co. Pp. 198.

JOHNSON, JAMES
    1899a   Isin Orişa Bibọ ni Ilẹ Yoruba. Exeter: James Townsend and Sons.
            Pp. 53. (Translated as Johnson, 1899b.)
    1899b   Yoruba Heathenism. Exeter: James Townsend and Son. Pp. 54. (See
            lengthy extract in Dennett, 1906: 243-269.)

JOHNSON, SAMUEL
    1921   The History of the Yorubas, O. Johnson (ed.). London: George Rout-
            ledge & Sons. Pp. lv plus 684.

KLIPPLE, MAY AUGUSTA
    n.d.   "African Folk Tales with Foreign Analogues." Ph.D. dissertation (1938),
            Indiana University. Pp. xxiv plus 973. (Ann Arbor: University Micro-
            films, 1964.)

KRONENBERG, ANDREAS
    1958   Die Teda von Tibetsi. Wiener Beiträge zur Kulturgeschichte und
            Linguistik, XII. Pp. xiii plus 160.

KRUG, A. N., AND M. J. HERSKOVITS
    1949   "Bulu Tales," Journal of American Folklore, LXII (246), 348-374.

LABOURET, HENRI, AND PAUL RIVET
    1929   Le Royaume d'Arda et son Évangélisation au XVIIe siècle. Travaux et
            Mémoires de l'Institut d'Ethnologie, VII. Pp. 62.

LADEMANN, GEBHARD, et al.
    1910   Tierfabeln und andere Erzählungen in Suaheli. Archiv für das Studium
            deutscher Kolonialsprachen, XII. Pp. 120.

LE HÉRISSÉ, A.
    1911   L'Ancien Royaume de Dahomey. Moeurs, religion, histoire. Paris:
            Emile Larose. Pp. 384.

LESSA, WILLIAM A.
    1959   "Divining Knots in the Carolines," Journal of the Polynesian Society,
            LXVIII (3), 188-204.

LIJADU, E. M.
    1908   Orúnmla! Hockley: Samuel E. Richards. Pp. 89 plus i.
    1923   Ifa: Imolẹ Rẹ ti Iṣe Ipilẹ Ìsin ni Ilẹ Yoruba. Exeter: James Townsend
            & Sons. Pp. 72. (First published in 1901.)

LLOYD, P. C.
    1957   The Itsekiri. Ethnographic Survey of Africa, Western Africa, XIII,
            Daryll Forde (ed.). London: International African Institute. Pp. 172-
            210.

LOMAX, JOHN A.
    1913   "Stories of an African Prince." Journal of American Folklore, XXVI
            (99), 1-12.

LOYER, GODEFROY
    1714   Relation du voyage du Royaume d'Issyny, Côte d'Or, Païs de Guinée,
            en Afrique. Paris: Arnoul Seneuze et Jean-Raoul Morel. (Not avail-
            able.)

LUCAS, J. OLUMIDE
    1948   The Religion of the Yorubas. Lagos: C. M. S. Bookshop. Pp. xii plus
            420.

MACDONALD, DUFF
    1880   Africana; or, The Heart of Heathen Africa, I-II. London: Simpkin
            Marshall & Co. Pp. xvii plus 301; xi plus 371.

MALINOWSKI, BRONISLAW
    1954   "Myth in Primitive Psychology" in Magic, Science and Religion. New
            York: Doubleday Anchor Books. Pp. 93-148. (First published in 1926.)

MAMET, M.
   1960   Le Language des Bolia (Lac Léopold II). Annales du Musée Royal du
           Congo Belge, Série in 8⁰, Sciences de l'Homme, Linguistique, XXXIII.
           Pp. 268.

MANSFELD, ALFRED
   1908   Urwald Dokumente. Berlin: Dietrich Reimer. Pp. xvi plus 310.

MAUPOIL, BERNARD
   1943   La Géomancie à l'ancienne Côte des Esclaves. Travaux et Mémoires
           de l'Institut d'Ethnologie, XLII. Pp. xxvii plus 686.

McCLELLAND, E. M.
   1966   "The Significance of Number in the Odu of Ifa." Africa, XXXVI (4),
           421-430.

MEEK, C. K.
   1925   The Northern Tribes of Nigeria, I-II. London: Oxford University
           Press. Pp. xviii plus 312; viii plus 277.
   1931   A Sudanese Kingdom. London: Kegan Paul, Trench, Trubner. Pp.
           xxxiii plus 548.
   1937   Law and Authority in a Nigerian Tribe. London: Oxford University
           Press. Pp. xvi plus 372.

MEEUSSEN, A. E.
   1962   "Lega-Teksten" in Africana Linguistica, (I). Annales du Musée Royal
           de l'Afrique Centrale, Série in 8⁰, Sciences Humaines, XLII, 75-97.

MERCIER, P.
   1954   "The Fon of Dahomey," in African Worlds, Daryll Forde (ed.). London:
           Oxford University Press. Pp. 210-234.

MILLIGAN, ROBERT H.
   1912   The Fetish Folk of West Africa. New York: Fleming H. Revell. Pp.
           328.

MONTEIL, CHARLES
   1932   "La Divination chez les Noirs de l'Afrique Occidentale Française,"
           Bulletin du Comité d'Études Historiques et Scientifiques de l'Afrique
           Occidentale Française, Année 1931, XIV (1/2), 27-136.

MÜLLER, Fr.
   1902   "Fetischistisches aus Atakpame (Deutsch-Togo)," Globus, LXXXI, 279-
           281.

NADEL, S. F.
   1954   Nupe Religion. London: Routledge & Kegan Paul. Pp. x plus 288.

NAPOLEON'S BOOK OF FATE AND ORACULUM
   [ca. 1925] London: W. Foulsham & Co. Pp. 191.

ODUM̧QLAYQ, A. O.
   1951   Iwe Ifa Kişe Orişa, Apa Kini. Lagos: Ijẹsha Royal Press. Pp. 31.

OGUMEFU, M. I.
   n.d.   Tales of Tortoise. Little Books for Africa, 26. London: The Sheldon
           Press. Pp. 32.
   1929   Yoruba Legends. London: The Sheldon Press. Pp. vi plus 87.

OGUNBIYI, Thos. A. J.
  1952   Iwe Itan Ifa, Agbigba, 'Yanrin Titẹ ati Owo Ẹrindinlogun. Lagos: Ife-
         Olu Printing Works. Pp. 104.

PARK, GEORGE K.
  1963   "Divination and its Social Contexts," Journal of the Royal Anthropologi-
         cal Institute, XCIII (2), 195-209.

PARKINSON, JOHN
  1909   "Yoruba Folklore," Journal of the African Society, VIII, 165-186.

PARRINDER, GEOFFREY
  1949   West African Religion. London: The Epworth Press. Pp. xii plus 223.
  1953   Religion in an African City. London: Oxford University Press. Pp. 211.
  1954   African Traditional Religion. London: Hutchinson's University Library.
         Pp. 156.
  1961   West African Religion. 2d ed. London: The Epworth Press. Pp. xv
         plus 203.

PARSONS, ELSIE CLEWS
  1917   "Tales from Guilford County, North Carolina," Journal of American Folk-
         lore, XXX (116), 168-200.
  1918   Folk-Tales of Andros Island, Bahamas. Memoirs of the American Folk-
         Lore Society, XIII. Pp. xx plus 167.
  1923   Folk-Lore from the Cape Verde Islands, I-II. Memoirs of the American
         Folk-Lore Society, XV. Pp. xxv plus 373; x plus 267.

PRICE, H. L. WARD
  1939   Dark Subjects. London: Jarrolds. Pp. 287.

PRINCE, RAYMOND
  1963   Ifa. Yoruba Divination and Sacrifice. Ibadan: Ibadan University Press.
         Pp. 18.

QUÉNUM, MAXIMILIEN
  1938   Au Pays du Fons. Us et Coutumes du Dahomey. 2d ed. Paris: Larose
         Éditeurs. Pp. 171. (First published in 1935.)

RATTRAY, R. S.
  1930   Akan-Ashanti Folk-Tales. Oxford: Clarendon Press. Pp. xx plus 275.

RIBEIRO, RENÉ
  1956   "Projective Mechanisms and the Structuralization of Perception in Afro-
         brazilian Divination," Revue Internationale d'Ethnopsychologie Normale
         et Pathologique, I (2), 3-23.

RYDER, A. F. C.
  1959   "An Early Portuguese Trading Voyage to the Forcados River," Journal of
         the Historical Society of Nigeria, I, 294-321.

SCHILDE, WILLY
  1940   Orakel und Gottesurteil in Afrika. Veröffentlichung des Ehemaligen
         Staatlichen Forschungsinstitut für Völkerkunde in Leipzig, Erste Reihe,
         XII. Pp. xv plus 333.

SCHULTZE, LEONHARD
  1907   Aus Namaland und Kalahari. Jena: Gustav Fischer. Pp. xiv plus 752.

SKERTCHLY, J. A.
    1874   Dahomey as It Is. London: Chapman and Hall. Pp. xx plus 524.

SKINNER, NEIL
    n.d.   "Hausa Folk Tales and Miscellanea, Being a Translation of Litafi Na
            Tatsuniyoyi Na Hausa, by Frank Edgar, 1924," I-III. (Typewritten manu-
            script.)

SOUTHON, ARTHUR E.
    n.d.   Ilesha—and Beyond! London: The Cargate Press. Pp. 126.

ŞOWANDE, FĘLA
    n.d. (c. 1964) Ifa. Yaba: Forward Press. Pp. 74.
    1965   Ifa. Odu Mimọ. Lagos: The Ancient Religious Societies of African
            Descendants Association. Mimeographed. Pp. viii plus 70.

SPIETH, J.
    1911   Die Religion der Eweer in Süd-Togo. Religions-Urkunden der Völker,
            Abteilung IC, Band II, Julius Boehmer (ed.). Pp. xvi plus 316.

STANNUS, HUGH
    1922   "The Wayao of Nyasaland," Harvard African Studies, III, 229-374.

STONE, R. H.
    1899   In Africa's Forest and Jungle or Six Years among the Yorubans. New
            York: Fleming H. Revell Co. Pp. 282.

TALBOT, P. AMAURY
    1912   In the Shadow of the Bush. London: William Heinemann. Pp. xiv plus
            500.
    1926   The Peoples of Southern Nigeria, I-IV. London: Oxford University
            Press. Pp. xii plus 365; xx plus 423; x plus 425-976; 234.

TAUXIER, L.
    1932   Religion, moeurs et coutumes des Agnis de la Cote-d'Ivoire. Paris:
            Paul Geuthner. Pp. 255.

TEILHARD DE CHARDIN, J.
    1888   La Guinée Supérieure et ses missions. Keer-lez-Maastricht: Collège
            Apostolique des Missions Africaines. Pp. 233.

TEMPLE, O. AND C. L.
    1919   Notes on the Tribes, Provinces, Emirates and States of the Northern
            Provinces of Nigeria. Cape Town: The Argus Printing and Publishing
            Co. Pp. 577 plus xiii.

THEAL, GEORGE McCALL
    1886   Kaffir Folk-Lore. London: Swan Sonnenschein, LeBas & Lowrey. Pp.
            xii plus 226.

THOMAS, NORTHCOTE W.
    1913-1914. Anthropological Report on the Ibo-Speaking Peoples of Nigeria,
            I-VI. London: Harrison & Sons. Pp. 161; vii plus 391; vi plus 199;
            vi plus 208; xi plus 184; viii plus 114.
    1916   Anthropological Report on Sierra Leone, I-III. London: Harrison and
            Sons. Pp. 196; 139; xxx plus 86.
    1918   "Ibo: Folk-tales," Man, XVIII (14, 25, 32, 43, 51), 23-87 passim.

TRAUTMANN, RENÉ
1927   La Littérature Populaire à la Côte des Esclaves. Travaux et Mémoires de l'Institut d'Ethnologie, IV. Pp. vii plus 105.
1940   La Divination à la Côte des Esclaves et à la Madagascar. Le Vôdoû Fa —Le Sikidy. Mémoires de l'Institut Français d'Afrique Noire, I, Pp. 155.

TREMEARNE, A. J. N.
1910, 1911. "Fifty Hausa Folk-Tales," Folk-Lore, XXI, 199-215, 351-365, 487-503; XXII, 60-73, 218-228, 341-348, 457-473.
1913   Hausa Superstitions and Customs. London: John Bale, Sons & Danielson. Pp. xv plus 548.

TUCKER, MISS
1853   Abbeokuta; or, Sunrise within the Tropics. London: James Nisbet and Co. Pp. vi plus 278.

VERGER, PIERRE
1957   Notes sur le culte des Oriṣa et Vodun à Bahia, la Baie de tous les Saints, au Brésil et à l'ancienne Côte des Esclaves en Afrique. Mémoires de l'Institut Français d'Afrique Noire, LI. Pp. 609.

WALKER, BARBARA K. AND WARREN S.
1961   Nigerian Folk Tales. New Brunswick: Rutgers University Press. Pp. x plus 113.

WESCOTT, JOAN
1959   Yoruba Art in German & Swiss Museums. Ibadan: Yoruba Historical Research Scheme. Pp. 43.

WESTERMANN, DIEDRICH
1921   Die Kpelle. Quellen der Religions-Geschichte, IX. Pp. xvi plus 552.

WILHELM, RICHARD, AND CARY F. BAYNES (Translators)
1951   The I Ching or Book of Changes, I-II. London: Routledge & Kegan Paul. Pp. xlii plus 395; 376.

WILLETT, FRANK
1960   "Ife and Its Archaeology," Journal of African History, I (2), 231-248.

WYNDHAM, JOHN
1919   "The Divination of Ifa (A Fragment)," Man, XIX (80), 151-153. (Reprinted in Wyndham, 1921: 65-70.)
1921   Myths of Ife. London: Erskine Macdonald. Pp. 72.